CU00747319

DAWNLAND VOICES

PUBLICATION OF THESE VOICES

IS SUPPORTED BY A GRANT BY

Jewish Federation of Greater Hartford

DAWNLAND
VOICES

AN ANTHOLOGY OF INDIGENOUS
WRITING FROM NEW ENGLAND

Edited by Siobhan Senier

JAIME BATTISTE

JUANA PERLEY

DONALD SOCTOMAH

CAROL DANA

LISA BROOKS

CHERYL STEDTLER

JOAN TAVARES AVANT

DAWN DOVE

STEPHANIE M. FIELDING

TRUDIE LAMB RICHMOND

RUTH GARBY TORRES

UNIVERSITY OF NEBRASKA PRESS | LINCOLN AND LONDON

© 2014 by the Board of Regents
of the University of Nebraska

Acknowledgments for the use of copyrighted
material appear on pages 683–90, which
constitute an extension of the copyright page.

All rights reserved
Manufactured in the United States of America

Library of Congress
Cataloging-in-Publication Data
Dawnland voices: an anthology of indig-
enous writing from New England / edited
by Siobhan Senier, Jaime Battiste, Juana
Perley, Donald Soctomah, Carol Dana, Lisa
Brooks, Cheryl Stedtler, Joan Tavares Avant,
Dawn Dove, Stephanie M. Fielding, Trudie
Lamb Richmond, Ruth Garby Torres.
pages   cm
Includes bibliographical references.
ISBN 978-0-8032-4686-7 (paperback)
ISBN 978-0-8032-5680-4 (epub)
ISBN 978-0-8032-5681-1 (mobi)
ISBN 978-0-8032-5679-8 (pdf)
1. Indians of North America—Literary collec-
tions. 2. American literature—Indian authors.
3. American literature—New England.
4. New England—Literary collections.
I. Senier, Siobhan, 1965–
editor of compilation.
PS508.I5D38 2014
810.8'0897074—dc23
2014009614

Set in Scala by L. Auten.
Designed by N. Putens.

CONTENTS

MALISEET

PENOBSCOT

WAMPANOAG

NARRAGANSETT

ACKNOWLEDGMENTS

More people than I can name, and certainly more than I could keep track of, helped during this project, from its initial conception, to finding and contacting writers, to tracking down copyright holders, to the final layout and presentation.

I can't quite describe what a great honor it was, and how humbling, to work with these eleven community editors. They are astonishingly brilliant knowledge keepers, and their commitment to sustaining their communities and traditions is breathtaking. Each one put in countless hours pulling this material together, teaching me about local literary traditions, and conveying the importance of this project to their friends and neighbors. Their expertise is tremendous, and they shared it generously and patiently.

Additionally, all of the living writers included here contributed much more than their own work: they solicited fellow tribal members for additional writings and put up with my endless questions about locations, language, and history.

Beyond the editors and writers, there were legions of smart and selfless people who talked with me on the phone or via email, and who helped me find other writings. Some sent pieces that I was unable to include here; others read over sections, proofread or copyedited chapters in progress, or participated in the often-circuitous search for rights holders.

The University of Nebraska Press deserves special thanks for supporting this project and indeed for its decades-long commitment to Native American literature. This anthology is long and in many ways unconventional for an academic publisher. It required rather more than the usual labor and negotiation among multiple authors, copyright holders, and other parties. Matt Bokovoy and his staff (Heather Stauffer, Leif Milliken, Sabrina Stellrecht, freelancer Joy Margheim, and others) were exceptionally flexible and understanding in working with first-time authors and accommodating a diversity of approaches to print literature while maintaining the high standards for which the press is known. Academic publishing is never lucrative, but the press and the tribal editors agree that any and all royalties from the sale of this book shall be distributed evenly among the following: the Penobscot Cultural and Historic Preservation Project, the Passamaquoddy Tribal Museum, Gedakina, Nipmuc Nation Project Mishoon, the Mashpee Wampanoag Museum, the Tomaquag Indian Memorial Museum, and the Tantaquidgeon Indian Museum.

Melissa Clark donated many hours of her time and expertise to creating a map of the territory described in this book. Mapping is tricky and political business, and in the end, the tribal editors were unable to agree on a single map of indigenous homeland in the northeast. I regret that I did not recognize this much earlier in the book-making process, but I thank Melissa for her generosity and refer readers to the many excellent maps that can be found on individual tribal websites.

I am undoubtedly forgetting individuals to whom I owe some sizable debt of gratitude, and I apologize sincerely to anyone I've left out: Kate April, Rocky Bear (Maliseet), Charles Brilvitch, Wendi-Starr Brown (Narragansett), Ana Caguiat, Amy Den Ouden, Thomas Doughton (Nipmuc), Burt Feintuch, James Finley, Jessica Fish, James Francis (Penobscot), Geneva Marie Gano, Maria Girouard (Penobscot), Rae Gould (Nipmuc), Joyce Heywood (Abenaki), Luke Joseph (Passamaquoddy), Robert Leavitt, Michael LeBlanc, Dyani Lee (Narragansett), Joan Lester, Drew Lopenzina, Margo Lukens, Pauleena MacDougall, Jason Mancini, Daniel Mandell, Rodger Martin, Donna Roberts Moody (Abenaki), John Moody, Tom Silver Fox Morse (Nipmuc), Wayne Newell (Passamaquoddy), Bonnie Newsom and other members of the Penobscot Cultural Heritage Preservation Commission, Robert Dale Parker, Dan Paul (Mi'kmaq), Micah Pawling, Shoran Piper (Golden Hill Paugussett), Paul Pouliot (Abenaki), Rick Pouliot (Abenaki), Dale Potts, Kathy Sebastian (Eastern Pequot), David Slagger (Maliseet), David Stewart-Smith (Abenaki), David Watters, Margaret Way, Hilary Wyss, Bill Yellow Robe Jr. (Assiniboine).

This project would not have been possible without the support I received as the James H. and Claire Short Hayes Chair in the Humanities at the University of New Hampshire. It would also not have been possible without the countless indigenous knowledge-keepers, past and present, who have kept these literary traditions alive. In a project this size, some omissions and errors have undoubtedly slipped through. I apologize sincerely, and assume full responsibility, for all mistakes.

DAWNLAND VOICES

Introduction

Siobhan Senier

Years ago, when I started thinking about this anthology, I had what I thought was a simple, practical need. I was hired to teach Native American literature, first at the University of Maine and then at the University of New Hampshire, and I wanted to include local authors. But that literature was maddeningly hard to find. Aside from two repeatedly mentioned early writers—the Mohegan minister Samson Occom and Pequot minister-activist William Apess—I kept hearing that "there just aren't any" Native American authors in this area.

Now, I had been taught in graduate school that "there just aren't any" is almost always a lie. So I kept looking. I did have company: like-minded colleagues, including Margaret Lukens at the University of Maine and Lisa Brooks (Abenaki), now at Amherst College.[1] With their help, I started finding writers: dazzling, contemporary poets like Cheryl Savageau (Abenaki), inventive novelists like John Christian Hopkins (Narragansett), powerful essayists like Donna Loring (Penobscot), and intriguing earlier writers like the diarist Fidelia Fielding (Mohegan) and the historian Lewis Mitchell (Passamaquoddy). I found, in fact, more indigenous New England authors than I could read, teach, or even count. More to the point, I found more than I could keep xeroxing for my classes, since works by these writers were very often out of print or unpublished. Hence the need for a ready compendium.

The idea of an anthology like this was apparently a new one. Acquaintances and even well-informed colleagues were usually surprised ("There's Native American literature *here*?"). Avid readers have at least heard that Native American literature exists, but some believe "it was all oral tradition." If they have read any Native authors at all, these are almost always from the Southwest or Great Plains. On shelves labeled "American Indian" in your local bookstore, writers from New England are almost always neglected.[2] That neglect, I soon learned, has deep historic and political roots and does damaging work to the indigenous people who still live here.

The myth of the "vanishing Indian" is very old, and by no means peculiar to New England: it has permeated American culture from *The Last of the Mohicans* to *Dances with Wolves*. But the myth exercises special force east of the Mississippi, where colonization happened earliest; and it takes a particular shape in New England, where European settlers have, from the beginning, been keen to install themselves as the "first" Americans.[3] Yankees like to believe that Native people "died off" (or "lost") early on and that those who didn't die were "assimilated" or have "very little real Indian blood." Few citizens are educated about the barrage of state and federal policies that have been consistently enacted and retooled, to this very day, to terminate Native communities in New England as well as across the rest of the United States: educational policies removing Native children from their homes and penalizing Native language use; land use policies aimed at breaking up Native collectivities; bizarre blood-quantum requirements claiming that Native identity "dissolves" with intermarriage.[4]

The writers in *Dawnland Voices* describe and challenge those policies in their own writings, appropriately enough, because writing has always been a key colonial tool. Historian Jill Lepore, for example, has traced how the earliest Puritan historians narrated (and renarrated) King Philip's War (1675–76) as the effective "end" of Native presence in the Northeast. In that same century, the state of Connecticut made it illegal even to use the name "Pequot" (O'Brien 31); other states followed with similar "detribalization" laws.[5] Soon, New England census and other records began recasting indigenous people as "colored," "mulatto," "French"—anything but "Indian"—in what some Native people call "pencil genocide."[6] And then local and town historians joined the effort. In *Firsting and Lasting: Writing Indians Out of Existence in New England*, Jean O'Brien (Ojibwe) reads hundreds of these town histories from Maine to Rhode Island. Year after year, she finds, local historians eulogized "the last of the tribe"—so enthusiastically and consistently, in fact, that they created a landscape "thickly populated by 'last'" members of a given "race" (113).

The New England case illustrates why the Australian scholar Patrick Wolfe has called invasion a "structure, not an event" (2). In settler colonialism, the colonizers keep invading: first physically, with war and disease; then culturally and ideologically, with more "humane" attempts to "civilize" indigenous people; and politically and economically, through policies designed to thwart tribal self-governance. As the authors included below explain, those policies currently take the form of state blockage of tribal economic enterprise (as in Rhode Island) and interference with tribal environmental protection of traditional homelands and waterways (as in Maine). If there is one thing the culturally diverse tribal nations represented in this volume have in common, it is the enduring popular conception that they no longer exist, or that those who would assert their heritage and rights are merely "casino-grubbing" or somehow standing in the way of modern economic "development."

Dawnland Voices thus joins an ongoing effort to help document and represent Native people's *continuous presence* in New England.7 As you will see throughout this anthology, indigenous New Englanders have had to say it again and again: "We're still here."

No anthology ever satisfies all readers, and no anthology is ever complete. But even among readers, teachers, and editors who know these things, anthologies carry a heavy burden. A classroom tome like the *Norton Anthology of World Literature* promises comprehensive coverage. The annual *Best American Poetry* series implies the highest standards of taste, plus national pride. Popular collections like the Chicken Soup series offer feelings of community with other people in similar straits: the grieving, the preteen, the dog lover, even the "executive" or the "prisoner." We might say, then, that anthologies have a politics, insofar as an anthology on your bookshelf, or your Kindle, does more than "introduce" you to a certain body of literature; an anthology can also confer membership in a particular group or a kind of distinction.

Perhaps this explains why Karen Kilcup, herself a thoughtful anthologist, has said there is no escaping this central fact: "an anthology creates a miniature canon, no matter how resistant the editor is to the vexed notions of goodness and importance" (113). Some anthologies self-consciously try to push back against this canonizing tendency. In *Reinventing the Enemy's Language: Contemporary Native Women's Writings of North America*, for instance, poets Joy Harjo (Muscogee) and Gloria Bird (Spokane) included many previously unpublished writers because they wanted specifically to represent women who had made major contributions to their tribal communities. A more recent collection, one that has greatly influenced the volume at hand, is Kristina Bross and Hilary Wyss's *Early Native Literacies in New England*, which encourages readers to look for Indian literature in unexpected places: in historic petitions, for example, and even in nonalphabetic forms like baskets.

Dawnland Voices tries to follow these books' lead. In particular, it redistributes the evaluation of literary "goodness" and "importance" to a much wider range of people than the usual editorial team or individual. Our team includes one non-Native college professor (me) and eleven Native American community editors—some of them academics, some community-based intellectuals, some elders, some rising stars. During the collection and selection process, all of us consulted with much larger networks of Native and non-Native writers, teachers, readers, and scholars. The resulting volume is thus extremely varied and includes a range of pieces that you might not usually see in a collection of "literary" writings: recipes, hip-hop lyrics, blog entries, children's poems.

There is a well-established tradition of literary "recovery" that depends on a dedicated researcher toiling alone in archives to unearth forgotten writers and republish their work for new appreciation. Many lost classics, especially by women and authors of color, have been rediscovered this way. Nina Baym scoured dusty library shelves for hundreds of nineteenth-century women's novels, many of which are now back in print and taught in literature classes thanks to her study *Woman's Fiction: A Guide to Novels by and about Women in America, 1820–1870* (1978). Henry Louis Gates likewise excavated African American treasures like Harriet Wilson's 1859 novel *Our Nig*—now republished, reexamined by other scholars, and recelebrated in Wilson's hometown of Milford, New Hampshire.

Besides the obvious baggage associated with the word "discovery" in the context of Native Americans in the United States, it does not really describe what happened as I compiled *Dawnland Voices*. Very occasionally, I did manage to find a forgotten Native author in an archive: the nineteenth-century Narragansett hymnist Thomas Commuck is one example. More often, when I brought such a "discovery" to Native people, they were either already familiar with that writer or far less interested in him or her than in some others, better known within their communities.

This is instructive, I think, for the current structures awarding "credit" to academics. For example, while academic and Native communities rightly honor Barry O'Connell for his definitive edition of the writings of William Apess, many Pequot and Wampanoag people actively remembered Apess and his work long before the 1992 publication of *On Our Own Ground: The*

Complete Writings of William Apess, a Pequot. Similarly, Annette Kolodny did something important by annotating and republishing Joseph Nicolar's 1891 *Life and Traditions of the Red Man* through Duke University Press in 2007, but Penobscot people had long been recirculating that book on and around Indian Island in Maine, sometimes selling ten-dollar xeroxed copies in the local gas stations and sometimes debating Nicolar's contributions to Penobscot culture and history. Academics, in other words, didn't "discover" these writers.

University-based scholars often think we know in advance what we want to ask of community collaborators, but if we are really willing to ask, and really willing to listen, they often take us in unexpected directions. Literary scholars have been, perhaps, a little slower to recognize this than anthropologists, who have a longer and deeper investment in fieldwork. Some of the best anthropologists, like Julie Cruikshank and Naomi Adelson, have found that their indigenous partners redirected and reshaped their very research questions. So I have tried hard to listen to Native people. For instance, I was interested in Commuck myself, partly because he wrote political letters in rhymed quatrains, but most Narragansett people with whom I spoke were more attached to the seemingly more homely writers of the 1935–36 magazine *Narragansett Dawn*. Wampanoag people at Mashpee, meanwhile, were entirely respectful of William Apess's historical work there, but it is Mabel Avant's poetry that they recite aloud at their community events. If you ask Abenaki people what books are important to them, they might show you old, well-thumbed copies of language primers by Joseph Laurent or Henry Lorne Masta. Passamaquoddy people often refer to Russell Bassett, published only on their tribal website, as one of their most beloved poets. This kind of tribal literature connects people to homeland, kin, and neighbors, to tribal language, histories, and traditions. In many cases these poems, novels, and essays are virtually unknown outside their communities—and (as Kolodny found when she annotated Nicolar) their "goodness" and "importance" are not always immediately transparent to outsiders.

Thus, even though it made for a more unwieldy, occasionally contentious, and infinitely *longer* publishing process, I enlisted the help of community editors. Academics who conduct what is now called "engaged" or "outreach" scholarship know that this is a serendipitous, unpredictable process, alternately frustrating and rewarding. I started by asking people I knew, usually Native scholars and writers I had invited to my classes and with whom I gradually built relationships over time, including Dawn Dove (Narragansett). In other cases, my closest contacts were unable to take on the editorial work themselves, but they put me in contact with knowledgeable people who could—for example, Stephanie Fielding (Mohegan) and Donald Soctomah (Passamaquoddy). In still other cases, I had to follow the chain of contacts much longer—sometimes for years, sometimes through blind phone calls to tribal historic preservation officers, sometimes even into email and Facebook. I connected with at least two wonderful editors—Jaime Battiste (Mi'kmaq) and Cheryl Stedtler (Nipmuc)—online long before I got to meet them face to face.

I wanted to organize this book by tribal nation because I have come to value the tribally oriented scholarship of writers like Craig Womack (Muscogee), who has said, very reasonably, that if you want to understand Native American literature, you had better know something about the tribal context from which it came.[8] This approach seemed to fit with what I was hearing from community members, too: Passamaquoddy people read very deeply among Passamaquoddy writers; Wampanoag people had detailed knowledge of the chronology of Wampanoag historians and poets; Narragansett people had a distinct sense of literary genealogy emanating from that 1935 magazine. In the table of contents, these tribal nations are organized more or less north to south, and readers unfamiliar with the territory can follow many of the locations that appear in the writings along almost any regional map. One virtue of this pattern is that it highlights some connections across communities: for instance, among Wabanaki peoples in Maine and between Narragansett and Wampanoag groups in southern New England.

I should note that my choice to organize the volume this way also created some exclusions. "Nations"—conceived of as ethnic/cultural entities that coincide with geopolitical borders—are modern constructs; as the Kanien'kehaka political theorist Taiaiake Alfred has pointedly remarked, "Neither the state-sponsored modifications to the colonial-municipal model (imposed in Canada through the Indian Act and in the United States through the Indian Reorganization Act) nor the corporate or public-government systems recently negotiated in the North constitute indigenous governments at all" (3). Put a little more simply, political designations like "Abenaki" or "Schaghticoke" are relatively recent arrivals and don't necessarily reflect the variety of bands and communities that consider themselves affiliated yet distinct. Moreover, the exigencies of book publishing, combined with the exigencies of the community-editor model itself, meant that some nations fell out altogether—the fault of the process, not any indication that these groups have no writing worth including. The Pequots, for instance—a huge omission in this book—are inundated with requests to "collaborate" with scholars, often hesitant to become involved with researchers they don't know well, and (as happened as this project came to deadline) simply oversubscribed with other work. Yet there is a considerable body of Pequot writing that reaches back before the monumental figure of William Apess and continues up to the filmmaker Rebecca Perry Levy. The bibliographies throughout the book are meant to direct readers to some of those omissions.

My original intent was to limit this collection to original writing, not transcribed oral tradition, and to writing in English, not in Native languages. Transcribed oral traditions have a vexed history, *especially* in anthologies; many of the most enduring "Indian" collections, like Jerome Rothenberg's *Shaking the Pumpkin: Traditional Poetry of the Indian North Americas* (1972), aren't really "Indian" at all but consist of loose "translations" of traditional narratives and other forms.[9] Leslie Marmon Silko (Laguna) once derided transcribed oral narratives as outright cultural theft, on the grounds that these traditions were either completely misrepresented in print or never should have been written down in the first place.[10] And then there is the whole genre of "as-told-to" American Indian memoirs, of which *Black Elk Speaks* is only the most notorious, which are often much more heavily edited than their non-Native "coauthors" have been inclined to admit.[11]

On the other hand, the community editors for this volume often insisted that transcribed oral traditions, and certainly Native-language texts, were among their most important literary productions. In some cases, Native people like Claudia Chicklas (Abenaki) have written down family traditions on their own. Others, like Jesse Bruchac (Abenaki) or Ella Sekatau (Narragansett), have retranslated earlier writings into their indigenous languages or created altogether new writing in those languages. Even some of the more "corrupt" texts by non-Native ethnographers, like Abby Alger's recordings of stories from Maine, sometimes appear in the bibliographies of this book, because they have been useful to Native communities, often reappropriated by them for purposes of cultural and linguistic revitalization.

One final editorial choice worth noting is my decision to organize the literature chronologically. I wanted to emphasize continuous presence—the reality that indigenous people have written, and written in English, since very soon after European arrival and have continued to do so, in every Euro-American form as well as some deeply "indigenous" ones. But readers will immediately notice large historical gaps in each chapter. Again, the absence (to take just one example) of very early Schaghticoke writings doesn't mean that Schaghticoke people weren't writing in the seventeenth century; it means only that the community editors chose to emphasize more recent work. Hopefully, readers will take these gaps as invitations to try and find, reprint, and reread that literature; at the very least, readers should be aware that the gaps tell us much more about Native people's access to (and perhaps interest in) the mechanics of publishing and preservation than they do about what Native people were actually writing at a given historical moment.

In choosing which texts to present, and how, I deferred to the community editors, though they varied in how they approached these choices. Some took almost total responsibility for collecting the writings. The outstandingly efficient Stephanie Fielding (Mohegan) put a notice in the tribal newsletter calling for submissions; she and I were also in frequent conversation about the evolving chapter with then-Tribal Librarian/Archivist Faith Davison and Medicine Woman Melissa Tantaquidgeon Zobel. In Maine, Donald Soctomah (Passamaquoddy) solicited contributions through his extensive interpersonal networks; Cheryl Stedtler (Nipmuc), working from her home in New Jersey, collected writing almost entirely via email, while also combing through her own extensive archives.

While some living writers (particularly those who are already published) asked the editorial team to choose which texts to include, we always encouraged them to submit pieces of their own choice. This method—which Lisa Brooks has called a "relinquishment of editorial control to the gathering place"—yielded some fascinating continuities, as in the Abenaki case (where many writers "home in" on the Connecticut River Valley), or the Wampanoag case (where writers return to particular events in colonial history).[12]

The Penobscots have a unique structure, an entire Cultural and Historic Preservation Department, which asks scholars working with Penobscot materials to come discuss their work in progress. So although Carol Dana, the Penobscot community editor, was relatively hands-off herself when it came to determining which texts were in or out, the Penobscot chapter benefited from input from a sizable group of knowledgeable and authoritative tribal members, who weighed in about which writers they felt best represented Penobscot history and interests.

In a few cases, community editors had distinct visions of what they wanted their respective tribal sections to accomplish. Joan Tavares Avant (Wampanoag) came to the project with a distinct historical mission, wanting to highlight the Wampanoags' continuous presence at Mashpee and Aquinnah; as such, she tended to gravitate toward historical writings. Two editors from up north, each working with some of the larger slates of *published* tribal writing, crafted chapters that emphasize tribal writing as a *nation-building* enterprise. Jaime Battiste (Mi'kmaq) is a legal scholar, and as such, he chose texts that demonstrate the continuity and power of Mi'kmaq law and sovereignty. Lisa Brooks (Abenaki), whose knowledge of early regional Native writing is encyclopedic, strategically selected texts underscoring Abenaki commitment to tribal homeland, community, language, and story. These chapters, and others, challenge the very shape of "New England" by showing how these tribal nations preexisted, and continue to traverse, state and national borders.

Not all Native communities have such well-oiled intratribal communicative structures or elders or junior scholars with the time and resources to coordinate a tribal anthology. This meant that some nations were not quite ready to be included, even though tribal members expressed interest and even though those nations have produced ample bodies of writing (e.g., Golden Hill Paugussett in Connecticut). This nearly happened with the Maliseet chapter, but Juana Perley (one of several Maliseet people with whom I had been in conversation with over the past few years) stepped in at the last moment to provide an introduction to the small slate of literature I had been able to amass with guidance from her and some of the other Maliseet writers included here.

Even where tribal input was the most widespread and vigorous (e.g., Mohegan, Penobscot, and Passamaquoddy), "tribal input" should not be taken to mean that any tribe has somehow "officially" signed off on the present project—nor, certainly, that every tribal member would agree with every selection or even approve of the direction of the tribal chapter overall. All of the community editors were keenly aware of the limitations of the anthology, particularly because we needed to set limits on the length of tribal chapters lest the book become too big to print, and finally because we needed to impose deadlines lest the book never appear at all. Under such constraints, everyone involved in this project readily acknowledges that the current selection is only a snapshot of much larger literary traditions—that, indeed, they were often working from the knowledge, memory, and agendas of a finite number of people, not from any "objective," definitive determination of what constituted the "best" writings. Karen Kilcup is probably right that every anthology, wittingly or unwittingly, creates a "miniature canon," but anthologists can at least remind themselves, and their readers: *It could have been otherwise.*

Many standard statements of editorial practice, particularly in academic books, give readers a sense of what to look for in terms of uniformity—where and how obvious misspellings were corrected, and so on. This was difficult in the present volume for several reasons.

Among the many forms of violence that Euro-Americans have inflicted on Native people, there is editorial violence. It isn't inflicted *only* on indigenous writers (Emily Dickinson's distinctive and indispensable punctuation was initially "corrected" out of existence), but editing has a particular, colonial baggage in Native literary history. One of the premises of this volume is that Native people began writing in English very early on, for purposes of cultural survival and self-determination; but it has to be acknowledged as well that they did so precisely because writing initially arrived as another form of colonial violence. Some of the earliest writings reproduced here (like the Dartmouth and Carlisle school letters) show how authorities often coerced Native people to write what they wanted to hear. By the late nineteenth century many writers, like Lewis Mitchell (Passamaquoddy), were being heavily edited, in ways that we can't always know or reconstruct.

Heavy editing and influence over content are also not peculiar to Native writing; *all* writing, Native or non-Native, is mediated. Anyone who has ever taught writing—or, for that matter, anyone who has ever written a sentence for another's inspection—knows this; but in practice, most writers and editors also find themselves newly surprised (and sometimes alarmed) by how readily "correcting" a text slides into changing its meaning. The writers and editors working on *Dawnland Voices* knew it too, and we had some interesting conversations, and occasional disagreements, about what to change, what to annotate, what to edit.

The bulk of this writing was initially unpublished or self-published in the form of small-run pamphlets through entities like Amazon or (increasingly) online; some were also originally disseminated through small, low-budget local newsletters. In turn, some of those were archived in small personal and tribal collections, sometimes as clippings or digital photographs without complete information about their provenance. Native communities, in fact, maintain remarkably good stewardship of their literary traditions—far better stewardship, in many cases, than the best-funded libraries and the most esteemed publishing houses—but they don't necessarily do it according to the mandates of those institutions. Some of the texts included below, then, lack some of the attribution of titles, dates, and other information that academics tend to demand.

Further, as noncommercial, community-oriented works with limited distribution, many of these poems, stories, and speeches contained most of the mechanical errors and inconsistencies you usually find in such publications. Where it was immediately apparent that errors were genuinely errors, the community editors and I made a first pass at correcting them, followed by professional copyeditors. My own wish was to make corrections with the lightest possible hand, so as not to sacrifice some of the aesthetic edginess that, personally, I have always found most challenging and interesting as a reader of Native American literature. Still, in some cases writers pushed back; so readers accustomed to the more uniform editing practices of university presses may be brought up short by some idiosyncratic choices across the collection—in capitalization or in poetic syntax, for instance. In other cases, some authors chose not to make their birth years known; still others preferred not to annotate certain Native-language terms, events, or locations.

Tlingit author Nora Marks Dauenhauer, who has worked with non-academic Tlingit community members to record traditional stories, has explained this dynamic usefully: she finds that community members are usually "eager to write down local traditions, but are not willing to learn and use a standard orthography," adding that, "[w]hereas literacy is perceived by teachers, linguists and folklorists as a purely technical matter, for members of the indigenous community it can be a profound emotional issue deeply bound up with group identity and self-concept" (Dauenhauer and Dauenhauer 13). Therefore, as much as possible we (community editors, copyeditors, the press, and I) tried to respect authors' stated wishes. If the author is living, we returned the piece to him or her for approval. Where the author is deceased, the community editors had the final say.

As all of these details about procedure might suggest, *Dawnland Voices* has been years in the making, and the manuscript and its individual submissions have gone through countless iterations. When I say we respected authors' wishes "as much as possible," I mean "as much as we could manage and control," given the large number of people involved in submitting, reading, formatting, and editing the text. Any writer who has published knows that from time to time undesired changes and errors slip through even the most scrupulous editing processes. I take full responsibility for any such changes or errors.

Once you deliberately involve even more than the usual hordes of people in the production of a book, you become acutely aware that everything—the table of contents, the arrangement of the materials, the editing—could indeed have been otherwise. In this sense the community editors and I were like teachers creating a course syllabus. Teachers have a finite number of days to cover a topic, so they are forced to make hard choices, always aware that there are other choices that could do just as well. Classes have to start at a certain point with a subject, after all, and teachers have to make decisions, justifying them as best they can. Most of the best teachers I know are continually revising their classes, and many even "de-center" them by inviting students to contribute readings and assignments.

Some of the community editors and I started to wonder: what if we could do this with a book? The rapidly expanding and shifting world of digital publishing is opening up (and complicating) just such possibilities for the dissemination of writing, for literary form, for conversations among authors and readers. As this book goes to press, a few of the editors and I, along with some of my students, are starting to experiment with web-based anthologizing. *Writing of Indigenous New England* (indigenousnewengland .com) promises to be a wonderfully rich and easy-to-use interface allowing writers, tribal historic preservation officers, local archivists, and others at different locations to upload materials of their own choice, annotating and editing them as they see fit.

We can think of *Dawnland Voices* as a hub and the website as offering different "spokes."[13] The first spoke is a collaborative bibliography. In the tribal chapters that follow, we offer bibliographies that help readers find further literature within particular tribal traditions. But bibliographies, of course, are infinitely extensible, so we have created a collaborative online listing available for additions, subtractions, and revisions from anyone who cares to log on (https://www.zotero.org/groups /indigenous_new_england_literature).

The second spoke (or set of spokes) is our online exhibit space, since the anthology itself is also extensible. In *Writing of Indigenous New England*, authorized editors and contributors can begin uploading the many texts we couldn't include in this book: letters from family archives, tribal newsletters, out-of-print poetry and fiction, even born-digital work. Our website uses the Omeka platform developed by George Mason University's Center for History and New Media; this platform allows curators to organize material by "collection" (in our case, by tribal nation) or by "exhibit." To date, I have found that an exhibit makes an excellent project for a class and a community partner: college students can provide the interpretive and technical work that a local historical society or tribal historian might need in preserving and disseminating materials. Our first exhibit—a collaboration between the Mt. Kearsarge Indian Museum in Warner, New Hampshire, and students in ENG 740: Native American Writing before 1800—focused on Abenaki baskets as texts. It is my hope that colleagues at other universities will partner with tribal historians, authors, museums, and other entities to produce new knowledge about regional indigenous literary traditions.

Finally, any book can be a hub for conversation and exchange among readers and writers, so another "spoke" of our online site involves social networking. One of the most enjoyable and enlightening parts of compiling this anthology was the part that, right now, most readers can't see: the conversations, questions, and debates that surrounded particular texts or editorial decisions. *Writing of Indigenous New England* has an online reading group (brokered at goodreads.com) where readers, students, tribal community members, and authors can "speak back" to the literature, explaining what makes it meaningful, even arguing with it and generating new writing in response.

In both print and online formats, regional indigenous writings could see their "afterlives" greatly expanded—to borrow a term from the literary historian Janice Radway, who has been writing about another marginalized body of work: 1990s girl "zines." Radway's assessment of these edgy, low-budget magazines resonates nicely with many of the texts contained in *Dawnland Voices*: she views them as "complex aesthetic performances that defy and disorient those who would try to make sense of them in conventional ways" (147). Like many other disempowered groups, Native American people will continue to write, often defining and promoting that writing in opposition to (or through sheer lack of interest in) academic ideas about what constitutes literary value. Still, while an academically sanctioned anthology may not be necessary for the existence of the tradition, we should still take seriously its capacity to "interject the voices and works of [Native people] into the legitimated precincts of knowledge production—that is, into magazines and books, libraries, and schools and universities" and, as such, to "render [them] not merely visible but audible" (Radway 145).

Hopefully *Dawnland Voices* contributes something to the visibility and audibility of Native American literature from New England. If there is one thing that everyone involved in this book seems happy about, it's that it is only the beginning of much longer projects and collaborations—hopefully with some of the people who are reading it today.

Notes

1. See *Studies in American Indian Literatures* 24.3 (Fall 2012), a special issue that Margaret Lukens and I guest-edited.
2. Some newer anthologies are doing a better job of acknowledging New England Native writers; see, for instance, Parker's *Changing Is Not Vanishing*. One fascinating older exception, heavier on New England selections, was *Literature of the American Indian* (1973), edited by Thomas Sanders and a Narragansett-Wampanoag man, Walter Peek. Another unusually capacious anthology was *Returning the Gift*—not surprising, as it was edited by Abenaki author and publisher Joseph Bruchac. The Cherokee writer-editor MariJo Moore is usually attuned to writers from around the United States and Canada; she included Carol Bachofner (Abenaki) in *Genocide of the Mind*. Thoughtful anthologies focusing on other regions of the United States include those by Hobson, Tigerman and Ottery, and Sarris.

3. For a discussion of vanishing-Indian mythology in the South, see Geary Hobson, Janet McAdams, and Kathryn Walkiewicz's excellent anthology of Native writing from that region, *The People Who Stayed*.

4. Jean O'Brien's *Dispossession by Degrees* explains in considerable detail how New England people's land bases were reduced. Eva Garroutte's (Cherokee) *Real Indians* provides an indispensable introduction to how policies like blood-quantum regulations have legislated indigenous identities.

5. See, for instance, Boissevain.

6. E.g., Miles 192.

7. Among historians, Colin Calloway has led the way, publishing several groundbreaking essays by colleagues in *After King Philip's War*. Among archaeologists, Robert Goodby deserves special note, along with the other researchers represented in Jordan Kerber's *Cross-cultural Collaboration*.

8. This is the argument Womack has famously made in *Red on Red*. Other scholars working in this vein include Weaver, Warrior, Justice, Kelsey, Lisa Brooks, and the writers in Janice Acoose et al., *Reasoning Together*.

9. See Parker, *Invention of Native American Literature*, 83ff.

10. Silko, "Old-Time Indian Attack."

11. On Black Elk, see DeMallie.

12. Lisa Brooks, personal communication, August 16, 2011. I borrow the term "home in" from an influential essay by William Bevis, who described the plots of many Native American novels as organized around a return to homeland.

13. Following Renya Ramirez's important book *Native Hubs*, I made a similar argument about the poetry of Mihku Paul (Maliseet) and Alice Azure (Mi'kmaq) in "Rethinking Recognition."

Works Cited

Acoose, Janice, et al. *Reasoning Together: The Native Critics Collective*. Norman: University of Oklahoma Press, 2008. Print.

Adelson, Naomi. *"Being Alive Well": Health and the Politics of Cree Well-Being*. Toronto: University of Toronto Press, 2000. Print.

Alfred, Taiaiake. *Peace, Power, Righteousness: An Indigenous Manifesto*. Don Mills ON: Oxford University Press, 1999. Print.

Alger, Abby. *In Indian Tents: Stories Told by Penobscot, Passamaquoddy and Micmac Indians*. Honolulu: University Press of the Pacific, 2006. Print.

Apess, William. *On Our Own Ground: The Complete Writings of William Apess, a Pequot*. Ed. Barry O'Connell. Amherst: University of Massachusetts Press, 1992. Print.

Bevis, William. "Native American Novels: Homing In." In *Recovering the Word: Essays on Native American Literature*. Ed. Brian Swann and Arnold Krupat. Berkeley: University of California Press, 1987. 580–620. Print.

Bird, Gloria, and Joy Harjo, eds. *Reinventing the Enemy's Language: Contemporary Native Women's Writings of North America*. New York: W. W. Norton, 1998. Print.

Boissevain, Ethel. "The Detribalization of the Narragansett Indians: A Case Study." *Ethnohistory* 3.3 (1956): 225–45. Web. 22 Aug. 2011.

Brooks, Joanna, and Samson Occom. *The Collected Writings of Samson Occom, Mohegan: Literature and Leadership in Eighteenth-Century Native America.* New York: Oxford University Press, 2006. Print.

Brooks, Lisa. *The Common Pot: The Recovery of Native Space in the Northeast.* Minneapolis: University of Minnesota Press, 2008. Print.

Bross, Kristina, and Hilary Wyss, eds. *Early Native Literacies in New England: A Documentary Anthology.* Amherst: University of Massachusetts Press, 2008. Print.

Bruchac, Joseph. *Returning the Gift: Poetry and Prose from the First North American Native Writers' Festival.* Tucson: University of Arizona Press, 1994. Print.

Calloway, Colin G. *After King Philip's War: Presence and Persistence in Indian New England.* Hanover N H: Dartmouth University Press, 1997. Print.

Cruikshank, Julie. *Life Lived Like a Story: Life Stories of Three Yukon Native Elders.* Lincoln: University of Nebraska Press, 1992. Print.

Dauenhauer, Nora, and Richard Dauenhauer. "The Paradox of Talking on the Page: Some Aspects of the Tlingit and Haida Experience." *Talking on the Page: Editing Aboriginal Oral Texts.* Ed. Laura J. Murray and Keren Rice. Toronto: University of Toronto Press, 1999. 3–41. Papers given at the Thirty-Second Annual Conference on Editorial Problems. Print.

DeMallie, Raymond J. *The Sixth Grandfather: Black Elk's Teachings Given to John G. Neihardt.* Lincoln: University of Nebraska Press, 1985. Print.

Garroutte, Eva Marie. *Real Indians: Identity and the Survival of Native America.* Berkeley: University of California Press, 2003. Print.

Hobson, Geary, Janet McAdams, and Kathryn Walkiewicz, eds. *The People Who Stayed: Southeastern Indian Writing after Removal.* Norman: University of Oklahoma Press, 2010. Print.

Justice, Daniel Heath. *Our Fire Survives the Storm: A Cherokee Literary History.* Minneapolis: University of Minnesota Press, 2006. Print.

Kelsey, Penelope Myrtle. *Tribal Theory in Native American Literature: Dakota and Haudenosaunee Writing and Indigenous Worldviews.* Lincoln: University of Nebraska Press, 2008. Print.

Kerber, Jordan E. *Cross-cultural Collaboration: Native Peoples and Archaeology in the Northeastern United States.* Lincoln: University of Nebraska Press, 2006. Print.

Kilcup, Karen. "The Poetry and Prose of Recovery Work." *On Anthologies: Politics and Pedagogy.* Ed. Jeffrey R. DiLeo. Lincoln: University of Nebraska Press, 2004. 112–34. Print.

Lepore, Jill. *The Name of War: King Philip's War and the Origins of American Identity.* New York: Vintage, 1999. Print.

Miles, Tiya. *Ties That Bind: The Story of an Afro-Cherokee Family in Slavery and Freedom.* Berkeley: University of California Press, 2006. Print.

Moore, MariJo, ed. *Genocide of the Mind: New Native American Writing.* New York: Thunder's Mouth Press/Nation Books, 2003. Print.

Nicolar, Joseph. *The Life and Traditions of the Red Man: A Rediscovered Treasure of Native American Literature.* 1891. Ed. Annette Kolodny. Durham NC: Duke University Press, 2007. Print.

O'Brien, Jean M. *Dispossession by Degrees: Indian Land and Identity in Natick, Massachusetts, 1650–1790.* Lincoln: University of Nebraska Press, 2003. Print.

———. *Firsting and Lasting: Writing Indians Out of Existence in New England.* Minneapolis: University of Minnesota Press, 2010. Print.

Parker, Robert Dale. *Changing Is Not Vanishing: A Collection of American Indian Poetry to 1930.* Philadelphia: University of Pennsylvania Press, 2010. Print.

———. *The Invention of Native American Literature.* Ithaca NY: Cornell University Press, 2003. Print.

Purdy, John L., and James Ruppert, eds. *Nothing but the Truth: An Anthology of Native American Literature.* Upper Saddle River NJ: Prentice Hall, 2000. Print.

Radway, Janice. "Zines, Half-Lives, and Afterlives: On the Temporalities of Social and Political Change." *PMLA: Publications of the Modern Language Association of America* 126.1 (2011): 140–50. Print.

Ramirez, Renya. *Native Hubs : Culture, Community, and Belonging in Silicon Valley and Beyond.* Durham NC: Duke University Press, 2007. Print.

Sanders, Thomas E., and Walter Peek, eds. *Literature of the American Indian.* Beverly Hills: Glencoe Press, 1973. Print.

Sarris, Greg. *The Sound of Rattles and Clappers: A Collection of New California Indian Writing.* Tucson: University of Arizona Press, 1994. Print.

Senier, Siobhan. "Rethinking Recognition: Mi'kmaq and Maliseet Poets Re-write Land and Community." *MELUS: Multi-ethnic Literature of the U.S.* 37.1 (2012): 15–34. Print.

Silko, Leslie Marmon. "An Old-Time Indian Attack in Two Parts." *The Remembered Earth.* Ed. Geary Hobson. Albuquerque: University of New Mexico Press, 1979. 211–16. Print.

Tigerman, Kathleen, and Jim Ottery. *Wisconsin Indian Literature: Anthology of Native Voices.* Madison: University of Wisconsin Press, 2006. Print.

Warrior, Robert Allen. *Tribal Secrets: Recovering American Indian Intellectual Traditions.* Minneapolis: University of Minnesota Press, 1995. Print.

Weaver, Jace. *That the People Might Live: Native American Literatures and Native American Community.* New York: Oxford University Press, 1997. Print.

Wolfe, Patrick. *Settler Colonialism and the Transformation of Anthropology: The Politics and Poetics of an Ethnographic Event.* New York: Continuum, 1999. Print.

Womack, Craig. *Red on Red: Native American Literary Separatism.* Minneapolis: University of Minnesota Press, 1999. Print.

MI'KMAQ

Introduction

Jaime Battiste

The Mi'kmaq have occupied the eastern coast and forests of Canada and the New England area, which collectively is called Mi'kma'ki, for as long as anyone can remember. The Mi'kmaq continue to transmit their knowledge, beliefs, customs, and practices through performances and oral traditions, based on storytelling, songs, ceremonies, symbols, and literacies, including wampum to record important teachings. Representing some of these legacies, I have sought to balance the writings in this section across the Mi'kmaw districts from New England, New Brunswick, the Gaspé Peninsula in Quebec, Prince Edward Island, Nova Scotia, and Newfoundland. As may be seen on a map, this territory is shaped like a crescent moon and symbolized as such on the Mi'kmaw flag.

Since at least the sixteenth century, Mi'kmaw people have been in contact with Europeans and have conducted diplomatic relations through treaties, compacts, agreements, and concordats with European sovereigns and other national powers. Much has been written and documented about Mi'kmaq from the viewpoint of Eurocentric scholars, but many of these sources are based on outsiders' perceptions about Mi'kmaq. Over the past generation, guided by Mi'kmaw scholars, Elders, students, and leaders, a Mi'kmaw renaissance has emerged, with many Mi'kmaw authors beginning to build not only on written history but also on Mi'kmaw knowledge and on traditions within Mi'kma'ki. In particular, the late Mi'kmaw author Rita Joe reminds us that it is important for Mi'kmaq to create writing, instead of just being written about.

This collection of essays, stories, poetry, and fiction was gathered with an aim of learning from the Mi'kmaw people through their words, experiences, imagination, creativity, and perspectives. Their writings demonstrate Mi'kmaw people's resilience under the suffering and humiliation of colonization as well as showcase Mi'kmaw talents. This work continues to show readers that Mi'kmaw knowledge and culture are current, dynamic, and gathering strength as contributions by academics, storytellers, and students build on Mi'kmaw teachings, voices, and visions.

Recognizing that "history" is a contested Eurocentric discipline, Mi'kmaq have understood their traditions in a different way, and this is a key theme within this set of readings. Mi'kmaw poets and their creative storytelling have also been instrumental in taking a moment in time and capturing it with a few poignant words. The late Rita Joe has led the way, inspiring a new generation of Mi'kmaw poets who continue to tell a new story for Mi'kmaq through poetry and creative writing. This collection can give only a glimpse of the poetry and other genres that circulate among Mi'kmaq.

Mi'kmaw academics have analyzed the colonial experience of the Mi'kmaq in five periods. The first is *precontact*, which marks an indeterminate time before the late sixteenth century, which in turn marks the beginning of the second period, the *contact period*. The third period is the *treaty diplomacy era* (1630–1796), in which Mi'kmaq diplomats advocated for and negotiated treaties with European settlers and royalty. The *treaty denial era* (1800–1982) is the fourth period, marking a dark time in our experience, when Mi'kmaw people were denied the rights that they had negotiated and when they often were the target of assimilation policies aimed at destroying the Mi'kmaq culture, language, knowledge, and ways of life. The fifth period is the *treaty recognition era* (1982 to present day).

During the first period Mi'kmaw people had their own governance structure, with an economy based on trade within our nations and an education based on survival and cooperation. Within Mi'kmaw teachings of this period are many stories that are viewed as fundamental to Mi'kmaq life. Undoubtedly, one of the most famous is the Mi'kmaw creation story, which contains many teachings about our holistic relationships with our families and our ecosystem. We have chosen a shorter version, translated and transmitted through generations and recorded by Keptin Stephen Augustine, a member of the Mi'kmaw Grand Council, which is the traditional governance structure of the Mi'kmaw people and continues to exist today despite years of oppression and discrimination.

Author Daniel Paul has been a passionate activist and advocate for justice for the Mi'kmaq to correct the history of oppression, assimilation, and cultural genocide. His book *We Were Not the Savages* has been a compelling resource for many Mi'kmaq and non-Mi'kmaq alike, revealing the dark legacy of colonial history that the Mi'kmaq survived. In particular, he works to create awareness of Governor Edward Cornwallis's 1749 "extirpation policy," which advocated the total annihilation of the Mi'kmaw people by placing a bounty on Mi'kmaw scalps. Regardless of this legacy, to this day Governor Cornwallis is honored as the founding father of Halifax and continues to have statues, streets, and buildings named after him.

During the treaty diplomacy period the Mi'kmaq entered into treaties with different European nations. Mi'kmaw laws, then, are important for understanding why so many different treaties were negotiated between the Mi'kmaw Grand Council and the British Crown. Treaty research has been a lifelong pursuit of James Sakej Henderson, and his introduction to the treaties makes it easier to understand the complex legal and historic framework within them. The largest essay within this collection is the story of the Mi'kmaw Grand Council relayed in the Covenant Chain. In one of the only works written down—and in English—by the executives of the Mi'kmaq Grand Council, the plight of the Mi'kmaq Grand Council and their continued struggle for justice is showcased.

Another important theme within this collection is the relationship between the Mi'kmaq and the territory now called New England, or Pastimkawa'ki, as we have come to know it. While the majority of Mi'kmaq live in Canada, they have always had a special relationship with New England. Perhaps the best illustrations of this are the Treaty of 1725 at Boston and the treaty with the newly formed United States signed in 1776 at Watertown. The Mi'kmaq at the time were considered a fierce threat and fighting force, and their knowledge of the eastern coast made them a great ally to any nation that planned to inhabit or defend newly created colonial settlements. Under the authority of these treaties, many Mi'kmaq sought a livelihood in New England, and with the federal recognition of the Aroostook Band of Micmacs in 1991, the relationships have been strengthened and continue today.

The treaty denial period is another dark period of cultural genocide for the Mi'kmaw people, when policies such as the Indian Act, Indian residential schools, and centralization were aimed at assimilating Mi'kmaw people and controlling their resources. This collection thus includes documented history on Indian residential schools and centralization, including an excerpt from the Grand Council's Covenant Chain. Isabelle

Knockwood's book *Out of the Depths* is a suggested reading for those look-ing for more information on the residential schools attended by Mi'kmaq.

The Indian residential schools, by eroding Mi'kmaw culture, stealing the language from many, and creating ongoing distrust of government and religion, have left a tragic legacy among victims and their families. Many survivors of the residential schools have experienced a syndrome that closely resembles post-traumatic stress disorder; as a result, several genera-tions of Mi'kmaq have grown up in households filled with personal and social problems. Centralization, which was built on the promises of better housing, health services, education, and welfare payments, decreased Mi'kmaw participation in the workforce and in traditional methods of sustenance such as hunting, fishing, and crafts. This has created among many in Mi'kmaw communities a sense of entitlement for justice to be served and for the government to fulfill promises made more than two generations ago.

The essay "Structural Unemployment: The Mi'kmaq Experience," by Dr. Marie Battiste, provides a brief look at the role centralization played the experience of Mi'kmaw people. This policy was meant to move Mi'kmaq into two centralized reserves in Nova Scotia, supposedly saving the federal government on costs of administering funding to the Mi'kmaq, but it also isolated Mi'kmaq in two reserves away from their traditional communi-ties and sustainable practices, while limiting their access to employment, resources, and other economic benefits. By doing so, the federal and provincial governments created a welfare economy for the Mi'kmaq and a dependence on government handouts for their day-to-day survival. Today the impacts of both the Indian residential schools and centralization con-tinue to affect Mi'kmaw people's self-determination and self-sufficiency.

The recent Mi'kmaw revival and successes of the Mi'kmaq in the treaty recognition era have been based largely on the Mi'kmaw treaties and the recognition of inherent Aboriginal rights. In 1929 the Canadian justice system was quick to dismiss the claims of treaty rights of Mi'kmaq in the *Sylliboy* decision; the recent trilogy of Mi'kmaw rights cases—*Simon*, *Marshall*, and *Sappier/Grey*—has recognized rights of the Mi'kmaw people and provided hope for a different future. Both the Constitution of Canada and the Canada Act of 1982 create a legal context in which the Mi'kmaq have been able to compel the government of Canada into negotiations based on Mi'kmaq rights.[1] Included in this Mi'kmaw collection, therefore, is the conclusion to my essay titled "Understanding the Progression of Mi'kmaw Law," which highlights how Mi'kmaw traditions and teaching have been used as the basis for a constitutional recognition and reconciliation of Mi'kmaw rights and explores the opportunities and challenges that lie ahead.

As Mi'kmaw people look ahead to a new era that involves treaty implementation and reconciliation with the various levels of government, an empowering education system is ever more needed. Of merit in higher education are the science and humanities courses that are now taught using traditional pedagogical methods along with contemporary Western systems. Elders have called this method a "two-eyed seeing" approach.

While several interpretations of history have been written by Mi'kmaw and non-Mi'kmaw men and women, the Mi'kmaq today are beginning to document their own oral traditions in creative forms such as film, photography, and art. The novel *Stones and Switches* by the late Lorne Simon tells the story of a young Depression-era Mi'kmaw man who seeks understanding of the world around him and of what it means to be Mi'kmaq at that time. And many new creative works are emerging, including documentaries like *The Spirit World*, by Keptin John Joe Sark of Prince Edward Island, and *The Spirit of Annie Mae* (Aquash), by Cathy Martin of Millbrook.[2] The oral history of the Mi'kmaq in its most beautiful form can also be found within Mi'kmaw music, by bands such as Morning Star, The Relatives, Eagle Feather, and A Tribe Called Mi'kmaq. It is important to remember that while the written word has been used by most academics, modern media have begun to help the Mi'kmaq preserve their oral traditions.

The final theme that this Mi'kmaw collection explores is the relationship between the Mi'kmaq and the New England area. This is a personal journey for me as well, as my mother was born and raised in Houlton, Maine. Many members of my extended family have lived and raised their children in the New England area, and some continue to live there today. Much like the tales of other Mi'kmaq who sought a better livelihood in New England, the last few pieces below focus on Mi'kmaq who chose to travel to areas of Massachusetts or Maine. Elder Elsie Charles Basque's story from "Here to There" is a short story that documents the journey of one family. Given that many Mi'kmaw families continue to live in the New England area, during my research I asked some of these families why they chose to live in New England, away from their ancestral homes and family.

Their stories tell of better economic opportunities, less discriminatory work environments, or wanting to be part of their own family's history in New England. Many Mi'kmaq have experienced greater educational and economic opportunities in cities such as Boston, Portland, or Bangor, which they feel they could not have found in Canada.

Today Mi'kmaq continue to do seasonal migrations to harvest the blueberries in Maine, a kind of rite of passage for many Mi'kmaw youth who took to the fields as soon as they were able. They did so in order to make money for the upcoming school year, for school clothes, or to support their families. For many, it is the way to pay off their cars or to get needed items that they could not afford otherwise. My own earliest memories of that time include being fourteen and working all day under the hot sun for two dollars per box of berries. I received my first paycheck for hard manual labor, which I then proudly used to buy my school clothes in Maine. I have fond memories of those days, staying in small cabins in Maine, without electricity or running water, being so sore from head to toe from bending over in the hot sun all day but eating well and enjoying the ancient camaraderie of communal friends and family. Like my ancestors, I spent summers in Maine, taking part in what they had done for generations before me. In his poetry Lindsay Marshall captures the experiences of so many who have gone to New England for generations to gain a temporary livelihood in those blueberry fields; however, for some, New England is not just a temporary location, but home. This ability of Mi'kmaw people—to be connected to homeland and kin even while living in and traveling to different places—is reflected in the works of the last two writers in this section, Alice Azure and Starlit Simon.

Chief Stephen Augustine

(Tribal Elder)

An elder of the Elsipogtog (Big Cove) First Nation in New Brunswick, Stephen Augustine is a hereditary chief on the Mi'kmaq Grand Council. He also serves as curator of eastern maritime ethnology at the Canadian Museum of Civilization in Quebec. In 2009 Augustine received the National Aboriginal Achievement Award for Culture, Heritage, and Spirituality. Of the selection below, he says, "My grandmother, who lived to be one hundred years old, passed this story on to me. This is part of the Mi'kmaq creation story." Chief Augustine wrote it especially for this volume.

Mi'kmaq Creation Story

In Mi'kmaq tradition there are seven levels of creation. These levels correspond to seven stages in the creation of the world. The first level is the act of creation itself. Some people would call it the Creator, but in Mi'kmaq culture it is more about the wonder and unfolding of creation. The word we use is *kisúlk*. This means "you are being created." Kisúlk is the Giver of Life.

The second level is the Sun, which we call Niskam, or Grandfather. When we stand in the Sun we cast a shadow. The shadow represents the spirits of our ancestors. Grandfather Sun puts spirit into life.

The third level is Sitqamúk, Mother Earth. Mother Earth gives us all the necessities of life through the elements of the earth: water, rocks, soils, plants, animals, fish, and so on. Mother Earth sustains life.

The fourth level of creation is Kluskap, the First One Who Spoke.[3] He is created from a bolt of lightning that hits the surface of Mother Earth. He is made of the elements of the earth: feathers and bone and skin and dirt and grass and sand and pebbles and water. An eagle comes to Kluskap with a message from the Giver of Life, Grandfather Sun, and Mother Earth. The eagle tells Kluskap that he will be joined by his family, who will help him understand his place in this world.

The first of Kluskap's family to arrive is the Grandmother, Nukumi.

She is formed from a rock. She brings wisdom and knowledge. The Grandmother is the fifth level of creation.

The next of Kluskap's family to arrive is the Nephew, Netawansum. He is formed from the sweet-smelling grass. He brings strength and can see into the future. The Nephew is the sixth level of creation.

The last of Kluskap's family to arrive is the Mother, Nikanaptekewisqw. She is formed from a leaf. She brings love for all her children, so that they will care for one another. She also brings the colours of the world. The Mother is the seventh level of creation.

As each member of his family arrives, Kluskap asks his fellow beings—the animals, the fish, and the plants—to sustain the Mi'kmaq peoples. Kluskap also calls upon the wind to fan the sparks left by the first bolt of lightning. This gives birth to the Great Spirit Fire. The seven families of the Algonquin peoples are formed from sparks that fly out of this fire and land upon the Earth. The Mi'kmaq are one of these families.

Grand Council of the Mi'kmaq Nation

Grand Chief Donald Marshall Sr., Grand Captain
Alexander Denny, Putus Simon Marshall

The leadership of the Grand Council is made up of three positions: the *kjisakamow* (grand chief) is the ceremonial head of state; the *kjikeptin* (grand captain) is the executive of the council; and the *putus* (wisdom) is the keeper of the constitution and the rememberer of the treaties.) The following essay, which originally appeared in the collection *Drumbeat: Anger and Renewal in Indian Country*, is a crucial piece of Mi'kmaq literary history, given that the Grand Council so rarely records its knowledge in writing, or in English.

The Covenant Chain

THE CONFRONTATION

Ironically, the morning of September 17, 1988, was a calm and beautiful day on Hunter's Mountain in Nova Scotia. Soon, however, over 100 of our Mi'kmaq harvesters and their supporters arrived to mark the beginning of what would be a most controversial two-week Treaty Moose Harvest.

Grand Chief Donald Marshall Sr. stepped forward and led the hushed group in a brief Mi'kmaq prayer to guide our harvesters.

Hidden from view, a short distance up the mountain road, scores of provincial game wardens and support Royal Canadian Mounted Police (RCMP) officers were waiting. Just three days earlier the Nova Scotia minister of Lands and Forests cavalierly declared that the Treaty Moose Harvest was "unauthorized." Orders were issued by the government of Nova Scotia to stop Mi'kmaq harvesters from carrying out our planned harvest of moose.

Despite public announcements that the Mi'kmaq would be charged, the harvesters proceeded up the mountain. At the centre of the controversy was the 1985 *Simon* decision of the Supreme Court of Canada, which unanimously ruled that the 1752 Treaty between the British Crown and the Mi'kmaq Nation was valid.

In a few minutes, the harvesters' vehicles were stopped and searched. A government helicopter circled the area; reporters and film media mingled between officers and harvesters. The line of vehicles with harvesters stretched as far back as the eye could see down the mountain road. The day would be a long one. One by one the cars were searched and weapons seized. The officers even seized the harvesters' identification and sanction cards issued by the Grand Council.

Six of our harvesters were charged under a provincial law. Despite the tension, the armed confrontation provoked no retaliation and was peaceful. This day marked the beginning of another long struggle for the Mi'kmaq to exercise a right. But the story does not begin with that day; the story goes back far into our history—to a time when a chain of covenants was made.

THE COVENANT CHAIN

Protection and allegiance are fastened together by links; if a link is broken the chain will be loose. You must preserve this chain entire on your part by fidelity and obedience to the great King George the Third, and then you will have the security of this royal arm to defend you. I meet you now as His Majesty's graciously honoured servant in government and in his royal name to receive at this pillar, your public vows of obedience to build a covenant of peace with you, as upon the immovable rock of sincerity and truth, to free you from the chains of bondage, and to place you in the wide and fruitful field of English liberty. The laws will be like a great hedge about your rights and properties. If any break this hedge to hurt or injure you, the heavy weight of the laws will fall upon them and punish their disobedience.
—Nova Scotia governor Jonathan Belcher addressing the Mi'kmaq at Halifax, 1761, at ceremonies renewing the Treaty of 1752

Freedom and liberty, confrontation, subjugation, resistance—all of these words describe the current situation in Nova Scotia as it relates to relations between the Mi'kmaq people and our settler neighbours. Despite protections afforded by international and domestic law, a people are forcibly dispossessed of their land and resources, their governmental institutions are intentionally destabilized, their children condemned to a bleak future based on poverty and dependency—all so that others can reap a profit. Some backwater Third World dictatorship? No, Canada (Nova Scotia). Such has been the history of the Mi'kmaq people.

A youth is convicted of murder and sent to prison. After serving eleven years of his term, it is found that he has been wrongly convicted. Could this have anything to do with the fact that he was a Mi'kmaq?

It took this event to spark the public outcry that led to the establishment of a royal commission to study the Nova Scotia justice system. Although at the time of writing, the Royal Commission's final conclusions have not been made public, much of the testimony given during the course of the proceedings pointed to consistent and racist discrimination against Mi'kmaq citizens on the part of the state's police forces, provincial politicians, and the judiciary.

Solemn and binding treaties are signed between nations. These treaties are recognized and affirmed in the Royal Proclamation of 1763, the Constitution Act of 1982, and upheld in a landmark 1985 Supreme Court of Canada judgment. But when the citizens of one of those nations attempt to exercise their rights according to the terms of the treaties, they are arrested and harassed. Could this have anything to do with the fact that they are Mi'kmaq?

The treatment of the Mi'kmaq has only recently been the subject of media and public scrutiny, but that is not to say that previously all was well. It just goes to show how little Canadians know about what actually goes on in their own country. It also explains why Canadians have traditionally let their politicians and governments get away with so much. In this chapter, we intend to introduce you to our history and to our current struggles, as a way of shedding some light on this dark corner of the public's consciousness. To understand how things got to be this way, we will have to take you back a few hundred years, to the times when there were no great numbers of non-Mi'kmaq in our traditional territories. It is only by taking the journey back that one can really get a balanced understanding of what is happening now and where things are going.

SELF-RELIANCE AND SELF-DETERMINATION

The Mi'kmaq are used to dealing with other peoples. Prior to the arrival of the Europeans, we carried on relations with other indigenous peoples throughout North America, among other things for the purposes of trade, alliance, and friendship. All such dealings were based on mutual respect and cooperation and formalized through the treaty-making process. The Mi'kmaq called this international law, the law of Nikamanen. Treaties are spiritual as well as political compacts that confer solemn and binding obligations on the signatories. The spiritual basis of the treaties is crucial to an understanding of their meaning, since it represents an effort to elevate the treaties, and relations among peoples, beyond the vagaries of political opportunism and expediency. They are intended to develop through time to keep pace with events, while still preserving the original intentions and rights of the parties.

About six hundred years ago, the Mi'kmaq people were invaded from the west by the Haudenosaunee (the Iroquois). After a number of fierce battles, the invaders were beaten back, and a treaty of peace was concluded. With peace restored, the nation reorganized itself: all of Mikmakik, our traditional lands, was divided into seven *sakamowti* (districts), and each of these in turn was subdivided among *manywikamow* (clans). Each clan was led by a *sakamow* (chief); a *sa'ya* (spiritual leader); and a *keptin* (war chief).

Together, the *sakamow* and *keptin* from each district formed one national council, the Sante' Mawi'omi (grand council or "holy gathering"), whose purpose was to advise the people and defend the country, This national confederation was first created in the tenth century. It was called Awitkativitik ("many families in one house"). The ancient symbol of this union, which can still be seen carved into the rocks around Kejimkujik Lake, is a ring of seven hills (the seven districts) and seven crosses (the seven chiefs), surrounding the sun and the moon (who together represent Niskam, the Creator).

The Mikmaw Nation is an alliance of many aboriginal peoples who inhabited Mikmakik. The meaning of "Mi'kmaq" is "the allied people"; "Mikmaw" is singular. "Mikmakik" means "the land of friendship" and covers present-day Newfoundland, St. Pierre et Miquelon, Nova Scotia, New Brunswick, the Magdalen archipelago, and the Gaspé peninsula of Quebec.

The leadership of the Grand Council is made up of three positions: the *lijisakamow* (grand chief) is the ceremonial head of state; the *lijikeptin* (grand captain) is the executive of the council; and the *putus* (wisdom) is the keeper of the constitution and the rememberer of the treaties.)

Mi'kmaq economy was based upon hunting, fishing, gathering, and farming, as well as trading surplus resources with other nations. This economic regime was founded upon the overriding principle of sustainable, responsible development to ensure long-term self-reliance and prosperity for our people. Through economic self-reliance we were assured social and political self-determination: the freedom and liberty to decide for ourselves the future of our people. We were also great travelers, having learned the art of sailing centuries before the arrival of the Europeans. In our boats we explored the North American seacoast from the frozen ocean beyond Newfoundland down to the Gulf of Mexico and what is now known as Florida.

The Norsemen may have ventured onto Mi'kmaq lands a millennium ago, but it was not until the 1600s that we experienced any sustained contact with European peoples. This was when the French established tiny settlements within our territories to engage us in the fur trade.

The relationship that developed between our people and the French was based on mutual cooperation and respect, and we had no reason to perceive any threat to our lands or our sovereignty. However, there was one very serious consequence of this contact: disease. It is estimated that at our peak, there were 100,000 Mi'kmaq. Once the new diseases and sickness brought to North America by the Europeans took their toll, however, our numbers on the coast were substantially reduced, and we began to move inland.

One other important change that came out of our contact with the French was in the spiritual realm. On June 24, 1610, our *sakamow*, Membertou, was baptized as a Catholic, and a covenant was made to protect the priests of the church and the Frenchmen who brought the priests among us. A great wampum belt 2 metres (2 yards) in length records this concordat. On the left are the symbols of Catholicism: the crossed keys of the Holy See, a church, and a line of text from the gospels written in our own language. On the right are symbols of the power of the Grand Council: crossed lances, an armed *keptin*, a pipe and arrow, and seven hills representing the seven districts. At the centre, a priest and a chief hold a cross, and in the hand of the chief is the holy book. Over the course of the seventeenth century, the whole of the Mi'kmaq people became Catholics and took St. Ann as their patron.

Perhaps it was inevitable that we would be drawn into the imperial competition between the English and the French that took place throughout Europe and North America during the seventeenth and eighteenth centuries. In any event, the Mi'kmaq did become key players in this struggle as it affected our territories: because of our strength, we could not be ignored.

In their haste to destroy French settlements, British forces crossed and devastated our country, and the lands of our allies of the Wabanaki Confederacy (the Penobscots and Passamaquoddies of what is now northern New England and the Maliseets of the St. John River valley in New Brunswick were the core of this confederacy; from time to time the Mi'kmaq Nation coordinated foreign policy with its members). As a response, we permitted the king of France to erect fortifications on our soil, and for a number of years we harassed British shipping from north of Casco Bay to the Grand Banks.

The tug of war began as early as 1621, when King James I of England "granted" part of the eastern seaboard to a Scotsman, Sir William Alexander, and it was dubbed "Nova Scotia." However, this action met with stiff resistance from the Mi'kmaq: we refused to enter into any treaty relationship through Alexander. The French convinced England to relinquish its claim soon afterward. In 1689, war was declared between Great Britain and France, and the following year the French at Port Royal in Mikmakik surrendered to English forces.

Neither the Mi'kmaq nor France's other indigenous allies recognized British sovereignty, however, and we continued the war until 1699. We believed that it was a matter of religious as well as political freedom, because at that time we were of the understanding that the English were "pagans." It was many years later, in 1761, that Kjisakamow Toma Denny told the British, "I long doubted whether you was of this [Christian] faith. . . . I declare moreover that I did not believe you was baptized; but at present I know you much better than I did formerly."

By 1713, with the Treaty of Utrecht, France was compelled to give up its claims to the Acadian peninsula in favour of the British, but it retained claims over Cape Breton, Prince Edward Island, and Newfoundland until 1763. Despite a drastic decline in our population during the previous century, the Mi'kmaq still had superior numbers to the Europeans that were present in our territories in 1713. At that time, there were maybe three thousand Acadians, a few hundred British and French soldiers, and almost no British settlers in Mikmakik. As a result, our loyalty was sought by the French, who depended on our help to harass the British, and by the British, who needed our cooperation to protect themselves from French attacks.

Because Anglo settlement began in earnest on the eastern seaboard of what is now the United States, relations between the British and the Mi'kmaq were profoundly affected by earlier developments in New England. Around 1640, the Massachusetts Bay settlers, who perhaps numbered in the thousands, began to expand into present-day New Hampshire and Maine. These lands were the traditional homeland of the Wabanaki Confederacy and the Mi'kmaq Nation.

Britain's professed policy was that it had to formally purchase tribal lands before settlers could take up legal estates. But repeated encroachments by growing numbers of settlers disrupted tribal land-use patterns, ownership, and economies.

It appeared that the colonists and the colonial governments were attempting to ignore the imperial instructions relating to the protection of indigenous land and resource rights. As a result, hostilities broke out during the 1670s. The Imperial Crown was forced to step in and provide assurances to the affected indigenous nations that their rights, under the stated imperial policy, would be respected. These assurances were formalized in treaties of peace, eleven of which were concluded with the southeastern Wabanaki tribes by 1717.

These arrangements, however, did not bind the Mi'kmaq or respond to their concerns regarding their territories in Mikmakik. In 1719, Great Britain appointed a governor for Acadia (Nova Scotia) and instructed him to engage our "friendship and good correspondence" through treaty. He was governor in name only, though, since he kept his office in Boston, 100 km (60 miles) away. In any event, at this time, the Grand Council refused to enter into any treaties with the Crown.

But the ongoing problem still existed: the imperial government and its laws could not maintain discipline among the land-hungry colonies. By 1722, armed confrontation once again flared up with the Wabanaki Confederacy. The Mi'kmaq joined in the battle and, in that year alone, our warriors took twenty-two British ships. England clearly had to focus its efforts on securing a more lasting arrangement. This was accomplished in 1725, when the leaders of the Wabanaki Confederacy—the Penobscots, Malecites, and Passamaquoddies—signed a treaty of peace with the British in Boston.

While they accepted nominal British sovereignty, they refused to surrender any more of their lands and only agreed to cease and desist from disturbing "existing" Anglo settlements that had been created in the 1690s. Subsequently, the members of the confederacy ratified this compact, including a distinct treaty of the Mi'kmaq district, Gespogoitg (identified in the 1725 Treaty as the "Cape Sable Indians"). However, having made no former treaties with Britain and wishing to remain non-aligned, the Grand Council of the Mi'kmaq Nation did not formally adhere to the Treaty of 1725.

The terms of the Treaty of 1725 conform to a pattern that had been established earlier. It was built on the law of Nikamanen, but it was the first formal treaty between the Wabanaki and the British Crown. For us, it served as a fundamental agreement on the nature of our relations, and it was to be renewed at appropriate intervals.

Parallel to this development, we continued to maintain our relationship with the French. Annual meetings with their representatives took place on Ile St. Jean (now Prince Edward Island), and France retained its naval base at Louisbourg, in Cape Breton, which had been constructed after the "loss" of Acadia in 1713. In 1743, hostilities were renewed between the imperial powers once again, ending with the defeat of the French at Louisbourg two years later. By that time, Louisbourg had become a vital French military and commercial base, with a population of about 3,000 souls. With the Treaty of Aix-La-Chapelle in 1748, England was required to return Louisbourg to France, and, as a result, the British began to build Halifax at Chebucto Bay on the Atlantic coast.

The Crown appointed Lord Cornwallis to "govern" Nova Scotia in 1749 and directed him to make peace with us. That same year, a Royal Commission of Inquiry into the legal rights of the indigenous nations in North America established the legal principle that the "Indians, though living amongst the King's subjects in these countries, are a separate and distinct people from them, they are treated as such, they have a policy of their own, [and] they make peace and war with any nations of Indians when they think fit, without control from the English."

Apart from the stationing of a few hundred soldiers at Annapolis Royal and Canso, almost no British settlement had occurred in Atlantic Canada prior to the establishment of Halifax. But this initiative, as well as British designs on other Nova Scotia locations, made it clear that they were intending to do in Mikmakik what they had already done in Maine and New Hampshire. On September 24, 1749, the Grand Chief of the Mi'kmaq declared war on the British, stating, "It is God who has given me my country in perpetuity."

By October of that same year, repeated attacks on British ships led Governor Cornwallis to issue a general order to "annoy, distress, take or destroy the Savages commonly called Micmacks, wherever they are found." But the Lords of Trade, Cornwallis's bosses, thought "gentler Methods and Offers of Peace" held greater promise, providing that "the Sword is held over their Heads." In August 1751, Maliseet, Passamaquoddy, and Penobscot representatives met with British commissioners at Fort St. George, objecting to unlawful settlements on their lands. The commissioners stated that the governor's "intention" all along had been to renew the Treaty of 1725 and went on to invite the tribes to meet in Halifax with Cornwallis.

Grand Chief Jean Baptiste Cope and his delegation came to Halifax in November 1752 to meet with Governor Cornwallis's replacement, Peregrine Thomas Hopson. After long discussion, it was agreed that the Treaty of 1725 would be renewed. Grand Chief Cope also said that he desired a new compact between England and the Mi'kmaq Nation. Hopson agreed. The Elikawake ("in the King's house") Treaty acknowledges the Mi'kmaq as British subjects and confirms their separate national identity within the United Kingdom. It also guarantees the Mi'kmaq the freedom and liberty to hunt, fish, and trade under the explicit protection of His Majesty's Civil Courts.

The Mi'kmaq agreed not to "molest" any existing British settlements but did not consent to any new ones. The symbol of this treaty, in our traditions, is an eight-pointed star representing the original seven *sakamowti* and the British Crown, with the Union Jack at its centre.

In the Mi'kmaq view, the Mi'kmaq Compact, 1752, affirmed Mikmakik and Britain as two states sharing one crown—the Crown pledging to preserve and defend Mi'kmaq rights against settlers as much as against foreign nations.

During the course of the next few years, various districts in Mikmakik ratified the treaty of peace, but things were far from over. The French continued to be in conflict with the English over commerce and settlement in North America, and Halifax was under siege by the Mi'kmaq and

Wabanaki. Fort Beausejour, a French fortress on the Chignecto Isthmus, was taken by the British in 1755. At the same time, French Acadians who did not swear allegiance to the English queen were deported, and many Mi'kmaq rose up in arms to protect the rights of their francophone neighbours. As a result, in 1756, Lieutenant Governor Lawrence offered rewards for Indian scalps and prisoners.

The imperialist struggle between France and England over North America, however, was in its last phase. The French fort at Louisbourg fell to the British in 1758. The capture of Quebec in 1759, and Montreal in 1760, put an end to France's designs in North America. With a view to consolidating their "winnings," the British acknowledged that relations with the indigenous peoples would have to be normalized. In Article 40 of the French Capitulation, Britain formally promised to protect the Indian property and rights in the New Prerogative Order. The Lords of Trade in London were keenly aware that the safety and future of English settlement in North America depended on the friendly disposition of the Indians. In 1760 they stated that settlement must "be done with a proper regard to our engagements with the Indians" (i.e., the treaties).

With European tensions resolved, the accessions to the Mi'kmaq Compact, 1752, began. Many of the Mi'kmaq districts again reconfirmed their commitment to the 1725 and 1752 treaties. By royal instructions issued to colonial governors in December 1761, British settlers were required by the Crown to remove themselves from any and all lands not lawfully obtained.

The new governor of Nova Scotia, Jonathan Belcher, announced in a 1762 accession meeting with the Mi'kmaq district chiefs who resided in areas that had been occupied by France that the king was determined "to support and protect Indians in their just Rights and Possessions and to keep inviolable the treaties and Compacts which have been entered into with them." Belcher's proclamation explicitly identified and reserved the territories still occupied and claimed by the Mi'kmaq, including the sea-coasts of the Unamaki, Epikoitik, Piktokiok, Sikiniktiok, and Gaspekiok *sakamowti*—altogether about two-thirds of the province as it was at that time.

Through the Royal Proclamation of 1763, King George III consolidated all previous policies related to the settling of Indian lands and settler conduct with the Indian nations. The proclamation stated unequivocally that the tribes were not to be disturbed in their use and possession of their traditional lands and that the only way in which such lands could be acquired was through treaty with the Crown. This statement was an early articulation of the Crown's trust responsibility to ensure that the Indian nations' rights and interests were safeguarded in the face of increasing settlement and competition for lands and resources.

Despite all of these commitments and guarantees, the settlers did not necessarily possess the willingness or the ability to ensure that the New Prerogative Order was implemented by the colonial governments and settlers. The reality that Britain was intent on settling North America, and reaping profits from its resources, undermined its stated policy of protecting the integrity of our nation: To this day we have been faced with the same schizophrenic approach to our rights as a people: in law, and at the level of rhetoric, our rights are recognized and protected; but in practice, because of immigrants' self-interest, we are treated as if we do not even possess the most basic of human rights.

TREATIES BROKEN: DISTORTING THE RELATIONSHIP

The appropriation of our land and resources continued. While France had come among us primarily to trade, the British planned colonization. There were no permanent French settlements in Mikmakik before 1605, and as late as 1686 the European population of Acadia was scarcely 900. Britain established its first major colony in our territory in 1749, and within a century Europeans outnumbered us in Nova Scotia. Many Mi'kmaq migrated to their ancient islands of Cape Breton, St. Pierre, Prince Edward Island, and Newfoundland to maintain their way of life. France had been, to a large degree, a guest who had never asserted any overt control over our affairs; Britain at once set about seizing our lands.

The commitment to let us retain the Catholic religion was also broken. All of our priests were expelled, and we were forced to rely on the French at the island of St. Pierre, off Newfoundland, for religious books. Our own *keptins* assumed the role of priests for many years after.

At the outbreak of hostilities between the American colonies and Great Britain, General George Washington, commander-in-chief of the revolutionary army, wrote to the chiefs and captains of Mi'kmaq Nation requesting military assistance.

On July 17, 1776, a mutual defence treaty was concluded at Watertown, and the Mi'kmaq became the first nation to formally recognize the United

States, which had proclaimed its independence just two weeks earlier at Philadelphia. By 1779, relations with Britain were restored and reaffirmed with the Crown at a meeting of the Grand Council that took place at Piktokiok.

But the peace between America and Britain left the English with only one naval base in North America, Halifax. To strengthen their strategic position, and to accommodate the many loyalists who moved north from the thirteen colonies, the British intensified their colonization of Mikmakik. This activity disrupted our economies and began to severely restrict our people's access to the land and resources that were so essential to their survival. By the 1790s, many of our communities were starving, and the commitments made by the Imperial Crown that settlement would only take place after lands had been formally surrendered by us seemed to be forgotten by the settlers.

At the same time, however, both Britain and the United States continued to recognize the special status of the indigenous nations, including Mikmakik. The first commercial treaty between the two states, known today as the Jay Treaty (1794), guaranteed our continuing rights to pass across the new border and engage in trade, as we had always done. This element was of particular relevance to us and to other nations such as the Haudenosaunee, whose traditional territories were split by the imposition of the international border.

Again, in 1814, when Britain and the United States concluded a treaty of peace to end the War of 1812, they guaranteed the restoration of all the rights and privileges previously enjoyed by the indigenous nations.

In the nineteenth century, the confiscation of protected Mi'kmaq hunting grounds began in earnest. Squatters, tolerated if not actively aided and abetted by local authorities, took up large tracts of our traditional territories without our consent or any form of compensation. Repeated representations to the Crown regarding these ongoing breaches of the terms of our treaties were either stalled or ignored.

Finally, in 1841, Kjisakamow Peminawit submitted a petition to the Colonial Office in London, and as a result, they reminded provincial officials that the Mi'kmaq had "an undeniable claim to the Protection of the Government as British subjects" and that we should be compensated for any losses. The province of Nova Scotia responded by agreeing to set aside 50,000 hectares (125,000 acres) of land as "Indian Reservations" for our use in 1842. Most of these lands were already recognized Mi'kmaq family estates.

We are still uncertain as to how this amount of land was decided upon, but it is clear that it had little to do with the actual areas of land that we were using and occupying at that time and nothing to do with our economic and social needs as a people. In any event, well aware that it had no authority to force us into abandoning our existing settlements, the province told London that it would "invite" the Mi'kmaq chiefs "to cooperate in the permanent resettlement and instruction of their people." We continued to live where we had resided and where we could, refusing to be confined to areas that we had not participated in selecting.

Soon it became clear that even this attempt at fulfilling the Crown's obligations of political and legal protection was inadequate. Only half of the 50,000 hectares were ever set aside and, by the 1850s, even this small remainder of our homeland was being settled illegally by Europeans. This had a catastrophic effect on our economies, since without adequate access to land and resources, there was little chance of putting food on the table or of generating surplus with which to trade.

Instead of expelling the squatters, as was required by the 1762 and 1763 proclamations, and by its own 1842 legislation, the province in 1859 required some of them to pay for the land they had illegally taken up. Few ever did. The Grand Council of the Mi'kmaq Nation wrote to the governor in Nova Scotia, challenging the constitutionality of "this extraordinary proposal to deprive them of th[eir] rights by entering into compromise with the violators of them," but it was not heard.

The wildlife resources that were the basis of our economy were hunted and fished out by settlers, our few farms were stolen, and we were reduced to living as itinerant woodcutters and peddlers of handicrafts. We suffered the same fate in Prince Edward Island and New Brunswick, which became separate provinces in 1769 and 1784, respectively, and in Newfoundland. New Brunswick began selling lands that we still reserved or occupied in 1844; in Prince Edward Island only one tiny island was left for our use by 1838. None of these actions was undertaken with our consent or formalized through imperial legislation, as was required by the Proclamation of October 7, 1763.

In fact, the imposition of borders and new administrative regimes had the effect of separating our people and undermining the Grand Council's ability to act as a cohesive unit. Our nation found itself confined within boundaries that had nothing to do with the way we had organized ourselves historically. But, despite the problems that this situation posed, we retained our tribal authority and continued to maintain the political structure of the Grand Council.

We retained our language and religion in the face of an overwhelming Anglo-Protestant majority and continued to meet as a whole people at Potoloteq (Chapel Island on Cape Breton) on St. Anne's Day each year. On the whole, we maintained our traditional communities, although their number decreased as our lands were seized by settlers or sold outright by local government officials.

The British North America (BNA) Act, 1867, united most of Britain's North American provinces under a single federal government and entrusted Canada with responsibility for "Indians, and land reserved for Indians," as well as "treaty obligations." However, it also appeared to give the provinces authority over the lands and resources within their boundaries that had been properly ceded by the relevant tribes.

In our case, this had a prejudicial effect on the matter of our traditional territories, since, from that time onwards, although Canada had the responsibility for upholding the treaties and protecting our rights and interests, it was the provinces (the successors to the land-grabbing colonies) who asserted that they held "title" to the land. To this day, the division of powers established by the BNA Act has been used as an excuse for nonfulfillment of the Crown's treaty commitments and as a pretext for preventing serious discussion on the land question.

POLITICAL REPRESSION

The remainder of the nineteenth century was a very difficult period for the Mi'kmaq people. Our collective attention was focused on day-to-day survival, with little time for anything else. During this time, the federal government began using its "powers" under the BNA Act not to protect our rights and interests but to destabilize our nation and to make it over in the image of the European. The twentieth century has proven to be a continuation of this trend, at least in terms of federal government policy.

"Elected councils" were introduced, in spite of the authority and jurisdiction of the Grand Council in New Brunswick, Prince Edward Island, Quebec, and Newfoundland, and a host of administrative procedures, which were intended to complete the destabilization program, were imposed. Although the government intended to undermine the Grand Council's authority with this initiative, we have adapted and developed a cooperative approach along with the elected councils. However, interference by outside agencies in Mi'krnaq internal affairs became even more pronounced than it once was, particularly on the part of the federal Department of Indian Affairs. Bureaucrats at the local, regional, and headquarters levels took it upon themselves to determine who was and who was not a Mi'kmaq; when houses would be built; how meagre reserve resources were to be utilized; how elections would be conducted.

This attempt at imposing an irresponsible and irrelevant form of indirect rule upon our people has proven to be an unmitigated disaster, made the worse because the unelected bureaucrats who continue to wield these powers are not accountable either to the Mi'kmaq or to the Canadian people.

At the same time, outside enforcement agencies began aggressively to restrict Mi'kmaq citizens in the exercise of their economic rights, particularly as they related to hunting, fishing, and commerce. We were told that any treaty rights we "may have had" were extinguished and that we had no legal basis on which to pin them. No recognition was given to the many and positive assurances we had received from the Crown regarding our rights, or even to our economic needs as a society.

From 1941 until 1953, a "centralization" program was initiated in which our citizens were coerced into moving onto two "recognized" reserves in Nova Scotia: Eskasoni and Shubenacadie. The intent of this program was ostensibly to make "administration" easier for the non-Mi'kmaq bureaucracy, but its effect was to take more Mi'kmaq citizens off the land, and to further undermine their self-sufficiency. The school at Wycocomagh and many Mi'kmaq farms were burned down by Indian Affairs as a means of ensuring that our people would relocate to Eskasoni. In the end, over 1,000 Mi'kmaq were displaced from their farms in various parts of the province and compelled to reside on what had become two acutely overcrowded containment centres.

Our youth were taken away from their families and forced to attend residential schools, where they were beaten to prevent them from speaking their own languages or practising their culture. The aim of the residential school system was to wipe out any sense of national identity on the part of youth, and replace it with European values and culture. It did not succeed in completely fulfilling these objectives, but it did serve to disorient and demoralize three generations of our people.

These efforts at dismantling our nation accelerated in 1960 when the federal cabinet decreed that the Mi'kmaq in Nova Scotia were to be divided into twelve separate "Indian Bands," to be dealt with as individual entities instead of a collectivity.

The ill-conceived and unconscionable strategy to destabilize our traditional forms of government, eliminate our culture, and ravage our economies has clearly been intended to terminate our rights, and our existence, as a people. But it has been met with ongoing resistance on the part of the Mi'kmaq. We have, of necessity, adapted to the new forces with which we must contend in our traditional territories, but always within the context of our collective aboriginal and treaty rights. Beginning in the mid-1960s, our people began to mobilize in new ways to defend the nation.

The unilateral imposition of policies and legislation affecting our people had to be dealt with. They needed assistance in coping with the morass of bureaucratic procedures and policies that were being spawned by the federal and provincial governments. In 1969, the Union of Nova Scotia Indians (UNSI) was formed to do just this. Since its inception, UNSI has worked closely with the Grand Council, the Mi'kmaq communities in Nova Scotia, and other Mi'kmaq institutions to preserve and enhance our collective rights.

Six years later, in 1975, the Native Council of Nova Scotia was established to represent the specific interests of those Mi'kmaq citizens who are not recognized as "Indians" by the federal government. It has always been the position of the Mi'kmaq that we know who we are. However, successive federal governments have seen fit to decide for us who is, and who is not, a Mi'kmaq, and this has had the effect of dividing our communities and creating a "second class" of Mi'kmaq citizens. The Native Council was formed to address the special needs of these people.

The Grand Council, UNSI, and the Native Council of Nova Scotia have developed a close working relationship with the objective of revitalizing the Mi'kmaq Nation and undoing the damage that has resulted from hundreds of years of outside interference and discrimination. It is only by building a strong institutional base that we can hope to renew the prosperity and self-sufficiency that our people once enjoyed.

However, the struggle has also been taken up on a number of other fronts. One of the most important of these is the exercise of our political rights as a people. The United Nations international covenants on Economic, Social, and Cultural Rights, and on Civil and Political Rights, both state very clearly that "in no case may a people be deprived of its own means of subsistence." Yet this is precisely what has been done to us.

HUNTING AND FISHING RIGHTS

The protection of our rights to engage in hunting, fishing, and commerce as embodied in the Treaty of 1752 is entirely consistent with the intent and the letter of these covenants, and yet, over the years, federal and provincial governments have made a conscious effort to deprive our people of their means of subsistence. The effects of these efforts are visible in all of our communities, where one of the primary sources of income is now welfare and where many of our citizens continue to be arrested and convicted for engaging in traditional economic pursuits and commerce.

The Treaty of 1752 is unequivocal when it speaks of hunting and fishing: "It is agreed that the said Tribe of Indians shall not be hindered from, but have free liberty of hunting and fishing as usual." We sought protections for our traditional economies so that we could provide for our children as we had always done. Today, we do not hunt and fish for sport; we engage in these activities to put food on the table and to generate revenue for our people. The recurring problem was that federal and provincial legislation was being used to prevent us from exercising our rights, and to wantonly harass the breadwinners of our communities.

Repeated efforts at negotiating this issue with the federal government had failed, and so a decision was taken by our leadership to pursue the matter through the courts. The case that was chosen involved James Matthew Simon, a Mi'kmaq citizen resident at Shubenacadie. In September 1980 he was stopped by members of the federal police, the Royal Canadian Mounted Police, and searched. Mr. Simon had in his possession a type of shotgun and shells that were not "permitted" under the Nova Scotia Lands and Forests Act and was charged with offences under that legislation. In defence of these charges, Mr. Simon cited the Treaty of 1752 and its hunting provisions.

The attorney general of Nova Scotia argued that whatever treaty rights "may have" existed had been extinguished. Since settler governments had succeeded in ignoring their treaty obligations to the Mi'kmaq for almost two hundred years, we assume he considered those treaties to be irrelevant. The Nova Scotia provincial court apparently agreed with the attorney general for the province, since they convicted Mr. Simon. His appeal was dismissed by the Nova Scotia Supreme Court. Ultimately, he sought, and was granted, leave to appeal to the Supreme Court of Canada.

On April 17, 1982, Section 35 of the Constitution Act came into force. It states that "existing aboriginal and treaty rights" are "recognized and affirmed." Although generally the constitutional amendment process was not satisfactory to the Mi'kmaq, it is acknowledged by us that constitutional recognition of the treaties was a positive step. In fact, it did have a bearing on the outcome of the Simon case.

On November 21, 1985, the Supreme Court rendered judgment and acquitted Mr. Simon of all of the charges laid against him. For the province, it was a significant defeat. For us, it was a vindication of many of the things we had been saying all along. The court found that the Treaty of 1752 is still a binding and enforceable agreement between the Crown and the Mi'kmaq people and that its protections regarding Mi'kmaq hunting rights override provincial legislation that interferes with these rights.

As important, the court ruled that the treaties must be interpreted in a flexible manner that takes into account changes in technology and practice. For instance, Mi'kmaq hunters could not be limited to using spears and handmade knives, as they once did and as the attorney general of Nova Scotia had argued. It was also made clear that this right extended not only to subsistence hunting but also to hunting for commercial purposes.

As a result of this decision, we knew that we were in a much stronger position to proceed with formalizing the exercise of our rights to the hunt. On Mi'kmaq Treaty Day, October 1, 1986, the majority of our leadership in Nova Scotia ratified a set of interim hunting guidelines as a first step towards this end.

The basis of these guidelines is a Mi'kmaq concept, Netukulimk, which includes the use of the natural bounty provided by the Creator for the self-support and well-being of the individual and the community at large. The guidelines covered safety and conservation considerations, as well as stating clearly that the treaty rights of Mi'kmaq citizens to hunt overrode existing provincial restrictions related to seasons, quotas, licences, and tagging and hunting gear and methods. At the same time, it was made clear that only those Mi'kmaq who followed the guidelines would be protected by the terms of the 1752 Treaty.

As a result of these events, attempts were made to negotiate a more formal arrangement with the other levels of government. However, they did not bear fruit, and today, the Mi'kmaq hunting guidelines are still in effect. Recent actions by the province of Nova Scotia do not lead us to believe that they are committed to dealing with this issue in good faith, and recent inaction on the part of the federal government to ensure that our rights are protected leads us to the same conclusion. In 1987, six Mi'kmaq citizens were charged with fishing "violations"; twenty-three were charged for hunting deer and moose; and three were charged in connection with commerce and taxation matters.

In the spring of 1988, Nova Scotia announced that the annual moose hunt would be taking place from October 3 to 7. Licences were to be granted to two hundred hunters by lottery. The Mi'kmaq were excluded from having any input into the development of this approach to the harvest. It totally ignored Mi'kmaq rights to the resource, and in fact, only two Mi'kmaq citizens won the "privilege" to hunt moose under the lottery system.

After much thought and discussion, our leadership decided to stage a separate Mi'krnaq moose harvest, to ensure that our communities had adequate access to the resource and that the harvest would be carried out according to the interim guidelines that had been developed.

Our moose harvest took place from September 17 to 30, 1988, in Victoria and Inverness Counties. It was supervised by the Mi'kmaq, and its focus was to provide Mi'kmaq citizens with the opportunity to harvest the resource for subsistence use.

The government of Nova Scotia took the position that this harvest was "illegal" and promptly initiated a propaganda campaign to discredit and intimidate our citizens. The harvest did proceed, but a total of fourteen Mi'kmaq hunters were charged with violations of the provincial Wildlife Act. Their cases are now before the courts. Subsequently, the province escalated its provocation by unilaterally announcing that any Mi'kmaq engaged in hunting anything pursuant to the 1752 Treaty would be prosecuted.

This experience calls into question the ability of the courts and the present political system to address the matter of our rights in a meaningful and lasting way. Despite the protections afforded to our treaties as a result of Section 35 of the Canada Act, 1982, and despite the enormous degree of effort that went into vindicating our rights at the Supreme Court level, we still find ourselves confronted by settler governments that refuse to recognize their own laws and their own courts.

The situation raises the question, if they don't play by their own rules, then should we? Although Canada prides itself on being one of the world's leading "democracies" and an advocate of human rights, we do not find much evidence of these things in our dealings with federal and provincial governments. Beyond this, it is clear to us that the problem is far more complex than court decisions or political will. It has to do with systemic discrimination and racism that are deeply rooted in the consciousness of the Canadian public and their institutions.

JUSTICE FOR WHO?

One important element of the 1752 Treaty had to do with the matter of justice. We knew that something had to be done to regulate relations between our citizens and settlers, but we also knew that the traditional Mi'kmaq justice system had to play a continued role in our own internal affairs. This called for a "two-legged" justice system based on the concept of cohabitation.

For incidents involving Mi'kmaq citizens on Mi'kmaq territory, the traditional Mi'kmaq justice system would apply. For situations involving settlers, the English justice system would be used. And finally, for matters that involved both Mi'kmaq citizens and settlers, the English civil justice system, with input from the Mi'kmaq, would come into play.

The Mi'kmaq refused to be administered under the political authority of the local settlers or under criminal law in connection with the administration of justice. Instead, the Civil Law of England—the fundamental principles of contract, property, and torts—was understood to be the appropriate basis on which to measure the conduct between Mi'kmaq and British people in Nova Scotia. This understanding is reflected in the relevant section of the 1752 compact and in the accession treaties that were ratified by the various districts of Mikmakik.

As with other understandings reached that had been confirmed by the terms of the treaty, this arrangement was implemented, but proved ineffective. In fact, with centralization in the 1940s, our traditional justice system was usurped by outside institutions and law enforcement agencies, and even in the settler courts we found that we were not permitted to enjoy "the same benefits, advantages, and privileges" as others, even though they had been guaranteed in the 1752 Treaty. This situation is most graphically illustrated by the experience of Donald Marshall Jr. at the hands of the Nova Scotia "justice" system.

Late one evening in 1971, in a Sydney, Nova Scotia, park, Sandy Seale, a black youth, was fatally stabbed. At the time, the incident aroused emotions throughout the local Mi'kmaq, black, and white communities. But it was only much later that the real implications of what followed would come to light.

Donald Marshall Jr. was eventually charged in connection with Sandy Seale's death. But, from the beginning, the conduct of the investigation into the killing was questionable. The two "eyewitnesses" to the crime gave testimony that appeared to be too consistent, and questions were raised about whether or not they had been coached on what to say. After the "eyewitnesses" had testified, other individuals came forward to the authorities, stating that one of them, John Pratico, was nowhere near the scene of the crime on the evening it occurred. These concerns were dismissed, not only by the Sydney police department, but even by one of Donald Marshall's own defence lawyers. However, in the end it was indeed confirmed that both of the "eyewitnesses" had been coached by the Sydney police and that they had given false testimony.

It later turned out that the two lawyers initially engaged in Marshall's defence did not make all reasonable efforts to fully investigate the possibility of his innocence: they did not carry out their own investigation and did not even conduct interviews with the alleged witnesses. No one seemed to doubt the fact that, since Donald Marshall was an "Indian," it was probable that he had committed the crime. He was finally convicted of manslaughter, and sentenced to life imprisonment. Despite his insistence, even after his conviction, that he was innocent, no appeal was allowed, because of the two "eyewitness" accounts.

Meanwhile, there were some people who were not satisfied with the outcome of the investigation or the trial. For instance, there were many unanswered questions about one Roy Ebsary, an old, eccentric character known to many residents of Sydney and its environs. He had been in the vicinity of the crime the night it occurred and had told then–chief detective John McIntyre not only that he had been with Sandy Seale and Donald

Marshall the night of the incident but that he had taken a swipe at Seale with a knife. John McIntyre did nothing to follow up on this admission.

Three years later, in 1974, Donna Ebsary, the old man's daughter, approached Sydney police with information that her father had indeed killed Sandy Seale. She spoke to McIntyre, who refused to even listen. The same information was provided to the RCMP, who, apparently, did not follow up either. The attitude of many of the officials who were handling this case is perhaps most succinctly illustrated by comments that were made by Robert Anderson, who was the director of criminal matters in the Nova Scotia Attorney General's Department at the time of Marshall's trial. Eleven or twelve years after the conviction, and after being appointed a county court judge, he was approached by Felix Cacchione, who at the time was working as Marshall's lawyer. Cacchione was concerned about some aspects of the investigation and was seeking information from Judge Robertson concerning the 1971 investigation. His response to Cacchione's presentation was, "Don't put your balls in a vise over an Indian." The implication was that Cacchione stood to compromise his future career prospects in Nova Scotia if he became known as an advocate of Indian rights and interests. (Mr. Cacchione is himself now a judge in the province.)

Ironically, Cacchione's experience and Robertson's comments were consistent with a pattern that had been observed way back in 1849. At that time, the Indian commissioner reported to the Nova Scotia Legislative Assembly that the justice system and the political process in the province could not be counted on to "protect" Indian interests and rights: "Under present circumstances, no adequate protection can be obtained for Indian property. It would be vain to seek a verdict from any jury in this island against the trespassers on the reserves; nor perhaps would a member of the Bar be found willingly and effectually to advocate the cause of the Indians, inasmuch as he would thereby injure his own prospect, by damaging his popularity."

The striking similarity between these events, separated as they are by over a century, demonstrates a certain insidious continuity in settler culture and attitudes and the degree to which discrimination and racism are part and parcel of the day-to-day reality in this province.

The criminal justice system is made up of a number of institutions and players, each a part of a system of checks and balances that is supposed to ensure that justice is served. All of these checks and balances failed Donald Marshall Jr. Some of this malfunctioning might be seen to be bad luck, but the consistent failure of the system in this case cannot be dismissed as merely coincidence. The fact that the system performed so miserably in this instance stems from one common thread: Donald Marshall Jr. was an Indian.

It was not until eleven years after Donald Marshall's incarceration that things began to change. At that time, Steven Aronson, Jim Carroll, and Harry Wheaton became involved in the case on his behalf and began uncovering the evidence that finally led to his release and to Roy Ebsary's arrest and conviction.

Even with this turn of events, the system still did not serve Marshall well. Compensation for the eleven years spent behind bars on a wrongful conviction was, at first, refused, then later granted after public opinion was brought to bear on the Nova Scotia government. Early calls for a royal commission into the whole matter were at first rebuffed as well, until finally the public outcry was so great, among Mi'kmaq and non-Mi'kmaq alike, that the province had to comply.

The evidence that came out during the course of the Royal Commission on the Donald Marshall Jr. prosecution damned not only the individuals involved in the case at all levels but the Nova Scotia "justice" system generally. It appeared that latently racist sentiments among the principals involved in the investigation and the prosecution played a large part in Marshall's wrongful conviction.

It also appeared that no one cared whether he was guilty or not, because he was a Mi'kmaq: certainly the evidence showed that many officials did not take the care in his case that they normally did in the course of their duties. The fact that he was an "Indian" made it easy for all to accept the likelihood of guilt and to slough off his personal situation as if it was of little importance, since after all, in the scheme of things, he was "just another Indian."

In effect, the cumulative body of evidence presented to the Royal Commission became an indictment of the whole Nova Scotia justice system. This is borne out by much of what emerged during the course of the commission's work, but in particular by the statements made by Judge Felix Cacchione.

He testified that the province did not display a sense of sympathy or responsiveness to Donald Marshall's plight but, instead, played "hard ball." No one involved in the administration of justice came to his assistance. Cacchione testified that one of the factors that led to this malaise on the part of the system was Marshall's race. He said that if Donald Marshall had been a prominent non-Mi'kmaq Nova Scotian, he would have been treated differently, and the whole matter would have been handled differently.

Eleven years after Donald Marshall Jr. had been convicted of manslaughter in the death of Sandy Seale, authorities were forced to admit what many had known and stated from the beginning: that he was innocent, and moreover, that he had been cruelly victimized. The so-called justice system failed him miserably, and his experience typifies what we, as a people, have been subjected to over the past few generations.

We trust that the outcome of this exercise will be a complete overhaul of the Nova Scotia justice system and a return to the arrangements originally contemplated in the Treaty of 1752. Tentative recommendations have been made to the Royal Commission regarding the ways and means of developing and implementing a Mi'kmaq justice system and how it would interface with the non-Mi'kmaq system. Our next steps will be determined by the Royal Commission's final recommendations, which are still in the process of being completed.

UNRESOLVED LAND RIGHTS FOR MIKMAKIK

A final word on the deviant nature of the justice system, as it affects the Mi'kmaq, has to do with the federal and the provincial governments and their approach to the land rights of our people. Earlier in this essay mention was made of the guarantees that were obtained from the Crown regarding the maintenance of our land base, with particular reference to the effect of increased settlement on our territorial integrity and traditional economies.

Since almost immediately after the signing of the 1752 Treaty, the Mi'kmaq have been seeking to resolve the matter of the ongoing theft of our land and resources. We met with little success, since clearly any steps that would lead to a more equitable sharing of land and resources in the Maritimes would be costly to those who now take for granted the benefits of their ill-gotten gains.

As recently as 1973, the government of then–prime minister Pierre Trudeau insisted that there was no such thing as "aboriginal title"—after all, who could conceive that non-whites would have land and resource rights to the territories they had inhabited since time immemorial?

But this position changed in the wake of an aboriginal rights case that originated in the Nass River Valley of British Columbia, with respect to the traditional territories of the Nisga'a people.

The Supreme Court of Canada considered the matter of aboriginal title in the *Calder* case, as it was called, and although the final judgment was inconclusive regarding that matter, it did become clear that the prior rights and claims of the indigenous peoples in Canada could no longer be dismissed so lightly, or in a cavalier manner. As a result, the federal government rethought its position, and, in August 1973, released a policy statement on the "claims" of Indian and Inuit people.

It now appeared that finally we had an opportunity to negotiate the issues that, for so long, no one except us had wanted to deal with. Because of the lack of treaty surrenders in Atlantic Canada and southeastern Quebec, the Mikmakik claims were considered "claims of a different nature" than the common-law aboriginal claims of British Columbia and the North.

In 1977, the Grand Council, through the Union of Nova Scotia Indians, made a formal application for land and compensation under the 1973 policy. This initial statement of claim has led to twelve years of fruitless discussions and countless pages of correspondence and documentation.

The reason is that, although all parties agree that we never surrendered title to our lands and resources, the federal government insists our rights have been somehow indirectly "superseded by law." The application of this nebulous and racist concept to the matter of our aboriginal rights can only be seen as one more example of the systemic and consistent discrimination that we, as Mi'kmaq people, have had to endure for centuries. The continued validity of the treaty and the Royal Proclamation of 1763 deny the possibility that the concept of "superseded by law" can be applied to us.

At the beginning of this essay, we outlined how the initial relations between the Mi'kmaq and the British Crown developed and the many guarantees that we sought and obtained from colonial authorities regarding our traditional land and resource base. There is no need to repeat them. The point is that, despite these guarantees, the dispossession of our land and resources and the marginalization of our institutions was allowed to proceed.

The province of Nova Scotia passed certain laws regarding the subdivision and sale of our lands, and indeed subdivided and sold our lands, but these actions were contrary to treaty commitments and to constitutional protections (the Royal Proclamation of 1763, for instance, has never been repealed and is appended to the Constitution Act, 1982).

In fact, "responsible government" did not exist in Nova Scotia until 1867: until then, the province was entirely controlled by prerogative instruments of the Crown, such as letters patent, instructions, and imperial proclamations. Today, Canada tells us that, because Nova Scotia sold off our lands pursuant to various legislation, our rights have been terminated by these actions and these laws. It does not seem to matter to them that the province's actions were outside of its competence and that they were inconsistent with, and contrary to, imperial directives of the time.

The reality of the matter is that our people have been forcibly dispossessed of their land and resources and had their economic institutions destroyed, without their consent and without any form of compensation. Meanwhile, others have benefited tremendously, and when they are called to account, they insist that because they carried out these acts, the acts themselves must be legitimate. The blatant hypocrisy evident in this kind of reasoning is astounding even to us, who have been compelled to deal with these attitudes for hundreds of years.

It should be of serious concern to Canadians that their elected representatives are so brazenly violating not only the treaty rights but the human rights of the Mi'kmaq people. Canada insists that our rights can be superseded by law. If indeed this is the case, then it must be a law based on genocide and exploitation, not on justice and equity.

This reality has serious consequences, not just for the Mi'kmaq people and other First Nations, but for all Canadians. On the one hand, if only aboriginal peoples' rights can be superseded by law, then Canada's public posture as a champion of human rights and equality rights is an exercise in deception, and subject to a cynical and selective application based on race. On the other hand, if it has nothing to do with race, and any government of the day can reserve the right to ignore its own constitution, treaties, and courts, then sooner or later they will do it to *you*.

Either way, the implications should be shocking to any reasonable Canadian. We are glad to have the opportunity to bring these matters to the attention of the public, since, as we mentioned at the beginning of this essay, for too long the truth has been suppressed.

It is time that these matters be brought out into the open, so that Canadian citizens can gain a clearer understanding of the conduct of their government and perhaps realize how unaccountable and arbitrary their "democratically elected" leaders really are.

There are many other issues we could mention, issues related to the fisheries, commerce, health, shelter, and education, but suffice it to say that there is much unfinished business between the Mi'kmaq Nation and Canada. After centuries of alternating neglect and oppression, we demand that our rights and interests be dealt with in the spirit of equity and justice. We are not asking for anything unreasonable, or anything that would be unfamiliar to the average Canadian.

However, regardless of whether or not Canada is ready to deal with us, we will proceed with the renewal of our nation, and we will continue to prepare for what must be done. In March 1989, an historic summit took place between the leaders of twenty-nine Mi'kmaq communities, representing over 18,000 of our citizens in the four Atlantic provinces and Quebec. This was the first time since 1776 that so many of our communities had come together to develop a common approach to land and treaty matters.

What came out of this summit was a Declaration of Mi'kmaq Nation Rights, which reaffirms the Mi'kmaq commitment to the principles of self-determination, sovereignty, and self-government. The declaration also states that our children have the right to be brought up in the knowledge of their language, history, and culture. And finally, it points to the fact that, as Mi'kmaq people, we must have a fair share of the natural, economic, and fiscal resources of this land called Canada. We are renewing the strength of our nation, which has for so long been in bondage, and we will succeed.

What we are seeking is the freedom and liberty to contribute positively to the future of our people and to our common future as neighbours in this great continent. What we require to do this is an equitable share of our traditional lands and resources and recognition of our inherent right to govern ourselves.

These are not alien concepts, and they are not threatening, as some would argue. They are based on the reality of the historical record and on the prevailing norms of international law that guide the conduct of nations in their relations with one another. The facts speak for themselves. We will let you draw your own conclusions.

Elsie Charles Basque

(b. 1916)

Elsie Basque attended the Shubenacadie Residential School between 1930 and 1932—years she recalled as "wasted." In 1937 she became the first Mi'kmaq person to get a teacher's certificate from the Provincial Normal College in Truro, Nova Scotia, and went on to teach at the Indian Day School in Indian Brook. In 1951 she moved with her husband, Isaac Basque, and their three children to Boston, joining a large expatriate Mi'kmaq community; Basque later began teaching for the Boston Indian Council. The family went home to Saunierville in 1984. Basque received an honorary doctorate from Nova Scotia Teacher's College in 1997 and another from St. Anne's University in 2005. In 2009 she was appointed to the Order of Canada. The following selection originally appeared in *The Mi'kmaq Anthology*, edited by Lesley Choyce and Rita Joe.

From Here to There

The '48 Mercury was packed to the roof—three kids, Hilda Joudrey, and me on October 21, 1951.

"Packed to the roof" pretty well describes the interior of that small car.

We were moving to Connecticut. And a family's needs had to be moved too, which meant not only clothes but bed clothes, etc. The etc. included Wilfred's new bike, which had been dismantled and tucked in somewhere between the pots and pans. There even was a "pee-pot" for Beverley tucked away in the back seat.

We were green, very green as far as travelling experience went. The day before, my good friend Irene (Gloade) had spent the day at our house baking goodies for us to take along for lunches. We had a box full of sandwiches, cookies, a cake, even an apple pie. Like I said, we were green—*very green* travellers.

Hilda Joudrey from Shubie was on her way to Peabody, Mass., to visit relatives. She had asked to accompany us. I liked the idea of an adult along to help with the children. In October 1951, Wilfred was seven, Brian had just celebrated his third birthday, and Beverley was thirteen months. Hilda was a godsend. I thought.

We had said our good-byes the day before. A bit sad about leaving our new house, but we were off to new beginnings. Adventure lay ahead—right around the corner.

Our first stop was on the side of the road somewhere in Cumberland County. We hauled out the sandwiches, the cake, and pie. Hilda had brought sandwiches too, but ours must have looked tastier and we shared with her. Then away we went again.

We had made good time considering that I had never driven two hundred miles from home. It was about five o'clock when we hit Saint John. That was our nemesis! Trying to find my way out of that eternal rotary, we got a flat tire right in front of a garage. The good Lord and St. Christopher were watching over us.

Cooped up in the car all day, we stretched our legs, went for a walk around the block. By the time we got back to the garage, the tire had been repaired and we were ready to be "on the road again." At the last minute, Hilda came running back to the car, carrying a sack full of goodies.

Hilda was a gratis traveller. In return she had promised to help with the children. All day long Wilfred had taken care of his little sister's needs in the back seat. Hilda had not once volunteered to assist in any way. I was somewhat annoyed but said nothing, hoping things would get better. After all, we were still a long way from Connecticut. I was sure everything would improve after our flat tire episode. But then Hilda shelled her peanuts, ate her grapes right under the hungry eyes of my children, and never once offered them any. That went down in my record book and I guess some forty-plus years later, it's still there.

Time to stop for the night. About half way between Saint John and St. Stephen we spotted the Half-Moon Motel and Restaurant. It was the children's first adventure in a motel, lots of exploring and chattering. Above all the commotion was the need to use the bathroom facilities—*now*. Hilda had already stationed herself inside the only bathroom.

When one's gotta go, one's gotta go. Several loud knocks, a few desperate "hurry ups," in what seemed like ages, Hilda finally opened the door. The surprise, the shock overwhelmed us. I can still see Brian pointing his finger at her and saying, "Who? Mom—who?" While we had been exploring, she had been busy too. She had applied layers of make-up and now resembled a lady of the night ready for action.

I was not about to be seen in public with her. I asked her to watch over

Beverley while I took my two little boys out to supper. On our return we brought a bowl of soup, crackers, milk, and cookies for Beverley. Hilda went out by herself. My disgust was mounting.

The next morning we set out on our second day of adventure.

It had been decided that I would drive to Boston with the children. Isaac would meet us at my sister Lucy's home in the Jamaica Plain section of Boston. I had been there in 1938. I had no idea of how to get there—from here—but I was on my way with three kids.

Immigration and Customs loomed just ahead. All we had for identification was a slip of paper from Mr. Rice, the Indian agent, stating our names, address, and that we were bona-fide Micmac people entitled to border privileges. As I look back now, years wiser (I hope), I realize that I talked too much. We were going to the States—to live—permanently—Isaac worked there. I was somewhat overly excited about the whole deal.

My excitement and happiness was short lived.

I quickly learned that persons leaving Canada, entering the United States as permanent residents, must apply for "green cards" right here and now. Proper IDs had to be issued. Pictures had to be taken. Picture-taking facilities were not available at the Immigration Office. That had to be done at a private photographer's in St. Stephen. Fortunately, the photographer was kind and understanding. That accomplished, surely now, we could proceed on our way. That is when I learned about "duty." I would have to pay duty on the car before I would be allowed to enter the United States. I can still hear the officer's stern voice as he pointed towards the ramp that led to the U.S. "If you so much as try to go across that ramp, I'll have you stopped and your car impounded."

What was I to do? I just had enough money to get us to Connecticut. Not enough to pay duty. We needed the car's contents, our dishes, our bedding. Isaac was at work, unable to contact. What to do?

I discovered that a train would be passing through on its way to Boston around 4:30 that afternoon. If I hurried, I might be able to get my children and belongings on that train. First, though, I had to find a storage place for the car. That accomplished, I went to a nearby furniture store where a kind Samaritan gave me a large carton, into which I literally threw the bedding, a few pots and pans. He helped me securely tie and tape the carton closed and got it to the railroad station in time for the train's arrival.

My dear little boys had been trying to take care of their sister, who had insisted on playing in the soot-covered yard. She had peed herself and her pretty pink overalls were black. Her whole little self desperately needed a bath. The train was coming down the track. We barely had time to purchase our tickets.

We must have been the most bedraggled-looking family ever to get on a train. Luckily, the end seat was vacant. It could be made into a bed for the children. First, though, I had to find clean clothes for my little girl and soap and water. She had been such a good little traveller. They all had. We still had adventure in our hearts.

In spite of all that went wrong that day, there was still a measure of light-hearted amusement in my soul.

I had noticed lots of open luggage, well, let's say, household items stashed in an alcove between the outside door and the seating area. Aha! Someone else was moving too. A small measure of comfort for the moment.

"All aboard," the train whistled, and we were on our way one more time.

The burly-looking conductor entered the passenger car near our seats, looked rather disgruntingly at us, took our tickets, and went on down the aisle.

The gentleman who owned the household items, which included a large galvanized wash tub and scrub board, was seated about three seats diagonally across from us. When he entered the train I noticed that he had something alive under his coat. With the conductor now directly in front of him, his hidden treasure, thoroughly resenting the restrained accommodation, began to adamantly declare its resistance by meowing in as loud a voice as a little kitten could. The conductor immediately made the traveller aware that animals were not allowed on the train unless in a carrier and also asked, "Do you own that pile of household stuff back there?"

The gentleman, who appeared to be Maliseet or Passamoquoddy, was on his way to Machias, a few stops down the road. With firm admonitions about using the train as a moving-van and a place for a kitten's toilet training. the conductor moved on. It wasn't long before the gentleman fell asleep. The kitten had a whole big train to explore. The conductor would make a few loud expletive remarks which would waken the man, who would rescue the kitten, and again it would snuggle inside his coat. As soon as he dozed off, however, the kitten would repeat its meandering. The conductor would get excited and again the kitten would be rescued.

This went on until we got to Machias, where the young man left the train with—as the saying goes—"his whole kit and keeboodle."

My tired little family was soon fast asleep. It had been a long, trying day. Some thirty-six hours since we had left Shubie. They were perfect travellers, totally unaware of the struggles and frustrations we had faced at Immigration. Many years later, this episode became the subject of testimonial required to establish "one country" relationship between Micmac/Maliseet nations and the United States. So, my frustrations that October day in 1951 became valuable information submitted to a policy review hearing in the 1970s.

Hilda! Where was Hilda? She, too, had bought a ticket to Boston and was somewhere on the train. I had long since given up on her being of assistance. Wilfred, at seven, was big brother, an assistant care-giver, and much more helpful than she.

We rode all night, rather peacefully. I had no idea where we were. Maybe some day, I'll take a leisurely train trip from Calais, Maine, to Boston, Massachusetts. That night in October 1951 will always be the most memorable.

Daylight came and with it the children awoke. Before long we were at the end of our route. We were at Boston's South Station. A telephone call to my sister's home brought my nephew to the rescue.

I had not seen my sister and her family in thirteen years. They had never met my family. The excitement was overwhelming.

Late that night, Isaac arrived. The children and I were excited all over again.

The next day, we all boarded a bus and late that afternoon we arrived at our home away from home in Willimantic, Connecticut. We were together and happy. Ready to start a new life in a new country.

Rita Joe

(1932–2007)

Perhaps the most beloved Mi'kmaq writer, Rita Joe received numerous awards in her lifetime, including honorary doctorates from Dalhousie University, Cape Breton University, and Mount Saint Vincent University; the National Aboriginal Achievement Award; and membership in the Order of Canada. In her autobiography, from which the selections below are taken, she describes her childhood in Whycocomagh, Cape Breton; her traumatic experiences at the Shubenacadie Residential School; and her marriage, writing, and family life on the Eskasoni Reserve.

From Song of Rita Joe

They say that I must live
A white man's way.
This day and age
Still being bent to what they say,
My heart remains
Tuned to native time.

I lost my talk
The talk you took away
When I was a little girl
At Shubenacadie school.

You snatched it away;
I speak like you
I think like you
I create like you
The scrambled ballad, about my word.

Two ways I talk
Both ways I say,
Your way is more powerful.

So gently I offer my hand and ask,
Let me find my talk
So I can teach you about me.

This is what it is like for the Native people of today. It is hard for you to see our face, and sometimes it is even hard for us to see ourselves. In the first poem in my first book, I wrote:

I am the Indian,
And the burden
Lies yet with me.

Twenty years later, I am thinking the same thing. The brave part is in taking on history and leaving your own story. Today I still say, "This is who I am. I want to share it with you." *Ta'ho'!* (So be it.)

I am just an Indian on this land
I am sad, my culture you do not understand.
I am just an Indian to you now
You wrinkle your brow.
Today you greet me with bagpipes
Today you sing your song to me
Today we shake hands and see
How we keep good company.
Today I will tell stories
Today I will play the drum and dance
Today I will say what is on my mind
For being friends is our goal.
Today I will show you I am just like you
Today I will show what is true
Today I will show we can be friends
Together we agree.
Today I will tell you about my race
Today I will share what is mine
Today I will give you my heart
This is all we own
Today I show.
Hello everybody, my name is Rita Joe.

Daniel N. Paul
(b. 1938)

Daniel Paul has had a long and distinguished career as a writer and activist. Like many of his colleagues represented in this volume, he has received numerous prestigious national awards, including the Order of Canada, an honorary doctorate from the University of St. Anne, and an honorary law degree from Dalhousie University. Paul founded the Confederacy of Mainland Micmacs, the *Micmac Maliseet Nations News*, the Mainland Micmacs Development Corporation, and the Micmac Heritage Gallery in Halifax. A prolific writer, he has published reviews and essays in the *Halifax Herald* and other venues; a forthcoming novel; and a monumental Mi'kmaq history, *We Were Not the Savages*, now in its third edition. The selection below is taken from that well-known book.

From We Were Not the Savages

MORE BOUNTIES FOR HUMAN SCALPS

When Governor Edward Cornwallis and his entourage founded Halifax in 1749, it was during a lull in the war with the Mi'kmaq. In fact, the Mi'kmaq greeted them with hospitality. One settler wrote home: "When we first came here, the Indians, in a friendly manner, brought us lobsters and other fish in plenty, being satisfied for them by a bit of bread and some meat."

However, at British instigation, this would soon change. At an early September 1749 meeting with the Mi'kmaq Chiefs, a British emissary restated the dictum given to their predecessors in 1715: submit to British rule unconditionally. He also confirmed their fears about the Colonial Council's new settlement plans for the province. This gravely alarmed the Chiefs and they reacted as could be expected. On September 23, 1749, the Mi'kmaq renewed their declaration of war against the British and began attacking military, shipping, and trade targets.

Geoffrey Plank lays bare what Cornwallis had planned if such occurred:

If the Micmac chose to resist his expropriation of land, the governor intended to conduct a war unlike any that had been fought in Nova Scotia before. He outlined his thinking in an unambiguous letter to the Board of Trade. If there was to be a war, he did not want the war to end with a peace agreement. "It would be better to root the Micmac out of the peninsula decisively and forever." The war began soon after the governor made this statement.

SCALPING PROCLAMATION OF 1749

After he had read the first edition of *We Were Not the Savages*, published in 1993, Charles Saunders, a columnist with the *Halifax Daily News*, sent me a congratulatory note dated February 2, 1994:

> Several years ago, I watched a panel discussion that had several minority members, including a Black and a Micmac. The Micmac representative said that Blacks were slaves in the early days of European colonization, but his people were lower than slaves. At that time, I didn't understand what he meant. What, I wondered, is lower than being a piece of property to be bought and sold like a horse or cow? Then, in the chapter of your book titled "The Edge of Extinction," I read about how your people were systematically starved to death. At least a slave gets fed, simply because the owner has a vested interest in keeping him or her alive to maintain the slave's value as property. So, thanks to you, I know what it is to be "lower than a slave"—to not even have value as human chattel or property.

At the beginning of 1749, in line with the statement contained in this letter, as far as British colonial society was concerned, the life of a Mi'kmaq had no value. Thus, they were accorded no civil or human rights. Even the blatant murder or robbery of one or many Mi'kmaq by a White man was not considered a crime and went unpunished. Such was par for the course across the Americas. At that time, the mass murder of the Red People of the Americas, which was often successful in exterminating entire races, was still common and done without fear of recrimination. In keeping with this well-entrenched European practice, in 1749 Nova Scotia's colonial government undertook an attempt to exterminate the Mi'kmaq.

Related to this and other abuses cited in this chronicle, the term "genocide" will be used, because it aptly describes the barbaric behaviour of the British in colonial Nova Scotia. Its use in this case is appropriate because the mayhem the British subjected the Mi'kmaq to meets every single definition listed in the United Nations Genocide Convention. Canada's conduct after 1867 also fits into several of its definitions.

The term genocide was first used to describe the extermination of most of Europe's Jews by Nazi Germany. It was later used by the United Nations in 1948 in the Genocide Convention to mean crimes against humanity, The "Convention on the Prevention and Punishment of the Crime of Genocide" was adopted by the United Nations on December 9, 1948. Article 2 of the Convention defines the word:

> Genocide means any of the following acts committed with intent to destroy, in whole or in part, a national, ethnical, racial or religious group, as such:
>
> (A) Killing members of the group;
> (B) Causing serious bodily or mental harm to members of the group;
> (C) Deliberately inflicting on the group conditions of life calculated to bring about its physical destruction in whole or in part;
> (D) Imposing measures intended to prevent births within the group;
> (E) Forcefully transferring children of the group to another group.

When musing over what you have already read and what you will read, please keep these definitions of the Genocide Convention in mind.

During my youth, I had often heard, in offhand or incredulous remarks, about the bounties which purportedly had been put on the heads of the Mi'kmaq in Nova Scotia by the British during the mid-1700s. Although I knew that bounties were put on certain animals, such as porcupines, from time to by governments I never really took these statements about bounties on the Mi'kmaq seriously because I couldn't imagine that a people who claimed to be civilized could propose such an evil plan. When [you are] young, it takes time to shed your innocence.

Then, around 1965, when [I was] attending upgrading courses at the old sugar refinery in Dartmouth with my brother Lawrence and the late Norman Brooks, a friend from Indian Brook Reserve, the truth began to dawn. And it dawned in a most unusual way. Getting out of school early one day, we decided to go to the old Piccadilly Tavern in Halifax for a few beers. After arriving, we bought our brews with the few bucks we could raise between us and then wondered where we could find a few dollars for a couple more. Norman and I looked at my brother, who was sitting across from us with his back to the wall, and told him we didn't know where he was getting his money from, but we knew where we were getting ours. This was because Lawrence was sitting directly under a reproduction of a proclamation for Mi'kmaq scalps signed by Governor Cornwallis.

After the joking was finished, I read the document and began to feel sick as I realized it was probably a replica of the original. However, at that time, I was still carving out a niche in life for myself and thus set the matter aside for the time being. Then, after going to work for the Department of Indian Affairs in 1971, I began to study up on the Indian Act, peace treaties, and other historical documents. It was during this time that I verified, to my horror, that on three occasions the British colonial governments of this province had in fact issued bounties for the scalps of Mi'kmaq men, women, and children!

Perhaps if I had known then about some of the horrors that had been committed by the English in the British Isles and elsewhere, I wouldn't have been so shocked by my discovery. But in school we had been taught a romanticized version of English history which ignored such horrors as those played out in 1746 at the battle of Culloden in Scotland. It was there that English troops, under the command of the Duke of Cumberland, engaged in atrocities such as locking thirty Scots in a house and burning it down around them; shooting and bayoneting the wounded; and slaughtering the retreating army. As if this wasn't enough, after defeating the Highlanders, the English added to their misery by forbidding them to wear their national dress, deporting many, and suppressing their Gaelic language. Knowing about such things as this might have helped to prepare me for the discovery I had made. On the other hand, probably nothing can fully prepare one for the barbarities perpetuated by one group of humans against another.

On October 1, 1749, demonstrating that he was well endowed with a heartless cruelty, Cornwallis convened a meeting of Council, consisting of Jean Paul Mascarene, Edward How, John Gorham, Benjamin Green, John Salisbury, and Hugh Davidson, aboard H.M.S. *Beaufort*, anchored in Halifax Harbour, and won approval for the following sadistic response to the Mi'kmaqs' declaration of war:

> That, in their opinion to declare war formally against the Micmac Indians would be a manner to own them a free and independent people,

whereas they ought to be treated as so many Banditti Ruffians, or Rebels, to His Majesty's Government.

That, in order to secure the Province from further attempts of the Indians, some effectual methods should be taken to pursue them to their haunts, and show them that because of such actions, they shall not be secure within the Province.

That, a Company of Volunteers not exceeding fifty men, be immediately raised in the Settlement to scour the wood all around the Town.

That, a Company of one hundred men be raised in New England to join with Gorham's during the winter, and go over the whole Province.

That, a further present of 1,000 bushels of corn be sent to the Saint John's Indians, to confirm them in their good disposition towards the English, and,

That, a reward of ten Guineas be granted for every Indian Micmac taken, or killed.

The horror contained in these words, because of their blind White supremacist views, probably escaped the English. The next day, without a hint of conscience, the following proclamation was signed by Cornwallis and issued:

Whereas, notwithstanding the gracious offers of friendship and protection made in His Majesty's Name by us to the Indians inhabiting this Province, the Micmacs have of late in a most treacherous manner taken 20 of His Majesty's Subjects prisoners at Canso, and carried off a sloop belonging to Boston, and a boat from this Settlement and at Chinecto basely and under pretence of friendship and commerce. Attempted to seize two English Sloops and murder their crews and actually killed several, and on Saturday the 30th of September, a body of these savages fell upon some men cutting wood and without arms near the saw mill and barbarously killed four and carried one away.

For those causes, we, by and with the advice and consent of His Majesty's Council, do hereby authorize and command all Officers Civil and Military, and all His Majesty's Subjects or others to annoy, distress, take or destroy the Savage commonly called Micmac, wherever they are found, and all as such as aiding and assisting them, give further by and with the consent and advice of His Majesty's Council, do promise a reward of ten Guineas for every Indian Micmac taken or killed, to be paid upon producing such Savage taken or his scalp (as in the custom of America) if killed to the Officer Commanding at Halifax, Annapolis Royal, or Minas.

Thus, at a cost to his Majesty's colonial government's treasury of ten guineas per head, and at a cost to his servants of their immortal souls, an attempt to exterminate the Mi'kmaq was under way. It was an action no civilized nation would countenance, nor could any nation that undertook it be called civilized. Such barbaric behaviour, under any set of circumstances, is unforgivable. In apportioning the blame for the issuance of this hideous document, it was Cornwallis who proposed it and thus shoulders most of the responsibility, but the Councillors share almost as much guilt because they approved the monstrous dictum.

Such inhuman behaviour was not new to Cornwallis. According to data enshrined in a book entitled *Culloden* by John Prebble, Edward Cornwallis was the Lieutenant-Colonel of Bligh's militia and was stationed in Scotland during the 1740s. Prebble's book details how Cornwallis and his troops helped put down the Scottish rebellion and fully participated in the barbaric mistreatment of the Scots. These events occurred after the English had looted and burned Achnacarry:

> The black smoke of burning Achnacarry was still coiling down Loch Arkaig when Bligh's went away, swinging toward Moidart with Culcairn's militia, "burning of houses, driving away cattle and shooting those vagrants who were found to be in the Mountains."
>
> Much of what they did was not reported, but John Cameron, Presbyterian Minister and Chaplain at Fort William, wrote down an account of it in his journal. He said that when the party camped for the night on the braes of Loch Arkaig, they saw what they thought was a boat on the shore. A party went down to examine it, and found it to be a large black stone, "but that they might not return without some gallant action, on meeting a poor old man about sixty, begging, they shot him." They also found an old woman, blind in one eye and not much more than a beggar herself, and when she would not say where Lochiel was hidden (if she knew), she too was shot. "This is certain," said Minister Cameron, "but what is reported to have been done to her before she was dead, I incline not to repeat—things shocking to human nature."

"Culcairn's," according to Cameron, "were responsible for these shootings, but the men of Bligh's did their share. They saw two men carrying dung to their bitter fields and these were ordered to come before Cornwallis. They came but on their way were foolish or thoughtless enough to look back at their field. The soldiers shot them."

Professor Geoffrey Plank, University of Cincinnati, relates a historic consensus about Cornwallis's performance during the rebellion: "Cornwallis's operation was remembered years later as one of unrestrained violence. Men were killed if they looked away when they saw his men coming."

Cornwallis displayed a lack of human conscience while doing his part to help the English army subjugate the Scots. In view of this, it can be concluded that the man had an inborn taste for the crimes against humanity he committed in Nova Scotia. Such an affliction is well reflected in the warped rationale he used to try to justify his monstrous edict. The incidents listed in the first paragraph of his scalping proclamation were acts of war carried out by the Mi'kmaq against military targets. They deserved a military response against Mi'kmaq Warriors, not Mi'kmaq civilians. Trying to use a few incidents such as these to justify condemning to death an entire race of people is reprehensible, even more so when one considers that some of these incidents are suspect and possibly no more than propaganda.

For instance, the wood-cutting incident falls into this category (it's also an incident that I've grown very weary of hearing about). It is alleged that it occurred in what is now Dartmouth, across the harbour from Halifax. The proclamation says: "On Saturday the 30th of September [1749], a body of these savages fell upon some men cutting wood and without arms near the saw mill and barbarously killed four and carried one away." The question this poses is: why was this group of "defenceless" Englishmen sent out into the forest alone to cut wood during a time of war without troop protection and thus left vulnerable to attack? If this was the case then it smacks of gross incompetence on a British officer's part. If the story is true and not propaganda, a more credible reason for them being sent out without troop protection is that they were not defenceless but as well armed as the Mi'kmaq and probably more so. This can be reasonably assumed because, as woodcutters, they had axes to cut wood with, which alone would have made them possessors of weapons as lethally effective, and probably more reliable, than most of the arms the Mi'kmaq had access to. In any event, because the English were assaulting the Mi'kmaq and stealing their territory, Cornwallis and his Council should not have been so affronted and reacted so barbarously when the Mi'kmaq fought back.

In fighting back to preserve their freedom and country, the Mi'kmaq paid a heavy price. The records indicate that the barbarous proclamation was very productive. The slaughter was indiscriminate—pregnant women, the unborn, the old, the infirm—there were no exceptions; even some Caucasians were harvested. As an indication of how many scalps were taken, Bates wrote:

> It is reported that . . . a party of Gorham's rangers one day brought in 25 scalps, claiming the bounty of £10 per scalp. It was strongly suspected that not all of the scalps were those of Indians, but included some Acadians too. The paymaster protested the payment, but was ordered to pay £250 anyway. . . . The records of Chignecto include several instances of extreme cruelty and barbarism by the rangers.

It was further reported that eleven Rangers disappeared around this time. Some believe that their scalps may have been among those presented to the authorities for payment. These sorts of accusations by other Caucasians against them are an indication of the infamous reputations and low morals of these men. However, whatever they did to one another, they must have found the scalp trade very lucrative in Nova Scotia, because many of the killers sent from the Massachusetts Bay Colony to carry out the intention of Governor Shirley's evil 1744 proclamation found the returns so good that they spent many years in the province. In addition, the practice was so widespread that many nonmilitary Caucasians used it to supplement their incomes.

In all fairness, it must be stated that during this period the French at Louisbourg were not without dirty hands. In retaliation for Cornwallis's proclamation, they issued their own proclamation for the scalps or capture of British soldiers. But, it must be emphasized, it was not for civilians and especially not women and children. Some Mi'kmaq took up the challenge and delivered such. However, mostly they brought in live military prisoners and collected a bounty for them.

Factually speaking, most individual Mi'kmaq conducted themselves in a relatively humane and civilized manner during this trying period. The few that were involved in the bounty trade committed some atrocities, usually under the influence of alcohol supplied by Caucasians. However, many of the atrocities that the Mi'kmaq were blamed for were in fact committed by the "friendly Indians" brought in by the English. The English had such a great relationship with these people that they were often their victims. Perhaps this was simply poetic justice.

The Mi'kmaq Nation, to its everlasting credit, even in the face of such horrific provocations as the 1749 proclamation, did not respond in kind and adopt a policy to attack Caucasian women and children. Although some apologists try to make a case to the contrary, no evidence exists whatsoever to support such a contention. Most of the prisoners they took were turned over unharmed to the French at Louisbourg and later released. The same could not be said for Mi'kmaq prisoners held by the English. Many were held indefinitely, while others were taken to Boston and hung. Cornwallis, in an October 1749 memorandum to the Lords of Trade, requested retroactive approval for actions he had already initiated. The memo provides further proof of his insincerity and treachery towards the Mi'kmaq:

> When I first arrived, I made known to these Micmac His gracious Majesty's intentions of cultivating Amity and Friendship with them, exhorting them to assemble their Tribes, that I would treat with them, and deliver the presents the King my Master had sent them, they seemed well inclined, some keeping amongst us trafficking and well pleased; no sooner was the evacuation of Louisbourg made and De Lutre the French Missionary sent among them, they vanished and have not been with us since.
>
> The Saint John's Indians I made peace with, and am glad to find by your Lordship's letter of the first of August, it is agreeable to your way of thinking their making submission to the King before I would treat with them, as the Articles are word for word the same as the Treaty you sent me, made at Casco Bay, 1725, and confirmed at Annapolis, 1726. 1 intend if possible to keep up a good correspondence with the Saint John's Indians, a warlike people, tho' Treaties with Indians are nothing, nothing but force will prevail.

There are three points in Governor Cornwallis's letter on which I'd like to comment:

1. Cornwallis cites everything but the real reason why the Mi'kmaq ended their brief cordial relations with the settlers. The omitted reason—and perhaps due to his biases he was unable to recognize it—was that they had discovered that the British had come to seize more of their land and establish more settlements instead of making a lasting peace. Therefore, their disappearance from the site of Halifax at the same time the British were evacuating Louisbourg was only coincidental. The declaration of war made by the Mi'kmaq Chiefs in response to the seizure of ancestral lands attests to this.

2. The statement Cornwallis makes, that "Treaties with Indians are nothing, nothing but force will prevail," provides a clear picture of the morally bankrupt people the Mi'kmaq had to deal with. His pretending to promote honour and good faith in dealings with the Mi'kmaq and other Amerindians while at the same time having no intention to act accordingly clearly reveals his own corrupt ethical standards and those of the system he represented.

3. The unfounded accusation he made against the missionary Le Loutre demonstrates both his religious bigotry and White supremacist beliefs. His contention that "De Lutre [sic] the French Missionary" was the cause of the Mi'kmaq disappearance from Halifax reflects both an abiding hatred for Roman Catholics and a firm White supremacist belief that Amerindians did not have sense enough to value their territory and fight for it without being goaded on by a White man. The truth is that the missionaries did try to assist the Mi'kmaq in their hour of need, but they were not, as almost unanimously characterized by the English, religious devils who held absolute sway over every decision the Mi'kmaq made.

To refute and place in perspective this opinion widely held by English colonial officials which insults the intelligence of the Mi'kmaq, let's examine the role of the missionary that the British hated the most, the Vicar-General of Acadia and missionary to the Mi'kmaq, Abbe Le Loutre. The following are two evaluations of his character quoted from *Challenge and Survival: The History of Canada*:

(1) He fed their traditional dislike of the English, and fanned their fanaticism. . . . Thus he contrived to use them on one hand to murder

the English and on the other hand terrify the Acadians. . . . Le Loutre was a man of boundless egotism, a violent spirit of domination, an intense hatred of the English, and a fanaticism that stopped at nothing.

Towards the Acadians he was a despot: and this simple and superstitious people, extremely susceptible to the influence of their priests, trembled before him. He was scarcely less masterful in his dealings with the Acadian clergy; and, aided by his quality of the Bishop's Vicar General, he dragooned even the unwilling into aiding his schemes. Three successive governors of New France thought him invaluable, yet feared the impetuosity of his zeal, and vainly tried to restrain it within safe bounds.

(2) It is not easy at this distance of time to appraise the character of Abbe Le Loutre. Accounts of his activities have come down to us from a period when national prejudices were intensified by the bitterness of the desperate struggle for the mastery of the North American continent. It was not strange that Cornwallis thought him a scoundrel. Nor was it surprising that the French authorities esteemed him a single-minded patriot. Parkman calls him the evil genius of the Acadians. . . . That he used his influence over the Micmacs to oppose the power of Great Britain is indisputable; that he incited his Indians to acts of barbarity is probable. But, even when this is established beyond reasonable doubt, it remains true that he used a weapon which was employed by both British and French without scruple during the several phases of the American conflict. It is noteworthy that when he became a priest he did not cease to be a Frenchman. As a Frenchman he caught a vision of a new Acadia, secure in its allegiance to his king and firm in its fidelity to the church. Had he succeeded, his claim to eminence would not be unacknowledged.

Instead of the monster depicted by English colonial authorities and many later chroniclers of history afflicted with racial and religious biases, Le Loutre was a humanitarian. He probably was affronted and appalled, as any decent human being should have been, by the inhumanities being committed against the Mi'kmaq and other Amerindians by the English. This line of thinking is confirmed by the fact that he tried in vain in future years to arrange a peace with the British that would have left the Mi'kmaq with enough land to preserve their status as a free and independent people.

This, in my estimation, is probably the only unbiased conclusion one can reach when evaluating his motivations.

When trying to understand the hatred the British had for Le Loutre, another factor must be kept in mind—their unwavering resolve to dispossess the Mi'kmaq of everything and to subjugate them absolutely. Anybody with the unmitigated gall to beg to differ with them was branded everything from bandit to devil. This was Le Loutre's folly.

Contrary to what English officials thought, men such as Le Loutre assisted the Mi'kmaq in trying to deal with the impossible situation given them, but he did not think for them. To think otherwise is a racist insult. The Mi'kmaq are intelligent human beings who survived quite well for thousands of years without having a White man to think for them, and I'm sure in this case they did their own thinking.

The other thing I wish to add here is that I believe the paternalistic and patronizing attitude adopted by many White historians towards the Amerindian intellect is a defensive measure. If they can convince themselves that the people their ancestors brutalized, dispossessed, and in many cases exterminated were little more than savage animals, then they don't have to face up to the horrors committed by these ancestors. After all, when you simply put down pests and varmints, who should complain?

In a memo dated February 16, 1750, the Lords of Trade responded to Cornwallis's letter. They approved of but were not overly enthusiastic about the course of action chosen, for they cautioned him:

> As to the measures which you have already taken for reducing the Indians, we entirely approve them, and wish you may have success, but as it has been found by experience in other parts of America that the gentler methods and offers of peace have more frequently prevailed with Indians than the sword, if at the same times that the sword is held over their heads, offers of peace and friendship were tendered to them, the one might be the means of inducing them to accept the other, but as you have had experience of the disposition and sentiments of these Savages you will be better able to judge whether measures of peace will be effectual or not; if you should find that they will not, we do not in the least doubt your vigour and activity in endeavouring to reduce them by force.

Many apologists have claimed that the cruelties inflicted upon the Mi'kmaq and other Amerindian Nations were for the most part local acts of depravity and not acts sanctioned by the European Crowns themselves. However, this reaction by British officialdom towards Cornwallis's proclamation proves that contention wrong. By not rescinding or condemning his inhuman proclamation, the Lords of Trade, policymakers for the British government, showed support, thus implicating the British Crown itself in the crime of genocide.

The Lords also put into writing the paranoid fear the English had of Amerindians. It is embodied in the worry they expressed that the bounty on the Mi'kmaq might, "by filling the minds of bordering Indians with ideas of our cruelty," somehow unite all the Amerindian Nations of the Americas against them in a continental war. The equivalent of such an impossible feat would have been the uniting of all the countries in Europe against an invader, which, based on their mutual dislike of one another, would have been impossible. However, what the Lords proposed might happen poses an interesting point. If the people of the Americas could have overcome their cultural differences and united, and if they had been heirs to a class-based, barbaric, and warlike history similar to that of the Europeans, whom they may have outnumbered, most of the citizens of Europe today might be speaking a language imported from the Americas rather than the other way around.

Back to reality. The scalping bounties also adversely affected the Acadian population, because many of them were part Mi'kmaq or were related to Mi'kmaq families by marriage. Many Acadians were also scalped by the bounty hunters simply because they were handy and hated. On several occasions Acadian Deputies protested to the Governor about the existence of the bounties. In his stint as Governor, Mascarene in one instance pointed out to them that the many Acadian inhabitants living close to the fort were doing so quite peacefully. Such remarks did not alleviate the fear and hatred the Acadians held for the Rangers.

On June 21, 1750, in what must have resulted from dissatisfaction with the number of Mi'kmaq scalps being brought in, Cornwallis and his Councillors raised the monetary incentive by proclamation to fifty pounds sterling per head. It's interesting that Gorham himself was part of the Council which approved the 1749 scalp bounty, and he was also a member of the Council in 1750 when the bounty was raised. One might be excused for concluding that he was in a conflict of interest.

How many Mi'kmaq were killed during the carnage following Cornwallis's proclamations is unknown, although some records mention scalps being brought in by the bagful. The government possibly did not keep a close count on the expenditures or charged it off as a miscellaneous expense, or kept an accurate tally but, after realizing the horror of its actions, destroyed the evidence.

In 1752, three years after the despicable proclamation had been issued, the colonial government ordered a temporary halt to bounty hunting in the province. At a Council meeting held at the Governor's house on Friday, July 17, 1752, it was resolved that a proclamation be issued to forbid hostilities against the Indians:

> By His Excellency the Honourable Edward Cornwallis Esquire, Captain General, and Governor in Chief, in and over His Majesty's Province of Nova Scotia, or Acadia in America, and Vice Admiral of the same.
>
> Whereas, by the advise and consent of His Majesty's Council of this Province, two Proclamations were, by me, sometime since applied, authority and commanding (for reasons set forth in the said Proclamations) all Officers, Civic and Military, and all of His Majesty's Subjects within this Province, to annoy, distress, take and destroy the Savages called the Mickmack Indians, and promising a reward for each one of them taken or killed;
>
> And whereas, for sometime past no hostilities have been committed by the said Indians against any of His Majesty's Subjects, and some overtures tending to peace and amity have been made by them, I have thought fit, with the advice and consent of His Majesty's Council to revoke the said Proclamations, and every part thereof, and further do hereby strictly forbid all persons to molest, injure or commit any kind of hostility against any of the aforesaid Indians, or any Indian within this Province, unless the same should be unavoidably necessary in defense against any hostile act of any such Indians towards any of His Majesty's Subjects;
>
> And whereas, since the said cessation of hostilities, and publicly known design of a conference to be had between this Government, in conjunction with the Government of Massachusetts Bay, with the

Tribes of Indians residing within, or bordering upon the said Governments, some evil minded persons regardless of the public need, and the good intention of the said Governments in their endeavour to effect a renewal of peace, and amity with the said Indians, and in violation of good faith, have, lately, in a vessel said to belong to Plymouth in New England, treacherously seized and killed near Cape Sable, two Indian girls, and an Indian lad, who went on board the said vessel, under given truce, and assurances of friendship and protection;

I do hereby, promise a reward of fifty Pounds Sterling to be paid out of the treasury of this Province, to any person who shall discover the author, or authors of the said act, so that the same may be proved before me and His Majesty's Council, of this Province, within six months from the date hereof.

If by reading this document anyone concludes that Cornwallis had suddenly become a humanitarian they should think again. The government of the powerful Massachusetts Bay Province wanted peace with the Mi'kmaq, and therefore he had no choice but to halt hostilities. In fact, the Massachusetts Bay Governor was probably instrumental in pressuring Cornwallis to later resign.

Even after Cornwallis rescinded his proclamations, many colonials still assumed the bounties were in effect and tried to collect for scalps brought in. None were prosecuted.

The three children referred to in the Governor's proclamation died horrible deaths. They were butchered alive. No serious attempt was ever made by the colonial government to find and prosecute the culprits. In view of Cornwallis's own record, it would have been just short of a miracle if there had been.

Cancelling the bounty was one of the last official acts that Cornwallis performed as Governor. Shortly thereafter, he resigned his commission and was replaced by Peregrine Thomas Hopson, who was sworn into office on August 3, 1752.

Although Cornwallis's barbarity is well documented, much of it by his own hand, up to the year 2000 no White jurisdiction had ever condemned him for it. In fact, only honours have been given by authorities in Nova Scotia and Canada to the memory of the author of the 1749 inhuman scalping proclamation. A statue of him is displayed in a park located across from the railway station in Halifax, and schools, streets, ships, a naval base, and so on have been named after him. In view of this, I ask, and will continue to ask, how can my country, which claims to be civilized, award such honours to a man who authorized ethnic cleansing? In my estimation the only award such an individual deserves is the gallows. From a civilized point of view, only a person subscribing to the same White supremacist beliefs that Cornwallis and Hitler subscribed to would believe that killing "inferiors" is incidental.

By 1752, through the horrendous death toll taken by genocide, disease, starvation, and war, the Mi'kmaq population had been reduced to approximately 20,000 destitute people. However, the English considered even this drastically reduced and impoverished population a threat to their security and sought ways to neutralize it, while at the same time affording the Mi'kmaq no chance to retain their land or their dignity.

Almost two and a half centuries later, in 1998, the Mi'kmaq reacted with outrage to an invitation from the City of Halifax to participate in its 250th birthday celebrations. The city wanted them to provide a canoe filled with Mi'kmaq Warriors to greet an actor portraying Cornwallis entering Halifax Harbour. Reacting to the People's outrage, Mayor Walter Fitzgerald issued this apology on February 1, 1999: "While we cannot change history, I sincerely apologise for any atrocities which were committed against the Mi'kmaq after the founding of Halifax in 1749." I thought then, at long last, there would be some official recognition that the founder of Halifax was a far cry from being the hero he has been depicted to be by many politicians and more than a few historians. Alas, it was not to be. On June 21, 1999, Fitzgerald proved that he had spoken with a forked tongue. On stage with him when he cut Halifax's birthday cake was an actor dressed up as Cornwallis, to whom the Mayor served a piece. In response to reporters' questions about this turnabout he replied, "The Mi'kmaq tribes killed a lot of White people, probably more than we did." When reminded by a reporter that Cornwallis had put a bounty on the heads of the Mi'kmaq, including women and children, [he] responded, "I think he did. I'm not sure about that." Some sincerity!

Thankfully, there is opposition building to such archaic views among the Caucasian population. The enlightened view expressed by Art Gallery of Nova Scotia guest curator Mora Dianne O'Neill to a *Halifax Herald* reporter on June 26, 1999, may well be that of the majority. When planning the 1999 Great Harbour Exhibit, O'Neill felt that the Mi'kmaq presence in Halifax from 1749 to the present had to be a prominent part of the display. To gather support for the Mi'kmaq part of the project she met with the Chiefs in February 1999. At the meeting she was asked by the Chiefs how she could justify Cornwallis's 1749 scalp bounty. She said she could not. Later, at a June 26, 1999, media tour of the exhibit, after having read about Cornwallis's brutality during the massacre of the Scots at Culloden, O'Neill added, "After that, there was no way I'd see Cornwallis hanging rather than from a rope."

Otherwise intelligent Caucasians have told me with a straight face that Europeans were on a civilizing mission when they came and stole the Americas. However, the barbarous methods the Europeans used in stealing the two continents leaves me with the impression that they were the uncivilized attacking the civilized. If what they did was civilized behaviour, may we never be civilized again!

Marie Battiste
(b. 1949)

Marie Battiste received her doctorate of education at Stanford University in 1984 and has additional, honorary degrees from the University of Maine–Farmington and St. Mary's College. She is now a professor at the University of Saskatchewan, where she also directs the Aboriginal Educational Research Center. In 2008 Dr. Battiste won the National Aboriginal Achievement Award. She is the author of numerous books and essays on indigenous education. The selection below appears in *The Mi'kmaq Anthology*.

Structural Unemployment: The Mi'kmaq Experience

In the 1930s the Department of Indian Affairs began to make efforts to better integrate the Mi'kmaqs into the Maritime economy and also to simplify the administration of the reserve system. It began to put into effect a plan to move all Mi'kmaqs living on Nova Scotia reserves to only two reserves in the province—Shubenacadie on the mainland and Eskasoni in Cape Breton.

In the course of encouraging this new settlement pattern, another major change was made in the resource base available to Mi'kmaq communities.

What happened at the Eskasoni reserve is a typical example of the process initiated by the Department of Indian Affairs. The reserve consisted of self-reliant farms supporting twenty Mi'kmaq families. The farms stretched to the shores of the Bras d'Or Lake, where there was an abundant inshore fishery. Forty square miles of wooded uplands provided sufficient hunting and trapping, firewood, lumber, herbs, and berries.

When the Department of Indian Affairs chose Eskasoni as one of the Nova Scotia reserves into which the Mi'kmaq would be centralized, conditions began to change rapidly. Within a few years the department had removed more than a thousand Mi'kmaqs from homes and farms elsewhere in the province and relocated them in tents and other temporary housing on the former cleared agricultural fields at Eskasoni.

Most Mi'kmaqs were reluctant to leave homes on other reserves and relocate to Eskasoni. As encouragement, the department promised a better quality of life on the centralized reserves: new houses, medical services, schools, grants to purchase seeds and farm equipment, as well as jobs in a lumber mill or in housing construction and opportunities for other employment.

Not all the department's inducements were positive. Local schools and farms on some reserves were destroyed; threats were made to burn churches; and the department offered some Mi'kmaqs the alternative of moving to Eskasoni or losing all government assistance.

Upon their arrival at Eskasoni, Mi'kmaq families, expecting a home and immediate employment in the promised lumber mill, in clearing land, or in construction, found they had to wait in a long line for everything. Federal money for housing was only enough to build the shells of houses, without insulation and inner walls. Many families lived in tents through the winter. When it became clear that federal money to finish the houses was not forthcoming, families moved in anyway, for they reasoned it was better than living in the tents.

While farming was encouraged, most of the land available was not particularly suitable for agriculture. The clearings and pastures which were promised were not provided—housing came first: when the houses were done then the fields and pastures would be cleared. When the housing construction ended, so did the jobs. Eskasoni was left with fifteen hundred people without incomes or jobs, little farmland, no mill, and as the result of new federal regulations, restricted hunting and fishing.

The department's vision of centralized reserve life was a failure, destroying the Mi'kmaqs' small farm, trade, and craft economy but not providing any replacement. After centralization, in the 1940s and 1950s at least thirty percent of male Nova Scotia Mi'kmaqs left Canada to seek employment in New England. Other Mi'kmaqs returned to their original reserves and attempted to restart their small farms.

James Sakej Youngblood Henderson

(b. 1944)

Henderson is married to Marie Battiste, with whom he has three children, including Jaime. In 1974 he received a juris doctorate from Harvard Law School and became a law professor who created litigation strategies to restore Aboriginal culture, institutions, and rights. During the constitutional process (1978–93) in Canada, he served as a constitutional advisor for the Mi'kmaw nation and the National Indian Brotherhood—Assembly of First Nations. A noted international human rights lawyer and authority on protecting indigenous heritage, knowledge, and culture, Henderson was one of the drafters and expert advisors who developed the principles and guidelines for the protection of indigenous heritage in the UN human rights fora. He has also been a member of the Advisory Board to the Minister of Foreign Affairs and the Advisory Committee to the Canadian Secretariat for the World Conference against Racism, Racial Discrimination, Xenophobia, and Related Intolerance (WCAR) within the Department of Canadian Heritage. Currently he is a member of the Sectoral Commission on Culture, Communication, and Information of the Canadian Commission for UNESCO; the Eminent Person Implementation Committee for Traditional Knowledge in the Biodiversity Convention Office; and the Experts Advisory Group on International Cultural Diversity. The following excerpt appears in *Honoring 400 Years: Kepmite'tmnej*, edited by Jaime Battiste.

Mi'kmaq Treaties

INTRODUCTION

After the Thirty Years' War between the Catholics and Protestants in Europe the Treaty of Westphalia (1648) created a new regime in international law of Europe. This treaty order divided Europe into Catholic and Protestant states. The states embarked on the establishment of a world order based on the secular sovereignty of states and on treaties, rather than under the Holy See. The change brought instability among the European monarchs who fought over acquiring jurisdiction over different parts of Mi'kmaki, and the Mi'kmaq were forced to defend their territories. This defense required the executives and delegates of the Grand Council and the chiefs to negotiate treaties with the secular states that claimed an interest in Mi'kmaki.

Under the Putuswagn traditions and the Aboriginal transnational law (Nikmanen law), the executive of the Grand Council of the Mi'kmaw Nation or their selected delegates were empowered to speak for the nation in the treaties and alliances. They were charged with creating and maintaining the centralized relationship with other nations and authorities. This was their unique role. However, the executive did not have inherent authority to enter into treaties that would automatically bind the district chiefs that comprised the Grand Council. Each of the Mi'kmaw districts had to consult with their families and ratify or renew negotiated treaties.

The Mi'kmaw treaties are about relationship and diplomacy. They are about maintaining and structuring relationships between diverse nations, Aboriginal and European. The treaties were a reflection of their spiritual heritage and their consensual traditions. They were concerned with creating a legal and diplomatic relationship with these nations. The relationship was conceived as a kinship relation, a "Chain in our Hearts," and a "friendship."

In 1726 the Council entered into treaty relations with the British Crown as allies of the Wabanaki Confederacy, by ratifying the central 1725 Compact with the Wabanaki and the Crown. In 1752 the Council entered into a direct Compact with the British Crown. It was known as Elikawake, being with the King's House. These two treaties are the center of the treaty relations and are surrounded by many ratifications and renewals by district chiefs and captains.

In the negotiation of the 1752 Compact, the Grand Chief explained the Mi'kmaw traditions. While he was empowered to treaty on behalf of the Mi'kmaw Nation, he had to return to the people, inform them of the treaty, go to the other chiefs and propose to them to renew the peace, use his utmost endeavors to bring the other districts to make peace, and return with their answers. This protocol was identical to that used in the 1610 alliance with the Church and in the Wabanaki Compact of 1725. It provided formal recognition of the treaty union with the British king with the Mi'kmaq "heirs and the heirs of their heirs forever."

The federated structure of the "Mickmack Nation" confused the European nations and colonialists. They were familiar with a king who conducted foreign affairs and entered treaties for the people without any consultation with his subjects or Parliament. It was not until 1760 that the British Crown's agent, Colonel Fry, revealed the federated structure of the Mi'kmaw nation and the need for separate ratification treaties with each district. These ratifications and renewals of previous treaties with each district created the "Covenant Chain," or the treaty federation with the Mi'kmaq Nation.

The Council and Delegates used wampum belts and strings, songs, and ceremonies to remember the terms of the compacts. The British used documents written by hand. These documents are found in the British and colonial archives, but many of the written treaties have not been found. In courts of law, the written documents have proven unreliable in incorporating the Mi'kmaw understanding of the treaties, so the courts have developed special rules to discover the Mi'kmaq understanding of the treaties. The following are treaties that were in the British Archives giving their understanding of the Covenant Chain of Mi'kmaq Treaties.

MI'KMAQ TREATIES AND COMPACTS

1610 National Treaty with Holy See of Catholic Church for all districts

1630 Treaty with Sir William Alexander for English King James I at Kespukwitk and Sipekne'katik

1638 Treaty with French King by Sikniktewaq and Kespekewaq representatives (still under research)

1646 Treaty with Innu and Algonquians

1725 Treaty ratified in 1726 and 1749 Treaties by all districts

1752 Treaty with imperial Crown of Great Britain ratified in 1753 by Kespukwitk district

1755 Treaty with Great Britain by Sikniktewaq district.

1759 Treaty renewing treaties of 1726 and 1752 by Epekwitk aqq Piktuk and Unamakkik

1760 Treaty renewing of treaties of 1726 and 1752 Treaty by Sikniktewaq, Sipekne'katik, Eskikewa'kik, Epekwitk aqq Piktuk, Unamakik, Kespekewaq

1761 Treaty renewing treaties for remaining chiefs of Piktuk, Unamakik (Ktaqtrnkuk), and Kespekewaq

1764 Treaty of Niagara with imperial superintendent Johnson of all districts

1776 Watertown Treaty with United States of America with all districts

1778 Treaty renewing peace treaties with Great Britain and Kespekewaq

1779 Treaty renewing treaty of 1726, 1752, 1760–61 with Sikniktewaq and Kespekewaq districts

1780 National Treaty with Odawa, Huron Alogonqian, Abenakis, etc.

1786 Treaty renewing treaties of 1726, 1752, 1760–61, 1778 with Kespeke-waq district

1794 Treaty with John Julian, renewing treaties with Sikniktewaq district

1796 National Treaty with Aboriginal nations at Kahnawake

Lorne Simon
(1960–1994)

An enormously talented young writer, Lorne Simon died in a car accident, cutting short a promising writing career. He was born in Big Cove and studied at the En'owkin International School of Writing in British Columbia. In his honor the Mi'kmaq Maliseet Institute in New Brunswick offers the Lorne Simon Award each year to a new writer. The following selection comes from his novel *Stones and Switches*. Set in the Depression era, it follows a young Mi'kmaq man, Megwadesk ("northern lights," in Mi'kmaq), through his struggles with poverty, racism, and conflicts between Catholicism and traditional Mi'kmaq spirituality.

From Stones and Switches

Suddenly Megwadesk asked, "Do you believe in that Bible stuff, eh? You know, all the miracles like Jesus raising the dead?"

"Sure, I believe in Jesus," Skoltch answered, not at all surprised by the question. He had been expecting something like this from Megwadesk. For such an uncanny fisherman, Skoltch thought, Megwadesk still asked the foolish questions of a youth.

"Can you believe in a god who'll make everybody rise stark naked 'n' all rotted on judgement day, eh?" Megwadesk continued. The growing sunlight made him bold. He could voice his secret horrors now.

"Sure, sure," Skoltch answered with feigned impatience. He was pleased, actually, for this opportunity to wax philosophical. A conversation with Megwadesk was always good for that. "But you shouldn't worry about them details! Let the white people worry about all that stuff! Nisgam gejidoq![4] We didn't have nothing to do with his murder! As far as I see it, on judgement day Jesus will come down on a cloud and he'll go to all the reserves first and tell all the Indians to just keep right on fishing, that's all! Then he'll get back on his cloud again and fly off to Trenton and go deal with the white people there, and everywhere else there's whites—and, by God, they'll pay for killing him all right, and for killing all the land and all the rivers and all the fish and leaving none for us! Amudj![5] They'll pay! Jesus was a fisherman! And don' you forget it! He knew where to set his nets, too—even better than you, I'm sure! He understands us! So don't you worry!"

Skoltch's comments annoyed Megwadesk. He told Skoltch, "You make Jesus sound like Gluskeb almost, eh, the way he'll help us and all."[6]

"Well, they're cousins, I think," Skoltch declared. "Or maybe stepbrothers! I forget right now how it was my dad put it! My dad was only good for stories, you know! But anyway, Gluskeb took care of us for a long time till he got tired, 'cause we were always making trouble for him, going to war with all kinds of tribes and everything like that! Gisulk, Mali![7] So Gluskeb needed a rest! Before he left, he called his cousin, Jesus, and told him to come on over and take care of us for a while! Sort of like babysit, I guess! So Jesus said, no problem, jinym![8] Remember, Malsum still had to be watched or else that devil would take over the world again! So Gluskeb knew somebody like Jesus had to be here while he went out west to sleep a bit!

"But Jesus was kinda lazy, see! He liked his wine too much, I think! Anyway, he stayed home and only sent his messengers to look after us! That's the priests and stuff! But you know how messengers are! Gluskeb never could leave anything up to his messengers, loon and rabbit! Nisgam gejidoq! If he did, they would make a mess of things! Eq![9] Bana total mess![10] So it's the same with these messengers from Jesus! Instead of just taking care of us and baptizing us and giving us decent burials, these priests turned around and invited all kinds of other people with them, see! Bana foolishness!

"So judgement day's going to come around just after Gluskeb wakes up and just before he gets back here! Gluskeb is going to shoot his arrow ahead of him and it'll land in the Minas Basin, see, to tell Jesus he can pack up his stuff and get ready to go back to his home! And Jesus'll get scared, see, 'cause he's let his messengers make a big mess of things here, and it's really all his fault 'cause he's been so lazy, see! Gisulk, eh! That's when he'll come around on his cloud and tell us to keep right on fishing and then he'll take all the other people together, even the dead ones—he'll call them right up from their Loyalist graves and all—and tell them, 'Listen here,' Jesus will say, 'either you go back with me or you go to hell.'

"Of course, you know how stubborn white people are! Many of 'em'll stand around their farms with their shotguns in their hands! Nisgam! They'll be just ready to kill Jesus all over again, if he so much as steps near their potato gardens! So poor Jesus'll have no choice but to send Satan after them! Satan'll come out of the water with his red cape and red whip and flog the laggards! Some clever ones'll manage to run away and hide in the swamps, though! Then Gluskeb'll come back and if there's any left over—shotgun or not—he'll take them by the scruff of their necks and throw them across the ocean, and tell them to stay there! They can hide from Jesus and Satan but they won't be able to hide from Gluskeb, that's for sure!"

Megwadesk did not find the story helpful. In his mind, either one believed in the old ways or one believed in the white man's Christian ways and yet there were many stories around which were a blend of the two.

"I've heard stories where Gluskeb and Jesus had contests and Gluskeb always won, eh," Megwadesk said. "First time I heard this one, though."

"Oh, yeah, Gluskeb always wins!" Skoltch said very seriously. "Dad told me them stories, too! Oh, there's hundreds of them! One time, some white guy came around here and wrote a couple down, but the old timers pulled his leg! Instead of telling him all the Gluskeb stories, they told him fairy tales, with Indians in them though, just to see if he'd write those down, too, and call them legends! Nisgam! And he did! So that's how much some people know! Ho! We're always pulling people's legs— and looking pretty serious when we're at it, too! But, anyway, about this Jesus and stuff! Meantime we got to go to church and all that just like a kid has to listen to a baby-sitter! But don't worry about all that judgement day stuff! It's just for white people really! That's why the priests are always going on about it, because they're guilty and they know it and it's always on their minds, bugging them like! So they go on and on about it! Me and you, we're okay and we'll keep right on fishing, either way! Personally, I wouldn't blink an eye if judgement day happened this afternoon!"

Skoltch coughed and then fell silent. His voice was hoarse from all the shouting. Talking down to people was exhausting sometimes.

"Oh, I'm not scared of that stuff, either. Don't get me wrong, eh," said Megwadesk. "I'm just curious 'bout what you think, that's all. But you don't really believe that silly story, eh? That's the matter with our people!"

"What's the matter? What're you talking about? Don't you know a good story when you hear one?"

"Too many of our stories are like that, that's all."

"Like what?"

"They're just like wishes that we keep holding tight to, eh, an' after a while all's we got's is wishes."

"What do you mean, 'wishes'? I'm telling you what my elders told me! It's like a story the prophets tell! It talks about what's gonna happen one day!"

"An' I say instead of wishing the white people'll just disappear one day and we'll all live happily ever after, we gotta start dealing with the facts, eh. Geez, we keep acting like we can just go on ignoring the real world, like we don't have to change someday 'n' start picking up ways of surviving in the white world!"

"That's not—"

"Sure it is! Sure, that's what it's about! Boys oh boys, just look at the story they tell about Old Set-Bol coming back to haunt the priest. They just wish the old priest could be scared. By something the way he can scare the people, eh, so they make this story up 'n' it makes 'em feel good—like it really happened. That's like justice for them. But, really, eh, it's just a fill-in for justice. It's all really 'bout wishful thinking, and nothing 'tall else! Nisgam nuduid, why do you think people believe in spirits and witches for, eh? It's 'cause they feel like they got no real power. So they need this magic power. If they can't get back at the whites for stealing all the land, then they'll say that the spirits like Jesus or Gluskeb or whatever'll get back at them one day! That's no different than anything else, either! If you do something wrong to another fellow in Messkig, 'n' you get away with it, like you don't pay a fine or go to jail or nothing, eh, then that fellow'll tell himself, *Well, maybe I can't do nothing but the spirits'll get 'im back 'cause what goes 'round comes 'round*.[11] Then he'll feel a little better. See what I mean? All these stories 'bout spirits 'n' medicine 'n' stuff is just a way of keeping our blinders on! We don't even see half—.

"So that's all you see in them stories, huh?" Skoltch cut in. "Then it's you who don't even see half of what them stories are for! First off, let me tell you that I don't act like I don't have to deal with the white world! I have to deal with them people all the time and some of them are real nice but lots of times they get away with things like throwing rocks at people and stealing land left and right! Okay, then! This story I told you tells me that we're not like them! We never went across the ocean and stole their land and told them they couldn't do this or they couldn't do that! So who's right? We're right! Now if we're right, does it mean that we should forget about our honest ways just because we're in a weaker position now? No, sir! I don't think so! Like I said in the story, we keep right on fishing and living the way God wants us to! We don't just turn around and be like them, stealing land, hurting people, taking kids away from their parents, breaking up families, destroying all the trees, being greedy, greedy, greedy! If they're right, then I'd rather be wrong! You see now what you missed in that story?"

"Well, let me put it 'nother way—" Megwadesk said but just then, the door opened and a brutal-looking middle-aged man with a twisted nose, a chipped eyebrow, and a lopsided grin swaggered in. His hair was dishevelled and there were branches stuck to his clothing in a manner that hunters sometimes wore to camouflage themselves in the woods.

"Here to see godmother Molly!" the fellow demanded, banging the door shut behind him. Megwadesk glared at him. Even from seeing only his back, he knew it was Rancid.

Lindsay Marshall

(b. 1960)

Lindsay Marshall has served as chief at the Potlotek (Chapel Island) First Nation in Nova Scotia, principal of the Unama'ki College at Cape Breton University, and as a Mi'kmaw poet laureate. In 1997 he published a book of poems, *Clay Pots and Bones*, from which the following selections are taken.

Clay Pots and Bones

Dear successive fathers:
Explain to me please, when did the
change take place, from owners
to wards of the selfish state?
Write down the reasons why
the land under our feet became
foreign soil in perpetuity.
Say again how the signers of
1752 lost as much as they
gained while the ink from a
quill pen rested in its
blackened Royal well.
What justification exists that
allowed our mounds to be
desecrated, clay pots and bones.
Rock glyphs painted over by
CFC-propelled paint.
Our songs and stories protected
by copyright and law, not in the
bosom of our grandmothers or
grandfathers of yesterday.
The cost of keeping us does
not reflect the real cost.
How many ghostly sails with

reeking holds did English
ports comfort in early fog?
Have you much experience in
the destruction of people,
besides us?

Mainkewin? (Are You Going to Maine?)

Do you remember Maine?

Do you remember telling everyone who would
listen that you were going to Vacation Land
picking blueberries?

Do you remember the taste of your first submarine
washed down with a cool Bud from the first store
you saw after you crossed the border?

Do you remember the cool mornings that enabled
you to get fifty plus boxes that first day at work
there in the barrens?

Do you remember where you went swimming to
cool off in the afternoons? Was it Schoodic Lake or
Columbia Falls?

Do you remember going back to the camp
after picking blueberries and seeing the filth
on your body?

Do you remember waking up the next day and
being unable to move without pain?

Do you remember working in the hot August sun
not worrying about the uv index?

Do you remember being up half the night treating
your badly burned red back and asking yourself,
"What am I doing here?"

Do you remember the excitement of getting your
first pay and spending it in Cherryfield, Millbridge
or Ellsworth?

Do you remember the Bay Rum Pirates, Canned
Heat Gang behind Grant's General Store?

Do you remember staying until the frost killed
the best berries of the season, the ones that were
promised to you by the leaseholder?

Do you remember hurrying to get home so the
kids could go to school?

Do you remember the trip home and someone
asking at the border, "All Indians?"

Progress

Handshakes, smiles all around, the
suits come in the band office
carrying their pens
Fast polite chatter, wet palms
hiding papers piled like a pyre
inside leather boxes with brass locks.
Minions of the queen mentioning her
thorny hat, this and that and the act
words spoken with no ahs or ays
The counselled Council listens
to the Concord pitch, its pros and cons
weighing each grain against each rock
Four plaque-like walls holding their eyes
Seeing nothing, new or different
since the last time
Mouthpiece spinning spiels, nods of non-comprehension
feathers combed not ruffled, patted nor struck
sign here, initial there, witness here

more handshakes dry palms wet again.
Saunter out the old Indian Day School now
band office, boxes go out with white blisterless hands
clutching pens like Cornwallis trophies
Black ink slowly drying with red splatters here, there . . .

Jaime Battiste
(b. 1979)

Jaime Battiste has a bachelor of arts in Mi'kmaw studies and bachelor of law from Dalhousie Law School. He is a First Nations and Mi'kmaq advisor, a constitutional and human rights advocate, and an advocate for First Nations youth. He has been on the national executive council of Assembly of First Nations and an assistant professor of Mi'kmaq studies at Cape Breton University and is now the legal advisor of the Grand Council of the Mi'kmaw Nation. He has published law review articles about Mi'kmaq law and Aboriginal and treaty rights and a book looking at the four-hundred-year history of Mi'kmaq diplomacy titled *Honoring 400 years: Kepmite'tmnej*. He was honored as a national role model by the National Aboriginal Health Organization. The following essay excerpt originally appeared in the *Dalhousie Law Journal*.

From "Understanding the Progression of Mi'kmaq Law"

Since the Court's recognition of aboriginal and treaty rights has affirmed the contemporary jurisgenesis of the Mi'kmaw creation story, the Crown and its agencies must acknowledge and establish a mechanism to implement treaty rights and constitutionally reconcile aboriginal rights of the Mawi'omi.[12] This process should be guided by Mi'kmaw oral teachings, legal traditions, and the constitutional framework, rather than be shaped by a policy framework developed unilaterally by the Crown. These teachings, traditions, and treaty are the origin of the constitutional relationship between the Mawio'mi and the Crown. They generate a *sui generis* relationship that is empowered by the core precepts of the honour of the Crown. This constitutional relationship has three distinct but often converging components: a respect for aboriginal law and tenure of the Mawio'mi, a mutual treaty relationship, and a fiduciary relationship embedded in imperial law. Any of these relations give rise to distinct constitutional obligations of the Mawio'mi and the Crown that inform the obligation of honourable governance.

Our history as Mi'kmaq has showed us that we have persevered through many obstacles and many misfortunes. As Mi'kmaq in Atlantic Canada we have our own indigenous laws, yet for a few centuries, as today, the courts and politicians have tried to persuade our people that these are not valid and must be abandoned. However, recent cases such as *Simon, Marshall,* and *Sappier-Gray* have helped to paint a different picture of our future. At the same time this trilogy of Mi'kmaq Supreme Court victories affirms our sacred teaching in the Mi'kmaq creation story. Recent cases have pointed out that our laws, embedded in our languages, are important keys to advancing our rights. While the courts have accepted the arguments put forward by Mi'kmaw people regarding the meaning of *sui generis* treaty and aboriginal rights, it is for us, as Mi'kmaq leaders, now and in the future, together with Mi'kmaq people, to truly define who we are for ourselves and what laws we seek to hold.

In the past the Mawio'mi has asked elected leadership at the band and organizational level to work together as a nation and not be divided by Canada's strategy of using Indian Act bands to carry out a band-by-band approach to negotiating. This advice was supported in the report of the Royal Commission on Aboriginal Peoples, which advanced a nationhood approach to problem solving as an answer to the multiple economic and political issues.

That said, it must be stated that there are many *Indian Act* chiefs who have urged working together and gaining capacity as chiefs working together on behalf of their nation. They, along with the Mawio'mi, argue that temporary solutions that ignore long-term problems will continue to lead us down the wrong path. The Harvard Project on American Indian Economic Development is one example of research conducted, showing how short-term nonstrategic decision making is characteristic of the standard approach of Native Nations. This approach has resulted in failed enterprises, highly dependent economies, and continued poverty and cultural stress. This is why different approaches must be taken that take into consideration long-term strategies that decrease dependency on year-to-year funding agreements.

The Harvard Project on American Indian Economic Development recommends a "nation-building approach." Part of that approach is having the "governing institution match indigenous political culture." This cultural match gives legitimacy and respect to the administration and the nation in the eyes of its membership. Greater respect for laws within that membership is a direct result, which means an improved and more efficient government model.

The cultural match model has its difficulties in terms of possible "what if" scenarios. The problem that many of our leaders point to in terms of creating custom codes that are based on Mawio'mi laws is that the approval of the minister of the Department of Indian Affairs and Northern Development is still needed to change existing citizenship or election laws. The minister, of course, could base any refusals on a whim or any reason at all, as well as on concepts that are Eurocentric in nature, such as principles of democracy or individualism. This argument is valid in that there are constitutional challenges to protecting our Mawio'mi laws and constitutional rights; however, we must not be afraid of temporary failure. Fear is not part of our constitutional rights; it is a product of racism and colonialization of our last five generations, which has resulted in cognitive imperialism. During the constitutional table discussion that is showcased in the documentary *Dancing around the Table*, the late Joe Mathias, a leader for the First Nations of British Columbia, stated, "Behold the turtle, it only moves forward when it sticks its neck out." The Mi'kmaq must learn how to overcome obstacles in the same way and must take risks and be bold to make progress and protect Mi'kmaq identity that consists of political integrity, language, and culture.

The Mi'kmaq have always adapted with the times and as we have evolved in other areas our methods of governance must also evolve. Yet it is important to remember that, as Mi'kmaq, we must keep those traditions alive that have set us apart from European or foreign settlers, for in those differences lay our aboriginal and treaty rights. By valuing our language, culture, and customs and by engaging and learning from our Elders and knowledge holders, we learn from our land and our ecology, keeping in mind the responsibilities of being Mi'kmaq and that these are delicate resources that need to be nourished and protected. We have lived for numerous centuries in Mi'kma'ki and our multiple generations have learned from our land, our place, our environment, and we have an immense knowledge that is useful today, as it will be tomorrow. Some of this knowledge we can share with others, and in so doing preserve and protect that knowledge for future generations. It can help us to understand the full effect of using the land and resources respectfully, without exploitation of the resources and the ecosystem.

By continuing Mi'kmaq learning we need to include research of the language through and with our Elders and knowledge keepers. More can be learned about Mi'kmaq values, customs, and traditions and about our indigenous laws for our everyday lives, whether as administrators or as leaders, as fathers and mothers. It is the responsibility of each of us to hold on to Mi'kmaw law and aboriginal and treaty rights. These are imbedded in responsibilities to retain the teachings, knowledge, values, and strength of our nation, for now and for the future. Our Mi'kmaq laws and our population should not be replaced by Canadian influences, which in a few generations would make it impossible to tell who we are and what sets us apart from others.

We must use creativity and teamwork to advance our rights and our rightful place within Atlantic Canada. In so doing, we will ensure our spot as a prosperous nation, and at the same time ensure that we as well as others remain respectful of our delicate ecosystem. We have yet to really reflect as Mi'kmaq how to move forward while ensuring that we adapt, evolve, and at the same time renew our traditional laws and values.

In concluding, it is important to acknowledge the value of the courts in helping to define for Canadians the law of the land, but we recognize that we cannot depend on them. Rather, it is up to us as Mi'kmaq leaders, scholars, lawyers, students, teachers, and experts to begin discussing reconciliation. As Mi'kmaq, how are we to move forward utilizing our strengths and centuries of experience in Atlantic Canada? Finally, we must not expect the federal and provincial Crowns, or the judicial system, to resolve our issues; we must look to our own teachings and balance our values, principles, and goals in a just reconciliation process. By doing so we can take the first step towards creating a better future not based on another culture's agenda or rules but rather on what we have always had within us.

Alice Azure

(b. 1940)

Alice Azure's recent writings have appeared in *Native Literatures: Generations; Yellow Medicine Review; Whisper n Thunder; I Was Indian: An Anthology of Native Literature; Visions and Voices: American Indian Activism and the Civil Rights Movement; Many Mountains Moving; Yukhika-latuhse; Mid Rivers Review;* and *Birthed from Scorched Hearts: Women Respond to War*. A Mi'kmaq Métis, her roots are in the Kespu'kwitk District of Nova Scotia. The St. Louis Poetry Center, to which she belongs, published her prize-winning poems in its annual chapbooks of 2007 and 2008. Her first book, and the source of the following poems, *In Mi'kmaq Country: Selected Poems and Stories*, was released in 2007 by Albatross Press. In 2012 her book *Games of Transformation* was named poetry book of the year by the Wordcraft Circle of Native Writers & Storytellers.

Repatriation Soliloquy

for Hunter Bear, Micmac Man[13]

The moment I saw you in that eye-popping oil painting—
forty inches wide by forty-six inches tall,
fiery red background framing your cowboy hat,
brim drawn down, further shading sun-glassed eyes,
pipe clenched in the corner of bear-jaws,
denim jacket drawn open across the relaxed expanse

of your white-shirted torso, elbows jutted outside
the portrait's border, open book balanced
in your right hand and
in the center of all this unnerving masculinity
sat two cups of your favorite drink, coffee—
that moment I knew I'd have to be the painting's caretaker.

My husband's lips tightened, face went ashen
as I paid the artist—your brother—his asking price.
Back home, the portrait, named Micmac Man,
got relegated to our basement den

where many nights I retreated,
beating my brains for understanding about why your image
should hold such sway upon my soul
like a Marlboro Cowboy gone amok,
sniffing the spoils of an unraveling animal—
easy hog-tying points. Then

I remembered your classroom style and teachings—
a great oak, unperturbed by winds,
always fighting for grass-roots people—
miners, migrants, Native Americans,
Black citizens caught up
in the Jackson, Mississippi, lunch counter boycotts.
Your family life bespoke a discipleship
of which I was incapable.
Thank God your detachment
from academic indoctrination

led me to ancient stories of Migoum'agi—
land of the Micmac—
how Kesoulk made Glous'gap, who, in turn taught the People
to thrive in a new creation.
Faintly I began to hear the sweet notes of a flute's song
nudging me towards that same country—beckoning me to
another beginning. One day I left
the material comforts of my home, your portrait in tow.

For nearly a decade your image hung central in my homes
from Rock Island to Washington DC and back to Chicago.
I called you a "marriage spoiler,"
for in your exalted position over my couch,
male visitors seemed to squirm, uneasy with
my MYTH —man in the house,
quintessential Indian Cowboy,
favorite professor,
clear-sighted justice worker—
all rolled into my inner MYTH of masculine psychology.

One man—Alec Azure—wasn't fazed.
He knew you as a compassionate friend,
was one of many who accompanied you on visits
to Fort Madison Penitentiary's Indian prisoners.

After we wed, he mildly suggested
the dominant red of your portrait's fine image
could brighten the interior of NAES College's[14]
fire-renovated white-drabness.
Opting for domestic harmony,
I donated you away to the college—
hung Micmac Man high in the central stairwell
where all of us who worked there daily passed
under your confident, laid-back calm.

After Alec passed to spirit—after I left the college's employ,
your portrait was removed down to the archives,
where you stayed until a decade later
when the time of your repatriation at last arrived.

It wasn't easy getting you out of that place
with me then living in southeastern Connecticut.
My Chicago friends—mostly women—said they'd help.
In the dark of night,
your portrait strangely astir,
they carried you out of NAES,
detached the canvas from its frame

staple by rusted staple,
rolled you up in bubble wrap
and sent you on your way
over interstate roads from Chicago to Pocatello.

Maybe it was a multiplier effect
of good medicine unleashed
by a Web-based tribute from your friends—
students, colleagues, comrades-in-arms, family and the rest
hundreds banded together—
that led to your release from that dark storage, from
the near lethal grip of Systemic Lupus.

On the other hand, as you once suggested,
your own Bear Medicine unrolled its Power,
returned you and Micmac Man to where you belong
front and center in that place you now sit—
will always sit—
among family and friends, enjoying camaraderie
and those cups of early morning coffee.

Mi'kmaq Haiku

Kejimkoojik[15]
cliffs, old sweet fern petroglyph
still keeping us calm

Someday I Will Dance

At Indian Summertime
When sugar maple, ash and oak
Turn the land to blazing hues,
When earth has given of her bounty,
They say you can see the People dance
Invisible yet present,
You can hear the People dance

In gratitude to Mother Earth,
Giving thanks to Spirit God.

Do they dance at old Saukenuk,
At the Capes of North and Blomidon?
Do their voices rise above Katahdin,
Around the harvests of Gaspé?

I've never seen them dance
Nor heard the People sing.
The realm of spirit things slips by,
Mystery seems to shun
This world of asphalt grids,
Concrete minds, anxious hearts
Strangers to the healing earth.

But today at Indian Summertime,
When Spirit God and Mother Earth
Unfold to me this season loved,
Today I know that

Someday, with the People, I will dance,
Someday, with the People, I shall sing.

Starlit Simon

(b. 1983)

The niece of Lorne Simon, also in this volume, Starlit Simon is from Elsipogtog (Big Cove) First Nation, New Brunswick. She earned a BA in sociology from the University of New Brunswick. In 2006 she worked at the Fredericton Native Friendship Center, where she created and wrote a newsletter, the *Mali-Mac Times*. Later she traveled through Canada and Europe, which led her to a new love: writing. She is pursuing her MFA in creative nonfiction at the University of Kings College and maintains her own website at starlitsimon.com. "Without a Microphone" was her first publication, appearing in *National Geographic Traveler* in March 2010. "In Quest of Road Kill" appeared in the *New Brunswick Beacon* online in February 2012.

Without a Microphone

The Celt is packed with Dublin locals and a few tourists who've heard of the place or have stumbled in to find a drink.

"You just never know who's gonna play here!" a Scottish man bellows to his friends who are crammed at the entrance. "You might even see the friggin' Edge."

Gradually the patrons maneuver through the room to their destination: the curved bar in the back. The pub is small but warm and welcoming, in part because a crowd has managed to squeeze their way inside this Sunday night. The long wood benches pushed up against the walls are filled with flushed, smiling faces, and the few barstools available have been given to women in heels.

The cobblestone floors flood with feet from all over the world. The Rattlin' Rogues perform covers and a few original tunes in the middle of the room, perched on split logs.

They take a break when a local opera singer, Anthony Kearns, drops in unannounced. He has a beer and mingles with the Rogues and some of the more familiar faces. Then he begins to sing without a sound check, without a microphone, without warning. The crowd hushes each other, and with the door to the bar open wide, the tenor's voice booms out into Talbot Street. The din quiets.

Some cry silently, moved either by his voice or by an excess of Guinness, but probably a combination of the two. This opera singer, seated on a log in the tiniest pub, has silenced the most drunken crowd as if he were on a grand stage in front of thousands of paying customers. This is The Celt, where musicians drop in unannounced seven nights a week.

In Quest of Road Kill

Zooming down the highway on a Saturday afternoon, I saw just what I needed for my latest hobby.

I pumped the brakes and swerved off the road.

"I don't want to ride with that thing. What are you going to do with it?" asked my boyfriend, Dan.

"I'll put it in the cooler," I responded.

"This is so sick," said Dan.

"This would make great reality TV," I said. No response.

"You know how you guys like those shows like *Swamp People* and *Man vs. Wild*? Well I bet there's an audience for road kill picking, eh?" I continued, hoping to pique his interest. I didn't.

I got out and jogged towards the carcass, stopped, then turned back towards the car. It was Dan's lucky day.

"You're okay," I said when I got back. "It was a raccoon, not a porcupine."

Almost every trip on a back road or highway throughout the summer of 2010 had me squealing onto the sides of roads. The results were always the same. The animal wasn't the coveted dead porcupine, the impact had destroyed the quills, or other scavengers had gotten to it before me.

But like hunters never forget their first kill, I can never forget the first porcupine I picked up off the side of the road.

The sky had a pinkish hue. It was getting late in to the evening. Three of my 11-year-old cousins and I were driving home after a day at Moncton's Magnetic Hill Zoo.

"A porcupine," I said excitedly, disrupting the kids' chatter.

"So?" said my cousin Knight.

"Aww," I cooed longingly. "He looks so good too."

"You're so weird," said Knight.

It was time for a little history lesson.

Porcupine quill work was a traditional Aboriginal art form found only in North America. The Mi'kmaq's quill work was so intricate and distinctive, they were often called the Porcupine People. Traditionally the quills were gathered without causing any harm. They'd simply follow the slow-footed animal, throw a blanket on it. It would release its quills into the blanket, and as Mr. Porcupine would waddle away the blanket would be cautiously removed.

Unfortunately, the art form was dying and traditional picking of quills most certainly was.

"We need to preserve this part of our culture," I said. "I need that porcupine!"

"Let's go back," said Knight.

"Yeah," chimed the other two.

The kids were thrilled to be involved in some sort of summer adventure, not realizing they'd just committed themselves to riding with a dead animal that had been stewing in the August heat for hours, if not days.

The cooler that was in my car before had been removed. It was Dan's way of trying to avoid what he'd been dreading all summer. I pulled in to the closest town, ran into their liquor store, and bummed several cardboard boxes.

I broke the boxes apart and lined the trunk of my car, then hurried back, trying pathetically to beat the rate of decomposition.

Knight and I laid a flat piece of cardboard on the ground and dragged the porcupine onto it by its feet. We each took two corners of the cardboard and lifted.

"Watch it," Knight yelled. "The blood almost dripped right onto me."

"Oh gross, that wet stuff's on my shirt," I yelled back.

For a second I felt like a rookie medic removing an innocent victim from a crime scene.

The half-hour drive home took an hour because of multiple breaks for air. I'd stop, and the kids would run out and gag, taking big gulps of fresh air.

The last break we took had me begging them to get back in the car because they wanted to walk home.

It was about 10 p.m. when I arrived at my mom's with the porcupine.

"I had a feeling you were up to no good," said my mom, peering out through the window.

"Can I pluck it in the garage?" I asked with the porcupine at my feet.

"She's crazy," I heard my stepfather say. "She's not putting that in our brand-new garage."

If anyone ever supported my bizarre ideas, it was my mom. I knew not to waste my time trying to convince my stepfather. Mom always trumped him when it came to household decisions anyway.

After some begging and bargaining she finally agreed. I started plucking at 11 p.m.

For hours I dealt with quills injecting themselves into my flesh and clinging on inside with their barbs, making them all the more painful to pull out.

My fingers were throbbing and bleeding, yet I continued on.

I felt an odd kin to an old neighbour's dog who seemed to come home every month with a fresh set of quills stuck in his face, never learning his lesson.

Halfway through the night, my mom brought me some rubber cleaning gloves. They were too awkward to grasp at the dainty quills, and often resulted in more pain to the tips of my fingers.

As the night went on, I wasn't sure if I could complete the task of plucking Pete (I had named him at this point.) Suddenly I remembered my brother.

Every Thanksgiving, he would have a mountain of turkey dinner on his plate. Every year after eating as long as he possibly could, he'd wind up pushing half the plate of food away.

"Your eyes are bigger than your stomach," my mom would always say.

The message seemed to ring through my ears to the wee hours of the morning.

After five hours and four small garbage cans filled with Pete's quills, there were still hundreds, maybe thousands of quills left on him despite the few bare patches.

At 4 a.m. I gave up and left a disheveled Pete sprawled on the garage floor.

I had burned sage and sweet grass all through the plucking process to try to snuff out the smell of death, but my mom said it lingered for days, giving her nightmares. She said the smell reminded her of funerals when the caskets were sealed, the seal never quite doing its job.

Dan, who had dodged the porcupine expedition, dug a hole in the woods the next day.

We carried Pete to the makeshift grave, dumped him in, and covered him up.

I said a little thank you to Pete, then went to sweep the maggots off the garage floor.

Notes

1. Section 35 of the Canada Act of 1982 recognizes and affirms the existing Aboriginal and treaty rights of Aboriginal people; and section 52 states that the "constitution is the supreme law of Canada, and any laws inconsistent are of no force and effect."
2. Other excellent videos about the Mi'kmaq are Alanis Obomsawin's (Abenaki) *Our Nationhood* and *Is the Crown at War with Us?*
3. Kluskap is also spelled as Gluscabe or Glooscap.
4. *Nisgam gejidoq!*, "God knows!"
5. *Amudj!*, "Yes!"
6. "Gluskeb" refers to Gluscabe, the culture hero also referenced in some of the Abenaki stories in this volume.
7. Gisulk, Mali!, "God, Mary!"
8. *Jinym*, "man" (a term of respect).
9. *Eq!*, "Yes!" (emphatic).
10. *Bana*, "simply."
11. Messkig is the fictional reserve on which *Stones and Switches* is set. The word means "large" in Mi'kmaq; in his own glossary, Simon remarks that it is "an ironic name for a reserve that has had most of its lands illegally taken."
12. A *mawi'omi* is a formal gathering.
13. Hunter Bear, also known as John R. Salter Jr. was Azure's graduate school advisor. He is the author of many articles and essays as well as *Jackson, Mississippi: An American Chronicle of Struggle and Schism*.
14. NAES, Native American Educational Services, was an accredited four-year college that had campuses in Chicago and Minneapolis and on the Menominee Reservation in Wisconsin and the Ft. Peck Reservation in Montana. Azure worked at the Chicago campus from 2000 to 2003.
15. Kejimkujik National Park in Nova Scotia is renowned for its petroglyphs.

Further Reading

MI'KMAQ AUTHORS

Augustine, Stephen Joseph. *Mi'kmaq & Maliseet Cultural Ancestral Material: National*

Collections from the Canadian Museum of Civilization. Gatineau QC: Canadian Museum of Civilization, 2005. Print.

Azure, Alice. *Along Came a Spider.* Greenfield Center NY: Bowman Books, 2011. Print.

———. *Games of Transformation.* Chicago: Albatross Press, 2011. Print.

———. *In Mi'kmaq Country: Selected Poems & Stories.* Chicago: Albatross Press, 2007. Print.

Barsh, Russel Lawrence, and James Youngblood Henderson. *The Road: Indian Tribes and Political Liberty.* Berkeley: University of California Press, 1980. Print.

Battiste, Jaime. *Honoring 400 Years: Kepmite'tmnej.* Jaime Battiste, 2010. Print.

———. "Understanding the Progression of Mi'kmaw Law." *Dalhousie Law Journal* 31.2 (2009): 311–50. Print.

Battiste, Marie. *First Nations Education in Canada: The Circle Unfolds.* Vancouver: University of British Columbia Press, 1995. Print.

———. *Reclaiming Indigenous Voice and Vision.* Vancouver: University of British Columbia Press, 2000. Print.

Battiste, Marie, and James Youngblood Henderson. *Protecting Indigenous Knowledge and Heritage: A Global Challenge.* Saskatoon: Purich Publishing, 2000. Print.

Butler, Audrey. *Radical Perversions: Black Friday?/Claposis.* London: Women's Press, 1991. Print.

Choyce, Lesley, and Rita Joe. *The Mi'kmaq Anthology.* Halifax NS: Nimbus Publishing, 1997. Print.

Cruz, Louis Esme, and Qwo-Li Driskill. "PUO'WINUE'L PRAYERS: Readings from North America's First Transtextual Script." *GLQ: A Journal of Lesbian and Gay Studies* 16.1–2 (2010): 243–52. Web. 9 June 2011.

Doyle-Bedwell, Patricia. "Mi'kmaq Women and Our Political Voice." *Atlantis* 27.2 (2003): 1–7. Print.

Henderson, James Youngblood. *Aboriginal Tenure in the Constitution of Canada.* Toronto: Carswell, 2000. Print.

———. *Indigenous Diplomacy and the Rights of Peoples: Achieving UN Recognition.* Saskatoon SK: Purich Publishing, 2008. Print.

Inglis, Stephenie, Joy Mannette, and Stacy Sulewski. *Paqtatek.* Vol. 1, *Policy and Consciousness in Mi'kmaq Life.* 1st ed. Toronto: University of Toronto Press, Higher Education Division, 1991. Print.

Joe, Rita. *Lnu and Indians We're Called.* London: Women's Press, 1991. Print.

———. *Song of Eskasoni: More Poems of Rita Joe.* Toronto: Women's Press, 1989. Print.

———. *Song of Rita Joe: Autobiography of a Mi'kmaq Poet.* Lincoln: University of Nebraska Press, 1996. Print.

Knockwood, Isabelle. *Out of the Depths.* 3rd ed. Halifax NS: Roseway Publishing, 2001. Print.

Marshall, Lindsay. *Clay Pots and Bones.* Sydney NS: Solus Publishing, 1997. Print.

Marshall, Murdena, and David L. Schmidt. *Mi'kmaq Hieroglyphic Prayers: Readings in North America's First Indigenous Script.* Illustrated ed. Halifax NS: Nimbus Publishing, 1995. Print.

Martin, Catherine. "Speaking from the Heart of Collective Memories." *Isuma* v. Web. 4 Aug. 2011.

McMillan, L. Jane. "Colonial Traditions, Co-optations, and Mi'kmaq Legal Consciousness." *Law & Social Inquiry* 36.1 (2011): 171–200. Web. 9 June 2011.

Meuse-Dallien, Theresa. *The Sharing Circle.* Halifax N S: Nimbus Publishing, 2003. Print.

Mi'kmaq, Confederacy of Mainland, Frederick Johnson, and Robert S. Peabody Museum of Archeology. *Mikwite'lmanej Mikmaqi'k / Let Us Remember the Old Mi'kmaq.* Halifax N S: Nimbus Publishing, 2001. Print.

Paul, Daniel N. *We Were Not the Savages: A Mi'kmaq Perspective on the Collision between European and Native American Civilizations.* 3rd ed. Black Point N S: Fernwood Publishing, 2006. Print.

Pellissier-Lush, Julie. *My Mi'kmaq Mother.* Charlottetown, P E I: RetroMedia, 2009. Print.

Peters, Jason. *Aboriginal Sport Heroes: Atlantic Canada.* St. John N B: DreamCatcher Publishing, 2011. Print.

Runningwolf, Michael B., and Patricia Clark Smith. *On the Trail of Elder Brother: Glous'gap Stories of the Micmac Indians.* Illustrated ed. New York: Persea Books, 2000. Print.

Salter, John R. *Jackson, Mississippi: An American Chronicle of Struggle and Schism.* 1979. (reprint) Lincoln: Bison Books-University of Nebraska Press, 2011. Print.

Sanger, Peter, and Elizabeth Paul. *The Stone Canoe: Two Lost Mi'kmaq Texts.* Kentville N S: Gaspereau Press, 2007. Print.

Sark, John Joe. *Micmac Legends of Prince Edward Island.* Charlottetown, P E I: Ragweed Press, 1988. Print.

Simon, Lorne. *Stones and Switches.* Penticton B C: Theytus Books, 1995. Print.

———. "Webs." *Stories for a Winter's Night: Short Fiction by Native Americans.* Ed. Maurice Kenny. Buffalo N Y: White Pine Press, 2000. 96–99. Print.

Smith, Patricia Clark. *Changing Your Story.* Albuquerque: West End Press, 1991. Print.

———. *Talking to the Land.* 1st ed. Lewiston I D: Confluence Press, 1979. Print.

———. *Weetamoo: Heart of the Pocassets, Massachusetts-Rhode Island, 1653.* 1st ed. New York: Scholastic Press, 2003. Print.

Tremblay, Gail. *Indian Singing.* Rev. ed. Corvallis O R: Calyx Press, 1998. Print.

ADDITIONAL READING

Alger, Abby. *In Indian Tents: Stories Told by Penobscot, Passamaquoddy and Micmac Indians.* Honolulu: University Press of the Pacific, 2006. Print.

Hornborg, Anne-Christine. *Mi'kmaq Landscapes: From Animism to Sacred Ecology.* Burlington V T: Ashgate, 2008. Print.

McKenna, Mary. *Micmac by Choice: Elsie Sark, an Island Legend.* Halifax N S: Formac, 1990. Print.

Nowlan, Alden. *Nine Micmac Legends.* Hantsport N S: Lancelot Press, 1983. Print.

Prins, Harald E. L. *The Mi'kmaq: Resistance, Accommodation, and Cultural Survival.* Belmont C A: Wadsworth/Tomson Learning, 2002. Print.

Prins, Harald, and Bunny McBride. *Genesis of the Micmac Community in Maine: And Its Intricate Relationship to Micmac Reserves in the Maritimes*. 1982. Unpublished report on file with the Aroostook Band of Micmacs, Presque Isle, Maine. Print.

Rand, Silas. *English-Micmac Dictionary: Dictionary of the Language of the Micmac Indians Who Reside in Nova Scotia, New Brunswick, Prince Edward Island, Cape Breton and Newfoundland*. East Hanover NJ: Laurier Books, 2007. Print.

Reid, Jennifer. *Myth, Symbol and Colonial Encounter: British and Mi'kmaq in Acadia, 1700–1867*. Ottawa: University of Ottawa Press, 1995.

Richardson, Boyce, ed. *Drumbeat: Anger and Renewal in Indian Country*. Ottawa: Summerhill Press, 1989. Print.

Tennyson, Brian Douglas, and Beaton Institute of Cape Breton Studies. *Cape Bretoniana: An Annotated Bibliography*. Toronto: University of Toronto Press, 2005. Print.

Tobias, Terry N. *Chief Kerry's Moose: A Guidebook to Land Use and Occupancy Mapping, Research Design, and Data Collection*. Vancouver: Union of BC Indian Chiefs and Ecotrust Canada, 2000. Print.

Upton, Leslie Francis Stokes. *Micmacs and Colonists: Indian-White Relations in the Maritime Provinces 1713 1867*. Vancouver: University of British Columbia Press, 1979. Print.

Whitehead, Ruth. *The Old Man Told Us: Excerpts from Micmac History, 1500–1950*. Halifax NS: Nimbus Publishing, 1991. Print.

Whitehead, Ruth Holmes. *Tracking Doctor Lonecloud: Showman to Legend Keeper*. Fredericton NB: Goose Lane Editions, 2002. Print.

MALISEET

Introduction

Juana Perley

Have you ever wondered why you see Maliseet/Malecite spelled two different ways? It is because the tribe exists in two different countries, the United States and Canada. The Malecite spelling is usually seen in Quebec. In the United States the community is referred to as a tribe, whereas in Canada it is referred to as a First Nation. Most of the Maliseet First Nations are located in New Brunswick province: Kingsclear, Woodstock, Madawaska, St. Mary's, Oromocto, and Wolastokwik 'Negoot-gook (Tobique).[1] There is a First Nation of Viger, located in Quebec, and the Houlton Band in Houlton, Maine. There are also numerous Maliseets living on Indian Island, Maine. They were adopted by the Penobscots when the Penobscots were obtaining their federal recognition.

I remember my first trip to Tobique. I was attempting to be recognized by the Canadian government so that I could obtain my tribal certificate. It is very curious that to be Native American you must be recognized by a government. It is the only American ethnic group that I know of that is required to have a document to prove ethnicity. This is one method that the governments use to control the Native American populations and their obligations to them. At one time, if a Maliseet woman married a white man, she and her children would no longer be considered Native American.[2] On the other hand, if a Maliseet man married a white woman, he and his children would not lose their Native American standing. As Andrea Bear Nicholas explains in her essay below, linguicide is a method of stripping culture from Native Americans; so too, this was a way of destroying a First Nation.

Tobique is the reserve where my great-grandfather, Gabriel Perley, originated. Gabe had left the reserve to find work in Greenville, Maine, as a guide, trapper, and snowshoe maker. Greenville soon became home for the Perley family. In the years to follow, Gabe and his wife, Philomen, did return to Tobique for weddings and baptisms. The first time I visited, I was very nervous, but I was welcomed by all. People knew about Gabe and knew that he left the reserve, but what had happened to him and his descendants was unknown. Jim Bear had come down to Maine to interview my sister and me after we inquired about tribal membership. He was a tribal member who worked as a liaison between the Canadian government and the tribe on issues of tribal memberships. He introduced me to Andrea Bear Nicholas, because at that time she was documenting various family trees. It turned out that Andrea and I were distantly related. She was able to point me to the archives where I could find documentation on Gabriel and Philomen Perley.

It does not matter if you have relatives living on the reserve. If you weren't there to sign the rolls then you were not considered a member of the First Nation.[3] According to the Canadian government, they had no documentation of Gabriel Perley ever being on the reserve. I was, however, able to find several documents that showed that he had lived on the reserve. After I submitted this documentation, the Canadian government started to lose various documents. It was at this point that I gave up.

There is a recurring theme in the following works, from Gabe Acquin's pictograph to Brenda Commander's 2009 letter to President Obama requesting assistance with the state of Maine over the Indian Claims Settlement Act. The short story "The Red Man's Burden," by my grandfather, Henry Red Eagle, also shows the frustrations and difficulties that many Native Americans faced then as well as today. Meanwhile, Shirley Bear's poignant poem "Fragile Freedoms" speaks to the vulnerability of the Native American world.

Mihku Paul's poem "Trade in the 21st Century" brings back my memory of staying at a working farm and bed and breakfast in Perth Andover. The owners knew that I was doing research at Tobique, but they had no idea that I was part Native American and that I had relatives living there. They were complaining about the high price of the potato baskets so painstakingly woven by Native people. Paul's poem, as all of these writings, brings to mind the adage about how much things have changed, but how much they remain the same.

Gabriel Acquin

(1839–1901)

Gabriel Acquin founded the St. Mary's Reserve in New Brunswick and became famous as a guide, hunter, and performer. Among the many dignitaries he hosted in his homeland was the Prince of Wales in 1860; Acquin later traveled to England, exhibiting his canoe and wigwam. Acquin's legacy is complicated. Historian Andrea Bear Nicholas has called his "a classic case of the colonized striving to imitate the colonizer in language, manners, and preferences, often to excess," contending that "by his excesses in abandoning traditional values of conservation, he contributed also to the demise of the ancient Maliseet way of life." Other Maliseet artists, however, have honored him, including the poet Mihku Paul (represented in this volume) and Martin Sabbatis, who produced a short animated film about Acquin for Fredericton's Cultural Capitals of Canada celebration in 2009. It seems important to include Acquin in a consideration of Maliseet literary history, given ethnographer Garrick Mallery's discussion, below, of his uses of *awhikhigan*, or birch-bark writings.

Pictograph

From *Picture-Writing of the American Indians*, by Garrick Mallery. Drawing courtesy of Chrestien Charlebois.

[This figure], scratched on birch bark, was given to the present writer at Fredericton, New Brunswick, in August 1888 by Gabriel Acquin, . . . who spoke English quite well. The circumstances under which it was made and used are in [his] words, as follows:

"When I was about 18 years old I lived at a village 11 miles above Fredericton and went with canoe and gun. I canoed down to Washademoak

Lake, about 40 miles below Fredericton; then took the river until it became too narrow for canoe; then 'carried' to Buctoos river; followed down to bay of Chaleur; went up the northwest Mirimachi, and 'carried' into the Nepisigiut. There spent the summer. On that river met a friend of my time; we camped there.

"One time while I was away my friend had gone down to the river by himself and had not left any wikhe'gan for me. I had planned to go off and left for him this wikhe'gan, to tell where I would be and how long gone. The wigwam at the lower-left hand corner showed the one used by us, with the river near it. The six notches over the door of the wigwam meant that I would be gone six days. The canoe and man nearest to the wigwam referred to my friend, who had gone in the opposite direction to that I intended to travel. Next to it I was represented in my own canoe, with rain falling, to show the day I started, which was very rainy. Then the canoe carried by me by a trail through woods shows the 'carry' to Nictaux Lake, beside which is a very big mountain. I stayed at that lake for six days, counting the outgoing and returning. As I had put the wikhe'gan in the wigwam before I started, my friend on his return understood all about me, and, counting six from and including the rainy day, knew just when I was coming back, and was waiting for me."

Chief James Paul

The art historian Ruth Phillips has found letters exchanged between Chief James Paul of the St. Mary's Reserve and Edward Sapir. The anthropologist, it seems, was putting pressure on Paul to re-create artifacts with what he deemed a veneer of authenticity—what he called "the style that the Indians used long ago before they knew anything about white man's ways," made without "white man's materials." Paul's response, dated 1911 and reprinted below, illustrates some of the complicated negotiations over culture, authenticity, and commodification that were common between Native people and non-Native collectors in that period and into the present day. In this, his letter has much in common with that of the Passamaquoddy scholar Lewis Mitchell to Charles Godfrey Leland, also included in this volume.

Letter to Edward Sapir, 1911

I am sending you two paddles. I don't think you have the Maliseet paddles and those I am sending, one of them is very old, but the other is not so old. You will take notice on one, there is some carving on it, that was done by some old Indian that had died long while ago. The oldest looking one is probably a hundred years old. I got them from a friend from Fredericton. He had them in his house for some time and never was used. I had to go to work and make him two new ones in place of the old ones that I got. On account I wanted them because they were so old. New paddles are worth $3.00 a pair. I am charg[ing] the half of what the new ones are worth so there will be no hard feelings between you and I. I think they are worth that to you on account they are so old but carved paddles it would be far much nicer what I make myself then what you see on that old one. I know you wouldn't feel like paying $10.00 a pair, but if you seen them after all fixed up, you would say that they couldn't be bought for $25.00.

Henry "Red Eagle" Perley

(1885–1972)

Easily one of the most prolific writers in this collection, Henry Perley (a.k.a. "Chief Red Eagle") published hundreds of short stories and essays in popular magazines, including *All-Story Weekly*, *Boy's Life*, *Open Road for Boys*, *All West Magazine*, and *Maine Recreation*. Born in Greenville, Maine, he traveled with wild west shows in the 1910s and 1920s, both within the United States and overseas to Europe; he also performed on Broadway and in silent films alongside such stars as Mary Pickford and Caesar Romero. In the 1930s Perley returned to Maine and began writing for pulp fiction magazines and Maine tourist publications. He was also a popular lecturer on Native American topics. The following story, published in *All-Story Weekly* in 1915, illustrates how Perley both used and revised the conventions of popular romance, dime novels, and westerns to create his own brand of fiction deeply rooted in the Maliseet homeland.

The Red Man's Burden

Peter Attean, better known as Wild Pe-al, confidently shoved his canoe into the friendly eddying swirl of a huge boulder and rested for a moment upon his pole. Calculatingly he measured the next pitch with a swift sweep of his eye, readjusting his load of hunter's supplies and traps a trifle, and braced himself for the struggle.

The water broke smoothly away from the head of the rapids, to be sucked with tremendous force into the chutelike passage formed by two boulders, to curl into a huge comber at the foot.

Cautiously he shoved his bow past the boulder until it was caught in the swift current and simultaneously swung the stern outward. Quickly catching another hold on the rocky bottom, he coolly held the frail craft motionless in the boiling maelstrom.

The onrushing water cleft the bow squarely and lapped hungrily at the gunwales as though resenting the intrusion; slowly the bow began to rise as he gradually increased the pressure; and finally, with a strong, steady heave that brought the veins out on his neck and forehead, he slid into the smooth water above.

Every year Pe-al started into the Maine woods on the 21st of September from Greenville, to be a self-made hermit for the seven long months in following his calling—the hunting and trapping of fur-bearing animals for their pelts. He made his headquarters at Loon Lake, across the Shallow Lake and Pagget Ponds, thence to Round Pond and Poland Stream, back to Loon Lake, a distance of about sixteen miles, with branch camps at Shallow Lake and Round Pond.

While there is no law controlling it, trappers' ethics forbade the transgression of one trapper upon the grounds of another; he may run a line across diagonally, but never run a parallel line or set any traps in the ponds, its tributaries or outlets, without the consent of the squatter.

So Pe-al felt monarch of all he surveyed as he leisurely paddled across the placid Caucomgomoc toward his camp four miles away.

Now and again his deep voice boomed into snatches of Indian song, for this to him was life; his Indian soul reveled in the surrounding landscape with its wavy, undulating outline against the soft, shimmering bank of fleecy clouds in the background; on every side multicolored leaves, already in their autumnal plumage, reflected their beauty in the deep, clear crystal of the lake's waters. He filled his lungs again and again in the very ecstasy of his joy, and his heart went out to all fellow beings, for he envied no man—he was in his element.

Millionaires may live in comfort and luxury, 'mid wealth and splendor; but for Pe-al Attean, give him this—the open sky for a roof, the soft, yielding ground for a marble floor, his rough garb for an evening suit, his old moccasins for patent pumps—and he would not ask more.

Suddenly his attention was arrested by the peculiar position of a dried limb. Instinctively he knew it to be a trap before he reached it. Sure enough, set cunningly in three inches of water, partly covered by mud and water-soaked leaves, was a No. 1 single-spring Newhouse trap, evidently set for muskrat. Scratched scrawlingly on the jaws were the initials H. le N.

With a muttered imprecation the Indian tore the snare from its fastenings and hurled it far into the nearby alders.

"Wonder how that came to be set there?" he muttered aloud. "It can't be that old Henri is away down here; nonsense. Still, it's Le Noir's mark."

Henri le Noir was a little, wiry French Canadian, known to everyone in northern Maine. For twelve years he had trapped in the vicinity of

Allegash Falls, some twenty-eight miles from the Canadian boundary; therefore Pe-al could not understand the initialed trap.

He drove the incident from his mind and resumed his way. Rounding the next point he would be able to see his camp, and he smiled in anticipation. As he shot past the rocky promontory into full view of the log cabin, he stopped paddling and uttered an ejaculation of anger.

Upturned on the beach was a blue-bottomed canoe that Pe-al knew to be Le Noir's, while curling spirally from the camp—his camp—was a thin thread of white smoke.

White hot with anger, the young Indian fairly lifted his canoe from the water with the mighty strokes of his paddle, his lithe, sinuous body half turned from the hips as he lent the force of his shoulders to the powerful muscles of his arms. The canoe grated on the beach, and without pausing to draw the craft up farther he covered the fifty yards to the camp on the run, threw open the door with an impetuous bang, and leaped inside.

"Get out of here, you Canuck!" he roared; "this camp is mine, and—"

He stopped in amazement, for instead of the swarthy little Frenchman, he encountered the deep, black eyes of a girl, now dilated in terror, her breast heaving as she leaned backward against a rude table for support. The full contour of her bare throat pulsed throbblingly against the shapely hand, lifted uncontrollably at the sudden outburst of the Indian.

"What is the matter?" she asked in French.

Pe-al shook his head uncomprehendingly; never had he been taken so completely by surprise, for the thought of a girl away up here in the wilds, so far from civilization, was so unusual that it fairly took away his breath.

He recovered and, doffing his black slouch hat, backed to the door.

"I beg your pardon," he said with a smile. "I thought it was old Henri who had set his traps on my line."

"He is my father," she replied, with a slight accent. "He is gone for some wood for make axe-handle; he will come back soon." Then raising her eyebrows she asked, "You wait?"

"Yes. I'll sit outside here until he comes, if you don't mind."

The rattle of tin dishes proclaimed her interrupted occupation; but once the rattle stopped and Pe-al, turning quickly, caught a glimpse of her face as she drew back from the half-open door.

With his big hunting-knife he whittled idly a piece of pine when he was startled by a peal of silvery laughter that rippled and shivered through the multi-colored leaves of the September wood like the carol of a bird. It suddenly ceased when he arose, but he caught the sound of half-suppressed giggles as the girl tried to restrain her merriment as the ludicrousness of the situation overcame the first shock of fright.

Pe-al concealed a smile with his broad palm, and turned to see Le Noir staggering under the five-foot butt of a sixteen-inch maple. He smiled in admiration, for it was no mean load for any man and Le Noir was small and nearly sixty years old.

With a grunt the Frenchman dropped the heavy piece to the ground, drove his ax into a nearby splitting-block, and for the first time, noted the newcomer.

"Quay, Pe-al," he grinned, using the Maliseet form of greeting. "I am glad for see you."

He knew nearly all the guides, as they frequently passed his camp in making the Allegash trip, and was on good terms with all on account of his guileless disposition and good nature, having a pleasant word for all.

"Quay," answered Pe-al, taking the proffered hand.

"What is de trub', Pe-al? You look mat."

"You'll have to get out of here Le Noir; you are in my camp and you have set your traps along my line. I can't have it. I've been here eight winters and expect to stay eight more. You'll have to get out."

A look of consternation spread over the features of old Henri at the first words of the Indian that turned to piteous appeal as he finished.

"No, no, no!" he cried; "don't mak' me go 'way, *mon Dieu*. I am ol' man. I will not bodder you; I ketch few fur; you will not miss heem; oop Canada way I cannot ketch mooch; maybe hunder' dollar wort' wan winter. Eet is small, an' I'm try here. Ple'se not mak' me go. Oh, *mon Dieu*."

He wrung his hands appealingly.

Pe-al did not speak. After all, it would matter but little; his Round Pond camp was in better condition than this one, and it would also give him an opportunity to try an undeveloped country to the westward.

Besides, there was the girl; she had emerged from the camp and now stood near her father, her lustrous eyes fastened on the Indian's face inquiringly. A flush mantled her cheek, mingling ravishingly with the natural rich olive, and a tiny dimple indented itself in the pure background as she half smiled.

Pe-al turned away, nodding. The little Frenchman devoutly crossed himself, and burst into an unintelligible mixture of French and English expressions of joy; and catching his daughter in his arms began a grotesque dance over the chip-covered yard, chanting weirdly in the peculiar monotone of the French Canadian of the border. It was this boyish spontaneity of the old man that won him so many friends.

Pe-al, too, felt a glow of gratification in his own breast. Suddenly Henri ceased his gyrations and with grave courtesy introduced his daughter with the Canadian disregard of gender.

"Pe-al, dis is my gal, 'Nita. His mothair she been a savage, too, lak you. 'Nita, dis been Pe-al Attean—she is dam gude wan feller."

Her eyes brimming with laughter, Anita nodded and disappeared into the cabin.

"*Oui*," smilingly jabbered Henri; "I am married Injen 'oman, but he is die two, t'ree year now. My 'Nita she is go school on Quebec and is finis' las' June. I am not want him for come up here, but he is like wood an'"—a cherubic smile illuminated his rough features as he caught Pe-al by the sleeve and whispered confidentially—"an she is lov' his ol' fadder."

The Indian paddled the eight miles to his Round Pond camp in a haze. From the bow of his canoe a pair of black eyes seemed to beckon him on, and unconsciously he would bend the stout maple paddle with the strength of his strokes. From that day Wild Pe-al was tamed.

In October a crew of forty woodsmen, under the leadership of Lew Morton as foreman, bateaued up the river and took possession of the lumber camps on the north shore of Caucomgomoc Lake.

They were followed two days later by twelve horses that were led through the woods from East Carry. This operation was controlled by Thomas J. Amberg, a wealthy contractor and lumberman, of Bangor, and was one of a series of five camps extending to Sourdahunk Stream on the Penobscot with headquarters at Cuxabexis Lake.

They immediately began the war upon the forest, the rhythmic *choc, choc* of their axes echoing and re-echoing through the autumn air.

Pe-al visited the camp, meeting many old friends who had been there the previous year, and was assured by Morton that his traps at the dam and along the Horserace would lie unmolested, as would those of Le Noir.

The short autumn days slipped by quickly and developed into the crisp, dry cold winter. Pe-al made his rounds every other day. Though there is a law to the effect that trappers must visit their traps once every twenty-four hours, it is not rigidly enforced.

On his way to the dam one morning Pe-al discovered that he had only two matches, and decided to stop at the lumber-camp to replenish his knapsack and snow-shoes. He stepped to the cook-house camp and tapped on the door with the handle of his ax. It was opened by Chef Marsh, who heard his request and responded heartily.

"Sure, Mike; I'd give ye my mother-in-law, Pete. How's things movin'?"

"Fair. Got an otter, a mink, and two muskrats yesterday. Any news?"

"Not much," replied Marsh. "Thomas J. blew in yisterd'y an' brought his son Roger an' another young feller with 'im."

"Is that so?" ejaculated Pe-al interestedly.

"Yep," went on Marsh; "the kid's big's a house—bigger'n Bob McClaggan. You know Bob—the P.I. chap that tends sled?"

"Yes, Bob was here last year," said Pe-al.

"Yuh, yuh," nodded Marsh. "Well, he's bigger'n him." Then angrily: "He's a big calf. Asked me last night if I didn't have somethin' he could use fur a napkin—a napkin; w'at do you think of that? I give him a dish-towel."

Marsh grinned in remembrance.

"Yer oughter seen 'im look at it. He wrinkled up his nose disgusted-like an' threw it clean 'cross the camp. I'll bet a dollar and a half he hain't up yet, an' I've gi'n 'em one call a'ready. Hey, French," he called to the curly-haired cook, "get 'em up an' tell 'em they git no breakfas' arter eight o'clock. I wa'n't hired to cook fer no college dudes. Say, Pete, why don't yer come in? It's kinder chilly."

"No, thanks, chef; I've got to be moving on. Where's Morton?"

As the Indian asked the question Morton stepped from an adjoining camp, designated as the office, closely followed by Thomas J. Amberg, a portly man with a decisive manner; a clean-cut youth of about twenty-two years, and another about the same age, whose herculean frame filled the door as he stooped to pass out.

Upon sight of the Indian he grinned, and with the aid of his hand trilled an imitation war whoop. Pe-al turned like a spring, a slow red flushing his swarthy cheek; his teeth came together with a click, and with narrowed eyelids he watched the approach of the quartet.

"'Mornin', Peter," greeted Morton consciously. "You know Mr. Amberg, of course."

"Good morning, Peter," said Amberg, proffering his hand, which Pe-al took. "This is Arthur Thieres, a clerk in my office, and this is my son Roger. Roger is a trifle undersized," he smiled, "but I am in hopes that he will grow. Boys, this is Peter Attean, trapper, guide, and all around woodsman."

Roger pushed forward and thrust out his great palm. "Glad to meet you, Attean—shake."

The Indian ignored the outstretched hand, nodded shortly, and half turned to go.

The corners of Roger's mouth dropped disagreeably.

"Huh," he snorted, "miffed, eh? Must have been my war whoop. I was only kidding on that yell. Can't you take a joke?"

"Not when it's an insult," answered Pe-al evenly.

"You don't call that an insult, do you?" demanded the young giant.

"I do," declared Pe-al; "not only to me, but to my people as well, and I resent it."

"Aw, that's all right, Peter," cried Amberg pacifically; "don't get sore at this big baby. He don't know any better. Come in and have some breakfast with us."

"Thanks, Mr. Amberg, I've had breakfast. I just stopped for a few matches."

Roger forced a sarcastic laugh. With his right hand he reflectively fingered his chin and surveyed the Indian as he stooped to tighten a strap.

"Resent it, eh," he drawled. "I must congratulate him on his fine sensibilities, Dad. It's quite commendable, you know, and—er—quixotic."

"Shut up, Roger!" commanded his father. "You have said quite enough, and your remarks are entirely unnecessary. You owe Peter an apology."

"Oh, but Father," protested Roger sarcastically; "he would resent it, you know; perhaps physically, and—"

"And if I did," said Pe-al stepping forward and confronting him with eyes that blazed, "I'd snap your caddish head off; and if you don't think I'm capable of doing it, I'll give you a demonstration right now. You—speak—again!"

He dropped the ax, and with a backward snap of his shoulders allowed the knapsack to fall, at the same time disengaging his feet from the snowshoes with a dexterous twist of his ankles.

Roger Amberg's season at right tackle on the U. of M[aine] team, a position where he had distinguished himself, had given him almost unlimited confidence in his ability to cope with any man; but there was something in the menacing attitude, in the cold steely glitter from the fathomless depths of the coal-black eyes that was quite unlike anything that the young giant had ever encountered. He read in that look a dormant animal ferocity, an indomitable spirit, an inexorable quarter to foe.

The tenseness of the situation held the little group breathless; no one attempted to interfere, and the two men gazed into each other's eyes for a full half-minute. Gradually the muscles of the Indian relaxed from their pantherish intensity; he slowly readjusted his snowshoes and picked up his ax. A grim smile flitted across his face as, without another word, he turned and proceeded toward the dam.

"Hell," exploded the older Amberg, "that man is half-savage yet!"

"Dad," announced Roger after breakfast, "while you fellows are going over the books I'll take a look at that Loon Lake spruce we spoke about. You can pick up my trail as soon as you get through. Just yell and I'll hear you alright, for I won't go far enough from the shore to get lost."

"All right," grunted his father without looking up from the books.

Roger slipped an automatic pistol into the pocket of his mackintosh, borrowed a pair of snowshoes of the camp clerk, and departed.

"Look out for that broken cross-bar," the clerk had warned, "or it may catch and flip ye."

An hour later Roger came into a little clearing and caught his breath with a little gasp of admiration, then hurried forward to greet Anita le Noir.

"Hello, little one," he leered; "who art thou and from whence didst thou come?"

The girl, startled by his appearance, did not answer.

"You mustn't be afraid of me," smiled Roger reassuringly. "Why, I'm your friend; that is, if you'll let me." Under his breath he murmured: "Gad, what a pippin."

Nita *did* present a pretty picture as she stood gracefully on her little snowshoes. A short corduroy skirt barely reached the tops of her ankle-length moccasins; over a blue flannel shirt she wore a V-neck sweater of white, while set jauntily on her daintily arranged hair was a white toque with a red tassel. In her hand she carried a little .22-caliber rifle. The crisp air had heightened her color, and with her wild surroundings she was the very personification of a modern Diana.

"Well, hain't you got a tongue?" cried Amberg in exasperation at her continued silence. "What's your name and how do you happen to be away up here?"

Instinctively Nita had experienced a violent dislike toward the youth at his first words, and though she realized that his questions were perfectly natural, she resented them. Her school training, however, stood her in good stead as she replied: "My name is Anita le Noir. Henri le Noir, the trapper, is my father, and we are staying in Pe-al Attean's camp just around that point."

"The Injun," muttered Amberg.

Aloud he said: "So you're staying up here in the woods with your dad, eh? Don't you ever get lonesome?"

"Sometimes I do a little," replied the girl, "but I have no other home."

"Oh, I say now, that's too bad. Why don't you get married?" he asked teasingly.

Nita blushed a rosy pink, but made no reply, and Roger, emboldened, advanced still closer.

"Say, you're all to the mustard," he said admiringly. "On the dead, you've got my goat already. You can call me to your fireside any time you like."

The young giant always prided himself on being a lady's man, and now thought he was making an impression on this simple child of the forest. So when Nita dropped one of her mittens he picked it up and held it behind his back.

"Now, before you get that mitten back you must pay a forfeit, the same as they did in olden times, you know; you must allow the cavalier to kiss you."

Nita made a grimace and started away, but Roger caught her by the arm. "Aw, wait a minute; don't go away. I was only kidding; now let's be friends."

The spirited girl wrenched her hand free, her body quivering with anger.

"Leave me alone, you big coward," she cried, "and give me that mitten."

Her action and words aroused Roger's pride and anger.

"By Jove, I'm going to kiss you anyway for that, my proud beauty."

Pe-al took advantage of every opportunity to visit old Henri and his daughter, and would often stay to dinner or supper with them. Upon these occasions Nita was all vivacity and smiles, and her hearty, contagious laugh would ring out like the tones of a bell at some quaint saying of old Henri or as Pe-al related one of his store of anecdotes.

As time wore on the Indian had found himself thinking a great deal of the half-breed girl. Her large, fawnlike eyes were ever present, and would shine out at him from the recesses of his cabin at night, along the spotted trail of his lines by day. His thoughts were full of her now as he hurried toward Le Noir's camp to visit them and incidentally to warn Le Noir of the proximity of Dan Turner, the game warden, who was making one of his monthly rounds; for he knew that the Canadian ignored the law and caught beaver, on which there is a heavy penalty.

With great strides he neared the point when he was startled by a scream. With a bound he made in the direction to see Nita struggling in Roger Amberg's arms, clawing and scratching at his smug face with the ferocity of a wildcat.

Amberg did not notice the approach of the Indian until he was less than ten feet away, nor could he ward off a right-hand swing that landed on the side of his jaw and nearly lifted his huge bulk from the ground. He arose dazedly to see Pe-al and Nita going in the direction of Henri's camp and quickly whipped out his revolver.

"Here, you cave-dweller, come back here," he cried, pointing the weapon unsteadily at the Indian's retreating figure. "Do you hear? Come back here."

Pe-al merely threw back his head and laughed.

Roger lowered the weapon and watched them disappear. His bluff had been called.

After notifying the Frenchman of the proximity of the game warden and leaving Nita to tell of their encounter with the stranger, Pe-al proceeded along the spotted trail toward his Poland Stream traps.

His heart was light, and though no word was spoken he read in Nita's eyes, in the pressure of her hand on his arm as they parted at the camp door, that she reciprocated his love. He swung his snowshoes lightly with the ease and agility of the woodsman, when his quick eye, trained to woodcraft, caught the gleam of the wicked eyes of a weasel gazing at him from a hollow log.

He fired from the hip, but the animal had disappeared before he had slipped his revolver from its holster.

Mingling with the report was a loud crackling of underbrush, and a cow moose broke through the branches of a fallen tree and swung into a shambling trot not thirty-five yards away. Subconsciously he drew a bead just back of the fore-shoulders of the animal when he was startled by a sharp report. The moose staggered ahead a few yards, pitched forward on its knees, and then crashed to the ground.

Dan Turner, Mr. Amberg, Lew Morton, and young Thieres burst into view to see Pe-al Attean advancing toward the fallen animal, revolver in hand.

"Well, Pete, I guess I've got you with the goods this time," chuckled Turner. "This means your guide and trapper's license and five hundred dollars, or wearing the yoke for four months with Sheriff Barnes, at Dover. All you guys will do it if you think you can get away with it, won't you? But you certainly had a nerve when you *knew* I was around. Good shot, too," he continued, as he bent over the huge beast—"right through the heart."

"But I didn't shoot her, Dan," protested Pe-al—"honest."

"Aw, tell that to Sweeney," laughed the warden. "I've got you good and hard. There's the moose that was alive not three minutes ago, as us four can swear. We hear a shot, and here's you with the weapon in your hand; Q.E.D. you're the goat. By the way, I'll just take that gun."

"But I tell you I didn't shoot her!" cried Pe-al. "I fired at a weasel over there not half a minute before this cow came into sight."

Turner burst into a loud guffaw.

"Shot at a weasel—with this? Pete, I thought you was a trapper, but by the Lord Harry any man who would shoot a weasel with a .38 ought to have his license taken away. S'pose you had a' bagged him, how much do you reckon you'd get for the pelt? And if you fired, as you say you did, not half a minute before this moose came into sight, why didn't *we* hear it? Got a silencer on this thing?" he asked sarcastically.

"But take a look around," urged the Indian; "maybe someone from the camp is out. Surely you will leave some tracks—"

"That you couldn't tell had been made today or last week," finished Turner. "We ain't had a snow-storm for two weeks, and furthermore, that was a revolver-shot, and it was shot out of this gun right here."

He tapped the revolver to give emphasis.

"I've got all the evidence I want, and you're my prisoner—now, now,

now, nothing doing. Tell it to the judge. I'm satisfied in my mind. Now, what will I do with that carcass?"

"I'll give you twenty-five dollars for it, Turner, just as she lays," offered Mr. Amberg briskly.

"You're taking advantage of me, Mr. Amberg," smiled Turner; "that meat is worth a hundred dollars if it's worth a cent. However, I'll take your offer. It ought to be bled and dressed tonight or early tomorrow morning, though. Here, I'll bleed it for you."

He stuck his hunting-knife into the neck; a spurt of crimson blood followed its withdrawal, and dyed the snow with the life fluid that only a few minutes before had been coursing through the veins of the forest monster.

"You might get Le Noir to dress it for you, Mr. Amberg," spoke up Morton, "and we can come over and get it in the morning."

And so it was arranged, Le Noir expressing great surprise at Pe-al's violation of the statutes.

"What for you do it, Pe-al?"

The Indian did not reply, but looked appealingly at Nita, and noted tears in her eyes.

"Even my friends won't believe me," he sighed.

Next morning, before the break of day, Turner and his prisoner started on the twenty-mile tramp to Northeast Carry, from whence they would take the stage across Moosehead Lake to Greenville and complete the journey by rail.

Amberg, Thieres, and Morton were to appear as witnesses, while Roger went along, as he expressed it, "just to see the Injun get his."

Pe-al was uncommunicative during the entire journey, answering only in monosyllables when addressed and maintaining an outward stolid indifference. He was lodged in the county jail overnight, while the news of his arrest spread throughout the villages of Dover and Foxcroft like wildfire, for the name of Wild Pe-al was known in every section of Piscataquis and Aroostook counties.

By Turner's advice he had engaged Arthur Snowden, a graduate of the law school at Bangor, and who had, during his short practice, made an enviable reputation at the county bar. He heard Pe-al's story through and slowly shook his head. "Looks pretty steep, Attean, but we'll do the best we can."

The Indian was to be arraigned at ten-thirty; at ten o'clock the deputies were forced to close the doors while a mob outside clamored for admittance. Young Snowden met him at the rail and slapped him on the back.

"We've got 'em, Attean," he whispered exultantly; "we've got 'em. And incidentally we're going to hand a surprise to somebody, too," he winked significantly.

The preliminaries were quickly disposed of, and the prosecution began. Turner was the first witness called. He described the facts already known—of their scaring of the moose and seeing her running from them; of hearing the shot and coming upon the prisoner with a revolver in his hand, and the dead moose a few yards away.

After the county attorney had dismissed him, and before he could leave the stand, Snowden rose to his feet.

"I would like to ask the witness a few questions, if it may please the court," he said. Permission being granted, he handed Turner Pe-al's revolver.

"I will ask Mr. Turner if that is the identical revolver that was seized from the prisoner."

Turner carefully examined the weapon.

"Yes, sir, it is," he announced.

"It is in the same condition as when you seized it, is it not?"

"Yes, sir; I only broke it to see that one shell had been fired," replied Turner.

"That's all, thank you," and Snowden sat down.

Mr. Amberg, Lew Morton, and Arthur Thieres corroborated Turner's testimony, adding nothing of importance.

The county attorney, deeming his case safe on the testimony of the witnesses, merely outlined the facts, and asked that the prisoner be given the full penalty and his license taken from him.

"He is a dangerous character and a menace to the county," he finished.

With the possible exception of his attorney Pe-al felt that there was not a person in the crowded court-room who did not believe him guilty, and his heart sank. Once he took a fleeting glance at the crowd, but saw there no expression of sympathy or friendliness—nothing save idle curiosity.

Snowden rose to his feet briskly. "Your honor, we will occupy only a very few minutes, but in those few minutes we hope to prove, and prove conclusively, that my client did not commit the act of which he stands accused."

The words created a stir in the little room, and the spectators leaned forward interestedly.

The young attorney picked up an oblong package that hitherto had lain upon his table and stripped off the outer layer of paper to disclose another wrapper of birch-bark bound with cedar-withes. Coolly and with deliberation Snowden cut the flexible twig and restored the knife to his pocket; there was not a sound save the crackling of the bark as he slowly undid the bundle and left it convenient to open quickly.

"My client does not deny that this is his revolver, in fact, he says it's the only one he owns. He does not deny that the moose was killed, nor does he deny that the testimony of the witnesses is anything but the truth."

"You will note, gentlemen, that this revolver is a double-action automatic of a .38 caliber." He ejected one of the cartridges and held it up in his finger. "You will also note that the bullet is a *soft-nosed bullet*, and will mushroom upon contact with animal matter. The bullet that killed the moose in question was a metal-cased bullet—and here is the proof."

He caught up the package and dumped the contents upon the table. From among its packing of moss and leaves he held up a piece of moose-meat cut from the side of the animal; embedded between two ribs, almost indistinguishable from the surrounding clot of dried blood, was a metal-cased bullet. Snowden pried it loose and handed it to the jury.

"It does not require a knowledge of firearms to see that that bullet was *not* fired from Peter Attean's gun."

The county attorney flashed to his feet.

"How do we know that the piece of meat came from the moose in question, and who killed the moose if not that man there?"

Young Snowden smiled and whispered in the ear of a deputy.

Those who were watching the prisoner saw a smile flit across his sphinx-like countenance as Anita le Noir was ushered into the room by a deputy sheriff, a single snowshoe under her arm.

She was duly sworn as a witness, and after asking a few preliminary questions, more to reassure her than for their bearing on the case, Snowden picked up the piece of moose-meat and asked:

"Your father took this piece of flesh from the moose, the killing of which Peter Attean is accused?"

"Yes, sir."

"You swear that, do you?" thundered the prosecuting attorney.

The girl's chin flew up as she flashed: "Yes, sir."

"Now, Miss Le Noir, you may tell us all you know of this case."

In her own quaint way Anita testified as follows:

"As soon as it was light enough next morning my father went out to skin the moose for Mr. Amberg and found the bullet, and then we knew Pe-al did not kill the moose. Then I followed a track made by a snowshoe that had a broken cross-bar. I have it here." She exhibited the broken bar and continued: "Near a tree, about fifty yards from the moose, I found—this." She held up an exploded cartridge. "Pe-al Attean did not kill the moose; the man that killed the moose is *him.*"

Her voice rose in her excitement, and she pointed a quivering finger at Roger Amberg, who had shrunk from the accusation as though it was the lash of a whip. His face went pasty-white and his jaw dropped vacantly.

In the commotion caused by the big student's collapse, Pe-al felt something warm creep into his brown palm and looked down to encounter Nita's big, black eyes brimming with happy tears. It required every ounce of his will-power to crush down the almost irresistible desire that assailed him to strain her to his breast, but he succeeded, and gave her fingers a little squeeze instead.

That night Turner was the last to bid the happy couple good-by as they prepared to take the train to Greenville on the first lap of the return trip to Caucomgomoc.

Roger Amberg had confessed in open court of how in a moment of excitement, he had shot the moose and had substituted a loaded cartridge, so that if called upon he could show a full magazine after he heard Turner accuse Attean. He saw a chance to clear, as well as revenge himself for the humiliation he had suffered at the hands of the Indian.

An automatic was taken from his pocket, the magazine of which carried ten cartridges with metal-cased bullets, and the shells were identical with that produced by Nita.

It was also brought out by Nita that he had worn the broken snowshoe, whose telltale bar had betrayed him. His father wrathfully paid the fine.

"Five hundred and twenty-five dollars to furnish a bunch of lumberjacks with moose-meat," he growled disgustedly, "and all on account of a big booby that ought to be shingled. Bah!"

He flung himself from the courtroom.

Pe-al was immediately discharged, and now as they waited for the six forty-five he smiled at the girl by his side, who wore a little band of gold on the third finger of her left hand, and smiled happily in return. They had been married in the court where, a few hours before, the bridegroom had stood a prisoner. Morton celebrated the marriage by getting ory-eyed, as he afterward expressed it.

"Wish you'd killa moose every day, Pe-al; every day in the year. Yes, an' I wish you'd git married ev'ry day, too."

Turner smiled. "Pete," said he, "you're the luckiest cuss that ever set a deadfall; but if it hadn't been for Mrs. Attean here we'd had you wearing that four-months' yoke instead of the lifelong yoke you've got now. By the way, how did you get here?" he asked the blushing, newly made bride.

"I snowshoed to North East Cary," replied she. "The man who runs the hotel there, and who is Pe-al's friend, drove me to Greenville last night, but we got there too late to catch the train you came on, so I came down this morning."

"But what about the snowshoe—the broken one you brought into court? How did you know that Amberg wore it?"

"I saw it when—" she stopped in embarrassment and looked up at her husband, who finished: "When he tried to kiss her." And he told the warden of the incident, which they had refrained from mentioning in court.

"The porcupine," blurted Turner. "Well, good-by, Pete. No hard feelings, I hope?"

"Certainly not, Dan. Why should I have hard feelings? It's through you that I've been made the happiest man in the great north woods."

"Whee!" yelled Morton; "me too!"

Shirley Bear

(Tribal Elder)

Born in the Tobique First Nation, Shirley Bear is a well-known writer, multimedia artist, activist, and traditional herbalist. She has exhibited her visual art in cities across Canada and the United States and has published her poetry and essays in numerous anthologies. She was also the subject of a short film, *Minqwon Minqwon*, directed by Catherine Martin (Mi'kmaq) for Canada's National Film Board in 1990. The poems below come from her book *Virgin Bones*.

Freeport, Maine

Gap, L.L. Bean and Patagonia
Freeport Maine

Children leading mum and dad
By the credit card

Blank faces, Brown races
Gap, L.L. Bean and Patagonia

Name brands, not cheap
All look alike, smell alike

Blank faces
Flashing neon eyes
Blank checks

Freeport Maine
Blank faces, White races
Blank checks

History Resource Material

Martin, Paul, Gabriel and Peter.
Arrogant men in long black robes,
baptizing and renaming.

"Because you are Soulless Savages,
We shall rename you. You should be
Saved. You shall be renamed!"

Isaac, Francis, Daniel and John.
These are names of priests in long
black robes, vicariously renaming
their children.

For God's sake.

Baqwa'sun, Wuli Baqwa'sun

Tilly Road, Tobique Reserve
I basked in the brilliant colours of the
maples and left old memories where
they live
in 1965 winter
      spring
            summer

Five ochre bones
you wrote: Two nights ago
I went to snowshoe in the moonlight
Baqwa'sun, Wuli baqwa'sun

I riffle through some old letters
you wrote: I never knew of these things
before I met you
and
I remember: God the father and his son
casting long shadows on the midnight snow
Grandmother's generous light
a man of the cloth, a cloth of wool
Baqwa'sun, Wuli baqwa'sun

Yesterday I filled my memory eyes
with the autumn colours

yellow orange red and brown
route 1-A: Houlton to Calais Maine
I gulped down the golden spread and
burped out old memories
in the moonlight on your snowshoes
God the father's son
leaving only the protruding skeletal
filigree after a warm spring and summer growth
leaving the old memories where they live

Kugh, kugh of your snowshoes
how gently you crept
into my life
playing gently on the ebony keys
bypassing all the ivory keys
man of cloth, cloth of wool
Baqwa'sun, Wuli baqwa'sun

The memories pan across this maple
brilliance of Lake Edwards Watercolour
fall of 1965
the autumn lake
the winter moon
the spring rain
the summer farewell
again in 1972
you're in Tibet
you write: I'm home, I'm home
you've shed your cloth of wool
the snowshoe etches prints
printing moonlit shadows in my memories
deep God the father's son
we leave old memories where they live

Today: October 1995
revisiting
letters long forgotten
after a windy night

the leaves have fallen to the ground
leaving only the protruding skeletal
filigree after a warm spring and new summer growth

September Morning

Wulustook runs shallow,
rippling softly in the morning sun.
Warm breezes caress
my feet, my hair, my heart.
Water hemlock looks harmless
against the azure sky.

Intense blue, deep indigo.
Secret memories run below
the surface of the current,
sparkle erratically
as the stars at midnight, cobalt
memories creating energy.

Sparkling stars on the
surface dance in the reflecting
light of the morning sun.
Rainbow virgins
dance
on the surface of
Wulustookuk.

Fragile Freedoms

Fragile Freedoms are the delicate balancing
acts played by the indian act politicians and the
canadian government bureaucrats in the plush
carpeted offices of the inner governmental
chambers, a game that affects the original men
and women who have survived unrecognized from

1492–1992, the games that continue to deny the
original people the right to self-determination.

Fragile Freedoms is the backlash that further
denied freedoms to the warriors at Wounded Knee
and Kanesatake.

Fragile Freedoms is the fragility of the paper
made from the disappearing grasses of the rain
forests of south america, the herb medicines of
the amerikan continent, the air that we breathe,
the water as it drips its final drops, our skin as it
slowly blotches and disintegrates from the radiated
pollutants in the air that affects this whole planet.

Fragile Freedoms is the delicate hope for the
possibility of making this time forward as the
beginning of healing.

Andrea Bear Nicholas

Dr. Andrea Bear Nicholas chairs the Native Studies Department at St. Thomas University in New Brunswick, where she developed the first Native Language Immersion Teacher Training Program based in a North American university. Language revitalization is her current focus: she is working on a massive collection of Maliseet-language stories and is also piloting a three-year adult Maliseet language immersion program at St. Mary's First Nation. Born and raised in New England, Dr. Nicholas is a member of the Tobique Community. She has published widely on Maliseet history, language, and culture. The following essay is excerpted and adapted from a piece she initially wrote for *Briarpatch*, an independent contemporary-issues magazine based in Saskatchewan.

Linguicide, the Killing of Languages, and the Case for Immersion Education

As defined by Tove Skutnabb-Kangas, linguicide is "the killing of languages without killing the speakers."[4] For the most part, Canadians and Americans are probably aware that linguicide was a central and overt policy in residential and boarding schools in both countries. Indeed, the stories of First Nations children being routinely punished in these schools for speaking their language, sometimes even with needles stuck through their tongues, are legion. While it is assumed that linguicide died with the closure of the last residential school in 1996, it continues as a covert policy into the present. As Dr. Roland Chrisjohn has stated, "Residential schools . . . never ceased operation; they merely changed their clothes, and went back to work."[5]

Though Indigenous children are no longer openly punished for speaking their languages, it is the power of dominant linguistic groups over Indigenous linguistic groups that continues to fuel linguicide by imposing a dominant language (English or French) on Indigenous children as the medium of instruction and by providing no option for education in the medium of the mother tongue.[6] By this means Indigenous languages are effectively ignored, stigmatized, and replaced or displaced. In the opinion of linguistic rights scholar Tove Skutnabb-Kangas, this form of education is "subtractive language education," since it subtracts from a child's linguistic repertoire instead of adding to it.[7] What makes it especially effective is that it separates Indigenous children from proficient speakers of their language during most of every day and requires them to function exclusively in an imposed and alien language.

Unfortunately, the core language programs in most schools for Indigenous children do not even begin to meet the challenge of maintaining or revitalizing Indigenous languages. Indeed, these programs are completely ineffective in creating fluency, even with the best of language teachers, since classes are most commonly only a few minutes a day while most of the rest of the day is conducted in the dominant language. So while teachers may never physically punish children or speak negatively about their students' mother tongue, the imposition of a dominant language as the main medium of instruction sends a subtle message that the Indigenous language is neither useful nor important.[8] Indeed, it is the subtlety of this message that makes it just as effective as outright punishment in destroying a language, if not more so.

Subtractive language education is also accurately called "submersion education" insofar as it submerses Indigenous children in both an alien language and an alien culture and expects them to sink or swim.[9] Too many end up sinking, and even among those who swim, they rarely achieve full proficiency in the dominant language primarily because they were never given the chance to become fully proficient in their mother tongue first.

As explained by Dr. Jim Cummins of the Ontario Institute for the Study of Education, the problem for Indigenous children forced to learn most subjects in the medium of a dominant language is that it generally takes about two years to become socially proficient in a second language but five years to become proficient enough to function well academically in a second language.[10] As a result, educators unaware of this disparity tend to label Indigenous students early in their schooling as "learning disabled" or worse, and it is these students who eventually tend to be pushed out of school. With only about 50 percent of Indigenous children completing school in North America, it is clear that the promise of equal access to education for these children has not been fulfilled and that the chief, but most addressable, cause is the imposition of a dominant language as the medium of instruction.

According to some researchers, the problem is more serious than just unequal access to education. Tove Skutnabb-Kangas and Robert Dunbar have linked submersion education to serious forms of mental harm, including "social dislocation [and] psychological, cognitive, linguistic, [and] educational harm."[11] Considering that First Nations in Canada and the United States have been subjected to submersion education for generations, it goes a long way to explain not only the disproportionately high rates of poverty, addiction, incarceration, and suicide that plague First Nations but also the social, economic, and political marginalization that Indigenous People worldwide have suffered.[12]

The links between these conditions and the common experience of submersion education have led linguistic rights scholars to conclude that the imposition of dominant languages as a medium of instruction is a "weapon of mass destruction."[13] As such, it fits the UN definitions of genocide and crimes against humanity.[14] While Canada and the United States may insist that they did not know their policies would have such destructive consequences at first, they can no longer plead ignorance.

THE ROLE OF LINGUICIDE IN COLONIZATION
AND LAND EXPROPRIATION

In the early years of colonization, the destruction of Indigenous languages in what is now North America was not considered essential. Traders needed Indigenous trappers to maintain their form of life on the land, and explorers needed Indigenous Peoples' knowledge in order to explore and map the land. Once European powers began competing with each other for land and resources, they established colonies as a way to solidify their claims. Led by a belief in their own cultural and racial superiority, colonial authorities routinely appropriated lands simply by granting them to prospective settlers without informing or compensating First Nations. Known as "settler imperialism," this genocidal process separated Indigenous Peoples from their food sources and regularly triggered resistance, which all too often served as a convenient justification for wars of extermination.[15] Either way, First Nations Peoples who survived quickly found themselves dispossessed, displaced, and powerless to seek justice or restitution.[16]

Once the colonial wars were over in North America, the project of expanding across the continent began in earnest on both sides of the border. Though Indigenous resistance was frequent and often fierce, authorities soon found settler imperialism to be a cheaper and more effective strategy than war.[17] Central to this process were the residential or boarding schools, which were charged with the duty of civilizing Indians by imposing English and eradicating Indigenous languages. Though described benignly as being in the best interest of the Indians, the real objective of this policy was much more sinister. So closely did language tie Indigenous Peoples to their lands that authorities focused on deliberately destroying First Nations languages as the key to severing ties between the people and their lands. The goal, of course, was purely material—to remove First Nations Peoples as barriers to settlement and thereby open the land and its resources to appropriation by the newcomers. While other strategies were employed to achieve the same ends, including the slaughter of the buffalo, the imposition of restrictive laws, and the establishment of reservations, linguistic destruction has formed the backbone of government Indian (and land acquisition) policies on both sides of the border, well into the present.

As in other parts of the world, this destruction of Indigenous languages serves powerful economic, political, and techno-military interests since it serves to disconnect First Nations Peoples from their lands and opens the door to unfettered exploitation and destruction of natural resources. Little wonder that linguistic diversity in the world is now said to be declining much faster than biodiversity, so much so that 95 percent of the world's languages are predicted to become extinct by the end of [the twenty-first] century.[18] Since submersion education is now linked to serious psychological, educational, and cognitive harms, its role in the impoverishment and marginalization of Indigenous Peoples can also be said to serve the powerful interests cited here. Indeed, as long as Indigenous Peoples continue to experience these consequences, it will serve, in turn, as a further excuse to keep them dispossessed well into the future. . . .

THE IMPORTANCE OF LANGUAGE IMMERSION
PROGRAMS TO DECOLONIZATION

Considering both the blatant and subtle strategies still employed to destroy Indigenous languages, it is impossible now to accept that language attrition is a natural process, or one achieved without agency. Indigenous languages are not being "lost." They are being systematically ripped from Indigenous Peoples through submersion education.[19] It is by understanding the deliberateness of the process, however unconscious or well-meaning it is claimed to be, that appropriate action can be undertaken to rectify the situation. Unfortunately, the window of opportunity for regenerating most of the precious Indigenous languages, such as Maliseet, will be gone in less than a decade unless massive policy changes and funding supports are instituted immediately to ensure that Indigenous children are given the opportunity to become fluent in their language.

With such harmful consequences now known to result from submersion education, there is little excuse for either the United States or Canada to continue to deny First Nations children the right to publicly funded education in the medium of the mother tongue. A key to achieving widespread support for this goal is to educate society not only about the negative consequences of submersion but also about the enormous benefits of mother-tongue-medium education. A short list of those advantages is as follows: (1) Immersion education is the best and most cost-effective means of learning to speak a language.[20] (2) Research has shown that learning to speak, read, and write proficiently in the medium of one's mother tongue actually enhances one's ability to speak, read, and write any other language.[21] (3) Full bilingualism or multilingualism tends to enhance academic achievement, not hinder it.[22] (4) Indigenous children educated a minimum of six to eight years in the medium of their mother tongue tend to outperform their peers educated monolingually in a dominant language.[23] (5) Within an immersion program there is less need to consciously teach traditional culture, values, and beliefs, since these aspects of culture are embedded in the languages. (6) Schools conducted in the medium of endangered languages go a long way to ensure that those languages will survive since they create fluent child speakers. (7) Such schools also ensure that the linguistic and educational rights of Indigenous children are respected, not only for those who already speak their language but also for those who may never have learned to speak the language of their community, their mother tongue, due to the processes described here.[24]

While initial costs of establishing immersion programs may be large, the overall benefits of immersion education are certain to be enormous insofar as improved school completion rates are known to correlate with lower social costs in terms of poverty, addictions, incarceration, and suicide.[25] In one cost-benefit analysis, for example, it was determined that it costs more to keep one person in prison for one year than it does to provide a private tutor to educate a person in the medium of his or her mother tongue for nine years.[26] For Indigenous Peoples themselves, the benefits of a populace thoroughly educated and proficient in their own language, culture, and history are well-recognized as a key to self-sufficiency, health, and ultimately, to decolonization.

Considering the harms of submersion and the benefits of immersion, both to dominant societies and to Indigenous Peoples, it is a travesty that immersion education for the First Peoples of this continent is not widely supported, especially when the benefits of bilingualism are so well-known. Hopefully, this article will help in the fundamental need to inform the public on both sides of the international border that the destruction of Indigenous languages is still actively being pursued and that urgent action is needed before it is too late, if this process is to be reversed. To this end, what is most needed is strong legislation at all levels of government supporting the right of every Indigenous child to an education in the medium of his or her mother tongue, at least where numbers would warrant it. Such legislation has worked both to save and to revitalize Indigenous languages elsewhere in the world. Why not here?

Chief Brenda Commander

(b. 1958)

In 1997 Brenda Commander was elected the first woman chief of the Houlton Band of Maliseet Indians, in which capacity she still serves today. She was raised in extreme poverty in Houlton, where her family worked picking potatoes and blueberries, among other jobs, to make ends meet. Commander began working for the Maliseets first in the education department, and then in finance. She has secured a position for a Maliseet representative to the Maine State Legislature (as the Penobscots and Passamaquoddies have long had). In her letter to President Obama, published in the *Bangor Daily News* on November 25, 2009, she joins a long tradition of Wabanaki leaders addressing colonial leaders in writing.

Open Letter to Barack Obama

MALISEETS WANT OBAMA TO COME TO THEIR DEFENSE

I commend President Barack Obama for recently holding an important meeting with the nation's tribal leaders. As chief executives of our respective governments, we both took oaths of office. While I swore to uphold the laws of my people, my obligations to the Houlton Band of Maliseet Indians run much deeper than law. I must do everything in my power to protect the Maliseet culture, ancient traditions, customary practices, and spirituality given to us by our revered ancestors. No group is more important to me and my fellow Maliseets in the continual struggle to retain our distinct character as a Wabanaki People than our children.

Our children truly are our present and our future. The Houlton Band of Maliseet Indians has struggled against great forces, especially the state of Maine, to protect and nurture our children.

In the 1980s and 1990s, Maliseet children involved with the child welfare system were being placed at alarmingly high rates with non-Indian families, threatening the existence of our tribe. Without aggressive intervention by our tribal government, we were in danger of losing an entire generation of children. What future does any people have without its children?

As we have battled the state of Maine to respect the Indian Child Welfare Act, the 1980 Maine Indian Claims Settlement Act, and our inherent sovereignty given to us by GheChe'Nawais, we have received no legal or political support from the United States, which has a trust responsibility to defend the Houlton Band of Maliseet Indians from harm. What we have accomplished to defend our right to exist as a sovereign people has come from our tribe and support from our Wabanaki neighbors.

Yes, we have received money. But what the Houlton Band of Maliseet Indians most needs from the president as the chief executive of the United States is for his government to cast off the political neglect we have experienced for the last 29 years since the signing of the Maine Indian Claims Settlement Act and instead become a concerned, dependable, and engaged ally as we face assaults on our sovereignty.

The Maine Indian Claims Settlement Act was not solely about settling our land claim against the United States. The act was about establishing a new relationship between sovereigns grounded in respect and trust. It was to be a national model, but it failed.

The United States has been conspicuously missing as we native people alone have struggled to have the state of Maine respect the intent of the settlement act.

The first treaty the fledgling United States executed was the Treaty of Watertown with my people and the Micmacs on July 19, 1776. When the nascent United States was facing a global superpower in the form of the British Empire, the Maliseet people answered the call, joining you in arms to secure your country's freedom. When we were not citizens and could not vote we came as allies to your defense in subsequent wars.

Now, we need this country to come to our defense in justly addressing the Maine Indian Claims Settlement Act. I ask that the president and this country act with honor through an engaged presence and participation in what the United States has committed itself to do.

Mihku Paul

(b. 1958)

Mihku Paul was born and raised along the Penobscot River in Maine and is a member of the Kingsclear First Nation in New Brunswick. She received a traditional education from her grandfather, a Maliseet elder, and also attended public schools. She holds a BA in communication and human development as well as an MFA in creative writing. A writer, visual artist, and storyteller, Paul paired the poems below with photographs and her own drawings in a multimedia installation, *Look Twice: The Waponahki in Image and Verse*, in 2010 at the Abbe Museum in Bar Harbor, Maine. Her first book, *20th Century PowWow Playland*, appeared in 2012, part of Bowman Books' Native New England Authors series.

The Ballad of Gabe Acquin

One hundred years ago and more
a boy was born within a shack,
where winter's biting wind and ice bore
witness to his family's lack.

His mother lay beside the lamp,
proud and breathless in delight,
while outside dogs began to howl,
then circle in, and fight.

She put the baby to her breast,
his greedy suckle strong.
And marveled at his coal black eyes,
his legs that were so long.

The midwife brewed a tea of herbs
and bid the mother take a drink,
while she sang songs from older days
and sat alone to think.

The father walked the river's skin,
frozen hard from shore to shore,

hunting for some food to eat,
meat to fill the cupboard store.

Three days would pass before he came,
hauling the carcass on his sled.
Venison to feed his kin
and the wife who shared his bed.

He took Matilda in his arms
and laughed to see the babe.
Your son came three nights past, she said,
and I have named him Gabe.

A cradle sat close to the stove
where scant warmth hovered in the air.
He never cries, she proudly said,
and eats just like a bear.

All through the seasons and the years
the boy grew tough and strong,
learning to fish and hunt and trap,
and never to do wrong.

The rez dogs loved him all his life.
He never felt their bite.
The people said it was a sign
that Gabe had second sight.

The river was his other home,
the woods he understood.
When others found no game to hunt
Gabe Acquin always could.

Quiet, watchful by the trees
his wiry frame bent to the ground,
his straight black hair beneath a cap,
he checked each track and made no sound.

Soon he followed as they fled
in shadows green and dark,

four-footed ones could not escape
once he had seen their mark.

When others came, *wenuche* men, rich
they asked for an Indian guide.
The people said Gabe Acquin's best,
From him, the game can't hide.

So each autumn came and went,
with Gabe a hired hand,
And every year he posed beside
the strangers looking grand.

Those men with rifles costing more
than Gabe earned in a year.
Boots so fine and polished
as they stood beside their deer.

And once they asked him to come up
and see the city sights,
all the buildings treetop high,
and all the brilliant lights.

They took him to the Old Government House,
a columned building made of stone
and posed while standing on the steps
but Gabe was told to sit alone.

White men lounging out in front
a photograph would show,
how they stood like they belonged
while Gabe sat down below.

One hundred years is long enough
to wait for someone to discover,
a man that knew the names of trees
who whispered to him like a lover.

He was a man who from his birth
heard the words of river and wood,

knew animals and all their ways,
took only what he should.

I found him in a picture
when I looked for my own story,
and he was staring out at me,
in his simple, fierce glory.

A Maliseet like me,
he was a member of my tribal kin,
I newly name him Muin; Bear.
They called him Gabe Acquin.

The Water Road

All journeys begin here, Madawamkeetook, home,
beside the good river, rocky at its mouth.

Stone shards, bone stratum
buried deep, our ancient cenotaph,
Old Meductic Fort, traceless memorial
on the shores of Wolastoq.

Now St. John.
The naming taken, baptized in ink and parchment.
They say he knew water transformation;
it gives life.

A thousand years and more, we paddled
the Old Meductic Trail; the water road.

Nomads, they called us,
citing "most ancient evidence" of our passage;
"the solid rocks have been furrowed
by the moccasins of the native tribes."

A signpost, our chalcedony flesh.
Blue veins you call Nature's highway,
the map flowing inside our bodies,

the Thoroughfare; Chepneticook lakes to
Mattawamkeag and onward to the Penobscot,
where a girl became a woman.

Her body craves the past.
Its water seeking the cool flow, ancestral memory,
where tributaries meet, flooding
undernourished roots that cling to her edges,
eroded year by year with forgetting.

Remember Meductic and the Water Road.
Birch bark, chert and bone melded with riverbank clay,
merging in the rippling shallows where canoes slide,
silent, among water lilies and pickerel grass.

Return

Last night I dreamed I heard the Earth groan;
felt her bone shift deep inside my skin.
I stood alone upon her shadowed spine
where ridges pronged with spruce emerge from stone.
Shimmering with iridescent spark,
a blade-edge moon hovered in the dark.

As a child I feared the stormy dark,
thinking I heard spirits howl and groan.
Outside my window lightning showed its spark,
electric motes cascading on my skin.
I lay in bed, my flesh felt turned to stone,
breathing deep to stretch my wrinkled spine

Hove up like some earthen spine,
Katahdin's peaks and cliffs rise in the dark.
Bouldered arms and ribcage carved of stone
communing with the mighty White Pine's groan,
Swaying with the wind against their skin;
anchored there beneath the moon's bright spark

A fire, dying, still gives forth a spark
igniting fallow memory in my spine.
The flames contained within this trickster skin
burn brightly, chasing nightmares from the dark.
I hear a woman's voice cry out and groan,
her restless heart bruising against stone.

The trail leads on past cedar, stream and stone.
Constellations light a distant spark.
The bear, Muin, lets out a growling groan,
stiffens midnight hair along his spine.
We two are travelers wandering the dark,
called to origin, trapped within our skin.

Muin and I cannot discard our skin
or change our muscled heart for one of stone.
He teaches me to welcome velvet dark,
guided by the moon's shape-shifted spark.
We traverse Katahdin's rocky spine.
I hear again the mountain's echoed groan.

My confused skin immersed in brilliant spark,
a steady warmth flowed gently up my spine.
Katahdin's song rose up from granite stone,
as sweet music replaced her beckoning groan.

20th Century PowWow Playland

In 1920, a centennial celebration,
time measured, commemorating that moment
when everything changed.
A separation, renaming territory, viciously tamed,
Carved and claimed, settled, the state of Maine.

Two faces stare out, children,
sepia toned, museum quality, pressed to pages.

Boy and girl frown before the camera's eye,
the rigid lens of history, a dangerous weapon.
Thirty years since that last great dance in the Dakotas,
when bullets traveled faster than
the light that traps these two;
gathering ghosts, supplicants buried their hearts,
died on frozen ground.

Captured sun blinds those young eyes,
lays bare the half-grimaced smiles.

Gone, the birchbark wigwam, the buffalo hide tipi.
Backdropped by a canvas tent,
the boy, dimpled cheeks smeared with "war" paint,
stands beside his sister, cousin.
Her banded braids hung with some cheap feather.

Children pose now,
War replaced by pageantry.
The wolf a legend, wearing the skin of a leashed dog,
and the cold warrior's eye, now closed,
steady hand empty, his battle cry now silent in
this fading picture, this 20th century powwow playland.

Trade in the 21st Century

When fiddleheads cost eighty dollars a pound
Will Indians get a fair price?
The chefs and gourmet menus abound
With fiddleheads at eighty dollars a pound.
Yuppies will search and search all the wet ground
And wonder in June why there are none around.
They might think the Indians aren't being nice.
When fiddleheads cost eighty dollars a pound
Will Indians get a fair price?

Notes

1. Maliseet people call themselves Wolastokiyik, after the St. John (Wolastoq) River that runs through their homeland.
2. For more on Canada's notorious Bill-c31, see Lawrence and Anderson.
3. For more on the history of tribal rolls and the ways they are used to exclude tribal members, see Garroutte.
4. Tove Skutnabb-Kangas, *Linguistic Genocide in Education—Or Worldwide Diversity and Human Rights?* (Mahwah NJ: Lawrence Erlbaum Associates, 2000), 311–18, 362–74; see also John Sutherland, "Linguicide: The Death of Language." *Independent* 10 Mar. 2002. Web.
5. Roland Chrisjohn, "Retaining Indigenous Students in Post-Secondary Programs: What Means for Whose Ends?," report prepared for the Council of Ministers of Education, Post-Secondary Education Project, Learner Pathways and Transitions, 1998.
6. R. Phillipson, "Linguicism: Structures and Ideologies in Linguistic Imperialism," in *Minority Education: From Shame to Struggle*, ed. T. Skutnabb-Kangas and J. Cummins (Clevedon UK: Multilingual Matters, 1988), 339–57.
7. See Andrea Bear Nicholas, "Education through the Medium of the Mother-Tongue: The Single Most Important Means for Saving Indigenous Languages: Rationales and Strategies for Establishing Immersion Programs," drawn from a symposium on Immersion Education for First Nations sponsored by St. Thomas University and the Assembly of First Nations, Fredericton NB, October 3–6, 2005, www.educatorsforimmersion.org.
8. Tove Skutnabb-Kangas and Robert Dunbar, "Indigenous Children's Education as Linguistic Genocide and a Crime against Humanity: A Global View," *Galdu Cala: Journal for Indigenous Peoples Rights* no.1 (2010): 1–3, http://www.e-pages.dk/grusweb/55/.
9. For a definition of submersion education, see Skutnabb-Kangas, *Linguistic Genocide in Education*, 582.
10. Jim Cummins, "Basic Interpersonal Communication Skills (BICS) and Cognitive Academic Language Proficiency (CALP)," in *Encyclopedia of Language and Education*, 2nd ed., vol. 2, *Literacy*, ed. B. Street and N. H. Hornberger (New York: Springer Science & Business Media, 2008), 71–83.
11. Skutnabb-Kangas and Dunbar, "Indigenous Children's Education as Linguistic Genocide," 2.
12. Skutnabb-Kangas and Dunbar, "Indigenous Children's Education as Linguistic Genocide," 3–4.
13. Tove Skutnabb-Kangas, "Non-Mother-Tongue-Medium Teaching for Indigenous and Minority Children Is a Weapon of Mass Destruction," UNESCO Executive Board debate, "Protecting Indigenous and Endangered Languages and the Role of Languages in Promoting EFA in the Context of Sustainable Development," Paris, October, 7, 2008.

14. Skutnabb-Kangas and Dunbar, "Indigenous Children's Education as Linguistic Genocide."

15. On "settler imperialism," see Norbert Finzsch, "'The Aborigines . . . Were Never Annihilated, and Still They Are Becoming Extinct': Settler Imperialism and Genocide in Nineteenth-Century America and Australia," in *Empire, Colony, Genocide: Conquest, Occupation, and Subaltern Resistance in World History*, ed. A. Dirk Moses (New York: Berghahn Books, 2008), 253.

16. See A. Dirk Moses, 'Genocide and Settler Society in Australian History,' in *Genocide and Settler Society: Frontier Violence and Stolen Indigenous Children in Australian History*, ed. A. D. Moses (New York: Berghahn Books, 2004), 34.

17. See Finzsch, " The Aborigines . . . Were Never Annihilated," 262.

18. Luisa Maffi, ed., *On Biocultural Diversity: Linking Language, Knowledge and the Environment* (Washington DC: Smithsonian Institution Press, 2001).

19. Skutnabb-Kangas, *Linguistic Genocide in Education*, xxxi–xxxiii.

20. William H. Wilson and Kauanoe Kamana, "'Mai Loko Mai Oka 'I'ini: Proceeding from a Dream': The Aha Punana Leo Connection in Hawaiian Language Revitalization," in *The Green Book of Language Revitalization in Practice*, ed. Leanne Hinton and Ken Hale (San Diego: Academic Press), 147–78; Jeanette King, "Te Kohanga Reo: Maori Language Revitalization," in Hinton and Hale, *Green Book of Language Revitalization*, 119–28.

21. Standing Committee on Aboriginal Affairs, House of Commons, Parliament, Canada, *You Took My Talk: Aboriginal Literacy and Empowerment :Fourth Report of the Standing Committee on Aboriginal Affairs* (Ken Hughes, chairperson) (Ottawa: Queen's Printer for Canada, 1990); Kimmo Kosonen, Catherine Young, and Susan Malone, *Promoting Literacy in Multilingual Settings* (Bangkok: UNESCO Bangkok, 2007), http://unesdoc.unesco.org/images/0015/001507/150704e.pdf.

22. Jim Cummins, "Language Proficiency, Bilingualism and Academic Achievement," in *Bilingualism and Special Education: Issues in Assessment and Pedagogy*, ed. Jim Cummins (Clevedon UK: Multilingual Matters, 1984), 130–51; Kathryn J. Lindholm and Zierlein Aclan, "Bilingual Proficiency as a Bridge to Academic Achievement: Results from Bilingual/Immersion Programs" *Journal of Education* 173.2 (1991): 99–113; Joanne Lauctus, "Bilingual Children Learn Faster: Study," *Ottawa Citizen*, April 24, 2000; Wayne P. Thomas and Virginia P. Collier, *A National Study of School Effectiveness for Language Minority Students' Long-Term Academic Achievement* (Santa Cruz CA: Center for Research on Education, Diversity and Excellence [CREDE], 2002), available at http://eric.ed.gov/?id=ED475048; Carol Benson, "The Importance of Mother-Tongue-Based Schooling for Educational Quality," background paper for EFA Global Monitoring Report 2995, UNESCO, Paris, 2004; Tracey Wade, "Eskasoni Elementary/Middle School," in *Sharing Our Success: More Case Studies in Aboriginal Schooling*, ed. George Fulford (Kelowna BC: Society for the Advancement of Excellence in Education, 2007), 144–48.

23. Rodney L. Brod and John M. McQuiston, "The American Indian Linguistic Minority: Social and Cultural Outcomes of Monolingual Education," *American Indian Culture*

and Research Journal 21.4 (1997): 125–59; J. Ramirez, S. Yuen, and D. Ramey, *Final Report: Longitudinal Study of Structured English Immersion Strategy, Early-Exit and Late-Exit Transitional Bilingual Education Programs for Language-Minority Children* (Washington D C: United States Department of Education, 1991).

24. See Andrea Bear Nicholas, "Linguistic Decline and the Educational Gap: A Single Solution is Possible in the Education of Indigenous Peoples," 2009, paper available from the Assembly of First Nations, Ottawa, or the author.

25. Francois Grin, "Economic Considerations in Language Policy," in *An Introduction to Language Policy, Theory and Method*, ed. T. Ricento (Oxford: Blackwell's, 2006), 77–94.

26. Ofelia Garcia, Tove Skutnabb-Kangas, and E. Maria Torres-Guzman, "Weaving Spaces and (De)Constructing Ways for Multilingual Schools: The Actual and the Imagined," in *Imagining Multilingual Schools: Languages in Education and Glocalization*, ed. Ofelia Garcia, Tove Skutnabb-Kangas, and E. Maria Torres-Guzman (Clevedon UK: Multilingual Matters, 2006), 3–47.

Further Reading

MALISEET AUTHORS

Bear, Shirley. *Virgin Bones.* Toronto: McGilligan Books, 2006. Print.

Commander, Brenda. "Maliseets Want Obama to Come to Their Defense." *Bangor (M E) Daily News* 25 Nov. 2009. Web. 21 Aug. 2011.

Nicholas, Andrea Bear. "Gabriel Acquin." *Dictionary of Canadian Biography Online* 2000. Web. 19 May 2011.

———. "Linguicide: Submersion Education and the Killing of Languages." *Briarpatch* 1 Mar. 2011. Web. 15 June 2011.

———. "Noel Bear." *Dictionary of Canadian Biography Online.* 2000. Web. 15 June 2011.

———. "The Spirit in the Land: The Native People of Aroostook." *The County, Land of Promise: A Pictorial History of Aroostook County.* Norfolk V A: Donning, 1989. Print.

———. "Warning about the 'Medicine Wheel', a New Age Hoax." 24 Apr. 2007. *Kisikew* (blog), http://kisikew.blogspot.com/2012/12/medicine-wheel-teaching-hoax.html. Web. 15 June 2011.

Paul, Mihku. *Look Twice: The Waponahki in Image and Verse.* 2009. Exhibit. Abbe Museum, Bar Harbor M E.

———. *20th Century PowWow Playland.* Greenfield Center N Y: Bowman Books, 2012.

Red Eagle, Henry. *Aboriginally Yours, Chief Henry Red Eagle.* Greenville M E: Moosehead Communications, 1997. Print.

Slagger, David. David Slagger Collection of Interviews (readings, transcripts, and recordings). Orono: Maine Folklife Center. 2008–2010. See http://umaine.edu /folklife/archives/collections/mf-153-david-slagger-collection/.

Tomah, Francis, et al. "Petition of Maliseets at Kingsclear, N.B., January 10, 1843." n. pag. Provincial Archives of New Brunswick, Fredericton. Print.

Garroutte, Eva Marie. *Real Indians: Identity and the Survival of Native America*. Berkeley: University of California Press, 2003. Print.

Lawrence, Bonita, and Kim Anderson. *Strong Women Stories: Native Vision & Community Survival*. Toronto: Sumach Press, 2003. Print.

Leavitt, Robert M. *Maliseet & Micmac [Mi'kmaq]: First Nations of the Maritimes*. Fredericton NB: New Ireland Press, 1995. Print.

Mallery, Garrick. *Picture Writing of the American Indians*. Vol. 1. 1888–89 ed. Mineola NY: Dover Publications, 1972. Print.

Parker, Everett. *Chief Henry Red Eagle: A True Moosehead Legend*. Greenville ME: Moosehead Communications, 2008. Print.

Phillips, Ruth B. "The Collection and Display of Souvenir Arts: Authenticity and the 'Strictly Commercial.'" *The Anthropology of Art: A Reader*. Ed. Morgan Perkins and Howard Morphy. Malden MA: Blackwell Publishing, 2006. 431–53. Print.

Potts, Dale. "Indian Storyteller in the Mainstream: Henry Perley of Maine and the Pulp-Fiction Market, 1910–1930." *Studies in American Indian Literatures* 24.3 (Fall 2012): 53–70. Print.

Teeter, Karl V., and Philip S. LeSourd. *Tales from Maliseet Country: The Maliseet Texts of Karl V. Teeter*. Lincoln: University of Nebraska Press, 2007. Print.

Upton, L. F. S. "Francis Tomah." *Dictionary of Canadian Biography Online* 2000. Web. 17 Aug. 2011.

PASSAMAQUODDY

Introduction

Donald Soctomah

They have proven that the Atlantic Salmon
has a genetic link to the rivers they return to
I think that the Passamaquoddy have a genetic link
to this ancient land, Land of the "Skicin"

We are the stars who sing, we sing with our light.
We are the birds of fire, we fly over the sky.
Our light is a voice. We make a road for the spirits, for the spirits to
   pass over.
Among us are three hunters who chase a bear.
There never was a time when they were not hunting. We look down
   on the mountains. This is the song of the stars.
—*Passamaquoddy song*

The Passamaquoddy have always respected the ocean, rivers, and land. Many stories have evolved from this respect through the years. Along Passamaquoddy Bay, the forces of nature are shown through the power of the ocean. In Lubec you can see the ocean water in the bay flowing into the Atlantic. With this view, you can understand why the ocean hunters would stop at this point to carry their canoe around this section of water. This is the home of the world's largest whirlpool. It's so deep and powerful it seems as though it could take you to the center of the earth.

Rocks, the shapes of creatures from the past, hold a special place in the hearts of the travelers. These rocks were where the Shamans held religious ceremonies, then inscribed messages on them for all to see. Where the Wenaukmees, legendary creatures from the past, left messages in the sand.

The St. Croix River is at the center of traditional Passamaquoddy land. Its meaning is immeasurable. Life depended on the annual run of fish though the river. Spring villages were set up at the river's outlet and its waterfalls to allow better access to fish.

Life in the very early days was not always this simple. It changed as the environment and the features of the land changed. In order to survive, the Passamaquoddy have experienced cultural changes since the beginning of time.

Traditional Passamaquoddy stories are handed down orally from generation to generation, and to me, this is more an accurate account of our past than the accounts of scientists. For me, my ancestral roots run deep here, and of that I am proud.

The Passamaquoddy bravely have been battling against assimilation into the European civilization. For centuries, the destroying forces have tried to crush the soul of the Passamaquoddy. In 1931 an elder man from Indian Township said, "Passamaquoddy must be tough to survive." Throughout Passamaquoddy history, survival was the name of the game. Even now, life expectancy is forty-eight years. Death rates far exceed those of the U.S. general population.

Cultural survival starts at home. The use of Passamaquoddy language has declined. I remember an elder woman from Pleasant Point saying to the children, "You cannot think the old way of the Passamaquoddy unless you speak it." The culture has been revived by leaders of the youth. A new era has come of a proud people, the People of the Dawn, the Passamaquoddy, the Skicin.

Passamaquoddy Tribal Words of Wisdom

MOTHER EARTH: A NATIVE'S PERSPECTIVE

You ask me to plow the ground.
Shall I take a knife and tear my mother's breast?
Then when I die she will not take me to her bosom to rest.

You ask me to dig for stone.
Shall I dig under her skin for her bones?
Then when I die I cannot enter her body to be born again.

You ask me to cut grass and make hay and sell it and be rich like the
     white men.
But how dare I cut off my mother's hair?

Sopiel Soctomah

(1755–1820)

Sopiel (or Selmore) Soctomah was appointed to serve as a scout for the Maine Militia during the American Revolution, and in this capacity he and fifty other Passamaquoddy men captured a British military ship. Also a wampum reader, he traveled to Quebec every four years to meet with the Iroquois at the Great Fire Council. Soctomah's son, Sopiel Selmore (below), carried on the tradition of wampum reading.

Wampum Reading

The first string of wampum beads were read, "We sent you this to open your eyes." The second string is read, "That you may see a great way." Then the third string is read, "That your ears may be opened to hear and fix yours hearts that you may have a right understanding to what I am going to tell you."

(1805)

Chief Francis Joseph Neptune

(1735–1834)

Like many other Passamaquoddy men of his day, Francis Joseph Neptune was directly involved in the American Revolution. He became known as the soldier who shot the commander of a British ship during its attack on Machias, forcing the British to retreat. Neptune is considered the last heritage chief of the Passamaquoddies.

Speech, 1813

Brothers, we your native Indian brethren, greet you and are happy to meet with you.

Brothers, soon after the beginning of the war, we called upon you and particularly upon the Committee of Safety of Eastport, to assure you of our attachment to our American brothers, and to testify our earnest desire and inclination to live in peace and amity with all neighbors, particularly our American brothers.

Brothers, we speak the language of our heart, as we have lived in friendship always before, so we will now and hereafter.

Brothers, the times are difficult, we will endeavor to support ourselves, yet occurrences may distress us, relief in such case would be acceptable.

Brothers, should you judge proper to appoint an agent to hear our complaints and administer to our relief it is very desirable.

Brothers, we should be happy if our father the priest assigned us might be induced to come and reside constantly among us, this would give us much comfort.

(1813)

Deacon Sockabasin
(1790–1888)

The son-in-law of Chief Francis Joseph Neptune, Deacon Sockabasin assisted the tribe in many negotiations and was fluent in French, English, and Passamaquoddy. He built the first timber-framed house at Pleasant Point when all other lodgings were wigwams.

Save the Fish and Wildlife and Return Our Land!

Passamaquoddy tribe of Indians, have from the commencement of the Revolutionary War in the year 1775 been faithful and steady friends to the United States and to the Government of this State—and that for the services we rendered this government the British government took from us all the land which we have occupied and improved for ages on the English side of the river St. Croix—and that by these and many other losses we have become very poor—and would beg leave further to state that the game and fish were formerly plenty in the forests and rivers and of great advantage to the Tribe—but of late years they have been deprived of this advantage by the fish in the rivers being mostly destroyed and little or no game being left in the forests or streams for hunting—therefore the Tribe humbly ask your Honorable Body to take their Governor and Tribe under the protection of the government of this State and grant to for the Tribe such assistance as you in your wisdom may judge proper—Your friends further state that they are in great want of a piece of woodland for the purpose of getting wood in the winter for the use of the elderly Indians, their women, and children, as they live on a point of land called Pleasant Point where they cannot procure wood, as all the woodland for the distance of thirty miles is owned by private individuals—Your friends further pray that a stop may be put to the destruction of the fish in the Schoodic River (St. Croix) and that such a law may be passed as will preserve and increase the fish in the said river and its branches—the Tribe further beg leave to represent that the wanton destruction of the game is detrimental to the public interest and very injurious to the Tribe therefore wish to represent that if not beaver, otter, or muskrats were allowed to be taken or destroyed by any white man except from the first day of April to the first day of May in each year that it would preserve the game and be of great benefit to the Indians—The Tribe would further state that at the commencement of the late war between this country and Great Britain they were offered lands and assistance by many in the English government if they would leave their possessions in this State and settle on the English side of the river St. Croix which offers were reflected by our Governor and Tribe considering ourselves as belonging to this State and as bound not only to this State but also to the United States both by the ties of duty and of friendship—All which we pray your honorable body to take into consideration and grant us such relief as you in your wisdom may judge necessary And as in duty bound will ever pray.

Joseph Stanislaus

(1800–1880)

An advisor to many chiefs in his day, Joseph Stanislaus was a man of great wisdom and a peaceful nature. An incident in 1835 around Eastport, Maine, shows how the Passamaquoddy Indians felt about the land. Stanislaus and some other men had taken birch bark to make torch lights for herring fishing; as they were leaving the forest, Ichabod Chadbourne, the non-Native "owner" of the land, approached them and started verbally abusing them. Stanislaus's words were initially reported in a highly derogatory fashion in the *Christian Examiner* in 1852 ("Shadbun no make 'em trees . . ."), but Donald Soctomah has rewritten that speech here to recapture what he perceives to be its original spirit.

You don't make the trees; you don't make the land; the Great Spirit makes the trees and land; Passamaquoddy don't steal bark. Indian land, Indian trees, Indian bark, Indian water. Great while ago the Great Spirit give this all to Passamaquoddy; white man steal Indian land and everything.

Sopiel Selmore
(1814–1903)

Chief Sopiel Selmore was the son of Sopiel Soctomah (p. 163) and a member of the Sons of the American Revolution. He was raised learning the old ways of his family as the traditional wampum keepers, and was the wampum reader at Sipayik. In 1870 he was one of the last two tribal envoys sent to Caughnawaga, the Mohawk village that served as the headquarters of the Wabanaki Confederacy. When he died, much of his knowledge would have been lost had it not been for the painstaking work of Lewis Mitchell (below) in reconstructing the wampum records.

Megaque's Last Battle

In the old times there was a certain Indian chief and hunter. He was so cruel and brave in time of war and his success in conquering his enemies and taking so many scalps was so great that he was called Megaque, the scalping man. In hunting seasons he always went to his hunting grounds with his warriors to defend and guard their hunting grounds from the trespassing of other hunters. He was well known by other Indians for his bravery and his cruelty to his prisoners. He conquered so many other warriors and tortured them that he was hated, and they tried to capture him alive. Some of the other warriors from other tribes gathered an army and marched to his hunting grounds when they knew that he could not escape from their hands. When they came near where he was they sent messengers to him and notified him of the approaching army; he was out hunting when they reached his camp, but they made marks on a piece of birch bark, a figure of an Indian warrior with tomahawk in one hand and spear in the other, which was put in a village of wigwams. When Megaque returned from his hunt and found someone had visited him during his absence, he also found the pieces of bark, which he read to mean a band of warriors. He had no time. He was so brave and proud he did not try to escape. In a day or two the band of warriors reached him. After fighting, when he killed many as usual, he was finally captured and taken to the enemy's country to be tortured. He could stand all the usual tortures bravely and sing his usual war songs while he was tormented. Finally he was killed.

Tomah Joseph

(1837–1914)

Tomah Joseph was a renowned birch-bark artist; he built on old tribal traditions of birch-bark mapmaking to create beautiful baskets, images, and canoes. His home was at Peter Dana Point, where he served as governor in the 1880s. He spent summers on Campobello Island, selling his artwork and working as a guide for summer visitors, including the young Franklin Delano Roosevelt. Donald Soctomah discovered the following letter to the Maine state government, written around 1895, in uncatalogued documents in the Maine State Archives.

The Power of One's Will

There were two Indian families camped away at some distance from the main village. In one lived a young man, and every night he would go to the other wigwams to see some girls. His mother warned him that he would come to harm, for there was danger abroad, but he never minded her.

Now, one night at the end of winter, when the ground was bare of snow, as he was walking along he heard something come after. It had a very heavy, steady tramp. He stopped, and saw a long figure, white, but without arms or legs. It looked like a corpse rolled up. He was horribly frightened, but when it attacked him he grew angry. The object, though it had no arms, fought madly. It twined round him; it struck itself against him, and thrashed itself, bending like a fish all about. And he, too, fought as if he was crazy. He was one of those whose blood and courage go up, but never down; he could die, but never give in till dead. Before daylight the Ghost suggested a rest, or peace; the Indian would not hear of it, but fought on. The Ghost began to implore mercy, but the youth just then saw in the north the break of day. Then he knew that if he could but endure the battle a little longer he should indeed get a great victory.

Then the Ghost implored him, saying, "Let me go, and whatever you may want you shall get, and good luck all your life." Yet for all this he would not yield, for he knew that by conquering he would win all the Spirit had to give. And as the first sun-ray shone on him he became insensible, and when he awoke it was as from a sleep. But by his side lay a large, old, decayed log, covered with moss. He remembered that during the fight he had seemed once to plunge his fist, by a violent blow, completely into the enemy up to his elbow, and there was a hole in it corresponding to this wound. He had torn away the other's scalp-lock, stripping the skin down to the waist; he found a long, hairy-looking piece of moss ripped from the end of the log to the middle. And all about lay pieces of moss and locks of his own hair, testifying to the fury of the fight.

He was terribly bruised and torn, but that he did not heed, for now he was another man, and a terrible one. His mother said, "I warned you of danger"; but he had conquered the danger. He had all the strength of five strong men, and all the might and magic of the Spirit; yes, the Spirit itself was now in him. After this he could do anything, and find game where no one else could. To conquer a ghost gives power.

To conquer the dead or to fight terrible spirits, to thereby absorb their power, and finally to keep them in a struggle until the day shines on them. But the chief cause of magic power among the Indians is that of Will. It manifests itself in many forms, mere courage being one. Thus the Wee-willmekq' confers supernatural ability or other favors only on those who are not afraid of it. The demon Log, as we have just seen, gives strength and prosperity to a man for simply fighting like a bull-dog. When the true magician "gets mad," and continues to get madder till the end, he is invincible. Allied to this is perseverance. The Rabbit is rewarded with skill as an enchanter merely for continuing to try. His very failures have this in them that he keeps on resolutely, though in a wrong road.

A very important part of *m'téoulin* is the materials employed. Among the Indians, very commonplace articles are employed indifferently. The magic consists not in them, but in the magician and his methods. He has had his dreams, or received, while alone in the forest, his inspirations, which have told him what to do. He takes the objects suggested, and with them performs his wonder works. Sometimes he tells others to do the same with the same things, but in this case he is still the motive force; it is *his* enchantment.

Lewis Mitchell

(1847–1930)

Lewis Mitchell is remembered and revered as an effective tribal representative to the Maine State Legislature. Below is an excerpt from a famous speech that he delivered in those halls in 1887, one that is widely circulated in books, historic exhibits, and school curricula in Maine today.[1] Additionally, Robert Leavitt and David Francis have reissued Mitchell's wampum records. Mitchell is said to have been the first tribal member to write in the Passamaquoddy language, using an orthography of his own creation. In the late nineteenth century he worked with Sopiel Selmore (above) to record wampum traditions. He gave the records to the anthropologist John Dyneley Prince, but they were lost in a fire, and Mitchell reconstructed these for Prince. Mitchell was an even more prolific writer than scholars have so far appreciated. His papers in the Library of Congress include hundreds of pages of traditional Passamaquoddy narratives, histories, letters, and other documents. His letter to folklorist Charles Godfrey Leland, just one of many in that collection, suggests something of the complicated mix of cultural pride and economic pressure that prompted him to write so much.

Speech before the Maine State Legislature, 1887

I was authorized by the Passamaquoddy Tribe of Indians to come here before you for the purpose of making known to you what the Passamaquoddy Indians have done for the American people, and how we have been used by the American people and how we used them. In 1775 or 1776, in the struggle between Great Britain and America, your people came to us for assistance. You authorized Col. John Allan to speak to us and you said, "He is our mouth, believe what he says to you." After many kind words and promises, Francis Joseph, who was the chief of the tribe at that time, accepted his offer. He promised to go and help his people gain their independence. Immediately he sent his captains to different parts of his country to notify his people to prepare for immediate war. In a few days Francis Joseph gathered an army of six hundred men. At that time, and many years before that, the Passamaquoddy Tribe was the headquarters of the Abnaki Nation.

Passamaquoddy Tribe can show you by a letter from Col. John Allan when he authorized the Passamaquoddy Indians to guard the coast from Machias to Passamaquoddy, and authorized them to seize the enemy's vessels. And according to his orders we can show you by the affidavit, Capt. Sopiel Socktoma [sic], with fifty others of his tribe, captured an armed schooner in Passamaquoddy Bay, and they ran her to Machias and gave her up to Col. John Allan.

We know the Indians who served in that war are passed out of existence, but the Passamaquoddy Tribe helped the Americans in that war, and the tribe is still in existence. Now we bountily ask your attention to help us by letting the Legislature examine the papers and refer them to Congress, if they see fit.

In the treaties of 1725, 1794, and Governor Dummer's treaty of 1727, and in the laws of Massachusetts and Maine at their separation, we were guaranteed the right to hunt and fish forever.

In the year 1854 or 1857 some dishonest person or persons presented a petition to the Maine Legislature, asking the State to sell the Indians' land—Indians did not need it—so the Legislature passed a resolve, that a certain piece of land, situated in the Town of Perry, owned by the Indians, would be sold by public auction, on such day, at Perry (they must have arranged everything so they wouldn't bid against each other) and that land was sold for the small sum of $500.00. The Indians opposed the sale of it. Now their firewood costs the Indians of Pleasant Point $1,500.00 a year.

If that land had not been sold, the Indians would not suffer for want of firewood. Thousands of cords of cordwood have been cut, and wood is on it yet. The land cleared by the Indians was also sold. Now we claim again that this is not right. An Indian agent himself bought this land afterward and again when we lost the claim on the Islands the case *Granger vs. Indians*, we not only lost the claim, but $2,500.00 out of the Indians in favor of Mr. Granger.

Just consider, today, how many rich men there are in Calais, in St. Stephen, Milltown, Machias, East Machias, Columbia, Cherryfield, and other lumbering towns. We see a good many of them worth thousands and even millions of dollars. We ask ourselves, how do they make most of their money? Answer is, they make it on lumber or timber once owned by the Passamaquoddy Indians.

How many of their privileges have been broken? How many of their lands have been taken from them by authority of the State? Now, we say to ourselves, these Indians ought to have everything they ask for. They deserve assistance. We are sent here to help the poor and defend their rights.

Now, this plainly shows us how much worse a people of five hundred and thirty souls are, stripped of their whole country, their privileges on which they depend for their living; all the land they claim to own now being only ten acres. If one or two men in this body were Indians, they would fight like braves for their rights.

Now look at yourselves and see whether I am right or wrong. If you find any insulting language in my speech, I ask your pardon. I don't mean to insult anybody, but simply tell you of our wrong.

Letter to Charles Godfrey Leland

Calais Sept 18 1884

Friend Leland,

I came up here in Calais with Sopiel Selma to see Mrs. Wallace Brown,[2] about the wampum, I write off a Sample for you,[3] what Sopiel ~~callest~~ calls it Indian International Salutation wampum used for that Purpose. it also used for Mourning and other Cerimonies. it was four Strings of it. I numbered the Strings and numbered the Different Colors of the Beads, Purple and White. You can do the painting yourself. I only tell you the number of Beads and colors, and we show to Mrs. Brown the Different kinds of wampum, that we can write off for you if you give us fair price for it. this writting is worth more than the songs and story writting. We [it?] should be a wampum of General treaty of peace made by all Indian tribes. this of course contains more information. Please let us know what can you afford to give for it as soon as you can, but in the meantime we writed it off. We can finished before we will hear from you. I also found in among the Passamaquoddies the have four Different kinds of Indian Songs first are Dancing Songs

Second, Molmamewi Songs

these Songs are sung in winter, when the Indians wants to kill the time in Long winter Evenings they gathered together in the wigwams, and each wigwam has a Clown called molmeehegan they carry Lots of Different articles to Susap? and Each Clown Recommending the article of its use in his Songs, this is very important.

thirds Salutation Songs, is used when Different tribes visit the others, and always were Recited and Saluted first in Songs and then . . . Wiqu cofaltin[?] or Public Supper or Dinner, they sung these songs before Eating.

fourth Lonely or Lonsome Songs

all these with words, the Price you offered me for Songs one Dollar for Every 600 Six Hundred words I also charge you the same for wampum writting, and of course Sopiel Selma wants something besides my Price for his trouble to telling me the words it takes him as long as the writting

Lewy Mitchell

Sylvia Gabriel

(1929–2003)

Sylvia Gabriel's baskets are in museums all over the country. She belonged to the renowned Gabriel family of master Passamaquoddy basketmakers, documented in the film *Gabriel Women: Passamaquoddy Basketmakers*. She was a founding member of the Maine Indian Basketmakers Alliance and a devoted teacher of the art. As the selections below show, she was also a talented poet; she circulated some of her verse in the tribal newsletters of the 1980s, but these are being publicly published here for the first time.

Wounded Be

How deep would you want the wound to be
and yet not really show?

We still carry the scars of old
and will 'til we die, you know—
they were handed down to us but
not on a silver platter;
by people who suffered needlessly
and didn't know what was the matter.
To live in the past is difficult when
the present seems the same—
and it looks like the future
holds in store, nothing but more blame.
Where are we all going and
what do we expect to gain by
rekindling old emotions
that only bring us pain?
Our efforts to get ahead and
find ourselves today,
are quietly shelved and abandoned
for the winds to blow away.
We'll pick ourselves up like a phoenix
and staunchly guard each day—
Then perhaps we will call on the Great
Spirit to come and show us the way.

From Dusk to Dawn

The golden sun is sinking
down behind the hill;
not a rustle, not a murmur;
everything is still.
Dusk approaches silently
and steals across the land,
to spread a blanket of darkness
with a swift but unseen hand.
The moon comes out to shine
on objects down below
and makes the shadows move about

like dancers to and fro.
Timid deer and frisky friends
all come out to play
and revel in the privacy
they rarely get at day.
All too soon the pinkish dawn
arrives in her sleepy way
to yawn and stretch and take a breath
before opening a new day.
With golden hair and sky-blue eyes
and gown of rainbow splendor,
lights the earth so we can see
nature and all its wonder.

Peter Mitchell

(1929–1978)

Another fascinating writer who submitted work to the Passamaquoddy tribal newsletters was Peter Mitchell, a World War II veteran from Perry, Maine. Mitchell was murdered, a case that—like several other homicides of Maine Native people during the 1960s and 1970s—remains unsolved. He wrote the following letter in 1966 and published it in one of the small, ephemeral tribal newsletters.

Open Letter to Americans

Look back into the story of our American nation, and see how much of our heritage has its roots in Indian culture. Look, and understand our pride in being Indian.

Study the ways of our tribe and try to understand why it is not always easy for some of us to fit our ways to yours.

We want to be friends with you, to be at home in your world. Many of us want to make our contribution to your industry, to your church and community life, for we understand that your world has to be our world, too. But as we adopt our ways to yours, we do not want to forget that we are Indian.

Some of us are sensitive, and some of us are shy. Sometimes our names may seem ludicrous to you. To us they have meaning and beauty, and we do not like you to laugh about them.

Please remember that we are just as different from one another as you and your brothers and sisters and friends are different from one another. Because some of us behave badly sometimes, do not decide that all of us are like that. Don't make of us that thing that you call a stereotype.

Let the lawmakers in our Congress know that as they pass new laws affecting our people and our land we want to understand these laws and what they mean for us. We want to share the planning of them. What we want is opportunity. We will do the rest.

Mary Ellen Stevens Socobasin

(1947–1988)

Socobasin was a teacher much beloved in the Passamaquoddy communities for her knowledge of and passion for sharing tribal traditions and language. In 1979 she wrote a bilingual story about a young girl, *Maliyan*, drawing on oral stories from tribal elders. The tribe reissued that story in 2000 on an interactive CD-ROM designed to facilitate language learning. The following poem, "Passamaquoddy Girl," has been widely reprinted in books, including *The Wabanakis of Maine and the Maritimes*.

Passamaquoddy Girl

A proud Indian girl grows up on the reservation
Takes a walk to the white community.
She knew nothing of "them."
She was greeted with laughter

She was treated unfairly
For she did nothing to "them."
She was called a redskin.
She looked upon herself saw only brown skin
She wonders what is wrong with "them."
She is called an Apache with a sneer.
She says, I am Passamaquoddy, eyes full of tears.
She asks herself what have I done to "them."
They make funny noises imitating her language.
She says to "them" I know two languages.
Doesn't that mean anything to you.
But to "them," they only understood one language.
The language of hate.
She asks herself what have I done to "them."
They don't know her. Still they condemn.
She committed no crime still they prosecute.
Stones of injustice are thrown at her.
Her heart starts to fill with bitterness.
She proclaims her hate for "them."
Years of ignorance go by.
Then she realized what was happening.
She was getting to be just like "them."
She says I am not one of "them."
I will not condemn all of "them."
For I am Passamaquoddy
A proud Indian woman.

Donald Soctomah

(b. 1955)

The great-grandson of Sopiel Soctomah (above), Donald Soctomah received his bachelor's degree in forest management from the University of Maine, where he later received an honorary doctorate. For eight years he served as the tribal legislative representative. He has written several books on the history of the Passamaquoddy Tribe and is now director of the Historic Preservation Office.

Skicin Love

Each day the bond within our souls gets stronger
Each time we travel to the ancestral sites we get a blessing from above
Each time we make love our bodies become one
Each time we look into each other's eyes I can feel the love growing
    deep inside . . .

Forever Tribal Love

Long time ago on Campobello Island, an island in the Passamaquoddy Bay on the Atlantic Ocean, was the summer village of the Passamaquoddy people. They always come to this spot for thousands of years; it was a good area for hunting and fishing activities. Here lived a young girl named Sipsis with her family; she made friends with a young boy name Posu; they enjoyed each other's company during the summers, but during the wintertime they separated to their family's hunting area deep in the forest. They looked forward to seeing each other during the summer, and after a few more years Sipsis had become a beautiful young lady and Posu a strong young man. But their families forbade them from spending time together. Finally Sipsis's family moved to another island across the Bay from Campobello Island to separate the two young loves. Each summer they would look across the Bay hoping to see each other and dreaming that the whales who swam around the island would carry them both to each other.

Years passed and time flew by; they each called to Gloscap to grant them a wish, and both asked that their love would last through eternity. He heard their songs of love and felt their passion, but their families did all they could to prevent this. One day Posu was walking along the shore and suddenly his wish was granted: he had become a large rock in the shape of a man looking across the Bay, and Sipsis on the shore of the other island at the same instant also became a large rock in the shape of a woman; she too was looking across the Bay to her love. Forever they would look across the Bay to each other as symbols of true love. Today on Campobello Island stands the Skitap Man Rock (called Friar's Rock) looking at Moose Island where his love also stands; she is known as Pilsqehsis Woman Rock.

During the War of 1812 the British warships occupied Passamaquoddy Bay; they fired their cannons at Skitap Rock for target practice but were never able to hit it. If you look at the ledge you will see the spots where the cannonballs hit. Pilsqehsis Rock was pulled over in 1900 by local fishermen, but the outline of the spot still shows the base of the rock. The story lives on each time this story is told.

Sacred Color Red

Of all the color seen by humankind
it is red that the Passamaquoddy Tribe holds sacred.
This is the story of how this came to be:
When native people were first made by the Great Spirit
he wanted to make the people special
to be close with nature and the universe.
One would not exist without the other.
The Great Spirit found a source of clay and mixed his blood with it
started to mold a man and a woman
then mixed the clay with the sacred plants.
Now when the sky turns red
something special happens in the tribal community:

people stay close to the village.
As a way to honor this color and the union of the tribal spirit to the
     Great Spirit
when someone dies, red ochre dust is put on the body
and on all the special belongings of the deceased.
Family and friends place the red ochre on their faces.

Vera Francis

(b. 1958)

Vera Francis of Sipayik is a storyteller, public speaker, educator, and activist dedicated to protecting and reclaiming Passamaquoddy homelands, including ancestral
territories in New Brunswick. In particular, she has been active in the fight against
liquid natural gas (LNG) development at the Pleasant Point Reservation, an issue
she recounts in the following piece, which she wrote in 2007 for an indigenous-
Chicano, web-based art project called Radio Healer. Francis has also written poetry
and published essays in magazines like *Cultural Survival Quarterly*. She has three
grandchildren: Dakota, Skylar, and Michael.

Technology Meets Ecology: Passamaquoddy Bay

THE HEARTLAND

Liquefied natural gas—LNG—is being pursued today as a "transitory" or
"bridge to the future" form of energy. Because of the questionable negative
public and private dynamics of LNG proponents such as Quoddy Bay LLC,
an Oklahoma-based energy company vying for access to Passamaquoddy
Bay, and the political backing given to such companies, language has
come into question . . . and, in fact, doesn't mean anything anymore.
When it is said that LNG is an effort to "displace oil and coal" and that
LNG is considered "cleaner," what is being lost in the public discourse
is, what exactly do "displace," "transition," "cleaner," and "bridge to the
future" mean?

Lost in these forms of language are tougher questions: U.S. clean energy policy helps the economy and protects wildlife, environment, refuge areas; but where do Native people's lands along political borders and public safety fall within these priorities? How does importing gas reduce U.S. dependence on imported oil? What about the cumulative effect that industrial overload (more than 100 ships per year are being proposed for Passamaquoddy Bay) has on complex, dynamic, and healthy ecosystems? There is clearly ample evidence that even with all the planning in the world a LNG carrier can break free from its mooring (see Elba Island).[4] Technology alone cannot guarantee against human error. As many fishers of Passamaquoddy Bay know firsthand, things happen much too fast with a four-knot current. What about those armed escorts for LNG tankers by the U.S. Coast Guard, not to mention the dense fog effect—when spoken in typical Down East dialect, it goes something like this—*socked in are yah?*

While a regional approach to the LNG terminal-siting process may soon be par for the course for considering cumulative impacts of the industry, current efforts to protect Passamaquoddy Bay and coastal lifeways from LNG, a hazardous and volatile cargo, are being sorely misrepresented. Before taking sides, explore what is really on the other side of the energy bridge—before making up your mind, fully appreciate the multidimensional character of this growing debate; be willing to learn the irrefutable facts.

In other words, the Passamaquoddy tribal community processes (however marred that they were) are not what ushered in the potential siting for LNG at Split Rock, Maine (a traditional and ceremonial gathering place). Poorly formulated environmental policy did that. I do think that until the populations most affected and left vulnerable by present-day attempts at nonrenewable energy development take control of the energy cycle and consumption—take control of the divisive efforts used to promote LNG—the perception that LNG is the Passamaquoddy Tribe's internal business, or that it is for its dissenters to quell, is faulty. Many around Passamaquoddy Bay have clearly rejected the notion of LNG using basic logic—it's simply irrational to operate hazardous facilities near any population, however remote its location. But that hasn't stopped LNG proponents from swindling coastal people's precious time and resources.

What's out-and-out missing from this debate, however, is a solution to help communities gain control over these fly-by-night outfits that operate more on predatory instinct and less on integrity, social responsibility, ethics, or even basic qualifications. Instead, entities like Quoddy Bay LLC are the ones actually allowed to control the local and national agendas—when, where, and how LNG will be proposed—even though they literally have no personal stake in the communities where LNG is being marketed.

In most business plans where safety, security, or even a small likelihood of harm exists, companies engage in a "risk return analysis," with the outcome concluding what the acceptable losses are—in human life, environmental degradation, economic upheaval. It is obvious that it is the Passamaquoddy people, and our neighboring communities, who will be the ones put at risk, with losses to our way of life, environment, economy, and future. And for what? The issue of financial rights for Passamaquoddy tribal members and their descendants were, after all, removed from the table as soon as Quoddy Bay LLC entered the scene. As discussed above, stacking the odds against rural, coastal, economically challenged, and indigenous communities is not sound environmental policy; it's environmental racism and discrimination.

We need to put the order back into this discussion, which is not only based on international law, responsible use of technology, and good science, but also depends upon social and cultural perspectives and ecology. Instead of relying on overly simplistic arguments that LNG is going to generate revenue for a municipal-based government, and thus create economic spin-off benefits beyond the reservation boundaries, learn the truth. A "risk return analysis" justifies people's dying for the business. Environmental justice principles always set the risk to human life at zero. Which is ethically right? No matter how we spin this, the only clean energy is renewable energy. No matter the point of view, the only thing spinning out of control are the developers for LNG. The longer this ad hoc approach—led by too few and their scores of public relations companies—is left unexamined by those whose policies have established it, the further away any effort for displacing coal and oil will be from our future.

Don't be fooled; each time LNG efforts have surfaced in coastal communities, it hasn't been by invitation. Quoddy Bay LLC was schemed up by a few individuals and outside companies. While a regional plan and programmatic environmental impact statements are significant objectives, everyone affected by inappropriate development needs to respond with the certitude of knowing what is truly at stake. The human, social aspects of community are, after all, an integral part of the environment.

The proponents' efforts to bring LNG to Split Rock are advanced through the values of material culture; sadly enough, this elevates individual rights over collective rights and operates by assumptions—growth is good, development is good, bigger is always better—that erode sovereignty and undermine cultural lifeways.

Absent a powerful watch over the quality of democracy in the entire energy cycle for LNG, Nulankeyutmonen Nkitahkomikon (We Take Care of Our Land) seeks a just transition to clean renewable energy sources and responsible use of technology, which can sustain economic development practices. Without first addressing the critical needs of an entire habitat, how could anybody adequately formulate a plan to grow the economy? We can each move to the front of this just transition by creating a new bridge that realigns visions for renewable energy with socially responsible energy policies and technology.

Dawna Meader
(b. 1959)

Meader's father was Passamaquoddy; however, she writes, "Native influence was removed from my life when I was six and my parents were divorced, and found again when I moved to Indian Township in the 1990s." She enjoys learning about her ancestors and her tribe's history and has always loved poetry and creative writing. The following poems appear in print here for the first time.

Gordon Island

The eerie silence of a sacred place
Speaks of atrocities to our race.
A place of sorrow, a place of loss,
Marked with mounds, and a lonely white cross.

To our people, it means so much more
Than a lonely cross upon the shore.
It stands to remember those who hate,
And a time they tried to obliterate.
Our ancestors' suffering was not in vain,
For here today we still remain.
The pain and suffering, the grief and tears
Are things not forgotten through the years.
They're in our songs, in our prayers.
They've been peeled from us like tainted layers.
So, step upon the sacred shore
Celebrate and cry no more.
We've overcome such trials thus far
With dignity and pride; it's how we are.
We may have forgiven the horror so wrong,
But we'll never forget. Our memory is strong.

Seasons

The seasons are changing
around us . . . inside us.
Like the changing leaves
vibrant with color,
so are my feelings
ever deepening.
A gentle breeze
called your love
blows on me,
from the west,
and like the leaves,
I let go,
and I swirl and twirl
through the air
until I finally land
with my feet
on the ground.

Then, like a breeze,
your love comes along
and sweeps me up again
swirling, spiraling,
over and over again
a constant cycle
a continuous circle
as is life.

Dream of the Hunter's Dance

I was not there, yet I could see
a magnificent sight to behold.
A hunter, a man, a warrior,
powerful yet silent and bold.
I watched as he lifted his face
and closed his eyes to the sun.
I felt his concentration.
With Nature he was one.
He cocked his head to listen,
then crouched and took his stance.
Breathlessly, I watched him
as he began to dance.
The feelings came upon me
in tumbling, rolling waves.
Primitive, raw, yet sacred,
a sensuous Indian brave.
I felt I was intruding
in his private, sacred place.
Although he couldn't see me,
my eyes couldn't leave his face.
Soft sounds came from his throat
as to his prey he called.
A soft answering grunt
came back in no time at all.
He poised to shoot his arrow,

made eye contact with the buck.
The deer just stood there frozen . . .
completely out of luck.
He walked to where it lay,
fell down upon his knees.
Arms spread wide he thanked
the Earth, the Sky, the Trees.
He didn't know he touched me
as no other had ever done.
I felt my soul drift toward him
and join with him as one.

Susie Mitchell Sutton

(b. 1963)

Susie was born in Eastport, Maine, and is Passamaquoddy/Iroquois. She has two sons whom she loves and adores, Peter and Tony, and considers herself "very lucky to have a husband like Butch." She dedicates this story, her first publication, "to her mom, Tuffy, and her sister, Rae-Lee, whom she misses dearly."

My Story of the Dragonfly and My Sister Rae-Lee and My MOM!

When my mom passed away in 2006, a friend of ours, Ed, put her life together on CD with Native flute music by my neighbor and friend Jan Michael Lookingwolf. Ed said that while he was making the CD and all the pictures were lying on the table this dragonfly appeared and was flying around the pictures as if to look at every one of them while he was working. Ed asked if a dragonfly had any meaning to me. I said, "Not that I know of right now."

The next day, we had a sunrise ceremony, very Native and spiritual, down by the elderly [center] where my mom's memorial bench is sitting now. We watched the sunrise over Passamaquoddy Bay, and it was the most beautiful sunrise I have ever laid eyes on in my life! Beautiful! We did some smudge and said some prayers to honor my mom and this new bench. All along the way, there was this curious seal who appeared to be watching over us, and this happened too when we scattered her ashes in Passamaquoddy Bay. She watched over us very carefully.

The next day we were off to Connecticut to meet my father, sister, brothers, nephew, and new family for the very first time. There was so much excitement for me to meet everyone. Well, we met my dad, Marilyn, and my brother Matt, and then we were off to meet my other family. We had a good dinner at Red Robin, and then off to my sister Rae-Lee's house. I just thought to myself, "It is *soo* beautiful." The first notice of any dragonfly was in the little dining area—two dragonflies in black frames. I thought to myself, "Cool!" As she was showing us her beautiful house, I noticed a theme of dragonflies, especially in her room. I told her the story of the dragonfly, and *it did mean something!* Well, at that moment when we were in her room, I knew for a fact that it was a connection to my mom and Rae-Lee meeting my sister, Dad, and the rest of the family! I said, "I know the meaning of the dragonfly: it showed me that I was supposed to meet my other family in Connecticut." And, to this day, I believe that dragonfly meaning.

When we left Connecticut, my sister, Rae-Lee, gave me a dragonfly pin—a pretty green one that I will cherish! That Christmas there seemed to be a dragonfly theme, 'cause the story was *sooo* cool! I got that beautiful dragonfly necklace from Butch and a beautiful hand-beaded pin from my uncle Dale who lives in Maine.

I lost my dragonfly sister Rae-Lee; she was taken away from us too young. There isn't a day that goes by that I don't think about her and my mom. I am reminded of them every time I see a beautiful dragonfly. That is my dragonfly story.

(2006)

Wendy Newell Dyer

(b. 1964)

Wendy Newell Dyer works as a freelance writer and photographer. She studied literature and professional writing at the University of Maine. She is a trained bereavement counselor for hospice, and she has been active in the prostate cancer recovery community since the passing of her husband, Bill. The following autobiographical essay is being published here for the first time.

A Warrior's Homecoming

I was adopted at birth, and I began the journey to find my biological parents in 1989, shortly before my twenty-fifth birthday, when the desire to know my genetic and cultural heritage became so strong that I was willing to go to any length to find my birth mother and father. I wanted to know if I had Native American ancestry, since I had been asked that question throughout my life but could never answer with any certainty.

I found both of my parents in a short amount of time. I wasn't surprised to find that I was of Passamaquoddy descent. I learned that my father is Wayne Newell, a well-respected Passamaquoddy tribal member, activist, educator, philosopher, and linguist. He was raised on the reservation near Eastport, Maine, known as Sipayik and has spent most of his adult life on the other Passamaquoddy reservation, Indian Township, near Princeton. My mother was raised in Perry but has spent most of her adult life in Virginia and North Carolina.

Once I knew my cultural heritage, certain things about my personality began to make sense to me for the first time in my life—like my connection to the land that has always been an important part of my daily spiritual practice. The forest and the natural world became my refuge when I was very young. The trees, the ocean, the birds, and the creatures of the woods were my closest friends. Observing and being immersed in the natural world helped soothe me through a difficult childhood. These things brought comfort to me as an adult, as I watched my husband's life slowly come to an end after a ten-and-a-half-year nonstop battle with prostate cancer.

It was because of this closeness that I have felt to nature, my desire to know more about the experiences and traditions of my ancestors, and my need to do something to honor my deceased husband's memory that I was led to participate in the Passamaquoddy Tribe's 12th annual Warrior Canoe Trip that took place in early August 2010. It was a journey by water that took me and my fellow paddlers from a purification ceremony at the Indian Township/Princeton bridge early one morning, down the St. Croix River to the ocean, and eventually to Split Rock, on the shoreline of Sipayik, the next afternoon, where we were greeted first by the drum and the songs of our ancestors, my father's voice welcoming us, and then by family, friends, and others who had gathered to witness our arrival.

I was privileged to become one of nearly 250 people who have made this journey since it was first taken twelve years ago. Passamaquoddy tribal historian and author Donald Soctomah and a friend came up with the idea to incorporate this ceremonial canoe trip that our ancestors had made for centuries into the annual Indian Day Weekend held each year at Sipayik. The trip has historically been a time of reflection and healing. It has been a time to remember and to honor our ancestors. This year's group comprised students, several college graduates, craftsmen, historians, writers, social workers, laborers, and tribal employees who had a variety of interests and accomplishments.

As we progressed down the St. Croix and eventually to the ocean, the bond that developed between us all is difficult to put into words. Many of the twenty-five people who made the journey are members of the Passamaquoddy Tribe, but not all. Some had lived on one of the reservations their entire lives, others had once lived there and moved away. Then there was me, and I have never lived on a reservation. Though we made the trip together as a group, there was an unspoken acknowledgment that we were each making the journey for our own reason. Several took the trip in memory of and to honor a deceased loved one.

We worked together as one unit, while at the same time we each had the space and time to drift off into personal thought and reflection. The experience of paddling for many hours down a river, away from the human-made world, renews the spirit as one reflects on the past, present, and future. Without the distraction of the human-made world that we live in, we were able to be still in the beauty of the natural world. We were able to leave behind the cares and worries of our everyday lives. We further bonded as we camped that night at Devil's Head near Calais, Maine.

As I journeyed, I thought about what the surroundings looked like before the modern world crept in and changed the landscape. I reflected on how things must have appeared to my ancestors a few hundred years ago. I wondered what they would think to be alive today to see all of the changes in the land and within society. I imagined them paddling down the St. Croix River without the smell of the paper mill in the background. I felt an emotional, mental, and spiritual healing take place within me as I connected with my ancestors in this ceremonial pilgrimage, as I bonded with my fellow travelers, and as I tried let go of the sadness and sorrow that I have felt since the death of my husband. I found acceptance with the realization that, for better or for worse, my life journey had brought me to that place and time. I have my own individual story of grief and loss, but within that story is one of perseverance and determination that was given to me by my ancestors. I was reminded of how my ancestors survived the many attempts to be wiped off the face of the earth.

I was told by someone in our group that because of their ability to adapt to the changes around them, our tribe, our culture, and our people have survived. In this human world full of personal and collective suffering, it was a comfort to be shown that personal suffering can come to an end when one chooses to accept "what is" and when one can embrace one's past without being crippled by it. On the trip I felt a deep sense of who I really am within my being. The experience was a homecoming of sorts for me as I made this effort to honor my cultural heritage and to take my rightful place in the history of our tribe. It was a time for me to let go of the painful experiences of my past, to embrace the present conditions of my life, and to look toward the bright future ahead of me. I draw strength from the knowledge that our tribe has been able to preserve the richness of our past, our traditions, teachings, songs, and dances, while we have been able to balance out the need to be productive members of this modern society. I was shown a strength within me that I had lost touch with, as well as a newfound joy for living. I look forward to the day when I can share this experience with my children and grandchildren so that they also might take a journey with our ancestors. I feel as if I have finally "come home" after a long and sometimes difficult life journey.

Russell Bassett

(b. 1967)

A respected writer from Sipayik, Russell Bassett has shared many of his poems, including those below, on the Pleasant Point Passamaquoddy tribal website (www .wabanaki.com). He has also been published in the collection *Timeless Voices* from the International Library of Poetry. Bassett ran away from home when he was five years old and lived with the attorney Don Gellers, who he says inspired him.

A Measure of Timelessness

Just as a river flows downstream,
There are events happening in and out of our lives;
The river goes in many directions
But goes along a fixed course,
And yet continues to flow endlessly.
Infinite is the time required
For the river to reach its destination; the end
Is not reached in any known time, and yet
All along at a fixed course are the twists and turns,
As every one of us, sometimes learning, learns,
Are the songs of Hiawatha,
And through an ebb and flow
Is to know and not know
That which comes and goes,
From the chant I come to bestow
Are the entities that take to make
So as not ever to forsake,
It's time to be shown.
As to pass at a glance, a mere chance,
Is done at a glimpse of an eye,
Without always knowing why,
That which occupies itself in silence.

Majestic Beauty

With new leaves in the trees
There are many worthwhile realities
Where life comes to life
To give beauty to that which thrives
And those gifts once unforeseen
From one to another extreme
To that which gives us solace
Not ever to be replaced
From the image in the mind
That binds us to our lost treasures
Without needing to know why
That is before your very own eyes
For that many smiles
That are not ever disguised
And a newness just begun
As the rising of the sun
Untamed rivers through my veins flowing
Unknown feeling in some way showing
Only to take notice of a majestic beauty
A magnificence plain to see

Of Life from Life

While I look not away,
I merely see this day,
As one shadow dance,
Many an even stance,
To one's own appeal,
A rare choice to conceal,
The real deal,
Of life from life,
A smile worthwhile,
In and of time,
In the ebb and flow,

One's humanness to know,
From genuine feelings to show,
And a warm inner glow,
Within a tranquil heart,
Being very much a big part,
Of goodwill to mankind,
As a way to find
Peace of mind.

One Aspect of the Journey of Life

As I plan to do what I must do,
I know not what may ensue.
In a world sometimes unkind,
I will be amazed at the things I find,
Only for a brief moment in time,
All the while,
Time continues to pass on by,
As I take notice of yet another day,
I realize there are many.
With each fleeting moment,
I get a sense of what came and went;
I capture important moments on a journey of life,
Moving through many phases,
Where no two moments are ever quite the same,
And subject to much change,
I often have to find time for a reprieve.
Out of much pain comes relief,
Less stress and a short letter of hope,
Strength and experience.

Kani Malsom

(b. 1969)

A Wabanaki sundancer from Sipayik, Kani Malsom says, "I lived in the sickness of drugs and alcohol, the sickness that hinders the growth of our people. The Creator took pity on me and gave me a dream to help me on this walk of life. The Creator showed me a better way to live my life. He showed me that red road, the sundance way of life. I no longer walk in that sickness."

To My Brothers,

June 3, 1996

We left Sipayik in search of ourselves
A search for our brothers and sisters of other lands
To find a circle of unity on the road colored red
Our circle unbroken became a hoop of many nations
Amidst soil blessed by many mountains capped by snow
Hand in hand,
The east joined the south,
The south joined the west
And so on . . .
The elders spoke words of knowledge from many moons past
Hearts listened, contentedly beating the same chants
Chants of strength, unity, and honor for all Native people
A sacred fire burnt, encompassed by cedar, sending scented
Smoke of tobacco above,
To Grandmother Moon who smiled proudly at her grandchildren below
Passamaquoddy men cleansed themselves, shared prayers
In a sweat of sage and twenty-eight rocks
Later, a circle of talk was held between the men
Visions, thoughts, and tears were shared for the people of their
    community
Healing for all, especially for Mother Earth and her children,

Was harmony—felt by all.
Forgotten knowledge was renewed, lost feelings were revived,
Families were missed

The Passamaquoddy men have returned now
To take care of their home, which is loved so much.
A place of wondrous beauty, where
Eagles soar high,
Deer spring through the pines, and
Porpoise swim.

We are the seventh generation of sons who have followed the sun to
    the
west and returned on the Red Road to a new dawn, with new dreams
    for
all, in honor of our Creator. This we shall never forget. TAHU.

Rolfe Richter

(b. 1969)

Rolfe Richter is a self-taught flute player who lives in Perry, Maine, and often performs around Eastport. He recorded a CD of his music, *Dreamwalk*, which contains more of his poetry. The poem below is being published for the first time.

Spring drew its first breath the previous day
as an Eagle flew my way.
I looked up as my spirit felt low
and hoped the Eagle would stay.
I felt Grandfather Sun give his warmth to my skin,
then saw the Eagle in play.
So I told myself to run and just follow the sky
as the Eagle flew my way.

I ran with Sister Wind to forget my troubles
still hoping the Eagle would stay.
Thinking of the breeze under his strong wings,
I saw the Eagle in play.
I stopped and he set on a tree close to me,
the Eagle I've seen today.
Our eyes then met and I saw beauty in his strength,
this Eagle who had flown my way.
As we stared, I realized his greatness
and the Eagle seemed to say,
"Learn to be wise and fly up your spirit again
like the Eagles you see on your way!"
It was then this winged brother soared high in the sky,
We both knew he could not stay.
And I ran again along the Great Mother feeling stronger
like the Eagle who flew away.

Christine Downing

(b. 1972)

Tina Downing is currently an elected member of the Pleasant Point Passamaquoddy Tribal Council. She also works in the tribe's Computer Technology
Department. This story, about her mother, Mary Theresa Downing (Lola), is her
first publication.

A Summer Day in Motahkomikuk[5]

It wasn't until I became a mother that I learned how strong my mom
was—and how amazing. One of my favorite memories of when I was
little was when my mom and I went out on a small adventure together.
We left the house in the morning. We walked up the road to a small
field. "Right here," she said, and when I looked down I saw a big patch

of strawberries. So we picked them and went back to the house. She took a glass and put the berries in it and added a little bit of sugar. She then took the bottom of a mixing spoon and mashed it all up. She told me this is what her mother use to do for her. She had me eat it, and boy it was good, so I ate it all up.

We left again to go to the spring to get fresh springwater. This time we took the car and made sure to bring all our empty jugs. "It's a little walk in the woods," she said. We walked to the spring and dunked our jugs in the water till they were all filled. "We will have to carry as many as we can, then come back for the rest," she said. So we did. Picking up our last jug on our way back, she asked, "Do you want some gum?"

"Yeah, Mom, I would love some," I replied.

She walked over to a tree and picked off this clump of yellowish stuff. She threw it in her mouth and a little while later she gave it to me. "What's this?" I asked.

"It's called *pokuwis*, which is spruce gum," she answered. "Just don't chew it too hard."

It was good. It didn't taste like store gum at all. We were back in the car and home to drop off our water. "What are we gonna do now, Mom?" I asked.

"Let have some lunch," she answered.

So she boiled some potatoes and fiddleheads, fried up some *pikseyis* and bologna, and some *tumahsis*. Everything was so good!! After lunch we headed down to the lake. I swam and she fished. A bunch of my friends came down and we played in the water till we looked like prunes.

Later, we headed out to my auntie's house. I loved going over there because she sang to me in Passamaquoddy and would tell me stories about my mom and her growing up. I never got to meet my grandmother, but the stories about her always amazed me. I could not imagine not having running water, lights, and all the things we have today. My mom and aunty started cooking, and I played outside. My uncle was always building something, so I went to bother him for a few minutes and then went back to playing. When it was time to eat, we all went inside, sat around the table, and ate. Everything was homemade with real ingredients—not from a box, like a lot of things we eat today. I was so full. We then went into the living room and I listened to them talk in Passamaquoddy and laugh while by the fire. I loved to watch the fire, but it made me sleepy.

My aunty asked me if I wanted to try the *bylu bylu*. I asked what it was and she told me it's like a swing. There were two ropes in the double doorway and she put a blanket between them and placed me inside. I think I fell asleep fast. I barely remember my mom carrying me to the car and, later, into the house. It was a good day.

Maggie Neptune Dana

(b. 1973)

Maggie Neptune Dana was born in eastern Maine into a family of hereditary leaders of the tribe and expert basketmakers. She presently serves on the Pleasant Point Passamaquoddy Tribal Council and works in the Finance Department. She wrote the following poems for the 1996 tribal pamphlet, *Passamaquoddy Community Vision*.

Coming Together

People of color
Blending as one.
Overwhelming completeness,
Stirring up the pain.
Wiping our tears.
The prophecies tell!

Hearts crying forgiveness,
Offering up our sorrows.
All sadness dissolves,
Hand filled with hope,
Respecting all beliefs.
Thankful for this day!

Bursts of realization,
Sacred thoughts begin.

Time stands still,
Our peace is present,
Serenity fills the air.
The little people are watching!

Singing tranquil songs,
Trying to relay the messages,
Sharing all we have.
Blankets of love
Surround us all.
Our ancestors are proud!

Spirits in harmony,
Drum piercing souls,
Expressions of dance,
Strutting their feelings,
Pounding rhythms echo to the deep.
The whales hear us!

Tears of happiness,
Vibrations of power.
Eagle feathers flutter,
Shaking Hoop hovers,
Our prayers are given.
All languages received!

Honoring to witness,
The Sacred wholeness.
Our Elders' wisdom,
People loving people,
Seeing at the joy.
My feelings are content!

Sacred Hoop Ceremony

Visions Fulfilled
Honored   Complete
Prophecies Unfold   White Buffalo Calf

Lures—
Nations United
Togetherness   Whole
Relations Embrace   Closeness.
Powerful Ceremony   Cleanses Spirit
Cedar Smudge   Sweetly Purifies.
Wiping The Tears   Forgiving
Sundance Songs   Heal   Strengthen.
A Woman Dances   Expresses   Great Pride
Spirits In Harmony   Sound   Integrity.
Prayers of Offering   Wellness   Guidance
Sacred Hoop   Overwhelmed   Faith.
Connectedness   Forgiveness   Love
Oneness   A New Beginning . . .
For All Nations!

Marie Francis

(b. 1975)

Marie Francis has been writing since a very young age, despite being discouraged by an early diagnosis of dyslexia. She graduated from Landmark High School in Beverly, Massachusetts. The daughter of Chief Melvin Francis, she now lives and works in Portland, Maine. "Diminished Dreams" is her first published poem.

Diminished Dreams

I look upon her,
She holds my answers, my future,
And my heart.
Her wisdom fades with
The crash
Of sand's time.

Her lost words are
Swallowed
By the waves
Of misconceptions.
Her man-made
Chiseled bounds
Keep her from soaring
To her enlightened highs.
Her cries fall deafly
On the horizon
Of onlookers.
Her voice dulls
With oncoming traffic.
Her love of beauty,
Life and death
Is gone.
I stand in wonderment.
I'm one of the few people
On the verge
Of extinction.
I'm melting away in this pot
Of modern-day life.
I cease to hear the songs
Of my past.
I'm chained to my dollar bills.
I scream for my culture,
But only on the inside.
What I am,
What I was,
And what I could be
Is gone.
I stand over the remains
And wonder
What insight she holds.

Natalie Dana

(b. 1985)

A descendant of Chief Tomah Joseph and a daughter of Nicholas and Annette Dana, Natalie lives at Indian Township, Maine. She is studying anthropology and archaeology with a minor in Native American studies at the University of Maine. These are her first published poems.

Listen

Listen,
      Do you hear it?
That soft cry on the wind
It is our ancestors crying
      Why do they cry?
They cry out, they survived for nothing
The pain, disease and death, all for nothing
We die slowly as they cry
      How are we dying?
It is our culture, our ways that are slowly dying
The ancestors are crying out for revival
      Can you hear it?
Listen. . . .

Fragmented People

We are a fragmented people
Scattered in the winds in all four directions
Time slowly eating away our memories
Memories that hold our language and our traditions
We are losing our elders
With them the knowledge of the past
Each new generation knowing less and less who they are

We are disappearing like the setting sun never to return again
Who are we? We who are a fragmented people
We are the Natives of this land
It is not war or disease that will kill us off
It is time and lack of interest in the old ways
Our people need to band together and renew the knowledge
Before it is gone forever
Only by remembering the past can we have a future
A future where we are no longer a fragmented people.

With This Pencil

Moving my pencil across the page
petals of a rose emerge. One by one
the petals form the rose only I can see.
Drawing the stem I cannot forget
thorns, for what is a rose without them?
As I finish my beautiful rose I
once again think about those thorns,
through them the rose teaches a lesson.
Roses teach that beauty comes with
a price, a price that most everyone will
pay to have them.
A price that I will not have to
pay as I look upon the beauty I have
created with this pencil.

Jenny Soctomah

(b. 1985)

Jenny served in the military in the Middle East. She is now a mother of three and is a descendant of Chief Tomah Joseph. Her father is Donald Soctomah, and her mother is Joyce Tomah. She says she loves to write her heartfelt emotions in her journal. The poem below is being published here for the first time.

The spirit is deep within us; from her we seek guidance,
Settle winds and the swift breeze always know where to find us,
We look to you to uncover our paths, our destiny we forever seek,
Looking here and looking there, never is she meek,
She holds our hands and tells us stories about the lands,
The river she says is a traveler always on the go,
The trees are the nurturer giving us the flow,
The animals are our friends and forever kindred souls,
The fire is a trickster wherever he shall blow.

   (2011)

Ellen Nicholas

(b. 1987)

Ellen Nicholas grew up in Sipayik. She received her BA in interdisciplinary fine arts at the University of Maine–Machias, and now teaches grades K-8 at the Beatrice Rafferty School at Sipayik Pleasant Point. She wrote the two poems below as companion pieces for her senior art exhibit at the University of Maine.

The Heart of Sipayik

The Broccoli Tree,
the heart of Sipayik, stretches out
between the local red brick school,
and the homes that dot the overshadowed land.
It soaks in the light from the sun
which peeks blindingly between boiling clouds that sweep across the
     dawning sky.
The tree trunk surpasses the tallest building
before it splits in two.
Its limbs twist themselves into an embrace,
with their mourning,
while the leafless branches reach across the sky with gnarled
fingers, searching the land for others.
Red-cheeked children run and play
in the schoolyard, fenced in by wire.
A man mowing his lawn waves his hat
at a crow that hops by, uncaring, on one leg.
Vehicles drive in circles around the small reservation,
blaring radios, kicking up clouds of dust.
The tree sways but not one sees.
Ignore the growling car engines,
the lawnmower's hum,
the squeals of children's laughter,
the cawing curses of a hungry crow,
and Listen.

Hear the tree sigh as the wind pushes by.
Hear the creaking of its old limbs
as the branches brush against each other in a caress—
Mourning until the day leaves bud and sprout
to dance in a rustle of back and forth, back and forth.
To the heartbeat of the land.

(2010)

Sipayik Reservation 1974

A crisp breeze whispers across the blank canvas of the morning sky. It rustles at the few remaining leaves on the giant broccoli-shaped tree that overlooks Pleasant Point. A few leaves shake free and fall to the ground in a twirling frenzy. The tree is the lone survivor. Once hundreds covered the land, but their roots and trunks were ripped from the earth to make way for state-paid houses.

The leaves crunch and crumble as a group of young kids with dark hair and light brown skin trample through the un-raked path. Their talking shoes quickly flap open and close, revealing holey white socks.

A grey-and-black striped cat slinks around the tree, keeping its distance from the shivering, smiling kids. Its muscles flex whenever the soft padding of the cat's paws encounter jagged rocks hidden beneath the decaying foliage. Down the road, coal smoke curls up from the exhaust pipe of a black Ford Falcon. As it drives down the dirt road the muffler backfires with a loud pop. The cat darts into the tall grass and disappears into an expanse of weeds and bushes in an overgrown cemetery that lies to the side of the monumental tree.

The black car pulls into a yard of a small, red-shingled house. Salt-and-pepper stubble covers the driver's square jaw that tightens as he frowns. Getting out of the vehicle, he slams the car door. He shakes his head as he walks to the small house.

The screen door of the house swings open and shut with a squeak.

"Goddamn Kirk," the driver announces.

Three children sit around a table eating cereal. They stop and stare at the large man with their mouths opened and spoons suspended in the air.

A woman wipes a dinner plate in a circular motion with a faded blue dishtowel. Her black hair, wrapped loosely around hair curlers, shakes with her movement. "What is it, Harrison?" she asks calmly as Harrison takes off his coat and moves to sit at the table. The woman goes on her tiptoes to put the dish away in the top cupboard shelf.

"Goddamn Kirk siphoned my gas again," says Harrison, "I filled it up last night, and I find it this morning goddamned empty!"

Two of the older children, a boy and a girl, exchange glances and smirk as they leave the table. They put on their jackets and swing their book bags over their shoulders. The younger girl waves to her siblings as she goes into the kitchen to get her father a bowl and a spoon.

The teenagers call out good-byes in Passamaquoddy, "Upc-cic!" with a giggle in their changing voices as they sprint out the door.

When the young girl places it in front of her father Harrison says thank you, "Woliwon tos," and fills his bowl with cereal and milk.

The young girl begins to collect her siblings' dirty dishes. Her white nightgown sweeps the tops of her bony feet when she moves to help her mother with the dishes.

"How do you know it was Kirk?" Harrison's wife asks as she grabs another dish. Behind small circular glasses a thin ring of blue separates the brown of her iris from the black of her pupils. Her eyes never leave the white porcelain.

"Joe caught him near his truck and that Mitchell boy, too." Harrison catches a dribble of milk on the side of his mouth with a cloth napkin. "The heathens," he says and gets up. He walks up behind his younger daughter, whose arms are immersed in dishwater, and bends to kiss the top of her head. His left hand moves to his wife's waist, and he uses his right to reach the top of the refrigerator to pull down a jar full of dollar bills and coins. He towers over both girls and the refrigerator.

"Need to fill up the goddamned car again," he says. His hand stirs around the rattling copper and silver coins to reach two crumpled dollar bills. Harrison's wife pushes her cheek out toward Harrison. He kisses it and leaves the house.

A red-brick church sits on the small cliff that overlooks the bay. Inside the little tower behind the crossed steeple, a bell rings in long monotone dongs. By the cement entrance steps is a white marble statue of Mary with her arms outstretched.

Across the street is the new, matching red-brick elementary school with large white letters on the front of the building proclaiming it "Beatrice Rafferty School," named after the nun who tragically died in the wooden church that caught fire one starless night. A nun holds open the front door to the school and hurries the children inside with her waving hand. The rope tied at her waist wobbles from the heavy movement of her large frame. Tufts of white and gray hair peek from under her wimple and veil.

The loud pop of the Ford Falcon's exhaust is sounded as it drives down the causeway toward Eastport, diverting the kids' eyes and haltering their progress to get indoors.

"Inside!" yells the exasperated nun with the cloudy hair.

In the hallway, a nun wearing thick glasses separates the children into different classrooms. A small boy says something in Passamaquoddy, which they're forbidden to speak in school. The nun overhears and smacks his bare arm with a metal ruler, eliciting laughter from the surrounding children. The school bell rings. The boy gives a crooked smile to the other children and enters the classroom rubbing his arm.

Bits of blue slowly burn through the whitewashed afternoon sky. A priest ambles down the road hugging a bible to his chest. He eyes the peeking sun through squinted green eyes, causing the crease in his forehead to deepen. His chestnut hair spirals in small strands on the back of his head. He taps his boots together at the school door, littering the black entrance mat with speckles of earth and pebbles before entering the building.

He walks down the long hallway, passing classrooms, listening to the symphony of children's voices, teachers' lectures, and chalk scratching the board. He reaches the cafeteria, preparing for First Communion study. The school bell rings.

Children rush out of class. Soon the long hallway is filled with chatter and a stampede of feet pushing toward the exit. The younger kids weave through the hall traffic. They enter the cafeteria with their book bags and coats.

The priest opens the bible and begins with a smile.

Clouds creep past overhead. The sun moves up and over the reservation, creating washes of red and pink that blend into the night sky. It descends over the thickly wooded area of Perry that boomerangs around the mudflats. The moon and the stars become brighter as the black of the night takes over. Streetlights lead the way for stray cats to roam the dirt roads of the reservation, while the trusting people of Pleasant Point turn off their lights and go to sleep with their doors unlocked.

The streetlight outside the red-shingled house blinks and goes dim. Moths retreat, heading for the next bright light down the street. A baseline of chirping crickets hides in the underbrush of the gulley. Somewhere down the street a raccoon clunks jars in a metal garbage can, searching for food.

Lacy white curtains dyed blue by the sliver of moonlight get pushed aside in one of the bedroom windows of the small house. The window slides open. Harrison's teenage daughter and son climb out, shushing each other's giggles and snorts. They creep toward the black Ford Falcon. The girl gets inside and throws the vehicle into neutral, then hops out to help the boy push the vehicle down the small hilly driveway.

Their shadows race to catch up with them as they run to the car. Martin starts the engine and they drive away.

"Goddamn Kirk!" the boy says, imitating his father, and the two laugh loudly with their faces flushed.

In the rearview mirror of the black Ford Falcon the reservation becomes a small silhouette with a cone shape of the broccoli tree shooting up into the midnight-blue sky. Orange streetlights glow dimly around the tree like fireflies. Pleasant Point disappears as they go around a turn. A thicket of pine trees surrounds them as they head toward Eastport to the gas station to buy beer.

Back at the red-shingled house, Martha, Harrison's wife, closes the kitchen curtain and laughs under her breath before heading back into her bedroom to go back to sleep.

Over Canada, the sun rises above mountains of trees, turning the sky and the land an orange hue. Rays of light pierce through the small openings of the broccoli tree's leaves, and a large tornado-shaped shadow from the tree looms over the graveyard. Broken tombstones and crosses lie scattered in the tall grass.

The screen door to the red-shingled house opens and shuts with a loud squeak and bang. Harrison walks down the steps toward his car, mumbling. Dew wets his black boots and sticks to them in little droplets. He wipes the driver's-side window with his red-flannel sleeve and peers in to look at the gas gauge. The thin orange arrow points to the quarter mark.

"That goddamned Kirk," he says calmly, banging the hood of the car with his squared fist.

He whispers and repeats, "Goddamn Kirk." Dandelions creep back up after being crushed under Harrison's feet as he heads back to the house. He slams the screen door shut behind him. The house erupts with children's laughter.

(2010)

Cassandra Dana
(b. 1992)

A descendant of Tomah Joseph and a daughter of Nicholas and Annette Dana, Cassy Dana lives at Indian Township, where she is director of the Passamaquoddy Tribal Heritage Museum. She is currently studying anthropology at the University of Maine–Orono.

Kci Woliwon

I am the voice that soothes you
I am the song of the bird
I am the silence of the night

Kci woliwon
Thank you for this gift
A tongue dying slowly
A language barely alive

Unknown words
Part my lips
A fish swimming in the sea
Leaves dancing in the wind

Children shift uncomfortably
Siblings look with admiration

Confusion
Eyes of cousins scouting
As God looks upon his Earth

Kci woliwon
Thank you
For the voice I have become
The words that will soon be lost
As the sun at night
No hope for light

Kci woliwon
Thank you for this chance
A chance to restore
A dog teaching a cat his ways

Notes

1. For a fuller version of the speech, see *The Wabanakis of Maine and the Maritimes* (c-46–c-49).
2. Brown was the wife of the agent to the Passamaquoddies, who recorded a large number of Passamaquoddy stories and songs.
3. The letter is accompanied by a pencil sketch of a wampum belt.
4. In 2000 a cargo ship crashed into the LNG pier at Elba Island, Georgia.
5. Indian Township, Princeton, Maine.

Further Reading

PASSAMAQUODDY AUTHORS

Bright, Sarah Stiles, and Wayne Newell. *Wind Bird: Gift of the Mist.* Orono M E: Maine Lakes Conservancy Institute, 2006. Print.

The Equinox Petroglyph Project. Machias M E: University of Maine, 2008. Print.

Francis, David, and Joseph Nicholas. *Chipmunk, a Passamaquoddy Boy in the Revolution: An Historical Novel.* Pleasant Point, Perry M E: Pleasant Point Bilingual Program, 1971. Print.

Francis, Vera. "Passamaquoddy Group Demands Delay of Liquified Natural Gas Terminal Construction." *Cultural Survival Quarterly* 28.4 (2004): n. pag. Web. 6 Aug. 2011.

———. "Technology Meets Ecology: Passamaquoddy Bay the Heartland." *Radio Healer* 2007. Web. 9 Aug. 2011.

Leavitt, Robert M., and David A. Francis. *A Passamaquoddy-Maliseet Dictionary Peskotomuhkati Wolastoqewi Latuwewakon.* Orono: University of Maine Press, 2008. Print.

————, eds. *Wapapi Akonutomakonol (The Wampum Records): Traditional Wabanaki Laws*. Fredericton NB: Micmac-Maliseet Institute, 1990. Print.

Pleasant Point Passamaquoddy Reservation Housing Authority. *Passamaquoddy Community Vision 1996—Passamaquoddy Tribe at Pleasant Point, Sipayik, Perry, Maine: A Design for Community Development*. Pleasant Point, Perry ME: White Owl Press, 1996. Print.

Sockabasin, Allen. *Thanks to the Animals*. Gardiner ME: Tilbury House Publishers, 2005. Print.

————. *An Upriver Passamaquoddy*. Gardiner ME: Tilbury House Publishers, 2007. Print.

Socobasin, Mary Ellen. *Maliyan (Mary Ann)*. Indian Township ME: Wabanaki Bilingual Education Program, 1979. Print.

Soctomah, Donald. *Hard Times At Passamaquoddy 1921–1950: Tribal Life and Times in Maine and New Brunswick*. N.p.: Passamaquoddy Tribe, 2003. Print.

————. *Let Me Live as My Ancestors Had 1850–1890: Tribal Life and Times in Maine and New Brunswick*. N.p.: Passamaquoddy Tribe, 2005. Print.

————. *Passamaquoddy at the Turn of the Century 1890–1920: Tribal Life and Times in Maine and New Brunswick*. N.p.: Passamaquoddy Tribe, 2002. Print.

————. *Save the Land for the Children, 1800–1850: Passamaquoddy Tribal Life and Times in Maine and New Brunswick*. N.p.: Passamaquoddy Tribe, 2009. Print.

Soctomah, Donald, and Jean Flahive. *Remember Me: Tomah Joseph's Gift to Franklin Roosevelt*. Gardiner ME: Tilbury House Publishers, 2009. Print.

The Wabanakis of Maine and the Maritimes: A Resource Book about Penobscot, Passamaquoddy, Maliseet, Micmac and Abenaki Indians, with Lesson Plans for Grades 4 through 8. Philadelphia: American Friends Service Committee, 1989. Print.

ADDITIONAL READING

Lester, Joan A. *History on Birchbark: The Art of Tomah Joseph, Passamaquoddy*. Providence RI: Haffenreffer Museum of Anthropology/Brown University, 1993. Print.

Prince, John Dyneley. *Passamaquoddy Texts*. Berkeley: University of California Libraries, 1921. Print.

————. *Passamaquoddy Wampum Records*. Philadelphia: American Philosophical Society, 1897. Print.

Spinney, Ann Morrison. *Passamaquoddy Ceremonial Songs: Aesthetics and Survival*. Amherst: University of Massachusetts Press, 2010. Print.

Walker, Willard. "Gabriel Tomah's Journal." *Man in the Northeast* 21 (1981): 87–101. Print.

PENOBSCOT

Introduction

Carol Dana

The Penobscot people live mainly on Indian Island across from Old Town, in Maine. The land holdings we retain today are in Williamsburg, Alder Stream, Carrabasset Valley, Steuben, and Lakeville. This is due to the Land Claim of 1980.

Our traditional route used to entail going to the coastal areas by canoe and staying there until August. Then we'd come back up the river and get ready for the winter. We used to go get wood in winter also and bring it back to the island from other islands. There are great hunting territories on the river and places where we could obtain ash for baskets. Sweetgrass came from the coast.

The river is so important to us. It was our highway and our food giver. The river is a part of us. Everything we had came from the land. Sometimes it is hard to put into words. One has to experience it, like getting into a canoe and traveling.

We have been in this area for thousands of years. Oral tradition was our main way of handing on teachings and values. Our culture hero was Gluscabe. There are many stories about him. He came and taught us how to live. He strove to create a balance in what was. He sometimes appears as a trickster himself. He interacted with the animals and gave us the dog. He derived most of his teachings from his grandmother Woodchuck. In many of these tales you can find what our values are through Gluscabe's adventures. It is said that he will return if you call on him. One way to do that is to build a fire by the water.

What we have today has been passed down to us by our elders, orally mostly, but also in written records. We had ways of communicating with each other along the trails. Evidence of this still may be found in the ancient petroglyphs. We etched in stone, left birch-bark maps, and drove sticks into certain areas to show the area was plentiful. We used rocks to indicate direction. We also used mnemonic devices, like wampum belts, to help us in our telling of certain events. These were used nation to nation.

Joseph Nicolar has left us a legacy with his recording of various tales of old woven into a contemporary style of speaking. There are many stories out there if someone takes the time to look for them. For instance, there is *Algonquin Legends of New England*, by Charles Leland, *Transformer Tales*, told by Newell Lyons to Frank Speck, and Abby Alger's *In Indian Tents*. These tales help us make that connection with elders that wouldn't otherwise be possible. As Penobscot people became educated, the stories were recorded, or they recorded themselves telling stories, which was the tradition of teaching. That's why Joseph Nicolar's work is so important, along with the stories that Molly Spotted Elk collected in addition to writing her poems. It connects us with our not so distant past in a way that is lasting.

Oral tradition is a personal way of conveying values and teachings. With oral tradition we kept things local by speaking to each other, whereas writing is more inclusive of others. There may have been a time when respect for the written word was broken due to the treaties. Native people also became exploited for their knowledge by outsiders, who wrote this knowledge down. In later years, writing was used as a way to save things. Writing is a lasting record that can survive time. It is one way our language has been preserved.

We have our dictionary and are compiling stories in Penobscot. Our language is related to Passamaquoddy, Maliseet, and Abenaki in Otenek. There is a language revitalization effort for Penobscot. It is difficult to get people on board because they feel they can't read it. One has to speak it to bring it back.

Recording writings today will be important in years to come for some young people. It's storytelling through time. It is a way of leaving a record about someone and events or teachings.

I became involved with this anthology through knowing Siobhan and her efforts. I tried to get Penobscot writers involved. We chose those willing to come forward and offer what they have. We also discussed our choices with the Penobscot Cultural Heritage Preservation Commission. No one agrees with every one of these writings. They belong to the authors.

Penobscot Governors and Indians in Council

Gale Courey Toensing, a journalist widely respected for her coverage of New England in the prominent newspaper *Indian Country Today*, cited the following petition in a 2009 article on Maine Indian leaders' appeals to President Barack Obama to protect them from state incursions against tribal sovereignty. The 1829 petition illustrates that such letters—including the one to Obama from Maliseet chief Brenda Commander, also included in this volume—have a long tradition. It is also reprinted on the website of the Maine Indian Tribal-State Commission, established in 1980 by the Maine Indian Claims Settlement Act, which attests to the endurance of its sentiments—the refusal to permit further theft of tribal lands and resources and the proud history of Native service in the American Revolution.

Maine State Power

In answer to the application made by John G. Deane, Esq., in the name of this State, that we the Penobscot Tribe of Indians will sell to the government of this State our two Townships, we say as follows: The white people have repeatedly asked us to dispose of our lands, and we have sold to them one portion after another till we have but very little left. The prospect is that in two or three generations there will not be enough for our children. To us it looks strange that white people knowing this should ask us to sell nearly half what we have left, when at the same time they have in this State so many thousand acres of wild land. If all their lands were cleared and settled, and consequently they wanted more, we should be willing to yield them a share of our own, for we are brothers, & one God made us all. Till this is the case, leave to us this little pittance, the miserable remains of the wide lands our fathers left us, enough to sleep on while we live & to bury us when we die.

And what do white people suppose we must think when we see they wish to take from us one piece of land after another, till we have no place to stand on, unless it is to drive us, our wives, & our little children away? But if so great & so free a country as this would exterminate us, we have no chance any where else; we or our children must sooner or later be driven into the salt water & perish.

But you say it is necessary that our Townships be settled, that there should be taverns on the military road.[1] Have not the Indians tried already to settle the Township you want most because they needed it for its advantages of farming, hunting & fishing? Our Governor undertook this.[2] Why did he not stay there? Because a bad white man, in his absence, by continually alarming his family, at last frightened his wife & children away.

Nor was this all. He had with great labor constructed an eel weir with which great lots of that fish were taken & and quantities of them salted down. This they destroyed. They also dug up & carried away his provisions, his pork, his fish, his potatoes, etc. Finally they burnt his cabins to the ground. It is treatment of this sort that has prevented the Indians hitherto from settling on some of their Islands, & on their Township. By & by they will try again. As to opening taverns on the military road, Indians have had talk among themselves sometime ago. They know that white men who travel that road must want taverns. They wish such men to be accommodated, & they have done last year & this present year what they were able by giving permits to white men to open a tavern at Matahwamkik Point, where it was most needed. Next year they will contrive with their Agent to have other taverns provided when and where they are wanted, so that travelers shall have no reason to complain on this point.

This we have done and are willing to do all that is reasonable to accommodate our white brethren. Why then do they seem as if they wished to reduce us to extremity? When the United States were fighting for liberty, Gen. Washington sent for the Chiefs of our Tribe, and gave them his promise that, if we would remain neutrals in the war, he would secure to us our rights. We have been faithful to our white brethren & all we ask in return, is, that their contract towards us should be just & reasonable.

Old Town
Nov. 5, 1829

Joseph Nicolar
(1827–1894)

Joseph Nicolar belonged to an illustrious Penobscot family: his grandfather was the hereditary chief John Neptune; his daughter Florence became a writer and activist. Another daughter, Lucy, married the Kiowa performer Bruce Poolaw and toured in the 1920s as Princess Watawaso. Nicolar's grandson (Florence's son), Charles Nicolar Shay, today maintains a small family museum on Indian Island. Like his Passamaquoddy contemporary Louis Mitchell, Nicolar served as a representative to the Maine State Legislature. He is best known for writing a book of Penobscot creation and contact stories, *Life and Traditions of the Red Man*, which he self-published in 1893. He also wrote short pieces for local newspapers under the signature "Y.S.," or "Young Sebattis," of which the following piece is one. Probably published in the *Old Town Herald* circa 1887, it was reprinted by folklorist Fannie Hardy Eckstorm in *Indian Place-Names of the Maine Coast* (1941).

The Scribe of the Penobscots Sends Us His Weekly Message

Some of the Names that the Indian Has Bestowed—Quaint and Old—Our Indian Correspondent Continues the Legends of his Race

Formerly members of our tribe on their annual trip to salt water for the purpose of fishing, etc., gave names to a number of places along the bay and river, which may prove of some interest to many persons living in those places.

Commencing at "Coo-cook-har-want-buk," "Owl's Head," we will ascend the west side of the river to our village. The name "Owl's Head" or the Indian name meaning the same, was applied to that promontory, now so well known to all entering the Rockland harbor from the south and was so called from its resemblance to the neck and head of an owl when viewed from the north side. About two and a half miles north of this place is "Ca-tar-gwan-tic," "Grand Landing," now known as the city of Rockland. This was always used as a landing place for those who were going south.

Canoes were generally taken out and carried across, that the "boisterous White Head" might be avoided, for the way around White Head was considered dangerous, also by carrying across into George's River two miles, a trip of fifteen miles was saved.

"Matar-kar-mi-co-suk," "High Land," was the name given to Camden on account of its mountains. Lincolnville was called "Mar-kurn-ta-quick," "Water ready for waves." The old Indians assert that the little bay is full of waves from whatever quarter the wind blows.

"Pa-qua-tan-ee," "out of the way," was applied to the spot where Belfast City is now located. This place was considered out of the regular course of travel. Sears Island, on account of a little sandy beach which can be seen from far away in the southern direction, was called "Warsumkeag," "Bright sand."

Now we come to the celebrated "Ar-quar-har-see-dek," "Stepping Ashore," now known as old Fort Point, where hundreds of pleasure seekers during the summer months enjoy the cool sea breeze, but in the olden times when members of the tribe visited here, they only stopped long enough to make the sign of their visit, showing which direction they were going, the number of their party and canoes, etc. On account of its being a marking place no one was ever allowed to mar or deface its outline by using it for a camping ground.

The reason for selecting this for a marking place, was because of it being the last prominent point, from entering the river from the bay, or going out into the bay from the river, and coming or going from the eastern or western shore all stopped here and made their marks. All the families of our tribe were known by a mark. Some were represented by animals, fish and reptiles, and others by well-known implements, the moon, sun, etc. Each mark showed the number in the family and the direction taken.

"Asick," "Clam-bed," situated a little west of Fort Point, is now known as Stockton and was always noted for being the first place where good clams could be found on going down river.

Verona Island was known by the name of "Ar-lur-meh-sic," "spawning island." The small river that flows into the Granite Quarries between Prospect and Frankfort was called "Que-que-mis-we-to-cook," "Duck River."

Our next stopping place was "War-li-ne-tuk," "Cove Brook," on the east side of the river north of Winterport. Then we crossed to the west side, landing at "Et-ta-li-tek-quan-ki-lur-nuk," meaning "a place where everybody runs up." Here we have a sort of high bluff, slightly sloping, produced by land slides. A cove is located on the one side, and at the base of the bluff there was a fine pebbly beach. This was always a noted sporting place and here they left the cramped position made necessary by the canoe of those times, and exercised by running up the steep sandy side of this bluff. It was always considered a great feat to run up to the top of this sandy bluff without stopping, as the sand gave way under the feet, and the steepness of the incline taxed the wind-power of the runner to the fullest extent. This was also a popular sporting place for all who wished to test their strength as well as a general race ground. And often large parties chose sides at "Kur-des-keag," put up a large amount of wampum and other valuables to be contended for as a wager, and started very early in the day that a large amount of time might be given to sports and that the superiority of the different factions might be decided. Thus a great amount of wampum and valuables here changed hands.

The name "Toul-bunt-bus-suk," "Turtle Head," was applied to what is now known as "High Head." Hampden River was called on account of a "slanting ledge," "Su-war-tep-skark." Then we stopped at "Kur-des-keag," "Eel River" upon which at its junction with the Penobscot River is now located in the City of Bangor. The river now retains the old Indian name somewhat Anglicized into Kenduskeag.

Up the river a short distance, at what is now known as the Red Bridge, was the "Devil's Track," "Majah-hundo-pa-mumptunque." Also here the Hathorn Brook was called "Pem-jedge-wock," "Current raggedly dropping down."

But returning to the Penobscot, at the water works, where so many beautiful salmon are taken every year by the sportsmen, the "So-ba-quar-ps-cook," "Sea-rock" was applied, and farther up, near Veazie we have "Wee-quer-gar-wu-suck," "Head of the tide." "Steep Hill," "Ar-quer-kek" was applied to Veazie, and what is now known as Basin Mill was called "A-ne-quer-sar-sa-suk," "Ant heap."

"Mur-lur-mes-so-kur-gar-nuk," "Alewive catching on the way," is now known as Stillwater Falls, and just above we have "Mar-tarmes-con-tus-sook," "At the young shad catching," and the next rips were called "War-sar-sump-qua-ha-moke," "Slippery ledge rips," and further on, at the bend of the river just before reaching Greatworks is "Bet-cum-ka-sick," "Round bend shoals." Then comes "Wag-ge-we-sus-sick," "Bad gall," now known as Greatworks. An old Indian once killed a sturgeon here, and finding a very large gall in the fish thought he must be bad.

Just before reaching Oldtown is "Tar-la-lar-goo-des-suk," "a place of painting," now known as "Shad Rips." Here the women were allowed to stop and paint themselves before entering the village.

Now we arrive at "On-ne-gar-nuck," "At the carry," on the Oldtown side; here it was always necessary to take canoes out and carry by what is known as Oldtown fall before paddling across to their village.

As there were but few stopping places on the east side of the river we will briefly mention them. Returning to the bay we have "See-bur-es-suk," "At the sea thoroughfare," now known as Vinalhaven; the "Cas-cu-nar-cook," "Crane Island," now known as Mark Island, opposite Camden, and "Pit-tow-be-gook," "Inland sea island," now called Long Island. Last, but not least was "Margi-bee-guar-do-suk," which the white man calls Castine. If we have not tired the readers of the HERALD this week with Indian names, we will give a few more in the course of two or three weeks. Next week we hope to interest them in a few more of our amusements.

Molly Spotted Elk

(1903–1977)

One of the most intriguing public figures of the early twentieth century, Molly Spotted Elk (born Mary Alice Nelson) left Indian Island when she was a teenager to dance in New York nightclubs and in Texas vaudeville. She got a starring role in *The Silent Enemy* (1930), a silent film in which she played an Ojibwe woman in love with a warrior played by Sylvester Long, another celebrity, then known as Chief Buffalo Child Long Lance. In the 1930s, like many other American intellectuals of color, she moved to Paris, where she danced and performed. She married journalist Jean Archambaud and fled France with her daughter during the war. Amid all of this, Spotted Elk was also an avid writer and indefatigable researcher. She wrote down traditional indigenous stories she had heard while growing up and was reportedly working on a novel when she died. Her poems—often idiosyncratic in their spelling, punctuation, and spacing—are housed in the Maine Folklife Center at the University of Maine–Orono; few have been previously published and most are undated.

We're In the Chorus Now

Aztec Days—
We are the famous Aztec Girls[3]
You've heard so much about
We're noted for our happy smiles
And for our dancing too.
Most everybody likes us
We hope you'll like us too.

As we go dancing
And old Kirk begins to play
You can hear them saying
The Aztec Girls are surely
Just the thing!

A Russian Mystery
> She was the lily, fair and white
> With golden curls and wistful eyes
> She was a fairy in the light
> A mystery, enshrouded in lies.

> Lilyan, whose lovely face
> A thing of beauty
> Led the line, to grace
> In loveliness and duty.

The Rascal
> Audrey, whose petite being
> And twinkling arts
> Childish outbursts
> And supple back
> Was the kid and acrobat.

The Singing Deceiver
> Mabelle, who was like a chameleon
> And whose tongue mellowed
> With bitter and sweet words.

The Gold Digger
> Ruth, whose shapely figure
> And superstitious nature
> Red-haired vamp we called her
> Had beaus from the smart set
> And friends from the ranches.

Her Pardner
> Jean, from old St. Louis
> A champ Charlestoner
> And St. Louis demonstrator
> A typical show girl who knew
> All stage language and tricks
> And rivaled a parrot for swearing.

An English Heather Bloom
> Violet; the teaser and vivacious

Whose personality beamed
And feet that could tap
Their size didn't stop
Any pep for a Tiller step—
One of the Hipp Girls
Who has fallen in love
With that light-haired Jackson
That witty newsman in front.

A Bit of Sweetness
Mabel; a lovely flower from New York
Her friendships and smiles
Are like haunting fragrance
That linger after she has gone.

Untold Charm
Charlotte, there's beauty in her
soul
And love shines from her
eyes—
Who still can blush and
graceful be
To those who know her well.

We Moderns
Betty, a damsel from San Antonio
Who can pet, and smoke and drink
And gain more jolly pounds
Than any one I've ever known
Yet who loves her Billy so
She doesn't know just what to do;

—A Rare Book—
Gicella is like a rare book
Bound in all that is worthwhile
By the leather of Intelligence
On whose pages one can find
Understanding, love and trust—
A ballerina, who some day

Will take her name to fame
Because its ballet, true she likes
And art to her is work and strife.

It was up in the morning
Rehearsal at ten
Down in the ball-room
of Gunter Hotel
First there was stretching
And limbering up
Until old Pop Mason
Yelled to begin.
It's this and that step
We'll do for today
In tempo, let's keep
We'll try it again.

"In line" goes the call
We drop into place
With faces at front
And eyes straight ahead
It may be a waltz
A buck and a wing
A Tiller routine
Or the latest thing—
Whatever the dance is
We pupils watch him
And soon be all doing
That very same thing.

Again and again
We'd have to begin
From where we just started
Beginning to end
Essence right and left
Then double essence right
Reverse the step
And give it pep.

Geegis

That you must seek the mountains and the snow
And grasp those worlds that gleam afar,
So that our child may glimpse a star
And learn of you, of heights, so she may go
Out to the rim of life's wide open sea
Singing, following you, the boundaries of a life.

Prayers are whispered that never leave the tongue
For love is more than words upon the lips—
Faith of a small child's rhyming prayer
And still, and still—you love us ever, still—
Her baby glee shall ever belong to me
Her childhood laughter of a girl
And smiles of luscious maidenhood
Beloved, father will ever belong to you,
And for us, the tears of her maturity.

[Untitled]

I'm free in the world of these carpeted hills;
I'm drunk with the scent of cedar and pine.
I revel in scenes of the snow-rocks and rills;
I feast where the gods of the great forest dine.[4]

[Untitled]

Some ten or few years so ago or more
When Old Town was a pretty spot
The lumber-men, drivers, wood-cutters too
Came down from Argyle in a bunch
On Saturday night wen pay day came
An' all got through—but jolly four
They always went an' always fought

Wen 'ere wus nothin' else to do
But on Thursday right after lunch
The jolly four and Harry Kane
Rushed into town straight to a bar
Down Old Joe Perro's—gay and free
After they drank a plenty
Off to the minstrels they go
Look in the dance at the City Hall
'Twas after midnight so by far
When they met the stranger Pete
A small nice looking foxy genty
From some 'ere West I guess—Ohio
Or some guys says out—St. Paul.

He joined the bunch an' drank a lot
An seemed a fine young rougher
'At all 'em boys jus took 'im in—
Well wen all the snow had fallen thick
An' everyone ditched fur this stranger guy—
Till it was o' a gal 'at got 'im in hot
An' turned his hide from green to tougher
Twas over Malie Danna—'ats the way it begin
Wen Stranger Joe from out the gals did pick
The prettiest Injun gal.

Baby Girl

Your two bright eyes they shine like diamonds,
I long to see your hair in curls.
I'd give the world to hold you, darling,
And to call you, baby girl.

I have the picture dear you gave me,
My Bible holds your little curl,
In dreams again it seems,
I hold you as I call you, baby girl.

You say you long to see your daddy,
I know you'll never prove untrue,
The years seem, oh, so long my darling,
Since I've been away from you.

You'll soon grow up to be a lady,
And go out in this great wide world,
Darling, when I meet you,
I'll still call you baby girl.

Tonight I see your face before me,
Your dimpled cheeks and teeth like pearls,
I reach to touch your little hand, dear,
But you're gone, my baby girl.

The Lost Soul of the Wilderness

I heard it long ago, as long ago
That long far cry of the panther
The querying hoot of the owl's "whoo"
The heavy beats of the cow moose's canter—
I thought I heard the whine of the fox
And the wailing howl of the lonely wolf—
Methought, there was the cry of Lox[5]
Far off—riding the back of the wolf
But all I really heard, was the sighing breeze
And the piercing cry of a diving loon,
And all I saw—were gaunt, and budding trees.
Beyond, the dying sun—above, a friendly moon.

The Dreamer—Moodas (The Dream Spirit)

Touched by his trembling hand, the wayside weed
Becomes a flower, the rusty spiked reed
Beside the mysterious stream
Is colored and clothed with beauty.

Spectrally, rising where we stood,
I see the old primeval wood;
Dark, shadow-like, on either hand
I see its eerie waste expand;
It climbs the green and rocky hill
It arches o'er the valley's rill,
And leans from cliff and crag, to throw
Its wild arms o'er the stream below;

Unchanged, alone, the same deep river
Flows on, as it will flow forever.

So timidly, so shy, I hear the low
Soft ripples where its waters go;
The wild-bird's scream goes thrilling by,
And cautiously on the river's brink
The deer are stooping down to drink—
I kissed the blue eye of a violet
And gone was the woodland phantom
Gone, where and how I did not know
And I walked on—with a dream alone.

Northern Lights

Liken to a timid fawn thou art,
        Oh! Wondrous maiden of the North!
With eyes that shelter moonlight,
Flashes fire and cradle mystery—
So fair of face—full of form,
Yet slender as an alder.
        There is music in your laughter,
Flute-like when it echoes,
In thy whisperings are heard
Lapping waters and the breeze—
In thine graces there traces
Native haunts and trails of lynx,

Soft-footed, swift, but surely—
Thou dwellest in the sky
Within a lodge of ice and cold,
        Oh! Phantom maiden of the North!
Thou art not real or mortal—
But here amid the forests
Dwells thine likeness there,
She, a vision full of life,
She, a tender sapling,
And with heart like unto thine.
Neeburban, dusky full-breasted sylph.[6]

Fred Ranco

(1932–2008)

Fred Ranco grew up on Indian Island during the Great Depression, enlisted in the U.S. Army near the end of World War II, and later joined the National Guard in Bangor. Like many Penobscots of his generation, he also worked for the Old Town Canoe Company. After marrying an Abenaki woman he moved to New Hampshire for forty years. He maintained a small Indian crafts shop in Albany and during this time met journalist Tara Marvel, who recorded his life story. The poem below appeared in the March 1979 issue of the *Wabanaki Alliance*, a Native American newspaper (1977–82) that covered regional politics and culture and was read across Indian Country.

The Avenger

To you, the great white hunters
Who shot off my buffalo.
And also for you the great bald eagle
Also had to go.

The eagle was our talisman.
The buffalo, our life.
You left us naught but empty land
You left us only strife.

My war bonnet's getting ragged
My teepee lets in snow.
I have no hides to patch it,
And no eagle feathers grow.

The great white buffalo, whose spirit
Once led our braves to game
You've driven far from our lands
Now, there's nothing the same.

There were buffalo that flourished
As far as your eye could see
Led by the white bull buffalo
For the other braves, and me.

Now, as you look upon the plain
All you see is dust on the land.
Like Egypt country overworked
And ended up as a pile of sand.

My ambition is so much greater
I vanquish all the deer
I'll poach them till they vanish
And no more will be here.

And then, you mighty hunters
You'll eat your lowly cow.
And roam no more on Indian lands
To you, I make this vow.

ssipsis

(b. 1941)

ssipsis (Penobscot for "little bird") was born on Indian Island in the Penobscot Nation and is well known for her writing and visual art. Some of her birch-bark etchings are on permanent display at the Penobscot Nation Museum on Indian Island; other works are at the Abbe Museum in Bar Harbor. ssipsis has also worked as a social worker and as an editor for the *Maine Indian Newsletter*. The pieces below first appeared in *Molly Molasses and Me*, a book she calls "a collection of living adventures" with her Passamaquoddy friend Georgia Mitchell, and in which she uses a great many Passamaquoddy terms.

Injun Laugh

I'm very glad to be here
And see lots of shiny faces
I come from long way up river
From the aboriginal people's places

I'm supposed to talk about ecology
Environment and tradition
And living the creator's way
Indigenous people's rights, legal fights
And bi-cultural education

I wish I could stay a long time
To talk about those things
But I worry that my place be gone
If long time I stay away

I would get restless and homesick
For my own nation
And I might shrivel up and die
For taste of moose and beaver

So maybe we be done with greeting
And get into the meat/heart of talk
So I can get back to native land

I'm very glad to learn about radiation
That they plant near my reservation
For that means some grow no hair
And their face is bare
And they light up in dark
So we can see who they are
And not shoot for bear

I learn about cyclamates, a chemical sweetener
The hard way

And that was about ten years ago
When a big Mack truck
Dump on reservation
All that soda pop that stores don't want
And so give Injun
They also give Injun diarrhea
And cancer and short life span
But we don't worry that white man
Don't care
Cause we just passing through
And we got better place to go

I laugh when history books say
That white man took Injun land away
Cause I still see land sitting there today
And white man tell us it's written
In their book who own land
Injun still laugh
Cause he no read book
And Injun know who owns land
And it written in Injun book

And white man teach us
In their school all those things

Including golden rule
And Injun laugh
Cause he no fool and he don't want
To be taught like a gol danged mule
And white man get mad
Cause Injun laugh
And they put us in jail
Cause we don't believe their book
But we don't worry
That white man don't care
Cause we just passing through
And we got better place to go
And white man try and try
To find Injun book
He cut down tree
He move mountain
He dig up grave
He look through garbage dump and shell heap
All time looking for Injun book
That prove Injun own land
And Injun just sit there and laugh
Cause white man still can't find Injun book

You know us Injuns walk freely on earth
You see some white folk never touch ground
All time feet is far away from earth
Those white folk never get kiss from earth mother
They got high platform shoes
Then they get in car with fifteen inches of rubber
And they get in car inside ten room house
And they drive in car on five inch of black tar
Out of concrete city
Into country
And back again
And still never touch earth
What they afraid of
They buzz around sky like pigeon

And whizz around ground like chipmunk
Where they going
As you know us Injuns walk freely
You know how much it cost for white man
To walk on Injun land
It cost them plenty
For moccasins that are fifteen deerhides thick
It cost them plenty
For houses that are ten wigwams wide
And it cost them plenty to move car that weighs
One ton boulder yes it cost them plenty

And they need their own river
Cause their skee wun smell[7]
And their mitch i gun stink[8]
And they got to mix it
One skee wun to fifteen miles of river
And they got no room to plant trees
And flowers to take that pollution smell away
Cause they fence in all that short grass
That even a rabbit would starve on
And you wonder why I ask about this white man
If they my brother and sister why they do not like
River, rabbit and blue sky
If they my brother and sister
Then I would say to them
Brother, I don't like some of those things you do
And if you don't stop doing those nasty things
I'm gonna get mad and throw water on you
And if that don't work
I'm gonna throw you into the fire
And if that don't work
I'm gonna tell my mother
And she's gonna ban you
From this side of the river forever

You know us Injuns we got lot of trust
There's the Livermore Savings and Trust

And the Androscoggin Banking and Trust
And the Merrill Trust
Our investment is in good name
So if Maine go broke
You know who to blame

Gewh Huz[9]

Recipe for muskrat stew entails more than the preparation of the menu, for it requires a lengthy lesson during a winter afternoon to juggle the native language of Molly Molasses, the Passamaquoddy, around the tongue into repetitive sounds, which sound funny at first, and very formal and then very familiar later on as we start cooking.[10]

I have been convinced that the language is music and the speakers sing their words. At the end of this chapter, I have set the recipe for muskrat stew on music paper.

Gewh huz, there is no English equivalent, for the word flows so in tune with the river as it swirls through the rushes that grow on the banks. Imagine the muskrat swimming, searching for the roots, and the river flowing over the glistening black head with its sparkling knowing eyes and the nose wriggling and smelling for the pungent medicine and food. It is said that the roots that the muskrat eats is the medicine which keeps colds and pneumonia at a distance. If one takes this medicine, one will be cured.

I think, if you eat the muskrat you are taking the ancient medicine, which is wholly the life of the muskrat. One cycle touches another. One keeps you in health and the other gathers your medicine. When the trappers bring you the cleaned and skinned muskrat, you are doubly blessed, for you have food and you have medicine.

Of course this is native and wild food. The meat is dark and rich with protein. Fat is there in separate white globules around the haunches, armpits, and stomach if the winter is mild. If the winter is harsh, then the muskrat will be lean and long and all the fat reserves gone. The muskrat will be spicy and smell like the roots it eats and the whole house will be filled with the heavy musk smell.

When cleaning the muskrat, the tail goes into the fire along with the fat and busy webbed feet that have swum the river, searching for food along the riverbank, digging and pulling roots. Some people like to eat the heads, the tiny succulent tidbits of brain, tongue, and fat cheeks.

When Gwug-gwug (Clarence Francis) and his wife Vi (Violet), came by to eat lunch one day, a respectful silence was felt around the table as the muskrat was eaten. We used our fingers to pry the small bones apart and suck the tiny morsels of meat from the rib cages, which look like a small fish trap. Beside our plates the pile of bones grew larger until at last our appetites were satisfied.

"Um, um, um. . . ." Final compliments to the muskrat. Cycles complete, coffee, cigarette, and lunch was done. The recipe that makes the lunch so delicious is such a simple one. The language lesson is more difficult and hardly silent. This is a lesson with much laughter and more stories and lessons within lessons. Molly Molasses is a perfect teacher, with patience and humor. The language must be perfect in pronunciation as well as perfect in understanding. When you learn the language you also learn history, medicine, social graces, conversation, and a sense of humor.

I must watch closely to her mouth and listen carefully with my ears and try very hard to bring those words to my own mouth. Slowly I must know where the sounds come from, the chest or the throat or the tongue or the teeth. With each experiment, I try again to place the sound correctly so it is right to Molly Molasses's ear. It is not enough to write the sound in phonetics or in English, because the sounds come from the whole body and not through tightly closed lips.

Ge nub ska ze tid psap nig.[11] If you were to read the phonetics, you would not know where the sound hits the right note, so placing the phonetic below the note will show how much higher or lower that sound will be, and how long it will be sounded. I hope.

Donna Loring
(b. 1948)

Donna Loring has had a long and distinguished career: Vietnam veteran, police chief, security director, activist, and politician. Following in the footsteps of John Neptune, Joseph Nicolar, and others, she served as tribal representative to the state legislature for approximately twelve years and has published a memoir about the experience. As tribal representative, she submitted the "Joint Resolution in Support of the United Nations Declaration on the Rights of Indigenous Peoples" (April 15, 2008); Maine was one of the first states to pass a resolution in support of this declaration. Loring authored and sponsored LD 291, described in the article below, which she previously published in the *New England Journal of Higher Education*. This law, which has provided for substantive indigenous input into the way Maine teaches—and thus views—its own history, has fostered many of the contemporary Wabanaki writings in this anthology.

The Dark Ages of Education and a New Hope: Teaching Native American History in Maine Schools

In 2001 I authored legislation that required all public schools in Maine to teach Maine Indian history. On June 14 of that year, Governor Angus King signed "An Act to Require Maine Native American History and Culture in Maine's Schools" into law—the first of its kind in the United States.

What makes the law unique is its requirement that specific topics be studied, such as: (1) tribal governments and political systems and their relationship with local, state, national, and international governments; (2) Maine Native American cultural systems and the experience of Maine tribal people throughout history; (3) Maine Native American territories; and (4) Maine Native American economic systems.

The most important piece of this legislation was the creation of a Native American History Commission to help schools gather a wide range of materials and resources to implement the law. This led to creation of the Wabanaki Educational Curriculum, which tells the story of the Wabanaki people of Maine from the Wabanaki perspective. It is leading us out of the "dark ages" of education. "Dark ages" because education has been a two-edged sword for Native people. On one hand, it opened opportunities. On the other, it harmed us physically, psychologically, and spiritually. It inflicted spiritual wounds upon Native people lasting for generations. We call these wounds "Soul Wounds."

Richard Henry Pratt, who founded the Carlisle Indian Industrial School in Pennsylvania in 1879, had a saying, "Kill the Indian and save the man." The intention was to kill the cultural core within Indian children through boarding-school education and forced assimilation that included prohibitions on speaking their Native language or practicing Native traditional religion. Justification for this came from the notion that Indians were less than human. This view is abundantly evident in the way Indians were depicted by the press at the time. Among many nineteenth-century cartoons of Indians, one in particular comes to mind. It can be found today on the cover of John M. Coward's book *The Newspaper Indian*, published by the University of Illinois Press in 1999. In this drawing we see a Union soldier who has just shot the Lakota chief Sitting Bull (1831–90). Depicted as half man, half beast, Sitting Bull has clawed hands and a lower body made up of the back end and legs of a buck deer. The caption of the original cartoon reads, "The Right Way to Dispose of Sitting Bull and His Braves."

Indians were simply seen as subhuman savages to be disposed of. Thus began Indian education from the white man's perspective: educate the Indian in white man's culture and values, and he will become for all intents and purposes a productive member of white society. Indian children were forcibly taken from their mothers and fathers on the reservations and were mentally, physically, psychologically, spiritually, and even sexually abused. Native people call this cultural genocide.

The first off-reservation boarding school in the United States, Carlisle became a model for schools in other locations, which echoed its efforts to forcibly assimilate Native American children. Canada also utilized residential schools, many operated by the Catholic Church. I have seen films and read books on the abuse these schools perpetrated on the Indian children in their effort to "kill the Indian." I recently read *Out of the Depths* by Isabelle Knockwood, which chronicles the trauma she and other Mi'kmaw children experienced at the Indian Residential School at

Shubenacadie, Nova Scotia. It is one of the most powerful accounts I have ever read. Knockwood, who attended the school from 1936 to 1947, writes,

> I remember a nun shaking a girl by the shoulders and yelling, "Look at me, look at me" . . . [even though] direct eye contact between child and adult was considered arrogant in the Native culture. We were being forcibly disconnected from everything our parents and elders had taught us. We sang songs in honor of Christopher Columbus who discovered America. Apparently our ancestors had been "discovered" by this white man who was lost on his way to find spices. No one told us that the Hurons shown scalping the missionaries in the textbooks wanted their children to learn and to keep their own Native spirituality and their own land.

In some ways the experience I had in the public and private educational system in the United States was like Knockwood's. I was never abused in the same way as the Indian children who were forced to go to residential schools, but the purpose was the same: to assimilate me into the white man's world. And I have learned well how to walk in that world.

I attended elementary school, junior high school, and one year of high school in Old Town, Maine, a non-Native community just across the river from where I lived on the Penobscot reservation at Indian Island. It was during those years that I learned what it was like to be discriminated against both overtly and subtly. Various students called me a "filthy squaw," and teachers who for the most part ignored me made a point of calling on me to answer questions pertaining to what they thought all Indians should know—such as which paw prints belonged to which animals. When I had enough of being treated like a second-class citizen, I asked my very religious, non-Native grandmother to get me into a religious school. I thought if I went to one of those schools I would be treated better and there would be no discrimination or racism. I was wrong on that count as well.

Like Isabelle Knockwood, I was taught a history centered on white men, such as George Washington and Christopher Columbus. I never had a class on Native American history. I had no sense of my own history or the contributions made to this country by my ancestors. My people and my race were made invisible by the educational system by the simple act of omission. I find it ironic that the First Nations of this continent not only were made invisible by the educational system but were disadvantaged and discriminated against because of it. I guess you could call the early years of "kill the Indian and save the man" the dark ages of education. Those dark ages have spilled into this century.

The failure to include Native American history in our educational system leads to low self-esteem among Native American students and a lack of respect among their peers. It also contributes to a low retention rate in high schools and colleges. Native Americans graduate high school at lower rates than all other ethnic groups and account for less than 1 percent of college students enrolled in New England, according to national data recently published by the *New England Journal of Higher Education*.[12] But Native American statistics are rarely included. Native people are left out of the history pages and are left out of research and statistics. I read the newspapers and listen to media reports that give statistics about various subjects, such as population growth or health issues. We are simply nonexistent.

Education is supposed to be a shining light of knowledge and a gateway to a better life. Why has this gateway opened only one way for Indian people, forcing us to learn only about white society? By omitting Native history, we continue to cheat countless students—Native and non-Native alike. Indian history is so interwoven into the very fabric of this country, from George Washington and the Revolutionary War through Andrew Jackson, with his Indian termination philosophy and his Indian Removal Act, and Chief Justice John Marshall, whose legal opinions based on the papal bulls "Right of Discovery" and "Manifest Destiny" have kept Native people in poverty because we cannot own our own land. Even though we could not own our own land, we have fought in every war to defend this country. Native people have the highest rate of military service compared to any race in the nation.

Every student in this country needs to know the full story of the First Nations. The Maine Native American History and Culture Act holds great promise for our state. While work to carry it to fruition is ongoing, it has already proven to be one of the most important bills in history for Maine's Native people. Eight years after the bill passed, there has been a renaissance in Native voices through Native-authored books, poetry, art, plays, museum exhibits, and documentary films. The fact that Native history is required to be taught in public schools in Maine has begun to give Native people a strong, clear voice, a voice that they never had. The state of Maine is slowly learning from these voices.

An honest, truthful, and inclusive educational system needs to emerge from the dark ages and into the light of full knowledge. Native history must be a required subject, not only in public elementary schools but also in colleges across this country. It needs to be part of the core requirement, not just a token program of Native studies or help for Native nations. It is time our story is told and the educational system unlocks that one-way gate and allows us to take our rightful place in the history of this continent. It is the right thing to do, and I guarantee the results will be amazingly powerful and healing.

(2009)

Carol Dana
(b. 1952)

Born and raised on Indian Island, Carol Dana has six children and nine grand-children. In 2008 she earned her MA in education at the University of Maine. She has devoted years to Penobscot language revitalization, working with linguist Frank Siebert on the Penobscot dictionary project during the 1980s and teaching Penobscot at the Indian Island School during the 1990s. At present she is the cultural historical preservation officer for the Penobscot Nation, where she has helped to produce several workbooks, videos, and other cultural materials. The following poems first appeared in her chapbook *When No One Is Looking*.

Penobscot Home Nation

Penobscot home nation is in the minds and hearts of the people

When he talks them old time tales of hunting, mysteries,
wendigo, and little people,
I know I am home.

When she's making medicine for someone in need,
When every act is done in that spirit,
You forget there was ever such a thing as greed.

When sun warms your body through the heart of the land
And smiles play on our children's faces
You can see the work of Gluscabe's hand . . .

We're Like the Moss on the Rock

We're like the moss on the rock.
A little clump, hanging on for life
at Panampsk.[13]
Will we forever be erased?
No, it is here our footsteps
we must trace

Back to the source.

Why must we die to live, live to die.
Would you want to kill us if we
reclaimed our land,
brought our many husbands, wives
and knives?

Caribou Lake Winter[14]

Megalibu run, snowflake fly,[15]
Forever changing, cold, dry.
In sun we walked a long way
We wanted to drop in our tracks
When every move must count
Life depends on it
Impeccable warrior
Don't speak
Shaman's power

Runs deep
Kthadin, Pamola, Atahando[16]
Attean, Susep, Nicola[17]
Were people on the move
Who laughed, loved, cried and died
Over eons of time
We're forever grateful to be
from Molasses Molly, Swasson, Susep
Francis, Neptune, and Dani.[18]
Here our tree roots grow
Strong and deep.

[Untitled]

Mother of three didn't know
wouldn't show the beginning of discontent.
In her housework sometimes she wondered where he went.
Mother of four knew the pain, when
it was with his old lady he had lain;
Her maternal wounds had hardly healed
when he asked for his pleasure she should yield.
Quickly he left her bed. To hers he went.
He expected and waited for consent.
Mother of five wasn't sure she could keep
hope and love alive.
"I don't care," said her posture, looks and clothes.
The next baby had a sickness which spoke to her
of the preciousness of life.
The sorrow made room for the depth of joy that comes
once you know strife.

Mother of six so haggard yet wise
Mother of six could never surmise
the trial and outcome of one year wanting
to be as free as her partner and as undisturbed.
She walked the coals of questions about the

splitting of a family, a baby or not, an other woman.
The absence of a heart, being, and spirit that once lent
so much strength.
(Which led to the linking of a spirit much greater.)
The crossing of a bridge in so many ways.
Mother of six didn't like going through fire
Mother of six has seen the folly of desire.

[Untitled]

Pensive in her rocking chair
stiff and straight faced.
The hard line of her mouth
I would wait to see crack
To know what was inside.
Sometimes I felt I should hide
from her sternness and harsh ways,
Although there were many days
she would talk and smile with her friends,
passing the while
speaking in Passamaquoddy,[19]
their eyes smiling with fun
when directed at me.
I wondered, now what have I done
to amuse them so?
I would be perturbed to no end
for some understanding.
Little did I know the ladies joked
about having fun, teasing, and sex.
They talked about human qualities,
What the neighbors said or done.
We were the age-old stream
of Indian people
Yet I couldn't participate
because of my lack of native language.

Children

Remember when we were kids
playing in our hiding places?
Still Indian Island afforded to us
wide open spaces.
The sun would shine to warm our bodies,
Life was free, beautiful, fun.
Let us not forget! little one.
Sheltered by our family tree
We laughed, played, most free.
Then we look at tomorrow and
the memory is but a patch of sunlight in a storm.

Life appears to be gloomy and dull.
It's a comfort to bring back the child.
To laugh, stop awhile and see
There is wonder.

A Walk to Ktadhin[20]

I walked an old path along the river
With moon in view and hawks rising
The warm breeze soothed my soul
And pine trees scented our steps in the sun
Sisters we were in strength and spirit
A silent understanding grew up,
Somewhere surrounding our common struggle.

I likened the physical act of our walk
To the spiritual act of everyday steps.
The river sparkled at our laughter.
Crows, hawks and songbirds greeted us.
Pains grew and subsided.
Prayers urged us forward.
Comrades lent help through water, food
and foot massages, coaxing encouragement.

We walked through rural towns
As hot hardtop roads tried to stifle us every day.
Uphill wore out our feet and hearts
Downhill toppled us forward
Bendin' our limbs in a peculiar way.

Endless roads with little people dotting the horizon
Tired, sweating, near hysteria we were.
Everything was funny until the pain came wild-eyed.
Heavy body, so hard to take care of,
Wish I could outwalk you.
Demanding to be fed, relieved, watered, rested
Fighting every step of the way to
Walk away the pain we feel.

Rhonda Frey

(1955–2009)

For many years the only Native American journalist in Maine, Rhonda Frey worked in television, radio, and print. She produced a radio show called *Indigenous Voices* for WERU, a community-supported, noncommercial station in Blue Hill, Maine. She also worked for the Penobscot Nation as a human resources counselor. As an activist, Frey fought to get the word *squaw* banned from public landmarks in Maine with the Offensive Place Names Act. The selection below is from one of two curricula she produced with the Abbe Museum in support of LD 291, An Act to Require Teaching of Maine Native American History and Culture in Maine's Schools, passed in 1991.

Growing Up with Stereotypes: A Native Woman's Perspective

Growing up, I don't recall hearing we were of a different culture. As a child I would dance in the summers at Chief Poolaw's teepee for the tourists, but even then I thought, "Everyone does this sort of thing in their communities"; this was just a way for me to earn money. Bruce Poolaw claimed to be a chief but wasn't. He would provide us with regalia so we could dance. We would take around a basket for donations. He would try to take half and give us the other half, but whenever his wife, "Princess Watahwaso" (also known as Aunt Lu), would find out, she'd give us the other half and tell him, "You make your money on the store, let the children have theirs." We loved Aunt Lu.

I really didn't know color, other than I saw a black person once and told my grandmother. She said, "Tourists"; that was her only explanation of colored people. I also danced traditional dances in the Indian Pageant—again thinking this sort of thing happened in every community. We were trying to raise money for our church. Thousands of people would attend and watch the pageant.

Then there was John Wayne. We used to watch some of the old movies on television. I knew that cowboys and Indians were different, but I didn't see color. I recall at times I would have a weird feeling at the end of the show, as if something just wasn't right, but I could never put my finger on it. Funny, though, when we played cowboys and Indians as children, nobody wanted to be the Indian, because they always lost; everyone wanted to be cowboys. I watched *The Lone Ranger* a few times, too, and felt that same weird feeling.

My rather rude introduction to the non-Native world occurred in the sixth grade, and I began to see the differences. Luckily for me, I used to walk over to the Herbert Gray School in Old Town for about three summers prior to starting sixth grade, to swim at their pool and spend the day with the local children. They knew me as Rhonda. When I entered St. Mary's School in Old Town there were several of my friends in the same grade and they were good to me. I began to see they didn't treat the other children from Indian Island as nice as they treated me.

After the first two months of school I really encountered my first slap in the face. One of the boys in my grade said that I stole something from him. I looked at him so surprised and said, "No I didn't, why do you say that?" I had always been an honest person and certainly didn't steal. He kept insisting that I did; I told the nuns I didn't. The nuns seemed to believe me, but it bothered me that he said that. I went to him later and asked him why he did that and he said, "Because you were trying to be somebody, I had to show you you're not, I had to put you in your place." I just couldn't understand. I went home and told my mother. She said, "The people over there don't like us." I then began to hear and see the differences; I found out that I was no good, that I was dirty—even though I showered every day or took baths, I was still dirty. I was trash. We were "the Others." I began to watch the "cowboy and Indian shows" with a more critical eye and realized the shows were trying to put us down. I began to resent John Wayne and any other show that depicted Indians. I learned all about the dirty word "prejudice" at a very young age.

Of course, what didn't help was that the Maine Indian Land Claims was at its peak and the banners in the *Bangor Daily News* screamed, "Hey Old Town start packing, the Indians are taking your land." Every time a banner of this sort appeared, or a story came out that was filled with half-truths and exaggerations, we as students in the Old Town school system would pay for it.

In junior high some of the teachers were mean to us. There seemed to be a double standard; one that was used to grade non-Native work and one that was used to grade Native work. Even the way we were approached, the teachers weren't as nice to us as they were with non-Native students. We were the unwanted children in Old Town. I was one of the best students at Indian Island, and within two years I went down to the lowest division in the eighth grade because it was so difficult to deal with hormones and the horror shows I saw whenever prejudice reared its ugly head. I escaped a lot of the problems by studying. By high school I was back on the honor roll, except if I had one of the teachers who didn't like Natives. I got into the habit of asking older children from the island what the teachers were like and tried to avoid "the bad ones." Bad ones were always trying to put us on the spot, would critically correct our work. We would nearly flunk a test because of a small error and they always managed to try to make us the example in their classrooms. I definitely tried to avoid those teachers.

I couldn't get away from stereotypes, even at summer camp. I attended a camp when I was about thirteen. My mother insisted I go because my younger sister was going and she wanted to make sure she was safe and not alone. I barely saw my sister during the entire two weeks. It was nice because there weren't any remarks made about color so I actually relaxed and had fun. When I attended the archery class, however, the instructor told everyone, "Rhonda doesn't need to be told how to shoot a bow and arrow, she already knows because she's Indian." All the other campers who attended the class were in awe of me because I could shoot a bow and arrow. I had never picked one up. What could I say? Luckily I hit the target; not a bull's-eye, but it was near. I didn't attend another archery class.

When I was in the ninth grade, a friend of mine from Indian Island talked me into going to an all-girls academy, the Academy of St. Joseph's in South Berwick. I really wasn't keen on it, but I knew I was with someone from home so I thought I'd try. I thought it would be nice to get away. We met about forty-five young women who were our age from all over the world. It was so nice to be accepted for who we were as individuals, without any racism. The girls used to ask each other about what it was like where they lived. My friend Adrian and I were asked about being an Indian and what was it like living on an Indian reservation. They asked us first about the teepees. Adrian and I were a little surprised by the fact that they didn't know much about Natives and Native life. When we heard this, we looked at each other as if we knew what we were going to say. We started telling them about reservation life. We told them we lived in teepees and that we only wore non-Native clothes whenever we left the reservation. We had an elaborate story about our teepees being two-story, with small teepees all around a big one. The smaller ones were the bedrooms, while the big one served the family as a dining and gathering area. We told them all the men in the village hunted together and would shoot buffalo and the women gathered berries and worked in the gardens.

We had them going for days and then felt we had to tell the truth. So we did. All the girls took it in stride; they were disappointed, but I think they were also relieved to hear we lived in houses, just like them! I went back home after two months; it was so hard to live there.

By the time I reached tenth grade, the problem teachers were nearly nonexistent. I don't know why; it wasn't as if the Land Claims had gone away. Perhaps I was able to deal with it better. I would know what they were going to say before they said it and avoided the ones who would try to put me on the spot. I became very quiet and shy. I would choose what class I would participate in depending on the way the teacher approached me. I also started choosing what I would listen to and what I wouldn't. My survival tactics must have helped because I graduated high school, but I was so emotionally exhausted. A lot of the children I grew up with on Indian Island dropped out of school because they couldn't cope. I still wonder how I got through—although thoughts of certain teachers and my favorite guidance counselor, special friends, and the books I loved to read come to mind whenever I wonder, and I smile because they were there to help.

My best friend, Paula, whom I met in the bathroom at Old Town High in my senior year, was a light in the dark tunnel, along with several other girlfriends who were not prejudiced, and some of the guys would talk to me and were my friends. Imagine, being happy because they were there for me? Not happy because of events in school, or the prom, or being involved in some of the clubs, all of which are a part of student life, a life I felt I could not participate in.

I just concentrated on my studies and, in doing so, my grades improved. As I did better, I was accepted a little more; however, even then, if I did as well or better than a non-Indian I was okay, the non-Indian student was still much better, but I was okay. During the times of the Land Claims, I was just glad to be accepted. I also heard that I was an "exceptional

Indian." I guess because I excelled. I never did understand what that meant. Someone else said I was an Indian of a different breed—I guess I was salvageable—I never asked what it meant, perhaps I didn't want to hear the answer. I would go away from these situations feeling weird, thinking, "Yeah, I'm different all right—I just put up with you."

Where I could, outside of school, I would hide the fact I was Native. Luckily we are like chameleons; many of us have light-enough skin to hide in plain view. I was afraid of the reaction. I found that, if someone got to know me first for who I was and then I told them I was Native, they would see me as Rhonda, who happens to be Native. If I didn't wait, chances were good they would see me as an "Indian" whose name happens to be Rhonda.

It wasn't just the Maine Indian Land Claims that contributed to the prejudice. I decided that since I knew children in the Old Town school system before I went to school there and it really helped cushion the blow of prejudice when I attended the schools, I would enter my son on a local hockey team before he left the island school. To me, it would serve two purposes: one, he would get to know local area students, and two, he was such a loving child, I was afraid he wasn't tough enough; I thought hockey would bring out a little more male aggressiveness. Little did I know, I was exposing my son to his first experience with racism.

There were mostly non-Natives on the team. My son said one kid in particular would give war whoops. The coaches didn't correct the kid, nor did they talk about respecting others. My son suffered for two years. He did manage to get back at the kid. My son said they had a scrimmage and he went after the other boy because they were on opposing teams that day. He slammed the boy into the walls and then tripped him. How do you correct the behavior of a child after he's taken so much abuse from another? He knows it wasn't nice and he wasn't a mean child; there aren't too many instances where he would outwardly display such feelings, but being ten years old and abused by this kid with adults watching was more than he could take—I am actually proud of him. He stuck with hockey for two years despite this kid, and for this I am so proud.

My son experienced a stereotype just recently. He is a case manager for a private nonprofit agency in Augusta and works with children at risk from age zero to five. He attended a workshop recently and was told Indian children, both infants and toddlers, head the top of the list of "at-risk" children. My son has two children who are toddlers and he's the best father any child could ever have; he was quite appalled because such statements indicate that all parents of Indian children are not capable of caring for their children. I'm upset as well; a true slap in the face.

I have found that Indian people are expected to know everything about being Indian. I went on an eight-day fellowship with other journalists. It was an environmental immersion program discussing issues from Maine to Canada. One presenter was from Bangor, Maine. He was talking about all these Native place-names. When he found out I was a member of the Penobscot Tribe, he expected me to know what all those place-names were. When I told him I didn't, he said, "What kind of Indian are you? You're supposed to know what all these names mean!" Wow—talk about being put on the spot and stereotyped. How am I supposed to know all the place-names if I haven't studied them? I didn't respond to him; that was my way of handling it, but perhaps I should have put him in his place. I guess I'm supposed to know everything there is to know about our language and other Wabanaki languages. I've had conversations with others who expected me to know every tribe in existence in the United States—there are over five hundred!

My mother was Passamaquoddy and spoke only Passamaquoddy until age five. My father, who was Penobscot, heard Penobscot spoken as a child but could not speak the language other than a lot of words or phrases. How am I supposed to know Penobscot?

I know some Passamaquoddy but my mother refused to teach us because she had such a rough transition into English. She was five years old and spoke only Passamaquoddy, but when she entered school, she was not allowed to speak her language. Whenever she did, she would be punished. She was forced to learn English, a second language—right on the spot. She was barely out of the toddler stage, still just a baby, but it was as if her Native language was wrong, and bad. The sad part is that most Passamaquoddy children went through this and, as adults, don't want their children to be put through the same cruel immersion program. So many of us have had to learn our language on our own. When I was older, my mother did begin to teach me some of the words, and I always managed to figure out what she was saying when she spoke in her language with her sisters.

An elder told me that what you do today can affect generations to come.

The pain has come down with the generations. In life, I walk two roads, the red and the white. The red, with all the rich culture and the old ways, and the white, with the ever-changing technology and mainstream ways. I lived my first eighteen years on Indian Island. When I moved into the white lands, it was different and it was a transition. One of the first things I noticed was that people in the more mainstream cultures don't have large families. Growing up, I knew who my fifth cousins were and they were family. In the mainstream, a lot of people I spoke to didn't know who their first cousins once removed were, let alone being able to call them family.

Growing up on Indian Island did have its funny moments. By the time I was a teenager, the shows for tourists stopped and the tribe no longer wanted to continue the pageants. Everyone, including myself, felt it was time to dance and celebrate our own culture for ourselves, not for tourists. When tourists came to Indian Island, sometimes they would roll down their windows and ask, "Where are the Indians?" Once I remember my friends and I telling them we were Native, we were right there. The guy responded, "Oh," and then drove away. There was such disappointment in his voice and in his face. I thought, next time I'll handle it differently.

The next time, just the next week, I told some other people who were looking for the Indians, they missed them; they went up river to hunt. They were disappointed and said, "Oh, we missed them." They asked when they would be back; I told them I didn't know. It could be weeks before they return. I couldn't believe they bought it. I heard the same "Oh," but it wasn't the same disappointment. I did this only once, feeling guilty about the lie.

John Bear Mitchell

(b. 1968)

An educator and storyteller, John Bear Mitchell works for the University of Maine's Wabanaki Center and has made numerous appearances on radio and television, particularly with Maine PBS. Mitchell wrote eight Ulnerbeh (Gluscabe) stories, including the one below, for the environmental education organization Penobscot Riverkeepers 2000. The *Bangor Daily News* ran the stories. The Penobscot River, home to the Penobscot Nation, has been subject to drastic pollution, particularly from the pulp and paper mills that surround the area. Penobscot people have been at the forefront of efforts to clean the river and educate the public about it.

What's It Like Today?

Chapter 7 from the Ulnerbeh series

Ulnerbeh was nearing the end of his journey, and many years had passed since he had begun his travels.[21] He missed everything old, everything he considered the way it used to be—should be. With each dip of his paddle, Ulnerbeh reflected upon his life. What has happened to this land? Why have so many people built large wigwams on the shores of the river? Why do people travel on land and not the waterways?

Ulnerbeh couldn't answer the questions that he was asking himself. "There is only one thing to do," Ulnerbeh thought. "I will travel back to Indian Island and visit the village my people called Burnurwurbskek.[22] I will walk the island's dirt paths; I will examine the village and talk to the young people. I need to try to understand this change."

Ulnerbeh portaged from the Kennebec River and made his way toward the Penobscot River to head north. He noticed many changes in the land, and smooth black paths disrupted the way he used to navigate. Noisy animals zipped by as Ulnerbeh tried to make it to safety. One fast-moving animal, the color of a strawberry, went by so fast that the wind it left behind almost blew the canoe off his shoulders; that is the one Ulnerbeh wanted to put one of his arrows into, but it was too fast. Oh well, maybe next time!

Ulnerbeh placed his canoe down on the bank of the Penobscot River. He sat down and thought about noises he was hearing while he prepared himself a lunch. "Why all these changes?" he thought.

While Ulnerbeh was preparing his canoe, a small black-and-white dog came sniffing—looking for something to eat. Ulnerbeh watched the dog slowly walk up to him—but not too close. The dog hunched over with his two front legs stretched out in front of him and placed his chin on the ground, leaving his back end and tail standing high above his head.

Ulnerbeh flung a piece of meat at the dog. The dog jumped high and made a complete turn before hitting the ground, then lunged for the meat. Instead of grabbing the meat and running somewhere to eat it, the dog tossed and tossed the meat as if he were playing a game. Every once in a while the dog would run close to Ulnerbeh, look up at him, and run toward the meat once more. "Chabootdez," Ulnerbeh yelled. "You sure act like a clown. I'll call you Chabootdez." Ulnerbeh found a new friend, a friend to travel with.

Ulnerbeh and Chabootdez paddled up river until they came to a large wall that spanned the river. "What could this be?" Ulnerbeh asked. "It slows the river down." Ulnerbeh took his canoe out of the water and portaged around the large stone wall, which held the river behind it. As Ulnerbeh continued his journey, he encountered another and yet another wall that spanned the river. But finally, after the fourth portage, Ulnerbeh saw it. There before him was the village of Burnurwurbskek. Only now it looked somewhat different. Ulnerbeh recognized the shape of the village, but it also had had many changes since he last visited it.

Spanning the river was a long bridge. Ulnerbeh realized that his people no longer needed canoes to get to the village. Where fields of grass once grew, there now stood large houses. Where small wigwams were once scattered, now were the grave markers for the tribe's deceased.

Ulnerbeh walked the smooth road on the lower part of the village, slowly making his way up to the hill, the hill where his grandparents once lived. The field where the children had played games was now flooded with water, and Ulnerbeh saw children in bright plastic canoes floating around as they learned how to navigate their canoes around obstacles.

Ulnerbeh saw some boys playing a game on a smooth black surface. These boys with no shirts on used a large ball, which they bounced off the ground and passed to each other; it looked like they were trying to put the ball through a hoop that was attached to a pole. Sweat was dripping off their faces and Ulnerbeh noticed that the boys had very short hair.

"Hey, kid," one boy yelled. "Want to play with us? We need one more person to have a team!"

Ulnerbeh didn't know how to play this game; he'd never seen it before. "No thanks," Ulnerbeh said. "I'll just watch if you don't mind."

So he sat with Chabootdez and watched the boys play the game, but it did look like fun! One boy would jump up and slap the hand of one of his teammates every time he got the ball to go through a hoop. Ulnerbeh decided to call him "Cikawiyal" because every time he made the ball go in the hoop he would tease the other players.

Finally, the game came to an end. Ulnerbeh decided to walk with Cikawiyal. "What do you call this village?" Ulnerbeh asked.

"It's called Indian Island," the boy said. "Hey, who are you? Where are you from?" Cikawiyal asked.

"I'm from an old place, a place where the ways are very different from the way they are now," Ulnerbeh said. "What do people do around here that tells stories about their ancestors?" Ulnerbeh asked Cikawiyal.

"Well, there are a lot of people who make baskets out of birch bark or brown ash trees. Others sit down and circle a drum and sing old songs from the past, as well as some songs we borrowed from other tribes."

"Really, songs are still sung here?" Ulnerbeh asked.

"Well, at least some of our old songs and dances."

"How are kids taught the ways of the old times? Do you still have storytellers here to teach the kids about the important history of this place and its people?" Ulnerbeh asked.

"We do have people here who tell or write stories, but we learn a lot of what we need to know at school. The school has two teachers who teach us. One teaches us our old language, and the other teaches us our history and teaches us about the way things were hundreds of years ago."

"What is school?" Ulnerbeh wondered silently to himself. "It must be an important place if this is where the kids learn all of this."

Ulnerbeh continued his walk with Cikawiyal and thought about the changes in this village since he last visited it. Ulnerbeh thanked Cikawiyal for his company and made his way back down to the river's edge. Ulnerbeh sat there looking at the darkened river and tried to throw rocks at the small mounds of foam that floated by his feet. Chabootdez lay down under a tree and watched the small splashes the rocks made as they missed their targets. Just then Ulnerbeh noticed a man dipping a container in the river and filling it with the water.

"What do you do with that?" Ulnerbeh asked.

"I'm keeping track of the river and what people are putting into it. Hopefully one day we will be able to eat the fish out of this river again," the man said.

"You mean the fish aren't good to eat?" Ulnerbeh asked.

"No, not yet anyway, but hopefully someday!"

Ulnerbeh couldn't believe this ever could have happened. Poison fish? Poison water? Things sure have changed! Ulnerbeh went back to his canoe and placed it in the water. Chabootdez jumped in and sat straight up, as if he were going to lead Ulnerbeh back to something familiar.

"Imagine that, Chabootdez," Ulnerbeh said. "Stories are still told, baskets are still made, and children still play games, but my people can't eat fish or drink safely from the river! Their way of life is very different from the way it used to be. The house, their language, and their games have changed. Look around, Chabootdez. The village is so different now. I can see that they are working hard to maintain their culture, but as they go about their daily routines, they are very different from the people I once knew. I wish them the best and hope they choose to hold on to the culture the old people were recognized by."

Ulnerbeh navigated his canoe around some twisted metal pipes and headed toward the future—an unknown place.

Sherri Mitchell

(b. 1969)

Sherri Mitchell was born and raised on the Penobscot Nation, Indian Island, Maine. She has worked as a program coordinator for the American Indian Institute's Healing the Future Program, is a participant in the Traditional Circle of Indian Elders and Youth, and is an alumna of both the American Indian Ambassador Program and the Udall Native American Congressional Internship Program. Sherri is executive director of the Land Peace Foundation and an attorney for the Native American unit of Pine Tree Legal Assistance in Maine. She is the recipient of the 2009–10 International Human Rights and Humanitarian Award for her research on nation-state complicity with human rights violations against indigenous peoples.

Nokomis Speaks: Message to the Seventh Generation

My grandson, for so long I have awaited this day. For this opportunity to sit with you, eye to eye, heart to heart, and breath to breath. I have longed to see your face, to touch your cheek, and to smell the sweetness of your breath. I have longed to hold you in my lap, to know how your head would feel nestled against my breast as I sang to you.

Grandson, take my hand, walk with me, and listen to my story. Let me tell you who I was, so that you can remember who you are.

We are of this land, Penahwapskek, the place where the white rocks come out of the water. We are of these people, the Wabanaki, the people of the dawn. You were born Awesus nuga; Kakagoose, bear and crow, medicine clans. The land that you place your feet upon contains my footprints; the air that you breathe contains my breath. In your blood, your DNA, you carry the wisdom of seven mothers' daughters and seven fathers' sons. You ARE the seventh generation. The circle ends and is renewed within each cell of your body. KNOW THIS. For just as I was responsible for carrying the seeds of your being within me, so too are you responsible for carrying the seeds of the seventh generation yet to come.

The blood that runs through you has nourished the soil beneath your feet. Millions have died to ensure that you would live. The road that you walk upon has been paved with the blood of your ancestors; do not dishonor them. Walk this red road with your head held high. Place your feet with certainty, knowing that the answers you seek lie within you. You are never alone. You carry a piece of us all in the matrix of your spirit.

The time that I live in is one of crises. As the caretakers of this Earth our people have been charged with a heavy burden. Many have lost their way, blinded by generational wounds that have been ingrained into the public psyche, deafened by the sounds of justifiable homicide and historical references to a people "destined to be conquered."

Warriors of today do not wear leathers, feathers, or war bonnets. Warriors of today wear business suits. They battle in the courtroom, boardroom, and before Congress. They are in our schools, our clinics, and our banks. They secure our future by preserving the past. They teach the truth of our history and inspire us to remember who we are in accordance with ancient kinship roles. They protect traditional lands, repatriate the bones of our ancestors, and secure funding for the health and well-being of our children.

Warriors of today carry the seeds for sustainable agriculture, they harvest medicinal plants and teach our young people how to survive with honor and respect for the Earth. They do not kill their grandchildren to feed their children. The warrior of today may look different from those listed in the history books, but their mission remains intact: to serve and protect their people and to ensure the survival of generations yet to come. It is this mission, this responsibility, that you must never forget.

My grandson, for so long I have wanted to stand beside you; to walk upon the banks of this river that has sustained our people for generations; to fish the waters that my grandfather taught me to fish; to navigate these islands that have provided us with shelter; and to tell you the stories of our legends and our myths. I have wished to sing you the songs of our people as you drifted off to sleep. To share the beauty of our language, to describe to you the magic of this world in a tongue that is ancient and true.

I have longed to share with you the threads of indigenous knowledge, sacred knowledge, passed down from generation to generation. To impart to you truths that stand the test of time, of honor, integrity, and a lifeway filled with respect. It is this sacred knowledge that teaches us of our connectivity to all things. It trains our ears to hear the voices of our children beckoning to be born, to hear the song upon the wind that calms our fears and the whisper in the trees that guides us along our path. It is the reassurance of the land as we place our feet along our journey. And the lull of the waters as they carry us off into the dream-time. Sacred knowledge teaches us of our place in creation, as children of our people, children of the Earth, and cocreators of this universe. It teaches us of Grandmother Moon and Grandfather Sun, of light and darkness, of hard work and rest. Sacred knowledge holds us in balance through the ever-changing tides of our existence, keeping us connected to each other and to all of creation.

My grandson, if you forget all else that I have shared with you today, I ask that you remember this: The gift that you have been granted, through the seeds of sacred knowledge, contains all of the wisdom of our collective past and the guidance needed to lead us to our place in the future. This gift will teach you all you need to know of who I was and will lead you to where you need to be for the seventh generation yet to come. My grandson, the time has come for me to leave you. Remember my words and know that each time you place your foot upon this land, or in these waters, that I will be with you, standing beside my grandfather and all those who have come before you.

Sky Woman

Turning my gaze I see her,
suspended in the night sky
swollen and red, eminent
cycling on toward a new beginning.

Blanketed by a sea of stars,
she is cradled in perfect balance.
Delicate Anima sits stable and glowing,

while her mate shoots wish-filled sparks
to fade into the night.

Cradled in a blanket of snow,
I watch them, understanding then
the harmony of their union.
Internal rhythm is churned, as
calmness replaces chilled trembling.

Exhaling my longing,
to fade into the night,
I feel myself spiraling,
cycling on toward a new beginning.

The Lodge

So here I stand alone,
cold wind on dampened skin,
having just stepped out of the womb.
Waiting, silent, anticipating my return.
Round two, once again embraced
by the giver of life, a child
I am free.

Back to this sacred place,
where confusion falls away.
Worries seep into the Earth.
The scent of cedar fills my head,
Grandmother sings her song
I am free.

No garments to flatter
this woman's body,
or false image to uphold.
No paint upon my face,
hair is loose, unbound
I am free.

Nick Bear

(b. 1985)

A proud father of three girls, Nick Bear has been involved in writing, acting, and performing for many years. He grew up on Indian Island but identifies with all four of the Maine Wabanaki nations. Of his poetry, he writes, "I like to create images with my writing that showcase my heritage and the things it has taught me, or imagine through my writing the things I can show others. To keep my people living well and strong for our future generations is one of the biggest reasons for doing what I do because I feel that I have the voice and ability to do my ancestors justice." These are Nick Bear's first published poems.

Dry Funk

Angry at the world, thirsty for juice I can't have
Alcoholic one word that makes me feel like getting trashed
Family don't help and if they did I'd know it
In my face from all sides those sons of bitches would throw it
I'm not pissed at them I'm just pissed with friends
Who don't give a shit about me or them selves
So they'll drink to the end
Of every bottle god damn I miss that the most
Tipping up a jug seeing who could chug till its ghost
Saying fuck it and fuck you fuck life and fuck who
Ever got in my way and wanted to fuck too
My mouth is filthy from all the drink it's sipped on
Liquor in my bloodstream so even when I'm dead
It lives on
Can't deny myself this one true affliction
Fuck that wack clothing line, son
I'm talking about addiction
When you sweat just thinking where your next drop is coming from
Heaven forbid if you got a job with a kid and another one
On the way I'm numb from the sway and can't find a day

Whiskey calling my name singing me old songs I loved to play
Your guts wrench up and you don't need a reason anymore
Just the fact that it's there and what are you waiting for
Tapping you like come get it I'm rapping just to forget it
Booze will never beat this Indian cuz I'm a never let it

gladly

Put your heart in the sky let it fly and sing sweet songs like a lullaby
Arms open life is water gotta jump in to feel it
The way it was meant to be felt
Knelt mind body and spirit
Collect the puddle that had no choice but to melt
Don't fear it
Embrace that
Misplaced and in fact noble strength
Still looks good with a crack
Still would if she could take me back
Be still until we can shatter that looking glass
Fuck this happened fast
What's great is it woke me up at last
Spoke up and yelled "it's me your future—ready to walk up my path?"
Is what it asked
Loud and clear—I'm now; you're so last year
How bout a bow cuz this is my stage dear
Ate slayed deer last night with my hands
Need that connection animalistic
You're sand
To my waves calm and cool with sunny rays
Some of these days feel like eternity
Laugh as I see nobody who is worse than me
You's a nursery I'm a hurting unit
Working on me is letting go of all the stupid
Worthless no function but destruction type things
That threw my ass like a swing set

Us just rings
In my head like Indian songs that touch your skin
It's like there's roots in my Tims, branches off my brim
Growing faster by the moment
Living right strike me like a god damn sin
So I own it

Treaty of 2010

Just signed an Act and now it's in effect
Cut all ties with the United Stolen States of Death
As a general, I rule—you're no longer welcome to our grounds
Which means removal of all life that don't come from something
    brown
Load up your boats gather the multiple herds
Leave behind the memories—we laugh as they all burn
Authority isn't a value that you need to leave us
Sovereign as a unit fuck your God
In We Trust
Keep the dollar signs and face cards of power
We live off the land you live on it and cloud the
Skies with obnoxious the combinations of toxins
Can't imagine an option to stop these concoctions
Load my bow with wrath and snap the string that cuts my skin
Warpath can't describe the method of declaration
In segregation we were set as decoration
But independence from this nation will give us collective inspiration
There isn't a settlement or treaty that hasn't impacted
Our way of living which in turn enacted
A reaction from us whether outrage or silence
Count our blessing even still because the ways of their whiteness
Never assimilated me
Skillfully place us—reservations can save us
All lines of bullshit fed thru commodities
Split community was made to keep white harmony
Harming me starving me of course this was robbery

This Law isn't justice it's just us
And allota need
Change isn't easy it's never worth it when it is
Mother Earth gave us herself and you acted like bastard kids
Treatment to symptoms never a solid cure
Eliminate what constricts us and then it's for sure
Business of racism is booming and still evident
Can't catch a break even with a Black president
But the faith is there that hope will overcome
Trust in the creator that there is someone to rise up from
Horizon or sunrise the waters that give us life
Can take it all away and cut us down like a buck knife
Fear not for the tribes of red and people of color across these walks
Because you never did to begin with expect a bill for these talks
So as I pass this document on to my close ones
Put my initials at the top and jam like a broke gun

february weather makes me feel like this

wake up and smell the colonization   assimilate to get degraded by
your own people   god forbid i have an education   does that mean we
aren't equal, wait let me ask the census committee maybe they can shed
some light on our plight or why they have the right to say who's more
white   what happened to our pride and when did it slide out into the river
like erosion eating at our islands   liquor at our livers or drug prescriptions
in lieu of feelings the ones that need them can't afford or get chastised
because their skin is brown in appearance   is it interference   should i
be the whistle blower? the referee in this match doesn't have the balls to
come over . . . that bridge . . . their stacked chips . . . our happy kids are
never in the same sentences even if we have the best representatives   the
facts are this   we are the bastard children in a paternal society nourishing
our mother with false sovereignty because america's idea of government
is a form of genocidal robbery   my drum my heart my songs my ark   if
i could sing away our blues I would with red flowers in daughter's braids
patience for warrior son's shades and send white entitlement so far that
minimum wage would look like an executive's yearly net pay—this I prey

with red fists I pray since I'm only guaranteed today I take every second as a gift the creator gave we as Nation don't need guns for fighting rezervations are crumbling without freedom   emancipation is a kaleidoscope of races colliding we should be uniting untying chains that are binding unwriting the lies they are hiding   we need to start living instead of merely SURVIVING

Notes

1. "[R]oad built during the Aroostook War passing through Indian land at Mattawamkeag to northern Maine" (*Indian Country Today* note).
2. The governor of Maine in November 1829 was Nathan Cutler. The governor of the Penobscot Nation at this time was John Attean.
3. Spotted Elk danced at San Antonio's Aztec Theater in the 1920s.
4. Spotted Elk's journal states that on February 17, 1929, she "read most of the day—in a poetic and fanciful mood," and wrote this poem.
5. From the Penobscot word for badger, *Alakso*, or "Indian Devil"
6. *Neeburban*, or Aurora Borealis, is a signature Spotted Elk used for these last two poems. In an epigraph before "The Dreamer" she writes, "yes, Molly was timid and shy when this was written. The poem sounds so childlike, I have never changed it. I lived close and near to Nature and I wrote many nature poems—and Indian ones—few I have ever shown—because I was timid and sensitive and was afraid people would laugh and call me silly, for trying to write poetry."
7. "Skee wun," human waste water. Passamaquoddy language (author's note).
8. "Mitch i gun," human waste. Passamaquoddy language (author's note).
9. "Gewh huz," muskrat. Passamaquoddy language (author's note).
10. Molly Molasses is ssipsis' friend Georgia Mitchell, a Passamaquoddy from Pleasant Point, Maine.
11. "Ge nub ska ze tid psap nig," big fat onions. Passamaquoddy language (author's note).
12. See "Trends and Indicators in Higher Education," *New England Journal of Higher Education*, Spring 2009.
13. "Panampsk" is an abbreviated version of *panawapskek*, or rock.
14. Caribou Lake is below Chesuncook Lake, near Millinocket and Baxter State Park, Maine.
15. "Megalibu" means caribou.
16. Pamola is a peak on Mt. Katahdin, named for a spirit who inhabited the mountain; Pamola tested young boys, who became shamans if they passed his test. "Atahando" means power.
17. Attean, Susep, and Nicola are old Penobscot family names.

18. Swasson, Susep, Francis, Neptune, and Dani are more Penobscot family names, including Dana's, which was originally "Denis," pronounced "Daney."
19. The poem is about Dana's grandmother, who was Passamaquoddy.
20. Inspired by a traditional story of Kesihlet, who ran moose from the peak of Katahdin to what is now Bangor, Penobscot Chief Barry Dana established the annual one-hundred-mile Katahdin Penobscot Run in the 1980s. In 1984 Chief Dana's mother and Carol Dana were the first two women to walk the event, which now combines running, walking, and canoeing.
21. "Ulnerbeh" is a Penobscot word that means "friend like a brother/sister."
22. Mitchell explains that "Burnurwurbskek means 'where the rocks come out of the water' and denotes that the village is where there are rapids near Old Town." Personal communication, November 11, 2010.

Further Reading

PENOBSCOT AUTHORS

Dana, Carol. *Return to Spirit and Other Musings*. Greenfield Center NY: Bowman Books, 2014.

———. *When No One Is Looking*. Greenfield Center NY: Bowman Books, 2010. Print.

Dana, Joe. *Place of the White Rocks*. Indian Island ME: Penobscot Cultural Heritage Preservation Commission, n.d. Print.

Frey, Rhonda. "Current Events in Stereotypes and Racism—Stockton Springs (Stereotyping and Racism Curriculum: Grades 8–9)." 2007: n. pag. Print.

———. "Growing Up with Stereotypes: A Native Woman's Perspective (Stereotyping and Racism Curriculum: Grades 6–8)." 2007: n. pag. Print.

Girouard, Maria. "The Life and Traditions of the Red Man." *Ethnohistory* 55.1 (2008): 174–75. Web. 25 May 2011.

Lane, Daniel. *Ice Goes Out*. Bloomington IN: AuthorHouse, 2004. Print.

Loring, Donna. "The Dark Ages of Education and a New Hope." *New England Journal of Higher Education* (Summer 2009): 16–17. Print.

———. *In the Shadow of the Eagle: A Tribal Representative in Maine*. Gardiner ME: Tilbury House Publishers, 2008. Print.

Maine Indian Tribal-State Commission. http://www.mitsc.org/. Web. 9 June 2011.

Mead, Alice, and Arnold Neptune. *Giants of the Dawnland: Ancient Wabanaki Tales*. Huntington Beach CA: Loose Cannon Press, 2010. Print.

Nelson, Eunice. *The Wabanaki: An Annotated Bibliography of Selected Books, Articles, Documents about Maliseet, Micmac, Passamaquoddy, Penobscot Indians in Maine, Annotated by Native Americans*. Philadelphia: American Friends Service Committee, 1982. Print.

Nicolar, Joseph. 1891. *The Life and Traditions of the Red Man: A Rediscovered Treasure of Native American Literature*. 1891. Ed. Annette Kolodny. Durham NC: Duke University Press, 2007. Print.

Ranco, Fred. *Muskrat Stew and Other Tales of a Penobscot Life: The Life Story of Fred Ranco*. Orono: Maine Folklife Center, 2007. Print.

Shay, Florence Nicola. *History of the Penobscot Tribe of Indians*. Orono M E: Florence Nicola Shay. 1933. Print.

Spotted Elk, Molly. *Katahdin: Wigwam's Tales of the Abnaki Tribe and a Dictionary of Penobscot and Passamaquoddy Words with French and English Trans*. Orono: Maine Folklife Center, 2003. Print.

ssipsis. *Molly Molasses & Me: A Collection of Living Adventures*. Knox M E: Little Letterpress, Robin Hood Books, 1988. Print.

———. *Prayers, Poems, and Pathways*. Knox M E: Robin Hood Books, 2007. Print.

ADDITIONAL READING

Alger, Abby. *In Indian Tents: Stories Told by Penobscot, Passamaquoddy and Micmac Indians*. Honolulu: University Press of the Pacific, 2006. Print.

Barringer, Richard. *Changing Maine: 1960–2010*. Gardiner M E: Tilbury House Publishers, 2010. Print.

Bourque, Bruce J. *Twelve Thousand Years: American Indians in Maine*. Lincoln: Bison Books-University of Nebraska Press, 2004. Print.

Bourque, Bruce J., and Laureen A. Labar. *Uncommon Threads: Wabanaki Textiles, Clothing, and Costume*. Seattle: University of Washington Press, 2009. Print.

Carroll, Lorrayne. "'To Remove the Fear': A Conversation with Charles Norman Shay about Joseph Nicolar's *Life and Traditions of the Red Man*." *Studies in American Indian Literatures* 24.3 (Fall 2012): 97–114.

Cook, David S. *Above the Gravel Bar: The Native Canoe Routes of Maine*. Solon M E: Polar Bear, 2007. Print.

Eckstorm, Fannie H. *Indian Place Names of the Penobscot Valley and the Maine Coast*. Orono: University of Maine Press, 1974. Print.

Hardy, Kerry. *Notes on a Lost Flute: A Field Guide to the Wabanaki*. Camden M E: Down East Books, 2009. Print.

Haviland, William A. *At the Place of the Lobsters and Crabs: Indian People and Deer Isle, Maine, 1605–2005*. Solon M E: Polar Bear, 2009. Print.

Kennedy, Kate. *Florence Nicolar Shay: Penobscot Basketmaker and Tribal Advocate*. Indian Island M E: Charles Norman Shay, n.d. Print.

Leland, Charles G. *The Algonquin Legends of New England; or, Myths and Folk Lore of the Micmac, Passamaquoddy and Penobscot Tribes*. Boston: Houghton Mifflin, 1884. Print.

MacDougall, Pauleena. *The Penobscot Dance of Resistance: Tradition in the History of a People*. Hanover: University of New Hampshire Press, 2004. Print.

McBride, Bunny. *Molly Spotted Elk: A Penobscot in Paris*. Norman: University of Oklahoma Press, 1997. Print.

———. *Women of the Dawn*. Lincoln: Bison Books-University of Nebraska Press, 2001. Print.

McBride, Bunny, and Harald E. L. Prins. *Indians in Eden: Wabanakis and Rusticators on Maine's Mt. Desert Island*. Camden M E: Down East Books, 2009. Print.

Pawling, Micah A. *Wabanaki Homeland and the New State of Maine: The 1820 Journal and Plans of Survey of Joseph Treat*. Amherst: Univ. of Massachusetts Press, 2007. Print.

Prins, Harald E. L., and Bunny McBride. *From Indian Island to Omaha Beach: The Story of Charles Shay, Penobscot Indian War Hero*. Gardiner M E: Tilbury House Publishers, 2011. Print.

Rolde, Neil. *Unsettled Past, Unsettled Future: The Story of Maine Indians*. Gardiner M E: Tilbury House Publishers, 2004. Print.

Siebert, Frank. *Penobscot Dictionary*. Indian Island M E: Penobscot Cultural Heritage Preservation Commission, n.d. Print.

Speck, Frank G. 1940. *Penobscot Man*. Orono: University of Maine Press, 1998. Print.

———. "Penobscot Shamanism." *Memoirs of the American Anthropological Association* 6 (Oct.–Dec. 1919): 239–45. Print.

The Wabanakis of Maine and the Maritimes: A Resource Book about Penobscot, Passamaquoddy, Maliseet, Micmac and Abenaki Indians, with Lesson Plans for Grades 4 through 8. Philadelphia: American Friends Service Committee, 1989.

ABENAKI

Introduction

Lisa Brooks

The petitions, prose, and poetry in this chapter originate from the waterways of Ndakinna, "our land" in the Western Abenaki language, from the survivors of hundreds of years of resistance and resilience in the lands now most commonly known as northern New England and southern Quebec. While part of the larger Wabanaki—people of the dawn, people of the east—"Abenaki" is the term that came to be used most frequently for (and by) those Native families who inhabited the vast network of waterways from Lake Champlain, the western "lake between" Wabanaki and Iroquoia, to the Kennebec River on the west, and north to the mission towns of Odanak and Wolinak on the St. Francis River, as well as to multinational towns above Kwinitekw and Kennebec such as Menassan and Megantic.

The people and places of the Abenaki "home country" are connected by these waterways. It is no surprise that the central character in this chapter is the "long river" Kwinitekw, the Connecticut River that flows from its protected headwaters in northern New Hampshire through the countries of Koasek and Sokwakik, and all the way south through Mohegan country to the sea. While today it is the boundary between New Hampshire and Vermont, a river inundated with dams, old mills, and both industrial and agricultural pollution, it was once a superhighway of the eastern country, one of the most fertile places in the world, a cradle of agriculture that hosted numerous falls for bountiful salmon. It is a river that gathered families together. Kwinitekw remains a place lodged deeply in oral histories, in fishing and planting stories, and in collective memory. As the river begins its long recovery, its history and its songs are also being reclaimed and reimagined, including, as you shall see, by the writers who have made it their touchstone. It may be fitting that one of the first pieces in this chapter, the Petition at No. 2, emerges from a time when Abenaki people were just beginning to use writing as a tool to defend, protect, and reclaim the river of their birth.

Abenaki people fought fiercely for more than a century against English expansion into their homelands. Following the capitulation of their French allies, devastating losses due to warfare and disease, and the divisive politics of the American Revolution, Abenaki families remained in mission villages in Quebec, in the marshes and uplands of old villages and new colonial towns, and in groups of extended families who traveled old north country routes, gaining subsistence in the old way, through hunting, trapping, fishing, gathering, and trade, as well as day labor, logging, and small-scale farming. As Abenaki hunter Tahmunt Swassen told Henry David Thoreau, his hunting territory spanned an expanse from the northern Maine woods, where they then were sitting by a fire, to the Adirondacks and north to Quebec. Tellingly, Thoreau revealed in *The Maine Woods*, Swassen could "write his name very well" and was concerned with a law he had recently read that recognized Wabanaki hunting rights in Maine.

Many of the ancestors of the writers contained herein traveled those same routes. While some remained very close to home, many families took the old superhighways of Kwinitekw, Molôdomek (Merrimack), and Kennebec south in the late nineteenth and early twentieth centuries, returning to old villages or traveling to Massachusetts and Connecticut to seek jobs, holding a persistent sense of northern New England and/ or southern Quebec as home. The late twentieth century has been a time of reconnection, with families moving back up north to renew ties with the families who remained. It has also been a time of reconstruction, as we put the pieces of the puzzle back together, exchanging our family stories. Writing has been an important tool in this process of recovery. Piles of documents and boxes of family photos fill so many living room corners, and they have been brought out time and again at kitchen tables, weaving images and written words into oral histories. The pages of those writings are stained with coffee, maple syrup, and macaroni stew, the lasting evidence of our interactions. Mothers, fathers, and grandparents now tell ancient stories at those tables to their children, nearly forgetting they first learned them from reading the books of stories gathered and relayed with great care by Joseph Bruchac. The language work of Henry Masta and Joseph Laurent, for years passed around as worn photocopies, now weaves its way through the poetry of Carol Bachofner and Cheryl Savageau, even as it is used in the teaching and revitalization of language by Jesse Bruchac and Elie Joubert. Writing has been instrumental to this work. We leave it to be seen what the next generation will do with the increasing number of tools that they now have at hand.

It is these family stories, kept carefully and sometimes relayed casually, that enable us to recognize each other. They travel through this entire collection. They are the "back story" behind the early petitions and letters. They appear as snippets of dialogue and narrative in the extraordinary language work of Laurent and Masta. They are relayed gracefully in the oral traditional prose of Claudia Mason Chicklas and Marge Bruchac. They undergird the vibrant journalism, poetry, and prose of Donna Laurent Caruso. They shimmer in the eloquent and evocative poetry of Joseph Bruchac, Cheryl Savageau, Carol Bachofner ,and Suzanne Rancourt. They are the stories that Robert Tahamont and the other Carlisle students were not allowed to write . . . at least not while they were *in* school.

We are connected through the bonds of kinship, friendship, mentorship, and sometimes through family feuds, but most importantly, to draw an unshakably eloquent phrase from Cheryl Savageau's poem "What I Save," we are bound to each other by "the water flowing through [us] that cannot be contained."

Samuel Numphow

Samuel Numphow was the son of the Patucket sachem Numphow, a convert and early leader of the praying town of Wamesit, located at the ancient fishing falls of Pawtucket, a considerable Pennacook town and central gathering place, especially during the spring fish runs, at the confluence of the Concord and Merrimac Rivers, a longtime gathering place for Pennacook people. Samuel Numphow acquired his writing skills at the preparatory schools of the Harvard Indian College. Although he did not attend Harvard, he went on to become a leader at Wamesit, following in his father's footsteps, and wrote letters relaying Penacook movements north during King Philip's War. Both Numphow and John Lyne were leaders at Wamesit during King Philip's War. Here they relate that they are joining their Penacook relations at the headwaters of the Connecticut River, in a protected region far north of the settlements, after their own village, which remained neutral, was attacked by "armed men," their "neighbors" from nearby Chelmsford. According to Daniel Gookin, who originally printed Numphow's letter, "They came to the wigwams, and called to the poor Indians to come out of doors, which most of them readily did, both men, women, and children, not in the least suspecting the English would hurt them. But two of the English being loaded with pistol-shot, being not far off, fired upon them and wounded five women and children, and slew outright a lad of about twelve years old, which child's mother was also one of the wounded" (482–83).

Letter from Numphow and John Line to Mr. Thomas Henchman of Chelmsford [Whom the Council had asked to persuade them to return]

I, Numphow, and John a Line, we send a messenger to you again [Wepocositt] with this answer, we cannot come home again, we go towards the French, we go where Wannalancet is; the reason is, we went away from our home, we had help from the Council, but that did not do us good, but we had wrong by the English. 2dly. The reason is we went away from the English, for when there was any harm done in Chelmsford, they laid it to us, and said we did it, but we know ourselves we never did any harm to the

English, but we go away peaceably and quietly. 3dly. As for the Island, we say there is no safety for us, because many English be not good, and may be they come to us and kill us, as in the other case. We are not sorry for what we leave behind, but we are sorry the English have driven us from our praying to God and from our teacher. We did begin to understand a little of praying to God. We thank humbly the Council. We remember our love to Mr. Henchman and James Richardson.

(c. 1675)

Kancamagus

New Hampshire residents and tourists know "Kancamagus" from the scenic White Mountain highway named for the Pennacook sagamore. He was the grandson of the famous sachem Passaconaway and the son of the sachem Nanamocomuck, who was born around 1636. Kancamagus himself married a woman from Ameroscoggin. Abenaki historian David Stewart-Smith says that "his English name, Hodgkins, is probably an anglicization of the old tribal name, or title, Hegen or Hegens."[1] Some New Hampshire histories celebrate Kancamagus as a mediator between Indians and white colonists. Historian Colin Calloway, however, describes him as the beleaguered head of the Pennacook Confederacy, who sought to protect his people from settlers' incursions by attacking Dover in 1689; he signed a treaty with settlers the following year, after his wife and children were captured. Kancamagus was also instrumental to building the ties among Abenaki communities that enabled resistance to English expansion, forming strong alliances between Penacook and Androscoggin, for example, where he was raised and married into a leadership family. His petitions, below, transcribed by Simon Betokom, the Wamesit scribe, show him attempting to forestall a conflict that New Hampshire governor Edward Cranfield wanted to foment between the Abenakis and Mohawks. It appears in Colin Calloway's *Dawnland Encounters* (96–97).

Petitions, c. 1685

May 15th, 1685.

Honour Governor my friend, you my friend I desire your worship and
your power because I hope you can do som great matters this once.
I am poor and naked and I have no men at my place because I afraid
allways Mohogs he will kill me every day and night. If your worship
when please pray help me you no let Mohogs kill me at my place
at Malamake Revir [Merrimack River] called Panukkog [Penacook,
contemporary Concord N H] and Natukkog [Naticook, contemporary
Merrimack N H], I will submit [to] your worship and your power. And
now I want powder and such allminishon shott and guns because I
have forth at my hom and I plant theare.

This all Indian hand but pray you do consider
your humble Servant
John Hogkins

May 15th, 1685

Honour Mr. Governor, now this day I com your house I want se you and I bring my hand at before you. I want shake hand to you; if your worship when please then you receve my hand then shake your hand and my hand. You my friend because I remember at old time when live my grant father and grant mother then Englishmen com this country then my grant father and Englishmen they make a good govenant. They friend all wayes, my grant father leving at place called Malamake Rever other name chef Natukkog and Panukkog, that one rever great many names, and I bring you this few skins at this first time I will give you my friend

This all Indian hand

John + hawkins Sagomor	*peter × Robin*
Simon Betogkom	*Gorge × Roddunnonukgus*
Joseph + traske	*Hope × hoth*
king + hary his	*John × Toneh*
Sama + linis	*John + Canowa*
wapeguanat × Taguachuashat	*John + owamosimmin*
old Robin +	*Natonill × Indian*
mamanosques × andwa	

Petition at No. 2, Kwinitekw, 1747

In the spring of 1747 an Abenaki raiding party posted an awikhigan outside an English fort on the "long river," Kwinitekw. The "petition" was signed by "Old Town, Chee Hoose, Penewonse, and Prik Fore English, in the name of & on behalf of others." The men gave their location as "Number 2 on Connecticut River," identifying for their English readers a recently constructed settlement in Abenaki space (at the contemporary town of Westmoreland N H). The petition was part of an effort to reclaim Sokoki (the south people of Abenaki country) towns on the Connecticut River during King George's War, or the "Anglo-Abenaki Wars." It was composed by a coalition of Abenaki men and one Mohawk man, who had strong kinship ties to the Connecticut River valley:

Gentlemen. Whereas there have been very grievous complaints in the province of —— with respect to ye support and maintenance of your frontiers in a time of war, we . . . have undertaken to free you from such an extraordinary charge by killing & taking captive the people & driving them off & firing their fortifications. And so successful have we been in this affair that we have broke up almost all the new settlements in your western frontiers: so that you need not be at one half the charge you were in the year past in maintaining a war in those parts: for now there are but little else besides the old towns, and if they will not fortifie and defend themselves; we think they ought to be left to our mercy. And for this good service that we have done the province, we humbly ask a suitable reward; but if your honours see fit we will wait till a peace is concluded and then receive it in presents. But in the mean time if some small matter of encouragement be given us we will go on to bring your frontiers to a narrower compass still & make your charges still smaller; but if your honours approve of this our design we humbly request of you to give us information whither it be more acceptable to you that we man your defeated garrisons our selves and eat up the provisions which your poor distressed neighbours leave in ym when they flee in their hurry & confusion or whither we burn up the forts with the provisions; for we assure you we find much more in them than we want for our own support whilst carrying on this business. Gentlemen however some may look upon us now yet we can assure you we are your very humble, obsequious servants.

Joseph Laurent
(1839–1917)

Laurent headed an illustrious family at Odanak, Quebec, where he himself served as chief from 1880 to 1892. With his son Stephen (also included in this volume), he established a well-known trading post at Intervale, New Hampshire, traveling there each summer to sell baskets. His 1884 *New Familiar Abenakis and English Dialogues* is still widely used by Abenaki people today in language preservation and instruction. It is also an important early Abenaki *literary* work, what Lisa Brooks calls "a journey map through Wabanaki space" (*Common Pot*, 249). In the excerpt below, as Brooks explains, Laurent starts at the city nearest Odanak, Montreal; moves north through Abenaki villages and rivers; west to the Haudenosaunee homeland; south through Wabanaki territories in what are now northern Vermont and upstate New York; and back east, up the Connecticut River and into the White Mountains, the heart of the Abenaki homeland. Finally, he extends his reach to Boston, Europe, and the larger world. "The language," Brooks writes, "was the map that Wabanaki families used in returning to and traveling through the space they still recognized as home" (251).

Preface to New Familiar Abenakis and English Dialogues

The primary intention, the chief aim of the Editor in publishing this book, is to aid the young generation of the Abenakis tribe in learning English.[2]

It is also intended to preserve the *uncultivated* Abenakis language from the gradual alterations which are continually occurring from want, of course, of some proper work showing the grammatical principles upon which it is dependent. Hence the many remarks and explanations which are to be found all through this book: *ciphers, italics, etc., etc.,* employed in view to extend its utility.

As no pains have been spared to render as easy as possible the learning of the pronunciation, and the signification of every Indian word inserted in this book, and that the Abenakis language contains no articulations that the English vocal organs are not accustomed to, the writer hopes that many of the white people will be glad to avail themselves of the advantage and facility thus afforded to them for becoming acquainted in some measure, and with very little trouble, with that truly *admirable* language of those Aborigines called *Abenakis*, which, from the original word *Wôbanaki*, means: peasant or inhabitant from the East.

May this little volume, which will learn the white man how the Abenakis vocal organs express God's attributes, the names of the various objects of the creation: beasts, birds, fishes, trees, fruits, etc., etc., and how extended are the modifications of the Abenakis verb, be welcomed by the white as well as by the red man, and its errors and defects overlooked with indulgence.

> *Sozap Lolô,* alias,
> *Jos. Laurent.*

Names of Cities, Towns, Villages, Rivers, Countries, Nations, &c., &c.

Molian.	Montreal.
Moliani.	A Montrealer.
Molini*ak*.	Montrealers.
Moliantegw.	River St-Lawrence.
Masessolian.	Sorel.
Masessoliani*ak*.	Sorellers.
Masessoliantegw.	River Chambly.
Madôbalodnik.	Three-Rivers.
Madôbalodni*ak*.	People or inhabitants of Three-Rivers.
Madôbalodnitegw.	River St-Maurice.
Palkinek.	Berthier.
Palkini*ak*.	Peop. or inhabitants of Berthier.
Pithiganek.	Nicolet.
Pithigani*ak*.	Peop. or inhabitants of Nicolet.
Pithiganitegw.	River Nicolet.

Wôlinak.	Becancour.
Wôlinaktegw.	River Becancour.
Padiskônek.	Batiscan.
O'bamasek.	Rivière du Loup (en bas.)
O'bamasisek.	Yamachiche.
Pamadenainak.	Lorette (Ind. Village.)
Pamadenaiak.	Indians of Lorette.
Kebek.[1]	Quebec.
Kubek.[2]	Quebec.
Kubeki.	A citizen (man) of Quebec.
Kuibekiak.	People or inhabitants of Quebec.
Kuibekiskua.	A lady (woman) from Quebec.
Kuibekiskuak.	Ladies of Quebec.
Kaanawagi.	Caughnawaga.
Magua.	An Iroquois (indian).
Kaanawagihnono.	The Iroquois tribe.
Otawa.	Ottawa.
Otawai.	A man (citizen) from Ottawa.
Otawaiiak.	People or inhabitants of Ottawa.
Koattegw.	Pine River.
Koattegok.	Coaticook.
Mamlawbagak.	Mamphremagog.
Môdôwa.	Mantawa.
Paliten.	Burlington.
Sôn-Halônek.	Plattsburg.
Salatogi.	Saratoga.
Nebizonbik.	At the mineral spring.
Kwenitegw.	River Connecticut.

Winoski.	Winooski.
Pasômsik.	Passumpsic.
Pamijoasik.	Pamigewasset.
Wiwninbesaki.	Winnipisaukee.
Wawôbadenik.	White mountain reg.
Wigwômadensisek.	St Hyacinthe.
Wigwômadenik.	Yamaska.
Kwanahômoik.	Durham.
Namakôttik.	Megantic.
Panaôbskak.	Penobscot.
Panaôbskattegw *or* Panaôbskai sibo.	Penobscot river.
Panaôbskaiiak.	People (indians) of Penobscot.
Kanada.	Canada.
Pastonki.	United States of America.
Pastonkik.	In the United States of America.
Pastoni.	An American.
Pastoniskua.	An American woman.
Iglismônki.	England.
Iglismônkik.	In England.
Iglismôn.	An Englishman.
Iglesmôniskua.	An English woman.
Plachmônki.	France.
Plachmôn.	A Frenchman.
Alemônki.	Germany.
Alemôn.	A German.
Spôniolki.	Spain.
Spôniol.	A Spaniard.

Illôdaki. (*pron.* -ak-ki.)	Ireland.
Illôda.	An Irishman.
Illôdaskua.	An Irish woman.
Koswaki. (*pron.* -ak-ki.)	Scotland.
Koswa.	A Scotchman.
Agômenoki.— (*pron.* ok-ki.)	Europe.
Wdagômenoki. (*pl.* -ak)	A European.
Alsigôntegw. (*local term*: Alsigôntegok.)	River St. Francis.
Alnôba.	An Indian.
Alnôbai phanem.	An Indian woman.
Wôbanaki.	An Abenaki (Indian).
Sigwnigan.	A reserve.
Alnôbai sigwnigan.	An Indian reserve.
Alnôbai lowôzowôgan *or* Alnôbawôzowôgan.	Indian costume.
Alnôba'odana.	An Indian village.
Plachmôni odana.	A French village.
Odana.	A city; town; village.
Ki, aki.	Earth, the globe, the world; country; farm; ground; soil.
N'-d-aki, w'-d-aki.	My farm, his (her) farm.
Kdakinna.	The globe. (*literally,* our earth, our globe.)
K'-d-akinna.	Our farm *or* ground.

---

[1] Pronounce "Ke-bek" as in French, *Quebec.*

[2] This *orthography* is an *imitation* of the English pronounciation. [*sic*, Laurent's footnotes]

Henry Lorne Masta

(1853–?)

Like Joseph Laurent and their relative Peter Paul Wzokhilain before him, Henry Lorne Masta transcribed and translated Abenaki oral traditions into written form. His *Abenaki Indian Legends, Grammar and Place-Names* was first published in 1932, but Abenaki people have continued to circulate and use the book for language revitalization, among other purposes—a fact driven home by Joseph and Jesse Bruchac's recent reissue of this primer through Bowman Books.[3] Masta's book is also much more than a "primer": as the passages below illustrate, it contains lively dialogues that reveal a good deal about Abenaki relationships to place, cultural beliefs, travel, and humor.

Natanis and Sabadis

NAT: My friend Sabadis can you tell me which is the river called Connecticut and its course?

SAB: Is it possible that you do not know Kwenitekw and its course!

NAT: It is true, it is because I have never lived around here very much.

SAB: Where then do you keep yourself?

NAT: I live mostly in Australia; now tell me if you please what I have asked you.

SAB: Yes, and very willingly too. You know that in our language a word beginning with the prefix Kwena, Kweni, Kweno or Kwen8 it means long and the suffix tells what is long.[4]

The suffix "tekw" means river.

Kwenitekw means *long river.*

Kwena plus Kwam means long stick.

Kwene plus gisgad means long day.

Kweni plus tbakad means long night.

But the English instead of saying Kweni-tekw-ok say Connecticut. However, the Indian is more to blame for this than anyone else, because he speaks too low and does not open his mouth wide enough so as to articulate his words properly.

NAT: Well is Kwenitekw really a long river?

SAB: Assuredly. It would not be so called if it were not so.

NAT: Where, then, is its source, course and mouth?

SAB: Its source is in New Hampshire; its course between New Hampshire and Vermont and across Massachusetts and Connecticut and empties into Long Island Sound. It is about 400 miles long.

Wijokamit and Ma8wat

WIJ: Hallo! Hallo! Cousin Ma8wat how glad I am to see you. You have been away quite a while.

MA8: Yes, it is seven years since I left this place and I thought, old as I am, it would be better for me to return to St. Francis [Quebec], that is where I belong anyway.

WIJ: Cousin what you say is right. How old are you?

MA8: I am past seventy-five years of age.

WIJ: Cousin, then I am older than you. I am seventy-nine years old. Cousin I would like to ask you something.

MA8: Say what you want, I am not busy now.

WIJ: Well, then I must first tell you my story though it is a little bit long. When I was about ten years of age, I went with Lol8 Ta8mont muskrat hunting and every day after supper he would tell me things of old. He was then eight-one years old so the things referred to must have taken place two hundred years ago. Our forefathers lived and died at this place where we are living, now called Odanak. They owned a few houses and many birch-bark wigwams. Once upon a time, while they were dancing and drinking "bitter-water" rum, a white man of great nobility came in there and for some time only observed the place and people, but at last asked permission to dance with them. He was so polite that they could not refuse to allow him to dance with them, but they soon remarked that he paid special attention to the women; when he spoke to the men it was only to encourage them in their frolic and drinking. For instance as soon as they were short of liquor he furnished the money for some more from St. Francois, across the river, but he did not drink much of it himself, and when that was all gone too, he told the man to go for some more liquor, and Joseph who used to get it said, "We have no money," and the gentleman said to him, "Make haste and get some more whiskey, you have some money in your pocket." And Joseph did truly find some in his pocket, and after that he got some more and more all night long, and strange to say, his pocket was never empty when he came back though it took all he had each time to pay for the liquor.

At dawn of the day the noble white man was still dancing with his coat on, something like a Prince Albert coat and through the slit the women and the men too, saw his tail and all said he is the devil, and while looking at him, he slowly disappeared.

Now, Cousin, I would like to know if the devil, as we call him, can assume any human form or the likeness of anything he chooses and whether there is something by means of which we can detect him?

MA8: Wijokamit, I will tell you my impression of the case. The devil can assume human form, animal form, and the likeness of anything. He can also speak any language to tempt persons and nations of the world, For instance he assumed the form of an animal when he tempted Eve in the garden of Eden. The looks of the serpent must have been very pleasing before his fall, since he succeeded in deceiving the first Woman. He not only assumed the animal form, but he transformed himself into an angel of light and went to heaven to tempt the holy angels. He was allowed to go there until the resurrection and ascension of our Lord, Jesus Christ.

The devil is a spirit and a spirit has no flesh nor bone, it follows that he has no horns, no cloven hoofs, and no tail, but he can make himself to look like a person, like a beast, etc., so if a person is seen having horns or tail, we may say assuredly,—"he is the devil."

Robert James Tahamont
(1891–?)

Robert Tahamont attended the Carlisle Indian School in Pennsylvania with Albert DeGrasse (Wampanoag), also represented in this volume. His school records indicate that he was fifteen when he arrived in 1906 from Lake George and that he graduated in 1911. For a few years afterward he sent some correspondence to the school reporting that he was living in New Jersey, working first as a baker's apprentice and later as a carpenter. The two pieces below, which appeared in the *Carlisle Arrow*, are as heavily mediated as any student writing. Carlisle pupils were encouraged to write relatively stereotypical accounts of "Indian legends" and to focus on nations other than their own.

Chief Teedyuscung[5]

The Indian has played a very important part in the history of our country, especially the early history. Had it been not for Teedyuscung, a friendly chief of the Delaware Indians, John Harris, the founder of Harrisburg, would have been burned at the stake as was the intention of the unfriendly Paxtang Indians. John Harris' grave may be seen in the River Park at Harrisburg, at the foot of the tree to which he was bound when the Indians were going to burn him. Since Teedyuscung's hospitality did so much toward the founding of Harrisburg, a portrait has been placed in the state Capitol building at Harrisburg in honor of this benevolent chief. Teedyuscung was born near Trenton about the year 1700 and died in Wyoming Valley, Pennsylvania, in 1763.

(May 27, 1910)

The Masquerade Ball

The masquerade ball given by a party of girls in the gymnasium on the evening of October thirty-first, was, according to a statement made by Supt. Friedman, one of the finest "getups" ever given by the pupils. The ball started at seven-thirty, when figures garbed in costumes of varied and fantastic appearance marched into the gymnasium. Clowns prevailed and amused the lookers on by playing pranks with what appeared to be a stuffed dummy representing a scarecrow; but soon the dummy became animated and walked around. He proved to be not a dummy after all, but was a senior who portrayed the character with great exactness. There were pretty maids dressed in costumes representing Red Riding Hood, Gypsies, Swiss girls; Scotch girls, and many other quaint characters. The boys represented Indians, monkeys, girls, darkies, tramps, rustic lassies and happy sons of Erin. After several dances . . . each found out who his partner was. After having found their right partners, refreshments consisting of pumpkin pie, apples and coffee were served. Good behavior was observed throughout the evening and after the "*Home Sweet Home*" waltz all adjourned carrying with them the memories of one of the most enjoyable social events in the annals of Carlisle. The prize for the best-dressed couple was given to Mrs. Deitz and Suzanne Porter; they were dressed in hobble skirts with enormous peach-basket hats. Texie Tubbs and Harry West were the winners of the prize-waltz.

(November 11, 1910)

Stephen Laurent

(1909–2001)

Like his father, Joseph Laurent, Stephen was an accomplished linguist. He spent thirty years working on an English translation of a French-Abenaki dictionary compiled in 1713 by the Jesuit missionary Joseph Aubrey; the book has since become a critical source for Abenaki language revitalization work. Stephen Laurent was born at Odanak and lived much of his life in New Hampshire, where he ran the Indian Shop at Intervale until his retirement in 1974. The speech below was originally printed in the journal *Vermont History* in 1955.

The Abenakis of Vermont

Paakuinogwzian, Nidobak! In other words, How do you do, my friends! Although the word "paakuinogwzian" really means "You look new to me," it is the nearest approach to the English greeting, "How do you do?" Well, it is safe to say that I probably look new to you also, and perhaps a little bit disappointing, especially if you read the January issue of *Vermont History*, in which it was announced that you would have at the July meeting a hereditary chief of the Abenakis. It is safe to say that many of you expected to see such an individual all decked out in deerskin leggings, shirt of buck skins, a feather headdress, and the rest of what is generally considered to be the Indian's regalia. Had you been told that this so-called hereditary chief had red hair, wore glasses, and looked as if he came from East Boston rather than from the Indian village of St. Francis, you probably would have said: "We don't have to go to the Historical Society meeting to see such an Indian: there are countless numbers of such Indians up and down Main Street in our own town." . . .

Because of its importance as a tool of historical research, it might be appropriate to say a few words about the Abenaki language and its characteristics. I shall later give you a sample of its sound as a living tongue by narrating two historical episodes in Abenaki and translating them into English for you.

Like all North American Indian languages, the Abenaki dialect belongs philologically to the group called *holophrastic*, from a Greek compound meaning that a phrase or an entire sentence or description is telescoped into a single word. The Indian mind delights in synthesis and compresses into one word both object and action, with all that modifies either object or action. For instance, the word *awanoch*, meaning *white man*, consists of *awani* and *uji*, or *who* and *from*. We are told that when first the Indians beheld the white man, they exclaimed to one another: "A wani uji?" "A wani uji?," meaning, "WHO is this man and where does he come FROM?" But they considered it a waste of time and breath to say the whole sentence. To the Indians it was sufficient to say just: "Who from?" Ever since then the white man has been called *awanoch* (pronounced *awanoots*), and it comes from that memorable day when the red and the white race met for the first time. Since the word *awanoch* was on everybody's lips, lacking a name for the white man, the Indians figured they might as well call him *awanoch*.

Another interesting example descriptive of Indian synthesis may be found in the remarkable word *skenekwati*, Iroquois for *the left side*. Actually it means, "the side from which the blood flows." That is worthy of notice since it would seem to indicate that the Indians had discovered the circulation of the blood even before the celebrated scientist Harvey propounded his theory. Skenekwati is broken down as follows: *'nekw*, flowing blood; *ati*, the side from; while the initial syllable *ske* shows return to the point of origin. In Abenaki, the word for *moon* is *nahnibossat*, "the one that travels by night"; for *northern lights* we have *abasandoganal*, "the lights in the shape of trees."

The coming of the Europeans demanded an expansion of the Indian vocabulary which they met by Indianizing strange terms or coining their own names for new objects. Strangely enough the St. Francis Indians, living amongst French-speaking people, Indianized the *English* word pancakes into Pongoksak; while the Penobscot Indians, surrounded by English communities, have instead Indianized the French word *des crepes* (pancakes) into *tayklapsak*. Trousers are called *peljes* from *breeches*; *vinegar* has been changed into *pinegal*. As examples of coined words, we have, for *umbrella*, *obagawatahigan*, or "the thing that makes a shadow"; the word for *rum* is *akwbi*, "bitter water," while a Prince Albert coat (or tuxedo) was called *papsigagihlonk pitkozon*, meaning "the coat with a slit in the back." One of the most amusing and characteristic examples of word Indianization is the Abenaki word for clock. Not realizing the usefulness of the clock but noticing that it was a noisy contraption which made quite a racket during the night as well as in daylight, they promptly called it *papizokwassik*, "the thing that makes a lot of noise for nothing." . . .

As stated earlier in my talk, the etymology of Indian place-names is of great importance to all students of Americana. Unfortunately, that is an exceedingly difficult branch of philology because of the fact that these Indian words have been so corrupted by the English. Sometimes the Indians themselves were at fault through either mispronunciation, faulty diction, or inadequate articulation, as a result of which there arose frequent misunderstandings and false conclusions. In his *Etymology of Missisquoi* Dr. MacAleer gives an amusing example illustrating how some white men would jump to erroneous deductions as regards the meaning of Indian words. He writes that there was a hunting lodge in the Adirondacks called *Nehasne*, and the owner told all and sundry that the meaning of this Iroquois word was "Beaver on a log." Doubting the correctness of that etymology, someone got in touch with Iroquois-speaking persons and was told that it was a common enough expression meaning: "There it is! There it is!" They explained his delusion thus: Probably the owner of this lodge had been out hunting beavers in the company of two Iroquois guides. They came to a beaver dam but found no beaver. Finally, one of the Iroquois espied a beaver squatting on the end of a log. Excitedly he cried out to his companion: "Nehasne! Nehasne!" and at the same time pointed to the beaver on the log. The white man, overhearing this, immediately concluded that it meant *Beaver on a log.*

The *Etymology of Missisquoi* is itself proof of what a will-o'-the-wisp chase etymologizing on Indian names can be. At the conclusion of the book, after having consulted innumerable maps, read countless volumes, corresponded with numberless savants in the field of linguistics, Dr. MacAleer concludes: "This study was undertaken with an unbiased mind and it is ended without predilection." In other words, after all was said and done, the meaning of Missisquoi was still a mystery.

The New Hampshire State Development Commission likes to assert that "Winnipesaukee" means "the smile of the Great Spirit." Actually nothing in that word even remotely suggests either "smile" or "great" or "spirit." There is the word *nebes* or *nepes*, meaning *lake* or *region* or *territory*. It is anybody's guess what the initial syllable means; therefore, no one can be dogmatic about the word and state as a fact that it means this or that.

The best that any etymologist will do is to hazard a guess. I once asked Dr. Speck, Professor of Anthropology at the University of Pennsylvania, how far back he had traced that erroneous etymology for "Winnipesaukee." He replied that he had come across it in the writings of the Jesuit Father Vetromile, missionary to some Maine Indians in the 1860s. In fact, one old Penobscot Indian named Lobal told him the following story and vouched for its authenticity: Once Father Vetromile was entertaining a visiting priest. Lobal and another Indian were paddling them lazily along the Penobscot River while the good Father was holding forth on the etymologies of this, that, and the other Indian name. When he came to the word "Winnipesaukee," he said, "Take the word 'Winnipesaukee,' for example. That means 'the smile of the Great Spirit'." Then he turned around to Lobal for confirmation. "Isn't that right, Lobal?" Lobal, drowsing over his paddle, assented with a nod, saying, "Yes, Father." When they reached their destination, the priests and the Indians parted company. Suddenly Lobal's partner upbraided him for supporting the Father in his error as to the meaning of "Winnipesaukee." Said he, "You had a good chance there to put an end to that nonsense about 'Winnipesaukee' meaning 'smile of the Great Spirit'." Lobal merely smiled and explained that it was such a beautiful afternoon, he was enjoying so the singing of the birds, the soughing of the wind in the trees, the skating of the insects over the water, that he just didn't want to spoil it all by starting an argument over something so inconsequential as the meaning of an Indian word. Lobal's viewpoint seemed to be: after all, if the white man liked to think that "Winnipesaukee" meant "the smile of the Great Spirit," what harm did it do? It wouldn't make or break the world whether "Winnipesaukee" meant that or something more prosaic like, let us say, pork and beans.

Claudia Mason Chicklas
(1926–2008)

Like a number of writers in this volume, Claudia Chicklas worked with the New England Native American Institute in Worcester, Massachusetts; for many years, she edited its newsletter. Her lineage included some prominent figures: distant ancestor Eunice Williams (the Englishwoman who famously married into the Mohawk Nation after she was captured at Deerfield, Massachusetts, in 1704); Mary Watso (grandmother), a renowned Abenaki basketmaker from Keene, New Hampshire; and Elizabeth Sadoques Mason (mother), one of the first Native American registered nurses. Chicklas herself attended the University of New Hampshire and raised four children. She published a history of Ware, Massachusetts, where she lived at the end of her life. Her daughter, Joyce Heywood, who generously contributed these pieces to this volume, has been working with historian Margaret Bruchac (included below) on a forthcoming chapbook of Chicklas's writings.

A Profile in Courage

The old deed, translated from French, reads, "To the present Thomas MSadokis, hunter, living in the Abenaki village known as Frances de Sales who by his presence acknowledges to have sold, transfer, quit, convey and part with——to Israel MSadokis, his son, hunter of said village who accepts as buyer for himself——to wit: a piece of land situated in L'Ile called L'Ile Mondu——in the parish of St. Francois.——In consideration of the price amount of one hundred ten dollars.——In the presence of Leonard Dugnan, shoemaker, of St. Thomas de Pierreville.——The mark of Thomas (x) MSadokis, of Israel MSadokis.

> *Signed Leonard Dugnan, shoemaker*
> *I. U. Pitt, Notaire 17 January, 1872*

This deed transferring an island from great-grandfather Thomas to grandfather Israel was, I believe, in anticipation [of] Israel's marriage, which was recorded on February 15, 1872. Father and son were hunters, according to the deed, though it was understood that trapper was a part of that occupation. The hunting territory assigned to the families of St. Francis were many miles to the north and in order to provide for their families, able-bodied men spent many months in winter on those lands, alone or in family clusters, hunting and running trap lines for beaver and other animals, which yielded cash when traded to the Hudson's Bay Company.

Between the date of his marriage and 1878, things did not go well for grandfather Israel. Trapping was poor, money was scarce and his family experienced sickness which took the life of his second son. And so, he and Grandmother Mary made the decision to go to the land of the Quanicticook. Israel was 32 years old, and without skills, except as "hunter."

Their journey took them down the Quanicticook to southern Connecticut state, but they found no home there, and started back up the river, reaching Brattleboro, Vermont, in 1880. A chance meeting with a man peddling soft soap on the riverbank where they were camped brought them to Keene, New Hampshire.

Israel's knowledge of the forests and wild animals was not adequate to provide a living for his family, but the resourcefulness and courage learned from winters spent alone in the north set him on another path, and Israel, hunter, became Israel, small-business man and farmer. In the time of Custer's famous last stand, the climate for acceptance of an Indian family was not overwhelming, but with developing powers of persuasion, he convinced the president of the local bank to rent him a foreclosed farm. Much of the land needed clearing, and grandfather needed a horse and the skill to work it. Trading his mastery of tanning pelts to a notable softness in the old way, he contracted with a local farmer for instruction and practice in working a horse. Obtaining baskets made by relatives on the reserve, he sold them door to door until he had enough cash to buy an old horse, and he began to clear the land. In contacts with local residents, he carefully gathered information on how to move the stones so prevalent in New Hampshire hills and made neat walls around his fields. From others, he asked about the care of fruit trees and obtained seedlings, with which he began his small orchard of apples, pears, and plums. Grandmother Mary was already skilled in the raising of beans and corn, and he brought her seeds and knowledge of other vegetables. Soon, they produced all the food they needed for their growing family.

Grandfather had another skill which he adapted to new use. In Canada, he cut black ash and from it prepared splint for making baskets. He found black ash growing in New Hampshire and knew the local chair factories manufactured splint chairs. Improving on the simple machine he used on the reserve to split ash, he began to supply the local factories with a high grade of splint. This business grew until he had to erect a small back-yard shop employing several men to satisfy the demand for his product.

Somewhere between [after] the time he made an X to complete the transfer of land in 1872, he mastered the reading of English. My aunts and mother relate how he regularly read to them from the Bible, translating it as he went along into the Abenaki language for Grandmother Mary. He became active in his church, and went as a delegate to a state convention. And he applied his religious and cultural beliefs to his everyday life. Anyone who was in his house at mealtime, peddler, beggar, or friend, sat at his table and shared the family food. A woman living nearby as a child, in her old age told my aunts that their father had regularly given her widowed mother food and firewood when they had none, thus literally saving their lives.

Grandfather came to this, which had been his native land, an immigrant. Like so many other immigrants, he called on a great depth of courage to leave the home he knew and face an uncertain future, and once here, to overcome prejudice and hardship to build a new and better life for his family. Grandfather and fellow immigrants, from wherever they came, were all examples boundless courage.

Aunt Mary and Uncle Frank

Aunt Mary, my mother's oldest sister, was born on the Odanak Reserve in Canada in 1877 and came to this country at the age of one. Her parents made the momentous decision to emigrate when Grandfather Israel's trapline no longer could provide a living for his family, and they eventually settled in Keene NH. Oral tradition, derived from my aunts (Mary's younger sisters) and my mother, who was twenty years younger than this sister, does not describe Mary's childhood. However, I know her formal education ended at the eighth grade.

The stories about Mary begin when she was sent to Boston to apprentice as a seamstress when she was about twenty-five years of age. While living in that city, she met a young man of thirty-three who was a native of Keene, and was in Boston to learn photography, and he began to "pay court" to Mary. Before they returned to New Hampshire, Frank asked Mary's hand in marriage, and when she accepted, he gave her a pearl ring and pin, to seal the engagement. However, when they returned to New Hampshire at the end of their training, Mary to live with her parents and the six siblings left at home, Frank to maintain the household for his sister and widowed Mother, they found his family firmly opposed to the Indian from the poor section of town.

Frank felt he was duty bound to provide for his mother and sister, in those days long before Social Security, and he also realized that Mary could not live at peace in the same household with his outspoken mother. Thus, they began a long courtship which only ended in marriage when his mother died seven years later.

All through those years Frank called on Mary, with Grandfather Israel's approval, each Sunday evening and upon such holidays as he could manage. Mary entertained her betrothed in the living area of my grandparents' home, which included the kitchen, a large dining table, and a few rocking chairs for guests. Mary, often in winter, bought the ingredients and baked scalloped oysters for Frank and herself. I still have the old baking dish she used. My mother could not remember a time when Frank did not come calling on Mary, and it was he who gave her her first and only doll. The other aunts recalled that Frank took them to Fourth of July celebrations and brought them fruit at Christmas.

During those years Frank and Mary, with the limited help that Grandfather Israel could provide, managed to acquire a piece of land next to that of her family. Later, Frank purchased a small unoccupied farmhouse situated a short distance away and had it moved onto their lot. It took him many months, using what money and time he could spare after caring for his mother and sister, to put the house into livable condition.

Mary and Frank were married in 1910, after a decent interval following his mother's death. Frank was forty years old and Mary thirty-two, and they finally moved into the house which had been so long in preparation. They could now begin to plan, instead of dream, for a future. Frank decided the house was not large enough to accommodate a family, and so embarked on a project to raise the roof, which would add four upstairs bedrooms to the living space. The bedrooms gradually emerged, but children did not.

Several years later, Frank became aware that his unmarried sister, to whom he had signed over their family home upon their mother's death, and who had insisted upon her ability to provide for herself, was in failing health and experiencing financial difficulties. Bearing in mind the unused space in their home, Mary agreed with Frank that they should take in his sister to live with them. They made the invitation, which was rudely refused. What made them think, she wanted to know, that she could for any reason live under the same roof with an Indian?

And so the four extra bedrooms were unoccupied throughout the lifetimes of Mary and Frank. It was only after their deaths that the house, which Frank left to my mother, was occupied by a family with children.

Joseph Bruchac III

(b. 1942)

One of the most prolific contemporary Native American writers, Joseph Bruchac has written more than one hundred books for readers of every age, including novels, poetry, and retellings of traditional indigenous narratives. In the late 1970s, frustrated with the marginalization of good Native writing, he and his wife, Carol, started the Greenfield Literary Review Center. Bruchac has helped innumerable Native writers get recognition and has published many important anthologies, including *Returning the Gift*. Bruchac is also highly sought after as a storyteller and musical performer. With his sons, James and Jesse, and his sister Margaret, he continues to work to sustain Abenaki literature, language, and culture.

From Bowman's Store

[T]here were always relatively few French immigrants to the New World and many more men than women. Intermarriage between French men and Native women was a long-standing French colonial practice. Children from such unions in other places often were acknowledged by their fathers and sent to France. In North America, though, among Native peoples who universally share a deep regard for women, the culture in which those children were raised was almost always the Native one. However, the French last names gained either through baptism or through intermarriage set the stage for later generations, when Abenaki people could call themselves "French-Canadian."

The relatively sparse French populations in North America also made the French even more reliant than the English upon their Native allies. Whether as mercenaries or as full partners in the enterprise, the Abenaki people would make up the bulk of the many French raiding parties and armies that would engage in two centuries of warfare along the New England frontier. . . .

By the late 1700s, the Abenaki people of western New England had discovered that their survival depended upon taking one of a few paths. They could fight—and many did so. They could flee—and thousands did flee, seeking refuge in communities that became small united nations, incorporating the survivors of dozens of tribal nations. Or they could become invisible. They could cease being visibly Indian, and, in small settlements in the hills and valleys, carry on their lives. Swarthy-skinned, called Gypsy or French-Canadian, they would hide their language and practice their customs only in private. If they were light-skinned enough, they could even pass as white. But they would still hold the secret histories in their hearts.

As a small child I saw it happen. I watched it in a movie called *Northwest Passage*. It documented the eighteenth-century raid of Rogers's Rangers on the "St. Francis Indians"—the Abenaki village of Odanak. Spencer Tracy played Rogers, and he led his men bravely north to attack that village of cowardly, evil, marauding Indians.

In the movie there was a giant drum—a drum such as never existed in real life—big enough to dance on, in the center of that imagined Odanak. The Abenakis played a song of war on the drum until the righteous rangers arrived and silenced its voice. The beat of that war drum and the music played behind it in the soundtrack of *Northwest Passage* is echoed today when the Atlanta Braves play baseball—and thousands of white fans, dressed in burlesque imitations of Indian clothing, wearing headdresses of chicken feathers and garish war paint, chant and swing their arms in the tomahawk chop. At the end of *Northwest Passage*, after finally making his way back to civilization (which always begins where the lives of Indians end), Spencer Tracy stated, "Sir, I have the honor to report that the Abenakis are destroyed."

I was only six years old when I saw that movie, sitting next to my grandmother. For some reason, my grandfather had refused to see it. People cheered when Spencer Tracy spoke those victorious words. I don't remember cheering and I don't remember my grandmother cheering. But she knew the work of Kenneth Roberts, the author of the book on which the movie had been based. "The book," she said as we left the theater, "was different."

I think she was trying to comfort me, for that movie had made me afraid. I was afraid of many things when I was a little child and I didn't understand why. Loud noises frightened me. Big people who moved quickly frightened me. The dark frightened me—not the dark itself, but what might come out of it.

Burial Places along the Long River

For John Moody[6]

1.

I will not tell you how we know them,
those places along the river bank
where the wash and bend of Kwanitewk
will again reveal to the touch of sun
ancient bones of ancestors who were placed
beneath the sacred hands of fire.
Those places are where our villages were.

2.

One day, I canoed there with a friend
whose honest mind has not been twisted
by that strange disease the white men brought,
a sickness of the heart that they think
can only be cured by gold—men who,

as their ancestors hunted scalps,
now despoil our graves to sell pots and bones.

The river was thronged with other travelers
their motorboats eager to get them nowhere,
and like awkward eagles overhead,
a flight of ultralights whirred and snarled—
lawnmowers suburbanizing the sky.

3.

We turned into a quiet backwater.
There a great horned owl perched on a low limb.
Old ones, we said, we know you are here.
Then that spirit owl spread its wide wings
and floated, silent as a feather's fall
leading us back to a bank of blue clay, to a place
where the wind became a flute song,
where memory and vision were so intertwined
that for a time I forgot the name I carried
into this century and remembered more
than I had known before.

4.

I will not show you or tell you where,
where our spirits remain along the Long River,
so many of them upon both shores,
where the lift of flood still makes soil sweet
for the roots of com, the sustainer of life.
Our old ones rest below our feet,
under the lodges where children dream
of a grandmother's voice, a grandfather's song
still heard in the night after breath was gone.
Our burials show where our villages are.

Ndakinna

You cannot understand
our land with maps
lines drawn as if earth
were an animal's carcass
cut into pieces, skinned,
divided, devoured—
though always less eaten
than is thrown away.

See this land instead
with the wind eagle's eyes,
how the rivers and streams
link like sinew through a leather garment
sewed strong to hold our people,
patterns of flowers
close to the brown soil.

Do not try to know
this land by roads,
hard lines ripped
through old stones,
roads which still
call for blood
of not just those who cross,
wild eyes blinded
by twin suns startling the night,
but also those who seek to follow
the headlong flow
atop that dark frost
unthawed by the sun—
though seasons and
the insistent lift
of the smallest seeds
seek, without ceasing,
space for the old soil.

Instead, let your feet
caress this soil
in the way of the deer
whose feet follow and form
trails through the ways
of least resistance,
knowing ridges and springs,
ways of wind
through the seasons,
the taste of green twig
and tender grass,
the sweet scent of rain
urged up from moist earth.

When you feel this land
when you taste this land
when you hold this land
as your lungs hold your breath

you will be the rattlesnake
always embracing earth with her passage,
you will be the salmon, a chant
whipped through the ripple,
you will be the deermouse,
small feet stitching the night,
you will be the bear,
thunder held in soft steps,
when your songs see this land
when your ears sing this land
you will be this land
you will be this land.

Carol Willette Bachofner

(b. 1947)

Carol Bachofner is Abenaki, Scottish, French, and English by birth. Her poems and essays have been published in *Genocide of the Mind: New Native American Writing*, *My Home as I Remember*, the *En'owkin Journal of First Peoples*, *Prairie Schooner*, *The 2008 Poets' Guide to New Hampshire*, the *Comstock Review*, *Maine Taproots*, the *Cream City Review*, CT *Review*, *Crab Orchard Review*, *Cider Press Review*, *Dogwood*, and others. She has an M FA in poetry from the Vermont College of Fine Arts and is the author of four books of poetry, most recently *Native Moons, Native Days* (2012), a collection reflecting Abenaki culture. Bachofner is the current poet laureate of Rockland, Maine (2012–16). "The Old Man's Walk" first appeared in *The 2008 Poets' Guide to New Hampshire*. The other poems below appear in *Native Moons, Native Days*.

Abenaki Divorce

Nkamosa   *Get out!*
Alemosa   *Go back!*
To your mother!

I leave a bundle
(his belongings, nothing else)
by the door.

Without fanfare,
I remit him back
        to where he started. *Nkamosa.*

If it were only that simple, that final.

16 years and I am finally rid of the last piece of him: a watch belonging
    to his uncle.
        It was time.

I still see his name
on the check he writes

every month. I'd prefer a credit card
payment   direct deposit   no handwriting.

To rid yourself of a
cantankerous man and all of his
detritus:

> *lay a line of blessed tobacco*
> *along the doors and windows;*
> *smudge yourself with sage and cedar,*
> *dance with your hair down*
> *at the moon's waning.* Alemosa.

Winter Bringer

Winter Bringer:
my name in tribal language, the moon bringing
winter, bringing me. Ice hangs outside
the delivery room windows, *pkwamiak,*
like teeth from an old smile, like drips of cream
down the sides of the bowl where gingerbread
soaks up five-hundred-year old snow.

In the Abenaki Manner

We turn to the sea, feel the tide pulling,
see something coming. We turn our hands in the earth
to the corn growing greener day by day,
spending time with her sisters, ready to feed us.

In our manner, *alnôbaiwi,* it is best to sleep with the head
in the east, making it easy to see the coming sun.
In our way, we are always facing something,
seeing what others don't see coming.

Naming Water

Gwantigok, Penobscot,
             Passamaquoddy, Pashipakokee,
long rivers, long through the land you flow
long through us will you flow,
flowing from where the rocks widen,
from where pollack feed us.

Piscataqua, Androscoggin, Cobbosseecontee,
             Olamantegok, Quahog,
where water lies between the hills
through the sheltering place,
to where sturgeon gather together
to red ochre river, color of our children.
Shellfish place, treaty-making place.

Sebastivcook, Seninebik,
             Skowhegan, Baskahegan,
our stories flow
through little channels,
bearing rocks and memories
from where salmon leap the falls
to broad open waters,

turning back to where wild onions grow,
with birch and ash along their backs,
long rivers of first light
through our families flowing:
Wazwtegok, Winoztegok,
             Zawakwtegw, Gwantigok.

             Ndakinna.

Wazôliinebi

Snow is water
that feeds us without walking

to the stream. *Beboniwi*, in the winter way,
snow lets us rest from the work we do,
from pulling corn and tomatoes
and canning squash that grew like hair
nourished by *wazôliinebi*
while we watched over them.
We turn in bed and listen to snow
whispering about corn.

The Old Man's Walk[7]

Franconia NH, May 2003

They (white men) say (declare officiously)
that sometime in the night (which night they do not know)
in the deep fog of the White Mountains,
The Old Man fell to his death
crumbling into Profile Lake.

In truth (so say the Abenaki, his relatives)
he has been struggling to go home
to his wife for years now. Under the watchful
protection of the fog people, he broke free
of the bolts and cables
that held him for decades.
Wlipamkaani, travel well,
Old Man, Grandfather of the Granite,
long-suffering husband, watchful ancestor.

There is a lot of falling being done these days,
but this old face did not fall. He took his long walk,
the walk we all take, alone, without fanfare
or time of death called by an attending physician.

I think he smiled, though he hadn't smiled
for a thousand years.
I think he smiled and called out *matosao*, enough,

trembled with longing for his wife and children,
and simply dove off the face of the mountain
into the mirror of time, into his own profile.

It is good sign that the Old Man decided to walk
the land again, free of the white man's cords of steel.
Ohn, hohn, Grandfather, *wligonebi*. . .
the water feels good against your brow.

Planting Moon Kikas

Plunging hands into warm earth
where worms have shed casts, have moved
and gone through every seed row,
we take care to plant
the way our ancestors taught, sisters
together for strength and company.
We lean on each other too, family stories wound
around and strong in the northeast wind that
blows off the sea, that tries our memory.

She is *wasawak*, squash.
You are *adebakwal*, beans.
Kakiknia, I am corn.

Burial Dress

Carefully   Prayerfully

Inside, outside   Sinew sewn

Our Ways   of   Old Days

Ash and Fire   Spirit home

Elk skin   Doe skin

Supple, softened   Forest grown

Breath dress   in   Death dress

Shell and Bead   Woman's own

Fingering   Fringing

Back, forth   Together alone

Gentle sway   of   Whitened frays

Platform and Pyre   Indian bones

Jibaaki

I want to enter the ground slowly,
sift down in ashy snow to the beach
when the sea is out.
I want you to burn me there
and watch the sun coming up
to get my spirit across the water
and into the sky, a process
not like *Bostoniwi* death rituals
with pink formalin replacing blood,
stitched up neck, wrist hidden
under the best outfit in the closet.

I want to be dressed
in the clothes I made, decorated
with shells I found, fringed around
the edges, like the sky in a storm.
Wrap me tight in my turtle blanket
so my arm won't suddenly jut out
scaring the partygoers. It's okay
to steam the lobster if you dig
a hole deep enough to meet
federal standards for public safety.
I think there might be rules
about burning an Indian woman
on the beach, even at low tide.

Cheryl Savageau

(b. 1950)

Cheryl Savageau (Abenaki/French) is a poet and visual artist whose work draws on family, traditional stories, history, and the land. She has been awarded fellowships by the National Endowment for the Arts and the Massachusetts Artists Foundation, and her work is widely anthologized. Her second book, *Dirt Road Home*, was a finalist for the Paterson Prize and was nominated for a Pulitzer Prize. She has taught at the University of New Mexico, the University of Massachusetts, Clark University, and the College of the Holy Cross. Her quilts, paintings, and assemblages have been on display at the Abbe Museum in Bar Harbor, Maine, and at the University of New Hampshire. Her most recent book is *Mother/Land*, the source of the first six poems below; the remaining three come from *Dirt Road Home*.

Poison in the Pond

I.

the skin on my arms burns
It is hot today and sticky
and poison is flowing
out of orange barrels
into the waters of the pond

my eyes burn my lips burn
my tongue is thick
I cannot swallow
my throat is
sore as strep

the fish are dying
turtles wash up on shore
the lilies shrivel
sweetflag blackens
cattails are ragged sticks

the floating island
has stopped wandering

but it is for our own good
they tell us and no one
leaves. we tough it out

those orange barrels
the bans on swimming
on eating fish

our lungs burn
the air is hot and thick

this pond used to want
to be a river
now it wants to be
a meadow

these orange barrels
will teach it who's boss

11.

the baby is born
wrong there is
something
wrong with the
baby something
is wrong

there are seizures
there is something
about the brain
the parents are
teenagers
did you take drugs
you must've taken drugs

pond water laps the shore

you can see straight
to the bottom

III.

not everyone is tired
tired when they go to bed
tired when they wake up
too tired to answer the phone
too tired to get dressed too tired
to fix a meal, to take a walk
not everyone is tired
but lots of us are

IV.

it is twenty years
since the poison
barrels floated on flint pond
some of us are in our twenties
some in our thirties
some fifty or older
we ache ache ache we can't
digest our food
we sleep but don't sleep
we push ourselves and crash
we lie in bed and watch tv
don't touch us our skin burns
there are bites from insects
nobody sees water
dripping on shoulders
when there is no rain our feet
run beneath our blankets like
dogs dreaming of the chase
our bones have
turned to sand

v.

it is for your own good
it is all in your mind
it is depression
it is a new disease
it is an old disease only
nobody

knows its name
it is inherited
it is a french-canadian disease
it is a woman's disease
it is all in your head
there's no such thing

vi.

here
take these
little orange pills
it's for
your own good

Smallpox

> ". . . some of us did not die"
> —June Jordan

i.

it is the animals' revenge
for being held in pens
bred for meat
and docility
we don't have it here

II.

it is not the big pox
syphilis
which they also
got from sheep
we don't have it here

III.

there is nothing small
about it
when it comes
the back aches,
the head hurts,
the body burns,
the skin erupts

IV.

as power often does
it comes in four
manifestations

the kind and distinct pox
the confluent
the purples
the bloody pox

it comes in four
manifestations

this does not surprise us

V.

in other places
where women
are healers

the pox has
whispered
secrets
in constantinople
in africa
women search out
the mildest cases
harvest liquid
from the pustules
scratch it lightly
into outstretched
arms

VI.

in boston
in london
people with
scratched arms
live

VII.

none of us
have scratched arms
none of us have
mild cases
we bleed beneath our skin
that sloughs off
our living flesh

VIII.

it is some small thing
in us that keeps us
close relatives
some small thing
it is our blood type

it is some allele
some collection of genes
it is in our blood
my relatives

IX.

I have measles
for the second time
it is because I am
indian I know
though no one
will say so
indians don't have
immunity I read it
somewhere lots of them
died will I die
I ask my mother
sleep now
she answers
there is a dark cloth
over the lamp
the light still
hurts my eyes
I am sleeping in her bed
outside the bedroom door
voices mumble
my ears
itch from inside
my skin
is tight and hot

X.

it is after
the bostoniak
doctors learn
to inoculate

it is after
the bostoniak
doctors learn
to vaccinate
it is after
they know how
to prevent it
that they give
the blankets
that will cause it

XI.

there is
no one here
left to take
care of the sick

XII.

some of us
don't die
some of us
don't
some of us
don't die

Where I Want Them

on the lids of my eyes on the nape
of my neck across the top of my
shoulder down the side of my
arm grazing the hair and over the
knuckle of each finger and then
the fingertips one at a time in
the center of my palm on the tender

inside of my forearm in the crease
of my underarm the hollow of my
throat between my breasts circling
each nipple circling my navel following
the line of my backbone to the small
of my back on the mound of each
cheek on the tender underside of my
ass on the backs of my knees on the
inside of my thighs on the lips of the
flower where you will find me
trembling

Swift River—Kancamagus

. . . for Lisa[8]

we pull off the road
to this place
where in summer
swimmers
loll on the rocks
like otters
grandmothers
and grandbabies
wade in the icy
shallows where
sand has been pounded
soft and teenagers
dive into deeper
pools and come
out shining
beaded with water

today it is just us
and we walk out
over the boulders

find one mid-river
and sit back-to-back

we have just driven
down the Kancamagus
from the high spot
that separates
the watersheds
one flowing east.
the other west and south
the directions of her
people and mine

We laugh to realize
she is facing west
I am facing east
we've done this without
thinking
someday someone will
find two women in rock
back to back
on this mountain
facing sunset, facing dawn

Before Moving on to Plymouth from Cape Cod—1620

. . . for Donna and John[9]

they find what looks like
a grave
what looks like a grave
a grave and they
dig it up
they find a grave
it looks like
a grave
and they dig

it up
they dig it up the grave
it looks like they
dig it up and
they dig it up and
it looks like
a grave and
they
dig it up

Amber Necklace

inspired by ants
I tasted the sap
that oozed in great drops
from the bark of the pine
it tasted like its needles smelled
like winter like mountains or early morning
too strong for more than just a taste too sticky
to roll into the ball I wanted to carry in my hands like
a golden marble. I worried for the tree
was it hurt? I asked *no just leaking* my father told me
it's made so much extra food
he told me how even in deepest winter
you will not starve in a pine grove
how there is always food within
how the sweet globules turned over millions of years
hard as stone how the insects were caught Inside
preserved forever
it is not the insects I want but the sweetness they signify
I am caught in the sweet amber
of my mother's hair
nourished
by the light and dark of her
yes and the sticky
the too hard to manage

the I can't get it
off my hands
I want it now
those moments
of petrified love
where we first find ourselves
caught
before we know
what will preserve us

Trees

—for my father, Paul J. Savageau Sr.

You taught me the land so well
that all through my childhood
I never saw the highway,
the truckstops, lumberyards,
the asphalt works,
but instead saw the hills,
the trees, the ponds on the south end
of Quinsigamond that twined
through the tangled underbrush
where old cars rusted back to earth,
and rubber tires made homes for fish.

Driving down the dirt road home,
it was the trees you saw first,
all New England a forest.
I have seen you get out of a car,
breathe in the sky, the green
of summer maples, listen for the talk
of birds and squirrels, the murmur
of earthworms beneath your feet.
When you looked toward the house,
you had to shift focus,

as if it were something
difficult to see.

Trees filled the yard
until Ma complained,
where is the sun.
Now you are gone,
she is cutting them down
to fill the front with azaleas.

The white birch you loved,
we love. Its daughters
are filling the back.
Your grandchildren play
among them. We have taught them
as you taught us, to leave
the peeling bark, to lean
their cheeks against
the powdery white and hear
the heartbeat of the tree.
Sacred, beautiful, companion.

Looking for Indians

My head filled with tv images
of cowboys, warbonnets and renegades,
I ask my father
what kind of Indian are we, anyway.
I want to hear Cheyenne, Apache, Sioux,
words I know from television
but he says instead
Abenaki. I think he says Abernathy
like the man in the comic strip
and I know that's not Indian.

I follow behind him
in the garden

trying to step in his exact footprints,
stretching my stride to his.
His back is brown in the sun
and sweaty. My skin is brown
too, today, deep in midsummer,
but never as brown as his.

I follow behind him like this
from May to September
dropping seeds in the ground,
watering the tender shoots
tasting the first tomatoes,
plunging my arm, as he does,
deep into the mounded earth
beneath the purple-flowered plants
to feel for potatoes
big enough to eat.

I sit inside the bean teepee
and pick the smallest ones
to munch on. He tests
the corn for ripeness
with a fingernail, its dried silk
the color of my mother's hair.
We watch the winter squash grow hips.

This is what we do together
in summer, besides the fishing
that fills our plates unfailingly
when money is short.

One night
my father brings in a book.
See, he says, Abenaki,
and shows me the map
here and here and here
he says, all this
is Abenaki country.
I remember asking him

what did they do
these grandparents
and my disappointment
when he said no buffalo
roamed the thick new england forest
they hunted deer in winter
sometimes moose, but mostly
they were farmers
and fishermen.

I didn't want to talk about it.
Each night my father
came home from the factory
to plant and gather,
to cast the line out
over the dark evening pond,
with me, walking behind him,
looking for Indians.

French Girls Are Fast

French girls are fast
I find this out
before I know what it means
Two days in the Irish-Catholic school
my mother thought would keep me safe from sin
and the name is following me around.
Frenchie, hey, Frenchie,
ooh la la
the Irish boys leer
staring at the roundness
I am not ashamed of
the Irish girls still properly flat
beneath their uniform jackets

I learn quickly to sneer
light my cigarette with a wooden match

flicked against the brick school wall
taste the smoke, roll it over my tongue
and exhale upward in a gesture
of exquisite boredom
I tighten my face, turn
to look them up and down
and spit out the prayer
of this place—
eat it, assholes

Years later it is a grandmother
who accuses me
and I hear it again
French girls are fast
who am I to say otherwise
my belly pushing outward
with her grandson's child

She admonishes me
not to rest my hands on my belly

You'll ruin the baby
touching yourself like that . . .

My hands fly away for a moment
like frightened birds
looking for another place to perch
then settle back down
She shrugs and turns away

Later she digs out a blanket
she bought at Niagara Falls
from those Indians, you know,
she tells me, shaking her head,
clicking her tongue
but the blanket is nice, she says.
you can use it

I will not tell her now
my father's family is Indian,

that the blood was mixed in me
generations ago
My hands accept the white wool,
finger the stripes
of red, yellow, black, green
I draw it over me, the child,
my unruly hands, feel my body slowing.
getting ready for the long push ahead

Donna Laurent Caruso
(b. 1951)

Donna Laurent Caruso worked for over twenty years in marketing, advertising, and public relations in the manufacturing sector in Massachusetts before becoming a freelance editor, writer, photographer, and publisher. She has written for newspapers including *Fitchburg Sentinel and Enterprise, Lowell Sun,* and *Indian Country Today;* for the latter, she has covered issues concerning many of the people and authors represented in this volume, including the Nipmucs' Deer Island Memorial and Jesse Bruchac's and Robert Peters's book publications. Caruso has also written for numerous nonprofit newsletters and has done a great deal of editorial work, including her assistance to Larry Spotted Crow Mann (Nipmuc), whose fiction appears in this book. She studied with prominent journalists at Suffolk University in Boston and attended Boston University's Graduate School of Public Communication. The story and poems below are from her first chapbook.

The Removal Period

People from a Native American cultural center from central Massachusetts were invited to participate in the first, and possibly last, pow wow at the Native American Indian Center of Boston (NAICOB). While the cultural center is primarily a meeting place, the Boston center serves hundreds of federally recognized Native Americans, providing health and employment assistance within a forty-mile radius of its building. Since the state-owned building was, in 2003, worth millions of dollars, its sale could bring much-needed revenue to the cash-strapped state. And so . . . there are plans to remove, relocate . . . displace, the Indians from the property. Managers of NAICOB *organized this pow wow to show that there is a lot of support for the building to remain in its current use.*

The little band of seven People from central Massachusetts traveled to Copley Square in Boston using the underground public transportation from Park Street, before they found that because of construction on the line, they had to go above ground and take a shuttle bus from Copley Square to their destination in Jamaica Plain. As they waited on the corner by the Boston Public Library in their finest clothes, bus after bus passed. Roy cracked jokes to Therese about how they wouldn't be late if the pow wow began on Indian time and that they would have already arrived over in Jamaica Plain if they had "moccasined it" directly along the Old Nashaway Trail (Route 2), as in days gone by.

The People eventually reached the event at NAICOB and were happy to be welcomed to the grounds to meet friends, dance, sing, eat, and buy from the vendors. The emcee at this pow wow was from the central Plains of North America (Turtle Island); he told the crowd that this was the first pow wow he had attended since his Grandmother died the year before and that his preparation *of the ground* for the pow wow helped him recover from the sorrow he felt for her loss. He shared with Everyone that his Grandmother had taught him as a boy how to sew star quilts. And so, as Therese danced Within the Circle, she prayed for all the Grandmothers who have been there to raise and to teach and to protect their grandchildren and thereby help save them in large and small ways. Roy and the other men at the Drum sang a special Honoring Song for her.

Therese and Roy needed to be home earlier than their other friends, so they set out alone for the return trip. Since she wasn't sure which bus to take, Therese motioned toward a bus and asked a driver whether he was headed to Copley Square. He affirmed that they had the right bus but stared intently at both of them. Therese realized too late, and with concern, that she had gestured with what was in her hand: an *ostawe onakara*, or mud-turtle rattle.

"Hey, I am Taino, from Puerto Rico," the bus driver offered. Therese had just learned the weekend before that Janie, one of the local pow wow dancers that she had admired for years, is Taino. "Our people hid in the mountains," Janie said, "even with wave after wave of conquerors. We are still fighting."

"So! Who are you?" asked the bus driver.

Now, Therese had not quite adjusted from leaving the protective, accepting environment of the pow wow grounds. Outside of the grounds, even today one does not usually state aloud one's tribal affiliation without being prepared to respond to questions and comments about blood quantum, the questioner's own "Indian princess" ancestors, casinos, or tribal recognition or to be concerned about whether northeast woodlands ancestors had fought one another. But here was a man who did not veil his identity: "I am Taino," *spoken aloud in Boston.*

"Well, he is Cree," Therese said to buy a little time by telling the bus driver about her First Nations friend. "And I, I am Pocumtuck."

Realizing that the bus driver had never heard of the Pocumtuck, Therese said, "you Taino folk aren't supposed to exist anymore, either." They all laughed and then, more seriously, the driver told them that *his* father is still resisting in the hills.

~

In addition to her *ostawe onakara*, Therese held three turkey feathers in a needlepoint wrap of a repeated yellow, blue, and green peacock eye that was executed on a twenty-four-point canvas with embroidery floss. She carries turkey feathers *and* needlepoint so that when she dances, both her Indian and English ancestors are held within her hands.

The turkey feathers were Gifted to Therese: on three consecutive morning walks when she first moved to central Massachusetts, she would see a low, dark mound on the trail ahead; when she reached the general area and examined the ground, she would find a turkey feather. Each morning she carefully brought the Gift home and placed it in the blue-green, flecked ceramic pitcher and bowl her brother made in the hospital after his tour of duty.

The once densely wooded hills where the wild turkeys gifted Therese their feathers once rose protectively above her forty-year-old neighborhood. The hills are now clear-cut of trees and the bedrock has been dynamited, however, to level the land for condominiums as well as to "take" the smoky quartz granite. It took the neighborhood oaks all these past forty years to mature enough to produce acorns. So the neighborhood enclave below the hills, full of front-yard oaks, has now become a harbor for the wild turkeys *displaced* by the condominium development and mining operation. As she drove slowly by a group of turkeys gathered on a front lawn recently, they seemed to feed desperately on the acorns. Therese was inexplicably reminded of the historical late-1800s photograph of the last of the Kansa Indian women digging for wild turnip even as the pony soldiers surrounded their men. Survival, not a gift of a feather to a newcomer, drove these lawn-dwelling turkeys. As she drove away, Therese thought,

The land, oh the land where I was gifted three feathers is gone! Perhaps, perhaps it will be all right if the Grandfathers (the stones), even with rearranged molecules, are hauled nearby and become the foundations for the new cell towers along the Mohawk Trail. Oh the People, my People, you who for thousands of generations stood on the hill now gone and signaled Our People on the top of the big mountain (Wachusett! Wachusett!) and from there signaled The People at the Harbor. For you, I pray the grandfathers have become a new rendition of the moccasin telegraph and I pray for the young construction worker from Arkansas who fell down, down, down while working on the new cell tower, his fall to newly deposited stone and gravel within view of my living room window, not at all "out in the middle of nowhere," as the city councilors want to claim.

~

Roy and Therese sat beside one another on the bus shuttle. Looking at her turkey feathers, she thought about how she had not embraced gift-giving the way some people are able to : she had been well-taught to accumulate, rather than to give away the things she doesn't need. Roy played with the mysteries of *his* cell phone, tried to call home. Therese watched the bus driver and marveled at how well he blended in with the city people, dressed as he was in a driver's uniform. Another bus blocked their way and everyone had to wait while the traffic built up behind them.

Their driver got out and helped convince the offending bus driver to move out of the way. When he returned to his driver's seat, Therese took note of his walk, his movement, his Indian way . . . and knew at once this Driver would never allow himself to completely assimilate, blend in *or forget.*

They finally approached Copley. Therese reached a decision. "This is from a sacred place," she said as she gifted the driver a turkey feather and passed it to him over the collection box. *"He need not know the sacred place is now only memory or that my brother is dead,"* she thought. "Thank you," the driver said with respect as he accepted the Gift. And Roy and Therese were gone, down underground, to catch the trolley to Park Street.

When they reached her car parked at Alewife, she asked Roy to drive the rest of the way home to Nashaway so that she could study her two remaining feathers and imagine the Taino fighting wave after wave of robbers. She imagined she could see the bus driver's father . . . *"I can see him . . . in the shadows . . . I can see him now, clearly . . . and I can see that he knows that a big old Pocumtuck woman and a little Cree guy have recognized and honored and gifted his son with a feather of the sacred wild turkey near the Harbor of Boston."*

The next day she brought her dogs to the beautiful meadow up on Alpine Drive in her hometown, named, she assumed, by settlers who mourned for the loss of their own alpine homeland. This land had been preserved in a conservation trust, she thought, so perhaps the landscape will not be blasted and hauled away. Therese would not let the dogs enter the woods that frame the meadow because it was the home of many deer. But she was drawn into the woods, absolutely could not help entering. Then she resisted the urge to roam and turned back to the car. There on the ground before her, nearly *blended in* with the rocky and muddy path, was a wild turkey feather. She picked it up, astounded by its size as well as by the Return of the gift and by her . . . *luck*. She brought the feather home and placed it with the others in her brother's blue-green, flecked ceramic pitcher. She knew the Circle was again complete.

They could, as Janie said, *go on fighting*.

(2004)

Nnd Haiku: A Trilogy

Red strengthens ocean
Current darkened, life ended
Dolphins mourn to whales

~

Ocean air slams coast
Firestorm burns, winds beat inland
Seeds wait centuries in cave

~

Shifting rainbow shawls
Sweetgrass braided, bundled, hung
Sage smolders in tree-ear bowl

(2004)

Abenaki Filmmaker Earns Luminaria Award

SANTA FE, N.M.—A Luminaria Award for Lifetime Achievement in Film
was presented to Aln8bak (Abenaki) filmmaker Alanis Obomsawin by
the Canadian Consulate at the recent Santa Fe Film Festival.

Obomsawin was born in N'dakinna (Abenaki for "our land") near Lebanon, New Hampshire, and returned in infancy with her mother to the
village of Odanak, the historical village of aboriginal refugees of southern
New England who fled north after King Philip's War.

One of Obomsawin's family members in particular has been credited
with naturally preserving her Abenaki culture by immersing her in story
and song as a child. Until she was aged nine, Obomsawin's second cousin
Theophile Panadis taught her the Abenaki lifeways. When the family
moved to an area without other tribal people, Obomsawin held on to
Panadis's teachings.

She became a professional singer-songwriter, performing at various venues around the world. Two producers from Canada's public film producer
and distributor, the National Film Bureau, heard Obomsawin's Abenaki
singing in 1967 on television and invited her to consult on an aboriginal
story film. She then began to produce her own material, creating more
than 30 documentaries.

Interestingly, it is the armed conflict between aboriginal Canadians
and the municipal, provincial, and federal Canadian governments that
is the subject of Obomsawin's most well-known documentary. Her four-
film series on the Oka Crisis of 1990 documents what the *Toronto Globe*

and Mail newspaper referred to as "the . . . most significant event to take place on Canadian soil since the Second World War."

In 1535 France claimed the aboriginal village of Hochelaga (known today as contemporary Montreal) as its own. In 1990 government and private plans to construct luxury housing and a private golf course on "the Pines," land that was disputed in a Mohawk land claim, brought about open conflict. Quebec police were replaced by units from the Canadian army after a police officer was killed in a raid to remove Mohawk people from their land. Journalists were evacuated or forcibly removed from the area.

Obomsawin stayed and shot her film without a crew, using slow speed on her sound recorder to stretch out her audio supply.

Unique "Native-view" methods of storytelling allow the Oka documentaries to explain for the first time how Natives are supported by other tribal peoples around the globe—describing to the world a people of pan-nationalistic, as opposed to imperialistic, belief. At the time of the events described, the closing by other Native supporters of the Mercier Bridge into Montreal brought world attention and understanding to the dominant culture.

The first of the series, *Kanehsatake: 270 Years of Resistance*, documented the uprising. *My Name is Kahentiiosta* followed; it is about a Kahnawake Mohawk woman who was arrested after the 78-day standoff. *Spudwrench: Kahnawake Man* profiles Randy Horne, a steelworker from the community. Finally, Obomsawin recently completed *Rocks at Whiskey Trench*.

Obomsawin also produced, wrote, and narrated the 2007 *Gene Boy Came Home*, about Abenaki Vietnam War vet Eugene Benedi. *Waban-Aki: People from Where the Sun Rises* is a documentary of conversations with people who still live in the village where she was raised. In 2003 she produced *Our Nationhood*, about the Listuguj Mi'gmaq who are determined to live off their traditional lands, and *Is the Crown at War with Us?*, about the Mi'kmaq of Esgenoopetitj, who battle for their fishing rights. Other films include *Incident at Restigouche* (police raid of another Mi'kmaq reserve), *Richard Cardinal: Cry from a Diary of a Metis Child* (adolescent suicide), and *No Address* (Montreal's homeless).

Obomsawin has received awards ranging from the Order of Canada to honorary doctorates.

Margaret M. Bruchac

(b. 1953)

Both a scholar and a performer, Dr. Bruchac is an assistant professor of anthropology and coordinator of Native American and Indigenous studies at the University of Pennsylvania. As a storyteller and musician, she has been featured at the First Nations Festival, Historic Deerfield, Old Sturbridge Village, and hundreds of other venues. Her book *Malian's Song* was awarded the American Folklore Society's Aesop Award. Her academic essays on Native history, material culture, and repatriation have appeared in *Indigenous Archaeologies: Decolonizing Theory and Practice; Captive Histories: Captivity Narratives, French Relations and Native Stories of the 1704 Deerfield Raid*; and *Museum Anthropology*, among others. As the 2011–12 recipient of both a Ford Fellowship and a School for Advanced Research Fellowship, Dr. Bruchac is working on a new book manuscript, titled "Consorting with Savages: Indigenous Informants and American Anthropologists" for the University of Arizona Press. The two selections below were published in *Dreaming Again: Algonkian Poetry.*

War Wounds: Sophie Senecal Goes to Washington

INTRODUCTION

Soldier's Certificate #208738, housed in the Civil War records in the National Archives, identifies my great-grandfather, Lewis Bowman, as follows: 5′ 8½″, dark complexion, black hair, and black eyes; born July 20, 1844, Canada (no birth certificate); occupation: farmer and laborer; resident of Porter's Corners, Town of Greenfield, Saratoga County; previous residences in Canada and Vermont. Enlisted August 29, 1864, as a private in Company E, Sixty-Ninth New York Infantry, serving under Commander Peter W. Sweeney; wounded by a Minié ball at Hatcher's Run, Virginia, and gunshot in left knee, right thigh, left arm, right hip; medical discharge August 14, 1865, aged twenty-one years.

Lewis Bowman earned a disability pension of twelve dollars a month for thirty years. The shrapnel in his body (as my grandfather liked to put it) helped to pay for the care of two wives, thirteen children, and a one-hundred-acre farm. In 1890 Lewis's mother, Sophie Senecal, began drawing a widow's pension of eight dollars a month based on her son's service.

Pension attorneys processed thousands of military claims each year, exacting their fees directly from the funds due to veterans and widows. Attorney George E. Lemon handled more than 125,000 claims, tending to many veterans of color who were too illiterate to get what was owed them without assistance. It is doubtful that his clients knew how much money their attorney was raking in; in some cases, Lemon interceded for clients he never even met. Lemon's dealings inspired legislation that reformed the system so benefits would go directly to veterans and their families rather than to lawyers.

What follows is an excerpt from a longer essay that imagines Sophie Senecal's trip to Washington to meet with attorney George Lemon, who negotiated the family pensions.

WASHINGTON DC, JULY 22, 1890

"There you go, Mrs. Bowman, just make your mark on this here line, and you can collect your government pay."

Attorney George Lemon, sweltering in his silk brocade waistcoat, topcoat pinching at his ever-increasing girth, beaver hat cocked rakishly to one side, leans across the writing desk, pen in hand. He works his cigar around to the other side of his mouth, scattering ashes. As the ashes whisper their way across the documents, Sophie Senecal sees the eye of the eagle in the U.S. seal blink—there—just for a moment. She slowly eases back into the unfamiliar chair, narrowing her eyes.

"What's the matter, missus? No speak English?"

Sophie is remembering the way the nuns taught her to speak French, recalling the easy way the traders at the markets toss around English words, and musing about the strange marks she used to see young Joseph Laurent making in his books when he should have been learning his catechisms. Then that eagle on paper catches her eye again, arrows in his claws, dripping blood. She glances up at Mister Lemon, the sharpness of her gaze cutting through the cigar smoke.

"Speak fine, Monsieur. Read? No read. You read to me."

Sophie lets her mind drift as the man spins out a story that she knows is not written in the marks scratched on that page. Lemon is waxing poetic about a "grateful government," our "Red Brothers," and an "ancient alliance," speaking in those strange tones that all the Bostoniak use when they are saying one thing and hiding another. When he gets around to actually reading the document, every time one of those "money" words comes up, Lemon reflexively reaches into his pocket, fondling loose coins with his stubby fingers.

Sophie is passing the time wondering about some things that have troubled her for a long time . . . why her mother sent her off to the nuns at St. Francois instead of off into the bush with her cousins, and why that foolish man Charles Bowman insisted on working for the railroad and stopped peddling baskets. It was better, living the old way. Sure, hard traveling. You followed the seasons and the rivers, and them borders didn't mean nothin'. You went on back down to Missisquoi in the spring, seeing the cousins that stayed around there year-round, spent time on the shores of Bitownbawk when the lake was just starting to warm up, then followed them old trails over the hills and south to Nebizonbik, the place of springs. When she was a girl there wasn't so many of them tourists you see now, swarming all over the old places. *"At least dey be willin' ta pay good money for baskets,"* she thinks.

Sophie reaches into her tobacco pouch and finds the cross that Sister Anne gave her, to keep her safe from the Protestants and heathens. She smiles at the childlike superstitions of the French. She can't wait to get out into the open air where she can light her pipe.

"You understand how this all works, missie?" Lemon is saying.

Sophie pulls her blanket closer around her shoulders and nods, encouraging him to keep talking. The sound of his voice allows her to keep her thoughts to herself. As Lemon drones on, she tries to remember how it was that her son ended up rooming with them Irish boys in Troy. Maybe it was the music. That damn French fiddle. Or the drink.

"Says here, on this here Army of the You-ny-ted States Cer-ti-fy-cate of Dis-a-bil-i-tee."

Lemon roundly pronounces out each syllable of the official words as if he is speaking to a child. One eyebrow raised is all it takes for Sophie to still his tongue.

"Hmph . . . well, your boy Lewis, he was 'wounded in battle at Hatcher's Run, Virginia, on the twenty-fifth day of March, eighteen sixty and five, caught a Minié ball in the left leg, gunshot wound in the right thigh, partial paralysis

of the knee, gunshot wound in the left arm near the shoulder . . .' pretty well shot up, I'd say. Half disability pay should manage. You live with your son, Mrs. Bowman?"

Sophie doesn't answer immediately. Her body is sitting in an over-stuffed chair in Lemon's stuffy office, but her spirit is out walking, again, in that place north of Nebizonbik, peeling the sticky sap from *mesazeso*, searching for *koaiagwodawas.* "Christ, you be a heavy boy," she remembers half dragging, half carrying Lewis to the shelter up near the Palmertown spring, on the old northern trail. Every muscle in her body ached with the memory of every sick person she'd ever tended, and those southern bullets made Lewis heavier than any of them. She recalls her warrior son sitting by the fire, wrapped in an old trade blanket, his rifle resting against the pine tree behind him, his mouth filled with the bitter yellow root-threads, *lasawiam*, to take away his hunger for Irish whiskey.

In an opulent lawyer's office in Washington, George Lemon refills his whiskey glass from a crystal decanter, swallows hard, and clears his throat.

In Sophie's memory, Lewis rises up from the fire, ready to set foot on the northward trail, leaving Yankee men and their wars far behind. Sophie shifts herself in the chair, her bones creaking, and speaks.

"No. Canada."

While Sophie parlays with Attorney Lemon, her son hears her thoughts, listening in the way the old ones used to do. On a farm to the far north, in the lower hills of the Adirondacks, old Lewis Bowman is standing in the front yard, leaning heavily on a cane, facing south as he watches his boys, Jack and Jesse, plant them twin maple trees. His wives, Mary and Alice, go bustling past, carrying water to the barn. Lewis nods to them and then chuckles, whispering under his breath. *"Wlioni, Nokomes, ktsi wlioni. I hear you, Mother. Now leave me be—I got horses and sons and women to tend to."*

Attorney Lemon smirks and responds.

"Your boy got around, didn't he? Canada, Vermont, Albany, Troy, now he's got himself settled onto a little farm up in Porters' Corners. Ain't that just north of Saratoga Springs? Now that's a real swell place, resort town, ain't it? Them Injun basketmakers used to camp out at the springs in the summers. Dirty heathens makin' them purty little baskets."

Sophie's eyes narrow ominously. But she shrugs, turns her face, and sighs. Lemon shudders involuntarily, hikes back his shoulders, puffs on his cigar, shakes out more ashes, and returns to reading the legal document. Sophie is wondering why she let her sister talk her into riding those belly-rolling, lice-infested, soot-drenched railcars all the way to Washington just to listen to this fat man speak. Hoping he is almost done, she catches him checking his watch.

"So, Mrs. Bowman, are we agreed then?"

Sophie reads the letters that spell her name and insists on a correction.

"No missus nothing. Senecal. You write M Y name on dat paper."

Lemon shakes his head. This ignorant Indian probably isn't even married to that man she called a husband, hell, maybe she's got another one waiting back in the bush after the first one died. No matter, it's just another mark, just another easy twenty-five dollars. He writes "Sophie Senecal, alias Mrs. Bowman," forges the name of his secretary as a witness, and then signs with a practiced flourish. He hands Sophie the pen. She carefully draws one line, then another. A crossroads. A claw mark. It has to be done.

Lemon pulls out his purse and starts counting out paper money, but Sophie's chin lifts and her voice rises, just enough to make her point.

"Nda. Silver."

George Lemon smiles and reaches into his pocket. These Indians and their silver—superstitious bastards. *"Maybe I should raise my cut,"* he thinks. *"Let's see, the allotment to widowed dependent mothers rakes in $10 a month, $120 a year . . . hell, my $25 cut ain't hardly worth the trouble. Gotta raise my rates."* He shrugs and counts out eight silver dollars, loudly rapping each one on the table.

". . . Five, and six, and seven, and that's eight. Paid in full! Now that's your first month, see. You'll have to march yourself on down to the Sheffield Post Office to collect this same amount every month, long as you're still standing."

Lemon laughs at his own joke and then stares into the smooth brown face of this woman who claims to be in her seventies and wonders if she ever worked a day in her life.

(November 2002)

Praying Spoils the Hunting

—based on excerpts from the Jesuit Relations

In 1642, the Jesuit Superior, Vimont,
complained of the wicked conduct
of the Algonquins above Trois Rivieres.
"There was nothing but superstitions among them,"
he wrote,
"naught but outrages and calumnies against our Christians."
The Father vigorously opposed the wildnesses of these Indians,
fearing his good deeds
earnest thoughts
and good prayers
were all for naught.

In 1642, the Algonquins of the Island complained to Vimont.
"It is a strange thing," said they,
"since prayer has come into our cabins,
our former customs are of no service."
"I have seen the time," said one
"when my dreams were true;
when I had seen Moose or Beavers in sleep,
I would take some.
When our Soothsayers felt the enemy coming,
that came true.
Now, our dreams and our prophecies are no longer true."
Prayer has spoiled the hunting.
Prayer has spoiled our dreams.
Prayer has spoiled everything.

Vimont characterized these losses
as God's rightful punishment for their unrighteousness.
"God is angry with you," he told them.
And they agreed.

"If you had stayed in your own country,"
they said to Vimont,

"without speaking to us of God,
we would not know him.
He would not say a word to us,
he would not know us,
he would not see us
and he would not look for us."

"Before you came here," said they,
"even the French did not say so many prayers;
they only made the sign of the Cross,
and even then, some did not know how."
"It is you who have said the prayers
It is you who have called God to us."

The prayers, they told him, had no regard for the weather.
The prayers did not stop for rain or snow.
The prayers did not pause for the cold.
The prayers did not lift a basket, haul a canoe, gut a deer, or catch a
    single fish.
The prayers did not feed the hungry.
The prayers scared the animals.
Yet every day Vimont was shouting for more prayers.
"It is a strange thing," said they, "that you cannot remain quiet."

The Father cautioned them.
"If I do not teach you
if I leave you in the quiet
if I abandon you
you will burn in Hell
and never find salvation."

Three centuries later,
the Algonquins
built a fine little church
on the site of the original Jesuit Church
which, like the Hudson Bay Post, mysteriously caught fire and burned
    to the ground.

Now, on foot, by truck, by boat, by snowmobile,
they come to that church in every season
to pray.
In flowing words
with drums and tobacco
with guitar and flute
with sweetgrass burning
they sing to Kateri Tekakwitha
they pray to Manitou
they call the game.
"We are grateful for your generosity
we pray for your patience
we thank you for your sacrifice."
They call their four-legged, winged, and finned relatives back into
    being
back into their dreams
back into their camps
just in time
for the hunting.

   (July 2009)

Suzanne S. Rancourt

(b. 1959)

Rancourt's *Billboard in the Clouds* was the 2001 recipient of the Native Writers
First Book Award. She holds a master of fine arts in poetry from Vermont College,
a master of science degree in educational psychology from s u n y, Albany, and a
certificate of advanced graduate studies in expressive arts: therapy, education, and
consulting from the European Graduate School, Switzerland. Rancourt is also a
certified facilitator and affiliate of Amherst Writers and Artists. She teaches writing
to a variety of special populations: victims of domestic violence, women veterans,
mental health patients, women in homeless shelters, incarcerated women and
men, learning disabled, and others. She is ranked in aikido and iaido and is an
armed services veteran. Currently she is the program development consultant
for Next Step Fine Arts Program for adult traumatic brain injury survivors in
Ballston Spa, New York.

Take From My Hair—Memories of Change

today
a rake drags across my forehead—
it is August.

we used to migrate
down the coast and up through the central mountains—
a many-tined people,
we'd "j" our way to the foot of Katahdin—
a wind-ribbon of people,
we'd scoop our sustenance into ash baskets
that tourists preferred to buy unstained
and without blueberries—
the times changed
our men bent as willows,
our women strapped with foresight

why now
do i look for blueberries?

i strain to hear my language
among the leathery leaves
among the trees and trails that
my grandmothers and grandfathers walked
i keep thinking that i see them
walking toward me, i keep thinking that
i feel them touching me when my back is burdened sore
or when my rake swings sluggish
there in the fields of rhythmic silence
i have time to think
and remember what i think
i recall

when i'd rather look
for a shadow to become one
with a stone wall
and low shrubs
on steep hills among
ledge outcrops
moss sundried
but at sunrise there is dew, by noon
everyone has gathered pounds
of purple berries that stay remarkably cool as
the cases of jostled soda
trucked over rutted roads in the back of rusted-out pickups
creaking through fields and fields of time
and hunched, brown backs
one arm braced on a knee
the other combs for berries
and we'd sway—elephant heartbeat—
as slow as the sound of dew-soaked pantlegs
walking toward us

no one liked to be the first in the fields
no one wanted
to tell the bears

a bigger beast
now walks the land

Thunderbeings

While gazing through a window for a split-atomic second,
my grandmother, was struck and killed by lightening.
Her left finger touching one of the four brass posters
as gently as one touches the cheeks of newborns
as though she had pressed a doorbell,
a button on an elevator—ascend please—
then the lightning arched and she crossed over
leaving a fingerprint
and a strong smell of uric acid.

Her name was Dorothy, an artist
taught by the nuns. She painted in oils
the light and dark of all things—
ships full sail on calm oceans—
I could not reach them, hanging on the wall,
so I'd pull a chair under these two paintings
one new moon dark, the other full moon light—
I would press my finger on each brush stroke, each sail
wondering where these ships were sailing
in my Memere's head.

Her name was Dorothy, a Parisienne farm woman, I was told,
who on bad days when the horse and carriage
couldn't make the hard scrabble to Mass
would open up the parlor and hold her own, chanting Hail Marys.

The next year the lightning
came back, took the barn, took the horses.
The bed, where my cooling Memere had lain the year before
was removed from the house, stored in the shed
until forty years later when I polished for days
the spokes and posters. A brass lamp of sorts
illuminated images of a woman
I never knew. I rubbed
until the chalky, thunderhead blue dissolved
and the metal shone lightening yellow.
For years I slept in this bed,

and often heard her
still humming in the brass.

Fanning Fire

Damn. I knew I should have vacuumed.
My mother always vacuumed
Despite five kids who always had five friends,
A couple of dogs, cats and my dad's work boots.

My mother was ahead of her time or in denial or
chose escapism or was simply drunk. I don't care. She played
with us kids on her clean floors, finally clean floors. She had a house
with clean floors. While she laid on her back
she would place her narrow feet on my hip bones
our fingertips touching—ground eagle, sky eagle—
wingspan to wingspan, "Fly, Suzy, fly!"

I soared beyond her rages and whipping yardsticks.

The grass on the middle lawn was thick like golf courses,
a carpet most plush by the brick fireplace
never mortared never made permanent
the snakes nested there.
Mumma and I sat there and the snakes would come.
"This is how you hold them" her hand steady and direct
her voice unwavering. We would take turns holding the snakes,
look them in the eyes and not be afraid
of their wild beauty.

Singing Across the River

"Fly, Mumma, fly!" that's what I said
fanning her face with a dance fan made just for her
and this moment. Final phase, we call it—
small droosy salt crystals formed around the creases of her nose.

It was my turn to sit with her.
It was after midnight. She and I had done all our talking.
She would not go to hell, she said, because she gave the priest
one last chance to forgive her.
She forgave him for refusing to administer her last rites.
"No," I said, "you will go home to the stars."

Early on Mumma and I found a purple pouch
that would be her travel bag. She agreed, she would travel light.
She and Dad, me, my sister, Aunts and brother agreed
that the bag would not ever be removed from her body. We made
a pact that no one, not even Dad, would look inside.
Mumma packed the things she wanted to keep in her heart.

I never looked in her pouch but I know
she took a cassette tape of me singing my own songs.

It is a complex thing
this singing spirits home.

Even When the Sky Was Clear

My father talked to the clouds.
He knew when the snow would come
how much and for how long,
what kind of rain
and the wind that would bring it.

I would watch him
through my mother's kaleidoscopic den windows,
immaculate and sparkling,
I'd rush from the table, crayons, or tv.
Or from my rock sentinels holding my hand-hewn poplar bows and
    spears
or while perched amongst and atop my White Pine, I'd watch,
or with my feet buried in the peak of the sand pile.
I would watch my father

stand in the center of the dooryard appropriately round
in red and black checkered wools
or in a tee shirt mottled with holes from cutting-torch sparks.
Everything still and listening,
except for an occasional Crow's caw or Blue Jay,
or the tiniest sound of the first few snowflakes landing
or the muffled hiss of blanketing fog in its subtle turn to pre-rain mist.

Even in the summer
he'd look to the clouds, to the sky
at dawn, at dusk.

Now,
I stand in a circle.
There's a Tree in the center dressed in brilliant colors,
sometimes, I leave sweet things there and let the shadows touch me.
There's a drum and singers,
sometimes, I hear them.
Sometimes, I don't
because I am singing to the clouds
in the language
my father
taught me.

When the Air Is Dry

the insects buzz and saw
through heat waves.
Pepere knows it's time
to work the fields.
he stares at the sun.

these memories are distant
yet as shadows leak through pine needles,
the way milk drips between the leaves of a table,
they continue to seep

into my heart and home
of hand-braided rugs
and rocking chairs,
through my mind
into my children's lives.

to be fluid as wind
that sprawls over silvery July grasses . . . I need . . .
but cannot smell the scent
of sweet, sweet, fresh-cut hay, again, and the sun
burns the nape of my neck.
I have stacked bales of green hay
into little pyramids dotting open pastures,
they wait for the Farmall with its wagon
and splintered racks.
the muscles on my back tighten over ribs, a runner's ribs,
living sinew, breathe and glide
over skeletal ridges and valleys
baling twine cuts my hands, blood arroyos to my fingertips
and chaff settled in my pants. I remember

the hay
always weaved its way
into my hair,
making a wreath of it—the hat, the hair—
our skin brittle as dry leaves from wind-kissed sweat

what is it that stops moving when the sun sets?
what is it that spins inside my head and in my belly?

a dragonfly's
holographic vision coats
my past and future
with the iridescence of unexplained knowing.

why am I just standing in the middle of the field?
I've lost sight of the tractor's sound
I'm no longer where the voices are
the sun pounds my childish panic into its descent beyond

the silhouette of trees.
I hear singing

I raise my hand
to grasp a wisdom
children lose
when language
is beaten out of them.

James Bruchac
(b. 1968)

Storyteller, tracker, and wilderness guide James Bruchac is the director of the Ndakinna Education Center and Nature Preserve in Greenfield Center, New York. Bruchac is the coauthor of several books with his father, Joseph Bruchac, and he also coauthored *Scats & Tracks of the Northeast* with Dr. James Halfpenny. Bruchac is presently working with Dr. Halfpenny on an animal-tracking and observation guide for children, to be published by Fulcrum Publishing. In recognition of their combined efforts in teaching others about nature, in March 2004 Bruchac and his father, Joseph, were awarded the 2004 Conservation Achievement Award from the National Wildlife Federation.

Tracking My Nature

As I travel around the country sharing stories and teaching about the wonders of the natural world I am often asked such questions as "How did this all begin?" and "What made you want to share with others?"

My answers lie in the various mysteries of tracking that have become such an important part of my life. As I tell my students, no two sets of tracks are exactly the same. Like the animals in the forest, we each create our own tracks and trails. While making these tracks, our experiences along the way define who we are and even what we are to become. So I can only truly answer those questions by looking back over the tracks I have made. It is a trail that has spanned all corners of this continent and even crossed the sea.

As a young boy growing up in the Adirondack foothills town of Greenfield Center I was always interested in the natural world. My first introductions to nature came from Native stories told by my father on long winter nights. Most often these Abenaki and Iroquois tales shared with my brother and me were ones that, like our ancestors, had deep roots in the land we called home. They included such characters as raccoon, bear, turtle, wolf, and deer. Whether it was Azban, the raccoon boastfully racing a giant rock, or a man betraying a promise to Deer Woman, my father's animated and often interactive tellings allowed the images and actions of each story to come alive in my head. Falling asleep on long winter nights, those images often filled in my dreams, making me long for the day I could actually see those animals in the forest.

As I grew older, like many kids in my rural town, I began to spend much of my free time outdoors. Luckily for my brother and me, just across the road from our house was ninety acres of forest owned by my grandparents. By the time I was ten years old I had explored every corner of it. Just as I had wished on those story-filled nights, at times I would even spot an animal—a grazing deer, a woodchuck, a trotting fox. Each was a moment of wonder.

I also couldn't help but remember those very stories that had made me long for such moments. One day, for example, an angry red squirrel chattered down at me while I sat at the base of my favorite pine tree. As a barrage of twigs and pinecones fell around me I thought of the story of Gluskabe and the giant red squirrel. Big Red Squirrel was once five times the size of Great Bear. But because he was so mean, threatening to destroy the human beings, our Abenaki hero Gluskabe shrunk Big Red Squirrel down to the size squirrels are today.

"Still to this day," Dad told us, "Red squirrel hates the human beings. Lucky for us, instead of rocks and trees now he only throws twigs, pine cones, and acorns."

Besides his knowledge of stories, my father also knew a lot about the forest and its animal inhabitants. Some things he'd learned from his Abenaki grandfather who raised him. Others came from his years at Cornell University acquiring a minor in zoology. In our woods or on any of our family outings into the Adirondacks, Dad would point out and name the trees and plants and, of course, the occasional animal sign. I still remember my first set of Awasos tracks.[10] During a camping trip to the Big Moose Recreation Area near Indian Lake, while pulling our canoe up to shore to set up camp, we realized that the riverbank was covered with fresh bear prints. Closing my eyes I can still see them now. They were perfect tracks, every toe, pad, and claw showing in the wet sand. They were the kind of tracks I dream of nowadays when leading plaster-ready groups into the woods.

Stepping out of the canoe, I watched and listened as my father carefully interpreted the story they contained. But as he did so, I was also remembering two Iroquois stories he'd told about bears. In one story a bear disguised itself as a human to bring the people medicine. A lodge of people who were generous and welcomed in a stranger were granted that gift. The second story, however, was not so comforting. It was the tale of the Man Bear, a monster that disguised itself as a human being to deceive people and eat them. Luckily, seeing a little bit of fear in both and my brother's eyes and mine, my father assured us that this bear meant no harm and had already gone happily on its way.

Another of my early connections to animals lived just half a mile up the road. It was my grandfather, Joseph Bruchac Jr., who was widely known as "the Adirondack Taxidermist." Since his own boyhood, my grandfather had hunted and fished in just about every corner of the Adirondacks. An eventual member of the Taxidermist Hall of Fame, he had a studio filled with hundreds of mounted animals—from squirrels and rabbits to alligators and grizzly bears. Through my childhood visits to his business, by the time I was ten years old I had gotten an up-close look at just about every animal in North America. Of course, once they had entered his doorway they didn't mind an occasional poke or two from a curious boy. During those visits and during holiday get-togethers my grandfather would tell stories of his hunting adventures. Whether looking at my grandfather's mounts or quietly listening to his tales, I yearned for the day when I could see these animals, alive and in the forest.

Recognizing my love for the woods, my parents sent me to Pine Island Camp in Maine for eight full weeks when I was twelve years old. Stranded on an island in the middle of Great Pond with no electricity or running water and with an old army tent as my new home, I was at first very homesick. In fact, my parents still have some of the letters I sent from camp—complete with the tear marks I made extra sure to circle with my pen. Luckily, I soon found myself kept too busy to feel lonely, with activities that ranged from sailboating, canoeing, archery classes, arts and crafts, and swim time to a host of wilderness activities. During that camp I learned even more about the outdoors, including such skills as map and compass, knot tying, and how to use your poncho to make a shelter or gather rainwater. I also spent my longest times yet outdoors during overnight hiking and canoeing trips. Along the way I got the chance to observe and track many animals, including bear and moose. In the end it was a great, growing experience. Getting me used to being away from home and helping me find my sense of self-reliance had been one of the secret plans of my parents all along. In the beginning, though, troubled by my many pathetic letters, they feared they'd made a mistake. Halfway through the summer they drove all the way to Maine, ready to rescue their heartsick exile. To my parents' surprise, instead of finding a weeping waif wishing to go home early, they found a self-assured son eager to finish the summer as planned. Although it was only eight weeks of my life, the amount of personal growth and self-confidence I gained during Pine Island camp proved pivotal in my later years—as well as that fall when I entered the dreaded place called junior high.

Like many kids, upon entering junior high school, things changed for me. In fact, along with many of the other kids from my town, I was made fun of by kids from the city schools. Some would call us names like "woodchucks" or "hicks." Luckily, I had the strength to ignore much of what they said. That resilience came not only from my experience at camp but from some of those old stories my father so loved to share—especially those stories about smaller characters, human and animal alike, winning against the greatest of odds. In those days smaller heroes were my favorites. Despite the fact I would eventually grow to a height of 6' 6", I was, in those days, small for my age. Of course, the years of martial arts training I had taken alongside my dad didn't hurt either. I would make it through the first few months of seventh grade. I even made a few new friends along the way. However, when I was with those new friends, I began to feel as if I had missed out. Most of them came from huge neighborhoods with lots of other kids to hang out with. They had color TVs and video games. Like many kids of that age I wanted so badly to fit in and "be like everyone else." That goal, in my young eyes, was almost shattered the day my father was asked to come to my social studies class and tell stories.

To this day, I can still remember how embarrassed I was when Dad stood in front of the class. Closing his eyes, he began with a traditional Abenaki greeting song. I sank deeper and deeper into my chair. It was, up to that point, the most embarrassing moment of my life. It was even more embarrassing than the time I ran into the boys' bathroom in fourth grade only to slip into a fresh pile of vomit. Although my classmates appeared to enjoy the stories my father told that day, I silently swore to myself that I would never tell those stories or (even worse) sing a song.

Over time, as I began to grow, I eventually got involved with school athletics, especially football and track. Combining the reflexes and balance I'd acquired through martial arts with my newfound size, I quickly excelled. With this new interest, I not only made more friends but had much more to do after school. By the time I got home from practices I was often very tired. The idea of going into the woods was no longer so appealing. During the weekends I also spent more and more time with friends, most often those who lived in the housing developments far away from any real forest.

My parents, always believing my trail was my own, never openly interfered with my decisions, even when they led me further and further from my roots. However, as they had done in the past, they did provide me with various opportunities. One such opportunity took place in 1983 at the Six Nations Indian Museum in Onchiota, New York. My father and several Mohawk friends had been invited for a weekend at the museum to work with tracker and wilderness instructor John Stokes. John had been traveling around the country teaching traditional survival skills, many of which he had learned while living among the Aborigines of Australia. Now, back in the states, John was eager to both teach and acquire even more skills, stories, and knowledge, especially by working with Native peoples.

During that weekend with John I learned many new skills, including the bow drill fire and how to use a throwing stick. Of course, we did lots of tracking, as well as some martial arts. John made all these skills, including the ones I was already familiar with, seem really cool. With a seamless flow of story and skills, John not only helped me appreciate things I had learned as a child but left me eager to learn even more. It was at that point that I began to see that being a little bit different isn't that bad. It could even be, as John gracefully illustrated, an advantage.

Returning home after that weekend, the woods were never again very far away. I even started to share some of what I had learned with my friends—especially survival skills, which conveniently fitted in with such macho movies of that time as *Rambo* and *Crocodile Dundee*. From time to time I would also take friends over to my grandfather's taxidermy business and show them the hundreds of furs and mounted animal heads. Sometimes my grandfather would even share a hunting tale or two. In his later years, having already survived a massive heart attack, my grandfather seemed to be even more happy to share. Unfortunately, at the very time I came to really appreciate my grandfather's knowledge, his time to share had become short. During the winter of my senior year, Grandfather Bruchac suffered his final heart attack. The death of my grandfather was a huge blow to everyone in my family in many different ways. Along with the sorrow that would be felt by anyone losing a loved one, I also felt a strong sense of personal loss. Before I was even born, my grandfather had tracked and hunted just about every large animal in North America. There was so much I had still wanted to ask. Now he was gone.

Despite this loss, the rest of my senior year went quite well, including receiving a scholarship to Ithaca College. Shortly before my high school graduation, just as it seemed I would once again move further away from the woods, John Stokes called to ask if I could help out with his youth camp for teenage boys. This camp, called "Hawkeye Training," taught tracking and survival skills as well as bringing in traditional storytelling. For the next six years I traveled every summer to New Mexico to work with John. During those camps, besides learning more skills, I became equally excited about teaching them. There was always a mix of kids, both Native and non-Native, and it was great to see others experience that same excitement I'd felt about learning the old ways. Whether it was teaching someone to build a survival shelter or sharing a story, I found that the more I helped teach, the more I wanted to learn.

Throughout my college years, those weeks I spent in New Mexico in a way also served as an anchor. Despite all the time I spent training for football and preparing for an eventual career that I thought would focus on exercise science, every summer I was in the woods with John and the Hawkeye students.

After finishing at Ithaca, I wasn't quite sure what I wanted to do. Then, in 1992, I was given a chance to travel to Africa with my father. I had spent my first two years of life in Ghana, West Africa, while my father was teaching there. Going back to Africa was a dream come true. During that trip to Mali I made some major connections. For one thing, I saw firsthand how traditional tales weave their way into everyday tribal life. I witnessed a traditional community working together to do everything from harvesting millet to raising their children. I also got to see the use of such skills as tracking in some unique ways.

Among the Dogon the reading of tracks, particularly those of the desert fox, is used to tell the future. I watched one evening as the tribal divinator made an elaborate design of small mounds, lines, and depressions in a squared-off area in the sand, leaving a trail of peanuts leading up to it before we left. The next day there were fox tracks everywhere. Kneeling down by them, the divinator carefully studied how each track landed on his design. In the end, those tracks told him that their village would have a good planting season and that my father and I would have a safe journey home.

That experience inspired me in a way I had never been before. I knew then I not only wanted to learn more about Native cultures, I also wanted to teach. This new inspiration eventually resulted in a return to school at nearby Skidmore College, where I turned past minors in English and history into a degree in American studies. While taking classes I took on the job of running the North American Native Authors Distribution Project, a division of my parents' nonprofit Greenfield Review Literary Center. The goal of this project was the promotion and sale of Native American–authored books through both a mail-order catalog and the Internet. Along with having the freedom to make my own hours, I also became very familiar with Native American writing, from the retelling of traditional tales to fiction, nonfiction, and poetry. With well over a thousand books by American Indian authors at my fingertips, I couldn't have asked for a better resource.

At the same time, with the blessings of my grandmother, Marion Bruchac, we also began to teach our own wilderness programs on our family land. These early school field trips made it clear that there were many interested in learning what we had to teach. Also, due to the rising demand for my father's storytelling, I from time to time began to tell a tale or two. Within a year or two I was traveling around the Northeast sharing many of the same stories I heard as a child, stories that in seventh grade I'd sworn I would never tell, stories that nowadays I too have retold and published in books.

A short time later my younger brother Jesse and I formed the Ndakinna Wilderness Project. Ndakinna is the Abenaki word for the Northeast. It literally means "our land." The original goal of Ndakinna was to bring together various knowledgeable people, many of them Native American, to teach wilderness skills and northeastern Native culture. Before long we were offering programs on our family land not only for students but also for such organizations as the National Wildlife Federation.

As well as teaching, I was once again spending much of my free time in the woods, perfecting my skills. Doing so, I made an interesting discovery. As I had been doing with my studies of Native culture, from time to time I would refer to books when tracking. To my surprise I found some major mistakes in several popular books on tracking. These mistakes included such things as describing too many toes on some animals and not enough on others and even more errors concerning animal trail patterns (gaits). Hardly any tracking books explained, much less showed, what I was finding on my own in the woods.

As a teacher who wanted to pass on the best and most accurate information to his students, I decided this would not do. Then, in 1996, while teaching at my second National Wildlife Federation Summit in Estes Park, Colorado, I met acclaimed tracker and naturalist Dr. James Halfpenny, author of *A Field Guide to Mammal Tracking in North America*. Although I was not yet familiar with his book, which soon became one of my most trusted literary resources, I formed a great impression of the man. Following one of his lectures, I approached Dr. Halfpenny to inquire about some of the problems I was having finding accurate information on gaits. With a twinkle in his eyes, he immediately got down on all fours and began to demonstrate with exacting detail every single gait I had a question about. During that week Jim and I sparked up a friendship that resulted in my first of many trips to track with Jim in his backyard—Yellowstone National Park. Those trips gave me the chance to track and watch many more animals I had dreamed of seeing as a child. There were wolves, mountain lions, grizzly bears, buffalo, pronghorn, elk. Each set of tracks led us to new experiences, such as the time we watched Yellowstone's Druid

Peak wolf pack get chased away by the Rose Creek pack. Later that same afternoon I heard the echoing howls of the Druid pack calling for one of their younger members who had been separated from them in the chase.

During my visits I accumulated dozens of stories while learning the ins and outs of the modern science of tracking from one of the world's leading experts. The practical application of Jim's cutting-edge techniques and terms improved my knowledge as a tracker threefold. It also greatly improved my abilities as a teacher with students who ranged in ability from kindergarteners to wildlife officials and professional biologists. At the same time I continued my work with John Stokes. After several more trips to New Mexico, along with a select group of educators from around the world, I became a graduate of his Nurturing the Roots Community Mentoring Program—a program aimed at helping educators integrate the knowledge of traditional cultures from around the world with their teachings about nature and community.

Over the years, as my skills as a teacher continued to grow, so, too, did Ndakinna. Each year we offered more and more programming. My grandmother encouraged us to make even more use of her property, including turning my grandfather's old taxidermy studio into what would become the Ndakinna Education Center. Although confined to a wheelchair in her later years, she too had a love for the outdoors. Because of this, she decided to put the majority of the family land into a conservation easement—the first in Saratoga County. Inspired by the many people she saw coming to learn on her land, my grandmother wanted to preserve it in a natural state for generations to come. Every time I had a youth program she liked nothing better than meeting all the kids before they went home. Each time I would return from one of my trips she would wait patiently for me to tell her all that I had done and seen, especially my adventures with various animals. Sometimes, in return, she would share a story or two about my grandfather or even my great-grandfather Jesse Bowman. In those years following her husband's death, my grandmother had become one of my closest friends. That gave me extra pride in the fall of 1998, when I was able to give her a signed copy of my first book, *When the Chenoo Howls: Native American Tales of Terror*, coauthored with my father. This collection of northeastern monster stories represented another type of lesson-story I heard as a child and still love to share, especially with slightly older kids.

In 1999, after a series of illnesses, my grandmother died. Shortly after her passing, I found out that she had willed the majority of the family land to my brother Jesse and me in the hope that we would continue our work. But there was something else that had happened to change my life. In my grandmother's honor, we renamed the land the Marion Bowman Bruchac Memorial Nature Preserve. It is truly Ndakinna, a place I still call home.

After years of collaboration, in the spring of 2001 Dr. Halfpenny and I released a coauthored book on tracking: *Scats and Tracks of the Northeast*, published by Falcon Books. It was soon followed by *Scats and Tracks of the Southeast*. Those books gave a major boost to my credibility as a tracker. That same year my book *At Home on the Earth* was published by Modern Curriculum Press. As part of their Earth Keepers series, this book chronicles our family's history leading up to the creation of the Ndakinna Education Center and the nature preserve named in my grandmother's honor.

Since that time thousands of people of all ages have visited our education center. The only thing that seems to grow faster than the number of programs we offer, whether it be our many youth camps, skills classes, nature walks, or cultural events, is the number of eager people who attend. Today my time in the woods, more often than not, is shared with students, some of whom are now blazing their own trails as instructors.

So there lies my story—a short version, anyway. Looking back over the tracks it made, I guess it all makes sense and leads straight to where I am today. As I continue my tracks into the future, as in the past, I am blessed by being able to still follow the many tracks of others. John Stokes, Dr. Halfpenny, my parents, grandparents, great-grandparents, and many more, past, present, and future, continue to guide me on this trail. It is a trail that now, as a teacher, I am marking for others. My only goal is that the trail I follow and leave behind be a good one as I continue to track my nature.

Jesse Bruchac
(b. 1972)

The son of Joseph and Carol Bruchac, Jesse has devoted himself to the revitalization of the Abenaki language. He maintains an invaluable Abenaki-language website at www.westernabenaki.com and frequently offers language classes, language camps, and innovative language pedagogies. Additionally, Jesse works with his father at the Greenfield Review Literary Center, publishing new and old indigenous authors under the Bowman Books imprint. An accomplished traditional flute player and storyteller, he founded the Dawnland Singers and has produced numerous CDS, including ones with his music and songs he has written in Abenaki.

Gluskonba's Fish Trap (Klosk8ba Adelahigan)

—as told by Jesse Bruchac in Abenaki and English

Gluskonba was going about.
Klosk8ba / Papemosat.
Gluskonba / was walking about.

His grandmother was fishing in the river and Gluskonba saw how hard
    it was for her to catch a few fish.
*Okemos / wd'al8ma / sibok / ni / Klosk8ba / w'wawalegop /
    w'zahagi8mak.*
Grandmother / she was fishing / at the river / and / Klosk8ba / he
    noticed / she had a hard time at fishing.

"It would be good to help my grandmother," he said,
"mawia / n'wijokam8gwa / Nokomes" idam,
"It would be better / if I helped her / my grandmother," he said,

"so that she will not have a hard time fishing."
"Wji / nda / w'zahagi8mako."
"in order that / not / she have such a hard time fishing."

So Gluskonba built a great fish trap across the mouth of the river.
Ni / Klosk8ba / wliton / adelahigan / ag8z8ghitegwak.
So / Klosk8ba / made it / a weir / across the mouth of the river.

Then he went out on the ocean in his canoe.
Niga / odosan / zobagok / wd'olek.
Then / he went / to the ocean / in his canoe.

"The ocean is going to run dry," he shouted. "All of you fish will die.
"Zobagw zigebasahla!" w'g8g8lewamek. / "mziwik / ki8w8 / namasak / k'machinabaji.
"the ocean / will become dry!" / he shouted. / "all / you / fish / you will die.

"But I have made it so that you will live, all of you fish who hear me.
"Kanwa n'kiziton wji ni k'pmoz8l8zibaji. / Mziwik / nigik / awanigik / k'nodamiba.
"But / I have made it / so / that / you will survive. / All / those / who / hear me.

"I have made my river so that it will always remain. Enter into my river and you will live."
"N'kiziton / n'zibomen / wji / majimiwi / ao. / Pidiga / n'zibok / ni / k'pm8z8l8ziba."
"I have made it / my river it / to / always / be. / Enter / my river / and / you will survive."

The fish heard his words.
Namasak / nodamen8p / w'klozow8ganal.
The fish / heard / his words.

"We must do as Gluskonba tells us or we will all die," they said.
"kd'achowibna / pidiga / w'zibo / ala / machina," / agm8w8 / idamen8p.
"we must / enter / his river / or / die," / they / said.

All the fish, from the smallest minnow to the salmon and the great sturgeon,
Mziwik namasak / wji / p8paami piwseso / namasiz / li / mskwamagw / ta / kchi / kabasa,
All the fish / from / the smallest / minnow / to / salmon / and / great / sturgeon,

swam into the mouth of the river. They entered Gluskonba's fish trap and filled it.

W'dakasmoak / li / z8ghitegwak. / w'pidigaak / Klosk8ba / adelahigan / li / psanton.

They swam / to / the mouth of the river. / they entered / Klosk8ba's / trap / until / it filled.

Then Gluskonba closed his trap and all the fish were caught there.

Niga / Klosk8ba / kbaha / adelahigan / ni / mziwik / namaskak / w'bithamen8.

Then / Klosk8ba / closed / the trap / and / all / the fish / they were captured.

Gluskonba went to his wigwam.

Klosk8ba / odosan / w'wigw8mek.

Klosk8ba / went / his wigwam to.

"I have done a good thing, Grandmother," he said.

"Nd'aloka / kagwi / kchi wligen / Nokomis," idam.

"I have done / something / great good is it / grandmother," he said.

"No longer will you have a hard time fishing.

"Nda nikw8bi k'zahagi8maw.

"Not / now / you have a hard time fishing.

"Now you only need go and pull out whatever kind of fish you need."

"Nikw8bi / ibitta / kd'achowi / m8ji / zibok / wji / gassidigek / wji / nama-sak / g8gagwi / k'kadi."

"Now / only / you need / go / river to / for / all different kinds / of / fish / anything / you want."

Grandmother Woodchuck went to see what he had done.

Okemes/ agaskw / odosan / namiton / kagwi / kizi / wd'aloka.

Grandmother / woodchuck / went / to see it / what / had / he done.

She saw the fish trap crowded full of fish of all kinds.

W'namiton / adelahigan / wz8mi / bsanto / wji / namasak / gassidigek.

She saw it / the weir / to much / filled / of / fish / of all kinds.

"Grandson," she said, "you have not done well. All the fish cannot live in a trap.

"Nosis," / idam, / "nda / k'z8baloka. / Mziwik / namasak / nda / kizi / wd'oz8l8zowiak/ kd'adelahiganek.

"Grandson" / she said / "not / you have done well. / All / the fish / not / can / survive / in your trap.

They will die. Then what will the people who come after us do to live?
w'machinaakji / Niga / t8niji / aln8bak / awanigik / paiak / kizi / niona / wd'alokaadit / kiz8wzoak?
They will die. / Then / what will / the humans / who / come / after / us / they do / to be able to live?

We have as many fish as we need now. Go and let them out."
Niona / kizi / waj8n8 / dabinamasak / wji / nikw8bi. m8ji / k'boniam8k."
We / already / have / enough fish / for now. Go / you release them."

Gluskonba saw that Grandmother Woodchuck was right.
Klosk8ba / wawtam / okemes / agaskw / wl8ma.
Klosk8ba / understood / grandmother / woodchuck / was correct.

"You speak truth, Grandmother," he said. Then he went and opened his fish trap.
"K'wl8ma, / nokemes," / idam. / Niga / odosan / ni / t8wdana / wd'adelahigan.
"You are right / my grandmother" / he said . / Then / he went / and / opened / his weir.

"I have made a new ocean for you all to swim in," he said.
"n'kiziton / wskisobagw / wji / mziwik / ki8w8 / w'dakasmibak," / idam.
"I have made / new ocean / for / all / you / to swim in," / he said.

Then all the fish went out of his fish trap. They went again into the ocean.
Niga / mziwik / namasak / sahosawg / wd'adelahigan. / Mina w'pidigaak zobagok.
Then / all the fish / they leave / his weir. / Again / they enter / the ocean.

To this day, because fish are foolish, they still swim into fish traps and get caught.
Nikw8bi, / wz8mi / namas / giwhlowadakaak / agm8w8 / askwa / dakas- moak / adelahiganek / ni / bitha.

Now / because / fish / they are foolish / they / still / they swim / into traps / and / get caught.

But ever since then, no one has ever managed to catch all the fish again.
Kanwa / nikw8bi, / nda / awanigik / kizi / bitho / mziwik / namasak / mina.
But / now / no / one / can / catch / all / the fish / again.

GLUSKONBA'S FISH TRAP

Gluskonba was going about. His grandmother was fishing in the river and Gluskonba saw how hard it was for her to catch a few fish.

"It would be good to help my grandmother," he said, "so that she will not have a hard time fishing."

So Gluskonba built a great fish trap across the mouth of the river. Then he went out on the ocean in his canoe.

"The ocean is going to run dry," he shouted. "All of you fish will die. But I have made it so that you will live, all of you fish who hear me. I have made my river so that it will always remain. Enter into my river and you will live."

The fish heard his words. "We must do as Gluskonba tells us or we will all die," they said.

All the fish, from the smallest minnow to the salmon and the great sturgeon, swam into the mouth of the river. They entered Gluskonba's fish trap and filled it. Then Gluskonba closed his trap and all the fish were caught there.

Gluskonba went to his wigwam.

"I have done a good thing, Grandmother," he said. "No longer will you have a hard time fishing. Now you only need go and pull out whatever kind of fish you need."

Grandmother Woodchuck went to see what he had done. She saw the fish trap crowded full of fish of all kinds.

"Grandson," she said, "you have not done well. All the fish cannot live in a trap. They will die. Then what will the people who come after us do to live? We have as many fish as we need now. Go and let them out."

Guksonba saw that Grandmother Woodchuck was right. "You speak truth, Grandmother," he said. Then he went and opened his fish trap.

"I have made a new ocean for you all to swim in," he said. Then all the fish went out of his fish trap. They went again into the ocean.

To this day, because fish are foolish, they still swim into fish traps and get caught. But ever since then, no one has ever managed to catch all the fish again.

Notes

1. David Stewart-Smith, personal communication, July 2011.
2. Laurent and other writers use the French spelling, "Abenakis."
3. Jesse Bruchac is currently retranslating Masta's book and cautions that Masta himself mistranslated a good deal of the Abenaki. Personal communication, July 2011.
4. The early Jesuit missionaries who recorded Abenaki rendered the nasalized, unrounded "o" as an 8.
5. Teedyuscung was chosen to lead the eastern Delawares after the Penn family stole over a million acres of their homeland in the 1737 "Walking Purchase." Having united the eastern Delawares, he helped negotiate the 1758 Treaty of Easton, agreeing to peace with the colonists in exchange for the right to remain in Pennsylvania's Wyoming Valley and a full investigation of the Walking Purchase. In 2004 the Delaware Nation tried unsuccessfully to sue for the return of some of those original lands.
6. John Moody is an ethnohistorian who, with his wife, Donna Roberts Moody (Abenaki), runs the Winter Center for Indigenous Traditions in White River Junction, Vermont.
7. Settlers called this formation "The Old Man in the Mountain" and mourned its so-called collapse in 2003. To Abenaki people, however, he left voluntarily, going home.
8. Lisa Brooks.
9. Moody; see note 6 above.
10. "Awasos" are black bears.

Further Reading

ABENAKI AUTHORS

Bachofner, Carol Willette. *Breakfast at the Brass Compass*. Rockland M E: Front Porch Editions, 2009. Print.
———. *Daughter of the Ardennes Forest*. Charlotte N C: Main Street Rag, 2007. Print.
———. *I Write in the Greenhouse*. Rockland M E: Front Porch Editions, 2011. Print.
———. *Native Moons, Native Days*. Greenfield Center N Y: Bowman Books, 2012. Print. Native New England Authors Series, vol. 7.

Brooks, Lisa. *The Common Pot: The Recovery of Native Space in the Northeast.* Minneapolis: University of Minnesota Press, 2008. Print.

Brooks, Lisa, and Cassandra Brooks. "The Reciprocity Principle and ITEK: Understanding the Significance of Indigenous Protest on the Presumpscot." *International Journal of Critical Indigenous Studies* 3.2 (2010): 11–28. Print.

Brooks, Lisa, Donna Roberts Moody, and John Moody. "Native Space." *Where the Great River Rises: An Atlas of the Upper Connecticut River Watershed in Vermont and New Hampshire.* Ed. Rebecca A. Brown. Hanover NH: Dartmouth College Press, 2009. 133–37. Print.

Bruchac, James. *Be Good.* Greenfield Center NY: Bowman Books, 2010. Print.

Bruchac, James, and Joseph Bruchac. *At Home on the Earth.* Cleveland OH: Modern Curriculum Press, 2001. Print.

Bruchac, Jesse. *Mosbas and the Magic Flute.* Greenfield Center NY: Bowman Books, 2010. Print.

———. "Western Abenaki Dictionary and Radio Online: Home of the Abenaki Language." *WesternAbenaki.com.* Web. 11 Aug. 2011.

Bruchac, Jesse, Joseph Alfred, Elie Joubert, and Jeanne Brink. *L8dwaw8gan Wji Abaznodakaw8gan / The Language of Basket Making.* Greenfield Center NY: Bowman Books, 2010. Print.

Bruchac, Joseph. *Above the Line: New Poems.* Albuquerque: West End Press, 2003. Print.

———. *Bowman's Store: A Journey to Myself.* New York: Lee & Low Books, 2001. Print.

———. *Dawn Land.* Golden CO: Fulcrum Publishing, 1995. Print.

———. *The Faithful Hunter: Abenaki Stories.* Greenfield Center NY: Greenfield Review Press, 1988. Print.

———. *Hidden Roots.* Greenfield Center NY: Bowman Books, 2010. Print.

———. *Long River.* Golden CO: Fulcrum Publishing, 1995. Print.

———. *March Toward the Thunder.* New York: Dial Books, 2008. Print.

———. *Ndakinna (Our Land): New and Selected Poems.* Albuquerque: West End Press, 2003. Print.

———. *Returning the Gift: Poetry and Prose from the First North American Native Writers' Festival.* Tucson: University of Arizona Press, 1994. Print.

———. *The Waters Between: A Novel of the Dawn Land.* Hanover NH: University Press of New England, 1998. Print.

———. *The Wind Eagle and Other Abenaki Stories.* Greenfield Center NY: Greenfield Review Press, 1985. Print.

———. *The Winter People.* New York: Dial, 2002. Print.

Bruchac, Joseph, and James Bruchac. *When the Chenoo Howls: Native American Tales of Terror.* New York: Walker & Company, 1998. Print.

Bruchac, Margaret. *Dreaming Again: Algonkian Poetry.* Greenfield NY: Bowman Books, 2012. Print.

———. *Malian's Song.* Middlebury: Vermont Folklife Center, 2006. Print.

Bruchac, Margaret, Siobhan Hart, and H. Martin Wobst. *Indigenous Archaeologies: A Reader on Decolonization*. Walnut Creek CA: Left Coast Press, 2010. Print.

Caruso, Donna Laurent. "Abenaki Filmmaker Earns Luminaria Award." *Indian Country Today* 23 Jan. 2008: n. pag. Print.

———. "Dream of a 'Monsta' at Plimoth Plantation." *Indian Country Today* 30 Oct. 2009: n. pag. Print.

———. "Language Keepers." *Indian Country Today* 9 Nov. 2009: n. pag. Print.

———. "Sacred Run and Sacred Paddle Provide Solemn Memorial for Massachusetts Natives." *Indian Country Today* 1 Dec. 2010: n. pag. Print.

———. *To Solder the Birch Bark*. Vol. 1. Fitchburg MA: Nashaway Publications, 2004. Print.

———. *To Solder the Birch Bark*. Vol. 2. Fitchburg MA: Nashaway Publications, 2011. Print.

Chicklas, Claudia, and Warren Bacon. *Ware: The Manour of Peace*. Ware MA: n.p., 1996. Print.

Czapla, Cathy. *Abenaki Ghosts*. Marvin SD: Blue Cloud Quarterly, 1987. Print.

Halfpenny, James, and Jim Bruchac. *Scats and Tracks of the Mid-Atlantic: A Field Guide to the Signs of Seventy Wildlife Species*. Guilford CT: Globe Pequot, 2006. Print.

Haviland, William A., and Marjory W. Power. *The Original Vermonters: Native Inhabitants, Past and Present*. Hanover NH: University Press of New England, 1994. Print.

Joubert, Joseph. *The First Council Fire*. Greenfield Center NY: Bowman Books, 2011. Print.

Laurent, Joseph. *New Familiar Abenakis and English Dialogues: The First Ever Published on the Grammatical System*. 1884. Greenfield Center NY: Bowman Books, 2010. Print.

Laurent, Stephen. "The Abenakis: Aborigines of Vermont." *Vermont History* 23.4 (1955): 186–95. Print.

———. "The Diet That Made the Red Man." *New Hampshire Archaeologist* 1955: 6–9. Print.

Laurent, Stephen, and Fr. Joseph Aubrey. *French-Abenaki Dictionary*. Portland ME: Grand Trunk Publishers, 1995. Print.

LeCompte, Nancy. *Alnobak: A Story of Indigenous People in Androscoggin County*. Auburn ME: Androscoggin Historical Society, 2003. Print.

Masta, Henry Lorne. *Abenaki Indian Legends, Grammar and Place Names*. 1932. Greenfield Center NY: Bowman Books, 2008. Print.

Parker, Trudy Ann. *Aunt Sarah Woman of the Dawnland*. Dawnland Publications, 1994. Print.

Rancourt, Suzanne S. "The Bear That Stands." *JME: The Journal of Military Experience* (Military Experience and the Arts) 3.1 (2013). Article 23, http://encompass.eku.edu/jme/vol3/iss1/23. Web. 19 Dec. 2013.

———. *Billboard in the Clouds*. Willimantic CT: Curbstone Press, 2004. Print.

———. "The Smell of Blood." *Blue Streak: A Journal of Military Poetry* (Military Experience and the Arts)1 (2013). http://militaryexperience.org/blue-streak-a-journal-of-military-poetry-vol-1/. Web. 19 Dec. 2013.

————. "Why I Don't Meditate." *Blue Streak: A Journal of Military Poetry* (Military Experience and the Arts) 1 (2013). http://militaryexperience.org/blue-streak-a -journal-of-military-poetry-vol-1/. Web. 19 Dec. 2013.

Ricard, Elaine. *The St. Francis-Abenaki Paper Trail 1790–1900*. Ottawa: Elaine Rickard, 2006. Print.

Savageau, Cheryl. *Dirt Road Home*. Willimantic CT: Curbstone Press, 1995. Print.

————. *Home Country*. Farmington ME: Alice James Books, 1992. Print.

————. *Mother/Land*. London: Salt Publishing, 2006. Print.

————. *Muskrat Will Be Swimming*. Gardiner ME: Tilbury House Publishers, 2006. Print.

Smith, Ashley Elizabeth. "Commentary: An Abenaki Anthropologist's Take on the Discipline." *National Association of Student Anthropologists e-Journal* 1.1 (2008): n. pag. Web.

Songbird, Abena. *Bitterroot*. San Francisco CA: Freedom Voices, 2000. Print.

Tahamont, Robert. "Chief Teedyuscung." *Carlisle Arrow* 7 Oct. 1910: n. pag. Print.

————. "Christmas at Carlisle." *Carlisle Arrow* 6 Jan. 1911: n. pag. Print.

————. "The Grasshopper War." *The Red Man* Sept. 1911: 29. Print.

————. "How the Term 'Fire Water' Originated." *Carlisle Arrow* 14 Oct. 1910: n. pag. Print.

————. "The Masquerade Ball." *Carlisle Arrow* 11 Nov. 1910: n. pag. Print.

Tsonakwa, Gerard Rancourt, and Yolakia Wapitaska. *Seven Eyes, Seven Legs: Supernatural Stories of the Abenaki*. Walnut CA: Kiva Publishing, 2001. Print.

Wiseman, Frederick Matthew. *Reclaiming the Ancestors: Decolonizing a Taken Prehistory of the Far Northeast (Wabanaki World)*. Hanover NH: University Press of New England, 2005. Print.

————. *The Voice of the Dawn: An Autohistory of the Abenaki Nation*. Hanover NH: University Press of New England, 2001. Print.

Wzokhilain, Peter Paul. *Kagakimzouiasis Ueji Uo'Banakiak Adali Kimo'Gik Aliutzo'Ki Za Plasua*. Quebec: Frechette, 1832. Print.

————. *Wawasi Lagidamwoganek Mdala Chowagidamwoganal Tabtagil, Onkawodokodozwal Wji Pobatami Kidwogan*. Boston: Crocker and Brewster, 1830. Print.

————. *Wobanaki Kimzowi Awighigan*. Boston: Crocker and Brewster, 1830. Print.

ADDITIONAL READING

Baker, Emerson, and John Reid. "Amerindian Power in the Early Modern Northeast: A Reappraisal." *William and Mary Quarterly* 61.1 (2004): 3–32. Print.

Caduto, Michael J. *A Time Before New Hampshire: The Story of a Land and Native Peoples*. Lebanon NH: University Press of New England, 2004. Print.

Calloway, Colin G. *Dawnland Encounters: Indians and Europeans in Northern New England*. Hanover NH: University Press of New England, 1991. Print.

————. *North Country Captives: Selected Narratives of Indian Captivity from Vermont and New Hampshire*. Hanover NH: University Press of New England, 1992. Print.

————. *The Western Abenakis of Vermont, 1600–1800: War, Migration, and the Survival of an Indian People*. Norman: University of Oklahoma Press, 1994. Print.

Day, Gordon. "The Identity of the Saint Francis Indians." *Canadian Ethnology Service Paper* 1 (1981): 237–47. Print. National Museum of Man Mercury Series.

————. *In Search of New England's Native Past: Selected Essays by Gordon M. Day*. Amherst: University of Massachusetts Press, 1999. Print.

Day, Gordon M., Canadian Museum of Civilization, and Canadian Ethnology Service. *Western Abenaki Dictionary: English-Abenaki*. Hull QC: Canadian Museum of Civilization, 1995. Print.

DeLucia, Christine. "Placing Joseph Bruchac: Native Literary Networks and Cultural Transmission in the Contemporary Northeast." *Studies in American Indian Literatures* 24.3 (2012): 71–96. Print.

Gallagher, Nancy L. *Breeding Better Vermonters: The Eugenics Project in the Green Mountain State*. Hanover NH: University Press of New England, 1999. Print.

Ghere, David. "The 'Disappearance' of the Abenaki in Western Maine: Political Organization and Ethnocentric Assumptions." *After King Philip's War: Presence and Persistence in Indian New England*. Ed. Colin Calloway. Hanover NH: University Press of New England, 1997. 72–89. Print.

Gookin, Daniel. *An Historical Account of the Doings and Sufferings of the Christian Indians in New England, in the Years 1675, 1676,1677*. 1836. New York: Arno Press, 1972. Print.

Haefeli, Evan, and Kevin Sweeney. *Captive Histories: English, French, and Native Narratives of the 1704 Deerfield Raid*. Amherst: University of Massachusetts Press, 2006. Print.

————. *Captors and Captives: The 1704 French and Indian Raid on Deerfield*. Amherst: University of Massachusetts Press, 2003. Print. Native Americans of the Northeast.

Lewis, Randolph. *Alanis Obomsawin: The Vision of a Native Filmmaker*. Lincoln: University of Nebraska Press, 2006. Print.

McAleer, George. *A Study in the Etymology of the Indian Place Name Missisquoi*. Worcester MA: Blanchard Press, 1906. Web. 6 Aug. 2011.

Moody, John. "'Absolute Republick': The Abenaki Nation in 1791." *Vermont Bicentennial Newsletter* Winter 1991: 6–7. Print.

Morrison, Kenneth M. *The Embattled Northeast: The Elusive Ideal of Alliance in Abenaki-Euramerican Relations*. Berkeley: University of California Press, 1984. Print.

————. *The Solidarity of Kin*. Albany: State University of New York Press, 2002. Print.

Senier, Siobhan. "'All This / Is Abenaki Country': Cheryl Savageau's Poetic Awikhiganak." *Studies in American Indian Literatures* 22.3 (Fall 2010): 1–25. Print.

Sevigny, P. Andre. *Les Abenaquis: Habitat et Migrations, 17e et 18e Siecles*. Montreal: Bellarmin, 1976. Print. Cahiers D'Histoire des Jesuites, no. 3.

Williams, John. *The Redeemed Captive*. Carlisle MA: Applewood Books, 1987. Print.

NIPMUC

Introduction

Cheryl Watching Crow Stedtler

Friends and family always roll their eyes disapprovingly, wondering, "Again? You're going up there *again*?" I never considered it to be more than their friendly concern regarding my countless trips up to Nipmuc country. Month after month, year after year they continued. Not until a friend prodded me did I really ask myself, *Why?* And I really had to think on it. *Because I like it* simply wouldn't do. What is it? Why am I willing to drive five hundred miles roundtrip "up there"? Sometimes, I need to do it. The "need" varies—something I need to do for a project, something I need to do for my own well-being, something someone needs me to do for him or her. But that's not it. What makes me crave it? Is it how I reward myself? It is certainly no vacation . . . more like an addiction. What is it? On one hand, it is very grounding; on the other . . . well, it is downright exhilarating. It is going home to a place where I've never lived.

When I first started making the trips to Nipmuc country (my true home, in my heart and mind), I went searching—for what, I am not sure. What I found was family, a huge family with all the trimmings: lots of love, laughter, sorrow, with a helping of conflict. Home was like a magnet. I journeyed home to experience, to reflect, to grieve, to share, to love, to fight—I went home to live.

My mission here is to introduce my family's writings to you. I really did not know where to begin. I found it difficult trying to take the diverse writings of my brothers and sisters and tie them up in a neat package. But in thinking about my journeys home, I realized the clearest answer: these are our journeys.

When we write, we journey. Sometimes we write in search of something . . . an answer or an explanation. Other times it is to revisit or reflect on an experience. We can walk the grieving path and express sorrow, and we can also dance the path of love. When things become all murky and muddled, we write to clarify, to navigate the muck. And we write to honor our ancestors, whether it be one particular person or en masse. All of these writings are personal journeys—that sometimes scream to escape. They swirl in our heads and in our hearts until a pen releases them.

Writers of other cultures journey in the same way, but these writings are through Nipmuc eyes. I respectfully invite you to journey with us and walk our path. *Aho.*

Wowaus

(James Printer, c. 1640–c. 1709)

Nipmuc people engaged with alphabetic literacy early on, in large numbers, and often in complicated, seemingly contradictory ways. One of the most famous early Nipmuc writers was Wowaus, also known as James Printer. Son of a sachem from Hassanamesit, Wowaus attended Harvard's Indian College and, beginning in 1659, worked there as an apprentice at Samuel Green's printing press. He was instrumental in producing the first bibles in the Massachusett language, which were promoted by the missionary John Eliot. During King Philip's War, Wowaus joined forces with Metacom himself; afterward he returned to his earlier occupation. He was the typesetter for Mary Rowlandson's famous captivity narrative. In later life he returned to Hassanamesit and taught there. His son Ami was a signatory to the deed that sold the last of the tribal lands at Hassanamesit in 1727/28.[1]

The first brief text below appeared as a note tacked to a tree in Medfield, Massachusetts; the original has been lost, but a number of scholars have attributed it to James Printer.[2] The second text appears in Mary Rowlandson's captivity narrative as edited by Neal Salisbury.

Note Tacked to a Tree, Medfield, Massachusetts, 1676[?]

Though English man hath provoked us to anger & wrath & we care not though we have war with you this 21 years for there are many of us 300 of which have fought with you at this town we hauve nothing but our lives to loose but thou hast many fair houses cattell & much good things

Ransom Note for Mary Rowlandson

For the Governor and the Council at Boston

The Indians, Tom Nepennomp and Peter Tatatiqnea hath brought us letter from you about the English captives, especially for Mrs. Rolanson; the answer is I am sorrow that I have don much to wrong to you and yet I say the falte is lay upon you, for when we began quarrel at first with Plimouth men I did not think that you should have so much truble as now is: therefore I am willing to hear your desire about the Captives. Therefore we desire you to sent Mr. Rolanson and goodman Kettel: (for their wives) and these Indians Tom and Peter to redeem their wives, they shall come and goe very safely: Whereupon we ask Mrs. Rolanson how much your husband willing to give for you she gave an answer 20 pounds in goodes but John Kittels wife could not tell, and the rest captives may be spoken of hereafter.

Ebenezer Hemenway

(1804–c. 1878)

Ebenezer Hemenway's mother was Hepsibeth Bowman Crosman, a descendant of one of the original proprietors of Natick, the "praying town" established by John Eliot in Massachusetts in the 1650s. Hepsibeth is reputed to have been a highly regarded figure in Worcester who baked prized wedding cakes. She married a mixed-race man, Jeffrey Hemenway. Their son Ebenezer worked as a janitor in Worcester City Hall and became one of the city's leading black citizens. As a representative of such a complex interracial family and community, he represents what the historian Thomas Doughton has described as "a world of dynamic nineteenth-century Native social practice [that is usually] 'unseen'" (208).

Written by Ebenezer Hemenway on the Death of His Mother, February 17, 1847

"So man lieth down and riseth not till the heavens be no more."

The last tear I shed was the warm one that fell
  As I kissed my dear mother and bade her farewell;
When I saw the deep anguish impressed on her face,
And felt for the last time a mother's embrace.
  Gone; gone; oh! thou art gone;
God bless thee forever—oh! bless thee, my son.

O I thought of my boyhood—thy kindness to me,
When youngest and dearest I sat on thy knee;
Of thy love to me ever so fondly expressed,
As I grew up to manhood unconscious how blest.
  Gone; gone; oh! thou art gone;
The Lord ever bless thee—oh! bless thee, my son.

Then I thought of thy counsels, unheeded or spurned,
As mirth had enlivened or anger had burned;
But oh! when my sickness all helpless I lay,

Thou didst nurse me and soothe me by night and by day.
   Gone; gone; yes thou art gone;
To the land of the bless'd, and the land of the free.

Ah! years of endurance have vanished, and now
There is pain in my heart, there is care on my brow;
The visions of hope and of fancy are gone,
And cheerless I travel life's pathway alone.
   Lone; lone—all alone
For there's none here to love me, to love me like thee.

My mother, dear mother; cold hearted they deem
Thy off spring; but oh! I am not what I seem;
Though calmly and tearless all changes I bear,
Could they look in my boson—the feeling is there.
Lone; lone—all alone;
There's none here to love me; there is no love like thine.

Worcester, Massachusetts.

My father was born Jul 15, 1737; died Aug 15, 1819. Age 82 yrs.
My mother was born Mar 25, 1761; died Feb 17, 1847. Age 86 yrs

Zara Ciscoe Brough

(1919–1988)

Also known as Princess White Flower, Zara Ciscoe Brough was descended from James Printer; her grandfather James Lemuel Cisco and her mother, Sara Cisco Sullivan, both led the Hassanamesit Nipmuc Reservation before Brough herself assumed that responsibility in 1959. She founded the tribal museum in 1962. Brough was a powerful businesswoman and civic leader. She studied engineering in college and was vice president of a technical consulting firm in Waltham, Massachusetts. Like many tribal leaders across New England, Brough also served in local organizations and town committees, including the Grafton Planning Board, to try to preserve and protect indigenous lands and resources. She helped establish the Massachusetts Commission of Indian Affairs and was the first Nipmuc Indian commissioner, from 1974 to 1984. The piece below appeared in the *Nipmuc Nation Newsletter* in July 2004.

Days of Hassanamesit

My grandfather Chief James Lemuel Cisco was born on the Indian Reservation on Brigham Hill Road in Grafton on June 30, 1846. He was the son of Samuel C. Cisco and Sarah Maria Arnold Cisco. He died on November 15, 1931 (my twelfth birthday). I dedicate this work on our family to him. What a person he was: quiet but authoritative—a true Chief, or Sachem, of the tribe.

He was the eldest of eight children. Today we have in the museum schoolbooks used by these children of long ago.

Is it a fine idea to present history by a vignette of one particular person when so many dominant people were involved? Maybe not. However, sometimes we must emphasize certain people, and in the case of James Lemuel Cisco, I emphasize a person who added so very much to current history and interests.

James Lemuel Cisco was born on the old homestead of the Arnold Cisco family. His father, Samuel C. Cisco, who came from Cumberland / Slatersville area of Rhode Island, was a Narragansett Indian chief but, as was the custom of the day, was listed in various documents as a "foreigner."

Samuel Cisco, my great grandfather, was a medicine man and herbalist. His wife was well known as a medicine woman, especially as a midwife. Great Grandpa was six feet tall, wore a straw pipe hat and hair down his back. Great Grandfather brought the Cisco branch of the family into existence in Grafton. He was a Narragansett chieftain. In the Massachusetts Indian census of 1860, he is listed as a "foreigner." This means that he came from "outside" or a distant (in those days) place.

The same document used the term "colored" to describe him. This didn't mean a black person or Negro but meant a person other than white. Today, however, it's difficult for many Indians to verify their heritage because this term was used as a "catch all." Sometimes deliberately, sometimes when the tribal connection was not known. But "colored" in old records just means "not white European."

It's said Samuel Cisco walked to Grafton in the 1840s, met Great Grandmother, Sarah Maria Arnold, and married her.

In 1853, a letter was written by my great grandmother, Sarah Maria Arnold Cisco, stating that she wasn't able to keep a cow and horse for her family. The cow was needed for the milk produced. The family's land was being taken from her little by little. Her letter was a request to help her to retain what little she had. She was being "crowded" just as it is felt presently: a squeezed in feeling. She had nine children, so certainly needed space.

There are many other letters of her era and later that tell of the turmoil in everyday life of their family.

Great Grandfather Samuel Cisco was a medicine man and Great Grandmother was a medicine woman. One of the stories my mother would tell is of Samuel Cisco going to catch a black snake for rheumatism belts and bands he would make.

He was over six feet they say, about six-foot four. He would go out with a long staff over his shoulder, in part to aid his walking and in part to help in obtaining the snakes he needed. Our men really didn't smoke, but tobacco was kept for other purposes, such as for helping to catch black snakes.

In Grafton, there was a part of town that was very wild: a large glacial area on what is now called Potter's Hill. Here he'd hide himself as snakes would sun themselves on the promontory. This out-cropping served as a sunning area for all sorts of snakes, including diamondback rattlers. They'd say it was a very dangerous place.

Great Grandfather Samuel Cisco would isolate or "segregate" the black snakes he wished to obtain. Then he would chew the tobacco into a wad. Poking a snake with a staff, when the reptile opened his mouth, he would throw the tobacco in. The tobacco would have a narcotic effect and the snake would keel over in a stupor. Great Grandfather would kill the snakes and bring them home slung over the staff he'd carry over his shoulder. Older relatives would remember this tall man coming home with large black snakes dragging on the ground.

Great Grandmother Sarah Maria Cisco was a good cook, so my mother would tell me, and she cooked good Indian food, dishes now often in confusion called "Yankee cooking."

At the time of my great grandparents' marriage in the mid-1800s, the area Indians lived just as their white neighbors. Many of our people were humble farmers who eked out a living, supplementing their provisions with wild game and fishing. And game and fish were still at that time abundant.

Today, if we had barrels of sugar, molasses, flour, bins of vegetables, meat, and fish, smoked and cured, we would consider ourselves well off. We all know it, too. A lot of changes have come in this modern age, like buying a pound of sugar at a time and going to a store for everything you need.

James Lemuel Osco, my grandfather, was born in the old family house on Brigham Hill Road. At the time of his birth in 1846, it had been divided in to two sides. One side was usually occupied by the Sarah Cisco's parents, Harry and Sally Arnold. The other portion was lived in by the younger couple, Samuel and Sarah Cisco, and, eventually, their family of five boys and three girls.

In addition to my Grandfather James Cisco, their family included sons William, Henry, Samuel, and Lewis Cisco and daughters Carrie, Sarah C. M., and Delia B. Cisco. William died at age thirty-two, Henry at two, Samuel at thirteen, Carrie at five, and Sarah C. M. when she was a child.

I myself was fortunate enough to know both Grandpa and Aunt Delia, who lived to quite ripe old ages. Grandpa was eighty-five when he passed on, and Aunt Delia was over seventy when she died. They passed away less than two years apart. Aunt Delia had been the youngest of her generation. But all the other great aunts and great uncles were long gone when my generation began.

When James Lemuel Cisco was growing up on Brigham Hill Road, all the farmable land was cultivated and planted to raise vegetables for the family and for use as barter for other necessities of life.

James Lemuel Cisco grew to be a strong man, both physically and morally. He assisted his father in farming. He hunted for game and his favorite fishing, which he never considered [unappealing] "tasks." Although much of the "Indian culture" was put away as nonsense in those years, he still retained many of the Indian habits and ways, particularly with the use of certain terms and his "fish dance."

The "fish dance" was done after a successful "catch" with a washtub of freshly caught fish in the middle of the kitchen floor. He would pass it off jokingly if someone asked "why?" but he never stopped doing it. As we recall it was usually Pickerel. Of course, the dance signified a "Thank You" to the Great Spirit for a successful catch: Chief Lemuel Cisco's Pickerel Dance! He was a very old man, in his eighties, when we saw him dance around the washtub for the last time.

Corrine Bostic

(1927–1981)

Like other southern New England Native communities, the Nipmucs have long incorporated African Americans and other groups. As historian Daniel Mandell explains in *Tribe, Race, History,* some families "could cross and recross ethnic boundaries as different generations followed particular ancestral ties to forge deeper connections to either the Nipmuc or the African-American community," but this did not necessarily mean "surrendering kinship ties to the other ethnic group" (67). Corrine Bostic acknowledged both her Nipmuc and African American ancestry, though as a writer she identified perhaps most strongly with the African American community around Worcester. During the 1970s she was a major figure in the Worcester County Poetry Association, serving on the editorial board for its *Worcester Review,* in which "Ballad for Bubba" appeared. Bostic also wrote plays, as well as a commissioned biography of Sarah Wilson, one of the city's first black schoolteachers and a prominent activist for racial equality. The additional poems below appeared as epigraphs to the chapters in Wilson's biography.

Ballad for Bubba

she laid her yellow ring
beside her sunday shoes,
and the only golden thing she kept
was the dream deep in her soul
as she said to her folks—
I'm goin' to march in The Big Parade.
For today's the day
when we have our say
when we march downtown
in The Big Parade!

(her poppa frowned and chided
his "uppidity" daughter's way,
and said, "They'd all be finished"
if she marched in The Big Parade!)

but her eyes gleamed
with a holy glow
they'd never seen before
that seemed to fall
a silver path windin' out the door!

how their hearts feared
as they glimpsed that road
and back to their second child
sixteen years . . . to The Big Parade
to march . . . a soldier proud!

singin': I'm on my way
to The Big Parade
and I shall overcome
and I shall overcome
O I'm on my way
to The Big Parade
and I shall overcome!

momma poppa
can I go go
march with Cindy-Lou?
ALL the kids at Carver Junior
are marchin' too!
O how I wish your brother John
were home to talk to you!
but he'll be home tomorrow
from Groton Theology School.
now you go pray to the Lord, my son
and he'll wash you
whiter than snow
whiter than snow, my son.

(and his father said, "If you don't
I fear, it's the iron bars
for you for you
I fear it's the iron bars for you!")

so Bubba was sent to church
to sing and pray
while Cindy-Lou went downtown
and marched in THE BIG PARADE!
yes, Cindy and Bubba parted
on the steps of the teemin' church
where folks rolled 'round
like a dark cascade
to surge the streets in THE BIG PARADE
singin', We shall overcome
We shall overcome
We are on our way in THE BIG PARADE
and WE SHALL OVERCOME!

now two black folk rockin'; wonderin'
saw light in the southern sky
the terrible retribution
of a fiery torch leap high!

Sweet Jesus, screamed momma
I fear I fear I fear
somethin's happened at the church
for in that red-red fire
I do believe I see I see
A.M.E. Zion's Spire!

they ran cryin' to the town
when they reached that place
found the church BLOWN open, and
among the tattered old prayer books
laid seven black children
Jesus overlooked.

as momma headed home again
in her heart she prayed
Sweet Jesus take Bubba to heaven
let him live with you always
and Lord bless us four

keep us close
now and evermore

back home she met her son, John
flyin' out the door
headin' back for THE BIG PARADE
PACKIN' A FORTY FOUR
shoutin': WE SHALL OVERCOME
WE SHALL OVERCOME
I'M ON MY WAY
TO THE BIG PARADE
AND WE SHALL OVERCOME!

Dedication to the Young: Cuttin' a Spoonful

ooo, oh, yeh, said the kids
finger poppin' to Brown's rasp,
a witness? a witness? a witness?
Do I have a witness?

Touchstones

Come from the soul's starlight
Come blazing opulent Dreamers
Come singing your brilliant songs
Come ever searching and building
Come for those before and after.

Slatemen

Do not pick the flowers!
The iron voice stills
The outstretched hand.
While just beyond the round garden

The tall pines rise and fall
Like green suns.

For Teachers: A Self-Reminder

teach them that you are
but a man.
teach them of before
but mostly of now.
teach them that Life
"is mostly grass with an occasional butterfly."
teach them that the summer darkness
has fireflies, and
that the stars' brilliance
is heightened by the night sky.
teach them to be dreamers.
teach them of King's journey
from Birmingham to Memphis,
of Christ's from Galilee to resurrection.
teach them that Buck Rogers and Flash Gordon
flew from the funny pages to the moon.
P.S., but most important: TEACH THEM BY EXAMPLE.

Richard Spotted Rabbit Massey

(1934–2012)

Richard Massey served on the Nipmuc Nation Tribal Council from 1997 to 1999. He also presided over the New England Native American Institute, based in Worcester, Massachusetts, and advised the Worcester Historical Museum on its representations of Nipmuc people and history. In addition, he was the elder advisor for Project Mishoon, a Nipmuc underwater archaeology project. He wrote his own tribute to Hepsibeth Crosman Hemenway, who was his fourth great-grandmother.

Hepsibeth Bowman Crosman Hemenway, 1763–1847

As a descendant of Hepsibeth I was told many stories about all of my Indian ancestors by my beloved Indian grandmother. The history of Native Americans is sad for all the Indian Nations. The Native people of southern New England have suffered for 300 years. Many were sold into slavery, and the male population was decimated by wars.

Hepsibeth was a descendant of Samuel Bowman, who was one of the proprietors of the town of Natick. This town was an attempt . . . to Christianize Indians into being more like their English neighbors. There were several of these villages in Massachusetts and Connecticut, but Natick was the first.

Shortly after King Philip's War, and due in part to racial strife with surrounding towns, the Bowmans returned to their original homeland of Worcester.

Hepsibeth is referred to in early newspaper articles as an Indian maiden from Packachoag Hill. She was half white, on her father's side. It was illegal for Indians to marry white people in Massachusetts and Hepsibeth is recorded on early town documents as Hepsibeth Bowman, daughter of Lydia Bowman. In 1789 Hepsibeth married Jeffrey Hemenway, a mulatto who had a distinguished Revolutionary War record. She was 26 and he was 53.

I am related to their daughter Lydia. One of my favorite stories of Hepsibeth is how on the first Independence Day she roasted a pig on the common and fed the people of Worcester. She was also well known for her wedding cakes.

Edwin W. Morse Sr.

(Chief Wise Owl, 1929–2010)

Edwin Morse served as chief of the Chaubunagungamaug (Dudley/Webster) Band of Nipmuck Indians from 1982 until his death, when his son, Edwin Morse Jr. (Red Fox), succeeded him.[3] He was instrumental in the band's (ongoing) federal recognition struggles. Like many Nipmuc leaders, Morse was also a prolific writer, self-publishing three books of his own, including a lesson book, an Algonquian dictionary, and a collection of traditional stories.

Chief Wise Owl's Prayer

Great Spirit, Great Spirit,
I pray for all my people each day.
I thank you for all the beautiful things you bless us with each day.
Our beautiful families, the rising of the sun, the harvest, from our
  gardens, from Mother Earth.
For warm rains that fill our lakes and rivers, to provide us with water
  to cool our dry throats, and fish to fill our hungry stomachs, we also
  thank you for the grassy meadows that feed our hungry creatures.
We thank you for the trees, with their leafy arms, that reach for heaven,
  to give us shade, and wood to build our homes, to protect us from
  the winter, and give us shelter.
Without the blessings from you, Great Spirit, and the comfort of your
  loving arms, and generous heart, all your children would perish.

Manittoo-oo Manittoo-oo
Nuppeantam askesukok wame ninnimmissinnu-onk.
Neenawun kuttabotonish wutche wame wunnegin teag nenenaauau wun-
  antam auwoh nashpe nishnoh kesuk.
Wuttiahein wunnegin nutteashinninne-onk ni wapeu, wutche ni nepauz
  newutche ni kepenum wutche tamokkeete-onk wutche okasoh ohke.
Wutche kesoosinneat sokanon ne mogquen nuttahein nipisse kah sepuash ut
  kittinnumoush auwoh kodtuppoo muppoochinau.
Neenawun kuttabotamish ni moskehuash wompaskeht ne meetsoo auwoh

kodtuppoo odasoowas newutche ni mehtug nashpe wunnepogqush mapit
ne muhquequn wuche kesuk ni magou auwohonkkum kah wuttuhqun
ut wekitteau nuttaihein ut ogqunneg auwoh newutche popon ut magou
auwoh wunhogki.
Weskeche ni noonantam kenauau manittoo kah ni kummon chanatamwe
wuche ne kuttaiheu womonna-onk muhpitnash kah nutahquontous
metah wame wuche ne kuttaiheu kenechannog pish mohtupohteau.

Kitt Little Turtle

(George Munyan, 1940–2004)

Kitt Little Turtle was the medicine man for the Chaubunagungamaug Nipmucks
at Webster, Massachusetts. He was also an illustrator and a prolific writer who
produced articles for the tribal newsletter, *Nipmucspohke*, and the *Webster Times*,
as well as language texts of his own. He provided artwork and several traditional
stories, including the "Nipmuck Legend" and "Legend about Hobbamock," for
the Concord Museum's 1988 *Native American Sourcebook*. The other writings here
have been supplied by Cheryl Stedtler.

Coyote Spirit

Sacred Brother, wise and brave . . .
Why have they made your hide their slave—
    humiliating your proud spirit
    parading gleefully in your skin?
Solemn ceremony reduced to masquerade
    too naïve to see the disrespect of their charade.

Your nation, like mine, has no worth
    to the greedy usurpers pretending to own even Mother Earth.
    Sacred Brother, Beloved Coyote, can we, like Christ
    say they know not what they do . . .
    and can we truly believe that on some distant day

their eyes will open, their hearts will melt
and they, too, will learn to truly pray?

I weep for you and for their blindness
and how little they know of love
Yet in my spirit I can only pity, not hate, them—
and make a simple offering to the Powers above
that when their treasure fades as their high position falls
then they will know the truth we have tried to teach them of.
I love you, Coyote, and all our relations . . . *Aho*

The above is written on behalf of a loved one who has been desecrated, disrespected, and mutilated for the pleasure of party-goers. With Coyote's help and guidance, LT.

Nipmuck Legend

Long ago our people depended on game and wild food that made it necessary for them to be constantly on the move.

During a period when food was very scarce, a young man had a vision in which a wise crow told him about a food that could prevent the people from ever facing starvation.

The youth asked the crow where this food could be found but was told that it was such a long journey that a man would never find it.

Then the crow told the man that he would bring this food to him, [explaining that] crows would always follow the people because this food was one of their favorite delicacies.

Several days later the man was walking in the forest when he heard someone calling him. Looking up into a tree he saw the crow that had appeared in his vision.

The crow flew to the man's shoulder and told him to hold out his hand. Opening his beak, the bird dropped three seeds on the man's palm. They were corn, beans, and squash—the three sisters. Instructions were given for preparing the soil and placing fish in the ground to feed the seeds. This would be women's work while the men did the hunting and fishing.

The crow's descendants still visit the villages at planting and harvesting time to get their share of corn.

Legend about Hobbamock

A most treacherous and hideous being, Hobbamock lurks in the night-time shadows. Some people will not go out alone at night for fear of an encounter with this frightful fiend. He is the Indian "bogeyman" and the equal of the European "devil."

Those who are in harmony with their fellow beings and seek the presence of Great Spirit in their lives have no cause to be intimidated by Hobbamock! Only self-styled witches and medicine people who abuse their gifts can be seriously endangered by this mischievous evil one.

Sometimes called "Cheepie," this malevolent phantom is a source of pain, sickness, and emotional distress. He frequently materializes in various grotesque apparitions, including impersonations of departed loved ones—or enemies. . . .

Strangely enough, sometimes "Hobbamock" was given or adopted as a personal name or title, as in the case of Massasoit's high-ranking Wampanoag Council member who served as ambassador to the Plymouth Colony.

The Heat Moon

Chikohtaekeeswush follows the Strawberry Moon, and by this time (early July through early August) the Three Sisters would be up and growing well, allowing the inland people to travel on foot and by canoe to the shore for ocean and shell fishing. There would also be summer festivities with family and friends from distant tribes and villages. A few elders would remain at home to watch the gardens and attend to everyday tasks such as picking and drying berries that would reach their peak at this time. Parts of those ancient paths are still identifiable and some of today's highways follow the same routes our ancestors took on their way to the coast.

Feasts and dancing would be a part of the thanksgivings and ceremonies that were as much a part of the Heat Moon as the fishing. Many young people would meet their future husbands and wives among the other youths gathered at the shores in Narragansett territory. Men did most of the fishing, except for shell fishing, which the women and youngsters could do while chatting and enjoying the salt air. Women also tended to the smoking and drying of the fish on green wood racks that would also serve as convenient carriers on the return trip to the villages when the annual "working vacation" came to an end.

As much as the trip was enjoyed, it was always good to get back home to share their experiences with the elders, store away the dried fish, and prepare for the Green Bean Moon (Ashkashki Tuppuhquam keeswush), which was fast approaching. It is always good to have a shore dinner or at least some clam or fish chowder during the Heat Moon, in remembrance of our ancestors, and to give thanks for another of Creator's gifts—the bounty of the seas and the cooling breezes that sometimes bring a breath of salt air all the way to the inland villages.

Nancy Bright Sky Harris

(b. 1952)

Born Nancy Virginia Jacobs, Harris has served as vice president of the Board of Directors for the Nipmuc Indian Association of Connecticut. She has sung with Native American drum groups since 1989, when she and her brother Everett Little Turtle Jacobs formed the Full Circle Drum Society in Connecticut. She was also the lead singer in a women's drum group called Red Clover; she appears on several CDs (*Full Circle Drum Society, Eastern Spirit, Jammin on the Powwow Trail*). Harris and her family are also accomplished traditional dancers.

To Carol and David with Love

September 10, 1994

Manit wame masugkenuk
Kuttabotómish yeu kesukok
Kuttabotómish nishnoh oaas pámontog
Kuttabotómish wuttoohqŭnash, nippe, kesuk, aukeeteamitch, séquan,
ninnauwáet,
pópon

Wunnántam ninnimissinúwock neemat, nummissis awetawátuock
Annumau wunnetu numwohtoüsh kenutcheganit paumpmaúntam
  womonittuonk
Wunnonkou unnukquom wunnetu
Saup monomansuonk annoóssüonk quoshodtuonk
Aho

[Grandfather Creator,
Thank you for this day.
Thank you for the animals.
Thank you for the trees, the water, the sky,
the seasons—
Bless these two people, my brother and
my sister in their marriage.
Help them to be happy and fill their
life with love.
Let their yesterdays be a dream
of happiness
and every tomorrow be a vision
of hope and promise.
Amen]

Woman of the Warrior

She waits, quietly working the job of two,
while her mate is fighting for their country,
for freedom in the land.
They do not understand the reason he was sent
risking his life, risking his family life, but he goes
because he has to.
He is a warrior and she is the woman of the warrior.
We will respect her and show her honor starting today.

When he returns, he is not the same,
for he has been in a war that was insane.
At times he has been quiet and withdrawn, and at times she's
put up with his rage and misplaced scorn.

She's put up with the nightmares both day and night of a war
long gone by.
She's the foundation that he builds his emotional strength on
and a comrade in arms. She has had to explain to the family
and friends why he acts that way.
She has earned her stripes and her right to stand by her man
on Veterans' and Memorial Day.
She's the most special person in the World—She's the mate of
a veteran.

Wind from Summer

There were times I didn't know you,
you were the cool one, the cute one.
You were the soldier that went away
that wrote letters, and got a few from me.
Then you came back;
I was glad that I didn't lose you.
As I grew up, I discovered that you were fun to be with.
The wind from summer can be warm.
The Native blood that runs in your body
is as warm as that.
Your sensitivity, your caring, your sense of humor
draws people to you.
I am proud of you my brother.

The Gifted Porcupine Roach Maker[4]

The Creator gives us all gifts.
Some of us are lucky to discover
what those gifts are.
There is a man and his lady that live
in New England.
He has this wonderful talent
to make the roaches.

There are many who want Jim's roaches.
When someone wears a roach,
he is a proud dancer.
He is representing his people, himself,
and the spirit within him
dancing on Mother Earth.
Jim will hand-dye the colors
of the hair to match the regalia.
He inserts the hair in small amounts
to guarantee the work is secure and attractive.
Jan is there beside him
to give him support and advice.
I am very proud to meet both Jim and Jan
and to have a original porcupine hair roach
made for my son.

Creator of Life

Grandfather Creator,
Hear my prayer.
I hear you in the gentle wind,
calling me.
I hear you in the sunlight,
see your quiet rays gently shining in my face.
I see your power in the night as the stars twinkle
their happiness as being part of my life.
Help us in our words, our deeds,
and help the love that you have for us shine on our face.
Aho.

Hear Your People

Grandmother Earth, Grandfather Sky,
hear your people.
Calling, calling in their prayers, in their dreams,

for direction.
We want to see a new sunset,
a new beginning for our children,
and of the next seven generations to come.
Guide us to the right path
and let our moccasins follow in your steps.
Aho.

There Was a Time

She sits on the hills among the yellow flowers, quiet and still, while the
warm rays of the sun lay gently across her face. She is so quiet; the
animals small and large walk by her unafraid. They know she is a
Native child and that in her heart are peace and respect for all.

She thinks of a time when her people had the whole world to choose
and when the sky and Grandmother Earth were one.

The colors were more vibrant then; turquoise, sky blue,
gray—beautiful fluffy clouds speaking to each other as they moved
with Brother Wind.

She is a little sad as she thinks of the horses that grazed in the deep
green grass. No more.
Now there are fences to keep animals out and in. Now, there is no
freedom for the horses.
Now, the colors of the sky are dirty from pollution, and the clouds look
angry at each other as they pass quickly.

She prays to Grandfather Creator to protect the animals who have
no control of where they are being forced to live. She prays to
Grandmother Earth to provide food for all and she prays to Brother
Wind to bring back the vibrant colors of the past. *Aho.*

Hawk Henries

(b. 1956)

An esteemed musician, composer, and flute maker, Hawk Henries got his start in the mental health field, working with children with autism and later with adolescents with substance-abuse histories. He learned traditional flute-making skills—using only hand tools and fire—after being forced to repair a beloved instrument given to him by his family. By the early 1990s he was working full-time as a flute maker and musician at powwows, museums, and schools. Today Henries is a sought-after performer; he has released two original CDs and his music has been used in numerous films and documentaries. He participated in the 2006 commemoration of Jamestown, Virginia, and was commissioned by the London Mozart Players to write a concerto for Native flute and orchestra, both events described on his website, hawkhenries.com, on which the entry below also appears.

Carrying the Flute

My bag is full of flutes: some from Bolivia, Java, Hawaii, Africa, Japan
Europe, Australia, and from Turtle Island. Which is your favorite,
Which has the sweetest voice?
Some are long and dark, some wide, some mottled.
Still others have been broken, working differently than originally intended.
There are light-colored, short, bristly voiced and smooth, high-pitched ones.
Which is the most important . . .
Each brings an enriching quality that adds
Fullness to my flute bag.

—from my CD *Keeping the Fire* (1999)

I was initially inspired with a deep interest in Native flute music in the 1980s. At the time I didn't know of any other traditional flute makers in New England, but I really wanted to learn and started to listen to the music of several traditional Native flute players. I looked for a flute of my own but couldn't afford the ones that called to me. Eventually my family gifted me with a flute, which inspired me to pursue a deep relationship with music and traditions that Native and many other Indigenous people hold in regard to the flute. By trial and error, I learned to construct the flute.

Over time I developed a deep sense of relationship with, and responsibility to, the flute and its power to remind us of our sacredness and our interconnection with everything in Creation. The flute's voice calls to the Sacred in every person and aspect of life, in ways that transcend words or normal consciousness. Everything is sacred. Every breath, word, action, thought is sacred. Washing dishes, going for a walk, cleaning the car—it's all a part of the same whole.

I think of instruments as important tools that can open doors because I think that they're alive. They do work. They voice certain tones, and combinations of tones, that create vibrations that affect us physically. They create a space of openness or, at least, a willingness to be in that moment and be open. Humor and laughter create these spaces also. Together they create a physical and social space where we can remember our connections to each other while exploring our differences as resources for new understanding and mutual awareness—instead of using them as weapons of divisiveness.

The flute's body and voice remind us of the interrelatedness, interdependence, and sacredness of all people and all of Creation. Flutes have a long history of articulating certain ideas for which words might not be adequate. Their bodies and voices are a profound manifestation of the life-giving power of the relationship between masculine and feminine energies—earth and sky, water and fire, humans and nature. When I'm looking at nature, trees, insects, birds, stones, and all the other things we live with seem to be engaged in the activity that they're intended to be engaged in. There's a relationship that exists between those things and what we could consider to be a respect for that relationship. There is a common thread that is honored and which enables the exchange and perpetuation of that life force that gives them their existence and that also connects them to each other. Each tree in the forest is unique and uniquely important to the well-being of the forest as a whole yet also shares profound commonalities with all other trees.

I feel that it's an important time for people to look beyond the exteriors of what we look like and what we do and try to recognize that Divineness lives within every person. When the flute is created or when I use the flute, it's my intention to try to articulate these ideas through the sound and vibration and physical building of the flute. The flute can help us to remember the Sacredness within each of us and the relationships that exist between us and all of Creation. Like everything in Creation, music and sound vibrate, and vibrations emit energy. Through vibration, this thing we call spirit, energy, goddess, god, whatever it is—this Great Mystery—moves through objects, tools, and things. To use the flute is my way of remembering our place as a part of everything else in nature and honoring our common source of life while celebrating our individual and cultural differences. To me, the greatest gift of the flute is its power as a tool for prayer and the healing that comes from remembering.

Common humanity, when I think of it, doesn't mean that we're all the same. Instead, it speaks to our origins, the source or place before our manifestation in this bodily form. I think that we all come from the same source. Our culture can limit how it is that we see ourselves, even when we're physically out of its usual context. Whether it's conscious or unconscious, it's a safe place because it's what we're familiar with—we think we know it, so we're comfortable with it. We might be physically in another space or place, but we carry that box with us. Common humanity allows us to see outside of that box. When people engage together in creative energy and creative activities, they can transcend or move beyond the definitions—the boxes—that we call culture.

Sometimes we exclude others' way of seeing or doing or believing because we don't avail ourselves of their way of being in the world, feeling that our own traditions or beliefs are better than others' ways. We create chasms in our relationships with each other, which can perpetuate a hurting cycle. It's my experience that a respectful exchange of music and musical traditions allows us to communicate with each other about our own ways of life, in ways more powerful than what we can share with words. Music can be a way to dialogue among and between Native and non-Native peoples. In my experience, these kinds of dialogues are critical to the preservation of Native traditions and to improving the world for future generations, through raising awareness and mutual understanding.

Cheryl Watching Crow Stedtler
(b. 1960)

Cheryl Stedtler is the director of the Nipmuc Nation's underwater archaeology endeavor, Project Mishoon, at Lake Quinsigamond in Worcester, Massachusetts. She founded and edited the Nipmuc tribal newsletter, *Nipmucspohke*. Additionally, she manages a website and several online communication groups for the Nipmucs. Stedtler is also a microbiologist, a journalist, a genealogist, and an elementary educator. She shares her Nipmuc culture and traditions with all ages. Her essay on Benjamin Brown first appeared in the *Nipmuc Nation Newsletter* (1.4, 2004). The poem "Full Circle" originally appeared on cassette jacket for Nancy Bright Sky Harris's *Full Circle*, a collection of traditional drumming by the Full Circle Drum Society. The other poems here are being published for the first time.

Honoring a Father and a Son

Deep in the Virginia forest, they crouched behind trees as bullets whizzed by their ears. The soldiers of Company I, 11th Connecticut Volunteer Infantry were just a fraction of the 60,000 Union soldiers at Cold Harbor that June day in 1864. It would be a tough, hard fight, and the men knew it. Many wrote out their names and addresses and sewed them to their uniforms the previous night, fearing the worst. Another wrote in his journal on the eve of the battle: *"June 3.—Cold Harbor. I was killed."*

Benjamin Brown was now a seasoned soldier. Enlisting in 1863, he had six months of service behind him. But the other battles were not like today. Trees cracked and fell against swarms of bullets; his comrades were dropping all around him. Then suddenly—a flash—and he was on the ground, a Minié ball through his jaw. The bullet had knocked out several teeth, fractured his jaw, and nearly severed his tongue. But Brown was driven. Dazed, he spat out the bullet, picked up his rifle, and pressed on. Shortly afterward a large tree toppled, pinning him and two men from his company against the bloodied ground.

Private Brown survived the Civil War and returned home to Woodstock, Connecticut, badly disfigured and several inches shorter than the day he enlisted. The tree that crushed him caused severe back injuries that left him hunched forward and disabled. Yet he lived to marry Ellen Lewis Brown and father nine children. His youngest child, Edward, would follow in his warrior footsteps.

Ed never knew his father, as Benjamin died shortly before his birth. He joined the Merchant Marines at a young age and later enlisted with the U.S. Marines in 1916. A few short months later, the younger Brown found himself in the countryside of England and France, at the heart of World War I. Sgt. Edward L. Brown's unit, the 67th Company of the 1st Marine Division, there fought the famous battles at Belleau Wood and Chateau-Thierry, where Marines earned the name "Devil Dogs."

Injuries from machine-gun fire and mustard gas eventually returned him to Woodstock, where he told a *Worcester Sunday Telegram* reporter, "Our corps took the brunt of the German advance in France and they tell us that we saved Paris. . . . I left most of my maties over there under the sod, as fine a lot of fearless lads as the U.S.A. ever banked on and I'm proud of the record."[5]

Brown married Violet Jackson during his tour in Southampton, England. When Brown was injured in France and sent back home, she became one of the first war brides to seek out her husband in the States. Together they had nine children, with my mother, Patricia, as the youngest.

These two men, father and son, never laid eyes on each other, yet they shared the same courage and honor. That same drive was passed on to them by their ancestors and shared by many of our Nipmuc relations.

Why did these men fight so heartily for a country that took so much from them? This has always been a mystery to me. It is nice to think that they were carrying on a legacy as caretakers of the land, protecting what was still their responsibility in their hearts and minds. It is equally appealing to think that they were standing up for their enslaved and oppressed brothers, knowing their ancestors shared a similar history. Nevertheless, the true answer cannot be known until we have all made the journey and are together again.

Benjamin no longer rests beneath a broken piece of a stranger's tombstone with his name scratched on it. Twelve years ago the government became accountable for their neglect. They placed a proper military tombstone at his gravesite in North Woodstock. He was honored with a military service as well as a private Native ceremony. Many Nipmuc stood in the pouring rain for him that day. They did not know him. They knew he was a Nipmuc and a warrior. That was all they needed to know.

Father and son have their feathers of honor. We dance for Benjamin, his son, Eddie, all the Nipmuc warriors that came before them, and those that will come after. We will dance to honor them until we can dance no more—because we can. Without their sacrifices, there would be no dancing. . . .

Aho.

Full Circle

I draw the line between need and greed,
sort the dilemmas of heart. . . .
I test the waters, bury remains,
dodge the poisoned dart.

How did my feet come to light
on such a cluttered path?
No crossroads warned of treacherous trails
or impending bitter wrath.

I look to the sun to find my way,
to the Moon and wingéd friends.
They trace the circle I've come to know
will bring me home again.

With quiet heart, I dance this path,
hear the strong and steady Drum . . .
certain that soon, when Manitoo wills,
Full Circle I'll have come.

Never Too Late to Dance

At 22, I grew my hair
wiggled my toes in mud
stood in the rain

wore no makeup
I watched the sun set, and then I watched it rise
I let the dog have first pick at dinner
He chose the steak and left me the bones
I smiled. He smiled.
At 22, I let the one within teach me
And now each day we dance together down the Red Road.

[Untitled]

Circle low
Circle high
Brother Hawk
Dance the sky

What lesson will you share today?
What wisdom will you bring?
Here below I watch the sky
To see you on the wing

Share with me what I don't see
Take me where you go
Carry my prayers to Manitoo
Kuttabotomish netomp. Aho.

Pressed

Parasitic
Analytic
Molding every line
Pressing
Undressing
Wanting to opine
Whining
Dining

Choosing
Schmoozing
Sowing compliments
Slanting
Panting
Cutting
Gutting
Reaping benefits
Printed.
Minted.
Set in stone.
Used.
Abused.
Left alone by my own kind.

Cheryll Toney Holley

(b. 1962)

Cheryll Toney Holley is the current Nipmuc Nation chief. She is also a highly skilled Nipmuc historian, researcher, and writer. She served on the Massachusetts Commission on Indian Affairs from 1998 to 2008. In addition to writing for the tribal newsletters, she maintains several blogs, including one for the Hassanamisco Museum, and also writes creatively. The historical essay below has been widely circulated on the Internet and among educational institutions.

A Brief Look at Nipmuc History

The people the English referred to as Nipmuc, or "fresh water people," occupied the interior portion of what are now Massachusetts and parts of Rhode Island and Connecticut. The original homelands included all of central Massachusetts from the New Hampshire–Vermont borders and south of the Merrimac Valley to Tolland and Windsor Counties in

Connecticut and the northwest portion of Rhode Island. To the east the homelands included the Natick-Sudbury area going west to include the Connecticut River Valley.

The people lived in scattered villages throughout the area, including Wabaquasset, Quinebaug, Quaboag, Pocumtuc, Agawam, Squawkeag, and Wachusett. Their economic and subsistence cycles consisted of hunting, gathering, planting, and harvesting in their seasons. These villages were linked together by kinship ties, trade alliances, and common enemies. They lived in *wetus*, which could be moved to other encampments. Often thought of as wanderers, they were instead careful planners and good stewards of the land upon which they lived.

There are scattered references throughout history to Europeans landing on the coasts of Canada, Maine, and the islands nearby. In 1497 John Cabot landed on Newfoundland, establishing new fishing grounds for northern Europeans. The French attempted several times to colonize the Canadian and Maine coastlines in order to capitalize on the fur trade. Deadly epidemics resulting from these encounters ravaged the Native population. Current scholars estimate a possible 80 percent mortality rate. Later, when the English began to settle the area, they took the vacant villages and abandoned cornfields as a sign from God that they were meant to supplant the Indians as the rightful inhabitants of the land. (Ojibway oral history tells that a sign was given and the people knew that a terrible thing was on its way to destroy the people. Therefore, they left and traveled west to new lands, taking the sacred fire with them until it was safe to return it to the homelands. They refer to the Indians in New England as the ones that stayed behind.)

The earliest contact between Nipmucs and the English was possibly in 1621 at Sterling, Massachusetts, where Nashawanon was sachem. The Nipmucs initially had friendly relationships with the Europeans. In one instance a Wabaquasset native, Acquittimaug, walked from his home to Boston carrying corn for the starving colonists. It is estimated that there were 5,000 to 6,000 Nipmucs when the Pilgrims landed at Plymouth in 1620. The bulk of the Nipmuc population lived along the rivers and streams connected to the Blackstone, Quaboag, Nashua, and Quinebaug Rivers.

In the 1640s the Reverend John Eliot of Roxbury began preaching to the Natives of Massachusetts, Rhode Island, and Connecticut. Between

1650 and 1675 he worked to establish "praying plantations," or villages to aid in the conversion of the Indian population. He felt that by removing them from their tribal villages and creating towns for them the Natives would eventually forsake their "ungodly" ways and emulate the English. In the towns the Native people were forbidden to practice their traditional ways, wore English-style clothes, lived in English-style homes, and attended the Puritan church. Eliot himself set up seven of the towns, known as the old praying villages: Wamesit, Nashobah, Okkokonimasit, Hassanamesit, Makunkokoag, Natick, and Punkapoag. Nipmucs and other Natives who joined these towns did so for a variety of reasons. Protection from Mohawk attacks, curiosity about English ways, economic survival, access to education, and the availability of food and clothing were some of the factors involved in Native people voluntarily moving to the towns. Natick was the first town and church to be established and Natives were trained there to serve in the other Indian churches. Word spread and Nipmucs further west set up seven more praying villages, known as the new praying towns. These included Manchaug, Chabanakongkomun, Maanexit, Quantisset, Wabaquasset, Packachoog, and Waeuntug.

Further encroachments by the English upon Indian land increased hostilities between the Natives and the English colonists. Some of the praying Indians forewarned the English of impending war with the Wampanoag leader Philip, son of Massasoit. In April 1675 John Sassamon, a Wampanoag who was an informer for the English, was found murdered. Two other Wampanoags were found guilty [of the murder] by the English and executed. The English blamed Philip for the [murder of the] men and accused him of planning war against the English. Philip escaped arrest by fleeing to Pocasset, where the village of his sister-in-law, Weetomoe, was located. Philip sought help from the Narragansetts but was refused. He then went into Nipmuc country, where many were anxious to follow him into battle. War had begun and the praying Indians chose to fight and scout for the English. In July 1675 representatives of the Mohegans traveled to Boston and pledged their support for the English.

English colonists began voicing their fears of Indian attacks. They believed that the praying Indians would join the war on the side of Philip. In August 1675 the colonial government made a decision to confine all Indians to five plantations: Natick, Nashobah, Punkapoag, Wamesit, and Hassanamesit. Any Indians found outside of these limits were subject to jail or death. This severely limited the Natives' way of life. They could no longer hunt, harvest, or trade.

The murmuring against the praying Indians continued, and on October 30, 1675, the colonists forcibly removed the residents of Natick to Deer Island in Boston Harbor. By the end of the year they were joined by [members of] the Punkapoags and the Nashobahs. The Hassanamisco Indians were attacked and carried off by the Nipmucs fighting for freedom in November of 1675. That same month the English fired upon Wamesit, killing innocent women and children. The Wamesits, besieged by both the English and their Nipmuc neighbors, asked the colonial government for protection and were sent to Deer Island as well. Before the end of the war even the praying Indians that spied for and fought on the English side were sent to Deer Island in Boston Harbor as prisoners of the war.

Philip was eventually killed, and the war ended nearly a year later. The praying Indians were released from Deer Island and allowed to inhabit only certain Indian towns: Natick, Dudley (Chabanakongkomun), Hassanamesit, and Wabaquasset. The Nipmucs who had resisted the English invasion were killed or sold into slavery, or they went into hiding, often with tribes to the north and west of Nipmuc country.

The English pushed further into Nipmuc country, determined to make permanent settlements in the area. To survive, many Nipmucs moved from the reservations and adopted English habits and dress. They still practiced seasonal mobility and itinerant trading, selling baskets, brooms, and herbs to the white settlers. Nipmuc men fought in Queen Anne's and King George's Wars in the 1700s and participated in the Abenaki resistance in the 1720s, but they fought against the Abenakis. Nipmuc men also served in the Revolutionary War on the American side. During the Civil War Nipmucs served in both the 54th and the 55th Massachusetts Infantry Regiments of the Union Army.[6] Increasing numbers of Nipmucs moved into the growing towns in search of work and mates. Serving in the wars caused a shortage of Nipmuc men, and therefore Nipmuc women began to marry non-Natives, especially African-Americans, in order to have children, continue the tribe, and enable economic survival.

Intermarriage between Nipmuc people continued as well. Records from the 18th and 19th centuries show multiple marriages between Nipmucs from Dudley, Natick, Woodstock (Wabaquasset), and Grafton (Hassanamisco). Although they lived further apart, Nipmucs continued to maintain kinship ties, receive annuity payments from the state, and establish Nipmuc enclaves away from the traditional reservations. Nipmucs, like other Indians in Massachusetts, were considered wards of the state. Indian commissioners and guardians were appointed over them to manage their lands and debts. Many of these guardians stole from the Nipmucs by illegally selling land to pay their own debts. In 1849 and 1859 the commonwealth commissioned a count of Indians and a report on their condition. These reports, the Bird/Briggs Report in 1849 and the 1859 Earle Report, are used to this day as evidence of continued interactions between Indians and the Commonwealth of Massachusetts.

In June 1869 "Indians and people of color, heretofore known and called Indians" became citizens of Massachusetts through the Massachusetts Indian Enfranchisement Act. The Massachusetts legislature tried to follow federal Reconstruction-era race policy and came to the conclusion that, since there were few "pure-blooded" Indians left and since the state had always been committed to freedom for the African-American, why not for the Indian? Unfortunately, the act threw open Indian lands for sale to non-Indians. Lands held in common were divided up, as in the case of Dudley.

In 1871 the last of the Dudley land was sold and five of the families were placed in a tenement house on Lake Street in Webster. The rest scattered, moving in with other Nipmuc families living in Woodstock, Worcester, Providence, and Hassanamisco. Worcester developed strong Indian enclaves in mainly African-American neighborhoods. Nipmuc activities became centered on the Hassanamisco Reservation. Events such as the annual clambake and elections on the 4th of July were times for Nipmucs to gather and discuss tribal business. In 1886 living members and descendants of the Pegan Band of Nipmucs (the Dudley Indians) each received $61.61 as their share of the proceeds from the sale of the Dudley reservation.

In the early 1920s a variety of pan-Indian movements, including the Indian Council of New England and the National Algonquin Indian Council, created increased opportunities for Nipmucs to practice and share traditional ways and to become politically involved in Indian issues. The Cisco family at Hassanamisco became tribal leaders and formed the Mohawk Club, which met in Worcester to discuss and plan educational, cultural, and social events. The name was later changed to the Hassanamisco Club, with meetings held both at the reservation and in members' homes in Worcester. Tribal leaders during this time included Sarah M. Cisco, James Lemuel Cisco, and Althea Hazard.

Annual clambakes and elections continued in the late 1930s, with Sarah Cisco remaining in the leadership position. In 1937 and 1941 she petitioned the Massachusetts legislature for pensions for Hassanamisco people and for the upkeep of the reservation. In 1938 she also filed a claim for the return of Lake Ripple, a man-made lake in Grafton, to the Hassanamisco people. During World War II things were quiet in Nipmuc country. Nipmuc men went to war, and the women worked in factories and raised children. After the war community gatherings resumed. Some of the events at Hassanamisco became open to the public, but meetings where tribal issues were discussed remained open to Nipmuc people only. Election Day continued, with tribal members spending the entire weekend camped out on the reservation. Requests for assistance were made to the Indian Claims Commission and the North American Indian League of Nations.

The Nipmuc Indian Chapter of Worcester formed in the 1950s amid disputes between Worcester Nipmucs and the Hassanamisco leadership. Among those active in the Nipmuc Indian Chapter of Worcester were William and Elizabeth Moffitt, Lillian Brooks King, Roswell Hazard, Mabel Hamilton, Carl Oscar Bates, Jessie Mays, and George Wilson. The chapter was formed to provide for the educational and cultural advancement of Nipmuc people with the hope of beginning other chapters in other cities. The split was soon mended, though, and tribal gatherings continued at Hassanamisco. The Annual Hassanamisco Fair continued in July, Massachusetts Indian Day was celebrated in August, and the Hassanamisco Council met regularly. In 1962 the Hassanamisco Foundation was created to ensure that the reservation would be preserved intact and that other provisions were made for the Cisco family line. Zara Cisco Brough became tribal sachem and assumed leadership responsibilities. Zara was actively involved in Grafton town politics and successfully won dredging rights to Lake Ripple for Hassanamisco. As sachem, she worked for the protection of tribal rights and the preservation of the reservation.

In 1974 the Massachusetts Commission on Indian Affairs was created, and in 1976 the Commonwealth of Massachusetts officially recognized the Hassanamisco Band of Nipmucs. Nipmucs from other family lines became more active on the Hassanamisco Council. Members of the Council of Chiefs included Walter Vickers, Joseph Vickers, Charlie Hamilton, George

Cisco, Peter Silva Sr., and Samuel Cisco. The Hassanamisco Foundation was amended to ensure that if the Cisco line ended the reservation would never leave Nipmuc hands. Zara made plans for "New Town," a 500-acre town on what is now Grafton. She petitioned the governor and the legislature for the state-owned land to create this Indian town, but the land was eventually given to Tufts University for a veterinary school.

The Chaubunagungamaug Band, under the leadership of Edwin Morse, formed in 1981 to revitalize the Dudley Band of Nipmucs. Land was donated to the Chaubunagungamaug for a reservation in Thompson on the original Dudley reservation. Walter Vickers was named head chief by the sachem, Zara, and the Hassanamisco Council in 1982. Later that year he conducted the ceremony to install Edwin Morse as chief of the Chaubunagungamaug Band. The Reno Report, researched and created by Zara and Dr. Stephen Reno, became the official petition for recognition in 1984.

The 1990s brought much activity, both good and bad. The Nipmuc Tribal Acknowledgment Project, begun in 1989, continued the important research for federal recognition and compiled a census of the tribe. In 1995 the Hassanamisco and the Chaubunagungamaug Bands came together to work toward recognition, thus uniting tribal members under one banner, the Nipmuc Nation. Unfortunately, the unification did not last long. In 1995 the Chaubunagungamaug Band split off from the Nipmuc Nation to attempt federal recognition on its own. The split was due to diverse factors, including the division of power and tribal roll guidelines. Several Nipmuc organizations were founded during the 1990s. The Nipmuc Indian Association of Connecticut was founded by Joan Luster to provide educational, cultural, and traditional services to Connecticut Nipmucs. Cheryl Stedtler began publishing the *Nipmucspohke* newsletter in 1994 to keep tribal members everywhere informed. In 1997 the Nipmuc Women's Health Coalition, headed by Liz Coldwind Kiser, was formed to educate and inform Nipmuc women and their families about health prevention, healthy practices, and traditional healing. To assist the tribe in economic and community development, the Nipmuc Indian Development Corporation was created in 1999 by a group of concerned Nipmuc people.

Despite the hardship and multiple setbacks, the Nipmuc Nation Hassanamisco Band in January 2001 received a positive preliminary finding on federal acknowledgment.

(2001)

Bruce Curliss
(b. 1965)

Bruce Curliss is well known as a powwow emcee and leading Nipmuc spokesman. He has worked and traveled extensively throughout Indian Country. He has served on the Nipmuc Nation Tribal Council as well as on the Massachusetts Commission on Indian Affairs, which he chaired. Curliss worked on the PBS series *We Shall Remain*, and he has directed his own film, *Survivor*. Currently he lives and works in Santa Fe, New Mexico.

"Authentic," Power, and Stuck in My Craw

Strange how one can wake in the morning and think the day is normal, or as close to it as any morning could possibly be. When all of a sudden—BAM—reflection hits and the thoughts are diverted and shifted, twisted, and focused on an idea. Let's take today for instance. I was waking as I usually do and grateful to be waking up, which meant I was alive (one of the things I'm usually grateful for). But right before I got up and out of bed the thoughts of the word "authentic" hit. Maybe it was inspiration or just recent conversations; maybe it was my deep-seated disdain for the word. Actually, I don't have a problem with the word "authentic"; I would suppose it's about the use and situations I have found myself in when it has been used.

Like most words, "authentic" has its origins, uses, and definitions. Yet when I look it up in the dictionary, the multiplicity of defining properties of the word itself, only one stands out and here it is from the *Merriam-Webster Online Dictionary*: "true to one's own personality, spirit, or character." I think of "authentic" as a word meaning original, factual, real, being a meaning that is mostly used when talking of objects, such as art or other inanimate things. However, my disdain for "authentic" occurs when people use it as a tool of power over another group, person, or animate object.

So this is what got stuck in my craw this morning, and as a way to understand why it causes me such annoyance, here I am writing about it. A little about me might help. I'm a Nipmuc Indian from Massachusetts; I served as a commissioner and the chair of the Massachusetts Commission on Indian Affairs; I have worked for national nonprofits with tribal communities all over the country, mostly in education, training, and youth development. I have served my tribe as a tribal council member, a powwow emcee, and lecturer and presenter on a multitude of topics related to my work and lifeway. I have had way too many experiences to write them all here, but I'm grateful and have been humbled by every one of them.

One might ask, at least I would: how and why does a single word create such bedevilment? For me, it's not just one word; as I mentioned above, it's about power. You could replace "authentic" with a multitude of other words that have been used to devalue, humiliate, and degrade people, communities, and lifeways, and even to conquer or extinguish cultures.

I can think of a host of examples when the term "authentic" has been used as a term of power. Maybe sharing a few would be helpful. In my professional career I have often had to put together research and materials for training, funding, or policy. On one such occasion when I presented my work to a supervisor, I was taken aback when the response was, "This doesn't sound right to me; can you verify this and make sure it is authentic?" At the time I didn't recognize the challenge to me or the idea of whose material might be recognized as authentic over someone else's. I prefer going to the source, the tribes themselves if possible, rather than a published scholar. In another situation I was asked for some very specific information for publication. The information was tribally specific and came from the tribe itself. Once again I was taken aback when my supervisor questioned the authenticity and even the source and went on to give examples of non-Indian scholars who had contradictions to the information I presented.

The last example is one that I run into far too often. I have had the opportunity to emcee many powwows over the years. I use the term "Indian" when describing dances, singing groups, and the people. Inevitably, someone or several someones will tell me that the term "Indian" is incorrect and that I should use the term "Native American." I will spare the expletives that I want to use in response (I'm a professional, after all). What I usually try to say is, "I use the term 'Indian,' and although that isn't what you may understand, it is what I know and how I identify the people whom I'm speaking of and how I identify myself." If a supplemental explanation is needed, I expound: "'Native,' by my understanding, is that if you were born there you are a native of that place. So, those born in America are native of America and therefore Native American. For me that just doesn't cut it. I may have been born here, but it's much deeper than that. 'Indian' doesn't quite cut it either, but that's how I identify."

It is just absurd that someone would question how one identifies. Yet someone has embedded the term "Native American" in the American psyche, that it's the right and "authentic" term to describe the authentic first Americans—hence removing power from one group and giving the other power over it in the most basic form of identification.

Looking back over these thoughts, I can't help but wonder if there truly is an authentic Indian experience. I find myself laughing inside, because "authentic" isn't stuck in my craw any longer. I have removed the proverbial thorn from this lion's paw. But what I do know is that "authentic" is just a word, like so many others that I choose not to pay attention to, because I understand its meaning and use. For some it's to gain understanding and for some a tool to challenge, and mostly it's a word used to exercise power and ego, a moving target based on the needs of the people wanting the truth to match their understanding of truth. For my "authentic" self, the definition is simple and right from *Merriam-Webster*: being true to one's own personality, spirit, or character. How about you?

Woman, Mother, Sister, Daughter, Lover

Woman, Mother, Sister, Daughter, Lover
I pray for you
I pray for me
I pray to Earth Mother
I pray for your understanding
I pray for I do not know

Woman, Mother, Daughter, Sister, Lover
I pray for you
Your love everlasting
I pray for me
Your inner beauty soft
I pray to Grandmother Moon

I pray for your understanding
I pray for I do not know

Woman, Mother, Daughter, Sister, Lover
I pray for you
Your pains I can never carry
I pray for me
You are strength that holds my spirit
I pray to Sister Corn
I pray for your understanding
I pray for I do not know

Woman, Mother, Sister, Daughter, Lover
I pray for you
My existence is only justified because of yours
I pray for me
Your nourishment so multifaceted
Woman, Mother, Sister, Daughter, Lover
I pray for your understanding
I pray for I do not know . . . I pray for I do not know

For Woman:

What would describe you?
Could the wind call Woman? Woman is already in the wind
Blowing soft gentle winds up from the south
Bringing warmth to a chilled spirit of man
Woman you are

What would describe you?
Could the ocean crashing call Woman? Woman is already the ocean
Not the crashing of water but the gentle mist
Every drop of mist says "Woman" and refreshes the spirit of man
Woman you are

What would describe you?
Could the birds call Woman? Woman is already in every song
Filling the air and ears of all those who can hear
Bringing peace and solitude to the spirit of man
Woman you are

What would describe you?
Could the poet write the word "Woman"? Woman is in every word
Filling every page and bringing life to all those who read them
Giving flight to the spirit of man
Woman you are

What would describe you?
Could anything more than the call—"Woman"—do this?
I know not the answers of your description
I know "Woman you are" is enough for my lack of understanding
This which releases the spirit of man
Woman you are . . .
Woman you are . . .

For Mother:

You are what gives life to all that is living—you are known to me as
    Mother
I sometimes question my existence—you are known to me as Mother
I sometimes question the love I give—you are known to me as Mother
I sometimes question the love I receive—you are known to me as
    Mother
My strength, my fortitude, my laughter—you are known to me as
    Mother
My anger, my solitude, my frustration, my peace—you are known to
    me as Mother
You have given to me the most precious of gifts; you have given me all
    of who I am
You have been through it all standing tall and supportive, never
    judging and always loving
You have more strength than the strongest of strong
I can only give you my gratitude, love and thanks and let you know all
    that I am and
all I can be is love
You are known to me as Mother

For Daughter:

My little girl, you are the best present of the best Christmas

They say: someday you will grow up and away
They say: someday you will replace my love with that of another
They say: someday you will hate me just for being
They say: someday you will love me just because
They say: someday you will be angry because I say no
They say: someday you will . . . just forget someday
Today: I write these words for you; maybe someday will be
Have patience with me, Daughter please have patience with me
Know I love you, know that my love can't be replaced or duplicated
Know you are my daughter, you will always be my little girl
Know that I am a man, and can't always see what you see
Know I revel in the joy of watching you grow
Know this, my little girl, you are the best present of the best
    Christmas . . .
and I love you

For Sister:

Sister—older or maybe younger
Sister—stronger or maybe weaker
Sister—bolder or maybe timid
Sister—you are my hero, you have gone first and set the standard
Sister—you show us all who Woman, Mother, and Daughter are
Sister—you justify it
Sister—you share your nourishment, give of yourself
Sister—you give selflessly, sacrifice often
Sister—you are the heart of all flowers in springtime bloom
Sister—I thank Creation for your existence
Sister—I remember you in all the prayers taught
Sister—you are my thoughts
Sister—you are my wishes
Sister—you are, and always will be, the inspiration to me

For Lover:

I use words to describe what cannot be described, only felt
Half my soul, half my being
Bringing balance, turning my balance upside down
Only to realize I'm now right side up

I think of waterfalls crashing, calm pools of water
Warm and soothing, all in the same breath
Lover, for love you are most important to my being
I have only one place for you
Never a pedestal—by my side—in front—never behind
I run to catch up when you are ahead
Your patience undeniable, as you wait for me and understand
Lover—if I could only put into words where I soar to when you are
   near or even in just a passing moment
Lover—you are truly Woman in all the ways that I can understand as
   man
Lover—your energy only to be held next to the Sun's always nurturing
   my heart and soul
Lover—you are more than lover, you are the true and indescribable
   meaning of love
Lover—you give man, this man, the most important task of his life
To love, to truly love

Larry Spotted Crow Mann

(b. 1967)

Larry Spotted Crow Mann serves as the Drum Keeper of the Quabbin Lake Singers, a sacred trust of the Nipmuc Tribe. He travels throughout the United States and Canada to schools, colleges, powwows, and other organizations, sharing his music, culture, and history. Mann appears in several documentaries: *We Shall Remain*, directed by Chris Eyre for P B S; and *Living in Two Worlds: Native American Experiences on the Boston Harbor Islands* and *First Patriots*, both produced by Aaron Cadieux. He advised Margaret Barton on her book *New England on Fire* and has published his own work in *Memescapes: A Journal of Contemporary Literature* at Quinsigamond Community College. He is currently completing a novel; the selections below come from his first book, *Tales from the Whispering Basket*.

From "Deal Me In"

Early in the last century, in the 1930s, my mother's family lived in the woods of northeastern Connecticut in an area just shy of the Massachusetts border. The land was rich with wildlife and dotted with clean lakes full of fish. Streams meandered through lush forests without dams or mills. Only narrow footpaths and dirt roads just wide enough for a single, occasional horse-drawn buggy interrupted the old-growth forests.

Carved of the heart of the mixed oak, ash, pine, and birch woodlands, and nearly hidden among them, were six cabins clustered within a half square mile of one another. This is where my grandparents, aunts, and uncles farmed, fished, hunted, and otherwise lived off the land. This was their home, as well as the home of our ancestors, since time immemorial.

Mother Earth provided everything they needed, so my grandparents rarely had to go into town. These houses weren't perfect or as good as our ancestors' longhouses or *wetus*, but the people did their best with the cabins. For instance, leaky roofs were a problem from time to time, and some of the local critters could get inside and take a meal for themselves.

Clean, cold running water was outside at the well near the cornfield. Kerosene lamps provided light, especially needed when walking to the outhouse in the dark of night. Grandma told us that one of the best memories of their cabin was the stone fireplace. So warm, cozy, and peaceful did she feel that just sitting near its warmth would bring her good medicine. She would snuggle into her quilt for hours, listening to stories from her elders of great mysteries and wondrous happenings, as well as life lessons to guide her.

The work was hard but everybody pitched in. They enjoyed life and took care of one another. Because of this they were fearless. No one ever had the need to talk about the Great Depression because their sharing allowed them to survive and the atmosphere around them was that of tenderness and joy.

One thing about Indian people is that they know how to have a good time and laugh, even when life is at its toughest. So, once a week, ever since anyone could remember, my grandmother said, the entire family would gather at Uncle Henry's cabin for the weekly card game. Now, Uncle Henry, like my Great-Grandma, knew how to use herbs, roots, and trees of the forest to cure and heal ailments. He was also connected to the Sprit World and would share stories and songs about our relatives from the past with the help of the family Drum. After Great-Grandma crossed over to the Land of Endless Spirits, they all relied on Uncle Henry for most of the healing.

Uncle Henry was tall—over six feet—and his skin was light brown like an autumn oak leaf. He combed his straight black hair back and it reached all the way to his shoulders. He was always smiling and was known as one of the nicest people you could ever meet. That's probably why the weekly card game was always at his place; he would never say no to it and never yelled at anyone about the mess left behind.

Of course, you can't have a card game without a feast to go with it. Everyone brought a little something. Some of their favorites, depending on the season, were venison stew, succotash, corn on the cob, fiddleheads, baked beans, and corn cake topped with wild berries. And of course there was plenty of bannock bread and coffee to last the people throughout the evening.

So on this particular day, as they have done since anyone can remember, my family held the weekly card game. All twelve of my folks played cards late into the night, laughing, eating, and joking with one another with friendly insults and jibes.

What a beautiful sight it must have been, and how glad I am that they told me all about it. Imagine! All my relatives sitting around that worn-down pine table in the kitchen. One of the legs was off by about two inches, and some of the old playing cards from years past were stuck underneath it to bring back its balance. The kitchen was very simple and rustic, no finished or stained wood there. Sturdy, handmade cabinets were mounted by the ice box and over the windowsill. A wooden barrel of flour rested by itself in the corner, lonely looking, except everyone knew its friendly contents. The shelves were home to Nipmuc storage baskets made by Uncle Paul and Aunt Hanna. Some had tobacco; some held herbs; and others, natural remedies that Uncle would use. The small, wood-burning stove sat by the back door, so as soon as you walked in, you would be captured by the aroma of the stew or bannock bread being turned in the cast-iron pan by an aunt. And the back plate on the stove was a permanent home for that old aluminum coffeepot.

Every now and then a relative would get up to grab some more bannock or go into the living room to stoke the fire to curb the chill from the spring air. That night, as Uncle Billy put another log in the fire, he complimented his brother Henry for his fine workmanship on the hand-carved bows and arrows that were mounted on the wall to the left of the fireplace, next to the fishing and hunting supplies and split-ash baskets.

Even though the game got intense at times, it was all in good fun. Uncle Paul would be "up" in the game and always thought he was the best player anyhow. Once in awhile he would send playful taunts to his wife, Aunty Hanna, to catch up. Uncle John and Aunt Nellie were very competitive and were working together on a strategy to out-do Paul. Uncle Billy would lose track of his hand sometimes because he would be retelling the family how he caught the biggest fish in the world. Aunt Doris and the rest of them struggled to keep up but still had fun. They never played for money, but they played with just as much vigor and excitement as if a lot of money was at stake. Uncle Henry didn't even care if he won or not, he was just always happy to have his family with him and to be surrounded by so much love.

Then out of nowhere there was a weird knock at the door. It was weird because everyone around there just walks in and says hello. The nearest town was 20 miles away and it was 11:30 at night, and nobody comes around after dark in those parts. The forest was so dark you couldn't see your hand in front of you. The knock caused a sudden pause from the laughter and chatter. Even the crickets and peepers outside took a momentary interlude from their singing. All the eyes in the kitchen abruptly turned to the door, then to each other in a nervous grin. They were all wondering who it could be. Uncle John had a rushing thought to himself that maybe it was the Indian Affairs agent coming to try and take their land. Aunt Doris reflected on similar fears that state agents were coming to rip away the children and ship them off to Carlisle Indian Boarding School.

Uncle Henry quickly sensed the unease in his family and said, "Ok, everybody. Let's relax. It's gonna be fine; let me just see who it is."

Heart in the Clouds

Heart in the clouds,
Traversing the fragmented sky—
The Binary Wind
Forces Earth to Cry.
Heart Burns down,
Like Tears of Ember,
Discharging from a departed plague,
Erupting from my Center,
Illuminating the Dreams,
Like diaphanous blood,
Cursed into existence
And transfused from above,
Like a diffused kingdom,
And removed from my Throne,
Destitute in a dark place,
False comfort in the womb,
Clouds become Heartless,
And gather to Cheat the Sun,
Like a viscous path,
Crossed and Undone.

The Crow

(In His Own Words)

I am the Crow,
Mystical as the Moon
And Dark as the Night,
Traversing through the Spirit World
On Shadow Wings of Flight.
Some have feared my Murky Hue,
Even called it a Curse,
But the Dimness of my Feathers,
Binds me to the Universe.
The Sun that you seek
Is Beauty we cannot hide.
The Glowing of my Feathers
Reflects the Light inside.
I'm the product of the Dream World
Transformed by Creator's Gift,
Sometimes Bird,
Sometimes Man.
The Ability
To Shape-shift,
The things I Foresee
Have Powerful Distinctions,
Like Earth, Fire, and Sky,
Guiding me to the Visions.
My Family Ties are Eternal and Strong,
Tight as a row of Corn,
Loving and Sharing with One Another,
From the moment we are Born.
My words have been misunderstood—
Sometimes, mistaken for a Caw;
But if you listen with your Heart,
I'm speaking Creator's Law.

Sarah "She Paints Horses" Stedtler

(b. 1997)

Sarah Stedtler, a high school sophomore in New Jersey, is the daughter of Cheryl Watching Crow Stedtler (above). Stedtler is active in the Nipmuc youth community. In her free time, she enjoys drawing, horseback riding, and Native fancy shawl dancing. She hopes to have a career working with animals. These are her first published poems, written when she was in the fifth grade.

The Fresh Water People

Nipmuc is what I am
Interesting to other people
Powwows almost every month
Means "fresh water people"
Unknown to most of the world
Care for all the creatures
Kind to Mother Earth
Shares knowledge

An Indian Gathering

Powwow
Traditional, fun
Singing, dancing, drumming
Lots of Indian heritage
Honoring, laughing, talking
Loud, amazing
Gathering

Indians

What are Indians?
    An ancient American
    A person of a certain tribe
    A people almost destroyed by Englishmen
    The first farmers
    Mistreated by others
    Victims of harsh stereotypes
    My heritage
    An honoring people
    The creators of many inventions
    A people who have hope
    Nipmucs, Wampanoags, Cherokee
That is what Indians are!

The Dancer's Foot

If I were a foot
And you were the ground
I'd touch you so lightly
There would be no sound . . .

Notes

1. Because Great Britain and the colonies did not switch from the Julian calendar (with the year beginning on March 25) to the Gregorian calendar until 1752, some older documents use double dating.
2. For a full accounting of the note and its history, see Jill Lepore, *The Name of War: King Philip's War and the Origins of American Identity* (New York: Random House, 1999), 96.
3. The Dudley Band uses the variant spelling "Nipmuck." Tribal members with affiliations in both communities (like Larry Spotted Crow Mann, also a contributor to this section) sometimes use the spellings interchangeably as a gesture of unity.
4. A roach is a traditional headdress.
5. *Worcester Sunday Telegram*, May 18, 1919.
6. The Fifty-Fourth and the Fifty-Fifth Regiments were "colored" regiments.

Further Reading

NIPMUC AUTHORS

Bostic, Corrine. *Go Onward and Upward: An Interpretive Biography of the Life of Miss Sarah Ella Wilson, a Prominent Forerunner of Worcester School Teachers, Based on Fact, Oral Reminiscence, and Written Recollections.* Worcester MA: Commonwealth Press, 1970. Print.

———. *The Horns of Freedom.* Deerfield MA: Deerfield Press, 1971. Print.

———. *Requiem for Bluesville.* Worcester MA: Shield Press, 1970. Print.

———. *Togetherness.* Worcester MA: Graphic Arts Center, 1980. Print.

Brough, Zara Cisco, and James E. Atchison. *Trails of the Nipmucks: Indian Love Call . . . Legends—Folklore and History of the Nipmuck Indians of Worcester County and Neighboring Tribes.* Olmstead Falls OH: Olmstead Falls Printing, 1975. Print.

Doughton, Thomas L. "Unseen Neighbors: Native Americans of Central Massachusetts, a People Who Had 'Vanished.'" *After King Philip's War: Presence and Persistence in Indian New England.* Ed. Colin Calloway. Hanover NH: University Press of New England, 1997. 207–30. Print.

Gould, Rae. "The Nipmuc Nation, Federal Acknowledgement, and a Case of Mistaken Identity." *Recognition, Sovereignty Struggles, and Indigenous Rights in the United States: A Sourcebook.* Ed. Amy Den Ouden and Jean O'Brien. Chapel Hill: University of North Carolina Press, 2013. Print. 213–36.

Nipmucspohke. http://nipmucspohke.homestead.com/index1.html. Web. 2 July 2011.

Spotted Crow Mann, Larry. *The Mourning Road to Thanksgiving.* Marble NC: Word Branch Publishing, 2014.

———. *Tales from the Whispering Basket.* Boston: CreateSpace, 2011. Print.

ADDITIONAL READING

Connole, Dennis A. *Indians of the Nipmuck Country in Southern New England 1630–1750: An Historical Geography.* Jefferson NC: McFarland, 2007. Print.

Izard, Holly. "Hepsibeth Hemenway and Her Portrait: A Native American Story." *Old Time New England: Journal of the Society for the Preservation of New England Antiquities* 77 (Fall–Winter 1999): 49–85. Print.

Mandell, Daniel R. *Behind the Frontier: Indians in Eighteenth-Century Eastern Massachusetts.* Lincoln: University of Nebraska Press, 2000. Print.

———. *Tribe, Race, History: Native Americans in Southern New England, 1780—1880.* Baltimore: Johns Hopkins University Press, 2011. Print.

Meserve, Walter T. "English Works of Seventeenth-Century Indians." *American Quarterly* 8 (1956): 264–76. Print.

O'Brien, Jean M. *Dispossession by Degrees: Indian Land and Identity in Natick, Massachusetts, 1650–1790.* Lincoln: University of Nebraska Press, 2003. Print.

Robinson, Barbara. *Native American Sourcebook: A Teacher's Resource on New England Native Peoples.* Concord MA: Concord Museum, 1988. Print.

Rowlandson, Mary. *The Sovereignty and Goodness of God: With Related Documents.* Ed. Neal Salisbury. Boston: Bedford/St. Martin's, 1997. Print.

Trumbull, James Hammond. *Natick Dictionary: A New England Indian Lexicon.* 1903. New introduction by R. D. Madison and Karen Lentz Madison. Lincoln: University of Nebraska Press, 2009. Print.

WAMPANOAG

Introduction

Joan Tavares Avant
(Granny Squannit)

As an Elder I'm empowered and proud to have the opportunity to bring together the voices of two indigenous tribes who were here ten thousand to twelve thousand years before the Pilgrims landed on our shores. We are the Mashpee Wampanoag ("People of the First Light") and the Wampanoag Tribe of Gay Head ("Aquinnah"). Our boundary locations are different, and we each design and follow our own Native nation-building in tribal governance, policy, leadership, and language preservation.

Mashpee, the original "Land of the Wampanoag," is located on Cape Cod, in southeastern Massachusetts within Barnstable County. Cape Cod is a peninsula extending from the eastern coast of Massachusetts into the Atlantic Ocean. The Aquinnah Tribe of Gay Head is located at the tip of Martha's Vineyard in Massachusetts. We live by the rhythms of Mother Earth and the oral stories and traditions that our ancestors and leaders left us with. I remember my grandmother Mabel L. Avant, Nokomis, telling stories before we went to bed or when we were sitting under the apple tree. When those stories were told at the library, most children were scared to walk home.

Oral history, traditional beliefs, respect for Mother Earth, and respect for the animals—all of these simply form how we live in our communities. As Vine Deloria Jr. (Standing Rock Sioux) explains, "People believed that each tribe had its own special relationship to the superior spiritual forces which governed the universe and that the job of each set of tribal beliefs was to fulfill its own tasks without worrying about what others were doing. Tribal knowledge therefore was not fragmented and was valid within the historical and geographical scope of the people's experience" (qtd. in Wilson 9). In New England, oral traditions helped us survive. As medicine man Slow Turtle (John Peters) told me when I wrote an essay last year for *Cultural Survival Quarterly*, "Each Indian understood what his or her responsibility was, to care for the land for seven generations to come. We all know that the earth sustains us by watching nature. The muskrat possesses the knowledge that he had in the beginning. . . . Today people would call such a story a legend. It may be. Legends are pictures that contain the truth that the spirit itself works through nature and that by reading her script we can conform our lives in harmony with the Creator."

Why are we still here? For some tribal members, this remains a mystery because of the European colonization imposed on our society. I say we are the first people—that's why we are here.

COLONIZATION

The Indian was a free person; they were trying to turn him into an English person.
—*Vernon Lopez (Silent Drum), Mashpee Wampanoag chief*

The reason WE ARE STILL HERE is because of the courage and perseverance of our leaders who took the brunt of colonization. When the Pilgrims landed in 1620, they came with a contract to settle the area known as Massachusetts Bay and New Plymouth Colonies. They noticed that the Wampanoag had not subdued the land the way they were accustomed to. English colonists saw their new home as a wilderness and set out to redeem it. They decided that they had a natural right to the land. The Mayflower Compact established the first basis in the New World for written laws, which were created to rule over the indigenous traditional societies as well.

In 1647 towns were required to provide schools and "keep watch and ward" over the Indians. The pedagogical framework instituted by the colonists was structured to indoctrinate young boys and adults to be teachers and ministers. According to the English theory, this process would bring Native people to civility. In 1658 the Massachusetts General Court provided what was referred to as home rule. Indian villages and plantations could choose their own magistrates to determine both criminal and civil cases, but not without the watchful eye of an appointed English magistrate, who was given the responsibility of setting the time and place of trial and who ultimately approved the decisions of

Native judges. In 1665 the court ordered that no Indian should at any time worship their "false gods" or "the devil." If any Natives should transgress this law, the powwow (religious leader) would have to pay twenty shillings.

In 1677 the General Court passed an act providing that all Indians who were permitted to live within the colony should be confined to one of four plantations: Natick, Stoughton, Grafton, or Chelmsford, with the exception of Indian children and servicewomen within English communities. Natives who violated the regulations and lived outside the reservations were sent to houses of correction, or prisons. Under the acts of 1746, 1753, and 1758, the Massachusetts General Court appointed guardians to observe Native towns such as Mashpee, Falmouth, and Middleboro. Readers will learn much more about this colonial history and its effects on our people in the Wampanoag writings below.

The destiny of our generations depends on how our children are prepared for the challenges of the future. Wampanoag people have always worked hard to preserve tradition and ensure that our children have the knowledge they need to survive. I believe that it is up to indigenous leaders and parents today to continue combating the evils of colonization so that preserving our traditions will be easier for future generations. Our children can hopefully follow the ways of our ancestors, as before contact.

MASHPEE, "LAND OF THE WAMPANOAG"

We name ourselves after the land we live with. Because not only are we breathing in, we are also drinking from the water that is flavored by that very land. Whatever is deposited in the soil is in that water is in us. So we are all one thing, and we name ourselves after the place that is our nurturing. That sustains our life.

—*Ramona Peters, Mashpee Wampanoag artist*

Mashpee measures approximately twenty-seven square miles. The year-round population is roughly fourteen thousand. During the summer tourist season the population triples.

For most of its early history, the land belonged to the Wampanoag, who were also known as the South Sea Indians. Mashpee is one of approximately sixty-nine original villages that composed the Wampanoag Nation, whose people spoke the Algonquian language. Before the 1800s Mashpee was called Massipee or Marshpee. It was established as an Indian plantation in 1637. In 1660 Mashpee was organized as a praying town. "Marshpee District" was incorporated under the British Crown in 1763, but the law was repealed in 1766. In 1834 Mashpee was incorporated for the second time as a district. In 1870 Marshpee was incorporated into a town; the letter "r" was deleted and the town since has been celebrated as Mashpee. Indigenous inhabitants, the Mashpee Wampanoag, are the first people to have lived here.

Chief Vernon Lopez (Silent Drum), now over eighty years old, remembers,

> When I was growing up in the town of Mashpee it was a wooded area with pitch pine, cedar, cranberry bogs, many wild medicinal herbs, and many edible berries. We fished the bays, rivers, and ponds, hunted the forests, planted gardens, and traveled our ancient ways. I remember an icehouse, one small store with penny candy, kerosene for lamps and other products, not so much though. There was one school, no school buses, a post office and library, Baptist Church, and the Old Indian Church. We didn't even own many cars as we see today. In 1930 there were only four cars and they were up on blocks in the winter. There was up-street and down-street.

Mashpee remained an Indian-dominated community until the early 1960s. From 1834 to 1962 all but one of the town selectmen were married to a Wampanoag. By the 1960s there was an immense population and cultural shift. The town became settled with more non-Natives than Wampanoag. Developers have built several resort and residential communities with golf courses, shops, and restaurants. By 1970 the Town of Mashpee became the fastest-growing town in the United States, changing the political way of living for the Wampanoag. Mashpee's economy became dependent upon construction, tourism, educational services, and seasonal visitors, leaving the Native Americans in trepidation. The Mashpee Wampanoag continue to persevere through strong self-determination, as has been done down through generations. We became federally recognized in 2007.

> Moshup was the first schoolmaster. From his home on the Cliffs he taught the people respect. . . . He also taught us to be charitable—for when he had great stores of fish he gave of his abundance.
> —*A tribal member*

Aquinnah Wampanoag have lived for about ten thousand years at Aquinnah (Gay Head) throughout the island of Noepe (Martha's Vineyard). In Aquinnah's tribal legend, Moshup is responsible for the shapes of Martha's Vineyard, the Elizabeth Islands, Normans Island, and Nantucket. From the entrance of his den on the Aquinnah Cliffs, Moshup would wade into the ocean, pick up a whale, fling it against the Cliffs to kill it, then cook it over the fire. The blood from whales stained the clay banks of the cliffs dark and red. The Aquinnah Cliffs are a sacred place to the tribe.

The Aquinnah tribal website reports the history this way:

> Some 400 years ago Europeans reached Noepe in sufficient numbers to leave a record, and by the 1700s there were English settlements over most of the island. Our presence was quickly felt, and between the dislocation from land dealings and the influence of disease, our populations were reduced and our territories constricted. By the 1800s there remained but three native communities on Martha's Vineyard: Aquinnah, Christiantown, and Chappaquiddick. Aquinnah being the most populous and organized, we were able to maintain control over our land, despite intense efforts by the Commonwealth of Massachusetts to end our existence. Over the past 100 years, more and more native land has been lost as changes in the local economy forced tribal members to sell their lands, move to other parts of the island, or to leave the island altogether. Aquinnah was at different times in history referred to as a "praying town," an Indian District, and an incorporated town. Throughout it all we remain a sovereign tribe.

In 1972 the "Wampanoag Tribal Council of Gay Head, Inc." was formed to promote self-determination, to ensure preservation and continuation of Wampanoag history and culture, to achieve federal recognition for the tribe, and to seek the return of tribal lands to the Wampanoag people. The Wampanoag Tribe of Gay Head (Aquinnah) became a federally acknowledged tribe on April 10, 1987.

About 485 acres of tribal Wampanoag trust lands are located in the southwestern portion of Martha's Vineyard in the Town of Gay Head, with parcels in Christiantown and Chappaquiddick.

Like the Mashpee Wampanoag Tribe, the Aquinnah Wampanoag Tribe holds an important place in American history, which has rarely been recognized or fully understood by the non-Native public. Since European settlement there have been few opportunities for tribal people share their perspectives on their lifestyles and the tribal history and material culture. The Mashpee Museum, the Aquinnah Cultural Center, and writings like those included in this book are some of the many ways that Wampanoag people make themselves heard.

Early Texts in Massachusett

In 2010 Jessie Little Doe (Fermino) Baird received a MacArthur Foundation award for her work on Wampanoag (Wôpanâak) language revitalization. Wampanoag offers a unique resource to Native scholars like Baird (and Helen Manning, who appears below), in that a sizable body of texts is *written* in the language. This is due in large part to missionaries like the Puritan John Eliot, who produced the first Native translation of the Bible, with the help of Native consultants John Sassamon and James Printer (Nipmuc, also represented in this volume). Meanwhile, Native people who were trained to read and write, ostensibly for religious purposes, used this new form of literacy for their own ends, as demonstrated in the legal documents shown here. The linguist Ives Goddard and anthropologist Kathleen Bragdon have painstakingly reproduced, translated, and annotated a wealth of these texts; what appear below are their English translations only, to give readers a sense of some of the content addressed—and the resistance expressed—in early Wampanoag writing.

Petition from Gay Head Sachem Mittark, 1681

I am Muttaak, sachem of Gay Head and Nashaquitsa as far as Wanemessit.[1] Know this all people. I Muttaak and my chief men and my children and my people, these are our lands. Forever we own them, and our posterity forever shall own them. I Muttaak and we the chief men, and with our children and all our [common] people [present], have agreed that no one [shall] sell land. But if anyone larcenously sells land, you shall take [back] your land, because it is forever your possession. But if anyone does not keep this agreement, he shall fall [and] have nothing more of this land at Gay Head and Nashaquitsa at all forever. I Muttaak and we the chief men, and our posterity, [say]: And it shall be so forever. I Ummuttaak say this, and my chief men: if any of these sons of mine protects my sachemship, he shall forever be a sachem. But if [any of] my sons does not protect my sachemship and sells it, he shall fall forever. And we chief men say this, and our sachem: if any of these sons of ours protects our chieftainship, he shall forever be a chief man. But if any of our sons does not protect our chieftainship and sells it, he shall fall forever. I Umuttaag, sachem, say this and my chief men; [this is] our agreement. We say it before God. It shall be so forever. I Ummuttaak, this is my hand [X], on the date September 11, 1681. We chief men say this [and] our sachem; this is our agreement. [We say it] before God. It shall be so forever. These are our hands [X—X—X].

I John keeps am a witness and this is my hand concerning the agreement of Ummuttaak and his chief men of Gay Head and Nashaquitsa, all [and] both. I Puttukquannan am a witness. I witnessed this agreement of Ummuttaak and his chief men of Gay Head and Nashaquitsa, both. No one forever [shall] sell it; they [shall] keep it. I Puttukquannan, this is my hand [X]. I Sasauwapinnoo am a witness. I witnessed the agreement of Ummuttaak and his chief men of Gay Head and Nashaquitsa, all [and] both. I Sasauwapinnoo, my hand.

Petition from Gay Head

SEPTEMBER THE 5, 1749

At Gayhead the poor Indians met together, we who are the proprietors. They made a humble petition, by vote, to you, the honorable Commissioners in Boston, and also the General Court. Humbly we beseech you, we the poor Indians who are the proprietors of Gayhead: defend us much more regarding our land at Gayhead. We need what [will] be better [for us] other years that [will] come. We would plant our gardens on [the land] that the Guardians have leased out for six years, from when it was first leased out on October the 20, 1747. And we become poorer and poorer, from that time until today. No longer do we have pasturage freely where our animals can feed, except if we rent pasturage, to this day. Previously it was not so. Before this new law came we had at all times enough pasturage and also gardens. Therefore we humbly pray that there may be released to us our land that has been leased out. We say we are weary of renting more pasturage. And this year we [shall] use everything they do not lease out, and another year the poor Indians [will] not have gardens. Therefore humbly we pray that this new law may be taken away from us, because before this new law came these Englishmen were unable to treat us as they pleased on this land of ours. Therefore we say [we] would [have] only the law of <u>our King George</u> used for us on this land of ours at Gayhead.

And we also say regarding this land of ours at Gayhead that has been leased out by the Guardians, that we are deceived regarding the money that comes [from it]. Every year there comes four hundred and sixty-five pounds. And also we have other meadows and there is a part of that they have also leased out for only £2-0-0. And also one other thing: the island meadow at Menemsha the English took away from us. And from all this money that comes, few men and also women and children have a share. This one year that has come each one, man and woman and children, had for the half year only £0-15-0, and also for the other half year each one has £0-14-0. And many people, men and also women and children, were not given a share from the money that came. And all the Indian souls at Gayhead, men and women and children, number about 165. And all the animals of us Indians at Gayhead number about 400—if the sheep could be counted that is how many would be counted. These have no foddering place freely, except if we rent pasturage for our animals, from that time when this new law came until today.

And this year the poor Indians of Gayhead have been given no money to this day and already for a long time. Many are starving. They have no food. And many times they go to the Guardians [and] seek money, [but] they are not given money or anything. And since this new law came to us we are even poorer. Therefore humbly we pray that this new law may be taken away.

Joseph Ponue	*Pilat Sauwamog*	*Elis Henry*
Jude Hossueit	*Phillip Wossonan*	*Mary Qunish*
Ephraim Abram	*Joseph Joel*	*Ezther Pomit*
Jeremiah Sauwamog	*Joseph Pomit*	*Markit Cottoote*
Jemes Tallmon	*Jonathan Akoochik*	*Sarah Paul*
John Akoochik	*Thomas Tohqun*	*Martha Henry*
Samuel Pomit	*Jonathan Elisha*	*Buthiah Pomit*
Isaac Hossueit	*Jeremiah Allmih*	*Ledey Ontukque*
Labon Hossueit	*Darcus Amos*	
Barapus Isaac		*Bettey Ekill*

Noah Kesuk

Mathew Ontukque　　　　　　　　　　　　<u>*Proprietors*</u>

　　　　　　　Zachary Hossueit,　<u>*clerk at Gayhead.*</u>[2]

　　　　　　　<u>*A true petition.*</u>

Petition from Gay Head to Commissioners of New England Company

You Mr. John Allen, we beseech you that you would make known our words, of us poor Gayhead Indians.[3] We say truly we need a judge at this place of ours at Gayhead. And we have heard, however, that you have appointed as a judge the [person] called Elisha Amos.[4] And we say if this should be done we shall be much more miserable. This Elisha Amos has robbed us of our gardens and also our fresh meadows and our land. And if then this [person] were to be a magistrate among us we shall lose all our land at Gayhead. Therefore we beseech you that you would take away this [person] from us poor Gayhead Indians, lest if he should do this work we would be much more miserable because of this Elisha Amos, just as the word of God says in Job 34:30.[5]

Alfred DeGrasse

(1890–1978)

DeGrasse attended the Carlisle Indian School in Pennsylvania, graduating in 1911 with Robert Tahamont (Abenaki, also in this volume). He was active in student leadership, serving as vice president of his senior class and treasurer of the debating society, the Invincibles, of which Tahamont also was a member. Although attending Carlisle was traumatic for many students, DeGrasse's writings express some pride. The *Carlisle Arrow*, for which he wrote the following pieces, reported that he attended commencement and school basketball games after his own graduation and kept in touch with the school by letter about his travels, including a trip to Texas and California.

About Poison Ivy

Poison ivy belongs to what is called the Rhus family of plants. When it grows in an upright position it is called poison oak. Poison ivy is found in most every locality—in the woods, along the road sides, in the swamps and in the meadows. The most common place it is found is growing on stone walls. The leaves are oval and pointed at the top. They are from four to six inches long and from three to five inches wide. The edges are sometimes notched, but are mostly found with plain edges. The upper side of the leaves has a lustrous color and the under side has a downy covering. The young leaves have a lustrous brownish color and are always found in groups of three.

The flowers are of a greenish yellow and grow in drooping clusters. The berries grow in small clusters like grapes. In late summer they are a light brown color and later on they change to white. Although ivy is poison the juice is extracted and used as medicine. When one is poisoned by ivy mix two teaspoons of pure carbolic acid, two tablespoons of glycerin and one-half pint of water, or rose water, and bathe the affected parts. Or rub the affected parts well with grindelia.

(1909)

The Legend of the Red Eagle

Once, a tribe of Indians was troubled by a large red eagle. Every one of the tribe was afraid of him. Finally, the chief offered a sum of money as a reward to any one who would kill the eagle, but none of them were tempted to kill the bird for such a paltry reward. So the chief, in order to make the contest more alluring, offered as a reward to any one who would kill and bring him the eagle the choice of his two daughters.

It happened that one day while some of the braves of the tribe were out hunting, they came across a hunter who was shooting buffalo with a magic arrow. When they saw the large number he had slain with his magic arrow they were sure he could kill the red eagle for them. They told him of the prize which would be given to any one who could kill the bird. He promised to be there on the next day. The band of warriors went back to camp confident that they had found one who could kill the eagle. That evening they related to the chief what had happened. There happened to be an Indian among the tribe who was exceedingly anxious to win the prize, either by foul or fair means, so he determined to go and meet the hunter with the magic arrow and capture it if possible.

He found him on his way to the village with the arrow. He bound him to a tree and took the arrow. After disguising himself, he went back to the village where he was heartily welcomed. Meanwhile, a squaw who was passing by the road, heard the cries of the hunter and went to him and set him free, and after telling her what had happened, he proceeded to the village.

Just before sunrise next day all the people gathered around to witness the shooting of the eagle. The hunter came with his arrows, and as the eagle rose he shot three arrows; but in spite of the magic arrow the eagle spread his wings and flew away. As the disappointed people were about to leave, the squaw who had set the real owner of the arrow free, rode up to them on a horse and told them of the happenings of the day before. The people were enraged, and they turned upon the thief and drove him out of the village and forbade his return.

The real owner of the magic arrow, having picked up the arrow on his way to the village, arrived there in the afternoon of the same day, and as before, all the members of the tribe gathered around at sunrise to see the eagle shot. The eagle came out at sunrise and after flapping his wings rose majestically and started to fly, but he had not gone far before the magic arrow brought him down. The people of the tribe were glad because they would never again be troubled with the eagle; and the hunter with the magic arrow won the hand of the chief's daughter.

(1911)

When I was a small boy I often heard my mother tell the story about my grandfather, Watson F. Hammond, a native Indian of Cape Cod, who was in the year 1885 elected representative to the Massachusetts State Legislature, being delegated to go on business pertaining to affairs connected with the Indian school at Carlisle.[6] I often wished, after hearing the story, that I could be a loyal son of Carlisle and to my surprise my time came when I enrolled as a pupil in 1904. From that time until 1911 I worked to attain the honor of being a graduate of one of the greatest institutions of its kind in the country. I have not had a chance to show what Carlisle has done for me, but just as soon as I regain my health I expect to do my part.

(1912)

Mabel Avant

(Mashpee Wampanoag, 1892–1964)

An important figure at Mashpee, Mabel Avant ran for tribal office in 1935, served as the Mashpee town clerk, and became a leading historian for the tribe. She devoted a great deal of time to sharing traditional stories; Joan Avant remembers children running to hear Mrs. Avant tell tribal legends. Mabel Avant belonged to one of the tribe's oldest families, the Pocknetts; with her husband, George Avant, she had seven children of her own. Today her house is preserved as the Mashpee Tribal Museum.

Avant wrote a poem, "Reveries of a Wampanoag Chief," that has become something of a Mashpee classic, often recited at public events and republished in Mashpee authors' books, including Russell Peters's history of the tribe and Earl Mills's memoir. Here we reprint instead "The Voice of Our Forsaken Church" (which also appears in Peters's book), a poetic reflection on that historic structure that is referenced by several other writers in this chapter. The interview below was first recorded by Lou Cataldo in 1958, transcribed by Earl Mills Sr. in 2007, and later edited by Joan Tavares Avant for inclusion in her book *People of the First Light.*

Interview with Mabel Avant

MABEL: First of all I think you will realize, all of you, that the People of Mashpee were here before; as I said in my pageant, the white people came across "the big sea water" to make our homes—their homes—with us. At that time the People were at Mashpee! And according to "Aunt Roxy Mye," our People in Mashpee were under King Chief Popmomett.

Now I can't, and have never, run across any history on that. But it is handed down that Chief Popmomett was over the Mashpee People; I suppose he must have been under Chief Massasoit. He must have been one of the . . . well, like a deputy is now but he was called Chief Popmomett, and he lived in Quashnet. He was buried in Quashnet, north west of the homestead of Aunt Roxy Mye, near John's Pond. And then she told me that Popmomett is a Pocknett. They first called them Pognet, Popment. The last of all the Pocknetts are from Popmomett! Note that down at the Old Indian Church, you will see "Popmomett" on the old grave stones there, east of the church. Then next to them, you you'll see the Pocknetts there. So that proves that they were from Popmomett!

LOU: Let me interrupt you here. You mentioned that . . . for history . . . I'd like to clarify who is the aunt, who are you referring to? Aunt Roxy Mye (1827–1914).

MABEL: This Aunt Roxy Mye was very, very old. She was an aunt of my father (Willard Pocknett) so she knows she's very old, because my father died—oh, I don't know. He'd be upwards of almost a hundred, I guess now?! He was 74 when he died, and he's been dead about 20 years or something like that!

LOU: If we can get some years and dates in here we can clarify for the sake of history.

MABEL: Well I couldn't tell you just how old (Roxy) would be now but she would be one of the oldest citizens at the time. And in fact, I think she was my father's great-aunt and not his own aunt. I know she was.

Two of the oldest in Mashpee were Aunt Roxy Mye and Aunt Rhodie Sturgis. Aunt Rhodie Sturgis died about 25 years ago and I think she was 96 then. I got a good deal of history from her because she came from the Attaquin family, and that's one of the oldest in Mashpee. They lived on Mashpee Lake, as did Aunt Rhodie Sturgis or Attaquin. She married an Indian from Herring Pond by the name of William Conant. Her second husband was a white man by the name of William Sturgis.

He came from either Hyannis or Barnstable. They believed in funny business. She told that this Indian Lady said, "I'm going to show you—I want you to see your next husband." She believed it and Aunt Rhodie believed it, and she made me believe it. She said that, this Indian Lady said, I'm going to put some kind of roots and herbs in this potion that I give you. And in this potion, these roots and herbs I'm going to put plenty of salt. In the night now—you mark my word—your husband will come to you! You put a glass of water on the table, and, she said, "Your future husband will come and give you a drink of water!"

She said she invited her friend over and said, "We'll both eat a part of the cake and we'll see now who our next husbands are going to be." And then she said, "In the night this white man, with a beard, came and gave her a drink of water. But the next morning they compared notes. So she said, her friend, she said, "Well, you know that I'm going to marry a colored man. It's not going to be a Mashpee man either," she said. "I saw him." She (Aunt Rhodie) said, "You know, this the funniest thing, but I'm going to marry a white man and he's got a beard." And it happened!

She went to Barnstable to work. Somebody knocked on the door. She went to the door and this white man stood there with his beard. Immediately, she recognized him. . . . After that he kept making excuses to come here. The woman she worked for said, "Now you know that isn't right! Rhoda, you must not encourage him!" Aunt Rhoda had a will of her own and was kind of snappy. "Oh, this is my own life and I'll do what I want with it." She went along with it for a while, and then she married him.

Of course, you probably know of Merwin Sturgis, of the *Standard Times*. He worked there for a number of years. A year or so ago he got through there, and I think he is now teaching in Bourne. Well he is a descendant of this Sturgis she married (also Eileen). He had children [from a previous marriage?]. Aunt Rhodie and William Sturgis had a son, William Sturgis, who married Tina Pocknett. They had a daughter, May Sturgis (Peters), who married Charles (Tod) Peters.

Aunt Rhodie told me that someone from Plymouth came down and married into the Attaquin family. It was against the rules of the Mashpee Tribe to take any white person's name. If he married a Mashpee Indian he had to take their name. Because I asked her how is it that Uncle Charlie had light eyes and how is it that Aunt Mary Attaquin had brown hair instead of black hair like my mother's. She said it was because this man from Plymouth married into the Attaquin family. Our white relations lived in Sandwich near the Shawnee Lake in a big house.

The first Powwow I had, I went down to Sandwich Dry Goods Store. There was this girl with blond hair who said, "Oh I wish I could come up to Mashpee." She said, "You won't believe me, but I have Indian blood!"

Mashpee was made into a District. It was first supervised by the Natives. Mashpee was incorporated in 1870. There were three Native selectmen. I think it was Attaquin and Amos? They did have overseers over them, and they were white. You probably know that Marstons Mills was named after one of the overseers. His name was Marstons and he lived near Doctor Higgins. The other one lived up just as you turn onto Route 150 into Mashpee. Another one lived where Dora Dickerson lives, near where Carter Whitcomb's place is now.

Minister Fish lived for many years in the parsonage, he presided over the church, but he wasn't very satisfactory. The Old Indian Church was given to us by a white society in England.

LOU: Please elaborate on that a little bit now!! There's no doubt in the minds of anyone that the Old Indian Church has history at heart.

MABEL: I'm so tired tonight that I can't hardly talk because during that storm last night, between those gusts of the storm, I was praying and my mind was on the Old Indian Church, wondering if it was standing. Praying for one more chance to see if we could get it back as it used to be.

LOU: Yes! For the benefit, here now, we can interject and say that there is a very, very dire need of restoration.

MABEL: It is in dire need of restoration.

LOU: Yes! At the present time is there an effort to restore it?

MABEL: Yes! And I'm very pleased to say that I got in touch with one of our people the other day. I was off the soliciting committee. Some of the younger people thought they could do a good job, so they put the older people off. There was a man by the name of Williams that left a fund that we now receive. We get this fund from Harvard College.

This church was first built on Bryant's Neck in Mashpee on Santuit Pond, central to Mashpee, which was more central then. Mashpee wasn't built up like it is now. People could come from Ashumet, Quashnet, Wakeby, and Ockry, that was down south Mashpee.

LOU: Well, do you recall the history? Was it built back in the early 1600s?

MABEL: Yes! Well there's a dispute on that, some say 1634, some say 1664? But I would say the later date is more like it.

LOU: It's the oldest Indian Church in the country?

MABEL: Oh yes, without any doubt the oldest Indian Church. Finally the white people took over the church. Aunt Rhodie said they had some trouble over that: and you wouldn't imagine anybody fighting over a church. The Indians went to the church but the whites locked them out. Minister Phineas Fish (non-Native) had control of the church. The Mashpees (meaning the Wampanoag) dragged him out of the church. He would not allow our Indian preacher, "Blind Joe Amos," to be ordained there; he had to be ordained somewhere else.

Then "Blind Joe" was allowed to come. They sent up to the state offices and tried to get the militia down, against the Indians. They said the Indians were rioting.

LOU: What time? How long ago was that?

MABEL: Oh, that would be over a hundred years ago, because Aunt Rhodie says she just about remembers it. In my day I can remember when the white people and the Indian people worked together very peacefully. A good many of them used to drive over from Santuit and all around the Mecca.

Well now, there is one thing they would ask us, what we ate. "You come down in the summers to work. Then you go home and there is no work in the winter, what do you eat?" I said, "We have potato bargain. That's the morning meal. That's just onions, potatoes, pork fat and water cooked up together and seasoned." Then I told this lady, "In the fall we have skunk." "Well," she said, "you know, Mrs. Avant, I thought you were a very honest person, but now I can't believe that. I can't believe you'd eat skunk!" I said, "Yes we do and it tastes very good!"

The lady asked a white man who came down, "Do white people eat skunk?" He said, "Sure, and I've eaten it myself, and it tastes very good." But you see you have to know how to take those "kernels" out, and after you do take the kernels out, it tastes like anything else. It tastes like rabbit. My mother used to have it every fall up until the time she died. She was also the "mail driver" from Mashpee to Sandwich.

LOU: But don't forget the deer; they lived on quite a bit of that, too.

MABEL: Well, you know, one of the older Indians was George Oakley. He came from Connecticut. He's a Pequot Indian.

LOU: Is that who the store is named for?

MABEL: Yes. Yes. However, he married my great-aunt Betsy Attaquin. He made a farm—where the USO building is located now—that became the Town Hall. He lived to be about 96 years old. I can remember him, and he was a very nice person. He never drank or smoked. He was one who used to cure the Mashpee herring.

He could cure better than anyone in Mashpee. He knew just what kind of leaves or herbs to use. He would have a certain amount of walnut, but I think they called it hickory, and sweet fern, just to "chill it" cool the fire down and make smoke—just about right. The older white people used to buy the herring. Mr. Howell over in Barnstable every year asked me, "Can you get me any of the herring like Mr. Oakley, Russell, Tom Mingo, Ed Amos, and Irving Oakley used to have years ago?"

MARJORIE WORRELL (from the audience): Ms. Avant, who was it that wouldn't allow the people of Mashpee to speak their language?

MABEL: That was a legislative act. I think you'll find it in the Mashpee Town office, because they have all the records there. Laurie Green showed it to me!

MARJORIE: Ms. Avant, could you tell us who is it that kept the Mashpee People from learning to read and write?

MABEL: Well, it was by a legislative act of 1789, "for the Regulation of the Plantation for prohibiting of the instruction of the Mashpees in reading and writing under the pain of death."

The Voice of Our Forsaken Church

I strolled by the church of my childhood
Our Old Indian Church at Mashpee,
And it spoke to me in a voice so tender
As it murmured so wistfully.

"I have shared your joys and sorrows
Welcomed you each Sunday morn
In the sunlight of the summers
And in the winter's wind and storm
Although I'm old I still remember,
The horse and buggies, I recall,
Filled with many happy faces
Of the families large and small.
Out of the trails they came to worship,

The spirit of sabbath they did not lack
As they traveled through the forest
Some with papooses on their back.

Out of the past a handbell is ringing,
Calling them to come inside
And they filled my pews and gallery,
How my old beams creaked with pride,
The old clock struck the hour of worship
A few dogs nestled 'round the stove,
Waiting patiently for their masters
To hunt in the surrounding grove.

Once more I see the dear old parson
Opening the Bible he could not see,
It was just a force of habit,
For he preached from memory.
Sightless eyes, yet so courageous
His soul took its flight so long ago,
Yet I never forget the Christian spirit
Of my beloved friend, Blind Joe.

I still can see the dear old Deacons,
One with flowing beard so white,
The other with a goatee trimmed so neatly,
Each Sunday they were a welcome sight
As they sat beside my pulpit
In their straightback haircloth chairs
With bowed heads and a loud 'Amen'
As the parson said the prayers.

Hark I hear the children singing
The good old hymns so long ago,
'Jesus loves me this I know,
Cause the Bible tells me so.'
Some with voices sweet and lusty,
Others out of tune,
They were all my children and I loved them,
But they left me all too soon.

It is now Communion Sunday,
The old deacon breaks the bread,
While the other fills the pewter goblets
With sparkling wine so red.
The members join hands and sing in chorus
Like angels' voices from above,
'Blest be the tie that binds
Our hearts in Christian love.'

Gone is the wooden water bucket
Filled with water to the brim
Clear, cold and so refreshing,
Brought from a nearby spring.
My old chandelier lamps are missing,
I'm alone in the darkness of night.
Alone with fond past memories
To compare with my present plight.

I am old, my sills are sagging,
I have reached the winter of life,
Through countless ages I've served you
And through many years of strife.
Now my pews are empty,
There's a lock upon my door.
Oh, that I might know the splendor
Of those good old days once more.

Time is fleeting oh my loved ones,
You are getting older too,
And I bid you be ever ready
And to your faith be true.

I have taught you how to love Him,
And I'll always be your friend,
Ever ready to protect you
While I linger to the end."

Helen Manning

(Aquinnah Wampanoag, 1919–2008)

Helen Manning was born to a prominent Gay Head family, the Vanderhoops. She spent summers on the island but went to school in Washington DC, where she lived with extended family. Manning continued on in the city through much of her young adulthood, working for the Bureau of Engraving and Printing as well as the Department of Labor. In 1956 she moved permanently back to Gay Head to teach in the community's one-room schoolhouse, like her mother and grandfather before her. With a master's degree in education, she also taught special education and reading at the Oak Bluffs School. Manning was beloved as a cook at Manning's Snack Bar, the restaurant owned by her husband's family. She was active in civic life, serving on the Martha's Vineyard Commission, the Gay Head selectmen, and the Wampanoag Tribal Council, among many other boards and committees. In her later life Manning was revered as a tribal historian, and in 2000 she published the book *Moshup's Footsteps*, from which the following selections are taken.

From Moshup's Footsteps

PREFACE

Over and over again one hears the comment, "Gay Head is not Gay Head anymore." I imagine, now that the town's name has been changed from Gay Head back to its original Wampanoag name, Aquinnah—land under the hill—some will say Aquinnah is not Aquinnah anymore. Yet from my perspective (a Wampanoag woman, born in Aquinnah) this special place will always exist because the Wampanoags, People of the First Light, have woven a spirit-filled fabric using the threads of history, culture, and legends to honor the story of the Wampanoag Nation—past, present, and future. I, and other Wampanoags living on Noepe, land surrounded by bitter waters, or as commonly called, Martha's Vineyard—hold the common belief that the kind and gentle giant Moshup created the island, taught us how to fish and catch whales, and is a presence in our daily lives. We believe we are the children of Moshup and by holding on to our beliefs and legends we have been able to reclaim our language, gain federal tribal recognition, and reacquire our Common Lands, including the Cranberry Bogs, the Herring Creek, and the face of the Aquinnah Cliffs.

I was born in Aquinnah on September 24, 1919. My father, Arthur Herbert Vanderhoop, is Wampanoag and my mother, Evelyn Moss, is African American, or as she would say in her day, *colored*. My father's mother was Josephine Smalley and his father was Cummings Bray Vanderhoop. His paternal grandmother was Beulah Salisbury and his grandfather was William Adrian Vanderhoop. William Adrian was of Dutch and [Surinamese] descent and met my great-grandmother here on Noepe when he was traveling up and down the coast on a merchant slave ship. Their meeting in the 1830s, subsequent marriage, and beautiful family of nine children began the Vanderhoops on Noepe.

My home has always been near the Aquinnah Cliffs, the most sacred place on the island. I live in a house in the shadow of the lighthouse's beacon, not far from Moshup's Den; and, just to be safe, I'd better say that I'm not far from Cheepie's mischievous ways. (Cheepie is our trickster, so I always acknowledge him or pay the consequences.)

As a child, when I looked to the east I saw six small houses and I knew every family living in each house. Now I can see over twenty houses and I still only know who lives in six of them. Growing up, if you were Aquinnah, well, that was synonymous with being a Wampanoag. It meant that your ancestors had lived here continuously for centuries before you.

Many non-Wampanoags are not aware that, before the 1600s, Wampanoags, and other Native Peoples of the Eastern Algonquin Nations, were visiting and residing on the island, enjoying its rich hunting and fishing rounds, for over 10,000 years. By the year 2270 BC, we Wampanoags had made Noepe our permanent home. When the English arrived, we lived all over this island. We had inland winter encampments, protected from the fierce nor-easters, and summer villages near fertile lands and good fishing grounds. With the coming of the English in 1642, we lost almost everything, including our land and language. That is how we ended up in Aquinnah, home of Moshup.

We first came to Aquinnah to escape the illness and disease that the English brought with them, to which we had no immunity. We came to Aquinnah because we were being displaced when some of our leaders, or Sachems, transferred the Sachemship to the English. The English cleared the land and put up fences and the majority of us were forced to leave. Others came to Aquinnah to escape the English missionaries' attempts to pacify us through Christianity. History has proven that we are survivors. Even though we almost lost our language, we never lost our culture. We have many languages besides our spoken language, including the songs we sing, the heartbeat of the drum, and our legends. We have never forgotten our legends.

When I was growing up in the 1920s, every family had chickens, a cow, a pig, and a vegetable garden and, most important, every family had a home. I remember eating fish, lobster, scallops, venison, chowder, cranberries, plum porridge made with milk, raisins and nutmeg, nocake (a traditional dish of parched fine-ground corn), and homemade ice cream flavored with coffee and fresh peaches. Even if you left the community to go whaling for years or to go to college, when you came home you had a place to live. Land was not at a premium like it is today.

For years Aquinnah was considered remote and inconvenient. We did not have a fine harbor. We did not have electricity and phones until the 1950s. Then there was the time in the 1970s and 1980s when we reclaimed our power and people were afraid to buy land in Aquinnah for fear they would lose it in our land claim. Of course, now it is almost an impossible dream for children born here to think they will be able to own land unless they are willing to pay a very high price. That is why the tribe fought to bring affordable housing to Aquinnah, so that our children could keep the dream of Moshup alive.

My mother and father ran a hotel and restaurant, the Not-A-Way, just down from the lighthouse. For electricity we had our own system with a series of car batteries, and for water we had a cistern to collect the rain water or we carried water up from the spring. The specialty at the restaurant was quahog chowder, lobster sandwiches, and lobster dinners with my mother's special mayonnaise, french fries, and apple and blueberry pies.

When I turned school age, my life changed in that I began to spend only summers in Aquinnah and we went to my mother's family, in Washington DC, during the school year. In those days when we traveled from the Vineyard, we took the boat to New Bedford, on to New York via a boat from Fall River, and then finally on to DC via train. It was a two-day trip. When my father arrived in DC at the end of the season, he would be loaded with cranberries, sausages, fresh pork, hazelnuts, and other bounty from Aquinnah.

When I returned each summer, one of my tasks was to be a lookout for the arrival of the order cart. About three times a week a cart carrying meat and other staples would come. Another vender had vegetables and fruit. There also was the ice man, with blocks of ice to keep our food fresh in ice boxes, since we did not have gas or electricity.

During my entire childhood, I wished that I could remain in Aquinnah. Even after attending Miner Teachers College, and working in Washington DC, I never let go of my dream of returning. In 1956 my wish came true. I discovered the town needed a teacher for the one-room schoolhouse: six grades, fifteen students. It was the same school where my mother, Evelyn Moss Vanderhoop, had taught. I qualified and it proved to be one of the best experiences of my life. I thank my creator every day.

CRANBERRY DAY AND CRANBERRIES

Moshup's wife, Squant, was the caretaker of the cranberry bogs and convened the first cranberry day. The cranberry is one of the few fruits native to North America; others include grapes and wild blueberries. It is widely held that the wild cranberry, or *sassamanesh* in Wampanoag, is rich in vitamin C and has medicinal and nutritional properties. Tamson Weeks, a Wampanoag herbalist, used cranberries to heal a variety of complaints, including blood disorders, stomach ailments, liver problems, scurvy, and fever. She also said a poultice of cranberries could cure cancer.

Cranberry day marked the end of the summer season and the time for families to move inland to winter camps and away from the winds of the sea. For over a century Cranberry day has been the second Tuesday in October; and, as recently as the 1930s, it was a time to prepare for winter. Prior to the 1938 hurricane, the harvest was sold in New Bedford and the proceeds used to purchase the winter staples of molasses, sugar, and flour. Extra money helped the elderly and the poor. The bogs were an important part of the economy, with harvesting taking up to three days. People would pitch tents, cook quahog chowder over fires, and at night a bonfire would be lit. Then people would tell stories, and there would be dancing to fiddle music.

All the natives of Gay Head would travel in their ox-carts, carrying a lunch time feast of baked chicken, pies and all the fixings. At noon everyone would spread their lunches out in the bogs and different families would invite others to share their meal. The people would begin harvesting at dawn; originally, most of the harvesting was by hand. The cranberry scoop, as we know it, was not yet used. Some harvesting was done using a long handled box with metal teeth which was raked through the vines so you would not have to get down on your hands and knees. (Leonard Vanderhoop's Cranberry Report)

LANGUAGE

The Wopanaak, or Massachusett, language is an Eastern Algonquin language, similar to Natick, Narragansett, Mohegan-Pequot, Montauk, and Ouiripi-Unquachoag. The language territory covers the coastal region of the Merrimac River, south Narragansett Bay, and Cape Cod. Before the arrival of the English, a written Wampanoag language did not exist. The language was spoken and passed on, generation to generation. Today, using historical documentation of the written language produced in the 1600s by missionaries and native speakers, and with the assistance of linguists and language classes initiated and created by Wampanoags, the people of Aquinnah and Mashpee are reclaiming our language. With the help of linguistic experts, a short- and long-term plan is being developed to see this ambitious project through to fruition. The Wampanoag Language Reclamation Project is much to credit for this great reclamation of this important aspect of our culture.

Frank James (Wamsutta)

(Aquinnah Wampanoag, 1923–2001)

This speech has been famous since Frank James first delivered it on Thanksgiving Day, 1970. Pilgrim descendants had invited him to appear at the 350th anniversary of the landing, but they un-invited him when they heard what he was planning to say. James went ahead and made his speech before hundreds of Native American protesters, kicking off the annual National Day of Mourning. The United American Indians of New England (U A I N E) continue each year to stage this powerful counter-representation to a remarkably enduring myth of Native Americans in New England. The speech has appeared in numerous anthologies and publications and is now widely available on the Internet.

National Day of Mourning

I speak to you as a man—a Wampanoag man. I am a proud man, proud of my ancestry, my accomplishments won by a strict parental direction ("You must succeed—your face is a different color in this small Cape Cod community!"). I am a product of poverty and discrimination, two social and economic diseases. I, and my brothers and sisters, have painfully overcome, and to some extent we have earned the respect of our community. We are Indians first—but we are termed "good citizens." Sometimes we are arrogant but only because society has pressured us to be so.

It is with mixed emotion that I stand here to share my thoughts. This is a time of celebration for you—celebrating an anniversary of a beginning for the white man in America. A time of looking back, of reflection. It is with a heavy heart that I look back upon what happened to my People.

Even before the Pilgrims landed it was common practice for explorers to capture Indians, take them to Europe, and sell them as slaves for 220 shillings apiece. The Pilgrims had hardly explored the shores of Cape Cod for four days before they had robbed the graves of my ancestors and stolen their corn and beans. *Mourt's Relation* describes a searching party of sixteen men.[7] Mourt goes on to say that this party took as much of the Indians' winter provisions as they were able to carry.

Massasoit, the great Sachem of the Wampanoag, knew these facts, yet he and his People welcomed and befriended the settlers of the Plymouth Plantation. Perhaps he did this because his tribe had been depleted by an epidemic. Or his knowledge of the harsh oncoming winter was the reason for his peaceful acceptance of these acts. This action by Massasoit was perhaps our biggest mistake. We, the Wampanoag, welcomed you, the white man, with open arms, little knowing that it was the beginning of the end; that before 50 years were to pass, the Wampanoag would no longer be a free people.

What happened in those short 50 years? What has happened in the last 300 years? History gives us facts and there were atrocities; there were broken promises—and most of these centered around land ownership. Among ourselves we understood that there were boundaries, but never before had we had to deal with fences and stone walls. But the white man had a need to prove his worth by the amount of land that he owned. Only 10 years later, when the Puritans came, they treated the Wampanoag with even less kindness in converting the souls of the so-called "savages." Although the Puritans were harsh to members of their own society, the Indian was pressed between stone slabs and hanged as quickly as any other "witch."

And so down through the years there is record after record of Indian lands taken and, in token, reservations set up for him upon which to live. The Indian, having been stripped of his power, could only stand by and watch while the white man took his land and used it for his personal gain. This the Indian could not understand; for to him, land was survival, to farm, to hunt, to be enjoyed. It was not to be abused. We see incident after incident where the white man sought to tame the "savage" and convert him to the Christian ways of life. The early Pilgrim settlers led the Indian to believe that if he did not behave, they would dig up the ground and unleash the great epidemic again.

The white man used the Indian's nautical skills and abilities. They let him be only a seaman—but never a captain. Time and time again, in the white man's society, we Indians have been termed "low man on the totem pole."

Has the Wampanoag really disappeared? There is still an aura of mystery. We know there was an epidemic that took many Indian lives; some Wampanoags moved west and joined the Cherokee and Cheyenne. They were forced to move. Some even went north to Canada! Many Wampanoag put aside their Indian heritage and accepted the white man's way for their own survival. There are some Wampanoag who do not wish it known they are Indian for social or economic reasons.

What happened to those Wampanoags who chose to remain and live among the early settlers? What kind of existence did they live as "civilized" people? True, living was not as complex as life today, but they dealt with the confusion and the change. Honesty, trust, concern, pride, and politics wove themselves in and out of their daily living. Hence, he was termed crafty, cunning, rapacious, and dirty.

History wants us to believe that the Indian was a savage, illiterate, uncivilized animal. A history that was written by an organized, disciplined people, to expose us as an unorganized and undisciplined entity. Two distinctly different cultures met. One thought they must control life; the other believed life was to be enjoyed, because nature decreed it. Let us remember, the Indian is and was just as human as the white man. The Indian feels pain, gets hurt, and becomes defensive, has dreams, bears tragedy and failure, suffers from loneliness, needs to cry as well as laugh. He, too, is often misunderstood.

The white man in the presence of the Indian is still mystified by his uncanny ability to make him feel uncomfortable. This may be the image the white man has created of the Indian; his "savageness" has boomeranged and isn't a mystery; it is fear; fear of the Indian's temperament!

High on a hill, overlooking the famed Plymouth Rock, stands the statue of our great Sachem, Massasoit. Massasoit has stood there many years in silence. We, the descendants of this great Sachem, have been a silent people. The necessity of making a living in this materialistic society of the white man caused us to be silent. Today, I and many of my people are choosing to face the truth. We ARE Indians!

Although time has drained our culture, and our language is almost extinct, we the Wampanoags still walk the lands of Massachusetts. We may be fragmented, we may be confused. Many years have passed since we have been a people together. Our lands were invaded. We fought as hard to keep our land as you the whites did to take our land away from us. We were conquered, we became the American prisoners of war in many cases, and wards of the United States government, until only recently.

Our spirit refuses to die. Yesterday we walked the woodland paths and sandy trails. Today we must walk the macadam highways and roads. We are uniting. We're standing not in our wigwams but in your concrete tent. We stand tall and proud, and before too many moons pass we'll right the wrongs we have allowed to happen to us.

We forfeited our country. Our lands have fallen into the hands of the aggressor. We have allowed the white man to keep us on our knees. What has happened cannot be changed, but today we must work towards a more humane America, a more Indian America, where men and nature once again are important; where the Indian values of honor, truth, and brotherhood prevail.

You the white man are celebrating an anniversary. We the Wampanoags will help you celebrate in the concept of a beginning. It was the beginning of a new life for the Pilgrims. Now, 350 years later, it is a beginning of a new determination for the original American: the American Indian.

There are some factors concerning the Wampanoags and other Indians across this vast nation. We now have 350 years of experience living amongst the white man. We can now speak his language. We can now think as a white man thinks. We can now compete with him for the top jobs. We're being heard; we are now being listened to. The important point is that along with these necessities of everyday living, we still have the spirit, we still have the unique culture, we still have the will and, most important of all, the determination to remain as Indians. We are determined, and our presence here this evening is living testimony that this is only the beginning of the American Indian, particularly the Wampanoag, to regain the position in this country that is rightfully ours.

Helen Attaquin

(Aquinnah Wampanoag, 1923–1993)

Like many of the Wampanoag scholars represented in this volume, Helen Attaquin worked for Plimoth Plantation's Wampanoag Indigenous Program and the Boston Children's Museum, for which she wrote the piece "How Martha's Vineyard Came to Be." Wampanoag elders and educators used these two programs, established in the 1970s, to shape tribal self-representation in Massachusetts in the decades surrounding the federal recognition struggle; they also used their positions there to produce a great deal of important writing. Attaquin, who came from a prominent Wampanoag family, had a doctorate in education and published her own book, *A Brief History of Gay Head*, in 1970. She was also recruited to contribute the essay "There Are Differences" to the collection *Rooted Like the Ash Trees*. Published in 1987, in the thick of Wampanoag recognition struggles, it expresses many of the painful complications experienced by indigenous people across New England.

How Martha's Vineyard Came to Be

Moshop was a man of peace who first lived on the elbow of Cape Cod. He loved to contemplate the beauty about him and would sit long hours tranquilly smoking his big Peudelee, or pipe, while he watched the clouds or stared out at the ever-changing sea. He was known as a just man and a kindly philosopher whose wisdom was unquestioned. He excelled in feasts of strength and bravery, which the envious attributed to magic. This caused malice and dissension to arise among some of his neighbors. After long consideration, Moshop decided he was weary of strife and discord. He would search out a new place where he and his followers might live in peace.

Along the marshes of Nauset on Cape Cod, over the dunes and through the forests, Moshop and his wife Squant and their people walked with the rising sun and the sun guided them toward land which was new to them. The shore birds flew up ahead of them. Pheasant and deer looked on with wonder, then scurried into hiding behind bayberry, sumac, viburnum, and wind-swept oaks.

At last, spent with walking, Moshop paused to look about him. As he slowly dragged one huge foot, water rushed in and a pool formed behind him. The pool deepened and became a channel and the tide swept in to separate a portion of land. That land became an island separated from Cape Cod by blue water. Soon his footsteps were marked by a chain of small islands, but it was the land that lay ahead which fulfilled Moshop's desire and became the beautiful island of all. Moshop named this largest island Capawack, or "Refuge Place."

From the westernmost high clay cliffs of Capawack, Moshop could see whales playing close to shore. There were forests edged by ponds of fresh water; sheltered fields for planting, and beauty wherever he looked. Never before had he gazed on such perfection. Truly the Great Spirit had led him here. This was the Refuge Place he had been seeking.

With housewifely concern, Squant set about preparing their first meal. Moshop pointed to nearby young trees and she pulled some of them up for firewood. Today there are no sizable trees on Gay Head, for Moshop's wife and children burned constant fires in their lodges. Smoke from these fires settled in a haze over the hills and today Old People sagely nod their heads and say the haze that often is seen comes from Old Squant's fire, or if the fog is unusually thick, then Moshop is smoking his pipe, or Peudelee.

Moshop provided the food for Squant to cook by wading out into the sea and catching a whale by the tail. Quickly he dashed it against the cliff so the blood ran down in a crimson stain. It ran down into the sea and stained the water red, as the water sometimes is stained today when the surf washes against the cliffs, which have red clay deposits.

As the family of Moshop and Squant grew in size, they continued to eat their meals at the edge of their cliff home, where they discarded the whale bones as well as bones of other animals. There were many bones and sometimes teeth of animals unknown in present times. These are still found today by sharp-eyed visitors who recognize them embedded in the cliffs or washed down on the beach.

Scientists say that the rise of the land ceased at that time, but it still continues today and the sea is constantly nibbling away at Moshop's land.

From "There Are Differences"

I am writing this as a Wampanoag from Gay Head on Martha's Vineyard island. I am writing this as one of The People, commonly miscalled American Indians or Native Americans. I am writing here as an American, a citizen of these United States. And I am writing as a person, a member of the world population. . . .

What has always seemed to me to be the most striking quality about primal peoples, such as American Indians, is their inclusive attitude toward both experience and human beings—a sharp contrast to the highly exclusive frame of reference which marks the world of the dominant Western cultures. . . .

If the traditional pre-Columbian Indian world was inclusive, how is it possible that in the past 100 years (and in the last decade of militancy especially) Indians have become so aggressively exclusive? How has it come about that countless Indians who grew up in isolation in Alberta, Texas, California, Virginia, or Maine are somehow excluded from Indian identity and must provide exceptional credentials in order to gain access to that geographically narrow strip of America, in the southwest and northwest, where so-called *real* Indians have treaty numbers or are on the rolls of reservations, which are themselves the creation of just the kind of obsessive exclusivity that is the basis of the Western mind?

This means that we have to address ourselves to some unpopular questions. Why don't non-Indians have the right to paint and write about Indian subject matter? How much power can we give certain long-standing centers of Indian elitism that lay down the law for the entire Western Hemisphere on the subject of who is and who is not a *proper* Indian? How can we retain tribal sovereignty and still support the identities of Indians from isolated, non-reservation areas? How do we alter that reservation attitude that urban Indians are somehow "less Indian" than they are? Why are there so many cruel jokes about blacks who are part-Indian? It is estimated that about 40 percent of the black population of the United States is part Indian.

Why are there so many unpleasant inferences about native people who "don't look like Indians" (whatever that very stereotypical phrase is supposed to mean)? Why don't we stop making jokes about Jewish Indians? We don't joke about Indians who are Christian—so why do we find it amusing that many Indians are Jews? In short, why is Indian and white humor so often marked by naïve racism, sexism, and stereotypical images? Why have Indians readily adopted the cruelty of the dominant society to their own ambitious purposes, to the obtaining of authority, power, and personal control?

Why is there an inclination to contest the authenticity of Native American painters, writers, actors, and spokespeople who have attained a newly acquired intellectual and artistic maturity?

Native American exclusivity and snobbery have caused enormous pain and confusion. Many Indians don't feel that they came by their Indian heritage honestly. They wait until they know you well before they confide that their parents were native people. Or they apologize for claiming Indian blood.

I don't know exactly how this terrible self-consciousness originated but it has obviously done a great deal to promote an elitism among enrolled, reservation Indians whose heritage is apparently, though not necessarily, more substantial than that of urban Indians. This self-consciousness has been used as a political weapon by Indians anxious to seize or maintain power on the basis of a self-serving definition of authenticity. And, meanwhile, the average person in the dominant society tends to take pleasure in the in-fighting, the name-calling, and the power plays of peoples and groups that learned how to fight dirty by watching the Western world. . . .

. . . Despite [the] problems that individual Indians share with other low-income and non-white populations, most Indian leaders see the key to Indian survival not so much in civil rights legislation as in the maintenance of a land base and of the governmental power of the tribal community.

To speak of equality of citizenship in the Indian view means to treat Indians only as individuals by ignoring and suppressing the group rights they possess as peoples. It is to recommend, they believe, a termination of Indian government, the confiscation of tribal property rights, and, as a consequence, the disappearance of many of the distinctive elements of native cultures. The survival of Indians as peoples with a unique political and cultural identity is the goal of the Indians' rights movement, and, while some characterize that as separatism, Indians tend to see this only as the continuation of their traditional existence. The radical step, in their view, is a political and cultural assimilation that can come about only when non-Indian America tries to coerce Indians into surrendering their rights.

. . . here in New England, and in particular this area of southeastern Massachusetts, the environment is entirely different. Here, the Native Americans were among the first of the native peoples to be exposed to the European influence. Hence, they have been assimilated into the prevailing society for over three centuries. In the ensuing process, their tribal identity was blurred, and their political, cultural, and economic lifestyle altered, perhaps irrevocably.

However, there has always remained within them the mental image of their past tribal affiliations and allegiances. The present-day search for one's roots has served to resurrect these tribal yearnings and has given a new meaning to their Native American past.

But, with all these similarities and yet differences, is it any wonder that the Wampanoags' (for it is of them that I speak) struggle for identity should perforce take a different path from that of other tribal groups? Is it so difficult to understand that the Wampanoags of today, caught between two worlds as it were, should sometimes seem to lose their way and become sidetracked? To me, it is all the more amazing that they have managed to assert their Indian identity while yet retaining their place in the American mainstream of life. They have done this without antagonizing either their native brethren or their non-Indian neighbors. But, then, are we not all "related"?

Russell Peters (Fast Turtle)

(Mashpee Wampanoag, 1929–2002)

As president of the Wampanoag Indian Tribal Council from 1974 to 1980, Russell Peters filed the famous Mashpee land claim that eventually led to federal recognition. He had a master's degree in education from Harvard and served in the Korean War. We have selected some short passages from his important history *The Wampanoags of Mashpee* that we feel complement the other authors' offerings in this Wampanoag section, explaining some of the most important events in Wampanoag history.

From The Wampanoags of Mashpee

1763

On June 17, the Governor [of Massachusetts] and the General Court agreed to the wishes of the Mashpees and ended the long-held control of the guardians. The petitions to the King of England, the Governor, and the General Court resulted in a "coalition" government with limited self-rule.

The new law stated, *"That all the lands belonging to the Indians and mullattoes in Mashpee be and hereby are erected into a district by the name of Mashpee, with the following privileges: that the Indian and mulatto inhabitants and proprietors of Mashpee be and hereby are impowered in the month of March, annually, to meet in the public meeting-house in said Mashpee, then and there to elect a moderator of said meeting and five overseers (two of said overseers to be Englishmen), a town clerk, a treasurer, they being Englishmen, two wardens, and one or more 'constables.'"* The ability to self-govern, even though limited, was an important step toward Indian self-determination.

Despite all these advances, the English made it clear to the Indians that no matter how educated or Christian they became, they would never be equal in English society. Thus, on the eve of American independence and democracy, the Indians struggled for basic rights and liberty.

1833

This was a significant year in the history of Mashpee. At this time the Indians were oppressed by both their guardians and their missionaries. There were numerous abuses, including the taking of wood by neighboring whites who regularly came into Mashpee (with the permission of the guardians).

The Rev. Phinneas Fish, a missionary and a guardian, not only ignored the Indians' spiritual and physical needs but was responsible for defrauding them as well.

Rev. Fish preached to whites from neighboring communities at the Old Indian Meeting House, leaving the Indian ministering to Reverend "Blind Joe" Amos, who preached while standing under a huge tree in the forest.

The petition to the Governor that was sent by William Apes and the tribal elders was signed by nearly one hundred people of the District.[8] They pleaded for quick relief from the injustices of the guardians and the missionaries. They asked for the right to rule themselves, to forbid anyone from cutting or carrying wood from the plantation after the first of July of that year, and to remove anyone who violated the rule.

In response to the petition, Phinneas Fish wrote the Governor blaming the whole thing on William Apes. He warned of serious trouble and asked the Governor to take immediate action to prevent an Indian uprising.

On the first of July, two brothers by the name of Sampson came in defiance of the Indian resolution and loaded their teams with wood. William Apes and a group of Mashpee Indians ordered the Sampsons to unload and leave. They refused, whereupon the Indians boarded the teams and unloaded the wood. The defeated Sampsons hurried off to get the courts to back up their practice of stealing wood.

This incident was known as "The Woodland Revolt." For his part in the affair, William Apes was sentenced to thirty days imprisonment in the common jail. When told by a man from Barnstable that his sentence was not half severe enough, Apes replied, *"In my mind, it was no punishment at all, and I am yet to learn what punishment can dismay a man conscious of his own innocence."*

The Woodland Revolt caused great consternation for Governor Lincoln, Fish, and the Sampson brothers since the press used the Revolt to publicize the plight of the Mashpees. William Apes, Blind Joe Amos, and the tribal leaders were regarded as heroes; public sentiment was on their side. The stage was set for the Mashpee Indians to once again govern their District.

1834

The Indian District of Mashpee was established on March 31. The hard work of William Apes, Blind Joe Amos, Israel Amos, Isaac Coombs, Ezra Attaquin, and many others paid off. A new governor supported the Act which returned power to the native people. No longer were the Indians of Mashpee subject to the oppressive regulations imposed on them by the Commonwealth. Although there were some conditions placed on them by the legislature, the Indians had more control over their lives than since the English landed at Plymouth in 1620.

The Mashpee Town Hall, a large building by Indian standards, was built in the center of North Mashpee. Inside, a large hall with a balcony served as the meeting place and social center of town. Off to the side was a small office with an anteroom where the selectmen and other town officials conducted their business.

Mashpee also built the North Mashpee School, a one-story, one-room schoolhouse, and began to take English education seriously.

The town hall, the school, and the trading post were soon joined by homes of a more permanent style than the wickups (wigwams) and crude buildings that many of the Indians lived in. The new center of town attracted people from all over the Cape who were looking for excitement.

A young Indian named Solomon Attaquin, who had made good money in the whaling trade as a skipper, returned to Mashpee and saw the potential for business. He began planning a hotel which would cater to the naturalists and the sportsmen who came to Mashpee to hunt and fish or to be as one with the Indians and nature. The Hotel Attaquin opened in 1840 and quickly became renowned as a sportsman's paradise.

1870

A committee appointed by the Legislature went to Mashpee and held a meeting on the abolition of the Mashpee Indian District and the creation of the town of Mashpee.

Many of the Mashpee Indians felt that they were not ready for such a bold move, especially with the neighboring whites covering Mashpee land. With this in mind, the Mashpee Indian District voted against the proposed change to its status.

Despite this rejection, the Massachusetts Legislature went ahead and drafted an act to incorporate the town of Mashpee. Cape Cod legislators lobbied strongly for passage of the act because many people were waiting to get their hands on Mashpee land.

On May 28, 1870, Chapter 293: An Act to Incorporate the Town of Mashpee was approved. Section 1: *The District of Marshpee is hereby abolished, and the territory comprised therein is hereby incorporated into a town by the name of Mashpee; and said town of Mashpee is invested with all the powers, privileges, rights, and immunities, and subject to all the duties and requisitions to which other towns are entitled by the constitution and laws of this Commonwealth. . . .*

1976

On August 26 of this year, the Mashpee Tribe filed its case in federal district court in Boston claiming ownership of the land in Mashpee that had been illegally taken from them.

The Mashpee Tribe named 146 defendants, including the town of Mashpee, New Seabury Corporation, the Cape & Vineyard Electric Company, the Commonwealth of Massachusetts, and all other non-Indian people who claimed ownership of 20 or more acres. The Mashpee Wampanoags clearly stated that they were interested in gaining control of the undeveloped land, not in evicting the present residents from their homes.

The selectmen of the town called a meeting and appropriated large sums of the town's money for legal defense. They hired the law firm of Hale and Dorr to defend the town against the Indian claim. James St. Clair, who represented President Nixon during the Watergate scandal, was principal counsel. He was joined by lawyers from the firm of Goodwin Proctor and Hoar. This firm represented the title insurance companies who stood to lose millions of dollars should the claim be successful.

The filing of the case sent shockwaves throughout the ranks of real estate developers and they quickly joined forces. They conducted weekly meetings to fan the flames of fear and uncertainty among the non-Indian people who owned homes in Mashpee. The tribe responded by amending their lawsuit to exempt homeowners from the claim. To further reassure them, the tribe supported congressional legislation to clear title to the land of homeowners within the town. Ironically, the developers opposed the legislation, since it would eliminate the support they had gathered from the homeowners.

During this period, President Carter arranged a meeting between his personal friend Judge William Gunter and the two parties in the suit to resolve the Mashpee Indian land claim. The Indians and their opponents met in the Situation Room of the White House. The Mashpee selectmen complained bitterly about the hardship to the "poor" white homeowners and the "destitute" developers who were unfairly suffering from the Indian claim to the land. Judge Gunter asked, *"How much will it take to settle this—one million, two million, or what?"* Russell Peters, president of the Tribal Council and Earl Mills, chief of the tribe, responded that they were not interested in a monetary settlement; the tribe wanted the return of its land.

The Indians' claim to the land never reached a hearing in court. Instead, the developers threw up a roadblock—they challenged the right of the Mashpees to bring such a claim into court. The developers claimed that the Mashpee Indians were not a tribe within the meaning of the federal Non-Intercourse Act and could not sue for the land.

The Indians requested a continuance so that the issue of tribal status could be determined by the federal Department of Interior, which oversees tribal determination. Judge Walter J. Skinner refused, and for the first time in history, a panel of twelve white jurors was selected to judge whether the Mashpee Indians constituted a tribe.

The trial on tribal status began in October of 1977 and lasted forty days. In addition to the NARF attorneys, the Mashpees were represented by Lawrence Shubow, an experienced trial lawyer, and assisted by attorney Ann Gilmore.

During the trial, Judge Skinner refused to define the criteria by which tribal status would be judged. He deferred setting any standards until all the evidence was presented to the jury. The tribe was faced with an almost impossible situation—it was their burden to prove they were a tribe without knowing the standards by which they would be judged.

One by one, historians, anthropologists, sociologists, Mashpee Indians, and non-Indians were called to the witness stand by both sides. Historical accounts of the Mashpee Indians written by white missionaries were read to the jury, while the one historical account written by members of the tribe in the 1800s was excluded by the judge as being "biased."

White anthropologists and sociologists were allowed to testify as "expert" witnesses and gave their opinions as to tribal status. When the tribe presented the testimony of an Indian expert witness, noted author Vine Deloria Jr., the judge instructed the jury to disregard his opinion as being too "loose."

When both sides had presented all their evidence, the judge instructed the jury as to what constituted a tribe. In so doing, Judge Skinner expounded on legal definitions that had been developed throughout history, adding a number of criteria of his own. He provided the jury with six questions which would decide if the Indians could sue for the land: the jury had to find that the Mashpees were a tribe on each of the six dates in history chosen by the judge.

After two days of deliberation, the jury returned its verdict. Using the criteria established by the judge, they determined that the Mashpees were a tribe in 1834 and 1842 but not in 1790, 1869, 1870, and 1976. The judge used these findings to dismiss the land suit, ruling that the Indians were not a tribe within the meaning of the Indian Non-Intercourse Act of 1790 and had no right to sue for the return of their land.

Anne Foxx

(Mashpee Wampanoag, b. 1950)

Long involved with a variety of tribal committees, including the Mashpee Wampanoag Tribal Council, Anne Foxx has worked for decades to educate the public about
Native American people in New England. She has served for over twenty years on
the Advisory Committee for the Massachusetts Center for Native American Awareness and has worked with the Higher Education Opportunities Program, assisting
tribal members achieving undergraduate degrees. Foxx received a BA in sociology
and an MS in human services from the University of Massachusetts–Boston, where
she has also taught about contemporary Native issues. She conducted the following
interview with Joan Tavares Avant around 2005 for a presentation in Santa Fe.

Historical Continuities in Indigenous
Women's Political Activism

JOAN TAVARES AVANT: My first thought as I look at your topic is that Native
Wampanoag women since Creation have been politically active by being
linked to the preservation of the well-being and quality of life for their
relatives and the extended family which equals community. Women
understood the natural ecosystems. They planted the gardens, made
the cloths. Historically they kept the community intact while their men
were out in the forest hunting or out in the bays fishing.

Traditional and contemporary gatherings such as Indigenous ceremonies, rituals, festivals, music, or dance have been organized or led
by the women. Women elders tell the oral stories. This is the educational teaching concept for their family and community.

Today as I look at the Mashpee Wampanoag community and other
Native societies the women continue to be politically involved. They are
leaders by way of ancestral teachings. They have revived the language,
maintain dance and song, are exhibitors of Native arts and crafts, they
organize cultural events, are elected as Wampanoag princess, and
continue being involved in Native activist movements. Women have
served as president of the Mashpee Wampanoag Council. Like the

corn, beans, and squash, and the quahog, have been our main staple for sustenance, our women's collected wisdom is what makes our Indigenous community persevere.

ANNE FOXX: What's the first thing you can remember about the female role in your community?

JOAN: Wampanoag women had and still have various traditional roles in the community. Naturally, there were individual families which made the community. But the women's roles led to community and I'll try to clarify this. I will speak from my own family experience and observation. It was important for my mother to manage and care of the family. Most often she was the employee, the nurse, the chef and family manager, ultimately preserving the domestic sovereignty. These services were highly valued. Grandmother was historian, medicine woman, and she told the stories. Her mother was the only mail carrier using a horse and wagon two generations back. Whatever activities were done or positions held by my mother and grandmother and other women, these roles were shared with extended family and tribal members. Your responsibilities were to care for the quality of life for all. It was "natural" inbred tasks and cultural values.

ANNE: What do you know about kinship ties and the clan system? Why do you think it was important, or not?

JOAN: Kinship ties as a clan mothers are responsible for issues the family clan may have. I do not mean this from a monetary perspective, that's not it all. As clan mother your duty is to be knowledgeable in the areas of health, education, and welfare of your relatives and tribal community. You need to know the resources available when there is a need. You should be well versed in the history of your tribe, understand family values and beliefs. Regardless of the need you should be ready to lend a hand. I'm the Deer Clan Mother for my family and feel it is very important to carry on this tradition.

ANNE: Have you been in any way "politically active" in the community? Did you voice your opinion about the tribe, environment, involve yourself in tribal communities or tribal council, run for town or local government office?

JOAN: Yes, being politically active for causes of your family and tribal people is what you have to do as a Wampanoag woman. My mother and grandmother taught me the skills and inspired me to do what

I've accomplished. As a very young girl I learned to cook and share the meals with community members. Two important values I learned at home were to share and respect each other. Catering Wampanoag meals is what I continue to do today.

I served as the Mashpee Wampanoag tribal president for three terms, director of Indian education in the Mashpee Public School District for the past twenty-five years, have been politically active in fighting against building and destroying the land and in saving our ancient ways in the Mashpee community, actively involved in organizing the Circle of Caring Group, which focused on social problems within the Native community, i.e., alcohol and drugs, youth programs. At one point I led a group against the sale of alcohol in one of our center stores near the Native community and believe it or not we won. I have sat on many local boards. I ran for school committee a couple of years ago and lost by 38 votes. I am an avid advocate for parents and students when there are conflicts or academic concerns in school. I share the Mashpee Wampanoag history and culture by way of writing newsletter articles and teaching a variety of workshops.

ANNE: In your opinion, in what ways did women's roles change before and after contact with Europeans? Or did they change?

JOAN: Understandably, after that contact, because Native women were at the mercy of European social structure, to some point their roles became somewhat compounded. However, our Native legends, oral stories, memories, and Wampanoag narratives throughout the 17th century and to the present day tells us that Wampanoag women continue to maintain and practice their traditional Indigenous roles with dignity. My answer is "NO." Indigenous women's roles did not traditionally change.

Linda Coombs
(Aquinnah Wampanoag)

Linda Coombs was born and raised at Aquinnah but married a Mashpee Wampanoag and has lived at Mashpee for over thirty years. A museum educator, she has worked for the Boston Children's Museum and Plimoth Plantation's Wampanoag Indigenous Program, for which she was the associate director between 1996 and 2008. The essay below appeared in Plimoth Plantation's own magazine, *Plimoth Life*. Coombs is now the program director of the Aquinnah Cultural Center. She is also a talented traditional artist, producing beadwork, decorative painting on deerskin, twined woven baskets and sashes, and other objects.

Holistic History: Including the Wampanoag in an Exhibit at Plimoth Plantation

Plimoth Plantation's current exhibit *Thanksgiving: Memory, Myth & Meaning*, like its predecessor, *Irreconcilable Differences*, is a very unique experience. It accomplishes what no other exhibit on the "Thanksgiving story" has ever achieved. Its purpose is twofold: to peel away layers of the Thanksgiving myth until it arrives at the truest history and to use not just a single author to present and interpret all aspects of that history, but to incorporate the actual voices of historic participants in order to achieve a much more complete history.

The development and presentation of *Thanksgiving: Memory, Myth & Meaning* are in keeping with Plimoth Plantation's recently stated objective to become a bi-cultural institution. The exhibit is manifest evidence of the museum's work toward attaining that goal.

What does it mean to be a bi-cultural institution? It might seem as if the museum has already achieved that goal since both English and Wampanoag educational programs reside under the same roof. However, just having the two races under one roof does not automatically accomplish our bi-cultural ideal. This is a gradual and ongoing process that must be consistently maintained and monitored. It is the process and not just the end result that is important—the process of the museum's two cultures working collaboratively when necessary, separately if that is what is needed, and recognizing when either is the appropriate method.

Thanksgiving: Memory, Myth & Meaning, in dealing with the Wampanoag, is much more than just about us. Whether exhibits, books, films, or learning products, there are many available venues of information about us—always done by someone else. Sometimes these are so inaccurate and fraught with stereotypes that they are unrecognizable to the very people that they are supposed to be about. For example, take one of the recent Hollywood films about Squanto. He was a Patuxet Wampanoag, Patuxet being the original name for what is now Plymouth. I am a Wampanoag person from Aquinnah. While Aquinnah is not Patuxet, I am also a person who has worked at Plimoth Plantation (on this old Patuxet ground) for more than two decades. Upon first viewing the Hollywood film, I thought I was watching one of those natives of the South Seas Islands movies from the sixties. It was a good ten minutes before I realized that this movie was supposed to be about my own people! While the actors were Native People from other nations, they did not look like the Wampanoag. Their clothing and ornament were nothing like I had ever seen in twenty-plus years of making outfits for the interpreters on the Wampanoag Homesite. Some of the Native language spoken was Micmac. Some was unintelligible to me. And the landscape looked like the rocky coast of Maine, for it certainly was not Patuxet.

It was truly a moment to appreciate the effort that it takes to make our museum historically accurate. And that effort is worth every second of time. Why? To me as a Wampanoag person, that movie was a hodgepodge of inaccuracies. (Hollywood had the opportunity to work with us for historical accuracy but chose not to utilize that advantage.) So many of the movie's cultural aspects were either made up (the clothing) or borrowed from other tribes (the language). It was the Frankenstein version of that particular piece of history. To the Wampanoag People it was insulting and downright ridiculous. It is also very damaging. So much of the Hollywood version is simply not plausible when placed against the yardstick for measuring historical accuracy. However, the audience may not be aware of the implausible content. They may accept what they see at face value—particularly if it matches other misconceptions that they already hold.

We at Plimoth Plantation work very hard to peel away layers of inaccuracies and sift through centuries of misconceptions and misrepresentations.

Again, why is this important? Because to represent, by whatever means, any group as accurately as possible is to show respect. It shows respect for people—both those of the past and those of today. What is the purpose of learning about different cultures, whether past or present? So that you can know what kind of houses they lived in? What kind of bowls they ate out of? What they made their clothes out of? How they raised their children? Whether they kept animals? Is that kind of knowledge and information the desired end result? NO. It most certainly isn't. Or at least it shouldn't be. All of those things are just windows into the lives of people. The point of learning about other human beings is not just to collect facts and information but to use that learning to build respect and understanding.

Thanksgiving: Memory, Myth & Meaning shows much respect for the Wampanoag. It is much more than about the Wampanoag. At the very first thought of the exhibit, the Wampanoag were included. From start to finish we were active partners in the planning, development, and execution of the project. In this case, it was not just the Wampanoag Indian Program staff involved, but the whole community. The Wampanoag People had to buy into Thanksgiving: Memory, Myth & Meaning or it could not have happened. The exhibit includes many examples of our handiwork and pictures and videos of Wampanoag People (much of the photographic material comes from an unforgettable two-day film shoot held in October 2000 involving 100 Native People from the Wampanoag and several other Nations). Most importantly, however, our voice is here: the Wampanoag perspective from the Wampanoag People. In the exhibit our presence and our voice are given equal credence to the others represented.

We're still here. And our history is carried through the centuries to the present day. Typically the telling of that story has ended with the arrival of the Pilgrims or after King Philip's War. This omission has served to erase us from history. Since the Wampanoag were not in actuality erased, we would simply add that which has been omitted—creating a more truthful, more accurate, and fuller view of history. Some people call this revisionist history, saying it weighs too heavily on the "side" of the Native People or that it is too controversial. I would ask those people to look back at the textbooks from their elementary school or high school—perhaps even college days. There are patterns in the historical writing. One reads all about the Pilgrims bravely crossing the ocean to found a brand-new country based on freedom, then comes the Revolutionary War, and then continued building of the new country, America. Where does one read about the Wampanoag? Where does one find what was going on with them while everything else was going on? Until very recently, when it came to textbooks and historical thinking, we existed only in the 17th century—when Squanto showed the Pilgrims how to plant corn, when Massasoit befriended the Pilgrims, and the "First Thanksgiving." Often our existence was only mentioned in our relation to (or in the service of) the English. Readers and students of history have been left with the image that we went completely away.

In point of fact, we didn't go anywhere. And most Wampanoag People still live right here in our original homeland alongside everyone else. For us there were not always easy times or good times. There were other epidemics (after the first, most devastating one of 1616–1618 in which the Wampanoag lost approximately half of our population, conservatively estimated at 35,000 at that time), wars, still further encroachment and loss of land, demeaning treatment by those of other races, and systems that worked to our disadvantage and were completely the opposite of our traditional ways. It is not always a pleasant story, but it is nevertheless a true one. It happened. And on that basis alone, the story deserves to be told.

To tell our story—to add it back into the historical record—is seen as a negative thing by some. Reintroducing what should always have been included is seen as "changing" history. We are not trying to change history. It happened. Not telling what happened does not change the fact of its happening. What we would like to change are the attitudes that keep us in that place of omission, where one part or "side" of history is perceived as the whole. It is not just a matter of Wampanoag People having the opportunity to tell our "side" of the story. It is a matter that all of us see the history of the 17th century (or of any time period) holistically. There are no sides, but only one whole story. This, then, is what *Thanksgiving: Memory, Myth & Meaning* articulates and accomplishes with sensitivity. This is what gives the exhibit its unique qualities.

Paula Peters
(Mashpee Wampanoag)

The daughter of Mashpee leader Russell Peters (see above), Paula Peters has worked as a journalist for the *Cape Cod Times*. She has also worked in education and outreach with Plimoth Plantation and currently does marketing and communications management for Wampworx, a contracting company she cofounded with her husband, Mark Harding. In 2009 Peters received a standing ovation at the Massachusetts Society of Mayflower Descendants in Cohasset, Massachusetts, for her address, "Wampanoag Reflections." Her piece on the wampum jewelry controversy originally appeared in 2002 on NewsWatch, an online collaboration between the San Francisco State University Journalism Department, the Native American Journalists Association, and other news organizations devoted to journalism by and about people of color. It has since made the rounds of numerous websites and online discussions.

Wampanoag Reflections

"This is a time of celebration for you—celebrating an anniversary of a beginning for the white man in America. A time of looking back, of reflection. It is with a heavy heart that I look back upon what happened to my People."

These are not my words. These words were spoken by the late Frank "Wamsutta" James in the shadow of the statue of Massasoit on Cole's Hill in Plymouth on Thanksgiving Day in 1970. They were part of a speech he was to have given several month earlier at a state dinner to launch the commemoration of the 350th anniversary of Plymouth Colony. But when the Aquinnah Wampanoag elder submitted the text for review it was cut and censored so savagely he hardly recognized the words as his own.

So Frank James refused to deliver the censored version and instead gathered Native people from across the nation to hear his unedited remarks on that cold November afternoon that would become known as the first National Day of Mourning.

When I was asked to come here today to address this audience as we can see 2020 on the horizon, I could not help but evoke the memory of Wamsutta and the courage it took for him to defy state officials and instead gather indigenous people for a solemn display of unity—refusing ever again to be silenced, making it possible for me to be heard.

In the nearly four decades since that event we as Wampanoag people, and indigenous people across this country, have come a long way—initially demanding and ultimately earning respect for our sacrifice, our history, and our enduring traditions.

For centuries our story had been told with a biased slant that portrayed us as either a noble savage or hostile heathen—neither depiction being true. But for many years attempts to correct stereotypes and misconceptions were met with resistance to a truth that might reflect poorly upon those who colonized our ancestral homelands.

No one was interested in hearing about how a 15-century papal bull, the Doctrine of Discovery, was used to strip the indigenous people of our rights and endorse a Manifest Destiny that would take our land from coast to coast. Without organized religion, a church and steeple, our spiritual beliefs were devalued and our culture banned—those who came here for religious freedom committing cultural genocide on the people who welcomed them as strangers and taught them to survive in a foreign land.

And yet in all sincerity I have had people tell me—isn't it an amazing thing that the treaty between the Wampanoag Massasoit Ossamequin and Plimoth Colony's Governor William Bradford lasted more than 50 years? To which I always have to remind them, a promise is supposed to be forever.

I recall as a child my father, Russell Peters Sr., telling me the time had come for Native people to begin to take back our culture and traditions. He told me he grew up in a time when it wasn't popular to admit that he was a Native American, but despite centuries of oppression, we would not forget who we were, we could not deny our heritage as Mashpee Wampanoag.

Today I am grateful to people like Frank James and my father, and people like Russell Means and Dennis Banks for their activism in starting the American Indian Movement, and for Leonard Peltier for enduring decades of wrongful incarceration—for keeping my Native pride alive and for enduring an era of civil rights for Native People.

By now you are probably all asking yourselves, what does all this have to do with this dignified gathering of *Mayflower* descendents? What on earth was Wigmore Pierson thinking inviting this woman to come and address our annual meeting?

I will tell you I am not here to make you feel guilty for the past injustices upon my people. Even while the *Mayflower* brought upon my ancestors intolerance, unspeakable dishonor, and people who took advantage of Wampanoag generosity and good nature, I do not hold this gathering responsible for those actions.

Quite to the contrary, I hold this gathering responsible for the future.

That I can stand here today and be recognized as the keynote speaker of this event without having had my text reviewed for censorship speaks volumes about how far we have come, but there are still miles to go.

At Plimoth Plantation, where as a teenager I started out as an interpreter in the Wampanoag Indigenous Program more than 30 years ago, today I am the director of marketing. I have a lovely view of Cape Cod Bay from my office window and a door that closes even while it is technically always open.

In Plymouth, where plans are under way to commemorate the town's 400th anniversary in 2020, I have been invited to serve on the local commission to plan the events. This time you can be sure that the Wampanoag story will not be neglected, or censored, and will instead be told with dignity. I can actually envision a day when a "National Day of Mourning" will no longer be necessary, as acknowledgement of our history from a balanced perspective will bring closure to old wounds.

It is something we work to achieve every day at Plimoth Plantation—to tell the bicultural story of the Wampanoag and the colonists in a way that is respectful and truthful to each heritage. While the *Mayflower* brought some regrettable consequences upon the Wampanoag, not everything that came over on that ship was ill-fated.

There were true friendships and trade that advanced technology for the Wampanoag in a way that enabled us to improve our ability to hunt, fish, and farm. We introduced wampum as an initial form of currency to our new European neighbors and traders, while beaver pelts made their way to European milliners to be turned into some of the finest hats in the land.

There was an exchange of culture and knowledge that enriched both the colonists and Natives and had great potential had it been esteemed. But what we cannot do is turn back the hands of time.

Those of you who take great pride in your heritage as descendants of the original passengers aboard the *Mayflower* in 1620 actually have a good deal in common with those of us who are Wampanoag.

We live in a nation where people have flocked from around the world for freedom and opportunity and dispersed into a melting pot of cultural diffusion but for some stubborn crystals of true matter. We are, each of us, people who refuse to relinquish the significance of our ancestry and instead cherish the preservation of the legacy of those who went before us.

We have today, in spite of the past, enduring alliances and special friendships as a result of the fated voyage of the *Mayflower*. Had there been no *Mayflower* there would be no Wig [Wigmore Pierson]—need I say more. No *Mayflower*, no friends like David and Fran Burnham and, especially significant, I would not have the blessing of two daughters who are at once card-carrying members of the Mashpee Wampanoag Tribe and apparently descendents of the Winslow family.

And so, moving forward, it is not lost on me how critical it is for us to embrace a future that honors and respects our history lest we be doomed to repeat the mistakes of the past.

As a young interpreter I was often frustrated by how much people did not know about the Wampanoag and how insensitive people could be, unwittingly making insulting comments reflecting what they had learned about Native people from comic books and bad westerns. But a bit of sage advice from an early mentor has carried me through many an uncomfortable encounter throughout my life. She told me that ignorance was like a wall of stone and that if I were to clench my fists and try to break it down, I would only walk away with bloody hands. The stones, she said, need to come down gently, one at a time, by patiently educating people about our true story. So each time I am in a room like this, I see the potential not to make enemies, but to take stones off the wall.

That being said, I want to close with these words of Wamsutta: "We still have the will and, most important of all, the determination to remain as Indians. We are determined, and our presence here this evening is living testimony that this is only a beginning of the American Indian, particularly the Wampanoag, to regain the position in this country that is rightfully ours."

Beware: Not All Terms Are Fair Game

As news writers we have come to expect that many of our stories will stir up a bit of controversy, inspiring healthy debate in our communities. But some stories are designed to inform, educate, and entertain in a rather benign way. We can relax while writing them and feel like we are doing a real service to a broad spectrum of the readership.

That is exactly what I believed I was doing earlier this year when writing a feature story for the *Cape Cod Times* based in Hyannis, Massachusetts. It was about Wampanoag tribal members on Cape Cod and the island of Martha's Vineyard reviving the ancient tradition of making wampum jewelry. The beads tediously hewn from chips of quahog shell were greatly valued and traded among the Algonquin tribes in the northeast for hundreds of years. The strands of beads became the first form of legal currency for colonists in the 1600s. The word *wampum* became synonymous with money even as glass beads and western-style Indian jewelry gained in popularity and the wampum jewelry tradition waned.

But in recent years the rich purple hinge of the hard-shell clam has emerged from the sea like a newfound pearl and Native artisans are sought after for the authentic article, wampum jewelry made by Wampanoag craftsmen.

No sooner did the story hit the pages of the *Cape Cod Times* than my editors received a call from a non-Native woman named Janet Rounsville, owner of Yankee Crafter's Inc. in Yarmouth, Massachusetts. Darn if she didn't trademark the term "wampum jewelry" and was irate the news article used the term amply and did not mention her name once.

While I am aware of several non-Native people who make wampum jewelry, and in fact mentioned some of them in the story, I had never heard of Mrs. Rounsville. But a quick check of the U.S. Patent and Trademark office website confirmed the woman had indeed trademarked the term.

As a member of the Mashpee Wampanoag tribe I was personally perplexed. I asked the trademark office, how could such a thing happen? How could a word and term of our language as common as cottage cheese be given over exclusively to a white woman and denied to us forever?

Believe me, as the tribe with the infamous distinction of having welcomed the Pilgrims in 1620, we are accustomed to having things taken from us. But our language, and specifically the word *wampum* and the jewelry made from it, has spiritual significance the likes of which Mrs. Rounsville will never realize. You see, when I called her to ask her if she felt any remorse for taking the word, she said absolutely not. As a Cape craftsman who also uses the quahog shell to make jewelry she applied for the term fair and square and now it's hers. She even advertised the application as required by law in the U.S. Patent and Trademark journal, which lands on the desks of lawyers and bureaucrats all over the country. The Wampanoag are not on the mailing list.

The process made the term hers all right, but Mrs. Rounsville wasn't going to be entirely selfish with it.

"If the tribe wants their word back, they can buy it from me," she told me.

Tribal attorneys have advised us we can challenge the trademark in court and would likely win after a costly battle, or simply continue to use the term liberally.

Wampum jewelry, wampum jewelry, wampum jewelry . . .

Robert Peters

(Mashpee Wampanoag, b. 1962)

Like many of the writers from Mashpee, Robert Peters draws heavily on two traditions: his Wampanoag heritage and his African American lineage. He is known for his visual art as well as his poetry, some of which appeared in his father, Russell's, book *The Wampanoags of Mashpee*. He wrote a children's book, *Da Goodie Monsta* (2009), based on a story his son told him. The two poems below are original contributions to this volume.

Grandfather

I pray that the Grandfather Spirit is listening
When we cry out for all the people, places, and things
We have lost

I pray that the Grandfather Spirit is listening
When we tell him we want to be our own people again
We are not happy living in someone else's world

We want you to make things the way they used to be
Bring back the woods and the water
The quahog, the tutuag, and the osprey
Bring back the crow who gave us corn
So many lifetimes ago

Make things the way they were
When there was only up street and down street
Edmonds Dreen, Noisy Hole, Big Bog

I pray that the Grandfather Spirit listens
When we tell him we want a place in the world
For our children and our children's children
All our relations

It is not enough to have a place, where we can die

I pray that the Grandfather Spirit is listening
When we tell him we need a place in the world
So that we can live

Red Sun Rising

A red sun is rising
Lifting with it red people
Lifting the spirits that live in the land
Ancestors emerge from trees, and rocks, and water

The birds, the fish, and the four legged ones
Are watching, listening, and sensing

      The   Red   sun   rise

They hold out their hands and wings and fins
And rejoice the return to places
Once called home

High above the noise of civilization
A hawk glides effortlessly
Far below a lone wolf
Makes her way through city streets tentatively
Grass pushes through concrete
Because there is a small crack
And there is light
And there is hope

There   is   a   Red   sun   rising

Through the trees and the clouds
Up up up into the sky
Shedding furious light onto the land
Sending darkness into shadow
Up up up
Until even shadow has no place to go

The   Red   sun   is   rising

Red people come running
Come dancing, Come singing

        Red   sun   rising

Is it so surprising?
We are still here

Mwalim *7)/Morgan James Peters

(Mashpee Wampanoag)

In his writing, storytelling performances, and music, Mwalim blends his black and Wampanoag heritages. His CD *The Liberation Sessions: Soul of the City*, a concept album based on the playlists of fictional radio station WBAR (Black Ass Radio), won ten nominations at the 2010 Native American Music Awards. His book *A Mixed Medicine Bag* features "original Black Wampanoag folklore," like the colonial allegory included below. Now living in Mashpee, Mwalim is an associate professor of English and African/African American Studies at the University of Massachusetts–Dartmouth, a playwright-in-residence at Boston's New African Company, and an historian for the Prince Hall Grand Lodge of Massachusetts.

From A Mixed Medicine Bag

TURTLE AND THE OAK TREE

Have you ever sat under an oak tree? I mean one of those huge old oak trees where the broken branches have about 80 rings. Well, if you ever see one, sit at the bottom of it with your back against that part of the trunk leading directly to the main root; close your eyes and breathe deeply. Then just sit and listen . . .

Long before the woods, lakes, and swamps became golf courses, shopping malls, and condominiums, but long after turtles got their shells, a turtle sat under a tall oak tree on the edge of a swamp. Every day around sunrise, this turtle would walk out of the swamp, make his way up the hill, sit under this tree in silence, and look off into the distance. As animals who didn't know the turtle would pass by, they would often think he was in a trance. The truth of the matter was that in spite of the little pair of pincer glasses that sat on his face, this turtle couldn't see a thing—at least, not with his eyes.

Yes, he was a blind turtle that the other animals simply called "Blind Turtle" (animals weren't much for being clever about names back then). Although Blind Turtle couldn't see the physical world, he was a turtle of great vision and insight. Once a week, when the turtle sat under the tree, he would speak. He'd tell stories and share his visions with anyone who might have been around (and there was always some animal hanging around). Animals, being curious by nature, often did go and visit the turtle in his silence and when he spoke. On the days that he spoke, animals would ask him why he sat in silence for so long. He would simply smile and say that he was listening to what the world was saying.

Of course, the animals didn't always see Blind Turtle as wise. At first, most of them thought Blind Turtle to be crazy or a fool and would walk away shaking their heads, figuring that he had gotten old and was losing his sense of reality. As time went by and more and more of Blind Turtle's visions came to pass, many of the animals realized that his visions were legitimate. Those animals would sit and listen, trying to hear what he heard, but all they heard were the birds singing, the wind blowing, the water in the stream running, the various calls and songs of the other animals, or their footsteps as they passed by on the road near the tree.

There was a meetinghouse a little further down the road where many of the animals gathered to listen to the preacher. By this time, snakes had formed the Snake Circle (which was really more of a coil) and were still trying to hatch their plots to control the lakes, woods, and swamps. The Snake Circle began organizing a council of overseers in an effort to keep order—teaching the proper and civilized ways of snakes. The snake assigned to oversee this area was a slimy little water moccasin named Phineas. When he slithered into the community and laid claim to the meetinghouse, he wasted no time in starting with his preaching about the natural inferiority of turtles, lizards, and frogs. He taught that only those who served and obeyed snakes might make it to the hereafter and while animals might not be able to become snakes, they could aspire to be snake-like. All things valuable and beautiful on earth rightfully belonged to the snakes, he would say. After all of this, many of the animals stopped going to the meetinghouse, preferring to sit under the oak tree with Blind Turtle.

Phineas began to notice how thin his congregation was becoming, especially when it was time to tally up the income from the collection plate. He soon learned that many of his congregation were now going to the oak tree to listen to Blind Turtle. It was one thing to lose members of the congregation because they didn't want to come to a meeting; it was something else entirely to lose them to a turtle. What could a turtle, especially a blind turtle, offer to the animals?

One morning, Phineas decided to slither down to the oak tree and see for himself what could possibly be so special about Blind Turtle. He hid down near the creek—just to the west of the tree—where he could see and hear without being detected. He saw Blind Turtle come out of the swamp and sit under the tree. As time passed, animals began to gather under the tree and sit with Blind Turtle. After a while, Blind Turtle began to speak about a bunch of visions that he had seen during the week and things that he heard in the wind . . . it all sounded like rubbish to the snake.

Blind Turtle began to talk about a vision of a lizard from another community who would come and provide help for them in a time of need. He suddenly stopped speaking, turned towards the creek, and called out, "Hey! You down there; yes, you . . . the snake. Why not come up and join us? It'll be a lot more comfortable here in the grass, under the shade of the tree." Phineas tried to lie still and pretended to be a branch, hoping that the other animals wouldn't see him. "I know you're there, snake. The voices in the wind told me you were there. It's okay, you can join us." All of the animals turned and saw Phineas lying flat along the creek, trying to look like a branch . . . until he sneezed. One of the animals began to snicker, which made a few of the other animals giggle, causing more to laugh out loud. Pretty soon, all of them were looking at Phineas eavesdropping on Blind Turtle, pointing and laughing at the snake as he slithered away in humiliation.

Things really began to take a downward turn for Phineas after that day. He was a laughingstock to all of the Snake Circle. Imagine, a snake sneaking to a turtle's meeting! Fewer and fewer animals came to the meetinghouse and Phineas discovered what an echo the building had. Meanwhile, more and more animals were going to sit with the turtle under the oak tree, waiting for him to share a few words with those who gathered. Finally, Phineas decided that he would pay a visit to Blind Turtle and see for himself what the animals' attraction to this turtle was. Phineas surmised that if this turtle really had any power, it was the manifest destiny of snakes to control it.

On a day when Blind Turtle was sitting under the oak tree by himself,

Phineas approached and asked if he could join him. The turtle nodded his head and continued with his meditations. Phineas sat quietly observing Blind Turtle as he continued to stare off into the distance in silence. After sitting in silence for what seemed to be an eternity, Phineas finally asked, "What are you listening to?"

"The voices," replied Blind Turtle.

"What voices?"

"The voices of those who went before and those yet to come."

"Where do you hear these voices?"

"All around us."

"I don't hear anything."

"The voices are on the wind. They whistle through the branches of the trees and the rustle of the grass. The voices are all around; just listen."

Phineas tried to sit and listen and all he could hear was a breeze in the branches and leaves of the oak tree. Then, just when he was ready to give up listening, he thought he heard some voices. He wasn't sure, but somewhere in the whistle of the breeze in the tree, he heard them talking! He sat and listened for a while but was too excited to really pay attention. At last, he had the power of this old turtle. Phineas began visiting Blind Turtle rather regularly and would sit under the tree with him. One day after a visit, he slithered back to his house where he wrote out a report to the Snake Circle about his discovery. Phineas's report caused quite a buzz (it sounded more like a hiss, actually) in the Snake Circle. As a result, he was soon regarded as an expert in dealing with the turtle population. The circle appointed a delegation of snakes to come and investigate Phineas's claim.

The delegation came out and decided to spend time at the tree with Blind Turtle. Most of them only heard the wind, but a few actually heard voices. Obviously, it was not just a matter of the turtle having any powers (he was just a visually impaired turtle). It had to have something to do with the tree. They decided to examine the tree more closely, but it appeared to be just a plain, old oak tree. They took leaf and bark samples of the tree and ran all kinds of tests. Finally, the delegation issued the following report to the rest of the Snake Circle:

After careful investigation and reviewing Phineas's claims about the oak tree and the turtle, some of us heard the voices that he spoke of. The turtle's ability to hear the voices can be explained rather simply: Turtles, being such simple and earthy creatures, can probably hear these voices because they have little else going on in their minds to distract them. We've come to the conclusion that the power that Phineas spoke of was the tree itself.

Based on this report, the Snake Circle appointed all existing meetinghouses that were not made of oak to be torn down and replaced with oak structures. They also changed the procedure of the meeting: the snakes and congregation would gather in the oak meetinghouses and sit silently waiting for the voices to manifest. As quietly as they sat, all they heard was silence.

Meanwhile, Blind Turtle and the other animals continued to gather under the oak tree. Blind Turtle gave thanks to the ancestors for their wisdom and guidance, thanks to the trees, bushes, and grass for conveying this wisdom, and thanks to the crickets and small birds who sat in the tree and conversed on the days that Phineas and the members of the Snake Circle visited the oak tree.

To this day, you can still find snakes silently sitting among a meetinghouse congregation waiting to hear the voices.

Notes

1. Mittark was the sachem at Gay Head from the 1660s to the 1680s. Nashaquitsa is land connecting Aquinnah to the rest of Martha's Vineyard. The Gay Head community was initially hostile to Christianity, but Mittark convinced them to allow a mission. David Silverman has published an analysis of this petition in *Early Native Literacies in New England*, ed. Kristina Bross and Hilary Wyss.
2. The petition was written by the minister Zachary Hossueit, one of the most practiced writers in the community.
3. This petition was also written by Zachary Hossueit.
4. Elisha Amos was Mittark's great-grandson. Daniel Mandell writes in *Behind the Frontier* that Amos "was unable to gain in Gay Head . . . even after he persuaded the English to appoint him as the enclave's justice of the peace" (103).
5. "That the hypocrite reign not, lest the people be ensnared."
6. Hammond was the first Native American in Massachusetts to hold this seat in the General Court of the Commonwealth. According to Simeon Deyo's *History*

of Barnstable County, Hammond was born in 1837 and married Blind Joe Amos's daughter Rebecca, with whom he had six children.

7. *Mourt's Relation* is a famous colonial account, written in 1620 and 1621 by the Puritans Edward Winslow and William Bradford, about the settlement of Plymouth and the "First Thanksgiving."

8. The spelling of his name has varied over time; Peters uses an older spelling, while scholars today more often use "Apess."

Further Reading

WAMPANOAG AUTHORS

Aquinnah Wampanoag Tribe. "Wampanoag Tribe: History & Culture." Web. 21 July 2011.

Attaquin, Helen. *A Brief History of Gay Head or "Aquinuh."* n.p.: Helen Attaquin, 1970. Print.

Attaquin, Helen, and Children's Museum of Boston. *Wampanoag Cookery.* Boston: American Science & Engineering, 1974. Print.

Avant, Joan Tavares. "Now, and Always, Wampanoag." *Cultural Survival Quarterly* 30.2 (Summer 2006): n. pag. Web. 29 July 2011.

———. *People of the First Light: Wisdoms of a Mashpee Wampanoag Elder.* West Barnstable MA: West Barnstable Press, 2010. Print.

———. "With Intent to Civilize." *Cultural Survival Quarterly* 3:1 (2010): n. pag. Web. 29 July 2011.

Baird, Jessie Little Doe. "Wôpanâak Language Reclamation Project." Web. 10 June 2011.

Bingham, Amelia. *Mashpee: Land of the Wampanoags.* Mashpee MA: Mashpee Historical Commission, 1970. Print.

———. *Seaweed's Revelation: A Wampanoag Clan Mother in Contemporary America.* San Diego: GGBing Publishing, 2012. Print.

Coombs, Linda. "The Flow of Time and Seasons: Wampanoag Foodways in the Seventeenth Century." *Plimoth Life* 4.1 (2005): 13–19. Print.

———. "Holistic History: Including the Wampanoag in an Exhibit at Plimoth Plantation." *Plimoth Life* 1.2 (2002): 12–15. Print.

———. *Powwow.* Cleveland OH: Modern Curriculum Press, 1992. Print.

———. Rev. of *Mayflower: A Story of Courage, Community and War*, by Nathaniel Philbrick. *Cultural Survival Quarterly* 31.1 (Spring 2007): n. pag. Web.

———. "A Wampanoag Perspective on *Colonial House.*" *Plimoth Life* 3.1 (2004): 24–28. Print.

DeGrasse, Alfred. "About Poison Ivy." *Carlisle Arrow* 23 Apr. 1909: n. pag. Print.

———. "The Legend of the Red Eagle." *Red Man* Mar. 1911: 297–98. Print.

———. "Letter about Watson Hammond." *Red Man* Mar. 1912: n. pag. Print.

Duckworth-Elliott, Stephanie A. *Poneasequa—Goddess of the Waters.* Franklin Park NJ: Wampum Books, 2009. Print.

Fermino, Jessie Little Doe. "You Are a Dead People." *Cultural Survival Quarterly* 25.2 (Summer 2001): n. pag. Print.

Goddard, Ives, and Kathleen J. Bragdon. *Native Writings in Massachusett.* Philadelphia: American Philosophical Society, 1988. Print.

Hall, Stacy Elizabeth, and Jannette Vanderhoop. *The Legend of Katama: The Creation Story of Dolphins.* Oaks PA: Island Moon Press, 2004. Print.

Manning, Helen. *Moshup's Footsteps: The Wampanoag Nation, Gay Head/Aquinnah, the People of First Light.* Aquinnah MA: Blue Cloud Across the Moon Publishing, 2001. Print.

Mills, Earl. *Talking with the Elders of Mashpee: Memories of Earl H. Mills, Sr.* Mashpee MA: Lulu.com, 2012. Print.

Mills, Earl, and Betty Breen. *Cape Cod Wampanoag Cookbook: Traditional New England & Indian Recipes, Images & Lore.* Santa Fe NM: Clear Light Books, 2000. Print.

Mills, Earl, and Alicja Mann. *Son of Mashpee.* Rev. ed. Tucson: Word Studio, 2006. Print.

Mitchell, Zerviah Gould, and Ebenezer Pierce. *Indian History, Biography and Genealogy: Pertaining to the Good Sachem Massasoit of the Wampanoag Tribe, and His Descendants.* North Abington MA: Zerviah Gould Mitchell, 1878. Print.

Mwalim. *A Mixed Medicine Bag: Original Black Wampanoag Folklore.* Mashpee MA: Talking Drum Press, 2007. Print.

Peters, Paula. "Wampanoag Reflections." *Massachusetts Society of Mayflower Descendants* 4 (Apr. 2009). Web. 29 July 2011.

Peters, Robert. *Da Goodie Monsta.* Cambridge MA: Wiggles Press, 2009. Print.

Peters, Russell. *Clambake: A Wampanoag Tradition.* Minneapolis: Lerner Publishing Group, 1992. Print.

———. *Regalia: Native American Indian/Small Book.* Marlborough MA: Sundance Publishing, 1993. Print.

———. *The Wampanoags of Mashpee: An Indian Perspective on American History.* n.p.: R. M. Peters, 1987. Print.

Plimoth Plantation. *Investigating "The First Thanksgiving": An Educator's Guide to the 1621 Harvest Celebration.* Plimoth MA: Plimoth Plantation, 2003. Print.

Soliz, Chester P. *The Historical Footprints of the Mashpee Wampanoag Indians.* Sarasota FL: Bardolf, 2011. Print.

Vanderhoop, Jannette. *Cranberry Day: A Wampanoag Harvest Celebration.* Gay Head MA: Wampanoag Tribe of Gay Head (Aquinnah) Education Dept., 2002. Print.

ADDITIONAL READING

Apess, William. *On Our Own Ground: The Complete Writings of William Apess, a Pequot.* Ed. Barry O'Connell. Amherst: University of Massachusetts Press, 1992. Print.

Campisi, Jack. *The Mashpee Indians: Tribe on Trial.* Syracuse NY: Syracuse University Press, 1993. Print.

Carlson, Richard G. *Rooted Like the Ash Trees: New England Indians and the Land.* Naugatuck CT: Eagle Wing Press, 1987. Print.

Clifford, James. *The Predicament of Culture: Twentieth-Century Ethnography, Literature, and Art.* Cambridge MA: Harvard University Press, 1988. Print.

Deyo, Simeon. *History of Barnstable County.* New York: H. W. Blake, 1890. Print.

Dresser, Thomas. *The Wampanoag Tribe of Martha's Vineyard: Colonization to Recognition.* Charleston SC: History Press, 2012. Print.

Lopenzina, Drew. *Red Ink: Native Americans Picking Up the Pen in the Colonial Period.* Albany: SUNY Press, 2012. Print.

Mandell, Daniel R. *Behind the Frontier: Indians in Eighteenth-Century Eastern Massachusetts.* Lincoln: University of Nebraska Press, 2000. Print.

———. *Tribe, Race, History: Native Americans in Southern New England, 1780–1880.* Baltimore: Johns Hopkins University Press, 2011. Print.

Silverman, David J. *Faith and Boundaries: Colonists, Christianity, and Community among the Wampanoag Indians of Martha's Vineyard, 1600–1871.* Cambridge: Cambridge University Press, 2005. Print.

———. "'We Chief Men Say This': Wampanoag Memory, English Authority, and the Contest Over Mittark's Will." *Early Native Literacies in New England: A Documentary and Critical Anthology.* Ed. Kristina Bross and Hillary Wyss. Amherst: University of Massachusetts Press, 2008. 164–73. Print.

Weinstein-Farson, Laurie. *The Wampanoag.* New York: Chelsea House, 1988. Print.

Wilson, James. *The Earth Shall Weep: A History of Native America.* New York: Grove Press, 2000. Print.

Wyss, Hilary. *Writing Indians: Literacy, Christianity, and Native Community in Early New England.* Amherst: University of Massachusetts Press, 2003. Print.

NARRAGANSETT

Introduction

Dawn Dove

As a Narragansett Elder I am often disheartened by the history of our relationship with the newcomers to this land. We as the Indigenous people of this place have become marginalized in our own homeland; therefore I come to this project with a heavy heart.

Why would one share one's deepest feelings with those who have massacred, enslaved, indentured, and generally terrorized one's people? I have a vision of this place before European colonization, before the theft of our lands. I read early European chronicles, which always speak of the handsome, tall, healthy Narragansett people. The histories speak of the bounty of the land and the waters. Then our people were massacred, enslaved, indentured, and terrorized. I have come to know that the European colonists came to take, that they have taken, and that they continue to take, as their greed is insatiable. It is a terrible history, a terrible genocide, and a terrible theft.

My Grandmothers spoke to me of the beauty of our land and the waters, as pain was visible on their faces—the pain of remembering what has been destroyed and stolen. In this project we are compiling the written words of our people, yet there has been a terrible miscarriage of justice. The written words of our people of long ago have not been held in honor by the colonizers. There are only a few written words of the Narragansett that have been preserved, so they have been lost on the winds of time. Yet we carry in our hearts the oral traditions, which have been passed on to us from one generation to another. Just as my Grandmothers passed those truths on to me I continue to share with my grandchildren so that the truth will not be lost. We know that the colonizers' histories, the words that the colonizers passed on, are lies and half-truths and a cover-up of the great injustice done to the Narragansett people.

We the Indigenous people of this land have been decimated by disease, murder, and trickery. I think of Roger Williams, who is always called the friend of the Narragansett, yet that relationship was one of treachery once the colonists gained more and more control of our lands. I was always told through our oral histories that we did not sell our land; we only let others share the space. Roger Williams himself wrote that "Caunownicus . . . was not I say to be stird with mony to sell his land to let in Foreignrs.[1] Tis true he recd presents and Gratuities many of me: but it was not thouhsands nor ten thoughsands of mony could have bought of him an English entrance into this Bay. Thousands Could not have bought Providence or Pawtuxit or Aquedenick or any other Land I had of him."

Keep in mind that 1675 was the year of the Great Swamp Massacre, a terrible conflagration—children and women burned alive, a terrible planned annihilation of a people. The Euro-American story was that it was a battle in which all the Narragansett were killed. Yet we survived. We, the Narragansett people, continue to exist on this land, the land the Creator set aside for us. Yet because the colonizers "won," they felt there was no need to teach about the Narragansett. Even to this day the state of Rhode Island does not require that Narragansett history be taught in the public school system. The Lie continues by teaching the children to call the Narragansett and all other Indigenous nations "Native Americans," so that students do not even realize that they are speaking about the Narragansett, the Indigenous people of this particular land.

When I recall the oral histories that have been passed down in my family and I read the historical documents of the colonizers I can readily see why the colonizers want to keep the Lie. The truth would make one weep. The truth is so horrific that it would make one want to turn a blind eye rather than face the atrocities that were committed against our people. So the Lie continues from one generation to the next, so that the colonizers do not have to face the truth of their wrongdoings. They would rather live the Lie than face the great injustice that has been inflicted on the Narragansett and that, for that matter, continues to be inflicted on them. The pain and trauma are great.

The historical trauma that my people suffer is great. We did not inflict this upon ourselves; this is the direct result of the theft of our land, the enslavement and indenture of my people by the colonizers. As a child I was always told that we have relatives in Bermuda, as a result of the enslavement of our people by the colonizers. Imagine, if you will, the heartbreak and devastation of those who were left behind as family members were shackled and sent off on a slave ship to faraway lands. Then think of the children who were forcibly taken away from their families and placed in colonists' families as indentured servants (virtual slaves), who could no longer hear the sweet, familiar words of their family, who could no longer learn their own traditions and cultural values. This historical trauma lives in the hearts and minds of the Narragansett today. As we walk on our God-given homeland, we can see how the colonizers through their greed and corruption have stolen our birthright. This pain, these scars, these wounds are so deep that they have yet to be healed. We are branded with the names of our oppressors: Babcock, Brown, Champlin, Hazard, Johnson, Nichols, Perry, Stanton, Thomas, Wilcox . . .

As you read these few samples of Narragansett writings I want you to hear the historical grief in our voice. Hear the anguish of students and parents of Eleazar Wheelock's students at Moor's School. The Narragansett have often petitioned the government to right the many wrongs committed against them, to no avail. In 1768 Tobias Shattock and his brother John sailed to Britain to ask the royal government to help protect Narragansett lands from the colonists. Today the Narragansett government seeks justice from the United States of America as the full weight of the state of Rhode Island's congressional delegates have joined forces in the racist and prejudicial *Carcieri v. Salazar* court case.[2] The state of Rhode Island has continued to oppress the Narragansett Nation into the twenty-first century. My heavy heart wonders when the Narragansett spirit of this land will be honored.

Letters to Eleazar Wheelock

(1760s)

The Dartmouth College Archives contains letters from at least half a dozen Narragansett people who attended that Ivy League institution's predecessor, Moor's Charity School in Lebanon, Connecticut. While scholars have historically played up Native writers' deference to Moor's founder, Eleazar Wheelock, some of these letters, like John Daniel's, are also remarkable for their pointed criticisms of Wheelock's exploitation of his students and the underlying racism of his missionary efforts. Others, like Mary Secutor's, seem heavily mediated (possibly copied over or even written by Wheelock himself, or another agent). Even letters like this, however, are interesting for their consistent expression of a longing for home. Tobias Shattock left the school with his brother John to join the fight against the dissolution of tribal lands under the tribal sachem Tom Ninigret and Rhode Island's colonial governors.

Charlestown [Rhode Island] the 30 of November 1767

Rev'd Sr,

I would now acquaint you that I always tho't your School was free to the Natives; not to learn them how to Farm it, but to advance in Christian Knowledge, which was the Chief motive that caus'd me to send my Son Charles to you; not that I've anything against his Labouring some for you, when Business lies heavy on you; but to work two years to learn to Farm it, is what I don't consent to, when I can as well learn him that myself and have the prophet of his Labour, being myself bro't up with the best of Farmers. I am willing he should continue with you two or three years longer to be kept to School. For what Learning you have given him, I'm very thankful for.
    From yr humble servant,
    John Daniel

Charlestown the 12th of October 1767

Dear Sr,

I understand that you said I might stay at Charlestown till next spring;
I am bound to except it a token of Friend-Ship that you allow so long
time to Visit my Nation. But this wou'd be a much longer visit than I've
a mind to make at present; I shall return home about Thanksgiving, if
it be agreeable to your mind.

I am in a state of Health through the goodness of God, and hope
you are in Health also.

from yr most obedient humble servant,
Mary Secutor

Lebanon July 28

Rev'd & ever Hon'd Sir

I am not insensable of my Obligation to the Doctor for his Patarnel
Cair over me ever sence I have been the school my faults have been
over look'd with tenderness when they have deserved severity—I am
quite discouraged with myself. The longer I stay in the school the
worse I am don't think I shall ever do any good to the Cause & it will
cost a great deal to keepe me hear, which will be spending Money to
no purpose. I have been more trouble to the Doctor than all my mates.
don't think I desarve the honor of being in your school, if agreeable
to the Doctor I should be glad to leave the school next week & be no
longer a member of it

Hon-d Sir I would beg leave to
Subscribe my self your
Humble servant
Mary Secutor

Charlestown the 2nd of October, 1767

Rev'd Sir,

I've got home well, and have found my Friends in Helth through
the goodness of God. I wou'd now Inform You that affairs which

Concern us about our Land, appears somewhat Incouraging. The Hon Andrew Oliver Esq. has wrote to our Governor concerning the Sachems conduct; and after a warm debate the Governer obtain'd a vote that no more Land shou'd sold, 'till his Pleasure was further known, and that he is Cited to appear to the next Assembly. Sr William gives Incouragement that something shall be speedily done in our favour. As soon as I can git the Advice of my Friends, I can give You a more Perticular account. Tis oweing to the bad conduct of the Sachem that I came from the School. In regard to my Bretheren I'm Determin'd to exert my self to do something in their favour, to save their Substance that they may live together, and injoy the rich Favours so lately bestow'd upon them. The Indians are very thankful that you wrote in their favour to Sr William, especially when they heard how agreeable the letters were to the Generals Mind. It appears to me that yr influence on the Indians is greater than ever, and if you keep to the agreement to take from our Tribe non but Such as are recommended by the Council, Your Influence will increase. That if we shou'd move to, or near Onida, we shall be of great service to you in promoting your worthy Design.

I dislike the behavour of Boys that goes from the School, and gives it bad Character. I've so much reguard for the School, that all the Boys that is sent to you from our Tribe, for the futer, shall by their Parents be given up to live with you 'till they arrive to the age of twenty one years, if you desire it.

In grateful remembrance of Friendship, & Civility, with cordial love to the Schoolmaster, I am (Rev'd Sr with great respects) your most obedient huml servt,

Tobias Shattock

Thomas Commuck

(1805–1855)

Thomas Commuck left his home in Charlestown in 1825, joining the second wave of Native people who moved to Brothertown, Wisconsin. According to Deloss Love, he married Hannah Abner and had ten children, and he became a prominent member of the Brothertown community, serving as its postmaster and a justice of the peace. Commuck's "Sketch of the Brothertown Indians," published by the Wisconsin State Historical Society in 1859, details his experiences. He is also known as the author of an 1845 hymnal, *Indian Melodies*. The two letters below, from the Rhode Island Historical Society, detail his efforts to sell a parcel of land in Charlestown to finance his emigration.

Letter to Wilkins Updike

Calumetvill July 14, 1837

Hon Wilkins Updike Esq

Sir the undersigned in compliance with the wishes of Moses Stanton of Charlestown R.I. takes this method to inform you that I am one of the very few full blooded Remnants of that Once numerous and Powerful Tribe known by the name of the Narragansett Tribe of Indians. My object in writing to you is to get your candid opinion Respecting a claim that I have to lands lying in the town of Charlestown R.I. I am the only legal heir to my grand father Joseph Commuck's farm. He has no son nor daughter, brother nor sister living and no other grand child except myself. He owned at his death a farm containing about 1.50 acres as I always understood. But I believe that Moses Stanton estimates it at only about 1.2 acres[.] Said land be it more or less descends in a direct line to me. For the last two or three years I have become anxious to sell the same so that I may be benefitted thereby. I think that it was in 1823 that I traveled into State of N. York and liv'd amongst the Brothertown Indians and was adopted into the nation as you know that all Eastern Indians have been by them the said Brothertown Indians being composed of various Eastern tribes or rather the descendents of such. At the time of my leaving the state of R.I. my grand father's farm was leased to Daniel Sekater a resident in Charlestown. Since the expiration of said lease I do not know many of the particulars respecting whose hands said lands have been in but I have understood that [Jerasha Hull]—a woman who claimed to be half sister to my grandfather has had possession of said land. She is now dead. I have written several letters to Moses Stanton who is well aquainted with the justice of my claim[.] [T]o him I would respectfully refer you for any particulars respecting my claim. Being but a mere lad when I left Charlestown I was but very imperfectly acquainted with the laws rules and regulations of said tribe—but as near as I can learn I think that I could not sell said land without getting a special act passed by the legislature of R.I. to that effect. I have written to the governor of the state of R.I. Day before yesterday I received his answer. He says he thinks that by petitioning the legislature of the state of R.I. I shall have a special act passed for my relief. There is one point which I wish to be particularly instructed in—because I think that it may have a very important bearing upon the question. That is Congress passed a law last winter [authorizing] that the Brothertown Indians be admitted as citizens of the U.S. to all intents + purposes + that they have the title to their lands in Wisconsin Territory secured to them in fee simple. You are no doubt acquainted with the Bill of which I speak and of all of its provisions. You will perceive then that I am soon to be a citizen of the U.S. and I believe that the Constitution of the U.S. provides that no man shall be deprived of his just rights. I wish you to give me your opinion on that point in particular—If you can assist me in selling said lands I will reward you amply for your trouble. I wish that you would consult with Moses Stanton on the subject and act in [concert] he being one of the principal council men in Charlestown—I think of coming down to Charlestown if it is necessary to endeavor to secure my just rights but the road is a long one and I do not wish to come until I am certainly informed whether I can sell or not—1600 miles cannot be traveled with a considerable sum of money to defray expenses + that is the distance that I should have to travel should I [come]. Moses Stanton urged me in two of his letters to write to you on the subject of my claim—and I have

now done so + if you will have the condescension to answer me—you
will please to direct "To Thomas Commuck Calumetvill. Calumet
County—Wisconsin Territory" I have the honour to subscribe myself
your Humble + Obedient Servant—Thomas Commuck

Mr. Wilkins Updike—Esq
South Kingston W.C.R.I.

Letter to Elisha Potter

Manchester July 11th, 1844

To the Hon
E. R. Potter Esq

Sir

1   Once more I ask, how do you do?
    Tis long, since I have heard from you.
    Which leads me (whether right or not)
    To think that you have me forgot.

2   Myself and family are well.
    Which I do with much pleasure tell.
    And when these feeble lines you view,
    I hope'twill be the same with you.

3   I often think with heaving breast,
    Of <u>Rights</u>, which <u>Wrongly</u> are possest.
    And often to have I implored,
    That they might be, to me restor'd.

4   I sougt your aid, you promis'd to,
    That you would try, what you could do,
    That you my case, would take in hand.
    And help me thus to gain my land.

5   I know objections have been brought,
    But all their weight, and force, is nought.

Justice, and truth, are on my side.
Although my Rights, have been denied.

6 Some say one thing, some say another,
Some slander, Father, me and Mother.
Some say, "They never married were,
Therefore he's not the legal heir."

7 I join the issue with them here.
And soon will prove my title clear.
I'll take the law of common sense,
Which legal is to all intents.

8 My Father liv'd with Mother dear,
Till Death grim monster did appear
And cut the silver cord of life
By which she ceas'd to be his wife.

9 Two affidavits I did send,
To Moses Stanton, my old friend.
Who says, "he left them in your hand,"
That you my case might understand.

10 Examine them and judge ye (whether
Or not) you'l see, it was together
They liv'd, 'till Death intruded there.
Therefore, I am the legal heir[.]

11 So here I let the matter rest
And hope you'l try and do your best.
And to reward you for your toil,
I with you will divide the spoil.

12 So please to write and let me know,
Which way my case is like to go.
Six weeks from this, I hope the mail,
Will bring your answer without fail.

13 So now I must come to a close
But let me first, one thing propose.

Which is, <u>Pray</u> <u>don't</u> offended be,
For writing in this style to thee.
I remain with true sentiments of Respect as ever, your Humble and
obedient Servant

Thomas Commuck

Hon Elisha R. Potter Esq
Kingston R.I.

P.S. in order to save postage as much as possible, probably we had
better write as often as we can. For I shall soon have to resign my
office as Post master, in consequence of my now being a candidate
for member of the House of Representatives of this Territory, the
election comes off in September next. This is something that I never
expected, and I objected against it all I could, but my friends in the
region are determined that I shall fill this important place, and if
Elected I shall have to stand it. T. Commuck

The Narragansett Dawn

(1935–1936)

Perhaps one of New England's most interesting tribal publications, the *Narragansett Dawn* may have been the first indigenous periodical in the northeast. It was published monthly between June 1935 and September 1936. The editor was Princess Red Wing, an artist and founder of the new Tomaquag Indian Memorial Museum, which still serves as a tribal cultural center in Exeter, Rhode Island.[3] In the wake of Interior Secretary John Collier's 1934 Indian Reorganization Act, Red Wing's first editorial proclaimed a "New Deal" for the Indian. Tribal members contributed poetry, essays, oral history recollections, recipes, and local news. Few copies of the magazine remain outside of private collections (including that of the Tomaquag Museum), but the University of Rhode Island's library recently made a digitized version of all issues available on its website.

Editorial (May 1935)

No white person can read the heart of the Indian as can a son or a daughter of the Red Man's own race. Judge these pages from the Red Man's views. These columns come not from the experienced pens of journalists, but from the hearts and firesides of Narragansett Indians, who have not forgotten the faith of their forefathers. Today we open for our public of all races, "the great unwritten book of the Narragansett, sent down from father to son," portraying from time to time, many old stories, folk laws, ideals, principles, and traditions, which we hold as a sacred heritage.

We have called this monthly booklet, *The Narragansett Dawn* because we are watching for the "sunrise of better times" in the "New Deal" with our fellow countrymen. To-day is our memorial dawn, when every true hearted, red blooded, Narragansett stands together on the hilltop of hope, and stretches forth his hands towards the sunrise, for—

> "We face east at sunrise, and west at sundown;
> Each hill has its memory holy,
> Each valley its historic lore

Each enobled by our heroes
Who worked in the good days of yore."

Since those "days of yore" we have passed thru a long night—for nearly sixty years, the Narragansett Spirit has lain dormant, while civilization advanced on their old hunting ground. The August meetings at the Indian Church in Charlestown, R. I., each year, have been the only star that has twinkled in and out, during this time. It was back in 1880 that our Indian lands were sold by a council of five men, who had hoped to prove themselves, the only surviving Narragansetts. But Narragansetts came from as far west as Wisconsin to prove their tribal blood. Rhode Island's General Assembly made a survey, recognized and paid about three hundred of these Narragansett Indians for their land, made them citizens of the U.S. and recorded the tribe as extinguished. It seems, they were, or they went to sleep. But you cannot keep a real man down forever. All the recording in the country can not change the blood or wipe it out. Rhode Island had three hundred, in 1880, of full blood, half blood, and quarter blood Narragansetts, the remnants of that once powerful tribe, who since that time have continued to live and to multiply upon their ancestral territory. They it is, who have kept the faith; for many live today, who in 1880 received their $15.43, as their share of Indian land in Rhode Island.

The stories of these allotments are in many cases very amusing. Some have banked that $15 for all these years. Many were children. Many have children, grandchildren, and great grandchildren. We find many have not married out of the Narragansett blood, and have never lived out of Narragansett territory. Some retained farms and homesteads in southern R. I., paid their duties and taxes, and still live upon land that has never been occupied by white men or black men.

In our recent investigation, we found one grandfather with fourteen grandchildren, another with forty-one descendents, my Mother has twenty-one at her family gatherings, while another has twenty-one grandchildren and one great grandson, bearing the name of four well known old Narragansett families, whose forebears lived where he was born. We also found in old town records that the old full blood families have married and inter-married until nearly everyone of Indian blood in historic South County of our state is related by blood or marriage.

In our young tribal organization we have registered two hundred and fifty-nine who have come thru that long night of oblivion. They have educated their children; some have attended colleges and trade schools and universities. They have tilled the land, worked in factories, built buildings and bridges. We have doctors, lawyers, schoolteachers, nurses, ministers, artists, poets, athletes, businessmen, mechanics, stone masons, carpenters and skilled laborers of all sorts. Some come to public notice from time to time as public nuisances, when civilized vices have downed them. The worst vice is liquor, or the Indians rightly called it, "firewater." Nearly every public offense among the tribe has its origin in firewater. Some years ago the well behaved Narragansetts sent an interesting petition to the Rhode Island General Assembly, asking them to prohibit the sale of liquors by Whites and Indians on the Indian Church Grounds in Charlestown.

Some come to the front as performers in many different ways. Some went to war. Now and then one comes to public notice, denouncing the rest of the tribe. Some tag the footsteps of white people as commercial bigots, and flounce their feathered war bonnets in this land of peace and plenty. We smile; because it was King Philip who said, "There is eternal war between us." The Narragansetts said, "Come let us dwell in peace; there is room for the pale face to lie down with his red brother." And they offered Roger Williams the peace pipe, the *Calumet*, which is our tribal totem now and forever more.

Mrs. Franklin D. Roosevelt says one is not a "snub" who refuses to pour at social teas for mere politicians. Wise lady. Therefore we two hundred and fifty Narragansetts, who were told to "go play in our own back yard" have resolved to clean up and make pleasant every Narragansett back yard. We have resolved to plant there, little seeds of kindness, beside big seeds of honesty, to keep company with the sweet flowers of brotherly love. We have elected scouts and officers to clean out the weeds of jealousy and backbiting, to clean up the thrash of sin, drinking, and poverty of body, mind, and soul. Our workmen have a hard long job, but they *will* make the grass green again in our back yards, and when our seeds bloom the flowers of our father's faith, our children will go forth and pluck the lovely red blossoms of courage, and generosity, the beautiful blue flowers of truthfulness and kindness, and the white purity of the divine "Lily of the Valley"—thus they find the heritage of the Narragansett fathers and mothers, and loyalty to our country in their own back yard.

The Boston Marathon (May 1935)

About twenty Narragansetts in ceremonial clothes, were at Hopkinton, on April 19th, to see the take off of their runner, Ellison "Tarzan" Brown. The party was escorted by Chief Stanton, President of the N. T. I. Athletic Club.

"Tarzan" was in good shape, physically, but had the sympathy of the whole tribe in the loss of his mother. Her last wish being that he run, we felt that he was brave to follow out this wish, irregardless of his mental grief. He had a graceful stride as he passed the 11th mile point, where the tribe cheered him and Chief Stanton, pacing along side, offered him water. "Tarzan" smiled and ran on, making a finish, the 13th man, and looking as though he could run a few more miles. Three cheers for Tarzan!

Editorial (August 1935)

The *home* of the Narragansett Tribe of Indians was and is today along the west shores of the Narragansett Bay in southern R. I. as far west as Watch Hill. Home to them in past years did not mean a fixed place, but a large area over which to roam in search of food and clothing. When the settlers came, our Narragansett fathers changed their conception of homes. Even then they were not fixed homes, in many cases. They would move to the woods in summer, putting up their long houses and teepees. Here they would gather herbs, berries, roots and barks; make baskets and mats. In the fall and winter they traveled, selling their wares, for they had learned the value of the white man's wampum, and liked to buy the modern things which civilization was bringing them.

At intervals throughout New England, there were homes or houses of more settled Indians, which sheltered all these travelers. Families oft times traveled. Mrs. Sarah Cisco Sullivan of Grafton, Mass., brings us an interesting picture of one of these centers or stopping places.

She says, "In those days the Indian used to travel fifteen to twenty miles a day. Coming through Grafton, this seemed to be the stopping place. I was a little girl then, but I remembered how grandma used to have the attic floor filled with mattresses, some times for men to sleep on. The ladies and girls slept down stairs.

After grandma, came father who also kept open house. Oh, how vexed

Mother would become, at times! There was always, it seemed, someone coming or going. Many came from Maine, New Hampshire and Vermont. After resting awhile and getting something to eat, they usually brought out the accordion and jew's-harp. Everybody sang and danced. Often neighbors came in, at these times. Indians came up from southern Rhode Island. One I remember quite vividly is Dr. Ben Nokay.

I think he should be mentioned as a man with quite a little education of his day. Traveling up and down the country, selling medicine as he traveled, he saw and learned many things. He always stopped at our house for a day or two rest and visit. All the old folks came in to visit with him. We children, enjoyed sitting around the fire listening to his stories of the different things he saw and heard, in the places he had traveled through, during the winter. Dr. Ben Nokay came all the way up from the Charlestown Reservation, selling his medicines en route and spreading good cheer. We still have some of his old pamphlets, advertising his medicines.

He spent the night wherever he landed at sun down and was always welcome and considered quite a 'ladies man' of his day. As I look back, he was really not half appreciated for he really did a great deal of good with his medicines. At times when the New England snows would be six to ten feet deep he would be held up in whatever place he happened to be, for days. There he would make up his medicines for the next lap of his journey. Dr. Nokay was always kind to us children and his coming was quite an occasion."

This little revelation gives a picture of Indians' hospitality, as well as those of traveling natures. There were others who learned early, the white man's idea of ownership of land, and settled and made homes. But like their white brothers of a few generations ago, many journeyed to the town and cities, leaving the old homesteads to decay, or be taken up by others. As we moved among old ruins in South County, R. I., this spring, it seemed the spirit of many old Narragansetts lured us. There was the old Peckham home site, where was born our present Sachem, and his brothers, whose Mother Kate Stanton was married to Albert Peckham, a relative of the historian's father.

There is the "Mollie Rodman" Estate of several acres of land and the houses gone, the cellar-hole filled with underbrush. Here and there stands an old half tumbled-down chimney. The marks of old fireplaces fill one's mind with many pictures of other days.

Old Daniel Sekator's place is as the last descendant left it. Here the Sachem's wife, then Clara Perry, was reared. The spirit of many old Indian families centers here and one feels the frolic of several generations around those firesides. It should be a historic shrine for all coming generations of Narragansetts.

The old Brown Homestead burned, but we have a good picture of it. The old Wilcox place is now owned by many wealthy people. Chief Pine Tree pointed out to us acres and acres of land, the site of his birth, the land of his grandmother's. A sort of sad pride filled his voice as his ageing finger pointed, "here were rows and rows of corn, how I hated as a child, to pull the weeds." Now the summer bungalows of wealthy white people reside there, where they too seek the calm and peace of our ancestoral hills. You cannot buy today, one square foot, for what seven hundred and fifty acres went for, in that section around Watchaug Pond. Home! The graves of our fathers! Land where our Mothers gave us birth. Home!

Another pleasant site is the old Babcock Homestead, which has sheltered several generations of Babcocks. Here, in Bradford, live Frank Babcock and his wife Stella Brown Babcock and their family. Mrs. Babcock is sister of Cassius Champlin, president of our present tribal council. She is mother of Mrs. Lewis Wilcox of Westerly, who is married to the son of Chief Pine Tree. She is sister-in-law to Mrs. Minnie Steele of Pawtucket who owns a lovely home on Mineral Spring Ave. of that city. She is aunt to Ellison "Tarzan" Brown, our famous Narragansett runner. Her cousins are too numerous to mention. We tell you these family relations to show you our tribal blood has married tribal blood and therefore cannot possibly be lost. If some of these old roofs could talk—they would laugh at some theories of the "vanishing American."

"Indian Meeting Day," by Fred V. Brown (August 1935)

It is on August meeting day,
    We gather on the plain,
From far and near, it's those who may,
    But Injuns are the main

From Hamlet, City hill and plain,
    You'll meet them in the way,
Their goal? It is the Charlestown Woods
    On Injun meeting day.
There are the Nokas and the Browns,
    And Babcocks by the mile,
The Peckhams and the Ammonses,
    And more to make you smile.
You'll find the Johnsons and the Steeles,
    The Reverend and the lay,
In Charlestown's wooded land and fields,
    On Injun meeting day.
And on our August meeting day,
    There are others with their pride
    Their autos hit the sandy grit,
    And they come right down in style
And others, too, I fain would say,
    Who couldn't stay away,
For e'er they'd rue, it would not do,
    On Injun meeting day.
It is the second Sunday,
    This meeting that's unique.
From babes to Mrs. Grundy,
    They make the chassis squeak.
And others with their pomp and pride,
    These boastful bucks are grave,
They're each the last one of the tribe,
    The only Injun brave.
When summer days are fading,
    And harvest days are near,
On Narragansett feting day,
    We hope to see you here.
Now if you're near or from afar,
    And time is short and fleeting,
Just oil the car, and hit the tar,
    And come to Injun meeting day.

There's Stanton, with his war whoop,
    And Clifford Brown, the scout,
Now if you get their nanny,
    Mayhap they'll put you out.
But come for pleasure seeking
    And leave at home your woe,
Just come to Injun meeting,
    And spend the day with Lo.

Narragansett Tongue: Lesson 11 (March 1936)

A fire and a home are closely connected. A fire is used for signs also. The greatest attraction in any camp is the campfire. The beginning of an Indian village was a fire. Spring is on the heels of winter and we begin to think of hikes and trips into the woods, while we plan for summer camps. The Narragansetts were wont to move into new quarters with the spring. In winter they often sought the warmth of the fir trees and the denser woods where they could obtain game. In spring they moved to the open hillsides where they could plant corn, and to the streams where they could fish. As they made a new camp we hear the chief giving orders, "Let us make a fire." (*Potauwassiteuck*)

The fire-maker or torchbearer shouts to his helpers, "Let us make a good fire." (*Maumashinnaunamanta*)

    Fetch some small sticks—*aseneshesh*
    I will cut some wood—*Npaacomwushem*
    There is no more—*Netashin*
    Where is the sachem?—*Tuckiu sachim?*
    Here he is—*Peyan*
    Lay on the wood—*Wudtuckquanash*
    Blow the fire—*Potauntash*
    There is a light fire—*Wequanantash*
    It grows bigger like many candle
        lights—*Wequanautiganash*
    I am cold—*Nuckqusquatch*

Warm ye—*Awassish*
I thank you—*Taubatne anawayean*
Cut some wood—*Ponamauta*
Here is some more—*Wonck*
Give me a piece of wood—*Wudtuckqun*
Your brother is come with him—*Weche peyan hee mat*
Alright make a fire—*Potawash*
Here is a light—*Wekinan*
They are all here—*Peeyauog*
Like a candle light—*Wequanautig*
It is a cold night—*Takitippocat*
Sit by the fire—*Mattapah yoteg*
Let us mend the fire—*Mautaunamoke*

Fireside Stories (July 1936)

SINCE 1880

I wasn't living in 1880, but there are many who lived then, and are still living, of the tribe who never received a cent from the sale, when in some cases a brother or sister did. History records eight families of full blood. How about those who did not come forward to be recorded? From the mouths of some come this story. The land was sold for $5000 and divided into allotments of $15.43. Many considered this too small an amount to come and collect. Many considered they had not sold their rights, and were still Indians, not American citizens. And it is said, that $1,500 of this money was never paid to Indians, and after a few years was turned into the schools of Rhode Island. "My, oh my," said the Keeper of Records, as we listened. "Wouldn't that make a nice big step towards our Community House, if we had that with its interest since 1880?"

JOHN ONION

Ever hear the story of John Onion? It has been told for many years. Old John Onion lived in the Charlestown woods near the old Narragansett Indian school house located about a mile back of the Indian church, on what is now called School House Pond. He came down to the pond to skate one bright cold night, feeling mighty frisky. He out-skated all the other lads, and vowed he could out-skate the devil. The other lads left him to his task. It wasn't long before he realized he wasn't skating alone. The faster and fancier he skated, this figure followed. He shouted but no reply. Soon he recalled his vow of the early evening, and John asked no more questions. Breathlessly he skated to make the shore, but the dusky figure skated by him and disappeared. John did not stop to remove his skates but skated right up the banks of the pond right through the woods, as fast as his legs could carry him, and on right into the house. He never after tried out-skating the devil.

Ella Wilcox Sekatau
(Tribal Elder, 1928–2014)

Dr. Sekatau was a respected medicine woman, ethnohistorian, and language teacher and was the tribal genealogist. She published several important Narragansett histories with Professor Ruth Wallis Herndon. In 1971 a small Rhode Island press published her chapbook *Love Poems and Songs of a Narragansett Indian*, from which the selections below are taken. She wrote as Ella Brown and dedicated the book to John Brown, who passed away in 1969.

I Found Him on a Hill Top

I found him on a hill top
Not knowing, uncaring, ill:
For pain had clouded eyesight,
His gentle voice ears did fill.

Almost immediately
Worry he put behind me:
Into his hand I was placed,
Assured that well I'd soon be.

Great One, above all others,
Healer of the people 'round,
To you my life and my love
I offer now; I am sound.

Life and Seasons Must Surely Change

Life and seasons must surely change:
Perhaps the whispering wind knows
Why the Fall must follow Summer.
Whis'pring she follows where warmth goes.

The roaring wind of winter
With its icy fingers must throw
Upon the winter scenes on earth
The deep, cold, white, unyielding snow.

Although the body must remain,
The heart can take wing and decide
To follow summer e'er southward
Where the whisp'ring wind does abide.

For the Children

By candlelight a note write I
About this night so cold
The flickering flame wavers
And lights with its fingers bold
The room in which I now sit
And think of the blowing storm:
Safe, comfortable am I;
It's nice inside and so warm.

Outside the wind blows harder;
The trees bend this way and that;
The white particles of snow

Fallen down, the earth does mat;
Nature's blanket that protects
Things in the ground (roots of trees),
Cold and white though it may be,
Death comes to things it can freeze.

The feathered ones gone to roost
Await the coming of day
Hoping that the storm subsides
And the wind goes on its way
To another, distant place;
Forage for food they must do:
Stay alive yet one more day—
No food found—they will freeze too.

Furred ones deep in their burrows
Know nothing for they all sleep
The winter through, so 'til spring
When wee frogs at night will peep,
Whip-poor-will, his lonesome cry,
Floating o'er the grasses green:
The hills will catch the echo;
And the wind remains serene.

Sometimes I Wish I Could Rage Like You

Sometimes I wish I could rage like you
And scatter my hurts like your rain;
But, oh no, humans can't do those things,
Afraid we'll be called not sane.

Well, I don't care a bit what others think:
When you come from your distant reign
I'll soar on your mighty wild winds
And tell not a soul where my thoughts have lain.

Oh, Storm King, where did you come from
With raging winds and pouring rain

Like my innermost thoughts and turmoil?
My soul must fly with you again.

Would that I could always be free
To exhaust myself without disdain
From my daily cares and human woes.
I must go forth to escape the pain.

Sure I'm Still Hanging Around

Sure I'm still hanging around;
What else do you expect of me?
What is wrong with a man like you?
I love you; why can't you see
That all these years I've tried and tried
To make you mine and mine alone?
I think if you will look around
You'll see the love that I have shown
For you whenever I could even tho'
I often did it in a funny way;
If you'd just open up your eyes
You'd see what my actions say.
Simply take me for what I am;
I cannot change how I'm made;
Whatever wrongs I've done in life—
Can't you see the price I've paid?
Here I sit forlorn and weeping,
A soul adrift, an empty shell,
By your unfair hate for me;
The thought consumes me: I live in Hell.

Paulla Dove Jennings
(Tribal Elder)

Paulla Dove Jennings is a member of the Dove family and served for many years as curator at the Tomaquag Indian Memorial Museum in Exeter, Rhode Island (founded by Princess Red Wing of the *Narragansett Dawn*, above). Jennings's mother and father, Eleanor and Ferris Dove, ran the famous Dovecrest Restaurant next door to the museum. A respected storyteller and educator, Jennings has also served on the Narragansett Tribal Council. She wrote a children's book, *Strawberry Thanksgiving*, illustrated by Wampanoag artist Ramona Peters. She has contributed the following speeches from her personal papers.

Speeches

I am Sunflower, daughter of War Chief Roaring Bull and Clan Mother Pretty Flower. We are Niantic and Narragansett. We are Turtle Clan, the keepers of history, tribal lore, and legends. On the day that I was born my father said, "Today I am a man, for I have a daughter!" Women are the givers of life, just as Mother Earth is a giver of life, so daughters are very special to Indian men.

The creator gave us everything we needed to survive and live well. He gave us food, medicine, homes, games, music, special skills, basketry to hold our food and supplies. He gave us the sun and fire to keep us warm. He gave us night so that we can see the stars, the milky way, and grandfather moon. He gave us rain to clean us and nurture us and help our gardens grow and quench our thirst. He gave us the ability and wisdom to respect all living things, the highest hills to the littlest bush to the brightest birds to the moss-covered rocks and the sweet spring water. He taught us to give thanks for all living things.

Then the strange people came across the big water. Some of our people allowed them to stay, for the creator had given us much and we knew to share the gifts. These people we taught to grow our food and hunt our animals: deer, moose, bear, rabbit, turkey. We taught them to fish and dig for clams. We even shared our medicines with them. And more and more of them came. They brought their pigs and cattle, their wheat, and the common cold and rats. They came with their beliefs in fairies and witchcraft. They came with the common housefly. We shared our corn, our land. They wanted more and more. They killed more game than they needed and cleared land that belonged to the four-legged animals and the two-legged and the things that fly and the things that crawl. They shot my people, burned their homes and gardens, enslaved my people, and still they wanted more. They finally wanted everything, but we still survived. Our people became cold and hungry, for the greedy new people from across the big water wanted everything.

But we are still here.

I am Paulla Dove Jennings of the Turtle Clan. I am Niantic and Narragansett. I was born in Providence, Rhode Island. My grandmother was clan mother, my father was the last traditional war chief of the Narragansett. My mother is Pretty Flower, the heart of my family and my extended family, which includes other Indians and several non-Indians. I was taught to respect all living things, Mother Earth, and my country.

My brother and I were taught that the Narragansett were a proud people, that they defended their homes with honor when those who surrounded us were dishonorable. I was taught that modern history as taught in school was written by non-Indians, with non-Indian values. Our grandmothers told my brother and me many stories that related our family histories and tribal history. We were told of our great-grandmothers and great-grandfathers. We were told of the forced sale of our tribal family lands in Charlestown. We were told of tribal gatherings, family traditions, tribal traditions, and legends with morals to guide us as we grew into adulthood.

Imagine the surprise and shock we faced when we began school.

1946

Surprise #1. At Thanksgiving, schoolmates suddenly sprout feathered headdresses.
Surprise #2. "All Indians lived in tepees."
Surprise #3. "The Pilgrims fed the Indians at the first Thanksgiving."
Surprise #4. "Indians made war whoops by putting their hands over their mouths."

1953

Surprise #1. "After King Philip's War in 1675, there were no Indians in Rhode Island."

Surprise #2. It's only okay to be Indian at Thanksgiving.

Surprise #3. "Indians *massacre* white settlers; white settlers *protect* their homes."

1955

Surprise #1. Classmates no longer ask you, an Indian, to their homes.

Surprise #2. At school dances, you are no longer asked to dance.

Surprise #3. Your civics teacher asks if you're going to graduate, because "you people seldom graduate from junior high."

Surprise #4. "Indians are dirty and sly, and scalp and torture."

1957

Surprise #1. Most Indian boys in Rhode Island are relatives.

Surprise #2. You seldom if ever get chosen for prom committee, yearbook, or class plays.

Surprise #3. The girl your fair-complexioned brother is taking to the prom backs out four days before the event when she learns you're his sister.

Surprise #4. Your grandmothers tell you the Narragansett/Niantic are a proud people.

THE EARLY 60S

Surprise #1. Black pride on the rise.

Surprise #2. Indians are the invisible people.

Surprise #3. Black people who have Indian and/or white ancestry no longer acknowledge it.

Surprise #4. You are the token minority working for the telephone company.

THE LATE 60S

Surprise #1. Indians become visible in Rhode Island for the first time since the 1930s.

Surprise #2. Indians demand the return of tribal lands across the United States.

Surprise #3. Everyone, black or white, has a great-grandmother who was a "Real Indian Princess."

THE 70S

Surprise #1. I tell my children the Narragansett/Niantic were and are a proud people.

Surprise #2. I tell them to respect Mother Earth and all living things.

Surprise #3. I tell my children it's okay to question school history books and tell the true story of our people and all Native Americans.

Surprise #4. Wounded Knee.

Surprise #5. At Thanksgiving, churches invite an Indian—in Indian clothes, please—to dinner. Children still wear feathers and headbands.

Surprise #6. Youth groups, scouts, and adults, black and white, still play Indian at parades and events.

THE 80S

After 35 years—a period when history has recorded *Sputnik*, men on the moon, heart and liver transplants, a cure for polio, commercial jet travel, TV dinners, *E.T.*, civil rights, Narragansett tribal recognition, and the return of tribal lands—the racism, attitudes, and history books still have not changed.

My people are the only people in the world judged by a non-Indian term called "blood quantum." We are the only race of people who are asked:

1. Are you a real Indian?
2. Full-blooded?
3. Live in a tepee?
4. But you don't look Indian!

Dawn Dove
(Tribal Elder)

Dawn Dove is a sister of Paulla Dove Jennings (above); she is also the mother of Lorén M. Spears and Eleanor Dove Harris (both below) and the grandmother of six grandsons and two granddaughters. She shares in the family mission of education, having taught history for many years in the Rhode Island public schools and devoted herself to Narragansett cultural preservation. In 1995 she founded the Dovecrest Cultural Center on the site of the former Dovecrest Restaurant and began developing educational programs and presentations. Dove is also a traditional dancer and storyteller and studies and teaches Narragansett language in Charlestown, Rhode Island. The following two speeches, which she has contributed from her personal papers, illustrate shared concerns with other Native educators and leaders represented in this volume, especially southern New England writers concerned with education and "Pilgrim" history.

Alienation of Indigenous Students in the Public School System

We are the people of Turtle Island. The Creator gave this place to us. This is the place that is our Past, Present, and Future. We give thanks to the Earthmaker, the One who made the people. We are thankful for all of the beauty that surrounds us. We are thankful to walk in Beauty. Our life, our existence, is wrapped up in the blanket of this beautiful Earth. Our children are the inheritors of this place, this land, this Mother Earth. Our children deserve to be allowed to learn in a way that allows them to grow in harmony, in balance, and with respect for their culture and traditions.

We need to look at the public school system to find out why so many of our Indigenous students drop out, are low achievers, or are in special education programs. We know that there is alienation in the school system, but what can we do to change our schools? Our students need to feel that their culture is accepted in the school environment. Without this acceptance, students lose self-esteem, their sense of self-worth.

How is it that Indigenous culture is not accepted, not embraced, by the school systems? I have come to believe that the non-Indian population has emerged (after these few hundred years of occupation of this land) from these same educational facilities biased and uneducated about the real history of the United States. I highly recommend the book *Lies My Teacher Told Me*, by James W. Loewen. The population at large has been lied to or misinformed about the history of this nation. And as long as these lies and myths continue to be told, racism, discrimination, and bigotry will continue to exist.

This same curriculum is presented to the Indigenous population. The same history that is presented to make mainstream America feel good makes Indigenous children feel alienated and powerless. I remember reading in grade school, myself, that all of the Narragansett were killed during King Philip's War. There I was, in that classroom, with my teacher negating my very existence. Our students should not have to go through that humiliation. I have tried to get the teachers in my history department at the Chariho High School to read Loewen's book, to no avail. If the adults—the teachers—do not want to look at the truth, how can we expect a change in our society? We don't want "feel bad" history, but we do need inclusive, truthful history. Our textbooks have so slanted the history of the United States as to present a one-sided picture. We have raised a society that does not even know that we, the Indigenous people of this land, still exist.

Loewen writes that "the process of rationalization became unofficial national policy" in the mid-nineteenth century (125). This has continued to be the policy of the United States' educational systems. The United States has been determined to acculturate or assimilate the Indigenous populations—in other words, to take the Indian out of the Indian. The educational system has been at the forefront in this effort. When we look at a school system that systematically negates Indigenous traditions, culture, and history—and at the treatment that has been meted out to Indigenous nations in the past and today—is it any wonder that Indigenous students are alienated within the school system?

If I could, I guess I would start to make a change by throwing out the social studies and history textbooks that continue to lie to all students by fact or omission. There is so much good research out there that we really can make a difference. Indigenous students need to feel that their history, which is a part of United States history, is valued. Students must feel valued and accepted in the larger public school system. Often our students feel isolated in that system.

The schoolroom teacher, the administration, and the greater community must begin to embrace the Indigenous student's culture, traditions, and history, if we are going to begin to erase feelings of alienation within the public school system. Often, I feel that the only time that the greater community is interested in my community, the Narragansett, is when we are having a powwow or are putting on a dance and storytelling presentation. In other words, as long as we are presenting "feel-good" local color it is acceptable. But when important political issues are brought to the table, very few are interested. It is time Rhode Island and other states begin to realize the harm they are causing our youth. Our students need to know that they and their families and their Tribal Nations are accepted within the states.

Indigenous students need to feel safe and accepted in the public school environment. If teachers and administrators continue to harbor racist or biased views toward the student's Tribal Nation, how can we not expect alienation? If teachers and administrators have not educated themselves on the values, culture, traditions, and history of the Tribal Nation, how can we not expect alienation?

Indigenous students must be made to feel they have a connection to the mainstream public school. The students must be made to feel as though their culture and traditions are valued within the school system. Two days ago, on April 11, 2002, the new principal at Chariho High School made the following announcement: "Rain Spears has just told me that today is Narragansett Federal Recognition Day, so let's hear it for Narragansett Federal Recognition Day." I felt great and I am sure Rain felt great, as well as all of the other Narragansett students at Chariho. It was also a teachable moment for my mainstream students.

This is the first time that I ever really felt that connection, but I am ready to work with the administration to help end Indigenous student alienation in the school.

In Order to Understand Thanksgiving, One
Must Understand the Sacredness of the Gift

The sacredness of giving must be recognized in order to understand Thanksgiving. Thanksgiving is ceremony. Thanksgiving is the thanks one offers the Creator. Recognition of the sacredness of the gift—*ahtuq* (venison), *munneash* (corn), *nayhom* (turkey), squash, beans, wampum—must be shown in our prayers of thanksgiving. This is the essence of the difference between the beliefs of the Euro-American and the Indigenous people of this land. We understood and understand that each of the creations of the Great Spirit, the One who made the Two-legged, God, is a sacred being. Each is equal in the sense that we are each created by God. The spirit of the Creator is within each of his creations, just as the spirit of the artist is within each of his or her pieces of art. We and all of the other beings—whether they are animal, plant, or mineral—the Spirit of the Creator is within each of us. We, the Indigenous people of this land, understand this concept; therefore we call the Standing Ones and the Four-legged our brothers. As we give thanks each day for the gift of life and the gift of beauty that surrounds us we understand that the Creator is with us. This Place is sacred. Our ancestors have walked here; our ancestors' words were spoken in this place—all of this is a gift from the Creator. So when we see a stand of trees our mind does not say, "Oh, I can make so much money per board"; no, we think "Oh, those Standing Ones are reaching to Sky World; let me give thanks to the Creator for His Spirit within the trees." We give thanks for the beauty we are allowed to see. We do not need to ask the Creator for anything, for it has all been given to us. The gifts surround us. We are part of the sacred Circle the Creator has given. If we walk in balance, in harmony, in beauty, all our needs will be met. Therefore we only need to give thanks to the Creator.

Our spirit and hope—the spirit and hope of our ancestors who first met the Europeans, and those generations since—have cried out in anguish because of the Europeans' lack of understanding of the sacredness of the gifts of Mother Earth. The Euro-American has continued to think of Mother Earth as a commodity. This sacred place held the gifts of Friendship, Respect, Honesty, Equality, and Justice. These gifts were not accepted by the new arrivals to this land in the 1600s. The Pilgrims had come looking for a new life but because of their greed they were not able to accept the greatest gift offered to them—brotherhood of humanity. This greed has continued to hurt not only the Indigenous people, but the Euro-Americans as well. Today we need only look at the newspaper to see the hurt that has befallen this land. The ozone layer is being depleted, the polar ice cap is melting, toxic chemicals are in the air, landfills are overflowing, social ills abound, nuclear waste piles up. The stealing of corn pits was one of the first indications of this greed and disregard for Friendship, Respect, Equality, and Justice that the Pilgrims showed in this land.[4] The most difficult part of the Great Lie was that the Pilgrims told themselves that the stolen corn was God's gift. In the Euro-Americans' desire to deny wrongdoing and to continue the lie, the true gifts of the Creator have been denied to our children.

As the Wampanoag men brought the gifts of venison to share with the Pilgrims that time many years ago, they understood the sacredness of the gift. Occasionally one walks among us and shows us the spirit of the old ways. The loving spirit, the one who shares, the one who gives the gifts of Thanksgiving. Thank you, Creator, for Father Sky; thank you for Mother Earth; thank you for the Four Directions; thank you for the *Wetu* (lodging); thank you for the water; thank you for the fish and birds; thank you for the *ahtuq*. The game, the fish, the shellfish, the berries, *Kutapatush* (thank you)! The one with the old ways shares these gifts with the elders of the community, with the widows, and the weak. He understands that the *ahtuq*, in a very sacred way, gives his life as a gift. A gift given in a sacred manner will bring goodness to the people. The *ahtuq* merely consents to return home with the hunter. All phases of the hunt are conducted with love: the hunter and the people love the *ahtuq*, and the *ahtuq* agree to give their meat so that the humans will not starve. As gkisedtanamoogk has stated in *Anoqcou: Ceremony Is Life Itself*, "There are ceremonies or thanksgivings directed to the hunting. We talk to the spirits of the Forest. We have Sweat Lodge Ceremonies. We have . . . ceremonies of the *ahtuq*. We are thanking them for life and asking them to feed us" (19–21). It is too bad that the Pilgrims did not understand and did not remember the 90 Wampanoag men [who attended the first Thanksgiving] in a good way, a "Godly way," for their giving had been done in a loving way, with the love of the Creator. The 90 Wampanoag men had shared the gifts of the Creator with the Pilgrims. Today the larger American society must remember the gifts so that Friendship, Respect, Equality, and Justice may live in this land for all of the people.

I remember when I was a child the exchange of gifts of the Narragansett. The father of a family brought home a bushel of oysters from the bay or an *ahtuq* after the hunt or potatoes from the garden. The father had a wife and several children, yet he did not say, "I must keep all of this food for my own family, for I do not know how hard the winter will be." The father knew his ability was a gift from the Creator. The father did a thanksgiving by sharing the gifts with the elders and the widows and the weak. The sharing, the giving, told the gifted that they were valued members of the community, they were loved, they were honored by the sacred gifts of Mother Earth, from the Creator. The 90 Wampanoag men were also offering this same sacred gift to the Pilgrims: the gift of Friendship, Respect, Equality, and Justice, the gift that would have made this country truly a land in which there was freedom and justice for all. Unfortunately the gift was refused because of greed and racism.

Let me share a story with you about a family of woodchucks that visited our family garden. We had all worked in the garden; I remember walking behind my father dropping two, three, or four seeds in each little indentation my father made in the earth or running to the well to help pull up a bucket of water. And I remember the excitement when the first leaves showed. My parents, my grandparents, my brother and sisters, aunties and uncles, and cousins would also come to work in the garden. It was a happy time. There was always corn, squash, and beans as well as pumpkins, carrots, onions, peppers, lettuce, melons, beets, and radishes. The garden was a work of love and thanksgiving. Daily my father would look to the east and give thanks for the rising sun and the many gifts that the Creator provided.

Then the trouble started. First it was just a few nibbles, then a whole head of lettuce. Our family began the lookout. We wanted to catch those woodchucks. They were eating our food; our hard work was being stolen! Finally, one day my brother spotted the woodchuck in the garden. My mother told my father to get his shotgun. The commotion was so exciting; my heart was racing. My father got the shotgun and began to load the bullets. We were telling him to hurry so that he could get that woodchuck. As we stepped off the porch and walked a few steps closer to the garden, we all stopped and watched in anticipation. Father spotted the woodchuck, and another woodchuck, and then . . . two baby woodchucks came into view. Nothing happened for a few moments, then Father took the shotgun from his shoulder and said, "Well, I guess there is enough food for both families."

That lesson of generosity and acceptance of the animal people as equal to ourselves has always stayed with me. This is the understanding of the sacredness of all families. The Spirit of the Creator is in all of his families, whether they are two-legged, four-legged, fly with wings, swim in the waters, crawl upon the earth, or are the Standing Ones, or other plants or minerals. In understanding Thanksgiving one must recognize the gifts that our ancestors offered to the Pilgrims. One must understand the Sacredness of all of God's creation. Just as my father knew the wood-chuck was "stealing" from our garden, the 90 Wampanoag men knew the Pilgrims had stolen from the corn-storage pits. The Wampanoag people felt that the Pilgrims needed the corn more than they did. In a sacred way the Wampanoag came to Plimoth to share the sacred gifts of the Creator.

John Christian Hopkins

(b. 1960)

An award-winning journalist, John Christian Hopkins has worked around the
United States reporting on Indian sovereignty issues, such as the infamous police
raid on the Narragansetts' smoke shop, which he covered in August 2003 for
the *Pequot Times*. He has published three novels: *Carlomagno*, a swashbuckling
adventure that imagines the son of Metacomet surviving as a pirate in the West
Indies; a western, *Nagocdoches*; and *Twilight of the Gods* (2012). "Tarzan Brown"
and "Sad Country Songs" appeared in his chapbook *Rhyme or Reason: Narragansett
Poetry*. "William O." is an original contribution to this volume.

Troopers Lead Attack on Narragansett Reservation

CHARLESTOWN RI—Twenty Rhode Island state troopers—backed by
snarling police dogs—stormed the Narragansett Indian Tribe's reservation July 14, knocking elders, women, and children to the ground as they
attempted to shut down the tribe's newly-opened tax-free smoke shop.

"It was like something you'd see in Mississippi back in the 60s," Narragansett Chief Sachem Matthew "Seventh Hawk" Thomas said of the
frightening melee. Thomas and seven other tribal members were dragged
away in handcuffs and face a variety of charges, including assault, resisting arrest, and disorderly conduct.

The tribe—locked in a decade-long fight to open a casino—opted to
operate a tax-free cigarette shop in June. But the tribe put its plans on
hold after Thomas met with Gov. Donald Carcieri, who promised to find
economic aid for the impoverished tribe. The governor said the tribe could
not legally open a smoke shop without state permits. The tribe contended
that it was a sovereign nation and could undertake economic measures
to support its 2,600 members.

After state-tribe talks stalled, the Narragansetts opened their smoke
shop on their Charlestown trust lands on July 12. The governor, visiting
family in Ohio, was quickly made aware of the situation.

The governor said he spent July 13 in numerous phone conversations with Thomas. Carcieri claimed the Narragansetts said they would close the shop if the governor stopped his opposition to a casino.

Thomas said that isn't so. He said the tribe asked that the governor allow the question of a casino on the ballot—to be voted on by the state's citizens, as the law dictates.

Perhaps dismayed by public polls which show statewide support for a Narragansett casino, state lawmakers have kept the issue held up—and off any state ballots. When it looked like the question would be on the 2002 ballot, lawmakers decided to set up an 11th-hour "study commission" to explore the advantages or disadvantages of gaming.

In 2003, the commission produced a report supporting a ballot vote—but concocted wording so clumsy and vague that any vote would face near-certain failure at the polls.

"We've played by the rules," Thomas said. "And every time we win, they change the rules."

The tribe's complaints are often supported by the legal history. Since 1988, when the U.S. Congress passed the Indian Gaming Regulatory Act, the Narragansetts have been embroiled in an attempt to open a gaming hall. Predictably, the state fought the tribe through the courts. By 1994 the tribe had prevailed in the legal war, with the courts declaring that the tribe—being federally recognized—could indeed benefit under IGRA.

Then Rhode Island Gov. Bruce Sundlun hammered out a compact with the tribe. As a show of good faith, the tribe agreed to let the question of a casino appear on the ballot. Mysteriously, a half dozen other "casinos"—which had never been discussed publicly prior—also ended up on the ballot. The tribe cried foul and asked that their ballot amendment mention the tribe by name. Sundlun, a Democrat, supported the tribe's request. The state's Republican Secretary of State ignored Sundlun and the tribe and worded each amendment exactly the same.

Voters, confused and unable to determine which initiative was the tribe's, voted down all the casino questions.

Sundlun then lost the gubernatorial election to Republican Lincoln Almond, who voided the compact and spent eight years battling the tribe.

By 1996, the tribe had again prevailed in federal court.

The state's last court opinion rested in Washington DC. But rather than risk a final defeat at the hands of the U.S. Supreme Court, state politicians and their congressional cronies cooked up yet another scheme.

In an election year, 1996, with a federal spending bill that had to pass—or else see government offices closed down—the late Sen. John Chafee attached a midnight rider declaring that for purposes of IGRA the Narragansetts' 1,800-acre reservation would not be considered "Indian land." That left the tribe under state jurisdiction as far as gambling went.

Today, the Narragansetts are the only one of nearly 600 federally-recognized tribes that cannot open a casino.

With federal grants being cut back, the Narragansetts have found themselves with less funding to support their community. An elderly housing complex stands unfinished off Kings Factory Road, a ghostly reminder of the hostility the tribe had endured at the hands of the state and neighboring town of Charlestown. The town and state have used the courts to block the tribe's housing plans—which require the land be taken into trust—citing a fear that the tribe will eventually use the 32 acres to build a casino.

Lack of adequate funding often leaves tribal members facing other problems; for example, medical assistance funding usually runs out before the end of the fiscal year. Sometimes tribal members have no choice but to suffer in pain and wait until more funding comes from Washington.

With a 44 percent unemployment rate, the tribe is facing some of its most difficult times.

"I have an obligation to take care of my people," Thomas said.

The tribe opened its smoke shop—which took in $17,000 before it was abruptly closed by state police. The state fears that the tribe's tax-free cigarette sales could cost the state $10 million annually in uncollected taxes. The state charges a $1.71 tax per pack of cigarettes sold.

The issue took a dramatic turn on the afternoon of July 14. Five plain-clothed troopers had entered the smoke shop. As if on signal, uniformed troopers and their dogs came rushing through the woods, converging on the smoke shop entrance. An elderly tribal police officer met the first wave, demanding to see any papers—warrants or injunctions. The troopers pushed by him, threatening him with arrest.

Caught by surprise, tribal members began screaming at the troopers, telling them to get off their land.

Bella Noka was in the middle of the melee as her husband—First Councilman Randy Noka—was among the first to be arrested. Her 15-year-old son was thrown to the ground and held there by several troopers. As

Bella rushed to her son's aid, two of the troopers turned on her. She was knocked down, one of the troopers kneeling on her back. "I tried to stay in a fetal position so I wouldn't get hurt," said Noka.

As Bella Noka was being arrested her husband, Randy, sat up—hands cuffed behind his back and a trooper holding him down—and yelled, "That's my wife! Don't hurt her!"

Longtime Councilman Hiawatha Brown and Chief Sachem Thomas struggled futilely to prevent the troopers from getting inside the smoke shop. Thomas was dragged down the stairs, where several troopers wrestled him to the ground. Brown was grabbed by the hair as three troopers tackled him. One savagely pressed his hands against Brown's temples.

Another tribal member, Adam Jennings, had his ankle broken. Women and children were sent scurrying for cover or were indiscriminately knocked to the ground.

"This is all over cigarettes," Randy Noka said as he was led away.

"The governor should be ashamed of himself," Thomas exclaimed as he was being placed in the back of a squad car.

Tribal Elder Myra Perry was beside herself. "Someone has to tell the truth about what happened here! This isn't right."

After his release from jail, Thomas insisted that the Narragansett Tribe was only trying to defend its sovereign rights.

"When those planes hit those buildings on September 11, Americans jumped up and were ready to grab arms. But if somebody attacks our sovereignty we're supposed to sit back and take it?"

The smoke shop stands empty now; a hand-painted sign expresses regret to any customers affected and urges those who support the tribe to show their loyalty by boycotting the state's lottery tickets.

Tarzan Brown

It was a drizzly April morn
there was thunder in the stride;
a man climbed Heartbreak Hill
a legend descended the other side.
The Boston Marathon
was the nation's greatest race;

and the Indian from Rhode Island
twice had claimed first place!
They called him "Tarzan"
legends about him abound
the greatest runner of his time
the Narragansett, Ellison Brown.
Some tales are fancy
while others all too true—
he lost a championship race
stopping to remove a shoe!
He never really trained,
with a spirit free and wild,
he had the will of a man
and the wonder of a child.
Sometimes he ran barefoot
or bit snakes in half;
once, to win a bet,
he even ate some glass!
A whirling pair of legs
uncanny knack to win
carried him from the woods
to the Olympics, in Berlin.
Tarzan was no quitter
he put on quite a show
winning full marathons
two days in a row!
Despite his victories
and fierce, Indian pride
he never beat the demons
haunting him inside.
On a steamy August night
behind a bar someplace,
the legendary Tarzan Brown
lost his final race.
A man can outlive his time
but a legend never will

So Tarzan will always be
topping out on Heartbreak Hill.

William O.

The brisk wind blew
His chores were through;
He longed for some fun
Young William O.
Had an hour or so
Before the setting sun.

Though recently it snowed
To Deep Pond he trod
Ice skates over one shoulder
He trudged through the woods
Carrying all his goods
Glad it wasn't colder.

He made it to Deep Pond
Laced his ice skates on
A smile upon his face;
Young William O.,
His face all aglow,
Was ready for a race!

Short or tall
He beat them all
He said, on the level,
"Out on the ice
I glide so nice—
I could beat the devil!"

During an eerie chill
Down from the hill
A figure all in black
Skated through the snow

Straight for William O.
Leaving not a track!

"Let the race begin,"
said the devil with a grin,
his skates began to slice.
Young William O.
Was the first to know
He was skating for his Life!

Howls came from everywhere
And sparks shot in the air
As the race was on.
But, bending low,
Young William O.
Was king at Deep Pond.

Cutting like a knife
His skates tore up the ice
He darted fast and low
Across the finish line
With the devil right behind
Came young William O.

Young William O.
Would never know
How he beat Old Scratch;
For the rest of his days
No hell did he raise—
Trying to avoid a rematch!

Sad Country Songs

I never thought those sad songs had anything real to say,
but I understand now that I stopped loving her today.
I heard a lonesome whippoorwill, saw rainclouds in the sky.
Now I know how it feels to be so lonesome I could cry.
When I said "I do," I did, but now the end has come

I don't know where to turn because I still miss someone.
Like those sad, country songs, I am bitter and blue
but I would be crazy for crying, or keep on lovin' you.
At the end of Lonely Street is where I will be
The last word in lonesome will always be me.
I've got those smoking cigarettes, drinkin' coffee blues.
I'm walkin' after midnight, feeling I was born to lose.
If you see me come along, better let me pass on by.
Say "what's wrong?," you'll be sorry you ever asked why.
I'll tell you of sad, country songs of suffering and pain
of stumbling, shivering, eyes crying in the rain;
of long, lonesome nights and shattered desire,
how I first fell into that burning ring of fire.
I'll tell you my story, how things went so wrong
leaving my life like a sad, country song.
I'll tell you someday, but it might take some time
to get over this poor ol' broken heart of mine.
So if you see a tear, please pay it no mind,
just a remainder of a long, lonesome time.
No worry 'bout me, I'll get along all right,
just need help to make it through the night.
I'm somebody that done somebody wrong,
trapped forever in a sad, country song.

Nuweetooun School

(2003–2009)

In 2003 Dove family member Lorén M. Spears opened the Nuweetooun ("Our Home") School on the site of the old Dovecrest Restaurant. The school offered tribal children, K–8, a Native-centered curriculum and environment. In 2009 the school suspended operations after severe flooding in Rhode Island caused extensive damage. It did, however, create a sizable archive of student, staff, and community writing, from which the following selections are taken.

Lorén M. Spears, Executive Director and Teacher

ROARING BROOK[5]

My memories here abound:
If I close my eyes
I remember my cousin Shawn around;
He fished night and day
He took me along
Even though I scared the fish away;

Grandfather, Chief Roaring Bull,
Always kept the brook clean
Every spring the brook's water was glistening and full
Roaring from Arcadia, over falls and rocks;
We swam all summer in the pool
We thought it was deep
Our memories fun-filled and cool
Next best place to the beach;
We explored the tunnels through and through,
Had a blast young and old
Caught fish and crayfish, too

Never ending places to explore for the generations of old
As well as the 7 generations more

So long as we heed nature's call:
Care for Mother Earth and her creatures
So that Roaring Brook can be enjoyed by all.

Dasan Everett, Grade 3

THE FOUR ANIMALS

Walk this earth every day,
They drink the water as they lay,
They sing and they play,
Having their own beauty.

THE THREE SISTERS

As the yellow corn grows tall,
The bean hugs it around.
The tan squash stays upon the ground,
Blocks the naughty weeds from the sun,
The three sisters work together
In the seasons of the warm weather and that's the
way they go so good together.

Darrlyn Sand Fry, Grade 2

[UNTITLED]

The creator made us all
Animals, people, forest, and waterfall

He walks in the sky
Clouds and rain swish by

He made the trees, earth, and sky, brand new
The stars, the moon, and the planets, too

His love is so bright
Like the sunlight

Laurel Spears, Grade 3

[UNTITLED]

Sky woman falling from the sky
She missed her father so
She started to cry
She met this lovely man
He can hunt he can, he can
He is very nice
He can make his own spice
Turtle Island is where they live
Respect and honor is what they give

Thawn Harris

(b. 1978)

Thawn Sherenté Harris, a popular storyteller in Rhode Island and beyond, lives together with his wife and their five children adjacent to their Narragansett lands, where they pass on the values and cultural lifeways of their people. He is a traditional dancer and singer and also plays the cedar flute and hand-drum. Harris received his bachelor's degree from the University of Rhode Island and was the first in his family to graduate from college. He has worked for the tribe as an environmental police officer and is now a tenth-grade advisor and teacher at East Bay Metropolitan Career and Technical Center in Newport, Rhode Island. At that school, in early 2011, he delivered the following speech. It is being published here for the first time.

Thank You, MET Colleagues, for speaking out against the Rhode Island Education Board of Regents' proposed three-tiered diploma.[6]
My journey into this world was a fight, one in which my mother and I battled together along with the hospital staff in an effort to free me from

my environment, an environment that was slowly strangling the life out of me, before it had a chance to begin. Throughout the years that followed I witnessed or was part of many fights.

I fought for the attention of my parents, being one of six. I fought for the attention of my parents, who were often consumed with alcohol and/or drinking buddies. I fought to keep the peace when there was tension between those around me. I often stood up to my peers in defense of my relatives who could often be seen staggering throughout the community, though there were also times in which I said nothing, in an attempt to meld into the crowd, to feel like I was not different, to pretend that my family life was normal just like those around me. At times like this I had to fight my feelings of cowardice, embarrassment, and shame. I had to fight those feelings of love I had for that person, despite the fact that they are consistently drunk, dirty, and disorderly.

Those around me could not understand the feelings of oppression that were rampant throughout my community, beaten in so deep that the scarring is still present many generations later. A proud people, yes; however, with a loss of the ability to truly live the way we are instinctually hardwired to live, our pride and strength are often misdirected. We are in denial, and alcohol is the shovel that helps to bury our insecurities, pain, and fears. Why deal with something when you could just bury your head in the sand and act like you don't know about it or you don't care about it?

I see this new three-tier diploma as another tool in the long list of this state's efforts to oppress those not of privilege. I can see future generations turning to drugs and alcohol in denial of the fact that a high school diploma is and was important to them, their parents, and the younger ones who look up to them. It is hard for me even to think about, because the implied result of such a system is disastrous. I am in awe of how our state can continue to discriminate and oppress people in broad daylight, without even the slightest concern.

I would like to say that I am impressed, honored, and grateful for all of my colleagues, who have been fighting so diligently, with ferocity and passion. Listening to you all speak out against injustice has touched my spirit, raising goose bumps on my skin. I am grateful to you all for myself, and those whom this would affect, who can't even bear to take on such a challenge.

Eleanor Dove Harris

(b. 1979)

The daughter of Dawn Dove, and the mother of seven children of her own, Eleanor Dove Harris continues the family tradition of education and cultural preservation. A traditional dancer, she is married to Thawn Harris and, like him, is a storyteller and traditional dancer. She graduated from the University of Rhode Island in 2006 and is now a tenth-grade advisor and teacher at East Bay Met School in Newport, Rhode Island. These are her first publications.

TGIF 1

This past weekend I had the opportunity to travel with my family to Chippaquasett (Prudence Island). Blessed with an Onondaga godfather who happened to marry a woman who is a direct descendant of Roger Williams (therefore her entire family owns summer homes on the island), I somehow came into the chance luck of having one week per summer to enjoy the beauty of the island with my family, as a gift to his goddaughter: Nipewasé (Clearwater).

As our school moves into small committees to more effectively take advantage of opportunities and experiences that would better foster true learning, and I take on this new role (or recapture an old role) of Social Reasoning Committee member/leader, I found myself contemplating social reasoning on many different levels over the weekend and why it is so vitally important.

Thinking through a nonviolence lens, social reasoning is about two truths and, more importantly, arriving at a higher truth through information gathering and sharing. As we all know, history is written by the victor, and in the case of this nation, the original peoples of this land continue to face horrific forms of oppression on multiple levels, most notably in the form of our histories; schools so wrongly portray indigenous people and/or underrepresent them in their teachings.

While on Chippaquasett (the only word my Grandfather Dove ever used to describe what is now labeled on maps as Prudence Island; it literally means place of separation, referring to its location in the Narragansett Bay), my family was moved by the fact that we were on sacred land, the same place where our great Sachems, Miantanomi and Canonicus, held council, while at the same time we were saddened to think of how exclusive this island is and that most Narragansett people would never in their life have the opportunity to walk these shores, hike the trails of this island, watch the deer run through the open, gather blueberries from the abundant bushes, fish off of the great rocks, or jump into the bay that was the lifeline of our people from the rocky beaches.

As we continued to travel around Chippaquasett, we came upon what is now known as Pulpit Rock, on which a great sign has been erected declaring that this is the rock on which Roger Williams preached to the Indians and traded for the island in exchange simply for their friendship. My four children were all with me, and they read this sign, and if it were not for my mother having historical knowledge and oral history from our elders, they would have accepted this as truth and that would have been their history lesson. My mother went on to share with us that Canonicus and his nephew Miantanomi, who shared Sachemship (a beautiful way to lead a people with an elder's perspective and the perspective of the next generation), held council at this very rock, that this was a ceremonial site, and that we must offer prayers of thanksgiving and leave an offering of tobacco in their honor and for their memory. The sign did not even say anything about the Narragansett, let alone these great Sachems; we were simply written off in history as the "Indians of this Island," as if we did not exist anymore. There we were faced with two truths and my children were able to be social reasoners, and they were able to question why this had been done to our people's memory. They left that site with a higher truth and an understanding of not just history but who and what they are as Narragansett people, and, unfortunately, the oppression that they will face their entire lives as the indigenous peoples of this land.

Our students need to have these very opportunities, similar to the model that we utilized for Columbus Day, the N-word workshop, and for our unit on genocide. They must have the chance to see the story from all sides; they must learn how to gather real information from reputable sources; they must have the opportunity to reason and to think socially and interact with their greater community in seeking a higher truth, become civic with their ideals, and realize that just because it is written, it is not always so, that we can rewrite history, if not in a textbook but in our hearts and in our minds. We can live our lives enriched with truth and not clouded by lies that have been passed down from one generation to the next. It is time for us to become socially responsible and encourage our young people to know who they are, what they are, and why they are.

As we move forward on our social reasoning movement, I feel that I must begin by addressing two social/historical inaccuracies. Canonicut (Jamestown) is pronounced Ca-nON-i-cut (like the book is ON the table, not like that mAN is cool), the *ut* at the end means "place of"; therefore, it means literally the place of Canonicus, great Narragansett Sachem. My grandfather also always referred to Jamestown as Canonicut, never by the new English name for this very sacred island of many Narragansett burial grounds. Finally, here we are in Newport, steps away from Miantanomi Park. Shouldn't our students know who Miantanomi was? Just some thoughts to get you thinking!

(2009)

TGIF 2

More thoughts on race . . .

My mother, similar to many mothers, saved a ridiculous amount of my schoolwork from nursery school on up. Often she will come upon a small pile and give it to me as some special gift that I should cherish. Honestly, I almost always throw it out after a few moments of reminiscing. There are a few pieces that I have held on to that have now found a home in my attic stuffed in a box, and two of those specifically stand out in my mind.

The first one was a writing sample that I created somewhere around 1st/2nd grade that was a clearly an assignment during a unit on Native Americans around the usual Thanksgiving time. All around the edges I had illustrated stereotypic "Indians" with feather headdresses, and my first two sentences were, "I like Indians. I think Indians are nice."

Here I was, this young Narragansett girl, sitting in a classroom full of non-Native students in a school system without any Native teachers in a building built on the blood of my ancestors, with the only knowledge of the indigenous peoples of this land being that "Indians" must be nice, because I am one.

The second piece is a self-portrait of myself created in 3rd grade, and I know for a fact that is was 3rd grade because I have drawn my full body (in cutout form) with small red-heeled shoes with a bright yellow dress and a black belt—the outfit I picked out for my first day of school. I remember this outfit so clearly because (a) the idea of having high-heeled shoes (although, they couldn't have been more than ¼ inch) was just too cool, and (b) I remember school shopping at T.J. Maxx and coming with my mom across this bright yellow dress and a woman (who was white) standing next to us saying, "Oh, that dress will not look good on your daughter with her skin coloring—you should give it to me for my daughter." Of course, my mother defended her baby girl, told the woman off, and proceeded to buy the ugly dress, telling me that I look beautiful in any and all colors!

But the reason this piece stands out is because I had illustrated my skin color far browner than I have ever been, even in my tannest summer! Which reminded me how many times people/children/teachers would ask me if my mom was indeed my mom and/or why I was so light-skinned, and that voice of a little Narragansett girl saying, "I'm not white—I'm Indian, we are brown!" Or people saying I look just like my dad because our skin color is similar, when really I look just like my mom. Or saying that my sister and I look nothing alike when really we look exactly alike.

My children attend the same school system that I did and both of my eldest sons have returned home from school with similar pieces of work. My stepdaughter recently illustrated a self-portrait in 8th grade in which she was very brown. My middle son has had arguments with classmates about his skin color being brown; both of my school-age sons have been called girls throughout their lives as their hair is in the traditional long-braided style; and this year my eldest son was believed to be a girl by his math teacher for almost the entire 1st quarter of school. The saddest piece is that we have all internalized these experiences, experiences that begin when we are far too young to comprehend. My stepdaughter recently had her very first boyfriend, and when she came home we asked her if he was Narragansett (as she attends South Kingstown's Curtis Corner Middle School, with a much larger percentage of Narragansett students) and she said, "No, I think he is black"; we then asked her what his last name is and she replied with a popular Narragansett family name. Her boyfriend is Narragansett; we know his family very well.

(2010)

Letter to California State University Administration, Faculty, and Student Body

As an educator and Native American I was horrified to read the article published in California State University's *Union Weekly* ["Pow Wow Wow Yippee Yo Yippy Yay," March 14, 2011] on the powwow hosted by the American Indian Student Council.7 My immediate thoughts are that without question the author of this piece is uneducated on Native American culture and history and, therefore, ignorant of the traditional ways of the indigenous peoples on this continent. It is shameful to think that the educational system of the United States is systematically continuing to oppress the first peoples of this land through the eradication of appropriate histories of said people, thus creating uneducated and ignorant graduates, citizens, academics, and professionals.

The word *powwow* comes from my people; the Narragansett (federally recognized sovereign nation in the state of Rhode Island); it comes from the word *pauwau*, meaning healing person (medicine man/woman). When colonization first began here in the east, colonists observed spiritual ceremonies and heard repeated reference to the *pauwau* by the people—leading them to mistakenly refer to the "event" as a powwow. Today, Native tribes, communities, and organizations all over the country host powwows as intertribal ceremonies, lasting anywhere from one day to week-long celebrations throughout the year.

In moving forward, it is my hope that issues of cultural sensitivity and diversity training will become of paramount importance on your campus in an effort to heal the clearly divided student population. Muckraking, sensationalist journalism is certainly not the ultimate goal of the *Union Weekly*'s efforts? I'm sure the mission is to deliver relevant and meaningful news without bias to the student body; unfortunately, this article fell short. Not only were the efforts of a student group not honored, but an entire people, their cultural lifeways, and religious beliefs were disrespected.

(2011)

The Pursuit of Happiness

(2005)

As this chapter has suggested, Narragansett people have often written collaboratively, whether as members of a student body, or as contributors to a periodical, or as members of a family committed to educating tribal youth and the broader public. In 2005 the Tomaquag Indian Memorial Museum received a grant from the Rhode Island State Council on the Humanities to produce a lecture series and booklet, "The Pursuit of Happiness: An Indigenous View: The Narragansett People Speak." The booklet included writings by many of the people represented in this volume, plus Chief Sachem Matthew Thomas and Medicine Man Lloyd "Running Wolf" Wilcox. We have chosen selections from Ella Sekatau, Dawn Dove, and Lorén M. Spears to complement some of the themes raised in the entries above.

Dr. Ella Sekatau and Dawn Dove[8]

FROM *WUNNIGIN NUWADCHANUMUNUWUT KUTTOOWONKONGASHUT* (HAPPINESS IN OUR OWN WORDS)

Manit Upeantamooonk
Man it up e an tam oo onk
The Great Spirit's Prayer

Nooshun keesuqut
Noosh un kee su qut
Our father in sky world

Quttianatamunach kooweesuonk
Qut ti a na tam un ach koo wee su onk
We honor your name

Peyaumooutch kukketassootamooonk
Pe yau moo utch kuk ke tas soo tam oo onk
Come your Great Land

Kutunantamooonk nee enatch ahkeeut neanee keesuqut.
Ku tu nan tam oo onk nee e natch ah kee ut ne a nee kee su qut.
Your will let that be so on earth as in sky world.

Numeetsuwongash asekesukokish assamainnean yooyoo keesuqut
Nu meet suw on gash a se ke suk ok ish as sa ma in ne an yooyoo kee su qut
Our food day by day give us to eat this day

Kah ahquontamaiinean nummatcheseongash
Kah ah quon tam ai in e an num match es e ong ash
And do not think about our wrongdoings

Neane matchenukqueageeg nutahquontamauounnonog.
Ne an e match e nuk que ag eeg nu tah quon tam au o un non og.
As wrongdoings pointed at us we do not think about.

Ahque sagkompagunniinean een qutchishonganit
Ah que sag kom pag un ni in e an een qut chish on ga nit
Do not lead us unto bad things

Qut pohquohwussinean wutch matchitut;
Qut poh quoh wus sin e an wutch match i tut;
But deliver us from wrongdoings;

Newutche kutahtauun ketassootamooonk kah
New utch e ku tah tau un ke tas soo tam oo onk kah
For to you belongs the Great Land and

Menuhkesuonk kah sohsumooonk micheme. Neenaj.
Men uh ke su onk kah soh sum oo onk mi chem e. Nee naj.
The power and the shining forth forever. Let it be.

The Nahahiganseck language holds the key to our self-preservation, to our happiness. We are who we are in accordance with how we believe or how we understand our universe to be. Our ancestors held on to our language for the seven generations yet to come, which is also our responsibility. The state and federal governments established policies of genocide and then assimilation—cultural genocide to end our existence as Nahahiganseck people, but our *Kuttoowonkongash* (words) still stand. We give thanks to our ancestors as we continue to share these *Kuttoowonkongash* with our children and the next seven generations.

We remember the Elders speaking. . . . The Nahahiganseck people have held on to their language for all of this time by holding on to words that various families held as sacred. A tribal Elder told me long ago that the language is not dead as long as one person knows one word. In our community many people have held on to words that have been passed from generation to generation. Our grandmothers told us that the Elders used to go to the Meetinghouse—the Indian church—to have gatherings where important issues were discussed and our language was used. The ancestors feared repercussions from the government for using our language, so they went to the sanctuary of the Indian Meetinghouse where they could freely speak—where the words of our ancestors could continue to live, and where those words of the past, the ancient dialects, could persist in most families.

Today we will use the evaluation of linguistics, which shows continuity. This continuity is extremely important, as our language holds our culture. My favorite concept is the kinship relationships that my father taught me. The children of my aunts and uncles are my brothers and sisters, not just cousins, as in American society. My aunt is *nukasoommes*, or "my little mother." My uncle is also translated as "my little father" (*noochese*), whereas my father is *noosh*, without the "-ese," which is the marker for "little." My father always called my sisters' children and my children *weet-ahtooag*—brothers and sisters—rather than cousins. In addition to these relationships, we can also understand our culture by the way the root of the words for mother, *-oohkas*, and father, *-oosh*, are used to denote soft (*nookhay*) and rough (*koshkay*). This is just a small example to indicate the importance of language in understanding our culture.

Indigenous languages help Native people to understand the cosmology of their ancestors. Only ancient words of a combination of dialects spoken male to male or female to female, or a general dialect spoken by all, can express our true feelings as the Indigenous people of the Nahahiganseck Nation and surrounding geographical area. To us this part of the Earth Mother is still referred to as "Turtle Island," or Mishitonnuppasog Munnohhan—not America. When we say *Okasu Aukee* a feeling deep within us stirs. Our emotions rise to great heights when our own words are used. When we walk the lands under the auspices of the Royal Nahahiganseck Sachemwock we hear the echoes of the words of the ancestors and the echoes of ancient drums we dance to. Only words in our own language can in reality express those inherent cultural ties. Our well-being as a People depends on cultural preservation and specifically on language preservation.

The Nahahiganseck tribal government can help with this critical need by supporting the Nahahiganseck language revitalization project. The tribal government can institute immersion teaching methods. The Nahahiganseck language must become a vital part of our everyday conversations. Nahahiganseck must become the language used at our community center, tribal meetings, council meetings, and ceremonies.

Lorén M. Spears, Narragansett/Niantic

FROM "PURSUIT OF HAPPINESS: AN
INDIGENOUS VIEW ON EDUCATION"

Our children are often expected to fail. It is a self-fulfilling prophecy. Our children are set up to fail by a system that demeans their self-concept, negates their identity, provides low expectations, tracks our students (into low, non-college-bound tracks), and does not acknowledge or respect their individual gifts. Nuweetooun School was created in direct response to these issues. Our children need an environment to learn, grow, and mature into productive, enriching, and respectful citizens of our communities.

Modern American education is overfocused on memorization of the facts and lacks the connection to the whole picture. Native students learn better in experiential and inquiry-based modes of education. They are not often in classes that afford the opportunity for such methods, as the

American system only allows their elite academic students to utilize them. Yet they are the models most beneficial for all students.

Tomaquag Museum is working to help educate public schoolteachers on how to teach Indigenous history and culture from a Native perspective: with continuity and integrity through our annual teachers' institutes, sponsored in part by the Center for New England Culture from the University of New Hampshire. These institutes have been very well received; however, more needs to be done for public education to meet the needs of our Indigenous youth. Many schools do not encourage or assist teachers to attend these types of conferences, nor do many provide teacher learning opportunities at their trainings that address Indigenous history and culture.

In 1935 Charles Caroll of the Rhode Island Department of Education wrote, "We believe that [in] the study of American history, overemphasis is placed on the Indians, who contributed very little indeed to American civilization. . . . If we were making a history syllabus we would wish in Rhode Island to relegate the Indian interest to a matter of a passing episode [of] less than 30 years in a history covering 300 years."

It has been thought that Indigenous history is of no value to the overall American history. In reality, there is no United States history without Indian history. Indian history has been and will continue to be interwoven in United States history. Although the message is not so overt as Mr. Caroll's words, Rhode Island's stand has not changed much. It is not required by the Rhode Island State Department of Education for schools to teach the history of the first people of this state, the Narragansett. However, just over the border in Massachusetts, it is state-mandated that all schools teach Wampanoag history and culture. Until each state in our union is required to teach Indigenous history and culture that includes the view of the Indigenous population, the true dream of American education will be unfulfilled.

There is a federal law called "No Child Left Behind" that many of you are probably familiar with. But you are probably not familiar with the laws that specifically pertain to Indian children. The public schools in this area that I have met with were not familiar with these special laws pertaining to the education of American Indian students. An executive order by the president of the United States reads, "It is the purpose of this order to assist American Indian and Alaskan native students in meeting the challenging student academic standards of the No Child Left Behind Act of 2001, in a manner that is consistent with tribal traditions, languages, and cultures."

In response to the lack of success of our Indigenous youth in public education, three years ago I began a journey to help our Indigenous children find their path in life that allows them to succeed in both worlds—our Indigenous community as well as the larger community of the United States. I founded the Nuweetooun School at Tomaquag Museum to address the needs of our Indigenous children and to provide a culture-based education that honors their learning styles, promotes high expectations, leadership, and lifelong learning. It is our opportunity for the Pursuit of Happiness through education that honors our culture, history, knowledge, and gifts.

The mission of Nuweetooun School is to educate all students in a respectful, stimulating, and engaging environment. Our program integrates core educational curriculum standards in Language Arts, Mathematics, Science, Social Studies, and Health with a concentration in Environmental Education and Native Culture and History.

We are committed to an experiential, integrated, and collaborative learning environment in which we strive to develop well-rounded, enthusiastic, and self-motivated learners. They experience education that embraces their learning styles, honors their multiple intelligences, and enriches their educational, social, spiritual, and cultural development.

Most importantly, we learn to honor others, honor ourselves, honor the earth, and honor spirit. We believe that each child has many gifts and talents. We want to develop their ability to become critical, analytical, divergent thinkers and problem solvers. We want to foster an environment that will allow our children to flourish in today's world with confidence, self-esteem, competence, perspective, initiative, imagination, and purpose. Nuweetooun School means "Our Home" School. It is a school with the nurturing environment of home. Our goal at Nuweetooun School is to teach the whole child, mind, body, and spirit, in a way that fires their imagination for lifelong learning.

Nuweetooun School has given students opportunities to explore themselves as Indigenous people, to explore their Native communities as well as how they fit in the larger community. The culture-based education instills pride and confidence and also preserves our cultural traditions for future generations. It builds community, leadership skills, and helps the students overcome the historical trauma that has befallen their families and themselves in a positive, self-affirming, and culturally connected way.

As a parent and grandparent, one is always looking to improve conditions for the next generation. My grandson spent six years struggling in public schools. He was identified as needing "special attention." When he entered Nuweetooun School, he was reading at a fourth-grade level. At the end of the school year he was tested and now reads at the eighth-grade level! His vocabulary and self-esteem have increased, and he looks forward to school each day. Thank you, Nuweetooun! —a Grandmother

My child has been given the opportunity to express himself through various educational activities at Nuweetooun. This experience resulted in a love of learning, cultural awareness, and an increase of academic success. —a Parent

One cannot put a value on the hope that is developed in a child when he/she finds a sense of self-worth and true value. —a Mother

In our school we are allowing students to use their own experiences to facilitate their learning. They use oral history to support their findings in history reports as well as help document and preserve this history for the future. Students learn from their elders, community leaders, and each other. They use their traditional skills, such as drumming, singing, dancing, storytelling, basketmaking, beadwork, flute, and many other traditional experiences to express their understanding of the world around them. Students utilize cultural resources, their language, the environment trade books, as well as technology, to learn about their world.

Our students act as docents at the Tomaquag Indian Memorial Museum. They present traditional drumming, singing, dance, and flute. They have exhibited their Eastern Woodland pottery in an art show as well as mounting several student exhibits in the museum, such as exhibits on "Fishing Weirs" and the "History of Cranberries: Pre-contact to Present Day." These experiences teach them public speaking and presentation skills along with content-area expertise in science, social studies, math, and language arts. These experiences teach them life skills that will prepare them for high school, college, and their life's work.

There are schools like Nuweetooun School that are taking the education of Native youth into their own hands. The Akwesasne Freedom School in upstate New York, for example, is a full language immersion school. All content is taught in their Native tongue. They fund their school though private fundraising, parent support, and other grassroots efforts. Nuweetooun School is funded by parent or family-paid tuition, individual donors, fundraising efforts, private foundation grants, and a federal special project grant facilitated by (Rhode Island) Senator Lincoln Chafee. There are other Native schools across the country trying to reach the needs of Native communities for quality education that fosters community, tribal leadership, embraces their cultural practices and history, teaches through experiential learning and process-oriented techniques, integrates tribal language, art, music, and sciences throughout the learning experience. We need many more until public education truly embraces us, our unique cultures, languages, histories, and our role in U.S. culture and history.

Indian education must be in the control of Indian people. Tribal governments must put educating their people as their utmost priority. Native educational systems that have succeeded in the past have been under tribal leadership, allowing for the education of their people to include tribal history, culture, and language, as well as inclusion of some western concepts or processes. The community as a whole must take an active role in the education of their people as well as an active role in celebrating their successes. Native governments often can't afford to educate their youth without outside funding, such as state and federal dollars. With these monies come restraints; we must gain control of the educational processes, methodologies, ideologies, and curricula in order to provide the quality of education our children need and deserve in order to be productive citizens of our tribal communities and truly gain our pursuit of happiness.

The pursuit of happiness begins with the education we receive from our families, our communities, and the educational systems that are put into place to support our individual and tribal community's goals. We must foster learning environments that allow our children to reach their full potential to become active members and future leaders of our tribal communities and also make positive impacts on the American community at large.

Notes

1. Most Anglo-American histories describe Canonicus as the Narragansett sachem who "welcomed" and "gave" Roger Williams the land for what is now Providence, Rhode Island. Williams's letter, written to an Assembly of Commissioners and dated November 17, 1677, can be found in the volume of his correspondence edited by Glenn LaFantasie (752).
2. In 2009 the U.S. Supreme Court ruled that the Department of the Interior could take land into trust for tribes "not under federal jurisdiction" as of 1934, when the Indian Reorganization Act was passed. The case was devastating for the Narragansetts and other nations who won federal recognition more recently. In the Narragansett case, the tribe wanted a thirty-one-acre parcel it had purchased for elderly housing to be protected from state interference. More broadly, the *Carcieri* case has been condemned across Indian Country (by such leading organizations as the National Congress of American Indians and the Native American Rights Fund) as a violation of Indigenous sovereignty and abrogation of the federal trust relationship.
3. Red Wing was sometimes referred to as Mrs. Ella Peek or Mary Congdon. According to the Tomaquag Museum, Red Wing was born Mary Ella Glasko and married first Walter Peek, then Daniel Congdon.
4. Many historians have recounted the Pilgrims' raids on Native graves and corn caches. See, e.g., Seale and Slapin (203).
5. Roaring Brook, part of the Arcadia Management Area in southwestern Rhode Island, abuts the Dovecrest property.
6. In January 2011 over two hundred people protested a plan by the state Board of Regents to increase the weight given to standardized test scores in granting high school diplomas. The proposal struck a nerve, especially in school districts representing lower-income and minority students.
7. The student paper, published at California State University–Long Beach, issued an apology on March 21 after receiving a wave of criticism in letters and email.
8. Dawn Dove calls this essay "a thoroughly collaborative effort," even when it reverts to first-person pronouns.

Further Reading

NARRAGANSETT AUTHORS

Brown, Ella W. [Ella Wilcox Sekatau]. *Love Poems and Songs of a Narragansett Indian.* Wakefield RI: Ariosto Press, 1971. Print.
Commuck, Thomas. *Indian Melodies.* New York: Lane & Tippett, 1845. Print.
———. Letter to Elisah Potter. 11 July 1844. Elisha R. Potter Papers. Box 1, Folder 12. Rhode Island Historical Society, Providence RI. Print.

————. Letter to Wilkins Updike. 14 July 1839. Elisha R. Potter Papers. Box 1, Folder 12. Rhode Island Historical Society, Providence RI. Print.

————. "Sketch of the Brothertown Indians." 1859. *Wisconsin Electronic Reader*. http://www.library.wisc.edu/etext/WIReader/WER0439.html. Web. 7 July 2011.

Hopkins, John Christian. *Carlomagno*. Franklin Park NJ: Wampum Books, 2010. Print.

————. *Nacogdoches*. N.p.: PublishAmerica, 2004. Print.

————. *Rhyme or Reason: Narragansett Poetry*. Greenfield MA: Blue hand Books, 2012. Print.

————. "Troopers Lead Attack on Narragansett Reservation." *Pequot Times* Aug. 2003: n. pag. Print.

————. *Twilight of the Gods*. Amazon.com: CreateSpace, 2012.

Jennings, Paulla. *Strawberry Thanksgiving*. Cleveland OH: Modern Curriculum Press, 1991. Print.

The Narragansett Dawn. 1935–36. University of Rhode Island Special Collections. http://digitalcommons.uri.edu/sc_pubs/5. Web. 8 Sept. 2006.

Wheelock, Eleazar. Letters received. Rauner Special Collections, Dartmouth College, Hanover NH. Print.

ADDITIONAL READING

Charlestown Bicentennial Book Committee. *Reflections of Charlestown RI*. Westerly RI: Utter Company, 1976. Print.

gkisedtanamoogk and Frances Hancock. *Anoqcou: Ceremony Is Life Itself*. Portland ME: Astarte Shell Press, 1993. Print.

Loewen, James W. *Lies My Teacher Told Me: Everything Your American History Textbook Got Wrong*. New York: Touchstone, 1996. Print.

Love, William Deloss. *Samson Occom and the Christian Indians of New England*. Reprint. Syracuse NY: Syracuse University Press, 2000. Print.

McCallum, James Dow. *Letters of Eleazar Wheelock's Indians*. Hanover NH: Dartmouth College, 1932. Print.

McDougall, Frances Harriet. *Memoirs of Elleanor Eldridge*. Providence RI: B. T. Albro, 1843. Print.

Pierce, Isaac. *Narragansett Chief; or, The Adventures of a Wanderer*. New York: J. K. Porter, 1832. Print.

Seale, Doris, and Beverly Slapin. *A Broken Flute: The Native Experience in Books for Children*. Walnut Creek CA: Rowman Altamira, 2006. Print.

Ward, Michael. *Ellison "Tarzan" Brown: The Narragansett Indian Who Twice Won the Boston Marathon*. Jefferson NC: McFarland, 2006. Print.

Williams, Roger, et al. *The Correspondence of Roger Williams: 1654–1682*. Ed. Glenn W. LaFantasie. Hanover NH: Published for The Rhode Island Historical Society by Brown University Press/University Press of New England, 1988. Print.

MOHEGAN TRIBE

OF INDIANS OF CONNECTICUT

Introduction

Stephanie M. Fielding

When Siobhan Senier, general editor of this anthology, asked me to pull together the products of Mohegan writers, I felt ill-equipped to carry out such a job, but then that never kept me from doing anything before . . . and there were lots of people to help.

I've been writing all my life, but I haven't lived in Mohegan all my life. In my early years, Mohegan was my glory. There were no other kids in my Hawaiian schools (apart from my brothers) who could claim Mohegan as a part of their heritage. Something I did often and loudly. It wasn't until 1999 that I came to Mohegan and physically joined the Mohegan Tribe of Indians of Connecticut, just as I had joined them spiritually so many years before. Until then I had lived all over the country and the world and had seen many wonderful and exciting places. Yet Connecticut filled me with the same sense of beauty and comfort that Hawaii, my first home, did. I felt the presence of my ancestors. It seemed like everything I had been doing had led me to this time when I could serve my tribe, and it consumed me.

When I lived in Nigeria one of my best friends there was a linguist, one of the top linguists in the world. We talked about linguistics and he explained exactly how my wee son would acquire his language. Amazingly, he did. It wasn't until thirty years later, when I was told that the tribe's language was being resurrected, that I began to understand how I might assist the tribe. I took advantage of the education program the tribe offered and went to school; at fifty-five I was living in the dorms at the University of Connecticut at Storrs. I was older than all except one of my teachers. I managed to get a four-year degree in two years, and then, after a year off, started at MIT for my master's in linguistics (where my mentor was three months older than my oldest child). Since then I have devoted myself to reawakening the Mohegan language. In the "spare time" I have while serving on the Council of Elders (an integral part of our government that serves, among other things, as the supreme court of the Mohegan Nation), the Mohegan lexicon continues to grow, and fresh editions of the *Modern Mohegan Dictionary and Grammar* continue to be republished online.

When Siobhan asked me to gather samples from Mohegan writers, I started by putting a call for papers in the *Wuskuso*, the weekly newsletter for tribal members. Then came the reading of *The Collected Writings of Samson Occom, Mohegan*, edited by Joanna Brooks (2006). Ms. Brooks did all the hard work of finding, transcribing, and putting into context the voluminous work of Samson Occom (1723–92). It was nearly impossible to pick a piece or two from his work. It was a thrill to finally get my hands on this book: it was the last book our dear Chief Ralph Sturges read before his death. I am happy to say that I gifted him that volume.

This reading was followed by *To Do Good to My Indian Brethren: The Writings of Joseph Johnson, 1751–1776*. Johnson and Occom were contemporaries, if in different generations. Johnson married Occom's daughter Tabitha. We contemplated publishing their correspondence, particularly Johnson's humble plea for Tabitha's hand in marriage, but we couldn't find Occom's positive response—although we know for sure there was one.

During the next century Fidelia Fielding started gathering the papers and writings of anyone who spoke Mohegan or Pequot, which are the same language. As the holder of the tribe's traditions for her generation and the last speaker of the Mohegan language, she felt it her duty to protect the language. In 1903 a Columbia University student, Frank Speck, paid a visit to Fidelia. He was so charming that at the end of their time together she gave him her collection of papers, including a number of her diaries. He was interested in the language, and none of the Mohegan youth were. Speck took the trove back to his professor, J. Dyneley Prince, and they came up with a word list, which they published. Then Prince sent Speck on an anthropological excursion out west, keeping Fidelia's papers in his library. While Speck was gone Prince's house caught on fire and everything in his library was destroyed. After Fidelia died in 1908 her adopted son, John, found her last few diaries and gave them to Speck. These were the diaries that Speck translated and published in the Bureau of American Ethnology reports.

Mary Virginia Morgan, born in 1897, was next on the scene, followed quickly by Gladys Tantaquidgeon, born in 1898. Both were prolific writers and it was again difficult to choose a selected number of pages from either of them.

All the remaining writers are contemporary Mohegans. Among them are four generations from one family, if we include one who passed away in 2005. They are Gladys Tantaquidgeon, who is the aunt of Jayne Fawcett, who is the mother of Melissa Tantaquidgeon Zobel and the grandmother of Madeline Sayet. Our selection is also graced by mother and son poets: Sharon and Eric Maynard.

The landscapes that these Mohegan writers present in their writings are fascinating, whether they are exploring their own psyches (Troffer), or their Mohegan parents' (Smith and Fielding), or the actual landscapes of their experiences on land (Fawcett and Tantaquidgeon) or water (S. Maynard), urban settings (Donehey), or reservation (E. Maynard), or the landscape of our culture (Sayet and Zobel). A love for Mohegan shows strongly, as does a compassionate eye for the land and its inhabitants.

Samson Occom

(1723–1791)

Samson Occom has become one of the best-known early Native American writers.
For a long time he was most famous for his work (and eventual conflicts) with
Eleazar Wheelock, who educated him at Moor's Charity School and then sent
him to England to raise funds for the school that later became Dartmouth College. Occom documented his disenchantment with Wheelock, and the poverty he
experienced as an itinerant Presbyterian minister, in "A Short Narrative of My Life"
(1768), a piece that has been widely reprinted and anthologized. Recently, however,
historians have deepened the image of Occom as a Christianized, exploited Indian,
revealing him as someone who fought hard for tribal self-determination. With
his colleague Joseph Johnson, also included in this volume, he helped found the
Brothertown community. The petitions below reflect Occom's deep commitments
to the Montauk people on Long Island (having preached among them for many
years and married one of their members, Mary Fowler), as well as to his home
community at Mohegan. The following excerpts appear in Joanna Brooks's *The
Collected Writings of Samson Occom*.

Montaukett Tribe to the State of New York

To the Great and Most Excellent Governor, and to all the Great Men Ruling
in the State of New York in North America.—

We who are known by the Name, Mmeeyautanheewuck or Montauk
Indians, Humbly Send Greeting

We are very Glad and Rejoice with you that you have at last got your
Freedom Liberty and Independence, from under the heavy and Gauling
Yoke of Your Late King, who has tryed very hard to make you Slaves, and
have kill'd great many of You, but by Your Steadiness, Boldness, and Great
Courage, you have broke the Yoke and the Chain of Slavery;—Now, God
Bless You, and Make you very great and good forever

We Montauk Indians, have Sot Still and have not Intermedled in this
Family Contention of Yours, because we had no Business with it, and
we have kept our Young men quiet as we Coud, and the People on both
Sides have Usd us well in general

Now, great and good Gentlemen, we humbly Intreat your Condescention and Patience to hear us a little Concerning ourselves.—

The Great and good Spirit above, Saw fit in his good pleasure, to plant our Fore-Fathers in this great Wilderness but when and how, none knows but himself,—and he that works all things Acording to his own Mind, Saw it good to give us this great Continent & he fill'd this Indian World, with variety, and a Prodigous Number of four footed Beasts, Fowl without number and Fish of all kinds great and Small, fill'd our Seas, Rivers, Brooks, and Ponds every where,—And it was the Pleasure of him, Who orders all things acording to his good Will, he that maketh Rich, and maketh poor, he that kills, and that maketh alive, he that raiseth up whom he will, and pulleth down whom he will; Saw fit, to keep us in Poverty, Only to live upon the Provisions he hath made already at our Hands—Thus we livd, till it pleased the great and good Governor of the World, to send your Fathers into these goings down of the Sun, and found us Naked and very poor Destitute of every thing, that your Fathers injoyd, only this that we had good and a Large Country to live in, and well furnished with Natural Provisions, and there was not a Letter known amongst them all in this Boundless Continent.—But your Fore Fathers Came with all the Learning, Knowledge, and Understanding, that was Necessary for Mankind to make them Happy, and they knew the goodness of our Land, and they Soon began to Settle and Cultivate the land, Some they bought almost for nothing, and we suppose they took a great deal without Purchace. And our Fathers were very Ignorant and knew not the value of Land, and they Cared nothing about it, they Imagin'd, they Shoud allways live by Hunting Fishing and Fowling, and gathering Wild Fruits—But alas at this age of the World, we find and plainly see by Sad experience, that by our Fore Fathers Ignorance and Your Fathers great Knowledge, we are undone for this Life—Now only See the agreeament, your Fathers and our Fathers made,—We hope you wont be angry with us in telling The agreed that we Shoud have only two Small necks of Land to plant on, and we are not allowd to Sow Wheate, and we as a Tribe are Stinted to keep only 50 Head of Cattle, and 200 Swine and three Dogs,—Pray gentlemen take good Notice, dont this discover a profound Ignorance in our fore Fathers, indeed we Suspect, Some Times, that what little understanding they had was Drowned with hott Waters before they made these Shameful agreements, and on the other hand, dont this Show, that the

English took advantage of the Ignorance of our Fore Fathers Woud they be Willing to be Servd so by us? Were we Cababale to use them So?—We fare now harder than our Fore Fathers—For all our Hunting, Fowling, and Fishing is now almost gone and our Wild Fruit is gone, What little there is left the English would Ingross or take all to themselves—and our Wood is gone and the English forbid us of getting any, where there is Some in their Claim—and if our Hogs happen to root a little the English will make us pay Damages, and they freequently Count our Cattle and Hogs,—Thus we are Usd by our English Neighbours—Pray most Noble Gentlemen Consider our Miserable Case and for God's Sake help us; For we have no where to go now, but to your Excellence for help; If we had but 150 head of Cattle and some Sheep and a few more Hogs we Shoud be Contented and thankful

This is all we have to Say at this Time, and Shall now wait to See your Pleasure Concerning Us—

(1785?)

Mohegan and Niantic Tribes to the Connecticut Assembly

To the Most Honorable General Assembly of Connecticut Convened at Hartford in May, in the Year of our Common Lord & Saviour Jesus Christ one Thousand Seven Hundred eighty and five years:

Your steady, close and faithful friends the tribe of Mohegan, and the tribe of Nahantick sendeth greeting. Sincere friends and brethren may talk freely together without offence. Such we concluded, the English of Connecticut and Mohegans, and Nahanticks are—

Your Excellency may well remember, that we sent a Memorial to the General Assembly, held at New Haven last October, requesting, not a Priviledge, which we never had before, but a Protection in our Natural Priviledges, which the King of Heaven gave to our Fathers and to their Children forever. When we received an answer or grant to our petition, we were all amazed and astonished beyond measure. What? Only half a sein allowed to Monooyauhegunnewuck, from the best friends to the best friends? We are ready to conclude, that the meaning must be, that in time to come we must not have only one canoe, one bow, one hook and line, among two tribes, and we must have taxes imposed upon us also, &c., &c. Whilst the King of England had authority over here they order no such things upon us. Alas, where are we? If we were slaves under tyrants, we must submit; if we were captives, we must be silent, and if we were strangers, we must be contented; or if we had forfeited our priviledges at your hands by any of our agreements we should have nothing to say. Whenever we went to war against your and our enemies, one bow, and one hatchet would not do for two tribes—And what will the various tribes of Indians, of this boundless continent say, when they hear of this restraint of fishing upon us? Will they not all cry out, mmauk, mmauk, these are the good that the Mohegans ever gloried and boasted of—Certainly we cannot hurt the public by fishing, we never had more than two seins in Mohegan and two in Nahantick and many times not one in Mohegan for over 15 years together, and we fish but very little in the season. We conclude your excellencies must have mistaken our request. And therefore we earnestly pray again, that the honorable Assembly would protect us in our Natural Priviledges, that none may forbid, hinder, or restrain us from fishing in any of the places where we used to fish heretofore.

Signed Samson Occom, Henry Quaquaquid, Robert Ashpo, Phillip Cuish, Joseph Uppauquiyantup, Issac Uppauquiyantu

(May 1785)

"The most remarkable . . . Appearance of Indian Tribes"

The most remarkable and Strange State Situation and Appearance of Indian Tribes in this Great Continent.—

Some Times I am ready to Conclude, that they are under Great Curse from God,—But When I come to look and view the nations of the World I Cant See that they are under Greater Curse than other nations, there are the Poor Negroes How long they have been in wretched and most Cruel Slavery thousands and millions of em,—and when I Come to Consider and See the Conduct of the Most Learned, Polite, and Rich Nations of the World, I find them to be the Most Tyranacal, Cruel, and inhuman oppressors of their Fellow Creatures in the World, these make all the confusions and distructions among the Nations of the Whole World, they are the Nations, that inslave the poor Negroes in Such Barbarous manner, as out do the Savage Indians in North America, and these are Calld Christian Nations You may See, Mr John Wesleys account of Slave Trade Now lets query—Who is under the Greatest curse he that inclines to such hardness of Heart, as to exercise the utmost Cruelty upon their Fellow Crea or they that are thus Tormented,—As for my part I Can not See So far, as to determine who are under the Graetest Curse of all the Nations I believe all Adamites are under a Curse As for this Life, it is as nothing, it is altogether uncertain

Shall now take notice of things peculiar to the Natives of this Country.—Indians, So Called, in this most extensive Continent, are Universally Poor, they have no Notion of Laying up much for the Future, they all live from Hand to Mouth, as the Common Saying is Chiefly by Hunting Fishing and Fowling; the Women Raise little Corn, Beans, and Pompkins, and pick Wild Fruts, and do other Drudgery; those that live among or near the White People, have Learnt, Some of them, to live a little in imitation of them, but very poor Still, they are good Serv to themselves, they will wory and Toile all Day to lose two Shillings & gain Six pence, they have no Patience nor Ambistion to appear Great in the World, they have no Notion of much learning, them that have had Some Learning made Little or no good Use of it many have lost all their Learning,—they Learn no trades, if any of them have Learnt, they follow it not—They have no laws or Regulations Neither in, every on des what is right in his own Eyes,—Yet in general they [were] kind to one another, and are not given to Lying, Cheating, and Steeling much what this way is Trifling But they are much for Drink Strong Drink, Yet I cant think that it is more Natural to them than other their manner.

(1783)

Joseph Johnson

(1751–1776)

Like Samson Occom, Joseph Johnson studied with Eleazar Wheelock, converted to Christianity, and became a minister and teacher in Native communities. Like Occom, he has been rediscovered as a prolific early Native writer, one who produced a wealth of journals, letters, and sermons. He worked closely with Occom in founding the Brothertown movement, and he also married Occom's daughter, Tabitha. Johnson's network included the Oneidas in New York and the Tunxis at Farmington, Connecticut. He died young (and mysteriously), before he could see the Brothertown community come to fruition. In the journal excerpts below, which share some thematic continuity with the diaries of Fidelia Fielding, also represented in this volume, we can see that even as he traveled and established roots in other communities (perhaps precisely *as* he established those connections), Johnson retained a lifelong commitment to Mohegan.

From His Diaries

Wendsday, the 18th of November A D 1772.

Notwithstanding the good Entertainments with which I was Entertained the Evening past, they asked me only Seven pence. It is about Sunrise, So I go. This morn, I Crosed the Hartford ferry just before nine. I payd only one Copper for my ferrage. I Breakfasted at the house of the Revd Mr Patten Son in law of the Revd Doctr Wheelock. I was recieved very kindly by him, and his wife, as if I was one of the family.

I tarryed in Hartford about 1 hour and an half, then I Sat out for to vizit the Farmington Indians. I went 3 Miles. There I was much at a stand whether to call at Famington or no, as my design was to go to the Mohawk Country. There I Stood at a Stand some time. At last . . . Came 3 men. I enqured of them, whether it was much out of the way, to go by Farmington, to go at Canaan, through Norfolk. They told me, that now it was the nighest way I could go from here. So I concluded to go by Farmington, the more because I was desired by the Revd Samson Occom.

So here I . . . I dined Seven miles from Hartford at a Tavern, where much people were Exerciseing in a Military way. I arrived at Farmington about 3 in the afternoon, dined again, at one Elijah Wiempy's. I. desired the Indians to meet together, that I might read the Revd Samson Occoms Sermon, Preached at the . . . of Moses Paul who was Executed the Second . . . of Septe . . . 1772 at N . . .

This afternoon I spent, that is the remainder at the house of Elijah Wiempey. This Evening Several Indians assembled themselves together at the house of Thomas Occurrum. I read the Sermon, which Mr Occom Preacht, at the Execution of Moses Paul; they heard with much Solmnity, after that we Sang, after that I spoke little of the goodness of God to all his Creatures, to us in a Perticular manner. Than I Acquainted them of a Proposal, which Mr Occom proposed Concerning my keeping a School amongst them if the School was void of a Teacher. They all rejoiced, to think of the Proposal. They Continued asking me if I could Content myself with them, so after we had Prayed; we Concluded the ensueing Day to go their overseer, to get his Approbation and to Confirm all. So we retired, much satisfied, in the Exercises of our Meeting, to our several homes. This evening, I tarry at Elijah Wimpeys.

Thirsday the 17th of December A D 1772.

Very pleasant after a Storm—Sun rises fair—this morn before breakfast I wrote from the original, an Extract from the girls Letter—after y^t went to the School—Dismissed at 12—began soon—Scholars behaved very well During the School time, but when we Came to dismiss by Prayer to God—I charged them to be Silent—Solemn Considering to whome we was Praying—as they had several times before been disorderly in time of worship—I threatend them and warned them faithfully Sundry times before. So at this time also—So after our minds were Composed we Prayed—but after Prayer—I was Enformed that 3 different Persons had been Disorderly—Alas how to be freed from the unwellcome task I Could not see So forth with I ordered them one by one beginning at the Eldest—to the Younger So faithfully I made them a Sad Example of Disobeying the School Orders.

Hoping from my heart—as this is the first—So may it be last in this
School so long as I Continue here—

I Spoke freely to all the rest—that they a warning take—for I assure
them that I will no Distinction make—

And what was inflicted on these 3 at this time was very lite—Their
Names are Elijah Wiempy Junr.—and Luke Mossock—& Lucy
Mossock—So now I am about to Prick out more Tunes for Samuel
Adams—

Well I remember home—O mohegan, O Mohegan—the time
is long before I Shall be walking my wonted places which are on
thee—once there I was but perhaps never again, but Still I remember
thee—in you is lodged my father & Mother Dear—and my Beloved
Sisters—and brothers—

Keep them in thy womb O Mohegan, till thou dost hear the Voice
of God—O Mohegan give up thy Dead—then no longer Prisoners
Shall they be unto thee—the joyfull hour is Approaching. My Soul
Come Meditate the Day and think how near it stands when you must
leave—this house of Clay—and fly to Unknown Lands.—Hast my
beloved fetch my Soul up to thy blest aboad fly for my Spirit Longs to
see—my Saviour—and my *God*—Mohegan is a lonsome place, oft
have I sighed—but sighed in vain—desired, but desired in vain—Cast
down—but no one to Comfort me—in destress—no one to relieve
me—no friend to open my heart and vent my Sorrows—I opened
my mouth to the open air—and told the Stones my Sorrow. Thus
o Mohegan have you treated me—and thinkest thou—I can forget
thee—or thy inhabitants—thinkest thou—or thine inhabiters that I
am desireing to be on thee or with them—far far from me be such a
thought—but Still there is a precious few in thee, which Causes my
mind often to Meditate of thee—Perhaps in due time I may once more
Come on thy borders—but first I have to go, to distant Lands; and far
Country—and Different Nations I have to walk through—before I see
thee. Thus O Mohegan I must bid you farewell, and Shut the door of
my Heart against thee—for I have a truer friend—to entertain in My
Heart—So good night—

Spent chief of this Evening in Pricking out Tunes—for Samuel
Adams.

I Begin this Day, on the following fare well to My Brethren the Farmington Indians.

Beloved Brethren, and Sisters one and all I Beseech you to attend unto me a little, while I take my leave of you, and I Confess, not with little Reluctance. Attend diligently, and hearken what a Departing friend has to say to you, before he depart, and you See his face no more, nor hear his Voice Sounding amongst you as Usual, Either Exhorting or weeping or making melody to God—no more will you hear Encouragments Proceeding out of his mouth, no more warnings to flee from the wrath to Come. No more will you See his tears of Compassion, and Sorrow, flowing from his pitying Eye, no more Entering your houses, seting at your tables, no more will he rest his weary head upon your Pillows. No more the Object of your tender Care, no more Can you Express your loves and tender Respects to his Pe[r]son, because he goes to be here no more. He leaves you, and wishes you all well, [from] the bottom of his heart, wishes your well being in this World—and in the Regions of bliss unmolested happiness in the Enjoyment of God through the never Ending ages of Eternity here after.

Well my dear friends, here we are once, more assembled, and Perhaps the last Opportunity, that kind Providence will afford me to Converse with you. First then: let us all be persuaded to Remember the Great Supreme Being who is the almighty God, and Everlasting King. Who is the Blessed, and only Potentate, King of Kings, and Lord of Lords, Who is the first and the Last, the only True, and living God, who is Cloathed with Honour, and Majesty—Before Whom, all things are naked, and open before his Eyes. Who Searchest the Heart of Man, but how Unserchable is his Understanding and his power is Unknown.

Who art of a Purer Eyes than to behold Iniquity. Whose Mercy Endureth for ever. Who is Slow to Anger, abundant in goodness, and his Truth reaches to all Generations—

What more Can I Say? Is not this the Supreme Being Who hath made the Heavens and the Earth? The Whole Creation is the work of his Hands. He ruleth among the Armies of Heaven, and among the Inhabitents of the Earth He doth what Pleaseth Him. He is our Creator Preserver, and Bountifull Benefactor. The Great I A M. The god of Abraham, Isaac, and

Jacob. This is He of whom I said let us all be persuaded to Remember. This is the God whom Our fathers Disobeyed, & Provoked, and were Ignorant of, and are Destroyed. But we their Children who have walked in the Steps of our fathers and more agrevatly Sinned against the great god of heaven & Earth, and trampled under foot the blood of the Eternal Son, of the Ever blessed god. We hard hearted, Stubborn, Rebellious, and Impenitent, Gospel rejecters and Gospel Sinners are yet Spared. O the amazing goodness, long forbearance of the great, Eternal God, towards us his Creatures we are yet the Speared Monuments of Gods Mercy. O then let us not only Remember but adore! Love, and live in the fear of Such a Being. Let his goodness lead us to Repentance.

O! the admireable Distinction Shewn to us, that we, in our Day have heard the glad tidings of Peace on Earth, good will towards men. Good tidings of great joy (it is writen) which Shall be to all people, for a Saviour is born, which is Christ the Lord: this great god of whom I Speak regardeth the work of his hands. Gods love is manifest to wards us in many Things in the Preservation of our Lives, healths, & Comforts of Life. But gods Love to Mankind is Most admirable & astonishing in the gift of His Son, to a lost, Undone Wretched, & miserable World. Hear, what this Blessed Saviour, who was born, who is Christ the Lord Saith, after he taught the Master of Israel, the Necessity of Regeneration! And fortold his Death! For he said as Moses Lifted up the Serpent in the Wilderness, (Signifying what death he Should die) even so must the Son of Man be lifted up. I Suppose you know it was set upon a pole, amidst the [people?] of Israel, that they who were biting of the [flesh of the?] Serpent might look upon it and Live. Well remember the brash Serpant. I Shall Say no more, but read to you the following verses: Christ said of himself even so must the Son of man be lifted up, that whosoever believeth in him Should not perish, but have Eternal Life. Then he Saith for God So loved the World that He gave his only Begotten Son. Thus we See the Manifestation of Gods Love towards us the Work of his Hands, by the gift of His Beloved Son, in whom He was, and is Ever well Pleased; through Name of His Son (Immanuel! god with us, Jesus, who is to Save his people from their Sins. Christ, the anointed of God.) is now Preached unto us the forgiveness of Sins. Our Ears have heard the heart reviving, & heavenly Proclamation, Sent abroad, Upon this Earth, unto all Nations—that whosoever will let him take of the water of life freely. Rev. XXII.17. And again for God So loved the world that he gave his only Begotten Son, that Whosoever Believeth in Him, Should not, perish, but have Everlasting Life. John III.16.

Letter to Samson Occom

Farmington. Oct 13th 1773.

Rev'd & Hon'd Sir [Samson Occom];

I know that my name is Joseph Johnson. Nevertheless I with a becoming humility would attempt to write to your Worthy Person. I am Sensable of my unworthiness, I remember all things. Be pleased to consider of me, and pity, and pray for me. O the folly of my ways. But what is past, is past. Rev'd Sir, by the Goodness of God I am, and have been well, and I hope you, and yours have been well like wise. This day, I Spoke with Mr. Benjamin Bellnap, of Johnston, Rhode Island.[1] He came out of his way, on purpose to See poor me. He is bound westward how far I don't justly know. He was very urgent to have me go to his Town with him when he returned. He Speak much concerning thee, and Sends much love, and Respects to you, by word of mouth. He had with him your Sermon, and my Letter which was reprinted at Boston.[2] I humbly beg that you would condescend to write me a few lines, and tell me your mind concerning a Letter of mine, which I wrote at Norwich, dated first of October, or rather tell me your Whole mind Concerning me, and my desires. I am Joseph Johnson.

It is Late in the Night, and I am weary, labouring Days, and had a meeting this Night. So I humbly hope that you will excuse, my brevity in Writ[t]ing. I assure you it is not for a want of Love to you, or yours, no. I hope that you will be pleased to write Large, and free, advise, encourage, Rebuke, and make manifest your Purposes. Sir, my mind is the Same, my Request is the Same, and if Providence permits, I Shall come down, Soon as I return, unless you write a Prohibition. As you Said take her as She is, I Say So be it, Just as She is, with all my heart.

But She is Thy daughter.

Fidelia Fielding

(1827–1908)

Fidelia Ann Hoscott Fielding is remembered as the last speaker of the Mohegan language, although many tribal members today are active in language reclamation. Fielding understood the weight of that responsibility, collecting anything that that was written in Mohegan-Pequot and keeping her own language alive by writing in her diaries. In 1902 she gave her collected works, including her diaries, to the anthropologist Frank Speck, then a philology student at Columbia. While Speck was away doing fieldwork, the house where Fielding's collection was stored caught fire and was destroyed. After her death, her adopted son, John Fielding, gave Speck four small diaries that she had kept in her final years. The source for most of Speck's writing on Mohegan-Pequot, those diaries are now in the rare books collection of Kroch Library at Cornell University. The diary entries below have been poetically transliterated by Stephanie Fielding.

Man's Relationship with God

God is good because he knows all things.
A person does not know but a little
unless knowing God.

God is very great, exceedingly good.
You must be good too,
then when you die
you will rest in heaven,
that says God.

You must not become weary.
If you become tired you must look to God,
then you will get strength.
Then you will be strong because
God helps you.

In heaven there does not come
anything that is not good,
because God cannot accept it,

That is why there came Jesus.
He came because people were
dreadfully bad. They are.

The great father gave his son
so that not all should die.

He was never bad.
He gave himself for bad people.
God's son's name is Jesus Christ.
Bad people killed him here on Earth.

He gave himself in order that all people
will go to heaven when they die.
Jesus died that we might live.

The Devil goes by running
so that he may catch all people.
The Devil thinks that the earth is his own,
people too. Nothing, yes!

Only for that Jesus Christ came.
He (the Devil) cannot do anything.
Jesus Christ will put the Devil from heaven
because he lied and wants Jesus Christ's place.
Jesus Christ will put the Devil in the fire,
just as the Devil knows.

Jesus Christ died that all people wanting to
can come to heaven.

The Truth of Tomorrow

Rain. Great rain today.
Maybe tomorrow I can go to Landing.
I cannot say because
I do not know, perhaps I will,
perhaps I won't.

Those people who can say much,
half of what they say is not true as they say it.

Weather

Early this morning the sun can see.
Nearly noon, the sun is hot.
The sun is warm, nearly night,
already it is night, the sun is gone.

Cloudy day. Great rain today,
already noon, rain all night.

Cold this morning, snow gone; clear
it is nearly night. Cold tonight, windy all day,
wind is strong tonight.

Clear rising today, only cold,
snow is falling, nearly night, snow is falling.
Snow is very much. I saw a fox this early
morning and a hound chasing the fox.

Snow is falling partly night, sun gone, night.
Sun rising, much fallen snow.
You can see the sun today,
nearly noon. Nearly night, it is warm.

Nearly night, cannot see the sun,
it was clear today, all snow.
Already noon, it is going to go and rain.
Night, rain. Tonight the moon is clear.

Sun is rising clear, warm today.
The sun is rising clear, already night.
The sun rising this early morning,

Sun rising this early morning cold;
snow gone, wind is strong here.
Night, sun gone, cold here.

The day has hurried away. Since not anyone
can get ahead of it, he must go fast.
It is windy. It goes by whistling.

God is good. I see another sun. Already noon.
Very cold for anyone not having someone.
Already night, all things will fall asleep
now that it is night.

Mary Virginia Morgan
(1897–1988)

An intriguing Connecticut public figure known as the Duchess of Noank, Mary
Virginia Morgan (Goodman) wrote over five hundred newspaper articles and
historical lectures. A former Groton teacher, she was civically involved with the
Daughters of the American Revolution and the Indian and Colonial Research
Center in Mystic. Starting in the 1970s, Morgan wrote the column "Noank Notes"
for the *Norwich Bulletin*, and she continued writing for a variety of magazines
and historical society newsletters until the end of her life. Although her columns
sometimes appeared little involved with Mohegan culture, in 1935 Morgan helped
repatriate some skeletal remains to Groton's Indian Memorial Burial Ground,
and she also spoke out against the Connecticut Welfare Commission in 1953,
when it proposed selling off the remaining reservations within the state. The
following address was provided by the Mohegan Tribal Archives and is reprinted
with permission.

Address at 100th Anniversary of the Mohegan Church

To have been asked to have a part in the 100th Anniversary of the Mohegan
Church affords me a very great pleasure for several reasons—chief among
them being the fact that my mother's earliest recollections center around
this spot and that my grandmother, Mary Fielding Story, worshipped here

in her youth and young womanhood and received in this very room those deep and lasting truths which guided her all along the Christian journey and fitted her for the place on high where the many mansions be.

Tracing beyond my grandmother I come in our family tree to Cynthia Tocomwas Hoscott and her mother Lucy Tantaquidgeon. Lucy Tantaquidgeon was my 3rd great grandmother, her daughter Cynthia Hoscott was my great, great grandmother, her daughter Mary Fielding Story was my grandmother. Our grandmother Lucy and our grandmother Cynthia gave the land on which this chapel stands. Lucy Tantaquidgeon's will drawn up in 1831, one hundred years ago, was in the possession of my grandmother Mary Fielding Story and is now among the family papers of my Aunt, Edith Story Gray. Since so many here tonight are descendants of Lucy Tantaquidgeon I will endeavor to read the time-stained and fragile document.

This year 1931 seems peculiarly fitted for anniversaries, celebrations and I rejoice that the descendants of the Mohegans who once owned all the land for miles around, seek to honor their forbears and those women of Norwich who were zealous for the salvation of the Indians, by holding commemorative exercises on this historic spot.

Particularly at this time we hear of many people searching the records for the names and deeds of their ancestors. Many of us here tonight have the blood of many tribes, many nations, coursing through our veins. Some of us can proudly trace back to lords and nobles of English name and fame to the Great French King Charlemagne or the Norman William the Conqueror. But let us all be proud of the line, the royal line of Uncas, our Indian ancestor. King he was of this tribe, ruler of his people, just as great and as important in the eyes of his council as William the Conqueror in the eyes of his barons and nobles. Let us always be proud of the fact that the real Americans were our Indian ancestors, the first discoverers of this beautiful land of ours.

True, the American Indians lost their land, their power and English civilization enveloped them and thus their identity has been lost in most instances. They were not fitted, either mentally or by experience to cope with the ways of the English. They were still in the Stone Age when the English came with their civilization and Christianity. They fought for their land, for their rights, for their former power just as every nation has done and will do to the end of time, but it was just another case of the survival of the fittest and slowly but surely the colorful panorama of the Indian faded away and the newer ways of life, English civilized life, came over them. Their children married Englishmen, their descendants became of mixed blood as every white person is. No Englishman can call himself a full-blooded Englishman for back in his ancestry will be found men and women of other lands. Again I repeat, let us never fail to look back with pride on our Indian ancestors. We have had noted men in our tribe. Few tribes or clans or families can boast a Samson Occum [sic]. Born in Mohegan on 1723, reared as any other young Indian boy in the pagan faith and savage customs of the tribe. He became converted to Christianity and deeply alarmed for his own lost condition during the great awakening of 1739–40 when Whitefield's fiery doctrine awoke the countryside from near and far. After his conversion he felt the great urge to preach the gospel with its glad tidings of salvation to his race. He went to Lebanon, the home of the Rev. Eleazar Wheelock, asked to be admitted to his school which he conducted in his own family. Occum could spell out a few words and knew his alphabet but that was the extent of his scholastic knowledge. So great was his thirst for knowledge that in four years['] time he was fitted to enter college. But his intense application to his studies impaired his health and this and lack of money sent him home.

Back he came to Mohegan and soon took up the familiar life of the Indian, hunting, fishing, making baskets and teaching a few of the boys. He continued his studies of theology and went about preaching to the Indians here and elsewhere. In 1759 he was ordained by the Suffolk Presbytery. Certainly Samson Occum had a varied and interesting career. At the age of 43 he was sent to England to solicit aid for the school started by Eleazar Wheelock for Indian youths. So we can picture this ancestor of ours, this son of the forest with ages of superstition behind him, setting forth on this great mission, the first Mohegan Indian of education and culture. An Historian writing of him says, "His features and complexion bore every mark of his race, but he was easy and natural in social manners, frank and cordial, but modest in conversation and his deportment in the pulpit was such as to command deep attention and respect. He was in England over a year and during that time preached between three and four hundred sermons, many of them in the presence of the king and the royal family and nobles. He impressed and interested the Earl of Dartmouth to such an extent that he gave a great proportion of the money collected to found the school, which is known the world over as Dartmouth College. All honor to our noble ancestor Samson Occum who was one of the founders. In many hymnals will be found his well known hymn composed by him, in 'Awaked by Sinai's awful sound.'"

Thus we find on history's pages the names of Uncas, Chief of the Mohegans, friend of the English settlers and in the annals of the Congregational Church history the name of the Rev. Samson Occum and among the proud names of Harvard and Yale we find Samson an Indian of Mohegan, founder of Dartmouth College.

Uncas! Occum! All our ancestors of the days long past, we, the last of the Mohegans, salute you!

(1931)

Gladys Tantaquidgeon
(1899–2005)

Gladys Tantaquidgeon, revered medicine woman, studied Mohegan traditions with such leaders as Emma Baker, Lydia Fielding, and Mercy Ann Nonesuch Mathews (Nehantic); she also studied professional anthropology with Frank Speck at the University of Pennsylvania. Speck is controversial among some Native people and anthropologists today, but in the selections below Tantaquidgeon speaks of him fondly. She also reveals her love of travel, which she pursued during her career, working around the country with the Bureau of Indian Affairs and the Indian Arts and Crafts Board. At home in Connecticut, she founded the Tantaquidgeon Museum with her father, John, and brother Harold. She published widely; the unpublished manuscripts below, typed and undated, were selected by Faith Davison and Melissa Zobel from among the Gladys Tantaquidgeon Papers in the Mohegan Tribal Collections and are used with permission.

See the Beauty Surrounding Us

I never could understand why so seldom is mention made of the wonderful forms of nature that lie so close to our view, almost within sight of our own immediate environment. Have our senses become so dulled by our occupations that we cannot see the woods, the seas, the skies just beyond the horizon of the metropolis or the work fields into which we are sunk? Or have our fancies been moulded and our perspectives of nature been distorted by the lust for achievement in covering great distances to enjoy what is so often not more thrilling as such experiences go far afield than experiences to be had nearby? Or perhaps it is the contagious urge of competition in voyaging afar, to conquer new realms of adventure in travel, since the Poles have at last been reached, the dim mysterious islands of the south, the stern rocky crags and barrens of the north and the mirages of western deserts, have been opened to the emotionless intrusion of the tourist. We learn hard the lesson of Rasselas the monk who wandered in a life-long quest to seek what he left at his own hearth.

Multitudes have sailed in and out of a familiar harbor through a panorama of islands rounded with crowns of moorland and grass, set in a visa of distant horizon rivalling the bays of the Mediterranean in the impressive though cold beauty of the northern zone, yet its islands set amid colors of sky and seas fully as stimulating in their influence upon the freed mind, as the famed approaches to the showplace harbors of the southern seas. Yet it is only Boston Harbor and Massachusetts Bay of which we write! Widening out eastward over waters gleaming under the early morning sun in October only a sodden heart could remain indifferent to its appeal to the sense.

And among the feelings aroused is that of wonder and historic curiosity in regard to the fancies entertained for the self-same scene long ago by the now almost forgotten aborigines who saw it before the Mayflower and knew it not only by eye and sense as we do and before we did, but knew it enhanced by poetic traditions which we do not know. What would the Old World historic shrines and scenes be without their traditions and classical associations? And what would the New World scenes be without their human traditions recited as the ancients knew them to lift our imaginations above the land and sea into the clouds? But where are the spokesmen for the age of legend of the natives? Who is to tell us now that the islands of the Massachusetts coast were the central scene of an epic, a national legend of an almost unknown tribe of natives? What link have we with the last, two centuries behind us now, to help us conjure up the sagas of sea and islands, of heroes, of whales, ~~or islands~~ of shoals, dunes and forests coming and going as the heroes will it? The following transcript is the answer. Glance over it and ponder the wonder that has happened to preserve the sagas of beautiful regions redeemed at the last moment and enjoy it. It is almost a miracle for the literature of the land.

An Affectionate Portrait of Frank Speck

It was during the summer of 1902 while vacationing with his family in Niantic, Connecticut, that Frank Speck first visited Mohegan in the town of Montville, Connecticut about 30 miles north of Niantic. The members of this small group trace their ancestry back to Chief Uncas who with a band of followers settled in this area in the early 1600s. The dome shaped mat covered lodges had long since disappeared and Speck found the Mohegan living in frame houses the same as their non-Indian neighbors.

Only one log house remained. It was occupied by Fidelia Hoscott Fielding who called it her "Tribe House."

Speck made the acquaintance of three Mohegan teenage boys—Roscoe Skeesucks, Edwin Fowler, and our brother Burrill Tantaquidgeon and they camped in a wooded area about 100 feet from the Norwich-New London trail, then a dirt road. He was anxious to meet as many Mohegan as possible and had heard of Fidelia, the last speaker of the Mohegan-Pequot language. It was generally known that she was not too friendly toward non-Indians but his young Mohegan friends agreed to take him to her little log house which was located about a mile east of where they were camping. She welcomed Speck and that was the beginning of a friendship which resulted in her telling him legends and words in the Mohegan language which he later published. A student in the Department of Anthropology at Columbia University, he and Professor J. D. Prince prepared a study based on Speck's findings which were later published.

I was too young at the time to have known of his research from my parents and other members of the community about his visits with Great Aunt Fidelia and others in the community. Everyone liked the personable young student and he was made welcome in all Mohegan homes.

My family lived in the old Tecoomwas-Hoscoat homestead where a young Missionary teacher held Sabbath and Day School classes for Mohegan children in 1827. It was her wish to have a Meeting House on the then Mohegan Indian Reservation and her prayers were answered when the Mohegan Congregational Church was built in 1831. It has always been a Community church—the Mohegan and their non-Indian friends and neighbors all working together. Also worthy of mention along with houses of the early 1700s is that of the home of the Rev. Samson Occom, a full-blood Mohegan who became a Missionary-Teacher and helped raise funds which were used to found Dartmouth College. Occom was said to have been the most outstanding Christian Indian of his time.

Great Aunt Fidelia liked my parents and Mother said that she visited our home probably because our parents did not show disrespect toward her adherence to tribal traditions. During one of her visits when I was just trying to waddle around (because I was too fat to try to walk) she named me Skeedumbic nana, "Indian Grandmother." She also gave me a belt of black velvet with banded designs that had belonged to her Grandmother, Martha Uncas. Mother kept it until I was old enough to appreciate it. It is a part of my Mohegan dress which I wear on ceremonial occasions.

At a family gathering, when I was about eight years of age, I recall having seen Aunt Fidelia there. She was of medium height; black hair parted in the middle and straight back; sparkling black eyes; high cheek bones and smooth copper skin. During the dinner she left the room and went out of the house. She said she was going to talk to "the little people." Those were the legendary "makiawisag" that she had told Speck about.

She died in 1908 at the age of 81. In 1936, a memorial stone was unveiled at the site of her grave in the Ancient Burial Ground of the Mohegan, Fort Shantok, now within the State Park area. Sponsored by members of the Degree of Pocahontas, Hartford, Connecticut, the Mohegan were joined by members of several neighboring tribes on the occasion. Following her death several diaries in the Mohegan language were found and given to Speck which he translated and included in his study entitled "Native Tribes and Dialects of Connecticut, 1928."

From the early 1800s the Mohegan, as well as other Tribes in Connecticut, were known for their excellence in the art of splint basketry. By the time that Speck visited the Mohegan only four were making baskets. A variety of shapes and sizes such as large ones for gathering vegetables; for storing food; smaller sizes for gathering berries and sewing needs such as thread, needles, etc. A great deal of labor went into the preparation of splints from the brown ash or white oak before actual weaving began. Many ash splint baskets of that early period were decorated by painting designs on sides and covers. Dots, curved lines, conventionalized florals were applied by crude brushes made by fraying the end of a small twig of birch or other soft wood, dipped in the juice of berries or roots. Many museums have collections of these painted baskets of that early period.

Our father, John Tantaquidgeon, was the last Mohegan basketmaker. His teacher was a full blood Mohegan, Jerome Bohema, and father passed along his skill to his son, Harold, who in turn has shared the art of basket making with students and campers. Using splint of brown ash and white oak he made large and small baskets. Many of his baskets dating from 1888 to 1934 are on display in our museum which he helped to build in 1931. Also on display are examples of wooden bowls, ladles, spoons and scoops of maple wood made by Tantaquidgeon. Some have designs carved by his son, Harold.

Skeesucks "Little Eyes" whose elders were well known in this area for their basketry and wood carving carried on the skills. Speck was instrumental in enabling him to attend the Pennsylvania Academy of Fine Arts, Philadelphia, Pa. We have a number of wood, stone, and bone carvings, bark baskets, and bows and arrows by craftsmen in our collection. Beadwork was not highly developed and Speck photographed several small pouches made of black velvet with floral designs done with colored beads.

Speck left no stone unturned and he spent much time with the elders in an effort to learn about and preserve any and all references to early life and customs. The results were meager but he was persistent. The only observance of the most remote ceremonial character was the Annual Brush Arbor or Wigwam Festival. This modified version of the ancient rite of many Eastern Woodland Indians was performed "to give thanks for the Corn Harvest." As children we were a part of the year long preparations for this event. Men and boys making objects of wood, stone and bone. The girls and women making small beaded bags, dolls, patchwork quilts, and aprons. The Mohegan were farmers and fishermen and they provided vegetables (mostly corn), meat and fish for the Festival. One ceremonial food was "Yokeag." One year old yellow corn kernels were parched and ground to fine meal. Every family had a wooden mortar and stone pestle and the men worked long hours in preparing this. Traditionally it was known as "Traveling Food" and was carried by hunters and warriors. It was believed that "it Nourished the soul as well as the body." A small quantity was carried in a leather pouch and could have been eaten dry or mixed with water. Was this the beginning of "Journey food" or "Johnny Cake?"

Ten or a dozen men would construct a brush arbor in the church yard, some fifty feet square. Crotched poles of oak were set in the ground about 10 feet apart. Other poles were placed across the top and sides to form a base over which gray birch saplings were placed. Entrance was gained through openings left in the east and west sides of the arbor. Everything was ready for the opening day which was the last Wednesday in August. Women had been busy making cakes, bread and pies. The men were gathering corn and potatoes and also oystering and clamming. Cooks were on hand early in the morning. Tables had been arranged the day before. Succotash and clam chowder were favorite foods. Visitors brought yokeag to serve as a cereal and served it on ice cream. So began a two day festival for the Mohegan and their friends. Some of our members appeared in

Indian dress. In later years the festival was held to raise funds for our Church. It has not been observed since 1938.

I was eleven years of age when Frank and his wife, Florence, came to our home in New London, Connecticut, and asked my parents if I could visit them in Philadelphia. I was pleased that my parents agreed to let me go. It was two weeks before the Christmas vacation when they were to come to take me on my first long journey away from home. At that time there was no through train service between New York and Philadelphia so we had a stopover in New York. They could not understand why I was not impressed by the sights of the big city. What they didn't know was that it was my maternal grandmother with whom I spent many [hours] of make-believe travel to big cities such as New York and Washington, D.C. In this land of imagination we attended many social events and met celebrities when I was about five years of age.

Needless to say I had a wonderful visit. Their Philadelphia home, the University of Pennsylvania, their many friends and their efforts to make me feel at home. Then followed visits to their summer home at Riverview, Cape Ann, Massachusetts, where I met more members of their family and friends. When the children of the summer residents heard that a Mohegan Indian girl was coming to visit the Specks they expected me to dive into the water and swim like a professional. To their amazement, I could not swim a stroke! Perhaps someone had told them that our family name Tantaquidgeon means "going along fast" (in the water or on land). Our ancestor, an aide to Chief Uncas, was said to have been "a fast runner." No mention of swimming!

Harold Tantaquidgeon refers to his friend, Frank Speck, as "one of the greatest. He was a man's man and was comfortable with those from all walks of life. He walked in my moccasins and I walked in his." A born naturalist—he was an avid bird watcher and usually had a snake (non-poisonous) around the premises in Swarthmore and his summer home in Riverview, Massachusetts. Fidelia H. Fielding gave him the name "Skook-een" meaning "Snake Man" in the Mohegan tongue. He had a snake tattooed on his arm done by his Mohegan friend, Roscoe Skeesucks "Little Eyes."

One summer while in Mohegan he visited me at a Boy Scout camp where I had built, with the help of Scouts and Counselors, a Mohegan Village. He had planned to stay over night and the camp director said that he would prepare sleeping quarters in one of the cabins but Speck preferred to stay in my longhouse. A painting he did of that Village scene is one of our prized possessions.

Visits to the summer cottage in Riverview were many and we spent many hours discussing many subjects. There were Indian artifacts to be repaired—baskets, wooden objects, and even a Penobscot birch-bark canoe. When asked how he wanted me to do the repairs, the answer was, "Do it your way."

On one occasion we went to Indian Island, Oldtown, Maine, to visit the Penobscot group. Upon arriving in Oldtown, Maine, we went to the landing on the Penobscot River where a row boat was used to transport passengers to and from the Island. Speck asked the fee and the Penobscot answered "Three cents for you, two cents for Indians." That trip was worth more than I can put in words. Woodland Indian culture came alive in that setting with my good friend and teacher, Frank Speck.

When Father John Tantaquidgeon and son, Harold, were building a small house to be used as a Museum Speck was deeply interested and supportive. We needed a place in which to keep our treasures, many of which were made and used by Mohegan Indians. That was in 1931 and since that time two rooms have been added where artifacts from the Northern Plains, Southwest, and Southeast are displayed. Speck, his children and grandchildren are listed among the donors.

Every year members of the family return to visit and relive some of the happy times when they were growing up. One year when the Specks were going to be away for several months their three children lived with our family. Frank Jr. attended a local Elementary school and Alberta and Virginia were taught by our sister Ruth. A small building in our yard (now a garage) served as the schoolroom. Harold served as custodian. They had fun playing with Mohegan girls and boys and going on picnics.

Members of our family visited the Specks in their Cape Ann summer home and also in Swarthmore, Penna. We recall many happy gatherings of family and friends in the home of Speck's mother in Rockport. His father-in-law, Albert Insley, well-known artist of the late 1800s era, lived in Swarthmore with the family for a number of years. He was a kindly gentle man and spent most of his time in his third floor studio appearing only at mealtime and then went out for his daily walk. I loved his beautiful paintings and our quiet chats.

Field trips to the several Indian communities in the Eastern Woodland area offered a variety of experiences. On some occasions the entire Speck family would be accompanied by several faculty members and students. This was true of the trek to Millsboro, Delaware, to join the Nanticoke in their annual observance of Thanksgiving. Representatives of many different tribes attended including members of the Powahatan Confederacy of Virginia. During our several days stay we were entertained in the homes of Nanticoke families. It can be truly said that Dr. Speck was instrumental in the revitalization of the Nanticoke people. During several visits I recorded notes on folk medicine which appear in "Folk Medicine of the Delaware and Related Algonkian Indians."

On the western extremity of Martha's Vineyard, the largest of a group of islands lying off of the southeastern coast of Massachusetts, is the home of the Gay Head Indians. The name was given to the area by early English settlers because of its high and varicolored chalk cliffs. The Speck family and I visited the community on several occasions and later I returned to continue research in surviving folk beliefs. In 1928 some 200 descendants of the Gay Head group were still living in the area where early writers, such as [Bartholomew] Gosnold, found them in the early 1600s.

The Giant Moshup was very much alive in the tales related by my informants. Moshup through his magic power could lure whales ashore and cook them over a huge fire at the top of the cliffs. Blood and grease dripping down from the whale meat colored the cliffs. He was so powerful that he placed large boulders in Vineyard Sound which were the cause of many shipwrecks. Then there was "Little Granny Squannit" whom no one ever saw, but it was believed that she lived along the shoreline. It was customary, when going out gathering plants, fishing or hunting to leave some bread and meat in a small basket somewhere along the shore for "Granny" to ensure "Good Luck." It was not uncommon to hear a fisherman remark "Old Moshup and Granny must be fighting because the sea is awful rough this morning."

A brief visit with friends to the Island a few years ago found the people and Cliffs as charming as back in 1928.

Jayne Fawcett
(b. 1936)

Jayne Fawcett is a lifelong resident of Uncasville and a grandmother of six. She received her undergraduate degree from the University of Connecticut and a fifth-year degree from Eastern Connecticut State University. She has served as vice chair of the Mohegan Tribal Council and chair of the Mohegan Council of Elders, as tribal ambassador, and as a tour guide at Tantaquidgeon Museum. For twenty-seven years she taught school in Montville and Ledyard, Connecticut, and she served as the first president of the Montville Indian Parent Committee, which secured the right for Mohegan Indian schoolchildren not to be bussed out of their community. She has served on numerous advisory boards, including for the Smithsonian and the Institute for American Indian Studies. She was also a board member of the United South and Eastern Tribes and a presidential appointee of President Bill Clinton. Selected by Falmouth Institute as an outstanding woman leader, she is included in their video series. The following poems are original publications.

Homeland

As a child I heard my father's mother talking about "going back to Canadie" whenever things went wrong. "Canadie" was her homeland. Where was mine? I knew the Irish could go back to Ireland, the English to Great Britain, and the blacks had a whole continent. Where was my home, my safe place?

Where is My World
My Kingdom Come,
The Home my lineage can claim as own for all their little whiles,
And passing say, "Your oyster, son,
This is the Heritage I give; bear it before you like a shield;
It will protect, oh, precious, someday ones, from all the sneering spears
Your heart may feel;
You're not alone."
Where is My Home?

A hundred and a hundred years ago I searched with ancient kin
The way to know,
But it was lost, and I lost too
In pathless woods unknown.
Wherein an owl cried,
And finally the lonely wolf replied,
"Pretend."
My Kingdom is, I find,
Pretending in quiet woodlands
Of my mind.

Attic Dawn

(There were a lot of old attics in Mohegan, and I found them fascinating.)

Half light finds a dreary aerie
Vacuuming a darkened floor.
Dusty shadows filter wary, errant beams across the door.
Quiet rest tomorrow's treasures with the nightmares of today;
Sliding spider, tireless, measures emptiness in silken whey.
Half light creeps,
And beetles tremble,
Wanders wisplike;
Wanders fey;
Peaceful nightdreams all dissemble
With the crushing rush of day.

Pan's Song

This poem was published in the *August Derleth Society Newsletter* by my husband and was a favorite of horror writer and poet Frank Belknap Long.

Once upon a hollow tube
Blazoned with a fairy-ring,
I watched a disappointment slip
Upon a hope of spectral string.

Its end, inevitable and just,
To rise and fall,
Up,
    To and fro;
Then downward it would go again, and
Go, and
    Go, and
        Go, and
           Go,
As flowered grief did pipe to it,
And plaintively a heart-song sing.
While deep in happiness I sat,
And plucked upon the fairy-ring.

Shantok

Side by side we lie together
Rotting in the dust,
My silent friends and enemies
Who hold the past in trust.
With frozen lid and vacant eye
We share camaraderie
With bone and must and sepulcher,
Worked stone and pottery,
And life is but a whisper passing
Softly, swiftly by,
A lullaby of restless winds, a broken dream, a sigh.

Faith Damon Davison
(b. 1940)

Faith Davison claims to be a "late bloomer." She and her youngest son received their bachelor's degrees in the same year, but from different colleges. She has worked at a multitude of jobs—from selling live bait and pumping gas, to arranging and cataloging over one hundred thousand images that were digitized at a major American museum, to driving oxen. Having earned a master of library science degree, she built the Mohegan Library and Archives, including rare books, documents, and map collections and the tribe's three-dimensional collections. She has been a frequent contributor to the tribal publication *Wuskuso* and has published numerous historical pamphlets for the library and archives, as well as several essays in the Norwich Historical Society's *9-Mile Square*. Davison retired in the summer of 2010, with plans to start work on a Ph.D. and tend to her luxuriant garden. Her selections here belong to a long regional indigenous tradition of food and recipe-writing. The recipes below are being published here for the first time.

Mohegan Food

As you probably know, before the settlers came, we didn't have butter, milk, cheese, beef, or lamb or pork. Nor did we have chicken. But we did have turkey, duck, geese, and venison, other game birds, and a whole lot of fish and shellfish. We lived on the shore in the summer, so we even dried and smoked fish and shellfish to preserve them for the winter. This saltwater bounty contributed the most protein to our diet. We would plant our corn near our summer villages so that we could care for the fields even while reaping the river's and ocean's reward. Massapeag was the one of the sites of our old cornfields.

We gathered fiddleheads and early sprouting skunk cabbage. We also dried the blueberries and wild strawberries and "fox" grapes to make our foods sweet. We collected cranberries from the area known as Miller's Pond and also from near the Ashbow cemetery.

We grew pumpkins, corn, field beans, squash, and some sunflower seeds. We also dried corn and parched acorn meat for a kind of flour. We had hazelnuts, butternuts, walnuts, and chestnuts. We also ate the roots of the Jerusalem artichoke and the water lily.

For seasoning we had juniper berries and sassafras, as well as sweet bay, black birch, and many wild plants that most people today no longer use. We did not have salt in the abundance that is used today but we often used maple and birch sugar to make our meat and cakes tasty, as well as the rendered fats from raccoons and bear.

We made clambakes using hot rocks and seaweed for the steam; we boiled our meats by using hot stones dropped into watertight vessels. And, of course, we roasted and broiled things over an open fire. We made our corn cakes on flat rocks near the hot coals from our campfires. Our popcorn was roasted on the cob, but we had no butter to make it doubly tasty.

Breakfast was our main meal, but we'd eat it after being awake for a few hours, and it could be of anything filling—not just cereals. Then we'd snack all day and have a light meal before bedtime. We always had a pot of some kind of food on the fire in case guests dropped in. If there was any food to be had in a village, no one would go hungry. Along with succotash (beans, corn, and whatever else we could put in the pot), we made *yokeag* (dried, parched cornmeal mixed with fat) and journey cakes. With a little imagination, you could be eating the same soup your grandmother ate when she was a girl.

Corn

ROASTED CORN IN HUSK

1. Peel down husks to expose kernels but do not detach—remove silk.
2. Rub kernels with oil or butter.
3. Turn up husks over the greased ear. Then soak in cold water.
4. Place corn on grill rack set as close as possible to the charcoal or gas flame. Roast for 20 to 25 minutes.

BOILED CORN

Plunge shucked ears of corn into pot of boiling water. Take out 6 minutes after it boils again.

JOURNEY CAKES
This recipe is quick and good!

2 cups water
2 cups cornmeal
2 teaspoons salt
2 tablespoons butter (We probably used animal grease.)
½ cup dried fruit (cranberries, blueberries, cherries) or chopped nuts

Preheat oven to 375. Bring water to a boil in a saucepan. Stir in cornmeal, salt, butter, and berries or nuts. Place in the bottom of a greased 8-in. square pan and bake for 25 minutes. Cut into squares and serve. Serves 6 to 8.

CORN PUDDING

Cook 2 cups of fresh corn kernels in ½ cup of light cream 15 minutes or so, or use a can of creamed corn.

2 eggs
¼ cup flour
1 teaspoon salt
½ teaspoon pepper
2 cups creamed corn
2 tablespoons melted butter
1 can (14½ oz.) evaporated milk

Preheat oven to 300.
In a medium-sized bowl, beat eggs with a whisk, slowly beating in four, salt, and pepper. Then add corn, butter, and milk, blending well.
Pour batter into 1½-qt. buttered casserole. Place casserole in oven over a hot pan of water.
Bake for 75 minutes or until a knife inserted into casserole comes out clean. Sprinkle with nutmeg if desired. Serve it hot.

SUCCOTASH

3 tablespoons of butter or minced salt pork
1 small onion, chopped
1½ cups shell beans (streaked, pintos, etc.)
1½ cups fresh corn kernels
½ cup water
½ teaspoon pepper
½ cup cream

In a large skillet, melt butter, or brown up minced salt pork until it gives up its fat. Add onion and cook until translucent.
Add beans, corn, water, and pepper. Cook, covered, for 10 or 15 minutes. Stir in cream and cook 5 minutes more. Serve hot.

Variations on the theme would be to add chunks of rabbit or fowl. You can also add sliced Jerusalem artichokes for extra flavor and to make a thicker consistency. There are no rules.

Beans

Leather Breeches, or Dried Long Green Beans
In the old days, green beans were strung and hung to dry in the sun. When hanging, they resembled breeches. Once dried, the beans would last until the next harvest. They were soaked in cold water before being used in stews and soups. Too tough to use as a side dish!

When the Pilgrims first landed at Cape Cod, they dug up dried corn and bean caches, holes in the sandy soil that had been lined with tightly woven mats to keep the contents dry. This food helped them survive through the winter.

THREE BEAN CASSEROLE

1 lb. dried soldier beans or great northern beans
1 lb. dried lima or pea beans
1 lb. dried kidney beans or black-eyed peas
1 large onion, chopped

1 clove garlic
½ cup catsup or tomato puree
1½ tablespoons cider vinegar
1 teaspoon dry mustard
¼ cup maple syrup
3 strips bacon

Pick through dried beans for any foreign objects. Put into large pot and
boil for 2 hours. Drain.
Preheat oven to 350.
Combine everything with the exception of the bacon strips in a large casserole. Lay the bacon strips on top. Bake for 90 minutes. Serve hot.

Squash

SQUASH SOUP

1 onion, chopped
2 tablespoons butter
2 cups chicken broth
Cooked pulp of 1 large butternut squash
1 cup apple cider
Salt to taste

Cook onion in butter until translucent.
Mix onion, squash, and ½ cup of broth in blender until pureed.
Pour pureed mixture into large kettle and add remaining broth, cider,
and salt. Heat and serve hot. Add some whipped sweet cream for looks
and taste.

CRANBERRY-STUFFED ACORN SQUASH

4 small acorn squash
1½ cups whole fresh or frozen cranberries
½ cup applesauce
½ teaspoon grated orange peel

½ cup maple or brown sugar

3 teaspoons hazelnut oil

Preheat oven to 350.

Cut each squash in half, seed, and trim ends so the halves will stand up in a baking dish.

Bake squash, skin side up, in the oven for 35 minutes.

Remove squash from oven and let cool.

Combine cranberries, applesauce, orange peel, sugar, and oil. Spoon mixture into the hollows of the squash halves.

Return squash, filling side up, to oven and bake for about 30 minutes. Serve immediately. Can be augmented with dollops of whipped heavy cream.

Pumpkin, like winter squash, can be used in a variety of ways—boiled, roasted, dried in thin slices and then ground like cornmeal. Pumpkin shells were used to cook the contents and serve with, and the seeds were roasted for a snack. Pumpkins were also stuffed with meats or other goodies after the seed cavity was emptied and then cookeJd beside the fire.

STUFFED PUMPKIN

1 medium onion, minced

1½ lb. ground meat

2 cups cooked wild rice

2 eggs, lightly beaten

½ cup chopped parsley

Salt & pepper to taste

1 small pumpkin with a lid cut off, cleaned and seeded

Preheat oven to 350.

Sauté onion and meat until browned.

Combine all ingredients except pumpkin in a large bowl.

Fill pumpkin with mixture and replace lid.

Put pumpkin in a baking pan filled with 1 inch of water.

Bake for 1½ to 2 hours, or until tender. Let stand 15 minutes before carving. Then remove lid and cut into slices.

Wild Rice

Wild rice isn't really rice at all, but the seeds of a marsh grass that grows around the freshwater lakes in the northern areas of our country. Each family has a place to harvest this bounty, and every family member helps in the laborious processing.

WILD RICE

1 cup wild rice
4 cups water
½ teaspoon salt
2 tablespoons butter
1 cup thinly sliced mushrooms
2 whole scallions, minced
2 teaspoons each dried parsley, sage, basil, thyme
Pepper to taste

Combine rice, water, and salt in a 3-qt. saucepan. Bring to a boil, reduce heat to medium, cover, and cook until the liquid is absorbed (about 45 to 60 minutes).

While rice is cooking, melt butter in a skillet, add mushrooms, and sauté until tender. Then add scallions and herbs and cook for 2 to 3 minutes more. Remove from heat.

Remove rice from heat and let rest for 5 minutes.

Fluff rice with a fork and stir in the other cooked ingredients.

Like the other recipes here, don't be afraid to try variations of ingredients. Use whatever is good and plentiful!

Seafood

STEAMED FISH AND WILD RICE

6 oz. wild rice
1 cup water
2 cups broth

2 large bay leaves

6 juniper berries

⅛ teaspoon each cloves, ginger, paprika

1½ lbs. of any mild fish, such as flounder, cod, buckies (shad), etc., cleaned and boned

Cook the wild rice in water and 1 cup of the broth.

While rice is cooking, put the rest of the ingredients except for the fish in the bottom of a large steamer. Bring to boil. Reduce heat and keep broth at a simmer.

Put fish in the steamer tray above the broth. Cook about 5 to 10 minutes, until fish flakes.

Serve over hot cooked rice.

CLAM OR MUSSEL CHOWDER

Shuck enough quahogs or mussels for 1½ pts. of meat, reserving and straining the juices. Chop up pieces that are too large.

3 oz. salt pork, minced

1 large onion, chopped

4 large cooked potatoes, peeled and sliced at an angle, then chopped (the thinner bits are going to dissolve and add starch to thicken up the broth)

A pinch each of sage and thyme

3 cups of broth, plus the strained juices of the shellfish

Brown off the minced salt pork until all the grease is rendered.

Add chopped onion and cook until translucent.

Add potatoes, seasonings, and shellfish meat.

Add broth and juices. Let cook gently on the back of the stove until serving. Make a double batch; day-old chowder is really good.

STEAMED MUSSELS

Remove the beards and steam up twice as many mussels as you think you will need for appetizers. Remove the top shells and spoon lemon butter and minced garlic over the meat in the bottom shells. If you are preparing ahead, at this point you will put in oven-proof trays, cover, and refrigerate. Heat (or reheat) under the broiler for a couple of minutes without burning the mussels. Then serve. Stand back—everyone loves these.

A variation could be steaming them in white wine and serving with shallot butter. Remember, Native Americans took advantage of all resources available to them.

Stephanie M. Fielding
(b. 1945)

Stephanie Fielding's aboriginal roots are in Connecticut in the East and Hawaii in the West. She has lived and traveled all over the world, including Baton Rouge, where she wrote for five city magazines, and Denver, where she wrote for another magazine. Fielding finally settled in Mohegan, where she became determined to help resurrect the Mohegan language. To this end, she earned an MA in linguistics at MIT, wrote the Mohegan grammar, compiled a dictionary, and built the *Mohegan Language Project* website. In 2008 she was elected to the tribe's Council of Elders. Fielding is the mother of three grown children and has five young grandchildren. She is the great-granddaughter of the late Mohegan chief Occum/Lemuel Fielding. The following pieces are original to this volume.

Remembrance

Rama sat up straight in bed. Eyes, wide open, looking into the dark. Tears coursing down her cheeks. It was a dream . . . only a dream. The relief was incredible, but she couldn't stop the tears. She put her face in her hands and sobbed.

"What's wrong, honey?" asked her husband, sitting up in bed and putting his arms around her. He was worried; she never cried. "Bad dream?"

She nodded, still weeping. He was relieved.

"Tell me about it."

"It was Cori. She walked by with her friends—she was about nine—and she didn't recognize me."

Muggy smiled but tried to quench it so she couldn't hear his smile in the dark. "But Cori's only six months old and she knows you already."

"I know. But I want her to always remember me."

"There is no way she's going to forget you. It was only a dream; let's go back to sleep."

Muggy snuggled Rama against his chest and finally the sobs stopped, her breathing evened, and more pleasant dreams filled her sleeping mind.

The next day at work, after debriefing his inspectors, Muggy called his daughter, mother of Cori, and set up their next visit. Stephie was happy to take a few days in Honolulu; the sugarcane town of Pahala on the southern tip of the Big Island of Hawaii was a little too quiet for her city-girl blood.

~

Of course, Cori never forgot her grandmother and grandfather. The monthly trips from Hawaii, the presents, the cards, the phone calls all were reminders of her much-loved grandparents. And when Cori, her mom, dad, and baby brother, Bill, moved to Pennsylvania the visits continued, though not as frequently, and everything else remained constant, including the memory of her grandparents. Her grandfather, who was known as one of the meanest men in Honolulu, was putty in her hands. He may have closed down a hundred bars, raided a presidential campaign fund-raising party, and arrested the governor's son for underage drinking, but he was a pussycat with his little granddaughter. If you walked into their house and it smelled like chocolate chip cookies, you knew Grandpa could be given the credit. Grandma hadn't cooked for nearly twenty years now. Instead she herded models and would-be movie stars. She also taught people to stand on their heads, increase their psychic abilities, and practice alternative healing processes. Both of them were totally unforgettable.

The irony, of course, was that the forgetting started nearly thirty years later, but it was not on Cori's part. That mysterious and dreaded disease, multi-infarct dementia, started stealing her grandmother's memory a piece at a time.

Rama and Muggy had moved to Connecticut along with their youngest son, Leo, to reestablish a connection with Rama's tribe, the Mohegans. In Connecticut they called her by her given name, Margery, variations thereof, or Leading Cloud, her Indian name. She wanted them to know that she was a healer, a contribution to the community, but the dementia was chipping away at her abilities and she couldn't sustain her classes or gather a following. Her beautiful presence was felt and appreciated at the powwows and outreach events. Her peaceful face framed by her flowing white hair was the perfect complement to her red buckskin regalia. But she was no longer recognized for her accomplishments.

After a while Stephie, now free of pesky husbands and enjoying her children as adults, joined them and, two years later, their oldest son, Pat, arrived. One evening as the five of them sat for dinner, a giddy realization passed over them that their nuclear family was reunited and, as Margery and Muggy approached their sixtieth wedding anniversary, all their children were separated but not yet divorced from their second spouses. An odd coincidence that only four of them saw any humor in. Margery couldn't follow most trains of thought far enough for any humor to emerge.

One day as Margery and Stephie were having lunch away from the house, Margery said, "That man . . ." She searched for his name but couldn't find it. "The one that lives downstairs."

"You mean Pat?"

"Yeah, him. Who is he?"

"That's Pat. Your son, Pat," Stephie answered, shocked.

"I don't think so," she said. "Pat is different from him. I think he's only pretending to be Pat."

"No," said Stephie gently, "it's Pat . . . our Pat."

After that Margery referred to Pat as *cousin*. She didn't say anything to him for fear his feelings would be hurt, but the estrangement continued. After a while she understood that everyone had accepted this tall, red-faced man as her son, but she admitted in private that the bond was just not real to her; she could not make the mother connection with her oldest as she could with her other two children.

Stephie was nervous that those gaps would widen when the kids started to arrive for the sixtieth anniversary celebration. Hunter, Pat's son and the youngest of the grandchildren, was first to arrive. Margery didn't recognize him. He was branded as "the kid," and the poor, well-behaved grandson was constantly reprimanded for doing normal things . . . like reclining the recliner. Maybe part of it was that he matched none of the photos that were scattered around the house. Photos of proud grandparents holding their fifth and last grandchild, playing with the two-year-old in the pool, and watching the nine-year-old open birthday presents. He was fourteen now and looking incredibly like a blue-eyed version of his father at four-teen, but he was unrecognized as the loved little one.

Margery started to prepare for the coming of Cori months before she arrived. When Stephie spent a few nights with them and slept in "her" room, Margery was beside herself that Cori would arrive and there would be no place for her to sleep. The tension mounted as she protected her granddaughter's nest from intruders, real or imaginary.

Bill arrived with his new bride, Neoni. The warm grandmother welcome embraced them both, even though days before she couldn't remember that Bill was married. Amber, daughter of Pat and third-oldest grandchild, got a big welcome as well, but the one she was waiting for was Cori. Her brown-eyed, golden child; the first grandchild to be nestled in her arms. Stephie hid a secret concern that, because Cori had put on weight, she would be unrecognizable to her grandmother. But when Cori stepped out of the car, followed shortly by her younger but considerably bigger brother, Leroy, the anticipation was as complete as the recognition. There was no doubt who this was, and the love that flowed between them was as fluid as water.

Throughout the week people slipped away and had to be renamed.

"Who is that sitting in the corner?" she asked at one point.

"That's Leroy. My brother, your grandson," Cori responded without a twinge of consternation . . . as though it were a totally understandable question.

"Oh, yes, the handsome one." Leaving everyone to wonder, if Leroy was the handsome one, what was Bill? What was Hunter?

That night Cori and her grandma had a long conversation downstairs on Cori's bed. Grandma was lucid in her conversation, if not in her facts. She wouldn't leave Cori for fear that someone would come in during the night through the cooling screen door and steal this precious child away. She stayed up a good deal of the night guarding her grandchild, the first night she had spent away from her marriage bed in years. The next day she looked fragile and yellow. Everyone convinced her that Leroy could protect Cori and that she needn't be there during the night. She agreed, with relief.

Cori's warm attention continued throughout the visit, and, when Grandma was feeling better, they went to Shantok for a walk. They walked together in the Mohegan burial grounds, where visions became clear and feelings unspoken were brought to the tongue. The love was thick, and the protection that once flowed from grandmother to granddaughter now happily flowed in the opposite direction.

The last day, Grandma was looking well and happy. The confusion and weakness that encompassed her the first days the kids had gathered was gone. Leroy made a delicious dinner and everyone talked and played until, one by one, they went to bed.

Grandma and Grandpa awoke at six to say goodbye to Cori and Leroy. Grandma was fine until Leroy said, "I love you, Grandma," as he held her in his great embrace. The tears started and increased when Cori uttered the same words.

"Don't say that!" she scolded.

"Do you want us to say mean things to you now, so you'll stop crying?" Cori teased.

"No," she admitted, "that would make it worse."

"We do love you, Grandma—and Grandpa too. And we'll miss you and never forget you," said Cori.

"Me, too," Grandma managed to choke out. But everyone realized that the promise she made in those two words, she might not be able to keep in this world.

(2002)

The Hoop

The fire beckons through the night.
Ancestors and future generations
Stand darkly with the trees.

The dance begins.
The hoop is passed
From hand to hand.
Hearts beat with the drums.

Every hand touches the hoop.
Every heart embraces its meaning.
Every soul connects in rhythm.

The music gets louder.
The beat is faster.
Pass the hoop!
Keep it going!

Frantic feet pound the earth.
Protecting hands cling to the hoop.
Let it go! It must go faster!

The hoop leaps skyward
Out of earthly control!
Thirty-two hands reach for it!

Thirty-two feet jump for it!

Suddenly silence!

Its flight comes to an end.
The hoop lies broken on the ground.
Pieces burn in the fire.

Bring the hoop.
Collect the pieces.
We must fix it.
It is who we are.

It is impossible!
It's gone forever!
It's your fault!
It's your fault!

From the darkness
In the darkness
Steps Eliphalet, he who I carried,

"The hoop must live.
Only your blood can repair it."
He turns and reenters the past.

A warrior steps forward
Knife in hand
Blood flows from his arm
Covering the hoop.

The hoop lies broken.
Another sheds blood,
But the hoop remains broken.

Again and again
Blood is shed
In the name of unity,
But the hoop remains broken.

The last steps forward.
Her blood flows as well.
Magically the hoop is repaired.

It was you!
You should have gone first!
Too much blood was given!
Too much pain was suffered!

Stop the fighting!

It was everyone!
Everyone's sacrifice was needed.
The Tribe is the many, not the few.

Without the many
No glory could be gained
For the good of the all.
It is who we are.

Everything is possible.
We are here forever.
It is up to us.
All must rise.

In the darkness
The generations to come
Applaud in silence.
Our ancestor.

Sharon I. Maynard

(b. 1953)

Sharon I. Maynard's Mohegan name is Accomac, which means "long view across the water." Living in close proximity to Long Island Sound all of her life has given her an appreciation for the sea. Before serving on the tribe's Council of Elders, Maynard spent fifteen years working on board the ferries that travel from New London, Connecticut, to Orient Point, Long Island, New York. Her writings are a product of her experiences on board those iron workhorses. These are original contributions to this volume.

Long Island Sound

A longing
Something primal
Without definition
The wide expanse
And far off horizons
Scape ever changing
Predictable
Yet unpredictable
Ebb and flood
Tides low and high
Rhythmic
Timeless
Witness to all of time
From the very beginning
Extending into the future
Yet always present
Waves breaking
The breath of the giant beast
Sometimes gentle, as in sleep
Sometimes labored as in anger
Or passion

Often peaceful
But never at peace
In this place of eternity
Begins an adventure
A journey
Into waters familiar
Yet uncharted

(2010)

A Winter's Morn

When it was cold, it was very cold. The kind of cold where your nostrils stick together with every breath and every footstep is heard crisply and clearly. The kind of cold where the bottom of your glasses sticks to the tops of your cheeks.

Early in the morning on a cold winter's day, the sunrise is miraculous in its arrival. It is reflected in the ice film on the water.

There is a steady clank, clank, clank of the pulley hitting against the flagpole. The flag is flapping gently but soon will be snapping as the sun reaches higher in the sky, awakening the wind and waves.

As the first ferry slips across the sound, plumes of sea smoke rise and hang in the air. Now and then a harbor seal bobs in the icy water, peering with giant baby eyes at the passing boat.

Ice hangs from the ramp and the control box where the potable water source sprays and drips down the frosty steel.

Small sparrows stop and drink from the only fresh water not frozen by the cold air.

Seagulls, impervious to the air temperature, fly aimlessly overhead, searching for the now-sparse morsels of anything edible, as all the tourists have long fled the now-icy shore.

A layer of ice still coats the bow and the rails, waiting for the crew to break it up and push it overboard. Too much ice makes the vessel top-heavy and unstable. Freezing spray is unavoidable during many of the crossings.

It seems that there are only three kinds of winter days: a day that is the calm before the storm, then the day of the storm, then the third day, when the storm clears out and the wind blows terrifically. The pattern repeats itself over and over until spring mercifully takes over and the calmer waters of late May and early June finally arrive.

Of course, this is the general pattern. There is no way to fully predict what each day will bring New England, and particularly southern New England, weather being what it is. The snow/rain line, a rogue wave here and there (yes, they exist), variable visibilities, and secondary low-pressure systems forming off the coast that team up with a myriad of other meteorological conditions provide not only challenges and dangers but also high adventure and entertainment in the form of sea tales that grow larger with each telling. It is good to remember that wave height is equal to observed height divided by two.

Many stories are factual, though, and the telling of them somehow relieves the anxiety of the experience. It is cathartic. Hearing the tale convinces you that it did indeed happen. It happened the way you remember it, and it was not some awful dream. It is small wonder to me, after experiencing some of the crossings, that sailors drink. And I have yet to find any of those men not to have a firm belief in something greater than themselves—converted by some powerful and/or frightening incident at sea.

These experiences—of winter morns at sea—are usually shared, and these shared moments join everyone, not surprisingly, together in a kind of camaraderie and brotherhood that is hard to replicate under ordinary circumstances. You never forget those people, nor they you.

(2010)

William Donehey

(b. 1955)

Bill Donehey grew up in Boston, Massachusetts, during the turbulent 1960s. After completing his three-year commitment to the U.S. Army in the early 1970s, Donehey drove across the country solo, writing and reading his works along the way at small-town gathering spaces and big-city open mikes. Donehey is well known as a writer at Mohegan, having been published locally, in addition to publishing pieces in *Writers Digest*, Poetry.com, and other outlets. He published a chapbook in 1977, *Whispers in Silence: The Interior Documentum*, using what he calls parallax poetry—interlinking poems that tell one story of his life and the memorable people of the street and high society that he has met. Now living in southeastern Connecticut, Donehey works for Mohegan Sun, the second-largest casino in the world, teaching and conducting seminars in process and performance improvement. He has contributed the following poems from his personal collections.

River

Set your heart upon a river
Let it float to places it's never been
Don't cheat yourself of feelings never felt
Draw again
From the hand you've been dealt

The source of pride
That wells inside
Denies
Thoughts materialized
Two hearts collide
From the remains you decide
Is it love or
Just filling the void inside

His Lover

Street man walks with hurried pace
Sunken eyes within a weathered face
Seeking solitude to engage in lovers' embrace
Caressing the bottle, kisses he tastes
His partner lies empty, beside him she waits
To be disposed of
Tossed in regretful haste
Discarded among collected waste
How many dreams has she chased?
The streets fill with the warmth of the day
Crosswalks make for his daily pay
Ambling from car to car
Hand extended
Spare change for food, maybe a candy bar
The light changes; the traffic must heed
Young man offers some sweet-smellin' weed
Street man refuses, "That I don't need"
Coins in the pocket, enough by now
He can tell by the weight
And thanks them all with a bow
Street man walks with hurried pace
Anticipating eyes within a weathered face
To encounter another lover's embrace; for her kisses he waits

Spirit Teacher

When I feel my heart beat
Within these silent walls
Echoing
Echoing
Lullabied to sleep
You come and fill my dreams
Awakening my spirit to walk the night

Gathering stars, bathing in moonlight
Free as never before
Will this time end
Can we pass through dream's open door
Walk with me
That we may grow
Walk with me
There are so many things
I wish to know

Freedom

As you stood on the edge of a feather
Expecting to fly
I stood alone wondering if I should wave goodbye
Or if I should run to a mountain top
To try and touch you as you go by

Where will you go . . .
What will you see . . .
Who will you be . . .

When you arrive and knock upon Freedom's door
Keeper of dreams and visions now yours
Freedom reveals what they said,
"Two spirits within you reside
One Jekyll, one Hyde"
Truth is, you reflect their darkness
Deep inside.

Lessons taught to me, bands playing in my head
I can only give what you ask for
Nothing less, nothing more
It's your dance
Take the floor
Lift your feet up off the ground
It's time to soar

Thoughts of yesterday
Future to come
Freedom's words
A new song to be sung

The Course of Love

Don't think you can direct the course of love
For love
If it finds you worthy
Directs your course

Sparrow

I journeyed to the land where the sparrow is king
Across mountains whose peaks
Grasp a sea of clouds in marriage
The halo for a king
My journey became one of torment
Saved by the sparrow, to rest upon her wing
She told of another life where people talk of wisdom
And how children still laughed, still would sing
We traveled many miles through canyons
Across deserts finally to the sea
The sparrow became my friend
Through the lessons she sang to me
She taught me the beauty of art
Through the eyes of wonder
Taught me of courage
With a voice of thunder
Laughter from a broken heart
When morning came
I rose from my bed
The silence of dawn crashing

The emptiness within my room filled
With the song of the sparrow
Ringing in my head

Again

Temper and disdain
The fractured mind believes it's whole
In cadence of respeak
Fragmented words unfold
Disillusioned by trepidation
Stories retold just to repeat
Now safe between the lines
Reading from page four to one
Recant and recount
The story is never done

Joe Smith
(b. 1956)

Joe Smith grew up in the Mohegan area of Uncasville. He is the son of Norma (Schultz) Smith and William J. Smith, grandson of Loretta F. Schultz (1900–82), and great-grandson of Chief Matahga (1862–1942). He was surrounded by a large family of Mohegan aunts, uncles, and cousins during his youth, and he served as the organist at the Mohegan Congregational Church during his high school years. Following his education at the Mohegan Elementary School and Montville High School, he attended Columbia University, where he earned a B A in English and an M FA in film history. He wrote for the *Columbia Daily Spectator* between 1975 and 1978 and also published in *Premiere* magazine.

After working in the film business in New York and Los Angeles, Smith returned to the Mohegan homeland in 2003, where he now works for the Tribal Communications Department, overseeing the production of the tribe's weekly newsletter, *Wuskuso*. "Fade into White" is being published here for the first time.

Fade into White

My mother hovers at the edge of the frame of the photograph—white, like a ghost. It hangs now in my dining room, rescued from a Native American past that grows faint in the wake of one of the world's biggest tribal casinos—but for me and many others, it's a past that will never disappear. The rest of the people in the picture are in color—not in a literal sense in this black-and-white photograph perhaps, but I can imagine the earthy tan shades punctuated by splashes of black, red, white, blue—maybe even purple. They were Indians. She did not want to be.

The town of Uncasville, Connecticut, is named after the famed sachem Uncas of the Mohegan Tribe, a man whose life has been popularized and heavily fictionalized. As I made my way in the world, the name of my place of origin inevitably got a blank stare or a giggle from a new friend or acquaintance. Sometimes there would be a glimmer of recognition from those who might have boned up on their James Fenimore Cooper.

At one time Uncasville must have been a great wild watery forest—on the banks of a river, near Long Island Sound, and not far from the Atlantic

Ocean. Some Mohegans must have braved those many waters—some even sailed to England in the seventeenth century to petition the Crown for the land. Others stayed put and were probably most content with familiar territory in the state that is often called—with a trace of derision—the Land of Steady Habits. In the very late part of the twentieth century, the tribe's lands were invaded by a new breed of men—moguls and managers of the gaming industry near and far. Mohegan Sun was the result, and the tribe will never be the same. The land that was once home to a stinking chicken roost in the summertime, and a nuclear parts factory in the Nixon era, is now a pleasure dome.

Back to the lady in the picture. As a child, she was fair-haired in more ways than one. Born to a Native and Irish American mother and a Swiss immigrant father, she emerged as a towheaded baby—courtesy of the genetic lottery. This set her apart from her darker siblings, and her father singled her out as his Aryan Princess. He reserved a ruder name for the other children. This family unit didn't hold together, needless to say.

But on the day that the picture was taken seven decades ago, the Indians on Mohegan Hill were having their annual summer celebration. The celebration was in sight of the church that the white Christian missionary Sarah Huntington had built in 1832 with three Mohegan women, just one part of a long line of matriarchal rule in the tribe that continues to this day. My mother lived in a Cape Cod house just a stone's throw from that church, and I try to imagine the ruckus that took place when Norma—the youngest daughter of Loretta Fielding Schultz—refused to put on her Indian regalia (her eldest sister, Roberta, was quick to remind people: "It is not a costume!"). As the husband and sons who lived with her later in life well knew, when Norma dug in her heels, you just best get out of the way and run for cover. I can imagine the little brow furrowing, the eyes flashing with anger, the head shaking with an emphatic no.

I try to imagine what her own mother thought that day. Born in 1900, Loretta Fielding Schultz was known for high spirits, friendliness, and generosity of time and spirit. All of her children are in the photograph, along with a cousin named Donnie, and she stands over them protectively. Little Norma has chosen to stand apart from that protective shade, to stand out in the bleeding, bleaching sunlight. Her white father is not in the picture at all, so in a way she chose to join him, to continue to be his Princess. She was unto herself, the "white" child in a white dress devoid of decoration or color. While standing to the right of the others, she stares into the camera. The viewer might read a wealth of emotions into a facial expression that is angry yet frightened, defiant but sheepish. She seems to fear the people around her, and to consciously stand apart. Whether the motive is self-protection or self-expression is hard to tell. Maybe she just wants to fade into white.

The holding back, the separateness of that moment, remained. When the Native American movement picked up steam in the 1970s, and when the Mohegans started mobilizing in the 1990s, Norma always held fast to her belief that "I Am Not An Indian," or, when she was in a more expansive and angry mood, "We Were Never Indians." She spoke for herself and presumed to speak for others—including her own sons. She would not include our names on the tribal rolls, and we were reinstated by the intervention of her siblings. When the casino became a reality and the promise of money came with it, she would have no part of the profits made off of those "boozing, gambling fools." (I couldn't add smoking to that list, since that was her Achilles heel, and the habit that eventually killed her.)

The evidence of her racial heritage was all around her—literally. To the left of her house was the Indian museum started by her cousins, the Tantaquidgeons. To the right of her house was that looming church steeple and the bell that rang and still rings to bring the Mohegans to church. Place-names all over her neighborhood and in the neighboring towns referred to the tribe. But she was her own person—as she so often said when I was growing up, "I Am An Individual," which is often taken to mean that you are not a member of the tribe—and she held to that idea literally and figuratively.

Growing up and standing separate from her brothers and sisters, perhaps she preferred to believe in those pop-culture images at the movies to define her race—those villainous, savage "redskins" who tried to knock John Wayne off his horse on the plains and in the desert. When confronted with the sight of a real-life Indian of the Southwest during a cross-country auto trip with my father during the 1950s, she locked the car door in fear. Oh no, she wasn't one of those Indians, that's for sure. But what if the man near the car had recognized something in her—some kind of kindred look, some remaining genetic connection between them that went back hundreds and hundreds of years? Would she have denied it? She was from the forest land of the Northeast, but she would be unlikely to tell you she was from a forest tribe. Perhaps she would have preferred to have been from the European forests that gave rise to her father—her fondness for Strauss waltzes and *The Sound of Music* certainly indicates a strong strain of favoring one side of her heritage and denying the other.

Nowadays, we might use a lot of D words to describe this behavior—"denial," "dysfunction," "depression." These are words that would have been foreign to her ears; she was a believer in God, but not in Freud.

For the son who carries on the memory of this peculiar behavior, all sorts of emotions are evoked by it. There is anger, there is sadness, there is even compassion, as all of us who grow to adulthood struggle to let go of blame and realize the terrible errors we can all make in relationships with our families. It is tempting to tie this all up with a neat little Freudian bow—to blame the racial divisions created by her father—but I have to believe there is another side to that, a certain pioneering spirit that sought to find its own way. It's the sort of spirit I inherited that propelled me away from Uncasville, only to return many years later, bound by a powerful connection that I am unable to explain.

By definition, a tribe is composed of members who feel they belong there—by blood, by circumstance, by sensibility. Although she connected to and cared about her family—her tribe, if you will—my mother was not afraid to stand alone in her white dress. For me, the memory does not fade.

(2009)

Melissa Tantaquidgeon Zobel

(b. 1960)

Melissa Tantaquidgeon Zobel is the tribal historian and medicine woman for the Mohegan Tribe. After receiving a BSFS in history/diplomacy from Georgetown University and an MA in history from the University of Connecticut, she traveled throughout New England as a storyteller for the tribe. In 1992 she won the first annual nonfiction award of the Native Writers' Circle of the Americas for *The Lasting of the Mohegans*, based on her research for the Mohegans' federal recognition case, which was successful in 1994. Shortly after that Zobel became the first American Indian appointed to the Connecticut Historical Commission. Zobel has written a biography, *Medicine Trail: The Life and Lessons of Gladys Tantaquidgeon*, and two novels, *Oracles: A Novel* and *Fire Hollow*. Her first young adult novel, *Great Bear Blues*, will be released in 2015. "The Window" is an original contribution to this volume.

The Window

Let me tell you about my morning.

The new moon hung low in the February sky, like a sickle or an icy smile. *Never wish on a new moon. Never view a new moon through a window pane. Never hunt on a new moon.* I heard those superstitions over and over again, growing up on the Mohegan Reservation in Connecticut. I ignored them. I was more interested in things that were real, like the woods. It was a good thing too; the other sixteen-year-old boys refused to include me in their snow snake contests, snowball fights, and other winter fun. My mother said it was because they thought our family was cursed, just because a couple of men disappeared on hunting trips.

Whenever my mother mentioned my father's final hunting trip back in 1909, her sparkling Indian eyes dulled down to lumps of coal and she said something creepy, like, "The devil is as smooth as glass." I did not believe in her white man's devil, or in my father's Great Spirit either. I believed in things you can touch and smell, like the woods.

But my mother didn't allow me to hunt in those woods. So before she woke up, I grabbed my axe along with the shotgun she kept by the door to ward off hobos. The week-long blizzard had mostly died down and it was at least fourteen degrees when I pushed out into the breaking dawn. It took forever to plough through the snow-heaped trails past the main cluster of reservation homes. It was a miracle that some of the older shacks remained standing after so much wild weather. I found myself picturing those frozen hills covered with old-time wigwams. Then I imagined them dotted with western tepees, painted with buffalo, elk, bear, and any other enormous game that can feed you for months.

Upon entering Hoscott's Woods on the edge of our territory, I was greeted by a skin-and-bones red fox pawing its way out of the crusted entrance to its den and a jittery woodpecker chipping ice crystals off the hole to its nest. Those crackling sounds reminded me of my mother's fried pork rinds, crisping up in the cast-iron pan on our wood stove. I had not heard that sound since we sold off the last of our livestock at the New London County Fair last August. That day, I recall my mother pointing to a man with smoky gray curls in a bright-green suit and saying to me, "You remember Mister Church. Go see him about a job, and never mind what your late father said about him." I was eleven when my father disappeared, and I did not recall him ever saying much about Church. Although he did often claim that wearing green was a sure sign of wickedness. Maybe that's why he always insisted that my eyes were hazel.

I never did talk to Church that day at the fair. Instead, I entered the hatchet-throwing contest and split the crimson bull's-eye right down the middle. The man in charge slapped a ten-dollar bill in my hand. My mother adjusted her fake pearls and said, "Looks like your father taught you at least one useful thing." Indeed, he did. After that, I did not hear another word from her about Mister Church—until yesterday, right before I smashed her Mason jar.

It was a good thing for me to get out of the house today after all that fuss, even if there was hardly any strength left in my shrunken arms and legs. As the clouds drifted across the frozen new moon, I considered what their shapes meant. A snake, an owl. Both were signs of trouble. Truthfully, I had hoped to see something I could eat, like a deer. One cloud did look kind of like a fish. The frigid wind sliced my cheeks and I swear it sounded like it was saying "sssoup, sssoup." I clutched my thin, gray flannel jacket around my neck. Every time I exhaled, a ghostly, frozen fog surrounded me.

I heard a sudden shriek and spotted a frosty-cheeked young boy on the trail ahead. His scrawny back and shoulders were all loaded down with a net and pole and cutting tools for ice fishing on the Thames River. He was shaking his head as hard as he could and staring at me like he had seen a ghost. I had no idea what I looked like because I had broken the only mirror in our house last month. Yet I did know that my wrists were no wider than my hatchet handle. Whatever I looked like, the fishing boy did not take his bulging eyes off me. So I turned down a different path, hoping not to frighten him further. The wind picked up and began to howl and my flannel jacket ballooned like a sailcloth. It lifted me toward the blustery sky as if I were one of my mother's angels. Only the lead weight of her shotgun kept me earthbound. I tripped over what felt like a log beneath the snow, and the shotgun barrel vibrated in my frozen hands. It reminded me of how alive the hatchet felt right before I split open the skull of our dog, Wiggy.

A lame cottontail slapped its paws across the frozen earth, nearly losing its balance on a hard patch of ice. I raised my gun, imagining what he would look like surrounded by diced turnips, potatoes, carrots, and all the rest of the food I didn't have. I squinted to take aim and then dropped the barrel when I heard a splashing sound coming from right behind the rabbit. I worried that it might be a child, fallen through the ice, or, worse, another hunter after the same thing as me. Pushing through a dense tangle of icy grape vines, I discovered a wide-shouldered buck lapping up frigid water trickling from a spring. His breathing grumbled, like my empty stomach. I envisioned turning him into bowls of steaming venison stew, sliced rib roasts drizzled with gravy, and thick steaks broiling on an open flame. Arching his robust neck in my direction, he examined me, shook his antlers like I was not worth the bother, and leapt away. I followed that deer's trail as closely and quietly as I could, gasping every time I snapped a twig or crunched my boots too loudly in the snow. After slogging breathlessly up and down half a dozen pine-covered hills, I got stuck in a tangle of briars, or maybe it was bare huckleberry bushes, hidden beneath a deep snowdrift in the gully. The snowfall was picking up, and by the time I freed my wool trousers, the sky had turned white again. I stared at the spot where I imagined the new moon to be and wished that the snow would stop. As soon as I did, I remembered the old saying, *Never wish on a new moon.* Honestly, I do not believe those foolish old sayings, but they still pop into my head.

I could hear the sound of the buck moving, but where was he? Goddammit, if I did not lose sight of him. I spun around and around till I nearly toppled over, but he was nowhere to be seen—not that I could see anything else, either. I could barely raise my head, the snow battered me down so. My feet were numb and it felt like I was floating. I must have collapsed and blacked out, because I opened my eyes to see a tan, white-tailed backside leaping over me. The sight of that deer sent my heart pumping again. I used my gun as a crutch to pull myself to my feet and struggled to keep sight of the animal through the wall of white that surrounded me. The deer was headed toward something large and boxy in the distance. As I drew closer, I saw the hollowed-out ruins of an old stone house. One side of the building was fully open, where one of its rock walls had collapsed. The buck strutted through that open area and stopped in the very center of the house to nibble on a hearty rhododendron. I crept closer. From behind a stand of snow-flocked cedar, I watched him saunter about what might once have been a living room.

This elegant stone house was hardly the sort of place you expected to find in Mohegan territory. Its sizable cut-granite blocks were set with raised joints, far surpassing the work of our best tribal stonemasons. Such fine craftsmanship was rarely seen anymore, even in the mansions of the wealthy textile manufacturers, shipbuilders, and bankers in the town of Norwich. These masons had installed just the right mix of rust, pewter, and milk-colored rocks, with the odd three-cornered stone set in here and there for effect. The arched front doorway was capped with a particularly fine round stone, surrounded by well-chiseled, pie-shaped wedges that combined to produce the image of a cold, dark midwinter sun. There were half a dozen rectangular holes on each of the three remaining sides, where the original windows must have been. A single window on the first floor retained its frame and all six-over-six New English windowpanes. I brushed snow off the glass and the paint on the frame peeled back in thin gray curls that reminded me of something, only I could not say what.

Through the window I saw that the buck remained calm and I raised my shotgun from the ground to my shoulder. The barrel bumped into something that clinked. I looked down and saw a Mason jar with a rusted lid sitting on the window sill. The deer was unmoved by the noise so I inspected the object. The jar contained a paper with *my* name written on the outside! I pried open the lid with my pocket knife, almost collapsing from the effort. The note inside said,

My dear son,

I dreamed of shooting a great buck in this place. Your Grandpa Ned had the same dream, but he never returned from his hunt. Your grandmother said it was because he ran off with a bottle of whiskey. Your Aunt Win said that the devil took him for his own. I think he just got caught shooting a deer here, and somebody didn't like it. I think this because I saw it happen in this window. Remember that old story I used to tell you about The Devil's Window that could show your family's past? I thought it was an Indian fairy tale. Apparently not. In case his fate should befall me, I am leaving you this note, so you will know what happened to me, and why I did not take you hunting with me today. I hope to bring home venison for supper.

Your loving father, Jacob

P.S. Get the hell away from this window!

I shook the letter from my hand as though it were a copperhead. Every muscle in my body spasmed and ached.

"Your father abandoned us just like your grandfather abandoned him." That's what my mother always said. What I remembered most about my father was that he prayed to the Great Spirit more than most Mohegan Indians and that he was forever drawing the curtains shut. I thought it was because there were no windows in the old-time Mohegan wigwams and he preferred the old ways—unlike my mother. She often said, "There is nothing better than a new house with big, sunny windows." My father did not agree but he managed to pay for a modest house with two windows by hauling firewood for Mister Church at Bright Angel Trading Post, located less than half a day's walk from the reservation. Once I caught him dickering with my father over payment for a slab of salt pork. Church snapped at him, "All payment is up front! Nothing is free." My father left empty-handed and swore all the way home. Then he shot our horse, Ole Joke. Six weeks later, after we choked down the last of that poor creature's musty broth, my father announced that he planned to set out on his ill-fated hunting trip.

He was a man caught between the new and old ways of making a living. There was nothing left to hunt but he didn't have a trade. Thanks to men like Church, our reservation was rapidly becoming just like Norwich, a hubbub of fast business where men jabbered about the price of lumber and women gossiped about the value of their neighbor's newest household goods. I once heard some of those Mohegan gossips say that my grandfather served in the Union army for a full year before my father was born. I try not to think about that. They also claimed that my grandmother was half mad with hunger when he returned from the Civil War, which is why he turned back around and immediately went out hunting, still dressed in his Union blues. I hated the thought that my Grandpa Ned survived that war only to disappear on a damned hunting trip.

"Your father was a coward like your grandfather. That's why he ran away," my mother said more times than I could count. I remembered those words as I lifted the shotgun in the buck's direction and rubbed my finger up and down on the cold metal trigger. Now I knew that my father had not abandoned me and my mother. As I pulled the trigger I pictured the last thing we did together—my father and I—the night before he went hunting. Knee-weak with hunger, we had stumbled into the woods to build a fire. We chuckled as the flames roared and danced in the air, pushing and smacking at one another like young brothers. My mother had hollered at us, "Those flames would be better served inside our wood stove, roasting a chicken, or even a measly rabbit to fill my groaning stomach." My father mumbled back something about how flames needed to eat too, and he sprinkled a pinch of tobacco on the fire. I can still smell the delicious buttery smoke of that burning broadleaf.

The next part of this morning's story is embarrassing. I pulled the trigger on the buck and nothing happened. That's right. No shot fired from my gun. It appears that the hobos could have robbed us anytime they wanted, because my mother chose not to keep her gun loaded! The buck looked almost amused as he walked away. Of course, there was still the window left to consider. Standing before it with my empty shotgun, I wondered if my father had really seen anything in it or if he had simply let his imagination run wild. His tales about the Devil's Window included one in which a man saw his mother pour boiling water on his baby sister, whom he had been told died of scarlet fever. In another story, a girl watched her father lock her mother in a shed with a starving raccoon, and that same man claimed his wife had run off with a Bible salesman. It did occur to me that in both of those cases the person looking in the window could have simply been *remembering* the incidents, and that the window was not magic at all. Maybe my father remembered hearing what happened to his father as well. As I said, I am not superstitious.

Still, I peered hard into that window. At first, I saw nothing except the reflection of the new moon. *Never view a new moon through a window pane.* I snapped my eyes shut for a second when I recalled that saying. I am embarrassed to admit that I could not help it. When I reopened them I was startled by what I saw in that glass: the image of a man in green slapping an Indian woman to the floor, right beside a basket containing a baby with green eyes, or perhaps they were hazel. A rush of bile surged into my mouth and the gun slipped from my numb fingers. I bent down to pluck it from the snow and my hand touched a pile of what felt like frozen wool. I lifted the stiff clump of fabric and the air took on a faintly moldy smell, like an open grave. There lay a Union army belt buckle, a Spanish-American War medal, and two human skulls, each containing a single bullet hole. I stood back up and noticed a flash of green in the corner of my eye. I hastily turned to inspect it head on and tumbled backward. A bullet whistled past my ear and a thunderous explosion sent shards of glass and wood splinters flying everywhere. I grabbed the hatchet from my belt and threw it toward the origin of that shot. It thwapped through the air and landed with a dull thud, a sound I knew from the day I sent Wiggy back to his maker with that same ax. I ran away, glancing behind me only once. I should have been relieved to see nothing, except that I did not even see the stone house.

Charging through the deep snow set my chest afire. At least I wasn't cold anymore. The ice-fishing boy again crossed my path. This time he was struggling to carry a large stick, weighed down with half a dozen spotted northern pike. He saw me frantically prancing through the snow and his face froze into a weird expression that reminded me of the time my mother ate a bad button mushroom. I slowed down and made an effort to calm the twitching in my cheeks and approach him coolly. That sure paid off. He hastily untied half of his hefty catch, broke a limb off a nearby white birch, tied three fish onto that stick, and tossed it at me without a word. I reached out my trembling fingers, ready to carry my treasure home, proudly, like I was bearing the tribal eagle staff in the Norwich Memorial Day parade.

My mother must have been watching for me through the window. She rushed out into the snow and grabbed the fish-laden stick from me. "Thank God you were only fishing. I was afraid you'd gone hunting!" she said, hugging the stick. "This is beautiful, like one of those victory flags after the Spanish-American War!"

This was the first real food either of us had seen in days and here she was dragging the white man's wars into it! I snarled at her, just like I had done last night, right after I smashed her Mason jar. Honestly, I don't know if I broke that Mason jar just because I hated the sight of one more empty jar in our house or because it reminded me of that Mason guy who burned down a bunch of Indian wigwams, way back. The history books say my tribe helped him do it. Maybe we did. Of course, we were illiterate back then and didn't write down our version of the tale—which is why I am writing this one down for you. Now you'll know the true story of what happened to me, however crazy it sounds.

Anyway, after I broke that Mason jar last night, my mother sat down on the floor and patted the broken glass shards like they were diamonds. "Don't worry," she squawked, "it's not my good crystal. You can just speak to Mr. Church tomorrow about getting a job. He helped me out once before, while your father was away killing Spaniards in Cuba."

I snarled at her words and began to sharpen my hatchet, rubbing it with a whetstone till my knuckles cramped up. I pictured the last time I saw my father and tossed a pinch of tobacco into the fireplace in his memory. It isn't that I believe in the old Mohegan superstitions. Some of them are definitely horseshit. Take that old saying *Never hunt on a new moon*. I knew that the new moon would be out this morning, and that I would have good day hunting.

Indeed I did. Oh, indeed I did.

(2010)

Alysson Troffer

(b. 1960)

Born in Connecticut but currently living in Golden, Colorado, Troffer has worked for years in technical writing and editing. She has written for the *Mercury*, a newspaper based in Pottstown, Pennsylvania, and for the *Inner Door*, a publication of the Association for Holotropic Breathwork International. At present Troffer is writing her first book, about her experiences with Somatic Archaeology, an alternative, Native-influenced healing method that involves unearthing and healing the history in the body. Her great-grandfather Lemuel Occum Fielding served as tribal chief from 1903 to 1928. The following is published here for the first time.

The Little Girl on the Hook

Except for the last time I dreamed about the little girl, the dream always unfolds in the same way. I am in the basement, alone, heading toward the small closet with no door. It's that time again, time for me to check on her body and make sure she is okay. I reach into the closet and pull the string dangling from the lightbulb to illuminate the cool, clean, dry space that is empty, except for the dead little girl hanging on the wall. I visually inspect her. I do not touch her in any way.

The little girl is about four years old. She is motionless, hanging on a hook by the back of her short-sleeved dress. Trimmed with white lace, the dress is abloom with large pink and white flowers. Her arms and legs hang loosely, unrestrained, from her body. Her dark brown eyes are open partway, looking down, and her almost-black, wavy hair neatly frames her pretty, baby-soft face. In contrast to her pearl-white skin, her rosy cheeks are still aglow. I feel reassured, satisfied. She is indeed okay. I am adequately fulfilling my duty to take care of her, to keep her safe in this moisture-controlled and temperature-controlled space.

Then I wake up. The dream lingers long enough for me to remember it, but there is no lasting emotional impact. I have vague unease about the dream. Concerned that others will suspect I'm emotionally disturbed, I don't tell anyone about it. After all, who in their right mind has dreams about dead little girls?

The last time I dream about the dead little girl, my husband, Tim, is in the basement with me. I feel guilty because I almost forgot she was there and that I needed to check on her. Tim is there for some other purpose. I go to the closet, turn on the light, and begin my visual inspection. As expected, nothing else is stored in the closet except the girl's body. I start by examining her face. A second later, her eyes slowly open wide. I step back from her and gasp. She isn't dead! Her face remains expressionless, but she moves her eyes to look directly into mine. With my hand covering my pounding heart, I inch closer to her and look deeply into her eyes. As I move, her eyes follow mine. My fear is intense, but I am glad she is not dead. Intuitively, I know that she is a good little girl. She doesn't mean to terrify me. It's just that, all along, I thought she was dead!

I call to my husband. "Tim! She's not dead! Do you see her eyes move? Do you see that?!" He rushes over to me. He closely examines the little girl's face and eyes. She looks at him, then returns her gaze toward me. Her head moves along with her gaze so that her face is directly across from mine. He shakes his head, doesn't see her movement. "She still looks dead to me." He walks away and returns to his original task. I am confused. Why can't he see that she's not dead? No matter. I know with certainty she's not dead.

I wake up as terrified as I felt in the dream. I don't want to return to the dream, so I force myself to stay awake for a few minutes. Despite the intensity of my fear, this dream feels very important to me, like it has so much to say.

If not for the six-week dream-reading workshop I had been attending at the time, I might have let this dream fade into insignificance. Instead, I asked for help from the workshop facilitator, Anne, and my fellow students as to the dream's possible meaning. By integrating my recounting of the dream, some details about my personal history, and the group's insights, we succeeded in discovering its message.

Anne began by asking me, "Can you think of some part of yourself that you had put to sleep long ago that might now be awakening?" According to Anne's dream-reading method, the various people who play roles in our dreams are almost always different aspects of ourselves. She suggests that when we have another person in our dream, we can ask ourselves,

What is the essence of the quality of that person? Then we can take that essence and use it to help us read the dream's meaning.

So what was the essence of this little girl? She was a "good girl," patiently waiting for the right time to emerge from her deathlike sleep. And when that right time came, presumably when she sensed I was ready for it, she wanted me to know, unquestionably, that she was, in fact, not dead. Over the years, I had never abandoned her, but I had done only what was required to preserve her. That was no longer enough. She did not want to be left for dead anymore.

I told the group that my husband and I had recently started marriage counseling. Early on, the counselor helped us determine our major focus: I needed to learn how to identify and express my needs to Tim so that I could have my needs better met in our marriage. Tim was, and continues to be, very motivated to meet my needs, but he does need me to communicate them to him. The concept of identifying my needs and then asking for them to be met has been foreign to me for most of my life. In hindsight, I see that I put my needs and feelings on a basement hook in early childhood. I was three years old when my mother suffered her first episode of severe mental illness, which many years later would be correctly diagnosed as bipolar disorder. She had repeated episodes throughout my childhood, too many to count. Though my parents loved me and my three sisters, our childhood was chaotic and crisis-driven. Emotional neglect was not uncommon. To survive, I became the "good girl" who was motivated by a compulsive need to please others, especially my mother, at the expense of my own needs.

From this dream reading, the parallel between my recurring dream and the pressing issue in my marriage became stunningly clear. My little girl—the aspect of me that constitutes my needs and feelings—was awakening. I could no longer keep her in the basement, out of sight and barely playing any role in my life. To save my marriage, I had to give my little girl all the attention she needed.

I have since learned that one's "inner child" is considered a metaphor for one's needs and feelings. My little girl helped me see the awakening of my needs and the desire—no, the requirement—to fulfill them. I have since taken my little girl off the hook. She is no longer in the basement, a mere museum artifact being preserved for safekeeping. She is finally a living, breathing part of my life. I ask her what she wants to do. I ask her how she feels about a decision I'm about to make. I embrace her when she needs comforting. We're still getting to know each other, but our relationship is blooming. Perhaps someday we will be so close that we will be one, and she no longer will feel like a separate part of myself.

I suspect that Tim in my dream didn't see my little girl's movement because it was up to me to awaken to my needs and feelings, not Tim. And even though Tim in my dream didn't see this movement toward positive change, Tim in my real life sure has. I am now more skilled at recognizing and expressing my needs. I have learned that honest self-expression without irrational fear of my husband's anger or disapproval is paramount to me. Asking him to change his behavior on my behalf is okay, as long as my request is reasonable. And there's nothing wrong with telling him that I really do like receiving a bouquet of fresh flowers now and then. These days, if I want something from him, I let him know. I don't get everything I want, but our dialogue is open and negotiation is always an option. And when I'm undecided about what I want to do next, he often asks me, "What does your little girl want to do?"

Not long after I took my little girl off the hook, I was looking through some of my parents' old photos. I came across one of a dark-haired little girl who was about four years old. She looked exactly like the little girl in my dream. She was me!

(2009)

Eric Maynard
(b. 1976)

Eric Maynard is involved in many Native American cultural and community activities. He is a graduate of Eastern Connecticut State University, with a BA in English and an anthropology minor. Eric is currently enrolled in the library and information studies graduate program at the University of Rhode Island (focused on archives and special collections). His interests include Native American studies, history, film, creative writing, and comparative literary analysis. The selections below are his first published works.

The Circle

Infant—
  without a parent to permit it to start playing
Child—
  without the warmth of its Mother, crying
Adult—
  without the Medicine it needs to live
Elder—
  without a blanket or a heart-beat

I left my hand-drum at the sweat-lodge today.

  (2009)

[Untitled]

Native American professor,

Doctor of Philosophy
Reading a paper out loud on the subject of
the Columbian Exchange:

What right do I have lecturing
about Indians I have never met, and only

Read about? Positioning myself as an
Expert. Historical expert.
Anthro-
Hypnotist.
Hypocrite.
Sycophant.

The students
They are my Elders, listening to my paper
Reading my eyes
Learning my lies.
Expert? Can they see I'm hesitant?
Telling them what they either
Already know and view with disdain
or outright ignore what experts say.
Because no one is an expert.

   (2009)

Madeline Fielding Sayet

(b. 1989)

Madeline Sayet spent her childhood in Norwich and Uncasville, Connecticut. She was brought up on stories, dreams, and humor and learned the importance of never forsaking any of those things. She spent her early years listening to the stories of her great-aunt, Mohegan medicine woman Dr. Gladys Tantaquidgeon, and her mother, current medicine woman Melissa Tantaquidgeon Zobel. This is her first published story. Since writing it, she received her BFA in theater from New York University's Tisch School of the Arts in 2010, the White House Champion of Change Award for Native American Youth in 2011, and her MA in arts politics from NYU in 2012. She now works as a director and performer based in New York, where she has directed the premieres of *Miss Lead*, by Mary Kathryn Nagle (Cherokee), William S. Yellow Robe Jr.'s (Assiniboine) stage adaptation of David Seals's (Huron) novel *The Powwow Highway*, and her own Mohegan version of *The Tempest*. Her work as a director and educator explores the complexities of identity politics in contemporary performance.

When the Whippoorwill Calls

The clock beats faster than my heart. Tiny crows have stamped their impressions all over the corners of my eyes. My fingertips glide mysteriously along my seventeen-year-old skin. . . . "One, two, three, four, five. Ha. Ha. Ha. Five. Five wrinkles," I mimic *Sesame Street*'s Count; "Today, children, we will learn to count to five, using old people's faces. What fun!"

People tell me not to fear time. That it is just an element, like anything else out of our control. Yet here I am, calculatedly observing each mark time has left on me. I am told not to fear the white man. That he is not a threat anymore. But I know better. Indian people. Native people. We will always be at war with the white man; but he has time on his side in the battle, forever spreading in numbers—as we hurdle toward extinction.

So tell me, how I am supposed to stand strong, when every day I see more and more of the white man in the mirror? My skin, two shades lighter than I feel, weighs me down. No one would recognize me as a

Native at first glance. "Don't act white," my mother orders. Um, helloooooo, look at me! What do you think I look like? My friends joke that no one could ever hate me more than myself.

Mom says that things change. They always change, and people always fear, but we shall remain. I do not know. The people and stories of the past are fading fast in my mind. Moshup the giant, Granny Squannit of the little people, and all the spirits I saw as a child were only a dream. Just another story now, drifting through time and space as it leaves reality, sifting below the earth. Mom disagrees. The elders always think they know better.

But what does anyone know anymore? Earlier today I met with the language specialist and my Medicine Woman Mama to look over some language-revival documents. As we were sorting through some of the newer discoveries, we came across an error in the translation of my Mohegan Indian name. I was named Blackbird, for the dozens of black birds flying in and out of the house when I was born. Yeah, I know it's weird, but I was named Sugayo Jeets, for the dark one who flies apart. But guess what? *Sugayo* is the word for an inanimate black object—not for a black bird. So what's my name, Mom, since I have apparently been living a lie? It's actually Suks-u-kok. She named me Suks-u-kok! Great. With a name like that I am guaranteed work in the porn industry. (Let's keep this private, shall we?)

Luckily there is an *alternative* word for blackbird: *Achu-ka-yihs*. Yes, it sounds like a sneeze, but it is better than Suks-u-kok.

As I stare out my window, sparkling flakes of wonder drift eerily down to the cold earth, forming forgotten heaps beneath the whitewashed sky. Covering the earth in corpses of nature's tiny miracles. Soon the sun will come and burn up all the icy dead left lying, but for now those snowflakes rest huddled together in silent winter stealth.

I hear the call of the whippoorwill and ignore it. I know better. It is just my mind playing tricks on me. It is no more the sign of one of the Makiawisug, the little people, than I am a real Indian. That bird would freeze in this weather. I would rather let it freeze out there than give in to my own deluded fantasies. I just want a night of dreamless sleep in this cold, forgotten place, where nothing lives but memories. Just give me that.

Morning comes too soon. Some pest is tapping on my window. I roll over and bury my head under my pillow. The tapping continues. Go away! I throw my pillow at the window. Whatever it is clearly is not getting the message. I will stay strong. I am not moving from my bed. Tap. Tap. Tap. I am going to shoot it. Whatever it is I am going to shoot it. It's getting louder. Tap. Tap. Tap. Fine! I'm getting up but only so that I can get a gun and shoot you, whatever you are!—

Resting daintily outside my window, dusted with snow and dew, is a tiny whippoorwill. I examine the bird curiously. "Ow!" The bird bit me.

"What was that for?" The bird makes a series of short chirps that bear an unmistakable resemblance to laughter. Before I can stutter a reply, it dashes in the window, through my bedroom door, and into the house.

"Wait! Come back here!" I chase the bird down the stairs, only to discover him resting on the front doorknob.

"All right, I'll let you back out." The bird flies onto my shoulder as I go for the doorknob. I am not entirely sure its intentions aren't to bite me again.

"I'm going, I'm going." I open the door, and the freezing winter air nearly knocks me down as I stare at the tiny creature, merrily mocking me. It flies over to my coat and then back to me. "Oh, I am *going*, aren't I?" The whippoorwill hollers back to me as it flies out the door.

"No, wait, it's too cold, how can you . . ." But he is gone. I grab my coat and run after him.

"Ahhhhhhh. Shoes! Shoes! Geez, bird, you forgot to mention that."

I leap out of my front door, yank on my coat and boots, and pause suddenly.

"What am I doing? Oh, I am listening to a bird. Yeah, that's really normal. Nope. I will not follow you little bird, or figment of my imagination, or whatever you are! I am going to go back inside now like a nice sane person and get back in my warm bed. Goodbye."

Suddenly the bird is back again and biting my ear.

"Ahhhhhhhhhhh!!!!!"

"What's wrong!?" My mother calls down from the upstairs window.

"There is a whippoorwill down here taunting me!"

"Well then it is probably your own doing."

"I will not listen to a bird! It is your fault I care what a bird thinks of me in the first place! If it wasn't for you and your crazy stories—"

"Achu! Go!"

"You even used my new name! How sweet of you! What happened to Suks-u-kok!?"

Suddenly the wind blows the door closed, and I am locked out in the cold. The bird is laughing again. Or whatever its annoying bird version of laughing is called.

Fine, I am following you. Are you happy now? I am going to follow a bird and end up lost in the woods somewhere. The whippoorwill zips off and I chase after it, slipping in the snow as I go. After what seems like hours (but is probably about fifteen minutes), it stops at a tree.

"Oh, a tree. You brought me all this way to show me a tree." By this point my usual charming sarcasm is getting more frigid, if anything. I mean, really Achu, why are you surprised by that? After all, you are following a BIRD, and birds live in TREES.

"Ow." The bird bit my nose.

"I really wish you'd stop doing that." The bird flies down to the base of the tree and calls out softly. The call is returned by another whippoorwill.

"Oh, has the snow kept you out of your home?" I ask, suddenly sympathetic.

In an attempt to help, I start pushing snow out of the way and discover an entryway. As I continue to remove the sloppy white mush from the path, the entryway grows wider and wider. The bird nudges my back.

"Huh? You want me to go in first?"

The bird nods. I laugh. "No way. I do not know what is in there. I could be eaten by a bear." The bird (yeah, the bird!) is clearly skeptical.

"Why don't you go first? If it doesn't bother to eat a tiny thing like you, then I am probably safe." The bird shakes his head at me and flies ahead. I shake my head at myself as I delve into the mysterious dark space beneath a tree.

"Look, bird," I mumble as I crawl, "I know you like eating bugs and all, but I'm not such a big fan of them, so if I am covered with creepy crawlers, I will not be too happy with you." The bird laughs.

Wait a second. That was not a bird laugh. That was more like the hahahaha of a person. I turn around uncomfortably and feel like such an idiot as the leathery-skinned boy staring back at me winks mischievously. I am suddenly aware that the dim, narrow pathway has opened up into a long, illuminated, cavernous tunnel. I scrunch my nose.

"You bird . . . you're not a bird?" He shakes his head.

"You're a—" And I immediately avert my gaze. Every Mohegan child knows that the little people will freeze you in place with their magic if you stare at them.

"If I was going to freeze you, don't you think I would have done it by now?"

"Wait a second. This isn't real anyway. I don't believe in you anymore. You're just a myth thingy."

"Now I might freeze you."

"Oh, snap."

"So watch yourself. And, you know, everything you say can't be sarcastic."

"Says the bird who just turned into a boy."

"You know what I really am, and I *will* freeze you. Now, follow me quickly. Granny wants to see you. She's worried."

I look at him quizzically but still follow. He leads me down long glorious tunnels filled with possessions taken from naughty Indians and, perhaps, nowadays from naughty white people too. Everything fits the details of the stories I have been told. And it is quickly becoming clear that this is not a boy, but a tiny man. But nothing can convince me that this is not a dream.

The little man looks over at me and laughs, "Why are you so determined not to believe?"

"It's not that I'm . . . I gave up believing a long time ago."

"Achu-ka-yihs, just because you stopped leaving us gifts in the woods doesn't mean we stopped existing."

'How do you know my—? Never mind, of course you do. Can I ask your name or—?

"Weegun."

"Wait. Nuh uhhhh. Like T H E Weegun. Like the Weegun who fetched Nonner Martha to help Granny Squannit in the stories?"

"Not exactly, a couple generations down, like yourself. But otherwise, yeah, that's me. Granny's little messenger. It is good to see you haven't forgotten everything."

"Well, I couldn't have forgotten that. I mean, the Makiawisug are . . ."

"I thought you didn't believe in us."

"Well, I didn't, I—I don't, but . . ."

"Follow me, in here."

And then I see her. Poised elegantly in the back of the dark cavern, her silver hair glistening in the soft candlelight. Her ancient hands lined with the strength of many years. Her eyes looking at me with such fierce concern, it makes my blood run cold.

"Achu-ka-yihs," she beckons to me. "Your ancestors have been worried about you."

"My ancestors? How do you—?"

"Martha, Fidelia, Gladys, and all your great-greats, you only need to listen to hear their whispered fears. Your family has helped me many times, so I told them I would see if I could help them. If I could help you."

"Me? I'm fine."

Weegun laughs at me. "Whaaat?" I whine at him.

"Weegun, it might be best if you left the room now." Granny calmly gestures to the door.

I stick my tongue out at him as he goes and am suddenly frozen that way.

"I warned you." He chuckles as he walks out.

"*Ih, int ean ehing ay ihhh,*" I moan as I stand there, frozen. Granny unfreezes me and beckons for me to sit down. I sit cautiously, wondering why such a powerful woman of legend would possibly deign to offer me a helping hand. Not that I need it, of course . . .

"Listen to me, Achu-ka-yihs. I was here when the white man first arrived on the shores of our lands and your people first feared the end. I will be here long after. But let me tell you something. That end has not yet come, and it is still a long way off. It is your job to listen, and save the stories for your children and your children's children."

I look down, ashamed. She cannot understand what it is like to be a white Indian.

"You have done nothing wrong. Do not tear yourself apart seeking to excavate each drop of white blood within you. You must embrace the past, your past, in such a way that can help the future. You have great work to do in this lifetime, and your behavior has all of your ancestors in a frenzy. Their spirits are shifting uneasily because they are worried your work will not be fulfilled."

"How can I possibly help my people?"

"You see my people," she explains, "they are small but mighty, just as the Mohegan people have always been. They can freeze you to the spot in the blink of an eye, but they also have fears. I need you to take your fears and turn them to good use. You are stronger than you think. You have all of the strength of your ancestors backing you. Think of those strong women, and find it in your heart to do what needs to be done."

"But how can I—?" I break down in tears. Granny Squannit of the little people, the timeless mother herself, cradles me to her breast as I sob and shake.

"You once believed in the magic of the woodlands," Granny reminded. "As was the ancient custom, you left baskets of gifts for my people. I need you to believe again."

"Granny, look at me; I look like every other white person. How can I . . ."

"The white man is part of our world now. You cannot escape the fact that he is part of who you are, but that does not mean you are any less Indian."

"No one can even tell looking at me that I am—"

"You are, and you know you are. Do not try to tell me you are not the strong Mohegan girl we raised you to be. Before you were even born, Chief Tantaquidgeon blessed you in your mother's stomach. You can use your understanding of the white man to help your people. Do not let them fade. Go out there and stop giving so much cause for your ancestors to fret themselves silly. Give them a reason to be proud instead."

She cups my face in her hands. Silvery strands of hair dance about her face like dainty serpents. "Do not give in to the white man in the mirror." Her long, soft fingers glide across my face, brushing back my hair, and she kisses my forehead gently.

"Go now, and do me proud."

"Granny . . . I . . . thank you." I let my fingers slip from the graceful palm of Granny Squannit.

She smiles back at me. "Weegun will show you the way out." And suddenly he is back. "But first, Weegun, perhaps you could show her around and teach her to remember." He nods and guides me away. As I leave, I hear Granny whisper, "*Niyayomo*. It is ever so." Weegun leads me into many chambers filled with the stories of my people and of the land before the white man came. Some truths long forgotten, but others amazingly still told aboveground just as they have always been. Then Weegun nudges me. "Come on, Achu. It is time to go . . . home."

Home, above the ground, to where there is no magic. The sun has already set. We walk home in the dark, cold night in silence. I am so scared of breaking the spell of wonder, I dare not make a noise.

Then we are back at my house. My old, ordinary house. No, not ordinary. It has housed my family for many years, and we are not ordinary. We are strong Mohegan people. As I turn to my door, Weegun catches my arm and whispers, "Achu, don't forget."

In a flash he is gone. Before I can even respond. I silently beg him to make sure I remember. As I enter the house, it smells sweetly of dust and sage from my mother's many missions to preserve the past and bless the future. It smells like Indian. I climb back up the stairs where I had chased the dainty bird. The bird who turned out to be a man, who showed me a world where spirits never fade. I hop straight into my bed, in all my clothes. I dare not disturb a piece of this day's majesty. I silently thank the Creator. As I lean into my pillow, I hear the whippoorwill calling, singing gently, to help me sleep.

"Thank you, Weegun. Thank you, Granny."

My dreams are filled with blood, loss, battles, and truths—past, present, and future. Dreams of the many wars for Indian Country. When I awake, the whippoorwill has gone.

"It was only a dream after all," I sigh, taking in my ordinary empty bedroom.

As the tears begin to well up in my eyes, I shove my hands into my jacket pockets carelessly. There is something there. I slowly pull out a leather cord. It is a necklace. On it are two stone birds, a black bird and a whippoorwill.

"Thank you, Weegun," I gasp, smiling, and I am half certain the whippoorwill chirps back.

I go to the mirror to tie the token around my neck. As I stare into it, someone different looks back. No longer haunted. Someone younger, and stronger, her deep brown eyes glimmering with hope. The two birds snuggle into my collarbone, safe; my dark hair wraps around my shoulders. I let a smile wind its way up my lips, my grandmother's smile, and my great-grandmother's, and my great-great's.

Behind me fresh snow is falling outside, on the clean white ground. Each individual flake dances brilliantly onward. Tossed back and forth by the wind, but still steadily dropping toward its destination, unaware of any change. Until, in the crisp morning air, it greets the other flakes below, having completed the same journey, as is their duty. After all, that is what snowflakes do and will continue to do until the end of time. Creating a blank slate for each lonely wanderer to stroll through and tell just one more story, to add its mark to this great planet the Creator made for all of its creatures.

A dark black bird lands on the snow. Its feet leave little etchings all over the once-blank surface. I turn to the window to watch him go, both of us unaware where the trail of footprints will lead him. *The dark one who flies apart.* The bird twitches his head lightly in each direction, then turns and looks up at me curiously. *"Achu-ka-yihs,"* I whisper. *"Uyuqôm."* Dream.

(2009)

Notes

1. Laura Murray's note: "Belknap, deacon of his church, had written to Samson Occom on May 4, 1773, requesting that Occom preach in his town, which lacked a settled minister."
2. Murray's note: "Occom's sermon and Johnson's letter to Moses Paul."

Further Reading

MOHEGAN AUTHORS

Davison, Faith Damon, and Jeffrey Bendremer. "Mohegan Oral Tradition, Archaeology and the Legacy of Uncas." *Bulletin of the Archaeological Society of Connecticut* 70 (2008): 3–14. Print.

———. "A World Transformed." Map supplement to "Jamestown: The Real Story: How Settlers Destroyed a Native Empire and Changed the Landscape from the Ground Up." *National Geographic* May 2007: n. pag. Print.

Davison, Faith Damon, and Melissa Fawcett Tantaquidgeon. "Mohegan." *Encyclopedia of World Cultures Supplement* 2002: 218–22. Print.

Fawcett, Jayne, and Gladys Tantaquidgeon. "Symbolic Motifs on Painted Baskets of the Mohegan-Pequot." *Key into the Language of Woodsplint Baskets.* Washington CT: American Indian Archaeological Institute, 1987. 94–102. Print.

Fielding, Stephanie M. *Mohegan Language Project.* http://www.moheganlanguage .com/. Web. 10 June 2011.

———. *Seven Cities and Other Journeys.* Greenfield NY: Bowman Books, 2014. Print.

Johnson, Joseph. *To Do Good to My Indian Brethren: The Writings of Joseph Johnson 1751–1776.* Ed. Laura J. Murray. Amherst: University of Massachusetts Press, 1998. Print.

Kimball, Carol. *Noank Notes: Newspaper Columns of Mary Virginia Goodman.* Groton CT: Groton Public Library, 1990. Print.

Occom, Samson. *The Collected Writings of Samson Occom, Mohegan: Literature and Leadership in Eighteenth-Century Native America*. Ed. Joanna Brooks. New York: Oxford University Press, 2006. Print.

Speck, Frank, and Fidelia Fielding. "A Modern Mohegan-Pequot Text." *American Anthropologist* 6.4 (1904): 469–76. Print.

Tantaquidgeon, Gladys. *Folk Medicine of the Delaware & Related Algonkian Indians*. Harrisburg: Pennsylvania Historical & Museum Commission, 2000. Print.

Zobel, Melissa Jayne Fawcett. *The Lasting of the Mohegans: Part I, the Story of the Wolf People*. Uncasville CT: Mohegan Tribe, 1995. Print.

———. *Medicine Trail: The Life and Lessons of Gladys Tantaquidgeon*. Tucson: University of Arizona Press, 2000. Print.

Zobel, Melissa Jayne Fawcett, and Joseph Bruchac. *Makiawisug: The Gift of the Little People*. Uncasville CT: Little People Publications, 1997. Print.

Zobel, Melissa Tantaquidgeon. *Fire Hollow*. Ward Hill MA: Raven's Wing Books, 2010. Print.

———. *Oracles: A Novel*. Albuquerque: University of New Mexico Press, 2004. Print.

ADDITIONAL READING

Bruchac, Joseph, and Fidelia Fielding. *Mundu Wigo*. Marvin SD: Blue Cloud Quarterly, 1978. Print.

Dyck, Reginald. "The Economic Education of Samson Occom." *Studies in American Indian Literatures* 24.3 (Fall 2012): 3–25. Print.

LeBlanc, Michael. "Putting on 'The Helmet of Salvation' and Wielding 'the Sword of the Spirit': Joseph Johnson, Moses Paul, and the Word of God." *Studies in American Indian Literatures* 23.3 (Fall 2012): 26–52. Print.

Love, William Deloss. *Samson Occom and the Christian Indians of New England*. 1899. Syracuse NY: Syracuse University Press, 2000. Print.

Oberg, Michael Leroy. *Uncas: First of the Mohegans*. Ithaca NY: Cornell University Press, 2006. Print.

Simmons, William S. "A Pequot-Mohegan Witchcraft Tale." *Journal of American Folklore* 16.61 (1903): 11–14. Print.

———. *Spirit of the New England Tribes: Indian History and Folklore, 1620–1984*. Hanover NH: University Press of New England, 1986. Print.

Speck, Frank G. *Native Tribes and Dialects of Connecticut: A Mohegan-Pequot Diary*. Washington DC: GPO, 1928. Print.

Speck, Frank, and John Dyneley Prince. "Glossary of the Mohegan-Pequot Language." *American Anthropologist* 6.1 (1904): 18–45. Print.

SCHAGHTICOKE

Introduction

Trudie Lamb Richmond and Ruth Garby Torres

We were very pleased to accept the request to be community coeditors of this anthology. We have both been active participants in Indian affairs and issues most of our adult lives, fighting for Indian rights and eliminating stereotypes and misconceptions.

Located on the western banks of the Housatonic River in northwestern Connecticut, the Schaghticoke Reservation, established in 1736, is four hundred acres of primarily mountainous, rocky terrain. The Schaghticokes are one of five indigenous tribes in Connecticut (along with the Paucatuck Eastern Pequots, Mashantucket Pequots, Mohegans, and the Golden Hill Paugussetts) who survived the impact of colonialism, war, and disease.[1] As readers will see from the selections below, Schaghticoke leaders also played a pivotal role in establishing a state Indian Affairs Council to benefit all Native people in the state.

Historically, the colony and then the state of Connecticut have held Indian lands in trust, often infringing on the tribes' sovereignty by assuming extraordinary control over land use. Reservation management has been bounced among a variety of state entities, including the General Assembly, state-appointed overseers, the Parks and Forest Commission, the Welfare Department, and presently the Department of Environmental Protection. At the same time, the state has also encouraged Indians to leave the reservation, hoping that when no one was left on tribal homelands, the state could get out of the Indian business. Thus, in the early twentieth century Connecticut had a law stating that if Indians left the reservation for more than six months, they had to request permission to move back.

Chief Howard Harris and his son, Irving, veterans of separate wars, likely felt the injustice of having volunteered to defend their country and now needing permission from the Connecticut government to use their own reservation for its intended purpose. In the 1960s Connecticut Native people, like those across the United States, experienced their own resurgence of Native pride and indigenous activism. The Schaghticokes elected a new tribal council in 1968, broadened representation on the council in 1972, and began the process of disengaging Indian affairs from the Welfare Department.

A failed attempt to establish a state Indian affairs commission in 1972 resulted in a new strategy of aggressive outreach and mobilization of the state's tribes and individual Indians. With the political support of a major labor union and the Connecticut General Assembly's influential Speaker of the House, William R. Ratchford (D-Danbury), the Connecticut Indian Affairs Council (CIAC) was created in 1973. Irving Harris was appointed the first Schaghticoke representative to the CIAC and acted as chair during its nascent years.

With the new CIAC came a new position of Indian affairs coordinator. This state employee acted in many capacities, one of which was liaison to Governor Ella T. Grasso's administration. Brendan Keleher was working elsewhere in state government when he was tapped for this position. Keleher was tireless in his commitment to assist the members of the CIAC in regaining Indian control of reservations and asserting tribal authority. He was an adept diplomat who gently worked the sidelines to support tribal leaders' work.

Today only a few families live on the reservation, with the majority of the tribe living throughout Connecticut. However, many tribal members continue to use the reservation for meetings as well as social gatherings or just to visit it. The people strongly believe that "our culture is in the land and the land is our culture." The following are written expressions—most of them published here for the first time—by tribal members representing the three major families: Harris, Cogswell, and Kilson.

Howard N. Harris

(1900–1967)

Schaghticoke leaders and other tribal citizens have historically written a great many letters to authorities in other governments. Between 1925 and 1932 Howard Harris wrote several to the state of Connecticut, including the one below, which comes from Trudie Lamb Richmond's personal papers. The superintendent, Arthur Parker, never did resolve Harris's request to return to the reservation. The son of Chief Jim Pan Harris, Howard Harris was a leading figure at Schaghticoke in the early part of the twentieth century, and he was chief at the time of his death. After he returned home from World War I, he moved to Bridgeport, then a booming industrial city, because there were so few employment opportunities near Kent. Despite economic hardship and the intractability of state officials, Harris continued to try to move his family closer to his homeland, eventually settling in Litchfield. At the end of his life he implored his relatives to take care of the reservation.

Letter to the Department of State Parks

Mr. Arthur V. Parker
Supt State Parks
Hartford, Conn.

December 15, 1925

Dear Sir:

In reference to my inquiry for the residence on the Schaghticoke Indian Reservation in Kent. I am an Indian born on that reservation. My Father's name was James Harris and he is the last full blooded Indian to die on the reservation. The place which I have in mind would be where my grandfather lived, which is located south of the cemetery and would be the second house.

My reason for making the application for this house would be to have a place to raise a share of my living and in which I mean to raise poultry, and so as to have a garden and live here in summer and later in all seasons, to spend the week [illegible]

I also want to say that the cemetery up there is in a very bad condition, you cannot locate a Grave there and this ought to receive attention. My father's grave is their [*sic*] but it cannot be Found. Will you please look into this matter as soon as possible.

Signed Howard N. Harris

Irving A. Harris
(1931–2005)

Irving Harris took seriously the exhortations of his father, Howard, to take care of Schaghticoke. After he was discharged from the U.S. Air Force in 1953, he moved back into his parents' Litchfield home. During the late 1960s and early 1970s—the heyday of the Red Power movement—he began reaching out to other tribal members, caring for the reservation's small cemetery, and agitating with the state. He was instrumental in the creation of the Connecticut Indian Affairs Council, and the letter below expresses the strong working relationship he developed with its first coordinator.

Letter to Brenden Keleher

August 3, 1977

Mr. Brenden Keleher
Connecticut Indian Affairs Council
Department of Environmental Protection
State Office Building
Hartford, Connecticut

Dear Brenden,

I feel a varied mixture of emotions saying farewell to you. What a wealth of memories, recollections, headaches and heartaches, warm friendships and common sacrifices we have shared. The loyal and dedicated service you have given, the understanding you have shown all the complex Indian problems in the state, and the wise counsel you gave us all in finding the solutions, make seeing you go, especially difficult.

I know all members of the Connecticut Indian Affairs Council have knowledge of the quality and importance of the service you have given and they all share my regrets and deep personal loss. The ties of these years are not easily broken. I know for a man with your interest and devotion, the decision to leave state service was a difficult one to make. You have the satisfaction of leaving behind a job that no one can quite fill. You have written the history of the Connecticut Indian Affairs Council. You were the catalyst for some of its decisions and the members can thank you for its efficiency and prestige. Never will we find anyone so faithful and dedicated to your job. For all these things, I thank you.

My wife and I wish you and your family well, and expect to call upon you soon again to aid our Indian Affairs Council needs. With every good wish for your future, I remain gratefully,
Yours in Brotherhood,

Irving Harris
Chief-President
Schaghticoke Indians of Kent, Connecticut

Trudie Lamb Richmond

(b. 1931)

Trudie Lamb Richmond has an MA in education from the Bank Street School of Education, and a MA in anthropology from the University of Connecticut. She retired in 2010 as director of public programs at the Mashantucket Pequot Museum after fifteen years. She was awarded the First People's Fund Community Spirit award for her lifetime work as an educator and storyteller. She has served for over twenty years on the Native American Heritage Committee. She has served on both the Schaghticoke Tribal Council and the Indian Affairs Council. She presented her paper on Eunice Mauwee in May 2011 at the University of Massachusetts–Amherst, where she was serving as the tribal historian in residence. The second essay below appeared in *Cross Paths*, a publication of the Mashantucket Pequot Museum.

Why Does the Past Matter? Eunice Mauwee's Resistance Was Our Path to Survival

Good afternoon. I am very pleased to be here and especially pleased to have the opportunity to introduce Eunice Mauwee, an important socio-cultural figure in Schaghticoke history. She lived to be 104 years old. Her life straddled two centuries. Born in 1756, she died in 1860. For all of us born after 1860, she became the grandmother to us all. It was Eunice's legacy of resistance that became our path to survival. This year's conference title, "Why Does the Past Matter?" is truly a multilayered question, determined by who is reporting the past. Therefore, I would like to begin with these thoughts regarding indigenous grandmothers to set the tone for my remarks and the conference theme:

> When we were young, it was our grandmother who gathered us around to tell us of many things; of how the world began, of where we came from; why we must respect all living things; of the wonders of the universe. She always told us of the old ways. And when we were told these things, these truths, we searched her face of many wrinkles and believed she must have been there, way back then, in the beginning, so vivid were her words and the pictures she created in our mind's eye. It

was only when we were much older that we realized that this was the way of the elders. Their words were the traditions being passed down from their grandmothers and grandfathers. The hypnotic quality of grandmother's carefully selected words healed us. Cured us, strengthened and enriched our lives—which we were committed to pass on. Trudie Ray Lamb (Logan, "Preface")

In researching the historical past of the Native people who have lived along the Housatonic River for many centuries, one quickly discovers that local historians' writings were filled with inaccuracies. Most did not recognize the importance of how these communities in the Housatonic River Valley were all related, which created a strong kinship from Schaghticoke all the way down to Long Island Sound. These communities all had a strong partnership with the land and their cycle of subsistence was regulated by generations of spiritual tradition. However, these traditions and values were threatened repeatedly in the eighteenth century by the imposition of colonialism and the pressures of Christianity. The encroachment of colonists from New England to the east and New York to the west contributed to the weakening of Native social and political systems in the region.

Native women and men were faced with difficult choices for survival: accommodate or boldly resist. However, to understand Eunice better one needs to understand the changing times in which she grew up and the survival choices that her father and grandfather had to make. Eunice was the daughter of Joseph "Chuse" Mauwee and the granddaughter of Gideon Mauwee, the last traditional sachem of the Schaghticoke people. Leadership is generally hereditary and a leader's powers are absolute. But the actual use of power depends upon one's ability as a diplomat. Mauwee was greatly respected and a man of many skills. He was a canoe maker as well as skilled at building sweat lodges. For a long time, it was Mauwee's vision and leadership abilities that enabled his people to survive. He welcomed other Native people as they fled upriver from the colonial settlers who were obtaining more and more land.

The nearby town of Kent was incorporated in 1736. Gideon, always looking out for the welfare of his people, approached the town officials and requested a school and teachers for the education of Schaghticoke children. Before giving a response, several Kent leaders visited Schaghticoke and reported that the Indian children were too "wild" to be educated and therefore refused any assistance. Gideon may have been disappointed, but he had other options. He had a strong bond with the people at Shekomeko, a Mahican village just twenty-five miles north of Schaghticoke. When he received word that the Moravians were building a mission at Shekomeko he went to investigate. He was drawn by their friendliness, which was in great contrast to the hostile attitude of the townspeople of Kent. He invited the Moravians to visit Schaghticoke.

Unlike the English, the Moravians were not only willing to work among the Native people but willing to live among them as well. Moravian missionaries remained at Schaghticoke for nearly twenty years. They kept daily dairies, which included descriptions of Schaghticoke activities. Although the diaries heavily focused on religious events and conversion, fragments of Schaghticoke culture were included from time to time and thus preserved. Moravian records provide an important glimpse of Schaghticoke culture and traditions. About the time that the Moravians were forced to leave, Gideon made the decision to move his son Joseph "Chuse" Mauwee and his growing family down closer to Long Island Sound, to the town of Derby, where he felt Joseph and his children would have a better chance of survival, learning how to live amongst the English.

The youngest of nine children, Eunice was born in Derby. She and her family had adopted many of the English ways, which is strongly reflected in the following story. As Eunice told it many years later, she recounted one of the most revealing events in her early childhood. She described how, when she was no more than five or six, she hid in fear when her grandfather, Gideon Mauwee, and several male Schaghticoke came to visit because their "wild" appearance frightened her. Apparently dressed in the "Indian" manner—perhaps in animal skins and adorned with tattooed designs on their bodies and faces—they had Eunice believing they were going to eat her. These "real" Indians were undoubtedly perceived as menacing to her, although an Indian herself.

As a young child, Eunice was obviously greatly influenced by colonial ways. However, when she married John Sutnux, a Narragansett, they moved up to Schaghticoke. Now living on the reservation, Eunice was not detached but began to appreciate traditional values and culture, and basket making became a livelihood. It is not clear whether or not Eunice learned basket making from her father or when she came to live on the reservation. She survived most of her life as a basket maker, traveling about the countryside selling her crafts. Making baskets brought her closer to the indigenous knowledge and values of her ancestors. She also taught her granddaughters. When she was too old to travel anymore, although she continued to make baskets, she stayed at home and passed down tribal history through her storytelling. Eunice was a sociocultural authority among her people. She was neither a leader nor a political force, but her basket making was symbolic of the transfer of power, of cultural knowledge and Schaghticoke identity. Eunice's baskets represent the "internal qualities of culture" and are preserved and exhibited in museums and homes throughout the country. Eunice was a "real" Indian.

Growing Up Indian (or Trying To) in Southern New England

In 1852 John DeForest published *The History of the Indians of Connecticut.* In his introduction he wrote, "It is but a little more than 200 years since the state of Connecticut, now inhabited by a populous, civilized and Christian community, was entirely possessed by a few barbarous tribes of a race which seems to be steadily fading from existence." DeForest also included a 1630 map of Connecticut showing the location of Native groups. It gives the impression that the area is not heavily populated. In fact, he describes the northwestern part of the state "as a desert," ignoring the presence of the Weantinock and Potatuck people, whose ancestors had lived there for several thousand years.

Historical silences have largely contributed to the invisibility of the indigenous peoples of southern New England. Local historians often reduce our existence to a few brief paragraphs. We are nearly always described in the past tense. Yet DeForest's book, still considered one of the most complete and accurate books on the history of Connecticut Indians, is filled with bias, as he trivializes and minimizes the existence of indigenous peoples. He emphasized the manner as to how Native people of the state were viewed and treated.

Lumbee Indian scholar Robert A. Williams Jr., in his book *Like a Loaded Weapon: The Rehnquist Court, Indian Rights and the Legal History of Racism in America,* writes that racism has been encoded in our language, even our legal prose. He points out that our highest court, the U.S. Supreme Court, has employed the language of racism in many of its most important decisions on minority rights, perpetuating and sanctioning the "language of racism, giving racism an authoritative, binding, legal meaning in our legal system." Williams describes the Marshall Model of Indian Rights, developed by Chief Justice John Marshall. Marshall, he says, relied upon the same language that the "Founding Fathers" had used regarding Indians; language full of negative stereotypes and racial images that justify the stigma of inferiority attached to people of color.

Indian people in southern New England were an invisible minority when I was growing up. The Schaghticoke Reservation is located in northwestern Connecticut on the west banks of the Housatonic River, the area that DeForest described as an "empty space" or "desert." My grandfather, William "Will" Cogswell, was born there in 1865. When he married my grandmother, an Indian from New Milford, they lived on the reservation. Most of their children were born there. They finally left the reservation and moved to New Milford, to a place called Second Hill, where there was an active community of Schaghticoke relatives and where it was easier to provide for a large, growing family: eight girls and one boy. My mother was the eighth child.

In 1983, about seventy-five years after my grandfather moved his family off the reservation, I moved to Schaghticoke to build my home. I was determined and driven to be there. At the time, I was one of five families living on the reservation. It was my home for nearly twenty years. And my life there was not without struggle. Sacrifice and an intense determination to sustain visibility on the homelands of my ancestors was the driving force. It was important to show a continued presence and to make the statement "We are still here."

I read somewhere that the way a society treats its children is a reflection of that society's values and mores. When I think back on my childhood, a flood of memories emerge, a mixture of good times and some very unhappy ones. I believe many of those youthful encounters impacted on the direction I chose later in life, filled with determination and resistance. Although I was born in Bridgeport, Connecticut, not far from where the Housatonic River empties into Long Island Sound, I grew up in a small town just twenty miles south of the reservation. When my paternal grandfather died, my father moved our family—my mother, two sisters, and myself—to live with his mother, so she wouldn't be alone in her large, six-bedroom home. It was a beautiful place in the country with fruit trees, a garden, and a big old barn that called out to be explored with its countless hiding places. But that bubble burst very quickly. I had to go to school.

And thus began a long, sometimes lonely, arduous journey crammed with perplexing, conflicting discoveries. I had been filled with such excitement at the idea of the move. It was starting a new adventure. But I was not prepared for the transition of moving from a busy coastal city on Long Island Sound with a diverse population to a small, quiet, inland town where everyone looked alike. I definitely was not prepared when I discovered that no one else looked like me or my family. Not that anyone ever discussed such a topic with me. I was just aware of the way I was treated—differently. There was an attitude that I quickly learned to recognize, which imposed a learned behavior. Although I didn't have words at the time for what I was experiencing, I was learning about social injustice, discrimination, inequality, and unfair treatment. Here are a few "discovery" stories I am willing to share.

I was in the third grade when we moved. The school was about two miles away. But my family was told that we lived too close to the school for me to ride the school bus. Because my mother and grandmother didn't drive and my father left for work early, I walked. I walked until I learned to ride a bike. I had walked to school when we lived in the city. But the school was only two blocks away and I walked with other children in the neighborhood. But this was a two-mile walk and I walked alone. I never saw another child while walking to school. And it was a long time before I made friends.

In the seventh grade, my class was given a writing project as a homework assignment. The day we turned our papers in, we had a substitute teacher, the principal's wife. She had that *attitude* that made me put my head down. Before the end of the day, she told me that I had to stay after school and rewrite my paper, because she didn't believe I had written it. I had never stayed after school before. And I was the only one. It was embarrassing and lonely. But these were things you just accepted. I don't remember the assignment. I don't remember what I wrote about. But I do remember her attitude and the feeling that emerged because of it. There were certain adults and even some classmates who would express that "attitude." These were things you learned to accept.

There were many other "discoveries" like that. But the one that topped the seventh-grade experience was during my senior year in high school. I was to be one of eight students selected to speak at our graduation. The teacher called each one of us up to her desk to select a specific ethnic group from a list she had compiled. We would be asked to research the group we had selected and then write about the contributions they had made to the rest of the world. I was so excited. Here was my opportunity to talk about American Indians, to talk about my people, to really *be* me. It would mean that the entire graduation audience and my family would get to hear me. But the feeling of such pride only lasted a fleeting moment. American Indians were not on the teacher's coveted list. I was told that American Indians had not many if any important contributions. That was one of the deepest wounds and one of the most difficult of all the discoveries imposed upon me. She had been one of the few teachers I had admired. How could she be so wrong? As quickly as she had given me recognition she had taken it away. But just like every other occasion, I did not speak up or protest. It was not acceptable behavior.

What saved me was the summertime, when I would visit or stay with my maternal grandparents. Their little house, with its three little bedrooms and double-seated outhouse, was filled with a noisy, active family of uncles, aunts, cousins, and other relatives coming and going all of the time. I was embraced and comforted. Most of the houses on Second Hill were inhabited by Indian families, and we were all related. And everyone had stories to tell, stories about rattlesnakes, hunting, powwow stories. Then there were the late-night stories that I heard while hiding under grandma's great, round oak table as the aunts and uncles played cards and talked about living in New York City.

The "discoveries" I experienced during those times were strong and positive. They created the identity I craved. They nurtured my mind and my heart. The house and the family overflowed with stories. The little parlor was filled with family photographs on the walls and a big book of photographs on the end table. But my favorite photo was of my grandfather squatting down, wearing the big western headdress of a chief! Yet he always proudly reminded the family that "we were Potatuck." I was especially drawn to that picture because he had legs. I was ten years old when he died and he didn't have legs. I always imagined that he had lost them fighting in the "Indian Wars." I later learned that he had suffered from diabetes and that was why he lost his legs. I also learned that he enjoyed wearing the big headdress on special occasions such as powwow gatherings and special parades celebrating the anniversary of the settling of New Milford. Folks paid attention and recognized him as a Schaghticoke Indian. "But where did the headdress come from?" I asked. "Oh, Uncle Archie sent it back from out west. He was on his way to Alaska to join in the Gold Rush, but they lost his steamer trunk in Seattle." But that's another story.

Paulette Crone-Morange
(1943–2004)

Paulette Crone-Morange was the tribal administrator/historian of the Schaghticoke Tribal Nation. Her mother was Catherine Elizabeth Harris, and her father was Paul Francis Velky. Active in the tribe's long struggle for federal recognition, she held a variety of political positions, including secretary of the Tribal Council, vice chair of the Tribe, and chair of the Tribal Housing Authority. Crone-Morange was also the first Native woman to chair the Connecticut Indian Affairs Council. The following is an excerpt from a history of the Schaghticoke Tribal Nation that she coauthored in 2004 with archaeologist Lucianne Lavin of the Institute for American Indian Studies in Washington, Connecticut. It is especially valuable because it contains citations from some of the earliest Schaghticoke writings.

From "The Schaghticoke and English Law: A Study of Community Survival"

The Schaghticoke Reservation is located in Kent, Connecticut. The Reservation was created by the Connecticut General Assembly in May 1736:

> This Assembly being informed that a parcel of Indians that sometime dwelt at New Milford are removed and settled on the west side of Oustunnuck River, in a bow of the west side thereof about three or four miles above New Fairfield, upon a piece of plain land there, and have

a desire to continue at said place; Whereupon it is resolved by this Assembly, that no person shall lay out any grant or farm on said plain piece of land without the special leave of this Assembly. . . .

The Schaghticoke Reservation presently encompasses about 400 acres of rocky ridge and narrow valley woodland between the western bank of the Housatonic River and New York state. The Appalachian Trail passes through its uplands, near the historically well-known Schaghticoke rattlesnake den.

At the beginning of the historical period the "western lands"—as present north-western Connecticut was called—were part of the Schaghticoke, Weantinock, and Mohican (aka Mahikan) Tribal Homelands. The word "Schaghticoke" is an anglicized version of the Algonquian word "Pishgatikuk," which means "at the confluence of two streams," according to Schaghticoke elder and culture keeper Eunice Mauwee (1756–1860), the granddaughter of the Tribe's first recorded sachem, Gideon Mauwee/Mauwehu.

The Moravian missionaries, some of whom only spoke German, mispronounced the Algonquian word as "Pachgatgoch." The Moravian mission at Schaghticoke was known by this name as well as by various spellings of Scaticook.

The Schaghticoke Homelands centered about the confluence of Macedonia Brook (aka Schaghticoke River, according to early Kent historian Barzillai Slosson) and Housatonic River, where the Tribe's winter/spring village was located (it eventually became a year-round settlement); they also included southern portions of the Webatuck River Valley. Schaghticoke lands stretched north and south along these waterways and along major Indian trails that connected tribal members with each other, with important subsistence resources, and with other Native communities.

Mohican villages were located to the immediate north and west at Weatogue in the present Town of Salisbury, at Wechquadnach in the present Town of Sharon, and at Shekomeko near present Pine Plains, New York; other Mohican villages were located farther north in eastern New York and in western Massachusetts. Mohican Homelands are thought to have extended as far south as the Roelif Jansen Kill. The Weantinock Homelands were located to the south and east of Schaghticoke.

The diaries of mid-eighteenth-century missionaries to Schaghticoke and Wechquadnach show that the Mohican and Schaghticoke practiced a seasonal round of group movements involving two central bases—a winter/spring village and summer/fall village. . . . Task groups from each base village would visit smaller, short-term camps scattered across the landscape to perform specific economic activities, such as fishing, hunting, maple sugaring, berrying, and collection of raw materials for basket, wooden dish, broom, and canoe manufacture. The fruits of their labor would be brought back to the base camp. Every summer/fall, the Schaghticoke also traveled down the Old Berkshire and Oronoke paths—Indian trails that followed the Housatonic River from Stockbridge in Massachusetts to Stratford on Long Island Sound—to collect finfish and shellfish. The main winter village of the Schaghticokes located in present south Kent soon became a major refuge for Native Americans representing a variety of tribal communities uprooted by Anglo colonialism. . . .

According to the Tribe's genealogists, the modern Schaghticoke Tribe consists of three major lineages: Mauwee-Harris, Mauwee-Kilson, and Cogswell-Coggswell, whose roots may be traced back to the Tribe's earliest sustained historic contacts. These occurred in the early 1740s, when a Moravian mission was built at Schaghticoke and the English began settling lands on the east side of the Housatonic River, which originally defined the town of Kent. It was not until the 1750s that the Township extended into Schaghticoke lands on the west side of the river, after the General Assembly had granted a lottery of those lands to private buyers. In their report to the General Assembly, the surveyors admitted that some of the lands had been "sequestered for said Indians." . . .

. . . In contrast to the coastal Indian Tribes, those in the upper Housatonic Valley adopted non-confrontational survival strategies for dealing with Anglo invasion of their Homelands. The Schaghticoke Tribe and its neighbors began to experience the effects of English colonization about one hundred years later than the coastal Native American communities. By that time, Christian missionaries, particularly those preaching the "new light" evangelical forms of Christianity, had become more successful in converting Indians for a number of reasons. Not all of these reasons were religious. As shall be shown, socio-political survival and Christian conversion were often closely entwined.

The disastrous Native American defeats in the seventeenth-century Indian wars in New England and in New York made it quite clear to Schaghticoke leaders that white superiority in weaponry and manpower made confrontational strategies obsolete. Non-confrontational strategies that rested on knowledge of Euro-American legal structure and social etiquette were the most pragmatic options if they wished to maintain tribal cohesion within their traditional Homelands. The Tribe quickly established a policy of pacifism, negotiation, and flexibility steeped in English law to successfully deal with the colonial and state governments. This policy was illustrated as early as 1756 in a Schaghticoke petition to the Connecticut General Assembly, and it has continued to this day. As the Schaghticoke once noted:

> We have always with cheerfulness, assisted and joined the English in all Expeditions against King George's Enemies and have never been Chargeable, Burthensome, [sic] or Troublesome to this Coloney by any Contentions that some other Tribes have Occaisioned [sic] and have always continued in this Quiet and peaceable Disposition with the English, encouraging the Settlement of the English near us by selling our lands for very trifling Sums, having Reserved part of these Lands, which we are informed have been sold sometime since viz in 1754 by order of the Assembly.[2]

Tribal leaders were quick to realize that Christian missions, with their schools and white benefactors, might provide the means for sustaining the Tribe's land base and its community. Missions were a source for Native education in English language and law. Eighteenth-century upper Housatonic Indian leaders petitioned colonial governments for the right to establish mission villages. Around 1740, Moravian mission villages were founded among the Mohicans in Sharon and across the border at Shekomeko near Pine Plains, New York. In 1742, Schaghticoke leaders petitioned the Connecticut General Assembly for a minister and a school to educate Schaghticoke children:

> Upon the Memorial of Mowehu, Cheery, and others [Indian Natives] we your Honours Comitte [sic] Humbly Beg Leave to Report that it appears to us that there are near thirty souls of the Indians on the Borders of new milford; who are apart of the Memorialists and that

the Good ends proposed by them may probably be in a Good Measure Answered by this Assembly ordering a suitable sum to be put into the hands of some suitable person or persons in new Milford, to be Improved to help support such of them as will attend the School in new Milford; and also to support them on the Sabath [sic] when they will attend the publick Worship there.[3]

The General Assembly eventually granted this petition, but by that time Schaghticoke sachem Gideon Mauwee had already invited the Moravians to set up a mission and school at Schaghticoke. The missionaries accepted the invitation. The Schaghticoke mission was active from 1743 until 1770.

Unlike traditional forms of Christianity such as Congregationalism, the Moravian movement was a potent force in tribal revitalization. Schaghticoke participation in the Moravian form of Christianity helped maintain their psychological sense of community and self-identity and brought economic improvements to the Reservation. Most importantly, several Moravian missionaries were Englishmen who provided schooling in English language, culture, and law. Unlike other Protestant missionaries, the Moravians did not attempt to detribalize and assimilate their Indian converts. . . . Mauwee sent his younger son Joseph (aka Chuse) to live with the Tomlinson family in north Derby (present-day Seymour). Joseph learned to read and write English and adopted English customs, such as Anglo clothing and Christianity. He eventually returned to the Reservation as a tribal leader, however, and helped to formulate and write tribal petitions to the General Assembly. In 1786, for example, Joseph is thought to have written a petition to the General Assembly in which the Tribe accused their court-appointed overseer of withholding medical aid and moneys from tribal land sales and rents, noted the loss of hunting and fishing grounds, and requested a tribal school:

A meating held by the Indians in Scatecook in Kent april the 13th A D 1786. . . . if it Might be that wee should have the Privilidge of Chusing our conservetter once a yeare and that settlements Maid Every year Each one to make their Payment on their one Deall Except what shall be paid in sick Ness the Rest to bee Paid in Money or Produce to Premote a Skool.[4]

Another Schaghticoke survival strategy was the employment of Anglo-American intermediaries to act on their behalf within English society. During the mid-1700s, the Moravian missionary functioned in this role, protecting the tribal members from the encroachment and activities of some of their less-ethical white neighbors. But the local English disliked and mistrusted the missionaries and spread rumors that they were spies for the French. Local shopkeepers and farmers who operated cider mills were particularly disgruntled because the Christianized Indians were teetotalers. Their abstinence from alcohol cut mightily into Anglo profits.

> We your Honours Comtee. Take leave to report in reference to the affaire commited to our consideration as followeth we are well Informed that there are Several Strangers, and we Suppose they are not of our Kings Subjects, but foreigners which are Straggling about the Inland parts of Fairfield County, and the western part of Hartford and some time in New haven county and that in a more espetial manner they are conversant with those Indians that inhabit at podertuck in woodbury, and those that live west of the Housatunick River westward of the Town of Kent, and that the common rumor is that one of those foreigners have told the Indians that his majesties Subjects in these plantations will be destroyed by the uroppions settled on the S.west and the north joined with the flat heads on the west, and we are also told that the School set up by this govert. Among the sd. Indians westward of Kent, was discoraged and put by thro' the Influence of one of sd foreigners, and that the Indians are more and more Estrangd from his majesties Subjects by theire means, and upon the whole we fear his majesties Interest may be greately Indangered by the sd Strangers; therefore we Recommend it to your Honours Consideration that the sd foreigners may be taken up and caryed before the Governour of this Colony and such other of the civil authority as his Honour shall think proper to call to his Assistance before whome such Strangers may be examined, and the Govr. And authority that he shall call in as above sd we hope will be desired and authorized to take such Methods and use meanes as may be proper to Secure his majesties Interest in these plantations, and that the Indians about us may still depend upon the British Crown all wich is humbly Submited by your Comtee . . . approved in Upper House and bill to be drawn up; concurred in Lower House.[5]

. . . In 1892 Schaghticoke tribal leader Truman Bradley petitioned the Court of Common Pleas to appoint George Bull and Luther Eaton of Kent as appraiser of the real and personal property of the Tribe as well as lands mortgaged with funds borrowed from the Schaghticoke Tribal Fund. The court agreed and ordered Bull and Eaton to report their findings to the court. They did so one year later, and it was included in the court's judgment.

These . . . petitions show that the nineteenth-century Schaghticoke community was still adhering to traditional Native ideas of tribal corporateness through communal action among members living both on and off the Reservation. They also show the Tribe's continued use of its eighteenth-century political strategy to work peacefully within the Anglo-American legal system to maintain its tribal identity, in this case through the institution of mediation.

The passage of the federal Indian Reorganization Act of 1934, which allowed Indian tribes to become self-governing entities again, was the catalyst for Schaghticoke political activism in the mid-1930s. The creation of the Indian Claims Commission under the act instigated the Tribe to resist Connecticut's anti-tribal policies and attempt to regain tribal lands previously lost through illegal land sales and encroachment, by initiating a land claim with the federal Court of Claims in 1936.

It was the first of several Schaghticoke land claims within the state and federal court systems that have continued to the present time. The second, revised land suit, known as Docket 112, was originally filed with the Court of Claims in 1949. The Court of Claims deferred to the Indian Land Claims Commission, where the land suit was filed and received its docket number in 1951. It was dismissed by the court in 1975 because the Tribe lacked the funds for an attorney to file a brief on their behalf. It is one of the main reasons the Tribe initiated its pursuit of federal recognition in 1987. Only federally recognized Tribes have been able to win such land claims and regain control of their ancient Homelands.

Ruth Garby Torres

(b. 1955)

Torres received her BS in general studies with a concentration in political science from Charter Oak College, New Britain, Connecticut. She was a Connecticut state trooper for twenty years and retired when she was accepted to Harvard University's Kennedy School of Government. She received her MA in public administration in 2011. Torres served on the Schaghticoke Tribal Council and serves on the Advisory Board of the Native American Cultural Center at Yale University. She is also an active member of Native American Indigenous Studies Association (NAISA).

Eulogy for Irving Harris

By way of a proper Indian introduction, I must tell you how I came to this place. My name is Ruth Garby Torres. My mother was Adele Harris Garby. My grandfather was Howard Nelson Harris. Irving Harris was my uncle and my godfather.

When I finally put pen to paper (or in my case, fingers to keyboard), the challenge in preparing this eulogy was not in finding words with which to remember Irv, but to limit them. Irv was many things to many people—son, brother, nephew, uncle, husband, father, grandfather, veteran, coach, coworker, friend, adversary, chief. His life touched all your lives in some way, maybe recently, maybe long ago. Irv was a good and dutiful son. For many of his adult years he lived with his mother, caring for her and her home—the home on Old South Road. The yard and outbuildings were impeccably kept. This is how Irv loved his mother.

Irv was a good and dutiful son. His father didn't drive and Irv often chauffeured his dad to visit relatives and to meet with other Schaghticokes at the reservation. Before Grandpa died he asked Irv to protect the land at Schaghticoke and to assume his tribal leadership responsibilities. This is how Irv loved his father. Irv was a good and dutiful brother and uncle to many children. He was one of seven children, number five in the birth order. His six siblings produced over thirty nieces and nephews for Irv.

Like all families, we gathered together for weddings, funerals, baptisms, birthdays, and family reunions. Many of these gatherings took place at the home of one of his siblings. It was not unusual for Irv to arrive at the event, put in a half-hour of socializing, and commence doing the yard work or some outdoor project. This was not only indicative of Irv's discomfort with idleness but it was the way that he showed his love and support. He was quick to send a check at Christmastime when some of our holidays looked lean. My childhood home was the beneficiary of just such assistance. This was how he showed his love—quietly and from behind the scenes.

Irv was a good and dutiful nephew. When his dad's brother returned to this area a few years before his death, it was Irv who shuttled Uncle Charlie to meet with family and to attend tribal meetings. Irv was thrilled that Uncle Charlie came to him in his last days. And Irv was honored to play a role when Uncle Charlie died and was buried where he had come home—at Schaghticoke.

I am always interested in how husbands and wives met. These are important stories to know and to keep alive. Until recently I never knew how Irv and Laurie met. Laurie told me that she first laid eyes on Irv when they were high school students. He was several years older than she was and she first spotted him on the school's basketball team. A few years passed. She was still in school when their paths crossed. Irv had graduated by then. Her flirtatious attempts were rebuffed by Irv one day when he told her to come back when she grew up. Many years later (presumably now a grown-up) Laurie had her first date with Irv, or Ernie as she often called him.

Their small talk included conversations about their upbringings and Laurie was describing the place where she lived her childhood. Her home was on Harris Lane in Litchfield, in a section I believe they call Harris Plains. "Isn't that a coincidence—that's your last name," she exclaimed to Irv. She told him all about the legend of Joseph Harris. According to Laurie, town historians say local Indians scalped this Mr. Harris and a plaque once hung near the location of the deed. "Are you a descendant of the famous Joseph Harris?" Laurie asked Irv. Without missing a beat, he answered, "No, I'm the one that did it."

I believe Laurie was the love of Irv's life. Without her in his life, Irv would have been an entirely different man. She was his gatekeeper: if he didn't want to talk to you, Laurie was the one who diplomatically prevented your access, actually preserving your relationship with her upset husband. She was his voice. Sometimes he had difficulty articulating the exact words he wanted you to hear or writing one of his many letters to various state agencies. Laurie brought form to Irv's thoughts and ideas.

Irv was a demanding father. He wanted his children to be the best. In the only way he knew how, Irv tried to bring out the full potential of his sons and daughters. Rachel says his theme song was the one made popular by Frank Sinatra: "My Way." Douglas recently reflected on his appreciation for his father and his understanding of how difficult it may have been for Irv when he married "the package"—mother and son. But for all of the demands, there was no doubt Irv loved his children.

And he loved his grandchildren. Those two boys are the only people I know who Irv allowed to literally walk all over him. Even on a bad day, while Irv lay in bed, these two kids would invade his room, get on the bed with him, and crawl up one side of him and down the other. Irv never even batted an eyelash. If you knew Irv late in his life, you would know it was a sure sign of love if he let you into his physical space.

Irv was proud to be an American. He was a veteran of the Korean War, having spent seven years in the Air Force. He recently told me that he originally intended to be a career Air Force man but other duties called. While he was able, he was an active member in the Veterans of Foreign Wars.

Irv retired from the state Department of Transportation or, if you are old enough to know its former name, the Connecticut Highway Department. "CHD" were the initials I remember emblazoned on the orange raincoat that hung on Grandma's back porch. In my current profession, I have watched many a highway-paving job. Each time I observed this work, I was reminded of a story Irv once told about a paving project. I was a young girl and I heard this story in "real time," soon after it happened. Apparently, during the paving process it is imperative that the materials are heated to a high temperature and remain hot during their application. This is crucial to the success of the job. On one project where Irv was present, a coworker fell down onto the hot, practically molten, asphalt. Although I don't recall all the details, I was left with the impression that this man had fallen from a piece of equipment and was not able to recover quickly. Irv grabbed a hose and sprayed the man with cool water to provide him with enough comfort to recover from the spill while the other workers assisted. At the end of the crisis, Irv's boss admonished him for ruining the paved surface. It was this criticism that inflamed Irv—that the boss would care more about the job than for the man doing the job.

There are probably hundreds of Litchfield boys that Irv helped shape into men. For many years Irv coached football. I have been told that Irv was a tough and exacting coach but also a fair one. One of my coworkers, a state trooper and father himself, was one of Irv's football players. He told me recently, "Even though it was many years ago and for only a few short football seasons, I still have lasting memories that I carry with me today and often refer to in my daily life." It was Irv's fairness that tempered the demands. Irv saw the potential in these kids and honed it to the max. As a result, they had many winning seasons.

Irv had friends and Irv had adversaries—he may have actually had an equal number of both. Oftentimes Irv translated life into superlatives. He thought, not in terms of mediocrity, but in extremes. Someone was the dumbest "bleep" he'd ever met or the best or the smartest. A few years back Irv was at the Mohegan Powwow buying food from two Indian vendors he had known for many years. He looked around the lunchtime crowd and proclaimed in his booming voice, "This is the best damn chili in the whole powwow." That was how he showed his love for his friends—in what I'd call a "back door" kind of way.

If you were an adversary, you might not have appreciated the superlatives Irv had for you. In the last couple weeks I've had occasion to communicate with some of Irv's adversaries as they learned of his passing. One of them wrote me to say that even though he and Irv had many disagreements over the years, it was never due to what he characterized as "the pettiness that permeates Indian Country now." We agreed that, delivery style aside, you always knew where you stood with Irv. He did not connive. He did not stab backs. He was up-front with you regardless of how uncomfortable he might have made you feel.

In closing, please allow me to share some thoughts about Irv as chief of the Schaghticoke Tribe and as an Indian leader at the helm during a turning point in Connecticut Indian history. I think Irv's deeds in both these roles will be his life's legacy. I've already mentioned that Irv assumed the duties of chief from his father. This was in 1967. American history reveals that this time period was a turning point for the whole country. We were suffering the Vietnam War. We were beginning to consider the civil rights of all citizens. The nation as a whole was finally awakening to the historical injustices that had been meted out in the name of the nation. A movement was afoot, a renewal, a revitalization. It was Irv (and he would hate that I am holding him up in the limelight now) who was the point man for this movement in Connecticut. He was the "Indian in the Gray Flannel Suit," as they called him at the state capitol. He learned how state government worked and who the players in the political process were. He also quickly learned how to work within this system to effect change. As a result of his initial effort, many Indian people and our supporters challenged the "business as usual" way that the state of Connecticut treated Indians. We coalesced to slowly transform official policy and eventually to positively impact the lives of Native people here.

A few years ago I had occasion to meet author and U. Conn. professor emeritus Robert L. Bee at a Pequot history conference. In 1987 Dr. Bee published a paper entitled "Connecticut Indian Policy: From Testy Arrogance to Benign Bemusement." I introduced myself as a Schaghticoke and Irv's niece. For the next several minutes he talked about Irv's impact on Connecticut Indian Country. In fact, in the paper I just mentioned Dr. Bee credits Irv as leading "the drive for major policy reform" in this state.

In her 1979 report for the Connecticut Indian Affairs Council, Mary Guillette also acknowledged Irv as the "leader of the movement to gain Indian control over their own affairs and over their own reservations" in Connecticut. And as recently as last week, Ed Sarabia, the current Indian Affairs Council coordinator, alerted the public to Irv's death. In his notification he wrote this summation: "[Irv's] efforts and accomplishments on behalf of Connecticut's Indian population will be felt for decades." He closed by saying, "Indian Affairs in Connecticut has lost a major force."

I would like to close with that thought as well. I thank you all for gathering here this evening to celebrate Irv's life. This celebration will end with a reading by a Schaghticoke tribal elder, an Indian leader in her own right, a former adversary and respected friend of Irv's, Trudie Richmond. Irv may not have wanted this much fuss over his death, but he chose this reading and this reader.

Aileen Harris McDonough
(b. 1975)

Aileen McDonough, née Aileen Harris Nagle, was born in Connecticut and learned about her Schaghticoke tradition and history from her aunt, Ruth Garby Torres, and grandmother, Adele Harris Garby. She earned her BA in English from Wesleyan University. Currently living in Rhode Island with her husband and two children, McDonough runs a writing and editorial consulting company called 3am Writers and is at work on her first book of fiction. The pieces below are being published here for the first time.

How I Became a (Paid) Writer

In college, I majored in English. That should explain everything, really, because most people's impression of English majors is that they have two options upon graduation. One is to pursue a writing career and starve, slowly yet eloquently, hooked on drugs and stormy relationships in a New York apartment. The second option was the one I heard more often when telling people my major. "Oh, you're going to teach?" Now, I have nothing against teachers or the venerable profession of teaching. But I have known since before college and the subsequent choice of major that I was not going to be a teacher. Teaching, I feel, is a calling, and it requires a vocation akin to joining a convent or the Secret Service.

Option Two thus stricken, I was forced to confront Option One, and I didn't like what I saw. I am a practical soul who loved the leafy suburbs where I grew up, disliking New York City except for day trips to the Metropolitan Museum of Art or the Radio City Christmas show. Like a certain charming former president, I tried marijuana but didn't inhale (honestly—I didn't even know *how* to inhale). Unlike that same president, I was faithful as the long, long day to all my harmless, clean-cut boyfriends throughout high school and college. So I could not see myself with hollow cheeks, hunched over pen and paper, lamenting the whims of a philandering lover as cockroaches scuttled across the floor.

A semiconscious plan formed in my mind around graduation: get a job in publishing, where I could enjoy the purity of literature (not the rose but near the rose, as they say). Then get married to a man who made enough money for me to stay home with our children, which is when I would find time to write, unencumbered by financial need and drinking in the daily inspiration of motherhood. Yes, Virginia, there is a Santa Claus.

Fast forward a few years . . . not that they weren't good years. They were the years when I met my husband and realized that the princely doctor/lawyer type of the original vision needed to be replaced by a guy with crinkly blue eyes who has the good humor to support me in the daily excavation of Who I Am Under All These Neuroses. I did my stint in publishing, met wonderful people, had five jobs in five years, and fairly skipped out into the parking lot when I was laid off from the last one on a crisp, sunny day in October.

Having babies, well—is it too clichéd to say that moms of little children don't have lots of time to putter around with writing? Let me sum it up this way: by the time I had my second child, my once-ambitious daily task list boiled down to these sparse requirements I crayoned on the back of a diaper package:

1. Keep children alive
2. Do a load of laundry (maybe)

After my layoff, which occurred in the middle of a recession, I kept up a halfhearted job search. To keep from going completely crazy, and to supplement my husband's earnings, I ran a business selling cosmetics for several years. I stumbled into that pink circus tent unwillingly, but I loved every minute of the ride. And although my parents were horrified at the seeming waste of tens of thousands of dollars in school tuition, it taught me a lot about people, how to run a business, and how to dream in bigger ways than I'd previously allowed myself.

So last year found me disillusioned with my big pink dreams, bored to tears with my beautiful babies, arguing with my good-natured husband, and broke. And my cleaning-lady-cum-guru asked me to do a flyer. "Hey, you know how to write . . . write me a flyer and we'll do your house for free next week." By the next week I'd had business cards printed up, and the week after I was looking up "how to incorporate a small business" on the Internet. My ever-supportive husband looked up gigs for me on

Craigslist, and my parents were . . . overjoyed when I cautiously told them the news of my new dream and my fledgling business.

What had scared me to even consider—making a living as a writer—suddenly became the most viable possibility for career success on the horizon. Before I got too scared, I got busy with a catchy tagline and a spate of networking events. Soon I had clients to meet, new website copy due, and a modestly swelling business checking account. But before I even had my first successful paid project, I had become a writer. It happened in a flash at a meeting, when a suited professional held out his hand and introduced himself. I grinned as I shook that hand and said, "Great to meet you! I'm a writer."

On Loss

THE DAY BEFORE NEW YEAR'S EVE

When you have an ultrasound and the tech doesn't talk, you know there's bad news. Usually they are so chatty, pointing out the tiny arms or legs, listening to the heartbeat, making little jokes, "Oh, the baby is sucking its thumb!" The ultrasound room, with its dimmed lights and warmed sheets, is like a womb of comfort where all you can feel is hope and promise and joy. But if they are quiet, a weird, thick silence seems to descend. As I lay there, all I could really think of was how uncomfortable the TSV always was, being annoyed that my tipped uterus was making everything so difficult to see.

And then I could see the baby, and it wasn't moving. Not one little bit. No little jabbing of newly forming hands and feet, no fluttering of tiny translucent heart. It huddled, opaque and still, against its cushion of my insides. It was nothing. The tech didn't say anything. And I didn't ask the question. I knew that the minute I heard her voice I would know for sure, there was something wrong. I'd sense the tightness and the fear in her voice, under the carefully established professional calm, and I would know that the baby was gone, that it was all over. So I didn't ask any questions. With growing horror I just lay and thought about physical discomfort and listened to the click-click as the tech measured here and there and made little notes on the screen. And a few moments later, when the tech left and brought back the counselor, I wasn't surprised at all when she said, "I don't have good news for you today."

My husband and kids were out in the bright, kid-friendly waiting room with its huge fish tank designed for children's entertainment and occupation, full of specimens right out of Disney—Nemo-lookalike clownfish, several bright yellow angelfish, even a big blue fish like the lovably, forgetful Dory. The staff felt terrible, so terrible that I found myself comforting them a bit: "Listen, I do have two wonderful children, really, I'm very blessed," I told them. "If this was my first time, you'd probably be picking pieces of me up off the floor right now." Grandparents—thank god for grandparents—came to help, to take the kids home as my husband and I were ushered out the back door. As much for us as for the others in the waiting room—not wanting our hearts stabbed with the sight of other pregnant couples, not wanting to infect others with our horrible luck.

THE NIGHT BEFORE NEW YEAR'S EVE

Now I am sitting in front of my computer because I don't know what else to do. My D & C "due to fetal demise" is scheduled for the morning. It's not a little abhorrent to think that I am sitting here with a dead child inside me. I really try to put that thought away when it comes because if I gave it much time, it would break me down into tiny fragments, little shaking, screaming pieces. So I'm glad that I don't have to wait too long to get this over with. But then I feel sad and sorry that tomorrow I will wake up in a recovery room and suddenly, almost magically, I won't be pregnant anymore. Although, as far as carrying a child that will be born, I am not pregnant now, and the morning sickness I am still having feels like life's supreme sick joke. I'm still nauseated and hungry enough to eat for two, but there are no longer two. One is gone.

THE DAYS AND WEEKS AND MONTHS AFTER . . .

One thing my experience has taught me is compassion. I now feel horrible about every stupid thing I ever said to people going through anything that I have never gone through, and I don't really want to talk to anyone unless they've gone through this. Because if they've never gone through this, the things they say usually end up on the following list.

Things NOT to say to a woman who has miscarried:

1. Ooh, I almost had that happen to me, so I understand exactly how you feel.

Please do not relate your story of "almost" having this happen to you. "Almost" losing a baby is like "almost" getting shot. You almost got shot? Well, I got shot. Top that. So you almost got shot and you think you can relate to how I feel. You remember all the awfulness of almost getting shot. The bullet whizzed past your head, your life flashed before your eyes, you were scared. Guess what you were so scared of? Having this happen to you.

2. It's Nature's Way.

Excuse me, but are you a biologist? How exactly do you know that this is Nature's Way? The one thing we do seem to know about miscarriage is that we know nothing about them. Doctors don't know why it happens, there aren't any clear-cut explanations, so everyone relies on this Nature's Way crap, which is another way of saying that I was carrying a defective baby so it's better that I lost it. Well, this was not some "blighted specimen." In my case, even though it was relatively early on, I had maternity clothes and baby clothes ready from my other pregnancies, and a room in progress. This was a dream I already had in clear pictures, of holding a baby and having a child. I had never had any problems before and had no reason to think I might have them. I loved being pregnant and felt great. There is nothing "natural" about having that end.

3. Oh, did you [drink coffee, get pregnant after age thirty-five, run too much, put your arms over your head, go to a chiropractor, eat queso fresca]?

It seems to be a total mystery as to why some women eat badly and climb mountains and have healthy babies and some women spend weeks with their feet on pillows mainlining folic acid and still lose their babies. For goodness' sake, there is a whole show on TLC or something about women who didn't even know they were pregnant and spent the whole nine months drinking martinis or traveling the globe or winning cheerleading competitions. So I think we can all agree it's something of a crapshoot and dial down the judgment, okay?

4. At least you have [other children, a nice husband, a good job, a new puppy dog].

Why, why, why, when people have experienced a devastating loss, do other feel the need to remind them of what they still have? I mean, I know why, it's to help you regain perspective and realize that life could be worse, blah, blah, blah. But all it does is make you feel worse, adding guilt over having negative feelings to the negative feelings. I actually felt guilty when I mourned losing two babies after I already had two children. Who was I to feel bad when so many women have none at all? Wasn't I grateful for my two beautiful children? What was I, greedy? After all, it was Nature's Way.

5. At least it was [early on, only your first one, in the summer], also known as "I know someone who had it worse than you!"

OK, if you have just had a miscarriage, your feelings are a complex jumble, but one feeling that usually persists is hope. There is a little piece of you that is saying, "I still want a baby. This is still possible." Horror stories are very damaging to that hope, and very depressing at a time when depressing is downright dangerous. Even if they seem to go over the victim's head at the time, they will be remembered later with fresh fear and grief. So please, do not tell someone who just had *one* miscarriage about your aunt's friend's cousin who had *nine*.

6. It's God's will/God has a plan/God knows best.

This one is especially popular with church sunshine committees and older people. And normally, I do agree that God has a plan and we are all part of it and that things do happen for a reason. But at the moment of the loss, I don't want to hear that. I don't want to think that God has some game board up there and I'm moving along the path like a little metal Monopoly shoe. Pass Go, collect $200 and a nice husband, buy a house, have two kids, time to pick a community chest card—oops! Have a miscarriage.

A YEAR LATER . . .

When I find out a dear friend has had a miscarriage, I have to sit with the news a few days before I can call her. I'm so afraid I will cry myself, hearing her heartache. I want to be strong for her, share my love and support. But it takes time. After a while, I do call her, and that's all I have to tell her. It takes time. Just time. But she will be all right. And so will I.

Wunneanatsu Cason

(b. 1980)

Wunneanatsu ("one who is good inside") is the granddaughter of Trudie Lamb Richmond, from whom she learned Schaghticoke history and culture, and the daughter of Erin Lamb Meeches, Schaghticoke Tribal Nation councilor from 1990 to 2003. The mother of four daughters and one son, she is currently earning her degree in education, with the goal of teaching American history. She wrote the following two pieces on her blog, *Hand Over the Coffee* (handoverthecoffee .blogspot.com).

I'm Off to See the Wizard

(SEPTEMBER 29, 2010)

It's days like today that it's hard being a military wife. Don't get me wrong, I wouldn't change being married to a military man. The military has done so many positive things for us, but there are just some days when all the sacrifices that you make pile up and weigh you down.

This deployment has had its pros and cons. While I miss the hell out of my husband, the separation has taught us to appreciate each other more. In this case, absence really did make the heart grow fonder. The extra money has provided a security that we've been unable to achieve in the past. I have learned things about myself, my strengths, and my weaknesses, and I've had to face and overcome numerous fears. I never realized before how much I absolutely depended on my husband. I think this deployment has helped Greg and me grow as human beings separately so that we can be better together.

That being said, some days can be unbearable. I am lonely and sad, depressed and overwhelmed. Some days I feel like I'm absolutely bipolar; I can be happy and in control one minute, then in tears and homicidal the next. I think with every deployment they need to issue Prozac to every military spouse, labeled "Use as needed on 'THOSE' days" . . . because I know we all have them. Days that everything breaks, the kids are sick, the dog puked on the newly shampooed carpet, and you realize that you forgot to pay the mortgage.

Today I am sitting curled up on my bed in my sweats, the windows open so I can watch the rain, LARGE cup of coffee on my bedside table, and textbooks all around me. My Aunt Peggy sent an email this morning that my Uncle Micky is having some complications and is struggling with his battle with cancer. I am having flashbacks to last year when we lost my Grampa Dave to cancer and I was stuck in Missouri, unable to be there for my family. Being a military wife means having to leave your roots to plant temporary ones wherever the military tells you to. It means your heart breaking because your family needs you and you're hundreds or thousands of miles away with a car that needs an oil change or the brakes done or whatever.

I just want to cook them a meal and bring it to the hospital or sit and have a cup of tea with my aunt. Instead, I sit in rainy Virginia thinking about all that I've missed in the past nearly 8 years that I've lived away. . . . I couldn't go to Jaji Hayna's funeral because I was in Italy and couldn't get a flight. When Aunt Barbara passed, I was 1,200 miles away with a sick baby. I wished I had gotten home more often to spend time with her. Grampa Dave passed the morning of my open house trying to sell that damn house in Missouri. Greg was already living in Virginia and I just wanted to burn the damn thing down and pack up my car and leave. Instead, I did what I had to do and I left the next morning. I drove straight through from Missouri to Virginia . . . 20 hours with 4 kids and 2 dogs, only allowed the kids to stop when I needed gas. Food, potty, and gas all in one stop. I was a woman on a mission. I nearly collapsed when I finally reached Greg. Being a military wife means doing what you have to do even though your heart is breaking. That includes PCSing [permanent change of station] and having to leave the best friends you've ever had, watching your husband go off to war and feeling torn when all you want to do is pick up and go but you know you have to stay.

Just added up with a term paper due for a class I think I'm going to fail anyway, Julia's eye issue, doctor's and dentist's appointments, school obligations for the kids, soccer, cheerleading, the list goes on. It's one of THOSE days.

I need to go see the Wizard of Oz. My brain is fried, my heart is broken, I need the Lion's courage to face another day, and I want a refund on these damn red slippers. No matter how many times I click my heels, they just won't bring me home.

So Hand Over the Coffee . . . I'll need the caffeine to fight off the Flying Monkeys and Midgets!

Deployments and Motherhood

(NOVEMBER 22, 2010)

One of our primary functions as a parent is to provide our children with a moral compass—to give them an example and guidelines of right and wrong. We all want our children to grow up to be compassionate, respectable, contributing members of society. Or maybe you want your kid to grow up to be a serial killer. Either way, they learn their ways, their foundation, from their parents.

If we teach them to lie, deceive, swindle, and just create drama in general, this is the world that we are creating for future generations. Now, as a mother of 4, I absolutely know how hard parenting is. There is no other job out there that is more draining, thankless, and yet rewarding and fulfilling at the same time. And no one knows like my children how imperfect I am in that job. I'm sure it's debatable at times whether they'd even give me a passable performance review. But like all mothers, I try and sometimes I fail.

But then I remind myself that it's not always the big moments and milestones in life that give you the opportunity to parent your child. It is the little moments, how you treat others and interact with the world around you, especially when you think they're not looking, that really shape their hearts and minds.

One of my proudest parenting moments was when I didn't think any of my children were around. I was pregnant with Julia . . . VERY pregnant. It was actually 3 days past her due date. Katherine was 3 and she and Greg had just dropped me off for an ob-gyn appointment. They were going to run a quick errand and come back. I got out of the car and they drove off. As I walked, I mean waddled, up to the building, there was an elderly woman with a walker who was struggling to get up over the curb and people were just walking around her. I walked up to her and asked if she needed help. She looked at me with such relief and grabbed my arm. I lifted her walker and helped her up the curb. I stayed with her as she shuffled down the walk and we went up the handicap ramp and into the building. She thanked me and I went on with my day, not thinking much of it.

When I got in the car an hour or so later, miserable because that stupid doctor wouldn't induce me until I was a full week late, Katherine immediately says, "Mommy, I saw you help that lady. That was very nice of you." I hadn't seen Greg loop the parking lot and pull out of a different exit. Katherine had been watching the whole time as I helped the elderly woman.

It was at that moment that I realized the magnitude of my role as her mother. I use that memory as my gauge for my actions as I continue on this horrifically, terrifyingly amazing ride of motherhood. How would I want my children to react in this situation? What do I want my girls to learn from this? It was these questions that got me through this deployment.

What do I want to teach my daughters about the power and emotions of being a woman? I want to teach them strength, courage, love, and independence. I want them to be able to face their fears and know that they can overcome any hardship. I hope this deployment has showed them those qualities in me. I hope they saw that we will have bad days—days when we are brought to tears and can barely get out of bed, days when anything that can go wrong will go wrong and days when it feels like the entire world is about to rain down on us. I hope they also saw that as long as we keep our head up and find the silver lining in everything, there are good days around the corner—days when the sun is shining and we have an adventure, days when we get a surprise letter or package in the mail from Daddy to lift our spirits, and days like tomorrow, when he will step off the plane and back into our arms.

This deployment has been challenging, but we have gotten through alive and stronger because of it. So as this long, excruciating deployment comes to an end, forget about Handing Over the Coffee . . . all I want is my husband.

Garry Meeches Jr.
(b. 1997)

Son of Erin Lamb Meeches and grandson of Trudie Lamb Richmond, Garry Meeches was thirteen years old when he began writing poetry. Garry is Schaghticoke on his mother's side and Ojibwa on his father's side. He is also a champion traditional dancer, having danced since he was five years old. Garry also loves to draw and paint, after his father, an accomplished painter. These are his first published poems.

Soccer

The green, clean cut grass
Grasps my feet as I run past.
A salty stream runs down my face
While I dribble the ball with grace.
I trust my team to be there
To protect the orb with all their care.
Our competitive hatred is strong
Even though they've done nothing wrong.
The flying black and white sphere goes in the goal
It was hit so hard it made a hole.
I took pride in my shot.
It was easy, because protect their goal they did not.
I am midfielder in the games I play.
It was like this all day, every day
Because there were many others.
We were no longer teammates, but brothers.

Polar Bear Poem

Her white fur
Blends with
Her frozen kingdom;

Her back is smooth
With but a single hump
Like a small hill;
Her round-black eyes
Are as dark
As the night sky;
When she dashes
She is like a jet,
Fast and powerful;
The snow leaps very high
After her, large puffs
Of white, clouds of snow

I Am (Inspired by George Ella Lyon)[6]

I am from Waterford CT
Home of the Lancers' football team
And home of Garry Meeches
I am from well-done steaks
Not liked by everyone
But liked by a lot

I am from my dad's paintings
And my drawings
Our art fills the house
I am from "I'll see you later."
I know not of goodbyes
For we meet each other again

I am from the Native Nations
It is unknown to most
It is the Old America

Senses: Hear

Those who cannot see
Aren't necessarily blind,
They view the world
With not eyes but ears.
They see the echoing bang of a gunshot
And the sweet-pitched song of a little blue bird,
The booming roar of a great tan lion;
Shouts and squeals of young energetic children.
They view the world,
With not eyes but ears.

What Never Dies

History
School
Friendship
Family
My cat
Libraries
Memory
Cockroaches
So you think you can dance
Disease
Robots
Love
Zombies
America

Build a Poem

Guitar
Tan, brown
Wooden, curved, lightweight
Plucking, strumming, playing, enjoying
Guitar is awesome to me

Art
Colorful, black & white
Drawing, pictures, sculptures
Sketching, capturing, erasing, building
Art describes emotions and life.

Notes

1. Per Connecticut General Statutes, Chapter 824, Section 47–59a.
2. *Indian Papers*, Ser. 1, vol. 2, 7 (1756), Connecticut Archives, Connecticut State Library, Hartford CT.
3. *Indian Papers*, Ser. 1, vol. 2, 241 (1742), Connecticut Archives.
4. *Indian Papers*, Ser. 1, vol. 2, 218–218c (1786), Connecticut Archives.
5. *Colonial War Records*, vol. 4, microfilm reel 204 (1743), 126, Connecticut Archives.
6. Lyon is a popular writing teacher who has used a "Where I'm From" prompt to encourage young people to write (http://www.georgeellalyon.com/where.html).

Further Reading

SCHAGHTICOKE AUTHORS

Crone-Morange, Paulette, and Lucianne Lavin. "The Schaghticoke Tribe and English Law: A Study of Community Survival." *Connecticut History* 43.2 (2004): 132–62. Print.
Logan, Adelphena. *Memories of Sweet Grass*. Washington CT: Institute for American Indian Studies, 1979. Print.
Richmond, Trudie Lamb. "Algonquian Women and the Land: A Legacy." *Rooted Like the Ash Trees*. Ed. Richard G. Carlson. Naugatuck CT: Eagle Wing Press, 1987. 6-8. Print.
———. "Dear Wunneanatsu." *Native Heritage: Personal Accounts by American Indians, 1790 to the Present*. Ed. Arlene B. Hirschfelder. New York: Macmillan, 1996. 121. Print.
———. "Growing Up Indian (or Trying to) in Southern New England." *Cross Paths* 2008: n. pag. Print.
Torres, Ruth Garby. "Now You See Us, Why You Don't: Connecticut's Public Policy to Terminate the Schaghticoke Indians." In *Recognition, Sovereignty Struggles, and*

Indigenous Rights in the United States. Ed. Amy Den Ouden and Jean M. O'Brien. Chapel Hill: University of North Carolina Press, 2013. 195–212. Print.

ADDITIONAL READING

Bee, Robert L. "Connecticut's Indian Policy: From Testy Arrogance to Benign Amusement." *The Pequots in Southern New England: The Fall and Rise of an American Indian Nation.* Ed. Laurence M. Hauptman and James D. Wherry. Norman: University of Oklahoma Press, 1990. 194–212. Print.

Bragdon, Kathleen J. *Native People of Southern New England, 1500–1650.* Norman: University of Oklahoma Press, 1999. Print.

Lavin, Lucianne. *Connecticut's Indigenous Peoples: What Archaeology, History, and Oral Traditions Teach Us about Their Communities and Cultures.* New Haven CT: Yale University Press, 2013.

Starna, William A., and Corinna Dally-Starna. *Gideon's People: Being a Chronicle of an American Indian Community in Colonial Connecticut and the Moravian Missionaries Who Served There.* 2 vols. Lincoln: University of Nebraska Press, 2009. Print.

SOURCE ACKNOWLEDGMENTS

"Mi'kmaq Creation Story," by Chief Stephen Augustine, is published by permission of the author.

"The Covenant Chain," by the Grand Council of the Mi'kmaq Nation, originally appeared in *Drumbeat: Anger and Renewal in Indian Country*, edited by Boyce Richardson (Ottawa: Summerhill Press, 1989), and is reprinted by permission of Andrew Denny, descendant of Grand Captain Alexander Denny.

"From Here to There," by Elsie Charles Basque, originally appeared in *The Mi'kmaq Anthology*, edited by Lesley Choyce and Rita Joe (Halifax NS: Nimbus Publishing, 1997), and is reprinted by permission of Marty Simon.

Excerpts from *Song of Rita Joe: Autobiography of a Mi'kmaq Poet*, by Rita Joe (Lincoln: University of Nebraska Press, 1996), are reprinted by permission of the University of Nebraska Press. Copyright 1996 by Rita Joe.

Excerpts from *We Were Not the Savages: A Mi'kmaq Perspective on the Collision between European and Native American Civilizations*, by Daniel N. Paul (Black Point NS: Fernwood Publishing, 2006), are reprinted by permission of the author.

"Structural Unemployment: The Mi'kmaq Experience," by Marie Battiste, originally appeared in *The Mi'kmaq Anthology*, edited by Lesley Choyce and Rita Joe (Halifax NS: Nimbus Publishing, 1997), and is reprinted by permission of the author.

"Mi'kmaq Treaties," by James Sakej Youngblood Henderson, originally appeared in *Honoring 400 Years: Kepmite'tmnej*, edited by Jaime Battiste (N.p.: Jaime Battiste, 2010), and is reprinted by permission of the author.

Excerpts from *Stones and Switches*, by Lorne Simon (Penticton BC: Theytus Books, 1995), are reprinted by permission of Theytus Books.

"Clay Pots and Bones," "Mainkewin? (Are You Going to Maine?)," and "Progress," by Lindsay Marshall, originally appeared in *Clay Pots and Bones* (Sydney NS: Solus Publishing, 1997), and are reprinted by permission of the author.

Excerpts from "Understanding the Progression of Mi'kmaq Law," by Jaime Battiste, originally appeared in the *Dalhousie Law Journal* (Fall 2008) and are reprinted by permission of the *Dalhousie Law Journal*.

"Repatriation Soliloquy," "Mi'kmaq Haiku," and "Someday I Will Dance," by Alice Azure, originally appeared in *In Mi'kmaq Country: Selected Poems and Stories* (Chicago: Albatross Press, 2007), and are reprinted by permission of the author.

"Without a Microphone," by Starlit Simon, originally appeared in *National Geographic Traveler* (March 2010) and is reprinted by permission of the author.

"In Quest of Road Kill," by Starlit Simon, originally appeared in the *New Brunswick Beacon* (St. Thomas University) and is reprinted by permission of the *New Brunswick Beacon* (http://www.newbrunswickbeacon.ca/19190/in-quest-of-road-kill/).

"The Red Man's Burden," by Henry "Red Eagle" Perley, originally appeared in *All-Story Weekly* (1915) and is reprinted by permission of Juana Perley on behalf of the family of Henry Red Eagle.

"Freeport, Maine," "History Resource Material," "Baqwa'sun, Wuli Baqwa'sun," "September Morning," and "Fragile Freedoms," by Shirley Bear, originally appeared in *Virgin Bones* (Toronto: McGilligan Books, 2006) and are reprinted by permission of the author.

"Linguicide, the Killing of Languages, and the Case for Immersion Education," by Andrea Bear Nicholas, originally appeared in *Briarpatch* (March 1, 2011) and is reprinted by permission of the author.

"Open Letter to Barack Obama," by Chief Brenda Commander, originally appeared in the *Bangor Daily News* (November 25, 2009) and is reprinted by permission of the author.

"The Ballad of Gabe Acquin," "The Water Road," "Return," "20th Century PowWow Playland," and "Trade in the 21st Century," by Mihku Paul, originally appeared in *Look Twice: The Waponahki in Image and Verse* (exhibit), Abbe Museum, Bar Harbor, Maine, 2010, and are reprinted by permission of the author. "Return" and "20th Century PowWow Playland" also appear in her book *20th Century PowWow Playland* (Greenfield Center NY: Bowman Books, 2012).

Lewis Mitchell's letter to Charles Godfrey Leland found in Box 372, Charles G. Leland Papers, Pennell Whistler Collection, Manuscript Division, Library of Congress, Washington DC.

"Passamaquoddy Girl," by Mary Ellen Stevens Socobasin, originally appeared in *The Wabanakis of Maine and the Maritimes: A Resource Book about Penobscot, Passamaquoddy, Maliseet, Micmac and Abenaki Indians, with Lesson Plans for Grades 4 through 8* (Philadelphia: American Friends Service Committee, 1989), and is reprinted by permission of Robert Socobasin.

"Skicin Love," "Forever Tribal Love," and "Sacred Color Red," by Donald Soctomah, are published by permission of the author.

"Technology Meets Ecology: Passamaquoddy Bay," by Vera Francis, originally appeared in *Radio Healer* (2007) and is reprinted by permission of the author.

"Gordon Island," "Seasons," and "Dream of the Hunter's Dance," by Dawna Meader are published by permission of the author.

"My Story of the Dragonfly and My Sister Rae-Lee and My MOM!," by Susie Mitchell Sutton, is published by permission of the author.

"A Warrior's Homecoming," by Wendy Newell Dyer, is published by permission of the author.

"A Measure of Timelessness," "Majestic Beauty," "Of Life from Life," and "One Aspect of the Journey of Life," by Russell Bassett, originally appeared on the Pleasant Point Passamaquoddy tribal website (www.wabanaki.com) and are reprinted by permission of the author.

"To My Brothers," by Kani Malsom, is published by permission of the author.

"Spring drew its first breath the previous day . . . ," by Rolfe Richter, is published by permission of the author.

"A Summer Day in Motahkomikuk," by Christine Downing, is published by permission of the author.

"Coming Together" and "Sacred Hoop Ceremony," by Maggie Neptune Dana, originally appeared in *Passamaquoddy Community Vision 1996—Passamaquoddy Tribe at Pleasant Point, Sipayik, Perry, Maine: A Design for Community Development* (Pleasant Point, Perry M E: White Owl Press, 1996), and are reprinted by permission of the author.

"Diminished Dreams," by Marie Francis, is published by permission of the author.

"Listen," "Fragmented People," and "With This Pencil," by Natalie Dana, are published by permission of the author.

"The spirit is deep within us . . . ," by Jenny Soctomah, is published by permission of the author.

"The Heart of Sipayik" and "Sipayik Reservation 1974," by Ellen Nicholas, are published by permission of the author.

"Kci Woliwon," by Cassandra Dana, is published by permission of the author.

"We're In the Chorus Now," "Geegis," "I'm free in the world of these carpeted hills . . . ," "Some ten or few years so ago or more . . . ," "Baby Girl," "The Lost Soul of the Wilderness," "The Dreamer—Moodas (The Dream Spirit)," and "Northern Lights," by Molly Spotted Elk, are housed in the Maine Folklife Center at the University of Maine–Orono and are reprinted by permission of Barbara Moore.

"The Avenger," by Fred Ranco, originally appeared in the *Wabanaki Alliance* (1979) and is reprinted by permission of the *Wabanaki Alliance*.

"Injun Laugh" and "Gewh Huz," by ssipsis, originally appeared in *Molly Molasses and Me: A Collection of Living Adventures* (Knox M E: Little Letterpress, Robin Hood Books, 1988), and are reprinted by permission of the author.

"The Dark Ages of Education and a New Hope: Teaching Native American History in Maine Schools," by Donna Loring, originally appeared in the *New England Journal of Higher Education* (Summer 2009) and is reprinted by permission of the *New England Journal of Higher Education*.

"Penobscot Home Nation," "We're Like the Moss on the Rock," "Caribou Lake Winter," "Mother of three didn't know . . . ," "Pensive in her rocking chair . . . ," "Children," and "A Walk to Ktadhin," by Carol Dana, originally appeared in *When No One Is Looking* (Greenfield Center N Y: Bowman Books, 2010) and are reprinted by permission of the author.

"Growing Up with Stereotypes: A Native Woman's Perspective," by Rhonda Frey, originally appeared as part of a curriculum developed with the Abbe Museum and is reprinted with permission from the Abbe Museum, Bar Harbor, Maine, and James Frey.

"What's It Like Today?," by John Bear Mitchell, originally appeared in the *Bangor Daily News* (2000) and is reprinted with permission from the *Bangor Daily News*.

"Nokomis Speaks: Message to the Seventh Generation," "Sky Woman," and "The Lodge," by Sherri Mitchell, are published by permission of the author.

"Dry Funk," "gladly," "Treaty of 2010," and "february weather makes me feel like this," by Nick Bear, are published by permission of the author.

"The Abenakis of Vermont," by Stephen Laurent, originally appeared in the *Vermont History Journal* (1955) and is reprinted by permission of the Vermont Historical Society.

"A Profile in Courage" and "Aunt Mary and Uncle Frank," by Claudia Mason Chicklas, are published by permission of Joyce Heywood.

Excerpt from *Bowman's Store*, by Joseph Bruchac III, originally appeared in *Bowman's Store: A Journey to Myself* (New York: Lee & Low Books, 2001), copyright 2001, 1997 by Joseph Bruchac. Permission arranged with Lee & Low Books Inc., New York NY, 10016, reprinted by permission of Tom Low.

"Burial Places along the Long River" and "Ndakinna," by Joseph Bruchac III, are published by permission of the author.

"Abenaki Divorce," "Winter Bringer," "In the Abenaki Manner," "Naming Water," "Wazôliinebi," "Planting Moon *Kikas*," "Burial Dress," and "Jibaaki," by Carol Willette Bachofner, are published by permission of the author.

"The Old Man's Walk," by Carol Willette Bachofner, originally appeared in *The 2008 Poets' Guide to New Hampshire*, edited by John-Michael Albert (Ossipee NH: Poetry Society of New Hampshire, 2008) and is reprinted by permission of the author.

"Poison in the Pond," "Smallpox," Where I Want Them," "Swift River—Kancamagus," "Before Moving on to Plymouth from Cape Cod—1620," and "Amber Necklace," by Cheryl Savageau, originally appeared in *Mother/Land* (London: Salt Publishing, 2006) and are reprinted by permission of the author.

"Trees," "Looking for Indians," and "French Girls Are Fast," by Cheryl Savageau, originally appeared in *Dirt Road Home* (Willimantic CT: Curbstone Press, 1995) and are reprinted by permission of Northwestern University Press.

"The Removal Period" and "Nnd Haiku: A Trilogy," by Donna Laurent Caruso, originally appeared in *To Solder the Birchbark*, vol. 1 (Fitchburg MA: Nashaway Publications, 2004), and are reprinted by permission of the author.

"Abenaki Filmmaker Earns Luminaria Award," by Donna Laurent Caruso, originally appeared in *Indian Country Today* and is reprinted by permission of Indian Country Today Media Network.

"War Wounds: Sophie Senecal Goes to Washington" and "Praying Spoils the Hunting," by Margaret M. Bruchac, are published by permission of the author.

"Take From My Hair—Memories of Change," "Thunderbeings," Fanning Fire," "Singing Across the River, "Even When the Sky Was Clear," and "When the Air Is Dry," by Suzanne S. Rancourt, originally appeared in *Billboard in the Clouds* (Willimantic CT: Curbstone Press, 2004) and are reprinted by permission of Northwestern University Press.

"Tracking My Nature," by James Bruchac, is published by permission of the author.

"Gluskonba's Fish Trap (Klosk8ba Adelahigan)," by Jesse Bruchac, is published by permission of the author.

"On the Death of His Mother, February 17, 1847," by Ebenezer Hemenway, is from the collections of the Worcester Historical Museum, Worcester, Massachusetts, and is reprinted by permission of Richard Massey.

"Days of Hassanamesit," by Zara Ciscoe Brough, originally appeared in the *Nipmuc Nation Newsletter* (July 2004) and is reprinted by permission of Hassanamisco Indian Museum/Nipmuc Nation.

"Ballad for Bubba," by Corrine Bostic, originally appeared in the *Worcester (MA) Review* and is reprinted by permission of the *Worcester Review*.

"Dedication to the Young: Cuttin' a Spoonful," "Touchstones," "Slatemen," and "For Teachers: A Self-Reminder," by Corrine Bostic, originally appeared in *Go Onward and Upward: An Interpretive Biography of the Life of Miss Sarah Ella Wilson, a Prominent Forerunner of Worcester School Teachers, Based on Fact, Oral Reminiscence, and Written Recollections* (Worcester MA: Commonwealth Press, 1970) and are reprinted by permission of Stephen Bostic and Diane Bostic-Morgan.

"Hepsibeth Bowman Crosman Hemenway, 1763–1847," by Richard Spotted Rabbit Massey, is reprinted by permission of Sherley A. Massey.

"Chief Wise Owl's Prayer," by Edwin W. Morse Sr. (Chief Wise Owl), is published by permission of Tom Morse.

"Coyote Spirit" and "The Heat Moon," by Kitt Little Turtle (George Munyan), are published by permission of Cheryl Watching Crow Stedtler.

"Nipmuck Legend" and "Legend about Hobbamock," by Kitt Little Turtle (George Munyan), originally appeared in *Native American Sourcebook: A Teacher's Resource on New England Native Peoples*, by Barbara Robinson (Concord MA: Concord Museum, 1988) and are reprinted by permission of Concord Museum.

"To Carol and David with Love," "Woman of the Warrior," "Wind from Summer," "The Gifted Porcupine Roach Maker," "Creator of Life," "Hear Your People," and "There Was a Time," by Nancy Bright Sky Harris, are published by permission of the author.

"Carrying the Flute," by Hawk Henries, originally appeared on the author's website, hawkhenries.com, and is reprinted by permission of the author.

"Honoring a Father and a Son," by Cheryl Watching Crow Stedtler, originally appeared in the *Nipmuc Nation Newsletter* 1, no. 4 (2004) and is reprinted by permission of the author.

"Full Circle," "Never Too Late to Dance," "Circle low . . . ," and "Pressed," by Cheryl Watching Crow Stedtler, are published by permission of the author.

"A Brief Look at Nipmuc History," by Cheryll Toney Holley, is published by permission of the author.

"'Authentic,' Power, and Stuck in My Craw" and "Woman, Mother, Sister, Daughter, Lover," by Bruce Curliss, are published by permission of the author.

An excerpt from "Deal Me In," "Heart in the Clouds," and "The Crow, by Larry Spotted Crow Mann, originally appeared in *Tales from the Whispering Basket* (Boston: CreateSpace, 2011) and are reprinted by permission of the author.

"The Fresh Water People," "An Indian Gathering," "Indians," and "The Dancer's Foot," by Sarah "She Paints Horses" Stedtler, are published by permission of Cheryl Watching Crow Stedtler.

Interview with Mabel Avant originally appeared in *People of the First Light: Wisdoms of a Mashpee Wampanoag Elder*, by Joan Tavares Avant (West Barnstable MA: West Barnstable Press, 2010) and is reprinted by permission of Joan Tavares Avant.

"The Voice of Our Forsaken Church," by Mabel Avant, is reprinted by permission of Joan Tavares Avant.

Excerpt from *Moshup's Footsteps*, by Helen Manning, originally appeared in *Moshup's Footsteps: The Wampanoag Nation, Gay Head/Aquinnah, the People of First Light* (Aquinnah MA: Blue Cloud Across the Moon Publishing, 2001) and is reprinted by permission of Jo-Ann Eccher.

"National Day of Mourning," by Frank James (Wamsutta), originally appeared on the United American Indians of New England website, www.uaine.org, and is reprinted by permission of Moonanum James.

Excerpt from *The Wampanoags of Mashpee*, by Russell Peters (Fast Turtle), originally appeared in *The Wampanoags of Mashpee: An Indian Perspective on American History* (N.p.: R. M. Peters, 1987) and is reprinted with permission of Ann Peters Gilmore.

"Historical Continuities in Indigenous Women's Political Activism: An Interview with Joan Tavares Avant," by Anne Foxx, originally appeared in *People of the First Light: Wisdoms of a Mashpee Wampanoag Elder* by Joan Tavares Avant (West Barnstable MA: West Barnstable Press, 2010) and is reprinted by permission of the author.

"Holistic History: Including the Wampanoag in an Exhibit at Plimoth Plantation," by Linda Coombs, originally appeared in *Plimoth Life* 1, no. 2 (2002): 12–15 and is reprinted with permission of the Plimoth Plantation.

"Wampanoag Reflections" and "Beware: Not All Terms Are Fair Game," by Paula Peters, are published by permission of the author.

"Grandfather" and "Red Sun Rising," by Robert Peters, are published by permission of the author.

"Turtle and the Oak Tree," by Mwalim *7)/Morgan James Peters, originally appeared in *A Mixed Medicine Bag: Original Black Wampanoag Folklore* (Mashpee MA: Talking Drum Press, 2007) and is reprinted by permission of the author.

"Letter to Wilkins Updike, 1837," and "Letter to Elisha Potter, 1844," by Thomas Commuck, are from the Elisha R. Potter Papers, Rhode Island Historical Society, Providence, and published by permission of the Rhode Island Historical Society.

"Editorial" (May 1935), "The Boston Marathon" (May 1935), "Editorial" (August 1935), "Indian Meeting Day," by Fred V. Brown (August 1935), "Narragansett Tongue: Lesson 11" (March 1936), and "Fireside Stories" (July 1936) originally appeared in the *Narragansett Dawn* and are reprinted by permission of the Narragansett Council of Elders.

"I Found Him on a Hill Top," "Life and Seasons Must Surely Change," "For the Children," "Sometimes I Wish I Could Rage Like You," and "Sure I'm Still Hanging Around," by Ella Wilcox Sekatau, originally appeared in *Love Poems and Songs of a Narragansett Indian* by Ella W. Brown [Sekatau] (Wakefield RI: Ariosto Press, 1971) and are reprinted by permission of the author.

Speeches by Paulla Dove Jennings are published by permission of the author.

"Alienation of Indigenous Students in the Public School System" and "In Order to Understand Thanksgiving, One Must Understand the Sacredness of the Gift," by Dawn Dove, are published by permission of the author.

"Troopers Lead Attack on Narragansett Reservation," "Tarzan Brown," "William O.," and "Sad Country Songs," by John Christian Hopkins, are published by permission of the author.

"Roaring Brook," by Lorén M. Spears (Narragansett/Niantic), is published by permission of the author.

"The Four Animals" and "The Three Sisters," by Dasan Everett, are published by permission of the author.

"The creator made us all . . . ," by Darrlyn Sand Fry, is published by permission of the author.

"Sky woman falling from the sky . . . ," by Laurel Spears, is published by permission of the author.

"Thank You, MET Colleagues . . . ," by Thawn Harris, is published by permission of the author.

"TGIF 1," "TGIF 2," and "Letter to California State University Administration, Faculty, and Student Body," by Eleanor Dove Harris, are published by permission of the author.

Excerpt from "Happiness in Our Own Words," by Ella Sekatau and Dawn Dove, originally appeared in "The Pursuit of Happiness: An Indigenous View: The Narragansett People Speak" (Tomaquag Indian Memorial Museum booklet, 2005) and is reprinted by permission of Dawn Dove.

Excerpt from "Pursuit of Happiness: An Indigenous View on Education," by Lorén M. Spears, originally appeared in "The Pursuit of Happiness: An Indigenous View: The Narragansett People Speak" (Tomaquag Indian Memorial Museum booklet, 2005) and is reprinted by permission of the author.

"Address at 100th Anniversary of the Mohegan Church," by Mary Virginia Morgan, is published by permission of Robert Soper on behalf of the Mohegan Tribe Council of Elders.

"See the Beauty Surrounding Us" and "An Affectionate Portrait of Frank Speck," by Gladys Tantaquidgeon, are published by permission of Robert Soper on behalf of the Mohegan Tribe Council of Elders.

"Homeland," "Attic Dawn," "Pan's Song," and "Shantok," by Jayne Fawcett, are published by permission of the author.

"Mohegan Food," by Faith Damon Davison, is published by permission of the author.

"Remembrance" and "The Hoop," by Stephanie M. Fielding, are published by permission of the author.

"Long Island Sound" and "A Winter's Morn," by Sharon I. Maynard, are published by permission of the author.

"River," "His Lover," "Spirit Teacher," "Freedom," "The Course of Love," "Sparrow," and "Again," by William Donehey, are published by permission of the author.

"Fade into White," by Joe Smith, is published by permission of the author.

"The Window," by Melissa Tantaquidgeon Zobel, is published by permission of the author.

"The Little Girl on the Hook," by Alysson Troffer, is published by permission of the author.

"The Circle" and "'Native American Professor . . . ," by Eric Maynard, are published by permission of the author.

"When the Whippoorwill Calls," by Madeline Fielding Sayet, is published by permission of the author.

"Letter to the Department of State Parks," by Howard N. Harris, is from the personal papers of Trudie Lamb Richmond and is published by permission of Ruth Garby Torres.

"Letter to Brenden Keleher," by Irving A. Harris, is published by permission of Ruth Garby Torres.

"Why Does the Past Matter? Eunice Mauwee's Resistance Was Our Path to Survival," by Trudie Lamb Richmond, is published by permission of the author.

"Growing up Indian (or Trying To) in Southern New England," by Trudie Lamb Richmond, originally appeared in *Cross Paths* (2008) and is reprinted by permission of the author.

"The Schaghticoke and English Law: A Study of Community Survival," by Paulette Crone-Morange, originally appeared in *Connecticut History* 43, no. 2 (2004) and is reprinted by permission of Lucianne Lavin.

"Eulogy for Irving Harris," by Ruth Garby Torres, is published by permission of the author.

"How I Became a (Paid) Writer" and "On Loss," by Aileen Harris McDonough, are published by permission of the author.

"I'm Off to See the Wizard" and "Deployments and Motherhood," by Wunneanatsu Cason, originally appeared on the author's blog, *Hand Over the Coffee* (handover thecoffee.blogspot.com), and is reprinted by permission of the author.

"Soccer," "Polar Bear Poem," "I Am," "Senses: Hear," "What Never Dies," and "Build a Poem," by Garry Meeches Jr., are published by permission of the author.

CPSIA information can be obtained at www.ICGtesting.com
Printed in the USA
BVOW07s0904030714

358072BV00002B/2/P